Citrix® MetaFrame®
Access Suite
for Windows® Server 2003:
The Official Guide

TIM **REESER**
STEVE **KAPLAN**
ALAN **WOOD**

McGraw-Hill/Osborne

New York   Chicago   San Francisco
Lisbon   London   Madrid   Mexico City   Milan
New Delhi   San Juan   Seoul   Singapore   Sydney   Toronto

The McGraw·Hill Companies

McGraw-Hill/Osborne
2100 Powell Street, 10th Floor
Emeryville, California 94608
U.S.A.

To arrange bulk purchase discounts for sales promotions, premiums, or fund-raisers, please contact **McGraw-Hill/Osborne** at the above address. For information on translations or book distributors outside the U.S.A., please see the International Contact Information page immediately following the index of this book.

Citrix® MetaFrame® Access Suite for Windows® Server 2003: The Official Guide

1234567890 FGR FGR 019876543

ISBN 0-07-219566-5

Publisher
   Brandon A. Nordin
Vice President & Associate Publisher
   Scott Rogers
Acquisitions Editor
   Francis Kelly
Project Editors
   Emily K. Wolman, Lisa Wolters-Broder
Acquisitions Coordinator
   Jessica Wilson
Technical Editor
   Bobby Doss
Copy Editor
   Mike McGee

Proofreader
   Linda Medoff
Indexer
   Valerie Robbins
Composition
   Carie Abrew, Tabi Cagan,
   Tara A. Davis
Illustrators
   Melinda Moore Lytle, Kathleen Fay
   Edwards, Michael Mueller, Lyssa Wald
Series Design
   Peter F. Hancik
Cover Design
   Pattie Lee

This book was composed with Corel VENTURA™ Publisher.

Alan Wood
Compassion, honesty, respect, inspiration, support, tolerance—without these I would accomplish nothing. For my wife, Carol—though she didn't make the world, she does makes my world go 'round.

Tim Reeser
To my wife, Lindsay, and my daughter Rebekah, who were beyond flexible over the last eight months and allowed me to focus on this work. To the incredible engineering team at ECC, who pulled together under tight deadlines to make this book a true technical marvel.

Steve Kaplan
To my son, Ryan, and my daughter, Alexis, for their support and inspiration. To my brother, Alan, for his pioneering efforts in making server-based computing work on an enterprise scale. And to my client and friend, Anthony Lackey, for showing us all how leadership, vision, and exceptional execution can successfully transform the IT infrastructure of one of the world's largest corporations.

Bobby Doss
With love to my wife, Tammie, and my daughter, Emily (and the baby on the way), for always supporting and loving me. Also, to my mom and dad, who taught me to work hard and always strive for the best! I've never been able to tell them all how much I appreciate them, so I thought I would start here.

Tim Reeser is Chairman, CFO, and cofounder of Engineering Computer Consultants, Inc. (ECC). ECC is a Microsoft Gold Partner in Enterprise Systems and a Citrix Platinum partner, and has been providing enterprise server-based solutions for eight years. Tim has written for *Windows.NET Magazine* and *Selling NT Solutions Magazine,* and has been a speaker at industry events such as Citrix Solutions Summit, Ingram Micro's Venture Tech Network, and various user groups and consortiums. He manages the day-to-day sales activities of the sales team at ECC, and has weekly meetings with server-based computing customers, providing constant and timely insight into the current state of business. Tim holds a B.S. in Mechanical Engineering from Colorado State University, and is MCSE and CSA certified.

Steve Kaplan is the National Director of Enterprise Accounts for Vector ESP, Inc. His former company, RYNO Technology, was named the Citrix Platinum Partner of the Year for the United States before being acquired by Vector ESP in 2001. He is widely recognized as one of the most prominent proponents of server-based computing, and helped pioneer and develop the Citrix ACE Cost Analyzer Tool. Kaplan has spent years as a regular columnist for three different channel magazines and has worked with multiple hardware manufacturers and ISVs to help them develop channel and market-positioning strategies. He was a general session speaker at the 2002 Citrix Solutions Summit and has sat on the advisory boards of several industry leaders including a position on the Microsoft Partner Advisory Council. He holds a B.S. in business administration from U.C. Berkeley and an M.B.A. with an emphasis in both marketing and finance from Northwestern's J. L. Kellogg Graduate School of Management.

Alan Wood is a Project Leader and Senior Engineer with Engineering Computer Consultants. In addition to his Microsoft certification, he is a Cisco Certified Network Professional (CCNP) and a Cisco Certified Design Professional (CCDP). Alan has over 25 years experience in designing, operating, maintaining, and troubleshooting networks and telecommunications systems ranging from military infrastructure to campus networks and teletypes to SONET. In the academic realm, he developed and taught college curriculum for Microsoft Windows NT Network Administration and Telecommunications Systems.

Bobby Doss is a Director of Enterprise Services for Vector ESP, Inc. Located in the Houston office, he has been with Vector ESP for four years and has worked in the IT business for the last seven. He's certified on every platform Citrix has released since WinFrame 1.8, and is both a Citrix Certified Enterprise Administrator (CCEA) and Citrix Certified Instructor (CCI). In addition to his Citrix credentials, he holds a number of Microsoft certifications, including being a Microsoft Certified Systems Administrator and a Microsoft Certified Systems Engineer (MCSE) on both Windows NT 4.0 and Windows 2000. Bobby has also been recognized for reviewing several Citrix training manuals in use at authorized learning centers around the world. He was educated at Abilene Christian University and the University of Phoenix. He and his wife, Tammie, have a daughter, Emily, and currently await the arrival of their second child in late April 2004.

CONTENTS

Part III

Implementing an On-Demand Server-Based Computing Environment

Part IV

Appendixes

FOREWORD

The previous edition of this book, *Citrix® MetaFrame™ for Windows® Terminal Services: The Official Guide*, sold over 13,000 copies—a big success for a technology guide. That was three years ago, when the server-based computing market was still young. Much has changed since then. We've been through a long economic drought, political upheavals, terrorist attacks, and wars. And through it all—in spite of it all, in fact—the server-based computing market has matured, growing explosively and globally.

Today, nearly 50 million people use our technology every day to access the on-demand enterprise, and more than 120,000 organizations around the world are Citrix customers. These include all of the Fortune 100 companies, 99 percent of the Fortune 500 firms, and 95 percent of the *Financial Times'* European 100. When the first edition of this book came out, the idea of centralizing computing on the server was visionary and futuristic. Lately it's become the norm since its benefits are so clear and compelling: ubiquitous, secure access for workers combined with more cost-effective and efficient management of enterprise applications for the IT staff. As a result, we've gone mainstream in a big way.

The authors of this book—Steve Kaplan, Tim Reeser, and Alan Wood—have had something to do with this success. The guide itself is useful and informative, as its success has shown, and the first edition helped many readers successfully implement server-based computing environments. Moreover, the authors represent two companies that are part of a select group of top-notch Citrix Platinum-level resellers. So they have contributed to our success and the increasing adoption of server-based computing with both how-to information and hands-on implementation. I am grateful to them and proud to contribute this forward to the second edition.

This edition comes at an exciting time for Citrix. Earlier this year, we announced the Citrix MetaFrame Access Suite, extending our flagship product, Citrix MetaFrame Presentation Server, into a complete system of integrated software products that we call access infrastructure for the on-demand enterprise. You will see these terms used throughout the book, along with the familiar server-based computing terms and concepts that remain at the heart of what we do. Combining cutting-edge and tried-and-true notions, the authors present the very latest on access infrastructure technology along with best practices derived from configuring hundreds of Citrix MetaFrame and Microsoft Terminal Server systems. While access infrastructure for the on-demand enterprise simplifies the complexity of information systems, successful implementation requires an organization's IT department to address a range of technical, educational, cultural, political, and internal marketing challenges. That's what this book is all about, and anyone planning to transform their company into an on-demand enterprise will benefit from reading it.

Mark B. Templeton
President and Chief Executive Officer
Citrix Systems, Inc.

ACKNOWLEDGMENTS

Although the three authors performed a majority of the writing and editing, many ECC engineers contributed significantly to the writing, figure and illustration creation, testing, and editing. Despite very hectic schedules on customer premises performing design and implementation work, these engineers carved out weekend and evening time to make this book happen. The engineers who contributed significantly to both the writing, editing, and testing include: Brian Casselman, Larry Henshaw, Travis Hevelone, and Ben Reeser. In addition, several engineers made contributions in the form of editing and technical testing, including Ken Lang, Kris Climie, Erik Ambrose, and John McMaster. Beyond the engineers, ECC's internal technical editor, Tracy O'Hare, spent many hours making sure our writing was readable and that we followed the appropriate Osborne guidelines.

Thanks also to Bobby Doss, a Director of Enterprise Services for Vector ESP, who handled the technical review of the book. Bobby's input truly added to the technical accuracy and detail that will make this book popular with the folks charged with implementing server-based computing at the ground level.

A significant amount of the technical material in this book was gathered from Citrix personnel, who were all very helpful. Special thanks though to Doug Brown for his work of art, *Methodology in a Box* (which we encourage anyone involved with an SBC project to read at http://www.dabcc.com) and for his permission to borrow content and ideas from his work. We also are indebted to Kevin West, Senior Director of Messaging for Citrix, who helped us both understand and better articulate Citrix' latest positioning.

A special thanks to Tony English, co-founder and President of ECC, who provided the inspiration to take this work on, even though the Army called him away to Iraq for the duration of the project. We look forward to his safe return.

And finally, we want to thank all of our customers who had the vision and courage to implement server-based computing on an enterprise scale, and who thereby helped create the access infrastructure industry and the foundation for the on-demand enterprise.

KUDOS FOR THE FIRST EDITION

The genesis of the first edition was an enterprise deployment of Windows NT and Citrix MetaFrame 1.8 for a Fortune 1000 company that began in 1998. While several books gave good information on how to set up and administer Terminal Services and MetaFrame, no one had yet written about the challenges, pitfalls, and methodologies required to make implementation successful on an enterprise scale. Citrix agreed to endorse the book as their Official Guide, and both the authors and McGraw-Hill/Osborne have been very pleased with the sales.

The feedback for the book was quite good, particularly for a first edition. Our primary criticism came from covering too much networking basics in the book. This second edition addresses that issue and has undergone far more review by experts from both Vector ESP and ECC, as well as from Citrix and Microsoft.

INTRODUCTION

> *Over the next five years, Russell will likely realize more than $5 million in savings from implementing Citrix software and an additional $4 million in future cost avoidance from outsourcing IT operations.*
> —Tom Hanly, Chief Financial Officer, Frank Russell Company

The complexity of information systems is driving the cost of enterprise computing out of control, frequently offsetting the business benefits derived from information technology. Consequently, in spite of continuing and rapid advances in IT, it is more difficult than ever before for IT organizations to provide consistency of service to all the places and people they must serve.

This is confirmed by a recent study of the U.S. Department of Commerce's Bureau of Economic Analysis, which found that in 1965 less than 5 percent of the capital expenditures of U.S. companies went to IT. Early in the 1980s, when the PC was beginning to proliferate, the percentage grew to 15 percent. A decade later, the percentage had doubled, and by the late 1990s, IT costs were nearly half of all expenses of American corporations. But the amazing thing about these huge budgets is that they haven't led to a revolution in innovation or productivity; typically, 80 percent of a company's IT spending today goes toward just maintaining existing systems.

What's driving all this? Heterogeneity. Each successive wave of computing—mainframe, minicomputer, PC, client-server, the Web, web services—has not superseded previous waves but rather has been piled on top of what came before. Moreover, the diversity and proliferation of access devices, computing platforms, software languages, networks, standards, and application infrastructures have further complicated the picture, making the cost of computing more variable and more expensive than ever.

IT organizations are coping with these technical, economic, and business challenges through consolidation. They are reducing the number of moving parts by centralizing and consolidating as much of the heterogeneity and complexity as possible to fewer data centers, servers, and networks. Their goal is to migrate to a model that allows them to improve the level of service they provide to the business. To accomplish this, many are moving the complexity of computing to a central place where it can best be managed, controlled, and evolved over time. This makes everything outside the data center simpler to manage and more cost-effective to operate. It also dramatically improves information security and resilience to technological and business interruptions.

Access infrastructure for the on-demand enterprise provides a consistent user experience across a wide variety of access devices and easy, secure, and instant access to IT services—from anywhere. It allows heterogeneity to be managed centrally, and shields the user from the complexity of accessing heterogeneous information systems. It knows the user's identity and presents an interface that dynamically adjusts to the specific user's device, location, and preferences.

The MetaFrame Access Suite provides access infrastructure for the on-demand enterprise, which is built upon server-based computing; applications are executed on central server farms running Microsoft Windows Server 2003 Terminal Services and Citrix MetaFrame Presentation Server. Users see only screen prints of their applications displayed on a wide variety of devices, including handheld PDAs, PC tablet devices, Windows-based terminals, Macs, smart phones, Linux workstations, and traditional PCs. This computing paradigm also goes by several other names (with some variations in meaning), including server-centric computing, application serving, thin-client computing, ASP services, and simply Terminal Services. By providing organizations with the ability to quickly deploy a wide range of applications to users, regardless of their location, bandwidth constraints, or device, server-based computing has changed the way many organizations work today. Just as importantly though, server-based computing has reduced or eliminated the requirements for both PC upgrades and remote-office servers, thus allowing many organizations to minimize their ongoing capital expenditures and dramatically slash their administration costs.

Server-based computing is great. It's happening. It's part of our strategy.
—Steve Ballmer, Microsoft President, from the *Wall Street Journal*, July 21, 1999

EVOLUTION OF AN INDUSTRY

According to Giga Information Group, in a report dated February 2002, nearly two-thirds of enterprise users surveyed by Giga have deployed server-based computing; 32 percent believe it is a strategic technology.

Citrix launched the industry in the late 1980s with the introduction of a multiuser OS/2 product called WinView. Over the last few years, a majority of large company IT departments have adopted server-based computing in some form to solve a variety of problems such as wide area deployment of applications, remote access, and access to Windows applications on non-Windows devices (such as UNIX and Mac desktops), but many of these deployments are tactical rather than strategic. This, however, is changing. As companies begin to experience the cost, efficiency, flexibility, and productivity benefits of the Citrix MetaFrame Access Suite on a tactical level, they are increasingly and strategically standardizing on Citrix access infrastructure over time.

Today, the server-based computing industry is enormous and includes scores of Windows terminal choices, bandwidth management devices, wireless connectivity options, and thousands of software partners, resellers, and consultants. Microsoft's incorporation of Terminal Services into Windows Server 2003, and its commitment to continue the rapid feature enhancement, usability, and partner community of Terminal Services is further validating server-based computing as a mainstream technology. We believe that with Citrix' ability to extend the Terminal Services application deployment foundation to enable the on-demand enterprise, and with the additional pressures of shrinking IT budgets, along with the need to ensure disaster recovery and comply with new, stringent government regulations, this rising tidal wave of computing change will continue to gain momentum and, in fact, will become a prominent paradigm in business computing throughout the next decade.

NOTE: Some readers took exception with our declaration of server-based computing becoming the new networking standard when we published the first edition of this book in July of 2000. Nearly 50 million people in over 120,000 organizations around the globe now utilize Citrix software, and 50 percent of surveyed customers consider Citrix their corporate standard for application deployment. We firmly believe that the overwhelming economic advantages make this continuing transition inevitable. Organizations that do not embrace the much greater efficiencies and strategic benefits that centralized computing enable will be at a competitive disadvantage.

In an enterprise implementation of Windows 2003 Terminal Services and Citrix MetaFrame Presentation Server, most applications execute at one or more central data centers rather than on individual PCs. This entails a paradigm shift back to mainframe methodologies, procedures, and discipline, while still utilizing technology and environmental aspects unique to the PC world. It requires a much more resilient, reliable, and redundant network infrastructure than in a conventional client-server WAN. Myriad decisions must be made regarding building this infrastructure as well as several ancillary items such as choosing the right terminals, prioritizing WAN traffic, consolidating storage, enabling redundancy, and migrating from legacy systems.

WHAT'S NEW IN THE SECOND EDITION

This book is a continuation of the first edition written three years ago by Steve Kaplan and Marc Mangus. Server-based computing technology has evolved significantly over the last three years, with the release of Windows Server 2003, Citrix MetaFrame XP Presentation Server, MetaFrame Secure Access Manager, MetaFrame Conferencing Manager, and MetaFrame Password Manager (which together comprise the Citrix MetaFrame Access Suite), along with myriad third-party applications and solution providers that have brought this technology into the mainstream and have resolved and automated a host of issues and complications. Server-based computing on an enterprise level has expanded and evolved into what Citrix calls the on-demand enterprise. Citrix is the market leader in access infrastructure that enables people to access enterprise applications and information on demand.

This second edition incorporates these changes. We take an in-depth look at Microsoft Server 2003 and the changes this product brings to server-based computing, the changes Citrix has brought with the Citrix MetaFrame Access Suite, and the shift that is underway towards webification and web aggregation (such as with Citrix MetaFrame Secure Access Manager). We have also updated all of the information on client deployment, security, third-party add-on applications, and overall management of a server-based computing environment to include all of the latest advancements and industry best-practice trends.

In addition to the technical changes of the last three years, the business climate has also been transformed dramatically. Waves of power outage problems on the west coast in early 2001 and the east coast in August 2003, and the events of September 11, 2001, have forced businesses to more seriously analyze their disaster recovery and business continuity plans. Hundreds of businesses lost data, and just as importantly, lost access to data for extended periods of time. No longer is it acceptable to simply have a plan for data recovery; organizations must also now have a tested plan for business continuity. Fortunately, some of the businesses affected in these crises utilized server-based computing, and were able to demonstrate the effectiveness of replicated server-based sites and user access from anywhere, anyplace, at any time.

The authors of this book have been evangelizing the virtues of server-based computing since its roots as thin-client technology. Our firms represent well over 2000 successful server-based computing installations at every type of enterprise from *Fortune* 50 to small businesses with only ten employees. Even with this broad success, however, we daily engage with organizations that have little or no knowledge of the powerful benefits of server-based computing. A significant number of enterprises still have not made the jump from looking at their IT infrastructure as a cost department, to looking at it as an automation and enabling department. Many enterprises are still hesitant to throw out what they believe to be the safe approach of continuing down the familiar (and unending) road of constant PC upgrading and maintenance.

Although this book will speak to those businesses that have not seriously considered server-based computing, its text is more specifically aimed at helping those who have made the decision and are looking for industry best practices and practical tips to find the greatest success with this technology.

> *Server-based computing has allowed us to build a more efficient yet technically cutting-edge environment. We use it to reduce Telco expenses, augment our VoIP solution, and increase company productivity via the virtual desktop. With Citrix, we can manage all these applications for 300 users with an IT team of four people.*
>
> —John Graham, IT Manager, Mountain West Farm Bureau

THE COMPOSITION OF THIS BOOK

This book provides the framework to design and implement a successful access infrastructure for an on-demand enterprise. Our focus is on using Windows Server 2003 Terminal Services and the Citrix MetaFrame Access Suite to accommodate hundreds or thousands of users running their desktop applications from one or more central data centers. We address the myriad technical, design, and implementation issues involved in constructing this environment, and assume readers already have a good working knowledge of networking and system administration for Windows Server 2003.

The book is divided into three main parts. Part I is an overview of enterprise server-based computing. This section reviews Windows Server 2003 Terminal Services and MetaFrame XP Presentation Server and includes justifications for enterprise deployments. Part II covers the design of an on-demand computing solution and ranges from planning and internally selling the project to providing guidelines for data center and WAN architecture, file services, remote access, security, network management, and thin-client devices. Part III covers the deployment of on-demand computing and includes project management, installation, automation, server farms, profiles, policies and procedures, printing, and migration methodologies.

In Appendix A, we present internetworking basics for those who would like a quick brush-up on networking concepts. Appendix B provides a methodology for building a spreadsheet-based financial model to analyze the comparative benefits of on-demand versus client-side computing. Appendix C includes a suggestion for creating a utility-like billing model for charging users for application hosting.

We include *Notes*, *Tips*, and *Cautions* to supply additional detail to the text. A Note is meant to provide information when the general flow of the discussion is concentrating in a different area or is not as detailed as the Note itself. A Tip is a specific way to do or implement something being discussed. A Caution is meant to alert the reader to watch out for a potential problem.

Writing a book about such a rapidly evolving technology poses a challenge. By the time this book is published, additional tools and practices will be coming on the scene. Fortunately, the methodologies and approaches we describe should be relatively timeless, and should prove very useful as you begin your own enterprise server-based computing project.

> *Citrix MetaFrame software has greatly improved our ability to provide educational services to our students and faculty and has increased our students' willingness to use them.*
> —Pete Oyler, Instructional Technology Specialist, West Shore School District

WHO SHOULD READ THIS BOOK

We have written this book to speak to two audiences: The business decision makers (that is, CFOs, CEOs, CTOs, CIOs, and IT Directors) who are evaluating enterprise IT options, and the IT administrators who are considering or will be implementing and maintaining a server-based computing environment. We recommend that the business decision-makers focus on Chapters 1, 4, 5, 7, 8, 10, and 19, as these chapters specifically address business issues. All other chapters tend to be more implementation- and technically focused, although we worked to keep them relevant and readable by providing a multitude of graphics, pictures, charts, and tables.

In addition to the audience just mentioned, this material will provide a compilation of best practices for enterprise deployment of on-demand computing, and thus should also appeal to the engineers and consultants of the 7000 Citrix partners and 21,000 Microsoft Solution Providers worldwide. IT and project managers can benefit from the sections on change control, customer care, and migration strategies.

INTERACTING WITH THE AUTHORS

We welcome your feedback and will incorporate appropriate suggestions into further releases of the book. You can contact Steve Kaplan at steve.kaplan@vector.com, Tim Reeser at Tim.Reeser@engcc.com, Alan Wood at Alan.Wood@engcc.com, and Bobby Doss at bobby.doss@vector.com.

PART I

Overview of Enterprise Server-Based Computing

CHAPTER 1

Introducing Server-Based Computing and the On-Demand Enterprise

Nearly 50 million workers in more than 120,000 customer organizations around the world use Citrix enterprise access infrastructure solutions every day. Access infrastructure is a category of enterprise software that consolidates previously separate types of access technologies in the areas of device and network services, aggregation and personalization, security and identity management, and presentation and conferencing. At the heart of access infrastructure is the server-based computing (SBC) model, which is the term we will use throughout this book. SBC utilizing Microsoft Terminal Services and the Citrix MetaFrame Access Suite is reshaping corporate computing by driving costs out of IT while increasing the utility and value of applications through universal (and controlled) access. In a 2002 in-depth research project, Giga Information Group determined that the average risk-adjusted payback for the firms participating in the study occurred within 11 months of deploying SBC on an enterprise scale. And while the economic justification for SBC alone is compelling, many organizations are transitioning to this architecture primarily to take advantage of other strategic benefits such as improved security, enhanced disaster recovery/business continuance, faster time to market, increased productivity, universal information access, regulatory compliance facilitation, and faster organizational growth.

In the 1990s, Citrix created the server-based computing category with the product now called Citrix MetaFrame XP Presentation Server, and then dramatically expanded its scope in March, 2003 with the introduction of the Citrix MetaFrame Access Suite. This suite enables organizations to utilize server-based computing on an enterprise scale to provide a geographically unrestrained and consistent user experience along with instant access to enterprise applications, information, people, and processes. The result is a single, integrated and consistent access infrastructure for the On-Demand Enterprise. This chapter introduces the concept of enterprise SBC. We consider the many economic benefits of SBC and the major industry trends that are accelerating its acceptance. We'll look at the four main functions of SBC solutions: application deployment, remote office connectivity, business continuity, and workforce mobility. We also consider other SBC advantages such as the ability to help facilitate compliance with government regulations and become more environmentally friendly. We analyze the main components of an enterprise SBC deployment, and discuss the process of designing an enterprise SBC environment, which we will build upon in the chapters that follow.

ENTERPRISE SBC

Creating an on-demand enterprise built on access infrastructure and the SBC model enables IT departments to deliver software as a utility-like service. Benefits include ubiquitous access to the latest applications from any device across any connection. As with a regular utility, though, users are dependent upon a central source for delivering their service. If something happens to the network, users no longer can fall back to running applications locally. In this environment, building a robust, reliable, and scalable architecture is obviously essential. The data center(s) must operate similarly to mainframe shops, with stringent change control, controlled access, and well-defined policies and procedures such as rigorous offline testing of all new applications before their introduction into the production environment.

An SBC infrastructure has other similarities with the mainframe model of computing. For example, IT control of the desktop and application standards, reduced infrastructure costs, and much lower staffing requirements are attributes shared with the mainframe environment. Unlike the mainframe model, though, SBC users do not have to wait six months in an MIS queue in order to have IT produce a report for them. Instead, they can create it themselves in minutes by using Excel or any application to which IT gives them access.

SBC thus combines the best of both the mainframe and PC worlds. It incorporates the inexpensive desktop-computing cost structure of the mainframe model while allowing users the flexibility and versatility they are used to having with their PCs. The matrix in Figure 1-1 compares the cost and flexibility of SBC with both mainframe and PC-based computing.

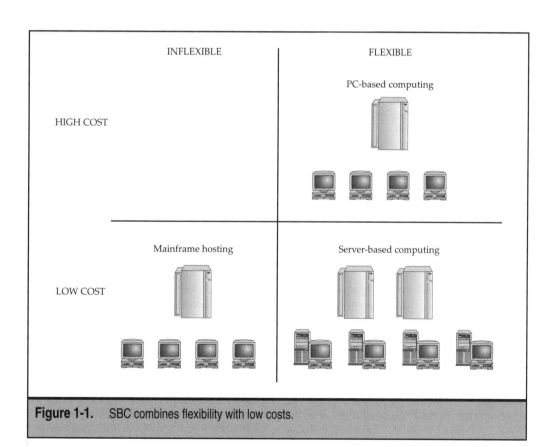

Figure 1-1.   SBC combines flexibility with low costs.

JUSTIFICATION FOR ENTERPRISE SBC

> *"MetaFrame grew from a remote access solution for a few employees to a key component of Lehman's enterprise infrastructure. By proving its scalability, performance, and flexibility under extraordinary circumstances, MetaFrame became an integral part of our IT strategy going forward."*
>
> —Hari Gopalkrishnan, Vice President E-Commerce Technology, Lehman Brothers

No company would transform itself into an "on-demand enterprise" because it's a cool phrase or a hot technology. There must be pain; that pain must be acute, and there must be a viable solution that can stop the pain. The pain many companies are feeling is the cost of IT complexity—80 percent of the typical IT budget today goes to just maintaining existing systems—combined with the inability of an increasingly remote and mobile workforce to access enterprise information where and when they need it. Migrating to server-based computing from a client-centric model simplifies complexity, consolidates hardware and software systems, cuts costs and increases access. This is the first step in becoming an on-demand enterprise where the IT staff is in control, information is available on demand, and the business can do much more with much less.

Economic Savings of SBC

Implementing an enterprise SBC environment is not inexpensive. In addition to the licenses, hardware, design, planning and implementation costs, SBC also requires a more robust data-center architecture than that of a distributed PC-based computing model. Nonetheless, an SBC environment is a much more economical alternative.

In an enterprise SBC architecture, the majority of resources are no longer expended on peripheral devices such as PCs and remote office servers and networks. Information processing, servers, and data are consolidated to central data center(s) where resources are much more effectively deployed. Wayne Patterson, chairman of Vector ESP, refers to this as achieving "economies of skills" because organizations can utilize a much smaller number of competent IT staff to manage their entire IT infrastructures.

Consolidating servers and storage to a central data center can significantly reduce expenditures on hardware and associated maintenance. Moreover, the process of centralization provides the architecture and economies to utilize more efficient types of storage such as network attached storage (NAS) or storage area network (SAN) devices. It also enables more efficient and economical implementation of software products such as AppSense and PowerFuse, which control what applications users are able to launch.

Personal Computers   Personal computers tend to have a maximum life span of only a few years for most organizations. Upgrading a PC is an expensive task that includes not only the cost of the machine and its operating system software, but also the expense of ordering, delivering, and configuring the PC. Data files often need transferring from the old unit to the new one, and the user suffers from downtime during the process. In an on-demand enterprise, personal computers typically no longer require upgrading since the applications are processed on central server farms. New users can often utilize inexpensive Windows terminals that are set up in minutes. Suppose, for example, that an organization normally replaces 2000 PCs every three years at a cost of $1100 each (including sales tax, procurement costs, installation, travel, and data transfer costs). By eliminating the refresh cycle requirement, SBC enables savings of $2.2M in capital expenditures every three years for such an organization. Chapter 7 and Appendix B both describe other costs associated with PC refresh cycles.

> *Our estimates had indicated expenses of over two million dollars to replace old hardware in Canada. By leveraging existing hardware with Citrix, we completed the whole project in Canada for only $400,000, saving the company more than $1.5 million.*
>
> —Louis Gilbert, Director of Data Center Operations, Air Liquide America

Homogenizing Clients   Citrix MetaFrame XP Presentation Server lets users run the latest Microsoft applications utilizing a wide variety of clients including Macs, most types of UNIX, Linux, many handheld devices, smart phones, DOS, all flavors of Windows, and even OS/2.

Fewer Laptops   Many organizations give employees laptops primarily to work between the office and their homes, or between remote offices. Because of higher up-front costs, higher failure rates, much higher maintenance costs, and lack of upgradeability, laptops cause a disproportionate amount of trouble and expense (relative to a desktop PC) to IT departments.

   In an on-demand enterprise, users see their personalized desktop and its applications no matter where they connect or which device they use. Thus, companies frequently avoid some of the expense of laptops by simply purchasing a Windows terminal for their employees to use at home. Employees can also access their applications through a browser from their own PC or from most Internet kiosks, further driving down the need for laptops. Only the truly disconnected worker needs a laptop, and with the new wireless WAN solutions offered by Sprint, Verizon, AT&T, and others, the disconnected worker will quickly become ancient history.

Administration

> *Thin continues to be in. A study by Gartner Group's Datapro unit has found that enterprises that have deployed networks based on thin clients...tend to extend those installations to other parts of the enterprise. "The staffing required to support fat client PCs is at least five times greater than for Windows terminals of PCs that are configured as Windows terminals," said Peter Lowber, the Datapro analyst who authored the report.*
>
> *—InternetWeek*, June 1, 1999

Since administration is the largest component of a PC's total cost of ownership, SBC saves organizations huge amounts of money by reducing IT staffing requirements. This comes primarily from the elimination of the requirement to push new applications to desktops. For example, Wayne Dodrill, Manager of Systems Integration for Concentra Health, a U.S. leader in occupational health care, noted that "Citrix access infrastructure solutions have helped us double our sites served, quadruple our applications deployed, triple our users, and reduce our help desk from 17 to seven—all while raking in an annual savings of over one million dollars in reduced hardware and bandwidth costs."

NOTE: ABM Industries is a Fortune 1000 company discussed later in this chapter that migrated entirely to a Citrix access infrastructure model. Prior to implementing SBC, the IT staff presented three alternative scenarios for migrating the company's 2500 Lotus Notes users around the country from R4 to R5:

> Scenario a) 24 months and $3.0M
> Scenario b) 18 months and $3.5M
> Scenario c) 9 months and $4.5M

After migrating company-wide to SBC, the actual time to upgrade to Notes R5 was only *18 hours with no added cost.*

Maintenance   The ability to eliminate user-caused problems such as loading misbehaving software applications or deleting icons results in greatly reduced PC maintenance expenses. When a PC breaks, it can often simply be replaced with an inexpensive Windows terminal.

Help Desk Support   The shadowing feature of MetaFrame XP Presentation Server typically enables fewer help desk staff to accomplish more through their ability to instantly and interactively "see" the user's screen. They can then provide remote support by taking control of the user's screen, mouse, and keyboard.

Help Desk Staffing   Password-related help desk calls account for nearly 25% of call volume on average, and businesses spend on average $200 per year per person on password management, including maintaining help desks that reset lost passwords. Citrix Password Manager eliminates the requirement for users to remember multiple passwords and therefore dramatically reduces the necessity for help desk intervention.

Help Desk Delays   Organizations often document the cost of providing help desk support. However, they seldom quantify the cost of lost productivity as users struggle to fix a problem themselves or wait for the help desk to handle it. Users too impatient or embarrassed to contact the help desk may waste other employees' time by requesting their assistance. SBC results in less user downtime by combining reduced hardware problems with easier and more effective access to help desk support.

Conferencing   Popular Web-based conferencing services commonly charge fees ranging between 25 to 50 cents per user per minute, which can easily run up expenses totaling thousands of dollars per month. Citrix Conferencing Manager enables real-time application sharing for both internal and external users, but at a one-time fixed fee. Therefore, the annual savings can be extraordinary, with a payback period often of only a month or two.

> *With session shadowing, we've been able to dramatically improve technical support for our users, and have improved response times to their requests by 90 percent.*
>
> —Patricia E. Plonchak, Senior VP and Director of Technology,
> Hudson Valley Bank

Employee Productivity   Work often stops when personal computers or applications are upgraded, repaired, or rebuilt. Incompatible software can require time-intensive repairs caused from DLL file and registry conflicts. Moreover, incompatible software versions sometimes require time-consuming data conversions to enable information-sharing among employees. On-demand enterprise users always have access to the latest application versions—standardized across the enterprise—from any device.

Training Costs   The resource-intensive logistics of a distributed PC architecture often limits an organization's ability to provide training on new applications or application upgrades, particularly to remote offices. MetaFrame XP Presentation Server's one-to-many shadowing feature enables remote training sessions for users throughout the enterprise. Users can shadow the instructor's machine while simultaneously participating in a conference call. This lowers the cost for training, meaning users can become more proficient and, thus, productive, reducing their requirement for application-based help-desk assistance.

Electricity   Windows terminals tend to use only about $1/7$th of the electricity of PCs. In states such as California with high electricity costs, the savings can run into tens or even hundreds of thousands of dollars annually for organizations with large quantities of PCs. Eliminating remote office servers can further reduce power requirements.

Eliminating the Need for Local Data Backup   Many organizations rely on users and on remote office administrators to do their own data backups, or they contract this function out to third-party services. SBC eliminates the time, risk, and expense associated with distributed data backups.

Remote Office Infrastructures

In a PC-based computing environment, even small remote offices often require not only domain controllers and file servers, but also e-mail servers, database servers, and possibly other application servers such as fax servers. An example of a PC-based computing environment in a remote office is shown in Figure 1-2. The remote offices also require associated peripheral software and hardware including network operating systems software, tape backups, tape backup software, antivirus software, network management software, and uninterruptible power supplies. Someone needs to administer and maintain these remote networks as well as ensure that data is consistently synchronized or replicated with data at headquarters.

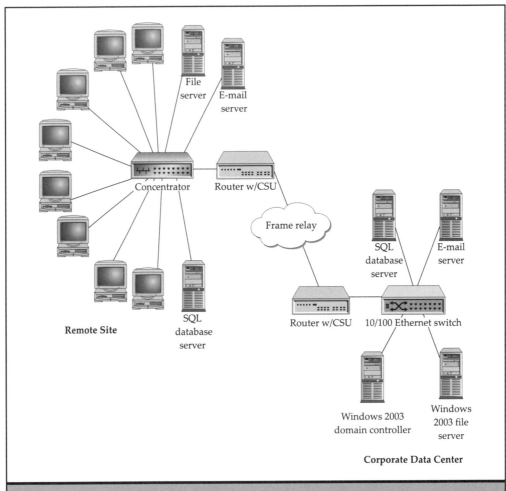

Figure 1-2. A typical remote office in a PC-based computing environment

In an on-demand enterprise, remote office servers and their peripherals can usually be eliminated entirely by running all users as clients to a central server farm. Both powerful and low-end PCs, Windows terminals, Macintoshes, and UNIX workstations can be cabled to a low-bandwidth hub and then connected with a router to the corporate data center through a leased line, frame relay cloud, or through the Internet utilizing the secure gateway component of MetaFrame XP Presentation Server or of a VPN product. Figure 1-3 shows a typical small remote office utilizing an on-demand enterprise with server-based computing.

Naturally, when the remote office servers and associated network infrastructures are eliminated, the corresponding support and maintenance costs are eliminated as well.

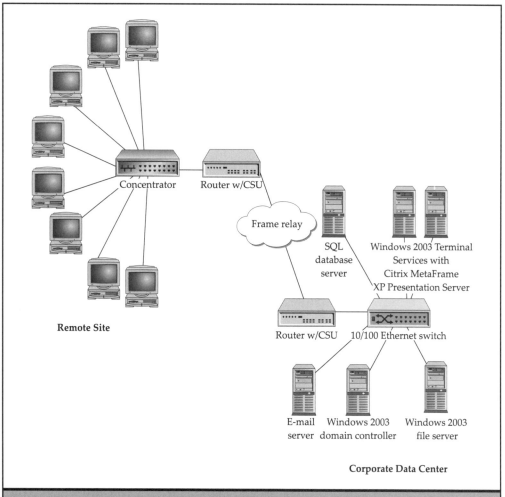

Figure 1-3.   A typical office utilizing enterprise server-based computing

Suppose, for example, an organization spends $17,000 every three years on upgrading each server in a remote office (including associated software, UPS, tape backup, travel time, network reconfiguration, and troubleshooting). These are fairly typical numbers. Suppose this company also spends $3000 per server per year in administration costs and $2000 per server per year in on-going maintenance. If there are 100 remote offices with an average of three servers per office, the company would then save $3,200,000 every three years just in remote office network expenses by migrating to SBC.

Remote Office Bandwidth It is not uncommon for an ERP package such as JD Edwards' One World to require 128KB of bandwidth or more per user, making it very expensive to connect remote office users in a PC-based computing environment. An on-demand enterprise utilizing Microsoft Terminal Services and MetaFrame XP Presentation Server requires only 10KB to 20KB of bandwidth per concurrent user. Rather than building a local area network (LAN) infrastructure at each remote office necessitating data replication with headquarters, the low bandwidth requirements enable remote office users to simply run all of their applications from the corporate data center. The secure gateway component of MetaFrame XP Presentation Server (similar to VPN solutions, though significantly lower in cost) enables employees to use the Internet as an even less-expensive bandwidth medium for enabling SBC.

Topologies

Fat-client PCs increasingly require faster LAN bandwidth of 100MB or even gigabit switching to every desktop. Users of PCs and Windows terminals operating in an SBC environment see only low-bandwidth screen prints. Although a fast server backbone is a must, legacy topologies of older 10MB Ethernet can typically continue to be used to connect client workstations with no degradation in performance.

Windows Server 2003 Migration

An on-demand enterprise simplifies Active Directory design and implementation by eliminating some, or all, of the requirement for remote office domain controllers. The MetaFrame Access Suite enables organizations to present the same Windows or browser interface to users as they would see when running Windows XP locally. Organizations can essentially upgrade all of their users to Windows XP without upgrading (and in some cases without even touching) a single desktop. Migrating to Windows Server 2003 within an SBC architecture is covered more thoroughly in Chapter 20.

Exchange 2003 Migration

Why would anyone ever deploy Exchange 2003 in any other manner than through SBC? Eliminating the requirement for remote office Exchange servers and the associated replication with headquarters slashes design, hardware, and implementation costs while enabling all workers across the enterprise to utilize a centralized Exchange server (or clustered servers) in the data center. This centralized deployment strategy lends itself to offering richer services to users such as Instant Messenger or Conferencing Server that are more challenging to deploy in a distributed fashion.

Network Management

Organizations often seek to simplify the complexity of distributing applications to desktops by utilizing management software programs. These packages, though, besides their tendency to be expensive, come with their own significant administrative headaches. They also typically lack the capability to distribute certain applications such as new operating systems. In the end, they remain dependent upon the memory and processing capabilities of the individual PCs as being sufficient to adequately run the new applications.

An on-demand enterprise requires no desktop distribution of hosted applications. The shift in emphasis from the desktop to the data center in turn simplifies asset management. It is also much easier to track true IT expenses because they are no longer hidden in various cost centers such as individual expense accounts and remote office contractor costs.

The administration tools of MetaFrame XP Presentation Server enable administrators to produce reports showing application usage by user, including the time online as well as server resources consumed. This information helps facilitate compliance with federal regulations such as HIPAA and Sarbanes-Oxley by providing an audit trail. It can also potentially reduce licensing fees for some software manufacturers. Network management is covered in Chapter 9.

Major Business Benefits of SBC

Beyond the economic savings provided by SBC, migrating to an on-demand enterprise enables a myriad of other benefits that enable organizations to conduct their business operations both more effectively and efficiently.

Application Deployment

The ability to rapidly deploy applications to all users on a wide variety of devices throughout the enterprise enables organizations to respond faster to their customers or bring new products to market more quickly.

> *Citrix MetaFrame XP Presentation Server and Microsoft Windows Terminal Services enabled us to reduce our transaction time for our primary advertising order entry application from minutes to seconds for our remote users. Furthermore, Citrix allowed us to quickly extend our headquarters' IT capabilities to our remote offices for a fraction of the cost required if we had chosen an alternative deployment method.*
>
> —Jonathan Hiller, CIO, *San Francisco Chronicle*

Today, we are seeing popular applications similarly driving the march into enterprise SBC. An organization's existing PCs, for example, may be inadequate to run a ubiquitous application such as Office 2003. Rather than spending the huge money and labor required to upgrade or replace existing PCs, an organization can implement MetaFrame XP Presentation Server and simply publish the Office 2003 icon to all users. If a transition is required, two different Office version icons can be published to users simultaneously.

Enterprise Resource Planning (ERP) and Customer Resource Management (CRM) applications, such as those offered by SAP, PeopleSoft, JD Edwards, and Siebel, are deployed much less expensively and more effectively in an on-demand enterprise. This was the case for California's Contra Costa County. When the Department of Information Technology received a mandate to implement PeopleSoft for the county's 360 human resources (HR) users, the county was faced with replacing many dumb terminals and upgrading most of the remaining PCs. They also would have had to undergo expensive bandwidth upgrades to 60 different buildings. The county instead set up a MetaFrame XP Presentation Server farm to deploy PeopleSoft, Kronos Time & Billing, Microsoft Office, Lotus Notes, and other applications to all HR users without requiring any PC or bandwidth upgrades. "My concern is lowering our cost of administration while providing a high level of performance and service to our customers," explained John Forberg, Deputy CIO of Contra Costa County. "Thanks to Citrix MetaFrame Presentation Server and Microsoft Terminal Server, we save about 180 hours of IT staff time each time we update our PeopleSoft application."

Universal Access   The web interface component of MetaFrame XP Presentation Server enables information, via both web and Windows applications, to be delivered through a browser-based interface. It gives users access to all of the information and applications that they need to execute their job responsibilities. This single point of access, and the bringing together of information in new ways, enables users to work smarter and faster, and make better, more informed decisions. MetaFrame XP Presentation Server enables users to enjoy the rich-client interfaces native to their applications delivered over the Web, and integrated with the other resources that they need. The web interface implementation is covered in Chapter 16.

Single Point Access to Multiple Server Farms   The web interface extension component of MetaFrame XP Presentation Server enables highly scalable application provisioning by aggregating application sets from multiple farms and multiple domains. Users need to authenticate with ID and password only once to access both MetaFrame XP Presentation Server for Windows and MetaFrame Presentation Server for UNIX applications from multiple server farms. This topic is covered more thoroughly in Chapter 16.

Collaboration   The delegated administration features of MetaFrame XP Presentation Server enable users, no matter where they are located, to work together on documents with different access rights depending upon their authorization. A sales manager, for example, might collaborate with a networking consultant and a salesperson to finish up a Word document late at night when all three are working from home.

Citrix MetaFrame Conferencing Manager is an enhanced collaboration tool that adds intuitive application conferencing to the MetaFrame XP Presentation Server. It enables teams to share application sessions, work together on document editing, and conduct online training regardless of the location of individual team members or the access devices or network connections they're using.

Embracing Corporate Standards   With SBC, control of the desktop shifts from the user to the IT staff, making it relatively effortless to implement corporate software standards. This reduces inefficiencies resulting from data-sharing problems and helps prevent duplication of work. It also enables IT to present a common user interface, whether Windows- or browser-based.

Unlicensed Software   The difficulty of preventing unlicensed software use in a PC-based computing environment can expose an organization to large fines because of the difficulty of preventing unlicensed software use. Citrix MetaFrame XP Presentation Server enables organizations to monitor application usage by employee.

Eliminating Games and Other Personal Programs   If desired, IT can completely eliminate the ability to load games or other productivity-sapping personal programs.

Reducing Virus Risk   Eliminating or restricting users' ability to add software via their local floppy or onto their local hard drive means that the network antivirus software should eliminate most computer virus problems. Centralizing all access into the network enables IT to implement products such as AppSense that can virtually eliminate the threat of macro viruses. This topic is discussed more thoroughly as part of Chapter 8 on security.

Helping to Prevent Theft of Intellectual Property   Since users see only screen prints of data, IT can more easily prevent employees from copying corporate information files. This can be important in staffing industries, for example, where applicant databases constitute the company assets and are frequent targets of theft by dishonest employees.

Eliminating the PC as a Status Symbol   Identical performance for everyone means that the PC loses its value as an organizational status symbol. The *personal* computer becomes the corporate computer. This eliminates the common, and very inefficient, tendency to shuffle PCs between users as new units are introduced. As a sense of entitlement to PCs is replaced by ubiquitous access to a personalized desktop, productivity replaces time-wasting bickering and PC redeployment.

Remote Office Connectivity

As a community bank, it is imperative for us to offer superb customer service at all locations. Citrix MetaFrame XP Presentation Server enables our employees at the branches to utilize our sophisticated systems at headquarters without the requirement for implementing an expensive wide area network infrastructure.

—Lee Wines, Executive Vice President, Bank of Walnut Creek

Employees in remote offices often feel like the company's "step children." They frequently do not get access to the same level of support and services as headquarters users, let alone access to essential databases or business applications such as ERP or CRM suites.

An on-demand enterprise gives remote office users the same capabilities that they have when sitting at headquarters. SBC makes remote office employees more effective because they can see "their" applications no matter which PC or Windows terminal they use and no matter where they use it. They have access to their applications and corporate information whether at home or at an Internet café on the other side of the world.

Users at remote offices are more productive because SBC enables them to access not only the corporate databases, but also the same network services—such as e-mail, color printing, and network faxing—as headquarters users.

Security   In a PC-based computing environment, corporate information is susceptible to loss or theft because it is stored on hard drives of individual PCs and servers distributed throughout the enterprise. In an SBC environment, all corporate information is housed in corporate data centers where it is secure, managed, backed up, and redundant. An enterprise SBC environment limits network entry points to the central data center(s). This eliminates the vulnerability that many organizations incur when they allow access to the corporate network through servers located in remote offices. Terminal Services 2003 includes built-in support for smart cards, enabling organizations to implement even greater security measures. Security is addressed more thoroughly in Chapter 8.

> **TIP:**   Here is an important question to ask when comparing SBC with PC-based computing: do you want your corporate data sitting on hard drives of individual PCs and servers distributed throughout your enterprise, or do you want it all to reside at your corporate data center where it is protected, backed up, redundant, and managed in a secure environment?

Messaging   SBC enables consolidation of e-mail servers in the data center, thereby eliminating the requirement for remote servers and replication. Data consolidation also makes it much easier to manage and access the data store.

Network Faxing   SBC vastly reduces the cost of implementing a network fax solution by enabling fax servers to be consolidated in the data center rather than be distributed at remote offices. Most fax server products such as industry leader Captaris RightFax are designed to run with Terminal Services and with Citrix MetaFrame XP Presentation Server. Employees can send faxes from their PCs and receive faxes directly into their e-mail program whether at headquarters, a remote office, or at home working through the Internet.

Facilitating Growth   SBC enables faster and smoother organizational growth by making it easy and efficient to open remote offices and assimilate offices of acquired companies into an organization's IT environment. Servers do not need to be configured and set up in the remote offices. Users only need low-bandwidth connectivity to the data center, and IT can then publish application icons to their desktops. ABM Industries, for example, acquired another company in early 2003. The IT staff had all users in five different offices online with ABM's systems in under a week.

Eliminating Theft of Fat-Client PCs   As organizations increasingly utilize Windows terminals instead of desktops and laptops, they remove the attraction for thieves to steal the devices since they are both inexpensive and useless without being attached to an SBC network.

Workforce Mobility

Citrix access infrastructure solutions extend access to a company's networked resources beyond the traditional office environment, allowing them to be accessed anywhere, over any connection, and on any device including wireless devices such as PDAs, smart phones, and tablet PCs. The low bandwidth requirements of Citrix MetaFrame XP Presentation Server often make wireless connectivity a practical part of an SBC environment without rewriting applications or implementing expensive infrastructure upgrades. In addition, Windows Server 2003 Terminal Services and MetaFrame XP Presentation Server fully support handwriting recognition. This should open up myriad opportunities for using wireless tablets while connected to the data center in several industries, including legal and medical.

Telecommuting   SBC users see only screen prints of applications, and the screen prints use very little bandwidth. Employees can effectively telecommute by dialing into the network or by coming in securely through the Internet utilizing the MetaFrame XP Presentation Server secure gateway component. A cable modem or DSL connection will often enable speeds equivalent to those obtained when using a fat-client PC at headquarters. Wireless WAN providers like Sprint, Verizon, Nextel, AT&T, and others provide, through the secure gateway, a secure, anytime, anywhere solution for traveling and remote users.

IT Flexibility

SBC gives IT departments flexibility in terms of adopting an application strategy without concern for developing a corresponding desktop deployment strategy. For instance, IT departments can purchase PCs or laptops without worrying about whether or not they will have the power and capacity to adequately operate a new set of unknown future applications. Even a seemingly simple task such as upgrading a company-wide browser version changes from a very time-consuming and expensive endeavor to a non-issue.

Business Continuity/Disaster Recovery

Only 6 percent of companies suffering from a catastrophic data loss survive . . . 43 percent never reopen, and the remaining 51 percent reopen only to close within two years.

—Disaster Recovery Journal, Fall, 2001

A PC-based computing environment has limited redundancy. A catastrophe at headquarters can leave hundreds or thousands of employees unable to do their work. Failure of a server in a remote office can mean a day or more of downtime until a replacement unit can be secured and installed. SBC makes it affordable to build redundancy into the corporate data center. Furthermore, Citrix MetaFrame XP Presentation Server includes server farm fail-over utilization of redundant data centers. If the primary data center fails, users can automatically be redirected to a secondary data center and continue working. If a disaster at headquarters or a remote office leads to displaced workers, they can securely access their applications and data remotely over the Internet from alternative locations—including their homes. This enables better continuity protection for all headquarters and remote office users than is practical in a PC-based computing environment. Disaster recovery and business continuance are covered in Chapter 19.

Environmental and Regulatory Compliance Benefits of SBC

In addition to the compelling economic and business justifications for SBC, there are also positive environmental and regulatory compliance benefits.

Supporting the Environment

Rapidly declining prices of new, more powerful PC models accelerate the rate of PC obsolescence. Over one hundred thousand tons of old PCs are junked each year, but dumping them in a landfill can cause lead, mercury, and cadmium to leach into the soil. Incinerating them can release heavy metals and dioxin into the atmosphere. SBC extends the life of PCs by often enabling continued usage until they physically break, and then replacing them with long-lasting Windows terminals.

Complying with Government Regulation

New regulations such as HIPAA, Sarbanes-Oxley, and California Senate Bill 1386 have important implications on how organizations conduct business. The information security aspects of these acts demand that organizations rethink their IT infrastructures, particularly whether they can afford the liability that is an inherent part of a distributed PC architecture. With an on-demand enterprise, all communication, documents, and workflows can both originate, and be stored on, central servers. Doing so ensures that corporate management always has copies of every stored document and is able to utilize software and hardware products to better protect and address the central information.

Industry Trends Accelerating Adoption of the On-Demand Enterprise

Three major industry trends are accelerating the adoption of SBC—and access infrastructure—as the foundation of the on-demand enterprise: Moore's Law, IT complexity, and IT consolidation.

Moore's Law

Moore's Law leads to a doubling of server performance roughly every 18 months without corresponding increases in cost. As more powerful Terminal Services/MetaFrame XP Presentation Servers support ever more users, the economics become even more favorable toward centralizing most organizational computing.

IT Complexity

The complexity of information systems is driving the cost of enterprise computing out of control, often offsetting the business benefits derived from information technology. Consequently, in spite of continuing and rapid advances in IT, it's more difficult than ever for IT organizations to provide consistent services to all the places and people necessary.

Each successive wave of computing—mainframe, minicomputer, PC, client-server, the Web, web services—has not superseded previous waves, but been piled on top of what came before. Moreover, the diversity and proliferation of access devices, computing platforms, software languages, networks, standards, and application infrastructures have further complicated the picture, making the cost of computing more variable and expensive than ever.

One of the most compelling attributes of the Citrix MetaFrame Access Suite is its ability to manage heterogeneity, enabling IT teams to centrally deploy, manage, and support secure access to Windows, web, and UNIX applications across the Internet, intranets, wide area networks, local area networks, and wireless networks. By centralizing access to applications and information, IT staffs can deliver, manage, monitor, and measure enterprise resources on demand. Citrix customers are able to run IT as a corporate computing utility, provisioning software as a service.

IT Consolidation

Organizations are coping with the technical, economic, and business challenges of increasingly complex information systems through consolidation. They are reducing the number of moving parts by centralizing and consolidating as much of the heterogeneity and complexity as possible to fewer data centers, servers, and networks. At the same time, they are trying to align IT with the business imperative of getting closer to customers by streamlining supply chains, simplifying business processes, and enabling expanded business models.

Their goal is simplicity. They are trying to migrate to a model that allows them to improve the level of service they provide to the business. To accomplish this, many are moving the complexity of computing to a central place where it can best be managed, controlled, and changed over time. This makes everything outside the data center simpler to manage and more cost-effective to operate. It also dramatically improves information security and resilience to technological and business interruptions.

> *McKinsey believes that companies can untangle most of their unwanted IT complexity by fo-*
> *cusing on five specific activities, which together will help them transform the way they use*
> *and manage IT, thus making IT organizations leaner and companies better prepared for the*
> *end of the downturn. These activities are to:*
>
> *Target the root causes of complexity.*
> *Instill a management culture in IT.*
> *Invest in consolidation.*
> *Reform the company's IT architecture.*
> *Plan for outsourcing.*
>
> — "Fighting Complexity in IT," *The McKinsey Quarterly*, March 4, 2003

The on-demand enterprise is the embodiment of this vision. An access infrastructure based on the SBC model provides simpler ways to give users a consistent experience and access to IT services—from anywhere, while lowering and stabilizing the cost of computing. Consolidating servers, storage, networks and IT staff is made possible by the capability of managing heterogeneity centrally. Users are shielded from the complexity of accessing heterogeneous systems, while still having a trusted connection that knows their identity and a user interface that dynamically adjusts to their specific devices, locations, and preferences. The quality of IT service levels is improved through end-to-end visibility of who, where, how, and when systems are used. It also enables enterprise organizations to deliver software as a utility-like service. We discuss how an IT department can create a utility-like internal subscription billing model in Appendix C.

Concerns and Myths About SBC

When considering implementing enterprise SBC, it is important to address concerns about network infrastructure reliability and single points of failure. We have also discussed SBC as if the only option were to utilize both Microsoft Terminal Services and Citrix MetaFrame XP Presentation Server software. We need to address concerns about using Microsoft Windows Terminal Services alone.

Network Unreliability

Enterprise SBC may be a new concept for your organization, but it is dependent upon your existing network infrastructure. It is senseless to take on an enterprise SBC project unless your organization is willing to make the necessary investment to bring your network infrastructure up to an extremely reliable and stable condition.

A history of network unreliability may have created user perceptions that they require their own departmental servers or must keep applications on their local hard drives to enable continued productivity in the event of network failure. In reality, users are becoming so dependent upon network applications, such as e-mail and browsing, that network failure means a loss of productivity in any case. Beyond this misperception, it is more prudent to spend a smaller amount of corporate resources building a redundant and reliable network than it is to devote a large amount of resources to maintaining an extremely inefficient PC-based contingency plan. SBC saves so much money on the client side that organizations should have the financial resources required to build world-class data centers and network infrastructures. Alternatively, they can utilize infrastructures already in place at established telecommunications or hosting companies. This option also generally makes it easier to utilize an existing data backbone to provide a secondary backup data center.

Single Point of Failure

Consolidating an organization's former PC-based computing environment into a central data center leaves remote offices, in particular, exposed to potential downtime risks they did not formerly face. A well-designed architecture utilizing the disaster recovery/business continuance capabilities of Citrix access infrastructure, as described earlier in this chapter, however, should significantly reduce cumulative organizational downtime.

Everything Is Becoming Web Based

Software manufacturers are increasingly writing Web-based interfaces to their applications. The reality, though, is that it is difficult to create a rich user interface in a web application. Even Microsoft's Outlook Web Access, for example, lacks the much richer interface of Microsoft Outlook. Most users prefer the dynamic and robust Windows interface to the static web-server HTML interface. Additionally, a browser requires a deceptively fat client in order to accommodate complex Java scripts and browser plug-ins. The browser, in fact, becomes an application that must itself be managed along with various plug-ins. This is complicated further by the use of embedded objects and client-side scripting as well as by applications that call other "helper applications" such as Microsoft Word, Excel, and Outlook. They may require specific versions of these helper applications in order to operate properly.

If the client-side browser is used to access business-critical information and applications, then security of the browser also becomes a concern. IT needs to develop methodologies for installing the numerous IE security updates and for locking down the browser and ActiveX controls.

When pressed as to why certain organizations would prefer Web-based applications, the reasoning is typically to lower total cost of ownership, to centralize application deployment, to simplify and enable cross-platform application access, to enable faster application deployment, and to lower maintenance at the desktop. But Terminal Services and Citrix MetaFrame XP Presentation Server provide all of those benefits today with legacy Windows applications, thereby avoiding the often underestimated expense and time involved in rewriting them for the Web.

Even when web applications are utilized, it still typically makes sense to deploy them from an administrative perspective, via MetaFrame XP Presentation Server where the browser is hosted on the server farms. Since a web application generally utilizes some combination of HTML/XML, client-side scripting, server-side scripting, and embedded controls to send data to the client device, deploying it via MetaFrame XP Presentation Server can help alleviate bandwidth concerns. A study by Citrix of a PeopleSoft 8 implementation showed that the average bandwidth consumption to the client desktop was reduced 57 percent by running the browser within a MetaFrame session rather than directly on the client workstation.

> *By deploying our Web-based physical therapy documentation application via Citrix MetaFrame, we were able to improve the performance of the application by reducing page refresh times from four seconds to less than one second. Prior to the use of MetaFrame, we were only able to roll out application updates two to three times per year. With MetaFrame, we are able to update applications nightly, if necessary.*
>
> —Wayne Dodrill, Manager of Systems Integration, Concentra Health Services

Citrix is committed to deploying all applications effectively through SBC. It makes more sense to implement SBC technology that will work for both Windows and web-based applications than it does to continue investing in a bloated PC-based architecture that is inefficient today and will be even more so in the future.

Microsoft Will Make Citrix Obsolete

> *As a key Microsoft partner and a trusted name in enterprise access, Citrix continues to deliver impressive product functionality that adds value to the Microsoft Windows Server Terminal Services environment, leverages the Microsoft .NET framework and allows customers to easily take advantage of their enterprise resources.*
>
> —Graham Clark, GM, .NET Platform Strategy & Partner Group, Microsoft

Microsoft is very supportive of Citrix and is a Premier Plus member of the Citrix Business Alliance. Indeed, Microsoft recognizes that Citrix drives a substantial amount of Microsoft software sales by freeing up organizational economic and staffing resources. This enables IT staffs to focus on the evaluation, selection and quality of implementation of applications rather than worrying about the delivery mechanics.

As with other Microsoft independent software vendors (ISVs), however, the challenge for Citrix is to continue adding value to Terminal Services. Thus far, the company has unquestionably succeeded. Microsoft views Terminal Services as an application delivery tool while the Citrix MetaFrame Access Suite is access infrastructure for the on-demand enterprise, enabling both managed heterogeneity and universal access. It is difficult, consequently, to imagine tackling an enterprise SBC initiative without the advantages the MetaFrame Access Suite provides in areas such as management, administration, presentation, disaster recovery, security, performance, user acceptance, conferencing, single sign-on, and IT consolidation simplification. The value that the MetaFrame Access Suite adds to Terminal Services is discussed more thoroughly in Chapter 3.

If, in the future, Microsoft or some other vendor makes MetaFrame Access Suite unnecessary, then only the software investment is lost. Although the cost of the MetaFrame software is not insignificant, it pales in comparison to the savings that companies are realizing by implementing SBC to create an on-demand enterprise. Such a solution is a serious and complex undertaking utilizing relatively new technology on constantly changing platforms. It is imperative that sacrifices not be made in the quality of the data center and networking infrastructure. This is also true for the MetaFrame Access Suite component. Delaying the decision to implement SBC in order to see what the future may bring means the continuation of large and unnecessary expenditures in the present.

COMPONENTS OF AN ENTERPRISE SBC ARCHITECTURE

An enterprise SBC architecture has three major components: one or more data centers, clients (at both the headquarters and remote offices, and possibly at home offices), and wide area network connectivity.

Data Center

The data center is the heart of enterprise SBC architecture. Not only are all SBC applications and corresponding data hosted in the data center, but 100 percent of the hosted application processing occurs within the data center as well. The major data center components include the MetaFrame XP Presentation Server server farm, file servers and/or network attached storage (NAS) or storage area network (SAN) systems, other application servers, host systems, a fast server backbone, and a backup system. Figure 1-4 shows a sample on-demand enterprise data center.

MetaFrame XP Presentation Server Farm

Application execution occurs on the servers running Microsoft 2003 Terminal Services and Citrix MetaFrame XP Presentation Server. Because of the high resource demands made on these servers as well as the challenges involved in configuring them to run multiple applications without DLL conflicts or other problems, it is prudent to utilize at least two load-balanced servers at all times. The MetaFrame XP Presentation Server load manager component is recommended over other solutions because of its ability to share server resources while providing good redundancy. If a user should be disconnected from the server, when she logs back in, the load manager will find the server in the farm where the user's session is running and reconnect her to it.

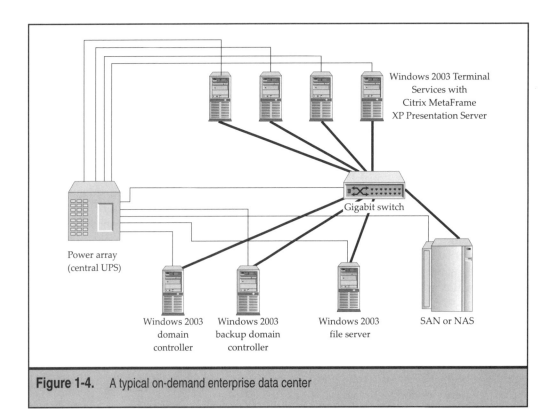

Figure 1-4. A typical on-demand enterprise data center

NOTE: Data is never stored on the MetaFrame XP Presentation Servers. Data is always stored on back-end file servers, application servers, NAS, or SAN systems.

File Servers

Typical file servers in an SBC environment run a network operating system such as Windows Server 2003 or Novell. The servers feed files to the MetaFrame XP Presentation Server farm, maintain directory services, store user profiles, and sometimes handle printing functions. For larger SBC implementations, a separate high-end print server should be dedicated to handle the printing function, as described in Chapter 18.

Storage Area Networks and Network Attached Storage Systems

In some SBC architectures, a storage area network (SAN) or network attached storage (NAS) will supplement the file servers, allowing organizations to store and access large amounts of data more efficiently. In others, the SAN or NAS may take the place of clustered back-end file servers and still provide mainframe-like reliability and redundancy along with superior performance and scalability. The best solution for your organization depends on both your application environment and user file-sharing needs. This topic is discussed more thoroughly in Chapter 5.

Application Servers

The rule of thumb is to have your MetaFrame XP Presentation Server server farm located wherever your data is stored. E-mail servers, SQL database servers, and all other application servers ideally should be located within the data center. At a minimum, they must be connected to the file servers and MetaFrame XP Presentation Server server farm through a fast backbone. The MetaFrame XP Presentation Server server farm hosts virtual Windows Server 2003 desktops (looking just like Windows XP desktops) for users throughout the organization (assuming they are not publishing the applications to a browser). While users see only screen prints of the applications at their workstations or Windows terminals, real data is traveling back and forth between the MetaFrame XP Presentation Server server farm and the file servers and application servers. An inadequate server backbone will cause an immediate data traffic jam that will result in performance degradation for all users. Application servers, including print servers, are covered more thoroughly in Chapters 5, 12, 19, and in Appendix A.

Host Systems

Mainframe and minicomputer systems should be housed in the data center where they can be managed along with the Terminal Services hosting infrastructure. This enables organizations to leverage both their data center environmental resources and their support staffs. MetaFrame Presentation Server for UNIX is covered in Chapter 12.

The Server Backbone

A fast backbone should connect the MetaFrame XP Presentation Server server farm, the back-end file servers, and all other servers in the data center. This backbone should be either switched 100MB Ethernet, FDDI, ATM, or switched gigabit Ethernet. As with all data-center components, a redundant server backbone is desirable. This topic is discussed more thoroughly in Chapter 6.

The Backup System

A backup system should enable automatic backups of all servers. Tapes should be rotated offsite. Remote electronic data backups by companies such as Evault and Iron Mountain can add still another layer of redundant data protection. This topic is discussed more thoroughly in Chapter 19.

Security

SBC enables enhanced security by centralizing data and network access. It is still essential to design and implement an enterprise security strategy. Citrix MetaFrame Secure Access Manager (another product in the MetaFrame Access Suite), third-party applications, firewalls, identity management, and authentication are some of the measures to consider. This topic is discussed more thoroughly in Chapter 8.

The Number of Data Centers

The number of data centers utilized depends upon many variables, including bandwidth availability and business and geographic segregation. For instance, if a corporation's European operations utilize entirely different software than U.S. divisions, and bandwidth is expensive between the continents, separate data centers make more sense than a single, central data center. In general, though, savings will be greater when data centers are consolidated. This is a result of the economies of scale realized by centralizing as much SBC hardware, software, and administration labor as possible. This topic is covered in Chapter 5.

Disaster Recovery/Business Continuity

A single data center, despite internal redundancy, leaves a corporation's headquarters and remote operations vulnerable to a single point of failure. One strategy for mitigating this risk is to utilize multiple data centers with fail-over capabilities. Another strategy is to use one corporate data center, and then contract with a disaster recovery provider to maintain a geographically distant facility that mirrors the MetaFrame XP Presentation Server server farm and other crucial components of the corporate data center. This topic is discussed more thoroughly in Chapter 19.

Clients

SBC users often work at headquarters, at remote offices, and at home. At times, they are in hotels or at customer sites. They utilize PCs, laptops, Windows terminals, tablets, and handheld devices. Increasingly, they use specialty display devices that incorporate the Citrix ICA protocol to take advantage of the inexpensive computing capabilities provided by SBC. Clients are covered in Chapter 7.

Personal Computers

PC users can access applications hosted at the data center in multiple ways. When PCs have a full-time connection to the data center (through Ethernet frame relay or the Internet), MetaFrame XP Presentation Server enables application publishing to either a Windows desktop or a browser. Employees see icons of both local applications (if any) and applications hosted on the MetaFrame XP Presentation Server server farm to which they have access. These icons can be part of their startup file, and it is not obvious whether they represent local applications or applications hosted by the server farm. Users who run all applications from the server farm may receive their entire desktop as a published application. The lower the number of local applications accessed by a PC user, the lower the administration costs. This topic is discussed more thoroughly in Chapters 4 and 15.

Laptops

Laptops typically run local applications when disconnected from the network. When connected to the network by a dial-up or wireless WAN connection, laptop users commonly launch a MetaFrame XP session. Extra training helps ensure laptop users do not confuse local applications with hosted applications. We have found that many employees of companies with SBC environments end up abandoning laptops except when on planes or in motels since they find it less cumbersome to use a PC or Windows terminal at both the office and home.

Windows Terminals

Nearly every major PC manufacturer, including IBM, Hewlett-Packard, and Dell, now makes Windows terminals. Many specialty companies, including Maxspeed, Neoware, and market leader, Wyse Technology, focus on building Windows terminals. Figure 1-5 shows one of the many models of Wyse Windows terminals. Windows terminals are typically display devices with no moving parts of any kind. They utilize a thinned-down version of Linux, Windows CE, or an embedded version of Windows XP. Windows terminals typically have built-in local-host emulation and, sometimes, browsing in order to offload these character display functions from the MetaFrame XP Presentation Server server farm. Some manufacturers, such as Wyse, also have wireless and tablet devices that enable users to access their complete desktop remotely.

Because Windows terminals often have mean times between failure measured in decades, their maintenance expense is extremely low. If a Windows terminal does fail, IT simply delivers a replacement unit to the user. The user plugs in the Windows terminal, turns it on, and sees his or her desktop. Unlike PCs, Windows terminals do not allow users to destroy their unit configuration by loading games, screensavers, or other potentially damaging software. This makes the Windows terminal an ideal device for telecommuters with families that like to share personal computers at home. It also significantly lowers the cost of supporting telecommuters. Windows terminals are discussed more thoroughly in Chapter 7.

Figure 1-5.   A Wyse WinTerm Windows terminal

Using a Browser Interface

As the Internet's pervasiveness continues to grow, more organizations prefer to utilize browser interfaces. With the web interface component of MetaFrame XP Presentation Server, organizations can use their browser to launch published applications from the server farm. The web interface component also enables an organization's customers and suppliers to launch authorized applications through a browser. Different users with different logins will see different applications. This topic is discussed more thoroughly in Chapter 16.

Wide Area Network Connectivity

MetaFrame XP Presentation Server requires between 10KB and 20KB of bandwidth per user session. This does not include additional bandwidth for large print jobs or for downloading or uploading files to and from a fat-client PC. When remote office applications are hosted at a corporate data center, they are completely dependent upon access to the MetaFrame XP Presentation Servers for all of their processing. An SBC architecture must include both adequate and reliable bandwidth connections along with redundant contingencies.

A frame relay circuit is the most popular connectivity method to multiple remote offices, though organizations increasingly utilize virtual private networks or straight Internet connectivity. Telecommuters, in particular, are using inexpensive fixed-fee Internet accounts to connect to corporate data centers. Bandwidth management is often desirable in order to prioritize ICA traffic. Bandwidth management devices from manufacturers such as Packeteer will prevent a user's large print job or file download, for example, from killing performance for the remaining users at a remote office. This topic is discussed more thoroughly in Chapters 6 and 17.

It sometimes makes more economic sense for regional headquarters and large remote offices to utilize their own MetaFrame XP Presentation Server server farms. This may also be true if the office uses software applications largely independent of, and different from, those employed at headquarters. Even in these scenarios, though, a common corporate database application, such as an ERP package, can still run off the MetaFrame XP Presentation Servers at the corporate data center. The regional offices can access this application by running the corporate ICA session within their own ICA session. This topic is discussed more thoroughly in Chapter 12.

DESIGNING AN ON-DEMAND ENTERPRISE ARCHITECTURE

A successful on-demand enterprise architecture depends upon a comprehensive project design. A detailed and in-depth plan needs to address all aspects of the migration to the SBC model, including data centers, disaster recovery, bandwidth, system management, policies and procedures, security, applications, migration strategies, clients, and support. Unanticipated problems will occur even with the best-laid plans. Diligent work up-front, though, will minimize the potential for problems and help ensure a successful implementation.

Windows 2003 Terminal Services is far more desirable and stable than a distributed PC-based computing environment, but PC users are often particularly unforgiving of SBC problems because they are initially reluctant to give up the "personal" part of their personal computers.

The considerable technical and cultural challenges make in-depth project and associated organizational change planning absolutely essential to a successful SBC implementation and on-demand enterprise architecture. The first step is to set up a proof-of-concept pilot to ensure that the crucial applications will run acceptably within an SBC environment. Next, assemble a project planning team to prepare a project definition document. The definition document should include the project goals, scope, roles, risks, success criteria, and milestones. The third step involves a comprehensive infrastructure assessment that both ensures support for an enterprise SBC implementation and enables a meaningful planning process. Finally, a comprehensive design plan for migrating from a PC-based environment to an SBC environment serves as a roadmap for the project managers and implementation teams. These steps are covered more thoroughly in Chapter 4.

ABM INDUSTRIES' ON-DEMAND ENTERPRISE IMPLEMENTATION

Deploying JD Edwards in our fat-client PC environment would have been prohibitively expensive. The tremendous cost advantages of Citrix enabled us to deploy all applications and networking services to our users around the country, even to those working in small offices or at customer facilities. We replaced our disparate and often overlapping regional IT processing with a unified corporate IT department and approach.

—Anthony Lackey, Vice President of MIS, Chief Technology Officer,
ABM Industries

According to Citrix, ABM Industries was the first Fortune 1000 company to deploy SBC for virtually all applications to every user throughout the enterprise. With annual revenues of over $2 billion and more than 62,000 employees, ABM provides outsourced facility services to thousands of customers in hundreds of cities across North America. In late 1998, management decided to implement the client-server version of JD Edwards' One World accounting system for all divisions. This would have required upgrading hundreds of PCs and many remote-office bandwidth connections. In addition, the company had nearly 1000 PCs that were non-Y2K compliant. Rather than continue the endless spiral of PC upgrades, Anthony Lackey, Director of Information Technology (he was promoted to Vice President of MIS as a result of the project success), built a strong case for embracing SBC throughout the enterprise.

ABM's rollout began only after months of in-depth design, planning, and pilot testing. They moved their data center from a San Francisco high-rise to a hosting facility that offered the advantages of high security and access to a much broader communications infrastructure. A redundant data-center hot site was set up in Scottsdale, Arizona, as part of a disaster recovery contract with SunGard, a business continuity firm.

Today, 50 top-end dual Dell servers running MetaFrame XP Presentation Server software in the data center support 2500 concurrent users at both the headquarters and at regional offices across the country. A Cisco gigabit backbone connects the MetaFrame Presentation Server server farm and other servers. All users store their personal and shared files on a network attached storage device, which includes more than a terabyte of information stored on its virtual Windows file server. Eighty percent of ABM's users work on Wyse WinTerms, while the rest use a mix of laptops and desktop computers running the Citrix MetaFrame XP Presentation ICA Client software. Figure 1-6 shows a schematic of the ABM access infrastructure architecture. At the time of this writing, ABM was preparing to pilot the new products of the MetaFrame Access Suite.

ABM Industries performed a detailed and conservative cost analysis that projected a minimum five-year savings of $19 million from switching their first 2500 users to SBC. The ABM Industries project will be referenced throughout the first half of this book as a case study showing the technical and cultural implications of transforming the distributed PC computing environment of a large organization into an on-demand enterprise.

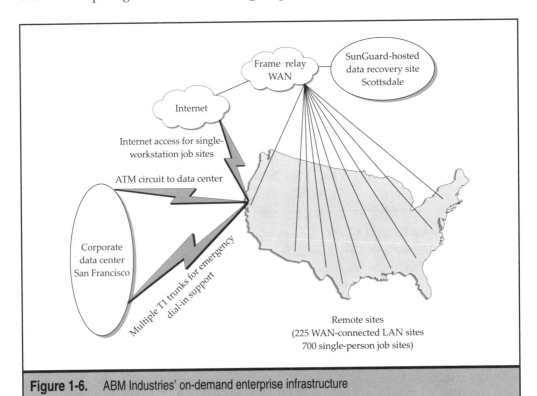

Figure 1-6.   ABM Industries' on-demand enterprise infrastructure

CHAPTER 2

Windows Terminal Services

Chapter 1 elaborated on how server-based computing (SBC) can solve a host of corporate IT problems and potentially save corporations significant money. Although Microsoft inherited the Terminal Services Code from Citrix, as described in Chapter 3, Microsoft has made a tremendous development commitment to the code since that time. Today, the Terminal Services component of Windows Server 2003 represents a very strong foundation for SBC. Giga Information Group, in their 2003 market overview, estimated that the SBC market would exceed $1.4 *billion* in 2003. Clearly, SBC would not be what it is today, nor hold the promising future parlayed in this book, without Microsoft's commitment to this platform.

When installing a Microsoft Windows Terminal Services solution into an enterprise, the methodology for administering and maintaining the system has more in common with a host-based or mainframe computing model than with a distributed PC model. In the traditional, centralized host architecture, dumb terminals provide a simple, character-based interface between the user and the host. Users can log on, run programs, read and write shared files, direct output to shared printers, and access shared databases. Furthermore, each dumb terminal session functions independently from other terminal sessions because the host operating system directs the communication between the host applications and the remote dumb terminal users.

The primary difference between Windows Terminal Services and a centralized mainframe or host architecture is the graphical nature of the Windows operating system. Host environments have traditionally been character oriented, requiring only a small amount of network traffic to travel over the communication lines between the host and the terminal. With Terminal Services, all of the graphical screen output and related input/output comprising mouse movements, keyboard commands, and screen updates must flow between the desktop client and the server.

In this chapter, we cover Windows 2000 and Windows 2003 Terminal Services. We discuss the many facets of the Remote Desktop Client (RDC) software and the Remote Desktop Protocol (RDP), including the differences between versions 5.0 and the new Remote Desktop Client for Windows 2003. We cover Terminal Services in the enterprise, including migration, domain considerations, and application considerations. Finally, we discuss licensing for Windows 2000 and Windows 2003 Terminal Services. Note that Terminal Services is the necessary basis for Windows-based SBC, whether or not Citrix MetaFrame XP is added to the solution. As we will discuss in Chapter 3, Citrix adds additional features and benefits to the Terminal Services included with Windows 2000 Server and Windows Server 2003 discussed in this chapter.

THE TERMINAL SERVICES FAMILY

Microsoft Windows 2000 and 2003 Terminal Services allow multiple users to log on to a Windows 2000 or Windows 2003 server, have their own desktop environment, and execute programs that stay resident. User logons effectively get their own protected memory space for applications and data. Users can have a Windows desktop and run Windows- based applications without the need to load the applications on their local PC. A server running Terminal Services can host hundreds of concurrent users (the specifics of server sizing will be covered in later chapters). In this chapter, we will use the generic term *Terminal Server* to refer to a server running Windows 2000 Server or Windows Server 2003 with Terminal Services enabled.

The client computing device used to communicate with the Terminal Server can be a PC or a specially designed terminal made to work with the Terminal Server display protocol. The PC or terminal runs a relatively small program that enables a logon and accepts redirected screen output from the Terminal Server. The Microsoft Terminal Services client program relies on a protocol originally developed for Microsoft's NetMeeting, called Remote Desktop Protocol (RDP). RDP is based on the International Telecommunications Union's (ITU) T.120 protocol. The T.120 protocol is a standard multichannel conferencing protocol that is tuned for enterprise environments and supports session encryption.

Terminal Services History—It Started with Windows NT 4.0 Server, Terminal Server Edition

Microsoft's Windows NT 4.0 Server, TSE, was the implementation of Citrix MultiWin (which will be discussed in Chapter 3) on the Windows NT 4.0 Server platform. Although Windows NT 4.0 is no longer officially supported by Microsoft or Citrix, it is worth discussing the beginnings of Terminal Services technology to further understand where it is today. For those still running Windows NT 4.0 TSE, we strongly recommend upgrading to Windows 2003 (see the upcoming "Windows 2003 Server" section for justification). If support for 16-bit applications is required, NT 4.0 Terminal Services Edition (TSE) is still necessary, as Windows 2000 and 2003 do not effectively support 16-bit applications.

Because of the MultiWin-inspired kernel of TSE, users could log on to virtual Windows NT 4.0 sessions with the same desktop and application look and feel of Windows NT 4.0 Workstation. With TSE, Microsoft created a separate code base for the operating system in order to overcome some of the memory management limitations of Windows NT 4.0 Server and to generally tune it for multiuser access.

Microsoft included their Terminal Server client, which is the client portion of the Remote Desktop Protocol, with TSE. This RDP client supported a variety of Windows desktops over TCP/IP networking, including Windows 95 and 98, Windows CE, Windows NT Workstation, Windows 2000, and Windows XP.

TSE Internals

In order to achieve the multiuser capabilities required in TSE, the Citrix MultiWin technology needed to be integrated into the Windows NT 4.0 Server kernel. This integration meant that several components, services, and drivers were added or modified in the original Windows NT 4.0 Server core operating system. Windows NT 4.0 components such as the Virtual Memory Manager (VMM) and Object Manager (OM) were modified to perform in a multiuser environment.

Virtual Memory Manager   The VMM in TSE mapped virtual addresses in the process's address space to physical pages in the computer's memory. In Windows NT, a process's address space was divided into two 2GB address ranges: *user* (process-specific addresses) and *kernel* (system-specific addresses). For the user address space, the VMM provided an individualized view of the physical memory to each process, ensuring that a call for system resources (a thread) within a process can access its own memory, but not the memory of other processes.

SessionSpace   The kernel address space in TSE was common for all processes within the system, thus providing a consistent means for accessing all kernel services. The fact that all processes in Windows NT 4.0 shared the kernel address space resulted in kernel resource limitations when supporting multiple interactive sessions on a single server. In TSE, these limitations were addressed by creating a special address range in the kernel, called *SessionSpace*, which could be mapped on a per-session basis. Each process was associated with a SessionSpace via a *SessionID*. When a remote user connected to Terminal Server, a new SessionID was generated, and all of the processes created for that connection inherited that SessionID and unique session space, as shown next. Other process groups, with a different SessionID, point to a separate set of memory-mapped objects and physical pages at the same virtual address.

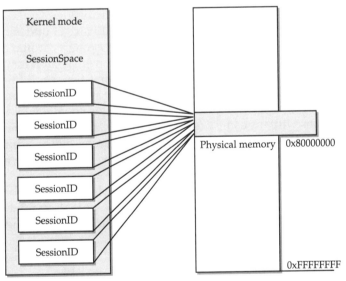

The Windows NT 4.0 Terminal Server made all objects required for multiuser capability virtual so that the applications and system programs from different user sessions do not collide. Every object name created within a session is appended with a unique identifier number associated with the individual user session (SessionID) that created it. For example, if a user started an application in the first session on the Terminal Server, the session would be seen as *session1* and the application seen as *application1*, as shown in Figure 2-1.

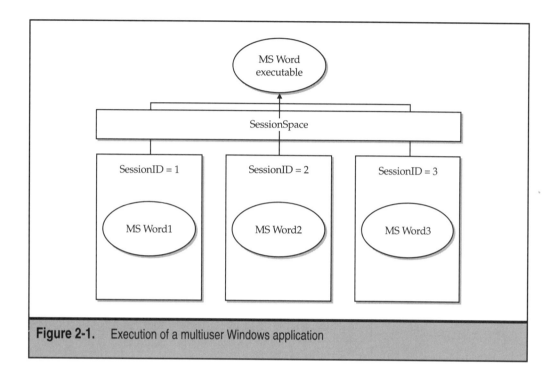

Figure 2-1.   Execution of a multiuser Windows application

The Remote Desktop Protocol was designed to support TCP/IP over LAN or WAN communication links. Due to the multisession nature of the protocol, a special user mode extension (RDPWSX), as depicted in Figure 2-2, is needed to receive all incoming client packets. RDPWSX manages sessions and calls WINLOGON to authenticate them. In addition, RDPWSX will validate the client license with the license server and negotiate client-server encryption keys.

Upon successfully establishing a session, the MultiWin subsystem gained control over session management. A virtual session was created by localizing a copy of WIN32K.SYS with all the necessary device drivers. The TERMDD (Terminal Server Device Driver) then provided the run-time environment of a session-specific protocol driver in order to service multiple client session requests. To support the mouse and keyboard commands sent to each session's copy of the WIN32K.SYS subsystem, the RDPWD (Remote Desktop Winstation Driver) was loaded.

The console session was always the first to load, and was assigned a special client connection ID of 0. The console session launched at system startup with the system-configured Windows NT display, mouse, and keyboard drivers loaded. The Terminal Server service contacted the Windows NT session manager (SMSS.EXE) and loaded the RDP user mode protocol extension RDPWSX to create two idle client sessions right after the creation of the console session. These two idle sessions listened on TCP service port 3389 for RDP protocol packets from the client.

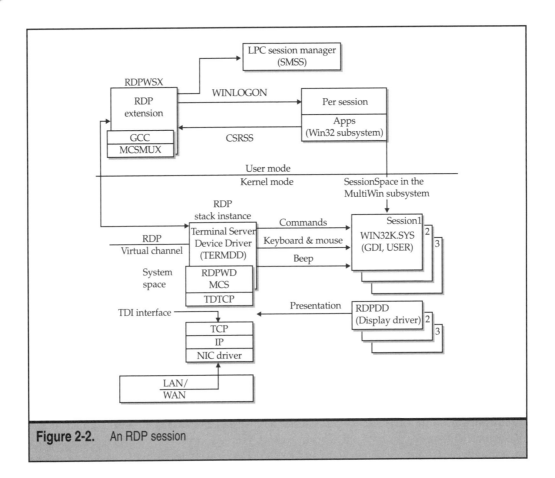

Figure 2-2. An RDP session

Code Sharing   Terminal Server also implemented memory *code sharing* (also known as Copy on-Write Page Protection). This feature allowed one copy of executable code, such as Microsoft Word, to be loaded into physical memory, and to have multiple users run the same copy of the program code. If a user loaded a private copy of a Word document, a separate memory space would be set aside and marked as read/write under the protection of Virtual Memory Manager. No other process could access this private memory space. This was extremely useful and efficient when a large number of users were using the same programs.

NOTE: Code sharing cannot be utilized in 16-bit applications, since they need to run inside a separate DOS VDM (Virtual Dos Machine). For this reason, approximately 20 percent more memory is used by 16-bit and DOS applications than by comparable 32-bit applications. In order to properly size the RAM requirement in TSE, a live functional test should be conducted to observe the total working set of memory consumed by a specific application, because many 32-bit applications contain 16-bit code.

Windows 2000 Terminal Services

In Windows 2000 Terminal Services, SessionSpace remains. The layout on the memory map has been modified to further tune the system and enable a common layout for all Windows 2000 systems, whether or not Terminal Services has been installed. The main modification is that SessionSpace has been reduced to 60MB and starts at the memory address location A0000000. Moving SessionSpace up to A0000000 allows all system drivers (win32k.sys), video drivers, and printer drivers to be loaded in a common virtual address location, whether they are accessed through a Terminal Services session or on a session without Terminal Services. Microsoft redesigned the memory mapping to eliminate the need for a separate version of the operating system to support Terminal Services, as was necessary with Windows NT 4.0 Server and TSE. Among other obvious advantages, service packs for Terminal Services no longer lag behind those for the base operating system as they did with TSE.

A new Windows 2000 service, appropriately called Terminal Services (termsrv.exe), is the controlling process in the Terminal Server architecture. It is primarily responsible for session management, initiation, and termination of user sessions and session event notification. The Terminal Server service is entirely protocol independent, so it can function using RDP or a third-party add-on protocol such as ICA from Citrix.

A user mode protocol extension provides assistance to the Terminal Server service. It is the responsibility of this component to provide protocol-specific functions and services, such as licensing, session shadowing, client font enumeration, and so forth. Each Terminal Server session protocol (for example, RDP and ICA) has its own protocol extension, providing a variety of services.

NOTE: For RDP, this user mode extension is called wsxtshar.dll.

Windows 2003 Server

Windows Server 2003 is now the flagship product for Terminal Services. Packaged with the release of Windows Server 2003 is a new client connection program. The new Terminal Services client, first released with Windows XP, is called Remote Desktop Connection (RDC) and provides substantial improvements over previous releases, including greater functionality through a simplified user interface. RDC can also be used to connect to a Windows XP Professional–based computer running Remote Desktop, and can be used to connect to previous versions of Terminal Services (Windows NT 4—Terminal Server Edition and Windows 2000 Server). RDC utilizes a new version of RDP and a new licensing model that provides for user and device licensing of Terminal Services and NT CAL's rather than just device licensing that had been required (see the "Licensing" section later in this chapter).

This licensing change represents a tremendous win for all Windows SBC environments, as it dramatically reduces the costs for environments where users have more than one device they connect from. For example, under the Windows 2000 licensing model, if a user connected to a Terminal Services server or farm from a laptop, desktop, and home computer, Microsoft required the user's organization to purchase three Windows Terminal Services client access licenses and three Windows 2000 Server client access licenses for this one user. Under the new per-user licensing, the organization will only need to purchase one license for that user.

Windows 2003 Editions Comparison

Windows Server 2003 comes in six releases and four named editions; Standard, Enterprise, Datacenter, and Web. The Web edition will run on small-footprint servers. As the name implies, this edition is for web servers only—systems running IIS 6.0 and web applications. This edition will make an excellent and cost-effective platform for web services such as MetaFrame Web Interface and MetaFrame Secure Access Manager, as discussed in Chapter 16.

The Standard edition is the general-purpose version intended for traditional Windows Server tasks such as file and print serving, security, and Terminal Services. This is the server upon which a Citrix MetaFrame XP installation is most likely to be based.

The Enterprise edition is a "hardened" version of the operating system. Microsoft has added a number of features to this edition to increase its value as an application server platform. We envision that this server will be used for three potential purposes: large Terminal Services Farms, clustering, transaction processing, or server consolidation.

Finally, the Datacenter edition is the "big iron" version of the operating system. It is designed for the most demanding application and availability requirements where hardware cost is not a concern. This version requires a minimum of eight CPUs in a system and can run on systems containing up to 32 CPUs. System administrators who covet the chance to work on a Windows "mainframe" will be running this.

As mentioned, there are actually six releases. The additional two are the 64-bit versions of the Enterprise and Datacenter editions designed for the Intel Itanium processor. Because of the emphasis by the Microsoft SQL Server team on 64-bit computing, these releases will be targeted at high-volume database or transaction processing applications, but not much else.

Table 2-1 compares the features of the four named editions.

REMOTE DESKTOP PROTOCOL (RDP)

In this part of the chapter, we describe in more detail how the Remote Desktop Client performs session management and other functions.

Feature	Standard Edition	Enterprise Edition	Datacenter Edition	Web Edition
Scalability				
64-bit support for Intel Itanium-based computers		+	+	
Hot add memory[1,2]		+	+	
Non-Uniform Memory Access (NUMA)[2]		+	+	
Datacenter program			+	
Maximum RAM Support				
2GB	+	+	+	+
4GB	+	+	+	
32GB		+	+	
64GB [3]		½	+	
512GB[4]			½	
Maximum Symmetric Multiprocessing Support (SMP)				
2-way	+	+	+	+
4-way	+	+	+	
8-way		+	+	
32-way			+	
64-way			+	
Directory Services				
Active Directory	+	+	+	½
Metadirectory Services (MMS) support		+	+	
Security Services				
Internet connection firewall	+	+		+
Public Key Infrastructure, certificate services, and smart cards	½	+	+	½
Terminal Services				
Remote Desktop for Administration	+	+	+	+
Terminal Server	+	+	+	

Table 2-1.   Windows 2003 Editions Comparison

Feature	Standard Edition	Enterprise Edition	Datacenter Edition	Web Edition
Terminal Server Session Directory		+	+	
Clustering Technologies				
Network load balancing	+	+	+	+
Cluster service		+	+	
Communications and Networking Services				
Virtual private network (VPN) support	+	+	+	½
Internet Authentication Service (IAS)	+	+	+	
Network bridge	+	+	+	
Internet Connection Sharing (ICS)	+	+		
IPv6	+	+	+	+
File and Print Services				
Distributed File System (Dfs)	+	+	+	+
Encrypting File System (EFS)	+	+	+	+
Shadow Copy Restore	+	+	+	+
Removable and remote storage	+	+	+	
Fax service	+	+	+	
Services for Macintosh	+	+	+	
Management Services				
IntelliMirror	+	+	+	½
Group policy results	+	+	+	½
Windows Management Instrumentation (WMI) command line	+	+	+	+
Remote OS installation	+	+	+	+
Remote Installation Services (RIS)	+	+	+	
Windows System Resource Manager (WSRM)		+	+	

Table 2-1.   Windows 2003 Editions Comparison *(continued)*

Feature	Standard Edition	Enterprise Edition	Datacenter Edition	Web Edition
.NET Application Services				
.NET Framework[1]	+	+	+	+
Internet Information Services (IIS) 6.0	+	+	+	+
ASP.NET[1]	+	+	+	+
Enterprise UDDI services	+	+	+	
Multimedia Services				
Windows Media Services	+	+	+	

Key: + = Feature included   ½ = Feature partially supported
[1] Not supported in 64-bit versions of Windows Server 2003.
[2] May be limited by lack of support by OEM hardware.
[3] Datacenter Edition's 32-bit version and Enterprise Editions 64-bit version both support up to 64 GB RAM.
[4] The 64-bit version of Datacenter Edition supports up to 512GB RAM.

Table 2-1.   Windows 2003 Editions Comparison *(continued)*

Session Connection

When a client initiates a session, the TCP/IP transport driver passes the request to the TERMDD program on the Terminal Server. TERMDD then passes the request to RDPWSX, which in turn signals the Terminal Server service to create a thread to handle the incoming session request. In addition, RDPWSX is responsible for initiating session negotiation with the client and capturing all necessary client information, such as compression, encryption level, client version number, and license details. As each client connection is accepted and assigned an idle SessionSpace, a new idle session is created. The session manager also executes the client-server run-time subsystem process (csrss.exe), and a new SessionID is assigned to that process. The CSRSS process then invokes the Windows Logon (winlogon.exe) and the graphic device interface (GDI) module (win32k.sys) to render the initial logon screen information and present it to the particular user SessionID, as shown in Figure 2-3.

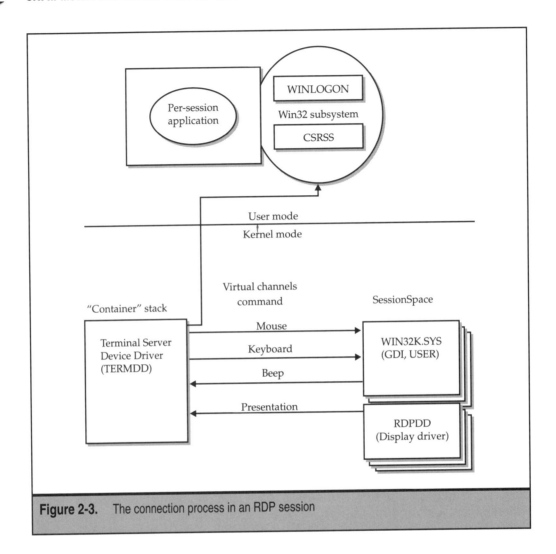

Figure 2-3. The connection process in an RDP session

NOTE: For use under heavy session logon activity, a registry setting can increase the two idle session numbers. The values are contained in the following key: HKEY_LOCAL_MACHINE\System\ CurrentControlSet\Control\Terminal Server\IdleWinstationCount\.

Network Load Balancing on Session Connections

RDC can utilize Network Load Balancing (NLB), available in Windows Server 2003 Standard, Enterprise, and Datacenter Server Editions, as well as Windows 2000 Advanced Server and Datacenter Server. NLB utilizes a round-robin approach for session connectivity to multiple Terminal Servers. NLB can detect downed servers, thus sending a client to one of the remaining live servers, and effectively eliminating a single point of failure if one server is down. Note though that this service is not the same as Citrix's load balance service, which utilizes server parameters rather than the network round robin that NLB utilizes. It is the opinion of the authors that NLB is not a sufficient tool for load balancing or effective redundancy in an enterprise server farm environment, but it may be sufficient for smaller environments (less than four servers in the farm).

Session Disconnection

When a user disconnects from an active session without logging off, the GDI stops taking commands from the user by stopping all drawing operations from reaching the display driver. A disconnected desktop object is created and represented in the Terminal Services Manager application (Start Menu | Administrative Tools | Terminal Services Manager), as shown in Figure 2-4.

During the disconnection timeout period, the RDP stack is unloaded, but TERMDD is still active because win32k.sys maintains an active handle to it for keyboard and mouse control. Before the timeout period expires, the user can be reconnected to the same session. The session disconnect process is shown in Figure 2-5.

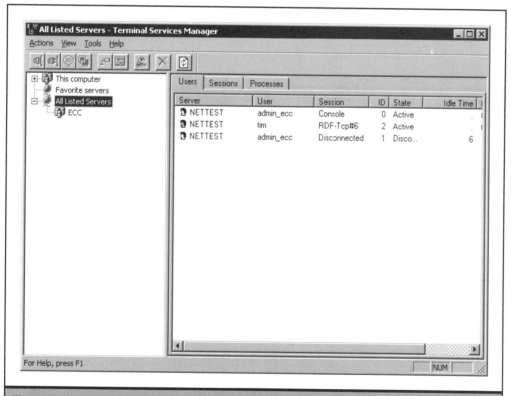

Figure 2-4.   The Terminal Services Manager application showing a disconnected session

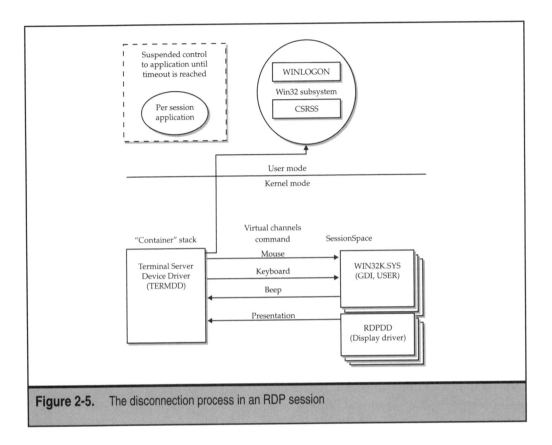

Figure 2-5.   The disconnection process in an RDP session

Session Reconnection

When a user initiates a connection to the same server, a brand-new connection is created. The RDP stack is loaded, and SessionSpace is assigned. The user is presented with a logon screen. Thus far, the process is identical to a new session connection. However, when WINLOGON scans the user ID and determines that the user has a disconnected session, TERMDD is instructed to perform a session reconnection. The user session is then switched back to the disconnected session.

Data Transmission

RDP packets are formed in the presentation layer of the Open System Interconnect (OSI) model. The packets are encrypted and frames packaged according to the requirements of the network protocol. Currently, only TCP/IP is supported by RDP. The RDP data content may include keyboard input and mouse movement coordinates, as well as graphical bitmaps and printer redirection output. The return RDP packet goes in reverse through the same protocol stack, is decrypted, and unwrapped, and the TCP/IP header information is stripped for the specific client session. Some of the data transmission optimization features of RDP include the following:

▼ **Intelligent encoding**   The redrawing of graphical images can be encoded to tell the client to redraw changes only since the last refresh took place. In other words, only the changes are sent.

■ **Glyph and bitmap caching**   A glyph is a graphical representation of a character. The RDP client automatically reserves a minimum of 1.5MB of memory space to cache the required set of glyphs needed in the display of common text. Bitmaps of different sizes are also cached in memory. Whenever a command is issued from the Terminal Server, the client can redraw the required text and bitmaps very quickly by extracting the elements from cache.

▲ **Bulk compression**   A client-side option optimizing a low-speed connection will turn on bulk compression, which can reduce the packet count by 50 percent.

Image Display

RDP uses a highly efficient encoding algorithm to encapsulate screen data, similar to the X-Window protocol. Most common or repetitive drawings are sent as a command rather than an actual bitmap. This method greatly reduces the amount of data required to paint a new screen or refresh an old one. Microsoft has published the exact bandwidth requirements to paint a common Windows screen, but lab tests from Mainstream Networks show that RDP 4.0 used up to 40 Kbps on a dial-up connection (with compression). There is a significant improvement in bandwidth utilization on the Windows 2000 version of RDP—version 5.0. These improvements continue with the Remote Desktop Client released with Windows 2003.

RDP updates the screen as follows. A user starts an application, which informs the GDI where and how to draw the application window. The GDI relays the command to the RDP display driver (RDPDD) by way of standard Win32 API calls. This is the same process used in a Windows NT system without Terminal Services, and is similar to the way a print job is rendered. The main API calls sent to RDP include the following:

▼ **TextOut( )**   This call results in the display of text information on a client screen. GDI informs RDP of the location and the glyphs (a graphical representation of a character). RDP tells the client which glyph to cache and which cache entry to use next time the same text is called for.

■ **PatBlt( )**   Pattern Block Transfer is used by RDP to tell the client how to draw a block of color. This translates into a small command and is the alternative to sending a block of bitmaps and consuming a large amount of bandwidth.

▲ **LineTo( )**   This command allows RDP to tell the client the beginning and ending coordinates of a 3-D beveling line. The line can be used to form boxes. This command can be as small as 6 bytes to complete a line drawing.

Windows 2000 Graphical Enhancements

RDP version 5.0 not only improved the protocol communication efficiency, it also expanded its feature set and offers some of the benefits contained in the ICA protocol.

▼   **Remote control**   This feature allows an administrator or authorized person to take over the screen, keyboard, and mouse movement of any user session running to the same physical machine.

■   **Clipboard redirection**   The RDP version 5.0 protocol synchronizes the server-side application clipboard to the client-side clipboard buffer. This allows applications running on the Terminal Server to cut and paste data to applications running on the client workstation.

■   **Client printer autocreation**   Local client COM and LPT ports can be remapped automatically from the server. The local default printer will be created in the Terminal Server session, and print jobs produced by applications running in a server session will be printed on the client's local default printer.

▲   **Bitmap cache**   Windows 2000 RDP provides additional persistent bitmap cache over version 4.0, which only used RAM cache. Upon successful bitmap transmission, the server instructs the client where to store persistent cache information. When the same data is needed again, only the location coordinate for this bit is sent to the client. This improvement is especially important in low-speed dial-up or wireless WAN connections.

Windows 2000 Terminal Services Client Architecture

Windows 2000 with RDP 5.0

With the introduction of Windows 2000, Microsoft significantly improved the capabilities of the core operation system to have Terminal Services integrated with all server platforms. Enhancements were also made to the RDP client allowing for better performance and additional features. The major advantages to this integration were the availability of standard services packs for Windows and Terminal Services and the requirement for software vendors to address compatibility with the multiuser environment. Between the releases of Windows 2000 Server and Windows Server 2003, Microsoft released Terminal Services Advanced Client (TSAC) which superceded the RDP client that shipped with Windows 2000. The TSAC, is based on the RDP 5.0 feature set, but comes in the form of an ActiveX control. The performance of the TSAC is comparable to the previous client, but offers far more flexibility in its deployment. It can be downloaded and executed within Microsoft Internet Explorer, or any application that can make use of ActiveX controls, such as those written in the Visual Basic or Visual C++ development systems. In addition to the downloadable ActiveX control, it is also available in the form of an MSI (Windows Installer) package, which looks and feels to the end user like the traditional RDP 5.0 client. Finally, the client is also available as an MMC snap-in, for administrators to use to assist with server administration.

Windows 2003 and RDC

Microsoft continues to improve functionality with the release of Windows Server 2003. The additional features of Windows Server 2003 allow integrated detailed control of security in a Terminal Services environment that previously were left to the creativity of the administrator and third-party applications. Remote Desktop Client (RDC) provides for better performance with streaming video, security, and client resource availability, and is now ported to the Mac OS X platform.

RDC using RDP now supports the following four operating system platforms:

▼ The Win32 platform, which includes Windows XP, Windows 2000, Windows NT, Windows 95, 98, and Windows Millennium (available for download at http://www.microsoft.com/windowsxp/remotedesktop/)

■ The Win16 platform, which includes Windows and Windows for Workgroups 3.11

■ The WinCE platform, which includes many new thin-client devices with WinCE running as the embedded operating system

▲ A Macintosh Remote Desktop Client (RDC) for MAC OS X (available for download at http://www.microsoft.com/mac/download/misc/rdc.asp)

Microsoft's design goals for RDC are to minimize bandwidth utilization, minimize memory usage, and speed up screen transmission. RDC represents a striking improvement over both RDP version 4.0 and RDP version 5.0 in both speed and features.

Table 2-2 shows a comparison of some of the major features of RDP and RDC.

Feature	Description	RDP 5.0	RDC for Windows 2003 and Windows XP
Clients	32-bit clients for Windows 95, 98, NT, 2000 and 2003	Yes	Yes
	16-bit client for Windows 3.11	Yes	Yes
	Windows CE–based clients	Yes	Yes
	Browser client	With TSAC	With TSAC
Transport protocol	TCP/IP	Yes	Yes

Table 2-2.   RDP Version 5.0 vs. RDC

Feature	Description	RDP 5.0	RDC for Windows 2003 and Windows XP
Audio	System beeps	Yes	Yes
Print stream compression	Compression of print jobs executed in a Terminal Services session	No	Yes
Terminal Services: slow link performance optimizations	Improved performance of high latency and slow throughput connections	No	Yes
Local printer redirection	Print to client-attached printer	Yes	Yes
Local drive mapping	Local client drive access from session	Yes	Yes
Cut and paste	Cut and paste between server session and client session	Yes	Yes
Remote control	Remote viewing and control of a session	Yes	Yes
Bitmap caching	Bitmap caching in memory	Yes	Yes
	Bitmap caching to disk	Yes	Yes
Time zone redirection	Remote client clock shows correct time, regardless of whether client is in different time zone from Terminal Server	No	Yes
Macintosh client	Client for Mac OS X	No	Yes
Preconfigured client	Predefined client with IP address, server name, and connection information	Yes	Yes

Table 2-2. RDP Version 5.0 vs. RDC *(continued)*

RDP Client Software Architecture

The RDP client software is installed on the server under the directory %systemroot%\
system32\clients\tsclient. The client disk creator program under Start | program | Ad-

ministrative tools ⏐ Terminal Server Client Creator will make the necessary disk set for distribution to client PCs.

When the Terminal Server client starts, the user interface calls the core API to set up a session with a server name or IP address. The default TCP/IP port is set to 3389. The security layer in turn calls the network layer to set up a socket with the goal of establishing a connection to the server. Once the TCP/IP connection is set up, the security layer starts to negotiate an encryption level with the server. Then the core protocol will negotiate bitmap cache, printer, and COM port redirection. Upon successful negotiation, an active session is launched, and the user is presented with the Windows logon screen. It is important to note that if the traffic is passing through a firewall, port 3389 must be open outbound from the client and inbound to the server.

Client Caching   Client cache is negotiated during session setup. By default, 1.5MB of RAM is set aside for bitmap caching. In addition, the RDC sets up persistent caching to improve communication speed over slow links. When a bitmap is to be sent to the client, the RDP device driver (RDPDD) compresses the bitmap image, then sends the bitmap across the network. RDPDD also instructs the client regarding which cache cell to store the bitmap in. When the client requests the same bitmap again, the server simply sends the cache cell reference number to the client.

The RDP client employs yet another technique to make use of screen cache in a remote control session. Windows drop-down menus make up much of the display. Most frequently used menus are cached in RAM when activated for the first time. Additional clicking on the same menu display will retrieve the screen cache from RAM rather then retrieving it over the network.

Remote Desktop Client Encryption   RDC supports three levels of encryption: low, medium, and high. Low-level encryption uses a 40-bit algorithm on client data being sent to the server. Medium-level encryption uses a 56-bit algorithm to encrypt data flow in both directions. Finally, high-level encryption uses a 128-bit RC4 two-way algorithm on both client and server. Terminal Services configuration on the server determines the lowest level of encryption allowed. For example, if the server enforces high-level 128-bit encryption, then only a 128-bit encryption client can connect to the server. However, if the server only requires 40-bit encryption, then 128-bit, 56-bit and 40-bit clients are all able to connect.

Remote Desktop Client Remote Control   Microsoft introduced remote control first in RDP version 5.0 with Windows 2000, and has continued to enhance it with RDC and Windows

Server 2003. Remote control allows administrators to view and take control of another user's session running on the same server. By setting special permissions in the Terminal Services Configuration/Connections (TSCC), help desk personnel can use the remote control feature to assist users by taking over their screen. To use the Terminal Services Manager (Start Menu | Administrative Tools | Terminal Services Manager), highlight the desired user, and click the Remote Control option. The screen resolution and color depth of the shadowing session needs to be equal to, or higher than, the shadowed session.

> **TIP:** Remote control in Windows Server 2003, unlike in Windows 2000, can now take over the server console session.

In a shadowed session connection, TERMDD establishes a *shadow pipe* in which RDP packets are sent to both the shadowing and the shadowed sessions, as shown in Figure 2-6. In this way, input is accepted from both sessions, and results are returned to both sessions.

> **NOTE:** If an administrator wants to remotely control a session from the server console, an RDP virtual session must be launched first, using the Terminal Services server as the "client." From inside the virtual client session, the administrator can then take remote control of a session.

Remote Desktop Client Session Administration The Terminal Services Configuration/Connections (TSCC) program can be used to control inactivity timeouts (when no activity is seen from the keyboard or mouse for a set amount of time). The same interface can also automatically reset a disconnected session when the disconnect timeout value expires. By default, these two values are not set. This means no timeout will be triggered when a user leaves the client session unattended or the session is otherwise disconnected. For security reasons, and to conserve server resources, we strongly recommend that a reasonable value be set for both of these parameters, as shown in Figure 2-7. A new feature with the Remote Desktop Client is session directory, which, when used in conjunction with the Network Load Balancing on a Terminal Server farm, allows users to reconnect to the specific disconnected session they've left within a farm, rather than just being directed to the next available server when they reconnect.

> **NOTE:** The systemwide session control in Figure 2-7 has the Active session timeout set for Never, the disconnection timeout set for 30 minutes, and the idle timeout set for two hours. These settings should be sufficient for most disconnect situations. Any adjustments of these values should be made according to company policy and user behavior. Generally, we do not recommend setting an active session timeout, as this will disconnect users who may be working.

For the settings in Figure 2-7, if a session detects no keyboard or mouse input for two hours, the session is disconnected. In this case, a user needs to log on to the system again

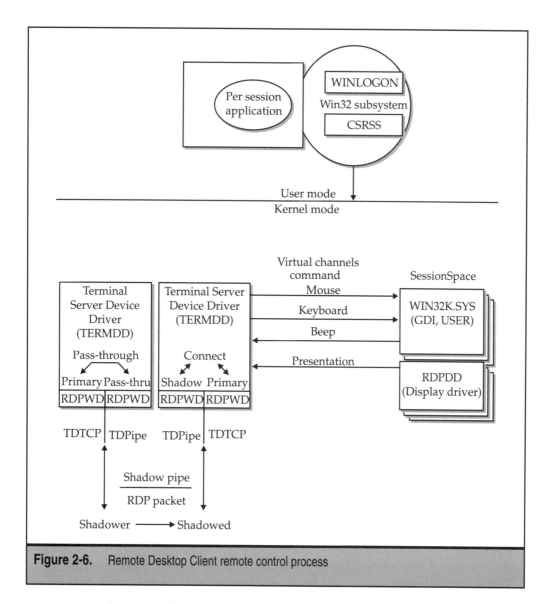

Figure 2-6. Remote Desktop Client remote control process

to connect to the suspended session, and no data loss is likely. If a user fails to log on within 30 minutes after the two-hour inactivity timeout however, the system will reset the disconnected session, and any data not saved will be lost.

New Features for Terminal Services in Windows Server 2003

The Terminal Services component of Microsoft Windows Server 2003 builds on the solid foundation provided by the application server mode in Windows 2000 Terminal Services, and includes the new client and protocol capabilities of Windows XP.

Table 2-3 lists the new features and benefits provided by Windows Server 2003.

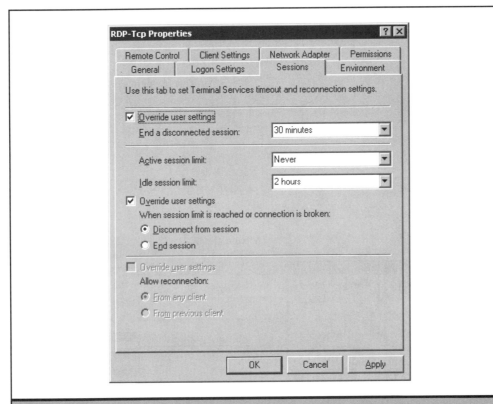

Figure 2-7. Setting timeout values for RDP sessions

Terminal Services licensing model and management improvements	Support has been added for the new user-based license model (device-based licensing and a hybrid approach utilizing both user- and device-based licensing are also supported). Additionally, improvements have been made to the Terminal Services License Manager Wizard, including a new Internet connection method for activating licenses, new error messages, and a new method for handling reactivation of upgraded Windows 2000 license Terminal Services.

Table 2-3. Windows Server 2003 New Features and Benefits

Printers	All printers installed on the client are visible to the server—including network printers. With Windows 2000 Terminal Services, only locally connected printers were redirected. Redirected printers are given names that are easier to read. For example, users might see "printername on printserver (from clientname) in session 9"; whereas in Windows 2000, they would have seen "_printserver_printername/clientname/Session 9." Printer redirection also works when connecting to Windows 2000–based servers. Printer driver mapping has been enhanced to provide better matching in near-miss cases. When a driver match cannot be made, the Trusted Driver Path lets you specify other standard printer drivers that you sanction on your Terminal Servers. The print stream is compressed for better slow-link performance between a server and client.
Client error messages	More than 40 new client error messages make it easier to diagnose client connection problems.
Security enhancements	The Terminal Server access model now conforms better to Windows server management paradigms.
Software restriction policies	Software restriction policies in Windows Server 2003 enable administrators to use group policies to simplify locking down Terminal Servers (and any other Windows Server 2003–based computer) by only allowing certain programs to be run by specified users. This built-in Windows feature replaces the AppSec (Application Security) tool used in previous versions of Terminal Services.
Session directory	Terminal servers can be organized into "farms." This configuration allows clusters of load-balanced computers to appear to their users as a fault-tolerant service. The new Session Directory feature in Terminal Services allows users to reconnect to the specific disconnected session they've left within a farm, rather than just being directed to the next available server when they reconnect. Session Directory can use the Windows Network Load Balancing Service, or a third-party load balancer, and the service can run on any Windows Server 2003–based computer. However, members of the Terminal Server farm must be running Windows Server 2003, Enterprise Edition.

Table 2-3.   Windows Server 2003 New Features and Benefits *(continued)*

FIPS compliance	An additional encryption level, labeled "FIPS Compliant," has been added to Terminal Server in Windows Server 2003. This level of security encrypts data sent from the client to the server, and from the server to the client, with the Federal Information Processing Standard (FIPS) encryption algorithms using Microsoft cryptographic modules. This new level of encryption is designed to provide compliance for organizations that require systems to be compliant with FIPS 140-1 (1994) and FIPS 140-2 (2001) standards for Security Requirements for Cryptographic Modules.
128-bit encryption	By default, connections to Terminal Servers are secured by 128-bit, bi-directional RC4 encryption—when used with a client that supports 128-bit. (RDC is 128-bit by default.) It is possible to connect with older clients using encryption lower than 128-bit, unless it is specified that only high-encryption clients are allowed.
Single session policy	Configuring the single session policy lets an administrator limit users to a single session, regardless of whether it is active or not—even across a farm of servers.
Terminal Services Manager	An improved Terminal Services Manager allows for easier management of larger arrays of servers, by reducing automatic server enumeration. This gives direct access to arbitrary servers by name, and provides for a list of favorite servers.
Slow link performance optimizations	Terminal Services optimized slow-link performance allows terminal client users to specify, via their user interface, the type of connection that exists between the client computer and the server. Based on this selection, Terminal Server dynamically adjusts desktop features to deliver the best possible user experience over the chosen network connection speed. This improves the remote desktop user experience over a variety of network connection speeds. The four options for network connection speeds are modem (56 Kbps, 28.8 Kbps), broadband (128 Kbps to 1.5 Mbps), LAN (10 Mbps or higher), and custom. The custom setting allows users maximum flexibility over what desktop features are disabled. These optimizations apply only when the user is connected remotely at sub-LAN connection speeds. At all other times, the computer has the full-featured desktop functionality. Clients running the following operating systems may utilize this feature: Windows XP, Windows 2000, Windows 95, Windows 98, Windows Me, and Windows CE.

Table 2-3. Windows Server 2003 New Features and Benefits *(continued)*

Time zone redirection	This feature allows a remote desktop session's time zone to be specified by the client computer's time zone. For example, an IT administrator who has deployed Terminal Services for a particular group of users located in several locations around the world can use Group Policy and Windows Management Instrumentation (WMI) on the server to turn on time zone redirection. This allows end users of Terminal Services to utilize their computer's local time zone rather than the time zone of the Terminal Services server. Clients currently capable of time zone redirection include Windows XP and Windows CE (Version 5.1).
Smart card sign-on	A smart card that contains Windows logon credentials can provide those credentials to a Windows Server 2003 remote session for logon. This feature requires a client OS that can recognize the smart card first: Windows 2000, Windows XP, and Windows CE .NET.
Ports	Client serial ports can be mounted to the server. This enables a variety of hardware on the client computer to be accessed by software on the server.
File system	Client drives, including network drives, are mounted inside the server session. This lets users open or save files on their own computers' disk drives, in addition to opening and saving files on the server.
Integration with Active Directory Services Interface	This feature provides the ability to script Terminal Services user configuration settings using the Active Directory Services Interface (ADSI). For instance, an IT administrator who upgrades a domain from Windows NT 4.0 to Windows Server 2003 can use ADSI to script the creation of user accounts within Active Directory and copy all user properties, including Terminal Services user configuration information.

Table 2-3. Windows Server 2003 New Features and Benefits *(continued)*

TERMINAL SERVICES IN THE ENTERPRISE

In this part of the chapter, we discuss some issues that will likely be encountered when adding Terminal Services to an enterprise organization.

Domain Considerations

The standard principles for installing a Terminal Server apply equally to Windows 2000 and Windows 2003 Terminal Services. If Active Directory is installed on the network, simply join the Active Directory domain. There is no longer a primary domain controller

(PDC) or backup domain controller (BDC) in Active Directory setup. For legacy support, a PDC Emulator will be created in the Windows 2000 domain controller when a Windows NT Domain client attempts to log on. Therefore, it is possible to mix TSE servers with Windows 2000 and Windows 2003 servers running Terminal Services.

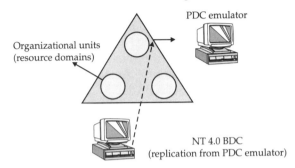

Migrating to Windows Server 2000 or Windows 2003 Server from an Existing Windows NT 4.0 PDC

If a Windows 2003 server is installed in an existing network that employs backup domain controllers, the new Windows 2003 server operates as a "mixed mode" domain controller. In this case, the Windows 2003 DC will be migrated first to Active Directory and will emulate a Windows NT 4.0 PDC. The old PDC-to-BDC security database synchronization will continue until all BDCs are migrated to Active Directory and "mixed mode" has been switched to "native mode."

Application Considerations

Most applications are written to run on a single-session platform such as Windows 95, 98, or Windows NT Workstation with a single user. Terminal Services requires significant changes to be made to the kernel and operating system to accommodate multiuser access. Because of these changes, both programmers and administrators must fully understand the issues and possible solutions in order to configure the system so that single-session applications can be executed in a multisession environment. We discuss some of the problems and possible solutions in this section.

Terminal Services makes special demands on how an application is written and how the application uses the Windows NT operating system. The Windows NT Registry is used by many programs to store variables during an installation, changes while the program executes, and changes that normally occur when users with differing logons access the application. On a typical Windows 2000 Professional workstation, an application may put data into the HKEY_LOCAL_MACHINE registry hive, assuming only one user will access the application at a time. On Terminal Server, this could prove disastrous, as changes to this registry hive would affect all users of this Terminal Server, not just the user executing the application making the change.

Many problems occur with applications that store local data constructs in global locations. In addition to separating global and local information in the registry, global and local file-based data constructs should also be maintained separately. For example, user preference files should not be stored in a main system directory (/%systemroot%) or program directory (\Program Files). Instead, preference files or other user-specific local data should be stored in the user's home directory or a user-specified directory. This consideration also applies to temporary files used to store interim information (such as cached data) or to pass data on to another application. User-specific temporary files must also be stored on a per-user basis.

Some specific issues that may cause an application to fail in a multiuser environment include

▼   **Incorrect registry entries**   Many applications write a global INI file to the system root for user-specific information. Thus, when one user changes or opens the INI file, other users may not be able to access the same file. Some applications add shortcuts to only the installer's menu during installation; because of this, other users may not see the shortcut. Still, many applications point the data files, temporary files, or cache files to the same location for all users. In this situation, only one user can run the application at a time.

■   **Changed object name**   An object created in a session is named differently. The application may not be able to find the object using the expected name or location.

▲   **Incorrect file and object rights access**   An application normally locates libraries and executables in the Windows NT %SystemRoot% directory. Multiple users accessing the same file may create file-locking problems.

The following are some other application problems and issues to be aware of within a multiuser Terminal Services environment:

▼   *Do not assume the computer name, MAC address, or IP address equates to a single user.* In the traditional distributed Windows client-server architecture, one user is logged on to one computer at a time. Thus, the computer name or Internet Protocol (IP) address assigned to either a desktop or server computer equates to one user. In the Terminal Services environment, the application can only see the IP or NetBIOS address of the server. Applications that use the computer name or IP address for licensing, or as a means of identifying an iteration of the application on the network will not work properly in the Terminal Services environment because the server's computer name or IP address can equate to many different desktops or users.

▲   *MS-DOS and 16-bit Windows applications require more RAM than native 32-bit Windows applications and may not execute at all in Windows 2000 Server or Windows Server 2003.* Windows runs an emulation layer called the Virtual DOS Machine (VDM) as a process on the 32-bit operating system. Although this memory requirement may not show up as performance degradation on a high-powered desktop computer running the latest Windows operating system with 64MB of RAM, it may easily show up on a system running Terminal Services due to the multiplier effect of many user sessions.

Multiuser Application Issues

You may encounter several possible issues when running applications under Terminal Services that were not designed to run in a multiuser environment. Some of the most important issues are summarized here. We will discuss these and other application-related issues in more detail in Chapter 13.

Application Compatibility Scripts

Many of the issues discussed so far have been addressed by the creation of application compatibility scripts. After installing an application, an administrator is required to run the corresponding script to resolve the issues mentioned. Windows 2000 shipped with 27 native Application Compatibility Scripts, and since then scores of software manufacturers have created additional scripts to provide users with fixes for their software in a multiuser environment. At the time of this writing, Windows 2003 only has four scripts in the Application Compatibility Scripts folder. Since Microsoft requires an application be multiuser compatible before it can be certified for Windows 2003, our assumption at this time is that a large majority of application vendors have simply included the scripts in their install process, thus alleviating the need for scripts. Obviously there will be some stragglers, so the need for Application Compatibility Scripts will continue for the foreseeable future. Application compatibility scripts are located in the %SystemRoot%\Application Compatibility Scripts\Install folder.

DOS and 16-Bit Windows Programs

After over eight years of Microsoft operating system support for 32-bit applications, it seems logical that all application vendors would have completed their software porting to take advantage of the speed, stability and interface changes. Win32 allows code sharing and thus runs more efficiently in a multiuser environment. If additional users need to access the same Win32 application code, a pointer is created that shares the same code from the original copy loaded in the kernel and user modes. Code sharing cuts down the total amount of memory usage when multiplying a large number of sessions. On the other hand, 16-bit Windows and DOS applications need to run in their own VDM, and so no code sharing is possible. Also, Win16 applications often require 16- to 32-bit conversion programs ("thunking" and "context switching") that increase resource utilization even further. Even with all of these obvious advantages, and nearly ten years to get it done, there are still a few poorly run software vendors who have not ported their software to a 32-bit code. We highly recommend running only 32-bit Windows applications whenever possible, even if it requires a large investment in moving to another vendor. Because Windows 2000 and 2003 are not well suited for DOS or 16-bit application support (although there are some instances where it works), if 16-bit or DOS applications are required, consider dedicating a Windows NT 4.0 TSE server to those applications, while building the rest of the farm around Windows Server 2003.

Effective Use of the Registry

In a multiuser environment, applications should store common information pertaining to systemwide operation in the HKEY_LOCAL_MACHINE section of the registry. Such information includes the path used to load application components, and what components are needed during execution. User-specific information, such as the locations of custom dictionaries (custom.dic) and user templates (normal.dot), should be stored in HKEY_CURRENT_USER. Some applications incorrectly store information meant to be user specific in HKEY_LOCAL_MACHINE.

Application compatibility scripts, Group Policies, and user profiles can all address an unused drive letter to the home directory of each user. REG.INI then changes pointers to this drive to each user's home directory environment variable. In this way, each user gets her own copy of an initialization file.

TIP: A utility in the Exchange Server Resource Kit, named profgen.exe, resolves common pointer issues arising from users trying to open the same e-mail post office box when a mandatory profile is used. This utility can be useful when enabling many users running Terminal Services to access the same Exchange server.

Application Install and Execute Modes

During installation, an application writes user-specific keys to the Administrator's HKEY_CURRENT_USER registry hive. Information such as Document Path and Autosave Path are missing from other users' HKEY_CURRENT_USER keys because they did not install the application. These keys are crucial in successfully using the application. Terminal Services provides a global Install mode to address this situation. During installation, the system is placed under Install mode by entering the command **Change User /Install** at the command prompt or by using Add/Remove Programs from the Control Panel. All user-specific keys generated by the application under the software hive are shadowed by a key hive in HKEY_LOCAL_MACHINE\SOFTWARE\Microsoft\WindowsNt\CurrentVersion\TerminalServer\Install.

This key hive is appropriately called the *shadow key*. Once installation is completed, the system can be switched back to normal execution mode by entering the command **Change User /Execute** at the command prompt. In the Execute mode of operation, the shadow key information is written back into each user's software key hive when the system finds that the keys are missing.

The same command addresses missing INI and DLL files in the case of 16-bit applications. These files are copied into each user's Windows directory (normally, *%homedrive%\%homepath%*\windows). This also applies to 32-bit applications if they use INI files. The *%homedrive%* and *%homepath%* variables are both solved when running chkroot.cmd and are replaced simply by *%rootdrive%*. The files that are copied to C:\WTSRV and C:\WINNT are copied to *%rootdrive%*\windows when a new user logs in.

User-Specific Application Data

Some settings, such as *DocumentPath* in the HKEY_CURRENT_USER Microsoft Word subkey, may only be created the first time the application is run. Therefore, the installer must execute the application in global Installation mode right after finishing the initial installation. By doing this, the system will generate these values and record them in the shadow key so that they can later be copied into each user's HKEY_CURRENT_USER registry hive.

NOTE: Logging in as a user and changing settings in an application can cause problems for any user running that application. Making a change while logged in as a normal user on a production machine to store a user's name and initials would cause all future users to see that user's name and initials when they edit documents. Thus it is important to find where these paths are stored and to script or add them to the shadow INSTALL key mentioned earlier so that all users only get the changes the administrator wants them to have.

Sometimes an application creates a path pointer to a common location for all users. For example, the Microsoft Office 97 installation program sets a document template pointer to C:\Program Files\Microsoft Office\Template. When multiple users try to update or open the same file, errors will occur. To address this situation, the administrator needs to search the registry and change the pointer to each user's home folder, such as H:\Office 97\Template, then create the correct directory structure for each user in the logon script *%SystemRoot%*\System32\usrlogn2.cmd. This file is called by the **usrlogon.cmd** (if this file does not exist, create it using a text editor) and add the following simple statement to accomplish this task:

```
IF NOT EXIST H:\OFFICE 97\TEMPLATE MD H:\OFFICE 97\TEMPLATE
```

NOTE: Most of the Microsoft Office installation issues discussed here have been resolved with Office 2000 and XP, or are easily resolved with the Office Resource Kit. These discussions still serve as an example of how to resolve similar problems with other applications.

A similar problem occurs when all users are directed to use the same cache files. The cache file pointer is set to a common location, such as C:\Temp\Cache. When multiple users attempt to write to the same location, the application will often halt, corrupt the cache, or simply crash the server. Again, the solution is to change the pointer in HKEY_LOCAL_MACHINE and HKEY_CURRENT_USER, then create the corresponding directory structure in each user's home directory to support an individual application cache.

File Security

Applications often store files in the system root directory. Security is normally set to Read-Only for regular users. When a user attempts to write to a file stored in this directory, execution of the application may fail. You can track down the particular file and reassign security to it by using the FILEMON utility (this freeware utility is available from Sysinternals at http://www.sysinternals.com). A better method is to relocate the file to each user's Windows directory.

Registry Security

Many issues arise due to registry security and incorrect use of the registry by legacy applications. REGMON is another tool available at the Sysinternals web site that administrators can use to track down registry keys that have the wrong security.

Application COM/DCOM Objects

The same application may create identical objects for multiple sessions. To separate the same object created by different sessions, a logon ID is appended to each object name. Session objects created in this way are called *user global objects* and are only visible inside the session in which they were created. If an object is created from the console, there will be no logon ID appended to the object name. This type of object is called a *system global object*. Because of this distinction, application objects to be used for multiple sessions should be generated as system global objects and installed from the console instead of a user session.

NOTE: Always install software from the console because of the issues mentioned earlier that arise from running applications in a session.

Memory Utilization

Some applications do not return memory to the system upon exit. This situation is exacerbated in a multiuser environment, and is difficult to track down when a large number of applications and users are involved. Although a nightly reboot with Windows 2000 or Windows 2003 should not be required if the applications are well written, real-world environments typically have at least one rogue application that is poorly authored. Many SBC environments implement a cyclical reboot program in order to clear memory and prevent memory leaks from causing erratic performance and server crashing. The frequency of the reboot depends on how active the memory utilization is. Citrix MetaFrame XPe has a reboot tool, and many of the resource web sites we list in the appendixes have example scripts as well.

DCOM Compliance

Most programs use traditional Open Database Connections (ODBC) to access network objects, such as a data source in a SQL database. To allow a common interface for communication between all system programs (objects) across a network, Microsoft developed the Distributed Component Object Model (DCOM).

In order to be certified by Microsoft as Windows 2000 or Windows 2003 compatible, an application must support DCOM. This ensures that software components can communicate and share functions over a network in an efficient and reusable manner. TSE inherited a subset of DCOM functionality from Windows NT 4.0. Therefore, some applications written for Windows NT 4.0 may not function properly under TSE's multiuser environment.

Microsoft has addressed this issue in Windows 2000. All DCOM activation modes are fully supported, as shown in the following:

▼ **Run as Activator** Local activation is the same whether Terminal Services is enabled or not. The server is activated on the same session as the activator.

■ **Remote Activation** When DCOM is activated remotely, the process is launched in a WindowStation with a special SessionID =0, not a session corresponding to the user. This modification preserves the implementation activity of a remote call.

■ **Run as Named User** The application is configured in the registry to run as a specified user. Local and remote activation of DCOM behaves in the same way.

■ **Run as Windows NT–Based Service** The application is configured to run as a service. This type of service is not tied to any session.

▲ **Run as Interactive User** The application is configured to run in the security context of the user.

LICENSING

Be sure to read all the way through this section, because the "Windows Server 2003 Licensing" section contains some great news that alleviates much of the licensing pain that SBC users have encountered.

In addition to the basic server operating system license required for every installed server, both Terminal Server RDP clients and Citrix ICA clients require two licenses to connect to a Terminal Server session. The first license is the standard Microsoft Client Access License (CAL) for accessing Windows NT files and print services.

The second license required to enable a client connection is a Windows Terminal Services License (TS CAL). If the session client is running on a computer with Windows 2000 Professional or Windows XP Professional when connecting to a Windows 2000 Server farm, it is not necessary to purchase a TS CAL for that client device or user. The server has a "built-in" pool of licenses it can provide to those client machines running Windows 2000 Pro or Windows XP Pro. In the case of Windows Server 2003, there is no "built-in" TS CAL pool. Owners of Windows XP Professional desktop licenses are eligible for free TS CALs, however. (Talk with your licensing provider to receive the free licenses as soon as possible since this offer from Microsoft is limited.) Although Windows NT 4.0 TSE does not enforce licensing, both Windows 2000 Server and Windows Server 2003 arduously enforce licensing of the TS CAL.

NOTE: There is a special provision for an Internet Connector in Windows 2000. This license mode allows 200 anonymous, concurrent users to access Terminal Services on a single server. However, the End User License Agreement specifically states that anyone affiliated with the owner of the license cannot use it (in other words, vendors, customers, employees, contractors, and so on cannot use the license). This rule makes the license restrictive to the point of being useless. Fortunately, the Internet Connector is being replaced as described in the upcoming "Windows Server 2003 Licensing" section.

Windows 2000 Licensing

Windows 2000 enforces the use of the Terminal Services CAL. During any attempt to connect to a session, both the standard CAL and the TS CAL will be checked. If either license is missing or invalid, the connection is refused. If the connection is granted, a temporary or permanent TS CAL is assigned.

NOTE: In a Windows NT Domain with Windows 2000 or Windows Server 2003 member Terminal Servers, Terminal Services licensing must be installed on a Windows 2000 or Windows Server 2003 member. When upgrading the Domain to Windows 2000 Server or Windows Server 2003 Active Directory, licensing must be reinstalled on a Domain Controller (DC). Failing to install Terminal Services licensing and the license codes on the new DC will cause a loss of terminal service capabilities (no license server available).

Windows 2000 Server comes with a license services server that tracks and allocates TS CAL licenses to clients at connection time. The license server needs to be installed on a Windows 2000 server and activated through Microsoft License Clearing House via a web browser, the telephone, or a process called Automatic Activation. When a client requests a connection to a Windows 2000 server, the request is forwarded to the central license server for validation. The license server uses the username and computer name to check for an existing license. If none is available, a new license will be issued to the client, and the connection is completed. If the license pool is exhausted, the connection is refused. A temporary license can be enabled that will expire after 90 days.

The significant issue with this licensing is that if a user connects one time from any device (a trade show kiosk, for example), a TS CAL is allocated (although it is not legitimate from the standpoint of the Microsoft Server 2000 licensing agreement to provide a license to a machine not owned by the person using it). Due to this execution of the licensing, the unclear license language, and technical problems (Microsoft provides no licensing option to deal with devices that aren't owned by the company whose user is using it), many customers found themselves continuously running out of TS licenses. In July of 2002, Microsoft responded to strong user feedback regarding the TS license execution by changing the licensing model slightly (via a hotfix patch) to allow the license server to expire leases after 90 days. To install this patch, install the Service Pack 2 Security Rollup package, or Service Pack 3 to your license server and all Terminal Servers in your environment.

TIP: After installing Service Pack 2 Security Rollup or Service Pack 3, uninstall and reinstall all TS licenses and reactivate them in order to complete this fix.

Licensing and Terminal Services Execution Modes

Windows 2000 Terminal Services can be installed in two different modes. The *remote administration* mode does not require a TS CAL. The purpose of this mode is to allow administrators to do server maintenance remotely. Therefore, certain restrictions apply to running in this mode. Only two concurrent client sessions are permitted. Server application compatibility services are also disabled, such as the global install mode. The *Application Server* mode is the mode utilized for Terminal Services in a server-based computing environment. This mode is not restricted like the *remote administration* mode and requires the TS CALs as discussed earlier.

Windows Server 2003 Licensing

Probably the single most significant reason to move from Windows 2000 Server to Windows Server 2003 across the corporate environment is the new licensing options. Although the execution of the license server is identical to Windows 2000, the licensing choices are dramatically improved. Following are the changes made to licensing with Windows Server 2003:

1. Windows Server 2003 provides a 120-day grace period for renewals as opposed to 90 days with Windows 2000 Server.

2. Windows Server 2003 supports a new license option—Per User licensing, as well as the Per Seat licensing supported in Windows 2000 Server (Microsoft has renamed it in Windows 2003 to Per Device). Additionally, a hybrid may be used (some licenses may be allocated per device and some per user). The Per User licensing will work best for environments where users have multiple devices that connect to the Terminal Servers (that is, a single user connects from a desktop, laptop, CE device, home PC, trade show kiosk, and so on). The Per Device licensing works best for environments where multiple users share the same device (manufacturing floors, hospitals, 24/7 offices, and so on). Note that with this change the temporary fix we discussed earlier in this section, allowing Windows 2000 to expire the leases every 90 days, has been eliminated.

3. The Internet Connector License noted earlier is replaced in Windows 2003 with an External Connector (EC) license called the Terminal Server External Connector (TS-EC) to address the need previously mentioned: to enable external users to access a company's Terminal Servers, without the need to purchase individual TS CALs for them or their devices. An example of an external user is a person who is not an employee of the company or its affiliates. The EC allows organizations to effectively provide Windows and TS CALs for entities not owned by them—for example, e-business customers or supplier partners—in order to give those entities access to their networks and terminal servers. The EC may be the best solution when business partners or customers need access to a server or group of servers. This may be the best solution when a small number of business partners or customers need access to a server or group of servers. This license mode allows 200 anonymous, concurrent users to access Terminal Services.

Licensing and Terminal Services Execution Modes

Unlike Windows 2000 Server, which had a dual mode Terminal Services component, Windows Server 2003 separates the remote administration and Terminal Services functionality into separate configurable components. Remote Desktop for Administration is enabled through a check box on the system Control Panel's Remote tab. Terminal Services is enabled by adding the "Terminal Server" component using the Windows Components portion of the Add/Remove Programs Wizard.

In addition to the two virtual sessions available in Windows Server 2003 Terminal Services remote administration functionality, an administrator can also remotely connect to the console of a server. A significant outcome to this change is that applications that would not work in a virtual session before, because they kept interacting with "session 0," will now work remotely. To connect to the console, administrators can choose one of the following methods:

▼   Use the Remote Desktop Microsoft Management Console (MMC) snap-in.

■   Run the Remote Desktop Connection (mstsc.exe) program with the /console switch.

▲   Create Remote Desktop Web Connection pages that set the ConnectToServerConsole property.

CHAPTER 3

Citrix MetaFrame Access Suite

Citrix MetaFrame XP Access Suite is a complementary product suite to Microsoft's Terminal Services (included with Windows NT 4.0 Terminal Services Edition, Windows 2000 Server, and Windows Server 2003) discussed in Chapter 2. Today, Citrix serves nearly fifty million users, facilitating a seamless user experience in heterogeneous computing environments, as well as application delivery across bandwidth-restricted connections.

Citrix MetaFrame Access Suite is comprised of five software products:

1. MetaFrame XP Presentation Server (MetaFrame XP)

2. MetaFrame Presentation Server for UNIX (MetaFrame for UNIX)

3. MetaFrame Password Manager

4. MetaFrame Conferencing Manager

5. MetaFrame Secure Access Manager (MSAM)

6. Citrix Password Manager and Conferencing Manager

Password Manager and Conferencing Manager are the newest members of the Citrix MetaFrame Access Suite. Password Manager provides a simple and elegant single sign-on solution for MetaFrame XP environments (although it also works in non-Metaframe environments), and Conferencing Manager provides an all-inclusive collaborative conference interface that leverages the shadow features of MetaFrame XP. These two products further enhance the user experience of the server-based computing environment.

In this chapter, we discuss the evolution of the MetaFrame Access Suite and dissect its Independent Computing Architecture (ICA) protocol. We also cover the enhancements that MetaFrame Access Suite brings to Terminal Services, including:

1. Secure, encrypted access for all enterprise users from any location, without having to open firewall holes. MetaFrame Secure Gateway provides a secure infrastructure by which users can access the SBC environment literally from anywhere, any time, any place, regardless of the firewall configurations (assuming the environment allows SSL [port 443] traffic). Although Terminal Services RDP traffic is encrypted, it requires that port 3389 be open both on the Data Center firewall and at the user's location(s).

2. True Application Load Management. Microsoft's built-in Network Load Balancing can be effective for environments with 100 users or less, but enterprise environments absolutely require a more robust and flexible approach to determining which users are placed on which servers under what circumstances.

3. MetaFrame Web Interface wizard-based deployment tool (formerly called NFuse). Not only does this tool provide an automated approach to deploying access to the SBC environment, but, just as handy, it provides an automated approach to deploying the ICA client itself. Conversely, the deployment and installation of the Remote Desktop Client with Terminal Services can be a daunting task when thousands of users need an update to the client.

4. Universal Access to applications from any client device, to applications on Windows or UNIX platforms. Although Microsoft now supports client access from Macintosh OS X and Windows clients, Citrix not only provides support for Mac and Windows, but also support for over 200 client operating systems, including most flavors of UNIX and Linux, DOS, and embedded devices.

5. Enterprise management tools. Citrix provides Resource Manager, Installation Manager, and Network Manager, as well as a host of embedded management tools that present administrators with critical information as well as the automation of enterprise SBC server environments.

Table 3-1 shows the value-add features that Citrix MetaFrame XP add to a Windows Server 2003 environment.

Application publishing	One-to-many shadowing	Customized billing reports	User collaboration
Program Neighborhood	Cross-server shadowing	Track user access to applications	Panning and scaling (handhelds)
Anonymous user support	Shadowing indicator	Centrally install applications	Pass-through authentication
Content publishing	Auto client update	Distribute service packs	Seamless windows
Content redirection	Universal print driver	Package customized install	Multimonitor support
Novell NDS support	Web-based client install	Web Interface for MetaFrame	Application save position
Delegated administration	Support for multiple farms	Non-Windows client access	End-to-end security
Centralized management console	Auto client printer detection	Integration with Network Management consoles	MetaFrame Secure Gateway
Connection control	Resource-based Load Management	Support for direct asynch	SSL/TLS 128-bit encryption
CPU prioritization	Schedule application availability	Client drive remapping	Support for digital certificates
Support for 1000+ servers in farm	Specify client IP range	Text-entry prediction	Socks 4 and 5 proxy support
Many-to-one shadowing	Application monitoring	Instant mouse- click feedback	SpeedScreen 4 browser acceleration

Table 3-1. Citrix ICA Value-Add Features

THE EVOLUTION OF METAFRAME

The Microsoft Windows NT operating system developed from a single-user operating system architecture and continued, for nearly a decade, only to be limited in certain applications by that fact. Windows NT provided real-time multiprocessing capabilities comparable to those of rival UNIX operating systems, but did not provide functions within its OS kernel to support concurrent multiuser access to applications hosted on NT platforms.

Given the dominant business computing architecture of the late 1980s and early 1990s, which featured increasingly capable desktop computers (so-called *fat-client* PCs) that provided much of the same processing as client-server applications, it may well be that the need for multiuser computing platforms (similar in concept to mainframe computing environments) was not of primary concern to Microsoft designers. In Microsoft's preferred computing model, information processing was conceived as inherently distributed and individualized: desktop computers were viewed as "peers" of server platforms. In fact, most early server systems were little more than highly configured PCs, typically featuring many of the same hardware components.

At that time, there was an interest in some niche areas for a server platform that would "host" applications and share them among several connected client devices, configured as dumb terminals. One such application was *remote access*: a technique by which one or more offsite users could access an application located on a corporate local area network (LAN). Ideally, the remote user would be able to perform useful work as though seated at a terminal directly attached to the LAN.

However, the mainstream architecture for business computing did not yet involve shared application use. Instead, the norm was a combination of Windows-based desktop computers, emphasizing locally stored and executed individual applications, and Novell, UNIX, or NT-based servers (or a combination of all of these) interconnected via a LAN, supporting client-server computing.

Multiuser Windows—MultiWin

The idea behind server-based computing on Windows NT can be traced to the X-Window System developed by MIT in 1984. By utilizing powerful UNIX servers, remote X-Window clients can send keyboard and mouse input to server-based applications running on central servers. The X-Window System on the server then tracks output from the applications and updates the appropriate remote client session screen.

The founder of Citrix Systems, Ed Iacobucci, originally conceived the idea of allowing different types of computers to run the same applications, even though they might not have the same operating system or adequate local resources. While working as head of the joint Microsoft/IBM design team on the OS/2 project, he approached both companies with the idea, but neither firm was interested. Iacobucci then formed Citrix Systems in 1989 and the technology behind the current Terminal Services was developed—MultiWin. MultiWin rode on top of the OS/2 kernel and allowed multiple simultaneous OS/2 sessions and desktops in a protected memory area for each individual user.

WinView

In 1993, Citrix shipped its first OS/2-based multiuser operating system, called WinView. WinView used the MultiWin technology and one of the first incarnations of a remote display client called Independent Computing Architecture (ICA). Citrix first worked to deliver multiuser extensions to the OS/2 operating system and subsequently worked on the delivery of applications across Novell and TCP/IP networks. Despite prevailing personal and client-server computing models, developers at Citrix believed that multiuser computing had a future, especially as applications moved off the desktop and "into the network." They convinced Microsoft that a market for multiuser NT could be cultivated and secured a license to add multiuser extensions to the NT operating system.

WinFrame

Whether or not Microsoft shared the Citrix vision of the future, the license agreement was certainly a "win-win" for Microsoft and Citrix. With the multiuser extensions provided by Citrix in the form of WinFrame, Microsoft would be able to answer criticisms from UNIX advocates regarding a purported "deficiency" of its server operating systems: they provided little or no support for multiuser computing requirements. If Citrix visionaries were correct, and a market for multiuser computing platforms could be cultivated, Microsoft would have a solution to offer that market.

Citrix WinFrame is a combination of Microsoft Windows NT 3.51 Server and Citrix MultiWin technology. WinFrame was a major upgrade to the OS/2-based WinView. At the time of its release, Windows 3.1 (and later, Windows 95) had become the desktop standard, and WinFrame surpassed WinView as a tool for installing and executing the standard corporate end-user applications.

Thin-Client Computing

In the mid-1990s, the argument for multiuser NT was reinforced by the findings of analysts such as the Gartner Group regarding the total cost of ownership of Windows PCs. Analysts claimed that fat-client PCs cost organizations between $7000 and $13,000 per PC per year in maintenance and support. This position touched off a firestorm of industry activity, mainly from longtime Microsoft rivals. The so-called SONIA set—an acronym for Sun Microsystems, Oracle Corporation, Netscape Communications, IBM, and Apple Corporation—led the charge to displace Microsoft PCs from corporate desktops, substituting their own "network computer" in their place. Despite the obvious self-interest inherent in the SONIA value proposition, and the subsequent failure of the network computer to take hold in the market, the underlying tenant of the SONIA argument took root. The Citrix concept of *thin-client computing* was introduced to the lexicon of modern business computing.

Thin-client computing advocates held that, as server capabilities grew, it was only natural for server hosts to become "fatter" and for desktop platforms to become "thinner." Application software, advocates argued, should reside on application servers rather than on individual PCs. Placing applications on a server would make them accessible by means of a variety of inexpensive client devices. The advent of the Internet and World Wide Web at about the same time reinforced this perspective. Many people adopted a view of computing in which all applications would be accessed via a universal, hardware-agnostic client such as a web browser.

Citrix Systems Synonymous with Thin

Citrix Systems, with its Independent Computing Architecture (ICA), emerged from the discussion of thin computing as the undisputed leader in a market it had long helped to facilitate. In an ICA-based solution, WinFrame-based application servers could host Windows-compliant applications, while end users, equipped with any of a broad range of client devices (whether network computers or Windows PCs), could access and use the applications over a network connection. Integral to the WinFrame approach was a remote presentation services protocol capable of separating the application's logic from its user interface, so that only keystrokes, mouse-clicks, and screen updates would travel the network. With the ICA protocol, Citrix claimed, the user's experience of the server-hosted application would be comparable in all respects to that of an application executing on the end user's own desktop PC.

Terminal Services and MetaFrame

Increased interest in the WinFrame solution encouraged Microsoft to license MultiWin, the core technology of WinFrame, from Citrix Systems in 1997 and to integrate the technology into its own operating systems soon after. As explained in Chapter 2, Microsoft first implemented MultiWin in a special Terminal Services Edition (TSE) of its NT 4.0 OS. With Microsoft's integration of Terminal Services, Citrix needed to raise the bar for scalability and management. This was accomplished with MetaFrame.

Introduction of MetaFrame 1.0/1.8

Unlike WinFrame, which had been a stand-alone product and a "replacement" operating system for NT, MetaFrame was an add-on to the Microsoft NT 4.0 TSE and Windows 2000 platform. One reason for the MetaFrame product was to continue to meet the needs of WinFrame customers who were interested in migrating their NT 3.51–based WinFrame environments to newer NT 4.0 TSE–based environments but who were afraid of losing application server connections with clients that were not supported by *Remote Desktop Protocol* (*RDP*). MetaFrame added ICA client and protocol support back into the Microsoft multiuser operating system offering, since ICA allowed for connectivity from many additional clients than RDP allowed.

MetaFrame XP

MetaFrame XP is the latest version from Citrix. With the release of Feature Release 3 (FR-3), XP is compatible with Microsoft's latest operating system: Windows Server 2003. In addition to the feature updates and changes, another very significant change that Citrix made with MetaFrame XP is the change in licensing; MetaFrame 1.0/1.8 Citrix required a server license for every server with Citrix installed as well as bump packs for additional users, while MetaFrame XP only requires one base license for each server farm (with bump packs for additional concurrent users). This change makes licensing far more flexible and convenient, and in most cases cheaper, as additional servers can be brought online as needed without additional Citrix software license expense (as long as no additional concurrent users are added).

With MetaFrame XP, customers have new version choices, including XPs, XPa, and XPe. All versions of XP are supported on Windows NT 4.0 TSE, Windows 2000 Server, and Windows Server 2003. MetaFrame XP supports full integration with Active Directory in Windows 2000 or Windows Server 2003.

NOTE: Following the release of Feature Release 1, Citrix stopped adding any additional features or enhancements to MetaFrame XP for Windows NT 4.0 TSE.

XPs is the standard version for Citrix servers for stand-alone point solution implementations with one to five servers. XPs feature highlights include MetaFrame Web Interface for MetaFrame, user shadowing, Secure Gateway, Universal Print Driver II, client time zone support, Novell NDS support, client device support, and full ICA client support.

Although more than one server can be used with XPs, it is rare, as applications cannot be load balanced across servers and any application publishing will have to be done separately on each server with different names.

XPa is the advanced version that includes all of the XPs features, with the addition of Load Management. This upgrade is designed for use in farms with 2 to 100 servers.

As shown in Table 3-2, XPe contains all the features included with XPa, as well as some additional features required for enterprise management. These extended features include Resource Manager, Installation Manager, Web Interface Extension for MetaFrame XP (formerly Enterprise Services for NFuse), a plug-in for Microsoft Operations Manager (MOM), and Network Manager. XPe is designed for 20 or more servers and accommodates multiple Citrix Server farms.

> *The centralized computing using MetaFrame XP provides us with the ability to completely customize which applications are provided to which users. This ensures that all users have access to the necessary resources required for their daily tasks. Software changes and upgrades are performed at the server effective instantaneously for all users. Overall, we have been able to expand and grow our IT projects ahead of estimated schedules with the seamless deployment of applications and minimum maintenance time required for our Citrix Farm.*
>
> —Michael P. Miller
> Network & Systems Administrator
> Primary Care Partners, P.C.

	MetaFrame XPs	MetaFrame XPa	MetaFrame XPe
UNPARALLELED MANAGEABILITY AND SCALE			
Advanced Shadowing			
Cross-server shadowing	X	X	X
Many-to-one shadowing	X	X	X
One-to-many shadowing	X	X	X
Shadowing indicator	X	X	X
Shadowing taskbar	X	X	X
Application Management			
Anonymous user support	X	X	X
Application publishing	X	X	X
Content publishing	X	X	X
Program Neighborhood	X	X	X
TCP-based browsing	X	X	X
Application Packaging and Delivery			
Centrally install and uninstall applications			X
Create logical server groups			X
Customizable project details			X
Delivery verification			X
Distribute service packs, updates, and files			X
MSI support			X
Package applications, files, and service packs			X
Package inventory			X
Packager rollback			X
Schedule package delivery			X
Server reboot support			X
Support for unattended installs			X

Table 3-2.   MetaFrame XP FR-3 Feature Grid

	MetaFrame XPs	MetaFrame XPa	MetaFrame XPe
Centralized Administration			
Active Directory support	X	X	X
Novell NDS support	X	X	X
User policies	X	X	X
Administrator toolbar	X	X	X
Centralized Data Store	X	X	X
Citrix administrative accounts	X	X	X
Citrix Management Console	X	X	X
Plug-in for Microsoft Operations Manager (MOM)	X	X	X
Citrix Web Console	X	X	X
Connection control	X	X	X
CPU prioritization	X	X	X
Windows Installer Support	X	X	X
Centralized License Management			
Centralized license activation	X	X	X
Enterprisewide license pooling	X	X	X
Plug-and-play licensing	X	X	X
Client Management			
Auto client update	X	X	X
Business Recovery	X	X	X
ReadyConnect	X	X	X
Web-based client installation	X	X	X
Network Management			
Access CMC from third-party management consoles			X
SNMP monitoring agent			X

Table 3-2. MetaFrame XP FR-3 Feature Grid *(continued)*

	MetaFrame XPs	MetaFrame XPa	MetaFrame XPe
Printer Management			
MetaFrame Universal Print Driver version II	X	X	X
Support for color and high-resolution printers with Universal Print Driver	X	X	X
Printer auto creation log	X	X	X
Printer driver access control	X	X	X
Printer driver replication	X	X	X
Printing bandwidth control	X	X	X
Resource-Based Load Balancing			
Instant load-balancing feedback		X	X
Load balancing reconnect support		X	X
Schedule application availability		X	X
Specify client IP range		X	X
Scalability			
Enterprise-class scalability	X	X	X
Cross-subnet administration	X	X	X
System Monitoring and Analysis			
Application monitoring			X
Customized reporting			X
Summary database and reporting			X
Perform system capacity planning			X
Real-time graphing and alerting			X
Server farm monitoring			X
Track user access to applications			X
User-definable metrics			X

Table 3-2.   MetaFrame XP FR-3 Feature Grid *(continued)*

	MetaFrame XPs	MetaFrame XPa	MetaFrame XPe
System Monitoring and Analysis			
Watcher window			X
ICA session monitoring			X
TOTAL"NET" LEVERAGE			
Web Application Access			
Web Interface for MetaFrame	X	X	X
Federal Information Processing Standards (FIPS) 140 security compliance	X	X	X
Support for RSA Secure ID and Secure Computing Premier Access second factor authentication solutions	X	X	X
Multiple server farm support	X	X	X
Application filtering and caching	X	X	X
Support for MetaFrame Secure Access Manager	X	X	X
Web Interface Extension for MetaFrame XP			X
ULTIMATE FLEXIBILITY			
Access to Local System Resources			
Auto printer creation	X	X	X
Automatic drive redirection	X	X	X
Client drive mapping	X	X	X
Clipboard redirection	X	X	X
COM port redirection	X	X	X
Performance			
Instant mouse-click feedback	X	X	X
Persistent bitmap caching	X	X	X
Priority packet tagging	X	X	X

Table 3-2.   MetaFrame XP FR-3 Feature Grid *(continued)*

	MetaFrame XPs	MetaFrame XPa	MetaFrame XPe
Performance			
SpeedScreen browser acceleration	X	X	X
SpeedScreen 3	X	X	X
Text-entry prediction	X	X	X
Seamless User Experience			
High-/true-color depth and resolution	X	X	X
16-bit audio support	X	X	X
Application save position	X	X	X
Auto client reconnect	X	X	X
Client printer management utility	X	X	X
Client time zone support	X	X	X
Content redirection	X	X	X
Multimonitor support	X	X	X
Panning and scaling	X	X	X
Pass-through authentication	X	X	X
Roaming user reconnect	X	X	X
Seamless windows	X	X	X
Win 16 multi-session support	X	X	X
Universal Connectivity			
Universal client access	X	X	X
Support for direct asynch dial-up	X	X	X
Support for TCP/IP, IPX, SPX, and NetBIOS	X	X	X
User Collaboration			
User collaboration	X	X	X
END-TO-END SECURITY			

Table 3-2.   MetaFrame XP FR-3 Feature Grid *(continued)*

	MetaFrame XPs	MetaFrame XPa	MetaFrame XPe
Security			
MetaFrame Secure Gateway	X	X	X
Delegated administration	X	X	X
SSL 128-bit encryption	X	X	X
TLS encryption	X	X	X
Smart card support	X	X	X
SecureICA 128-bit encryption	X	X	X
SOCKS 4 and 5 Support	X	X	X
Ticketing	X	X	X

Table 3-2. MetaFrame XP FR-3 Feature Grid *(continued)*

MetaFrame XP is Active Directory compliant. Thus, Active Directory groups may be used to configure permissions and users. Citrix does not change or add to the schema of Active Directory, and MetaFrame allows single sign-on for Active Directory, Novell NDS, and Novell e-Directory environments.

Web interface for MetaFrame is provided by Citrix, with all three MetaFrame XP versions to publish Windows applications to web pages on intranets and the public Internet. This tool also allows customization so that a number of applications can be combined into an "application portal." Additionally, MetaFrame Secure Gateway provides a secure method of application access delivered directly to the end user via a browser, over SSL, providing increased security while reducing problems with Firewall and VPN configurations.

With MetaFrame XP, access to applications can be provided across a variety of networks, including wide area networks, remote access dial-up connections, local area networks, the Internet, and wireless networks. Over 200 types of clients, including Windows PCs, Windows terminals, UNIX workstations, handheld devices, network computers, and numerous others, are supported as ICA clients. These client choices improve dramatically on the RDP client support inherent in Windows NT 4.0 TSE, Windows 2000 Server, and Windows Server 2003.

INDEPENDENT COMPUTING ARCHITECTURE (ICA)

ICA is an architecture for server-based computing that competes with and/or complements other architectures such as Microsoft's Remote Desktop Protocol (RDP) and Sun Microsystems/X-Open's X-Window protocol. All of these architectures share in the goal to provide a means to extend resources, simplify application deployment and administration, and decrease the total cost of application ownership.

With all of these server-based computing architectures, applications are deployed, managed, supported, and executed completely on a server. Client devices, whether fat or thin, have access to business-critical applications on the server without application rewrites or downloads.

For everything that ICA, RDP, and the X-Window System have in common, they vary significantly from each other at the component level. Since very little new development is currently being done with the X-Windows System, we will focus our comparisons on ICA and RDP, although the "MetaFrame for UNIX" section provides a brief discussion on ICA versus X-Windows.

ICA Presentation Services Protocol

As depicted in Figure 3-1, the ICA presentation services protocol transports only keystrokes, mouse-clicks, and screen updates to the client. The protocol has been demonstrated to operate consistently with 20 kilobits per second of network bandwidth and provide real-time performance with 30 kilobits per second for office automation applications. This enables even the latest 32-bit applications to be operated remotely across low-bandwidth links while delivering performance comparable to local execution on existing PCs, Windows-based terminals, network computers, and a host of evolving business and personal information appliances.

The ICA protocol was designed with low-bandwidth connections in mind, making it a robust performer on both large- and small-capacity links. Moreover, the ICA protocol responds dynamically to changing network, server, and client operating conditions. It takes advantage of available network and server resources and adapts automatically when conditions are more restrictive, often without generating any noticeable changes in the end user's experience. Much of the performance of the ICA protocol can be attributed to the use of intelligent caching and data compression techniques, and to technologies such as SpeedScreen. ICA is a non-streaming protocol, meaning that if a user's screen has not changed and they have not moved the mouse or keyboard, no traffic will be passed. This feature can substantially help larger environments operating over a WAN link as many users will not be using any bandwidth at certain instances, allowing much better utilization of the bandwidth as a whole.

Citrix MetaFrame enables us to deploy Windows applications to our students in both a very cost-effective and expeditious manner. This is true whether they are working on a PC or Windows terminal on campus, or working offsite using an Internet connection.

—Tony Holland,
Director of Computing Services,
Stanford Business School

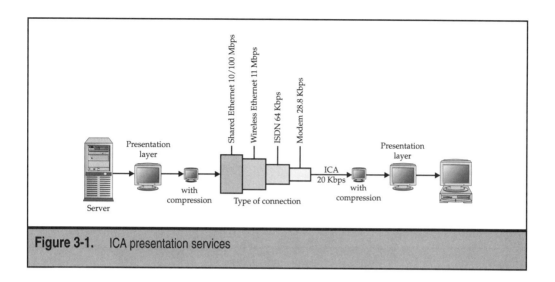

Figure 3-1. ICA presentation services

SpeedScreen

SpeedScreen is a technology for improving the performance of application delivery across ICA links. It improves performance by reducing the amount of data that must traverse an ICA connection as an end-user interacts with a MetaFrame server-based application. SpeedScreen targets the repainting function of a hosted application. With many applications, entire screens are repainted with each keyboard entry (or mouse-click) made by the end user. SpeedScreen uses an intelligent agent technology to compare information previously transmitted to the ICA client with information that is about to be transmitted, then transmits only the changed information. This is visually represented in Figure 3-2. By limiting repaint operations to specific sections of a screen affected by user interaction, the amount of traffic that must traverse the connection is dramatically reduced. Citrix's latest release of SpeedScreen, SpeedScreen 4, also called SpeedScreen Browser Acceleration, specifically focuses on major performance and usability improvements for end users connecting to published applications that embed JPEG and GIF images within Microsoft HTML pages. Supported applications include Internet Explorer v5.5 or later, Microsoft Outlook and Outlook Express.

With some applications, bandwidth consumption may be reduced by as much as 30 percent through the implementation of SpeedScreen, while total packets transmitted may be reduced by 60 percent. The result is lower latency in the network and better application performance for the end user—especially across low-bandwidth connections.

With the SpeedScreen Latency Reduction (SLR) manager, the end-user experience can be enhanced in two ways. First, local text echo can be enabled to give immediate feedback by having the local client render the text. The normal way text is transferred when using MetaFrame is by sending the keystroke to the server, which is processed and then rendered back to the client. This is convenient for users that type quickly, as even the slightest delay can be annoying. Second, SLR can provide for instant feedback for mouse-button clicks.

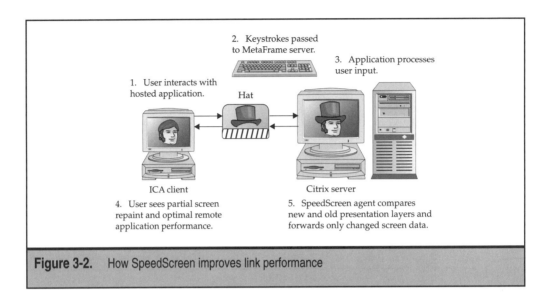

Figure 3-2. How SpeedScreen improves link performance

Connectivity Options

A broader range of connectivity options are supported by MetaFrame and ICA than by RDP, so a more diversified set of users can access and utilize hosted applications. Figure 3-3 depicts the connectivity options enabled by ICA, which include dial-up, ISDN, multiple LANs, wireless LANs, numerous WANs, and the Internet. RDP, by contrast, is limited in its support to only TCP/IP LAN/WAN environments.

Additionally, using MetaFrame and the ICA protocol breaks the barriers imposed by RDP by extending application access beyond Windows PCs. The ICA protocol supports more than 200 clients, providing flexibility in access options far surpassing that of RDP.

The ICA Client Environment

In addition to the contributions of MetaFrame and the ICA protocol to application delivery performance, MetaFrame also enhances the basic multiuser client-server environment. MetaFrame XP embodies numerous innovations designed to facilitate a broad range of hosted application environments. Considerable effort has been invested by MetaFrame XP designers to enable all applications, whether remote or local, to operate and interoperate as though they were local to the end user. This approach increases the user's comfort level and decreases the required training time.

The MetaFrame ICA Desktop

The MetaFrame ICA desktop is designed to provide a user experience that is on par with a Windows PC running locally installed and executed applications. MetaFrame enables complete access to local system resources, such as full 16-bit stereo audio, local drives, COM ports, and local printers, if available.

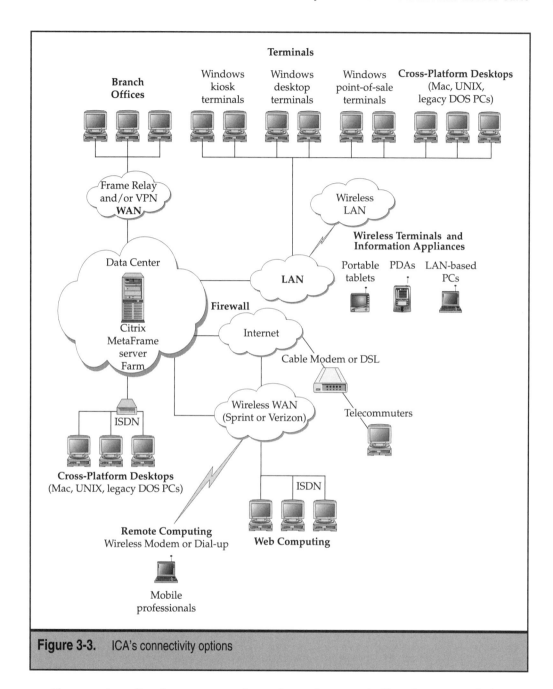

Figure 3-3.   ICA's connectivity options

The mapping of local resources can be performed automatically or by means of administrative utilities. Specialized client capabilities such as modem dial-up are also supported.

Additionally, mapped resources can be shared with the MetaFrame server, if desired. Configuration of these mappings is built into the standard Windows device redirection facilities. The client mappings appear as another network that presents the client devices as share points to which a drive letter or printer port can be attached.

Seamless Windows

Of course, not all MetaFrame XP implementations utilize a full-fledged "remote desktop" model (one in which there are no applications locally installed on the client). Indeed, in many environments where MetaFrame XP is deployed, clients are themselves Windows PCs configured to provide a mixture of some locally installed applications and some remotely hosted applications. *Seamless Windows* is a feature of MetaFrame designed to accommodate this scenario.

Seamless Windows is a shorthand expression referring to the capability of the Citrix ICA Win32 client to support the integration of local and remote applications on the local Windows 95, Windows 98, Windows NT 4.0, Windows 2000, or Windows XP desktop. When configuring a connection to the MetaFrame XP server, an administrator or user can simply select the Seamless Windows option to enable this function.

With Seamless Windows, the user can gain access to hosted applications without having to load a remote desktop environment. While connected in a MetaFrame XP server session, the user can gain access to local applications using the Windows taskbar. Icons for both local and remote applications can be installed on the local Windows desktop, and both local and remote application windows can be cascaded on the local desktop.

Multiple Keyboards   The Seamless Windows environment supports the definition of multiple keyboards to facilitate command entry in local and remote application environments. This prevents specially mapped key combinations used by MetaFrame (such as ALT-TAB) from interfering with similar key combinations used by locally executing applications.

Windows Clipboard   Seamless Windows supports the use of the Windows Clipboard in conjunction with both local and MetaFrame-hosted applications. Users can cut, copy, and paste information between applications running remotely on the server or locally from the desktop. Rich text format cut-and-paste is fully supported.

NOTE: The local/remote clipboard is part of MetaFrame XP's overall solution set. It can be used independently of Seamless Windows or Program Neighborhood.

Program Neighborhood

Building on the concept of a Seamless Windows environment, MetaFrame also delivers an easy-to-use method for accessing remotely hosted applications. Similar in concept to the Microsoft Windows Network Neighborhood, MetaFrame pushes links to published applications into a client-based Program Neighborhood facility.

In operation, Program Neighborhood presents application sets to MetaFrame client users. An *application set* is a user's view of the applications published on a given MetaFrame server or server farm, which that user is authorized to access. A single user- authentication operation (usually initiated when the user launches Program Neighborhood or a

MetaFrame-hosted application displayed in the Start menu or as an icon on the local desktop) identifies the user to all MetaFrame servers. Based on the user's individual or group account parameters, the Program Neighborhood is populated with an application set containing each application configured for the specific user account or user group. Published applications appear as icons and are preconfigured with such properties as session window size, color depth, and supported level of encryption, as well as audio and video appropriate to the user and his or her client device.

Program Neighborhood technology is especially useful as a means to quickly publish hosted applications that are intended for use by groups of users. Users can click the Program Neighborhood icon on their Windows desktop (or click the corresponding entry in their Windows Start menu) to review a list of hosted applications available for use. No special client configuration is required to launch and use these published applications.

MANAGEMENT FEATURES

The primary management tool for MetaFrame XP farms is the *Citrix Management Console* (*CMC*). The CMC is a Java tool that provides the user interface to control permissions, licensing, published applications, the load management feature of XPa, and the advanced features of XPe for both resource management and network management. The CMC is also the interface to monitor and manage printers, users, and servers. Java was chosen rather than using the Microsoft standard of the *Microsoft Manager Console* (*MMC*) for cross-platform compatibility. With the introduction of FR-1, Citrix made available the *Citrix Web Console* (*CWC*), which is not as feature-rich as the CMC, but is more convenient to use at all times.

The CMC can provide a significant load on the server farm if not used properly. It is recommended that the auto refresh feature not be used, especially in larger farms. It is also important to publish or use the CMC from the *Zone Data Control* (*ZDC*) *server.* Zone Data Control is further explained later in this chapter. The information that the CMC needs is located in the database on the ZDC, therefore if the CMC is run from a server other than the ZDC server, the server needs to download the information from the ZDC and this adds one more link to the puzzle. Another way to increase efficiency in using the CMC is to create folders within the CMC to categorize published applications and servers. This allows the CMC to refresh without gathering more information than is needed. Another method to reduce load on the CMC is to use the command-line tools that only query very specific data, and thus use the CPU and network bandwidth efficiently.

With MetaFrame XP Feature Release 3, Citrix released the MetaFrame XP Management Pack for MOM. This is a plug-in for Microsoft Operations Manager (MOM) that allows administrators to effectively manage the health and performance of MetaFrame XP servers from the MOM console. Since this interface is not Java based, it tends to be faster and less resource intensive. For users who are already using MOM for server management, this will make a great management tool.

From a client management perspective, MetaFrame XP brings to the administrative tool kit the Automatic ICA Client Update utility and a tool called ReadyConnect to facilitate rapid application deployment. Together, these features can save administrators many hours of tedious client configuration tasks.

The Automatic ICA Client Update utility provides the means to update Citrix ICA client software centrally, from the MetaFrame server itself. The latest versions of ICA client software are identified by the administrator, who then uses the update tool to schedule download and installation on appropriate client devices. This utility reduces the need to travel from client to client throughout the enterprise in order to install and configure the latest version of ICA client software.

ReadyConnect enables client connections to be predefined at the server. By capturing ICA client connection data, including phone numbers, IP addresses, server names, and other connection options, applications can be mass-deployed throughout the enterprise with speed and agility. Users can access applications across predefined connection points through a simple point-and-click operation.

NOTE: While these tools are convenient, we recommend that Web Interface for MetaFrame be used instead to deploy and manage client versions and configurations. This technique will be thoroughly discussed in the "Web Interface for MetaFrame" section of this chapter and later in Chapter 16.

Zone Data Collectors

Understanding zone data collectors is critical to optimizing larger farm performance. *Zone data collectors (ZDC)* are used to keep information within a server farm up-to-date between member servers and other ZDCs. Every server farm has at least one zone that is set up by default. The trick is to design the right number of zones in a farm so that each ZDC does not get overloaded with traffic from its member servers. In larger farms with 50 or more servers, the ZDC is best served by a MetaFrame XP server that does not accept ICA connections.

Generally, zones start degrading performance between 100 and 300 servers, depending on the number of logins, applications served, and changes in server load. Performance can be maintained in larger farms by creating additional zones. The trade-off of adding more zones is the open link (and thus the bandwidth required) to maintain updates between each ZDC so that all updated data can be propagated throughout the farm. For optimal performance, it is best to keep the number of zones to a minimum, but still keep each zone small enough to be efficient.

The ZDC tracks data that is dynamically collected from the farm to include server load, license utilization, and session information. The more static data for a farm is maintained by the IMA data store including total licensing, published applications, administrators, permissions, server names in the farm, and trust relationships.

The ZDC is chosen with an election process. The variables used for the election process are first the software version, second the administrator-defined preference, and third the host ID. The important thing to keep in mind is that the software version overrides even the administrator-defined preference. Because of the amount of communication that takes place between ZDCs, we do not recommend setting up zones that cross WAN links. The zone traffic data that is sent across WAN links is not manageable within Citrix, but appliances like the Packeteer PacketShaper can manage this bandwidth utilization.

Independent Management Architecture

MetaFrame XP introduced the Independent Management Architecture (IMA) to replace the ICA browser service. IMA is a tremendous improvement over the ICA browser with respect to speed, scalability, and reliability of enterprise server farms.

IMA contains two components. The IMA data store is responsible for keeping information about licenses, published applications, load-balancing parameters, printer options, and security. The IMA protocol is responsible for communications between MetaFrame XP servers that maintain accurate information about server load, license usage, and user connections.

The IMA service runs on all MetaFrame XP servers to communicate with the Citrix Management Console, other MetaFrame XP servers, and the IMA data store. Each Citrix farm has one IMA data store connected to an ODBC database. The databases that are presently supported are MS Jet (FR-3 replaced Jet support with MSDE support), Microsoft SQL Server 7 or later, IBM DB2, and Oracle 7.3.4 or later. Additional licensing is required from Microsoft, IBM DB2, or Oracle if MSDE is not used. Each server downloads its configuration updates each time it is started (when the IMA services start); it also checks for changes every ten minutes. When an administrator is doing testing and maintenance, it is sometimes necessary to have more immediate response for changes. This can be done by executing the dsmaint recreatelhc command from a command prompt on the MetaFrame XP server. When each server queries the IMA data store, it only downloads relevant changes, which reduces the amount of traffic on the network. The local server stores this data in its Local Host Cache. This is helpful for increasing performance of local queries, and the data is retained for 96 hours in case of communications problems with the centralized IMA data store. the zone data collector is also involved in this communication and will be addressed in the next section.

Access to the data store can be done via "direct" or "indirect" mode. Direct mode means that each server directly accesses the database using ODBC, whereas in the indirect mode the servers aggregate queries through one MetaFrame server and it communicates to the data store. When using MS Jet (or MSDE in Feature Release 3) for the data store indirect mode must be used because of performance and locking issues. Direct or indirect mode can be used with SQL, IBM DB2 or Oracle. For small farms (50 servers or less), MSDE can work but has the disadvantage of requiring indirect mode (single point of failure), is much more likely to get corrupted data, and can be a performance bottleneck. For farms that are mission-critical and larger than ten servers, using direct mode with SQL, IBM DB2, or Oracle is recommended. The SQL, IBM DB2 or Oracle server does not need to be dedicated to the data store, since these databases support more than one database per server, assuming, of course, that sufficient server resources are available.

Data store replication is a concern in larger farms. When a server queries the data store (especially over slow link speeds) other servers could timeout and cause problems. SQL, IBM DB2, and Oracle contain integrated replication capabilities that are effective in solving this problem (the dual-commit model is recommended). When planning the resources for the data store, a good rule of thumb is to allocate about 200KB of disk space for each MetaFrame XP server.

Resource Manager

MetaFrame XPe is required when using Resource Manager (RM). This product equips administrators with a full-featured management tool suite for analyzing and tuning Citrix MetaFrame XPe servers. RM adds real-time monitoring, historic reports, and a central repository of usage information and statistics to the MetaFrame product suite.

Resource Manager keeps data for 96 hours with an internal database (15-second server snapshots) and integrates with Microsoft SQL and Oracle databases to store long-term statistics. The local database will utilize about 7MB of data for each metric to maintain data for 96 hours. The local database is only compressed when the IMA service is started; this provides one more reason to script reboot the MetaFrame XP servers every 24 to 48 hours. The link http://www.citrix.com/download contains a group of predefined free crystal reports available for use with a Microsoft SQL/Oracle database.

While monitoring the server statistics, RM can send out e-mail, pages, or SNMP traps when predefined loads are met (for example, when CPU utilization reaches 60 percent, RM can send the Citrix administrator group an e-mail). RM uses metrics to define monitored parameters, alert thresholds, and configurations. Metrics, once defined, can be applied to servers or published applications. Hundreds of example metrics are included with the RM installation. Citrix recommends, for performance reasons, not to have more than 50 metrics per server.

The farm metric server is the central server that manages all of the metrics on each of the servers and published applications. By default, the first server in the farm to have RM installed on it becomes the farm metric server, although this can be moved by the administrator at any time. Better performance can be achieved by having the farm metric server on the same machine as the zone data collector. RM can be installed on a second server in the farmer, which will automatically become the backup farm metric server for use if the primary goes offline. The metric data can be stored on the same SQL or Oracle server as the IMA data store if the server has sufficient resources. The database connection server is responsible for communicating with each MetaFrame server and the summary database (SQL or Oracle) if data needs to be retained past 96 hours.

Each defined metric has six possible states:

▼ Green indicates the metric is operating within acceptable limits.

■ Yellow indicates the metric has exceeded the time and value limit.

■ Red indicates the yellow limit has been exceeded and administrator action has been executed (e-mail, page, SNMP traps, and so on).

■ Blue indicates a new metric that is not completely defined.

■ Grey indicates a metric that is paused (snooze) for a predetermined amount of time; in this state, data is still collected, but alerts are not processed.

▲ Black is a sleep state; data is still collected, but alerts are not processed.

Network Manager

Network Manager (NM) is used for limited management through SNMP and to view MetaFrame XP statistics from HP OpenView, Tivoli NetView, and CA Unicenter. This tool can be useful for companies that have existing SNMP management software. NM is a component of XPe only. Since security can be compromised through SNMP, security is a primary configuration concern. If possible, SNMP should be left read-only (the default setting for Window 2000/Windows Server 2003) and all MetaFrame XP management should be done through the CMC or MOM plug-in. If it is critical to restart, terminate processes, disconnect sessions, log off sessions, send messages, and shut down, SNMP requires read-create or read-write permissions. In this case, SNMP should be locked down by limiting these SNMP privileges to only the IP address of the SNMP management server. SNMP is discussed in further depth in Chapter 9.

Installation Manager

Citrix Installation Manager (IM) is designed to automate the application installation process and facilitate application replication across MetaFrame XP servers throughout the enterprise. Through the use of IM, applications can be distributed across multiple servers in minutes rather than days or weeks. IM is available as a part of MetaFrame XPe only. IM is fully integrated into the CMC.

IM is especially useful in organizations utilizing more than 10 MetaFrame XP servers, or having numerous and frequently updated applications. In these environments, the automation offered by IM can yield significant cost and administrative time-savings.

IM contains two components: the Packager and the Installer. With the Installer deployed to all Citrix servers in the enterprise, the Packager makes replicating applications a simple two-step "package and publish" process.

The Packager runs on its own PC or server, while the Installer runs as a background service on each MetaFrame XP server and is transparent to the user.

The Packager provides the administrator with a wizard that supports the step-by-step process of installing and configuring an application. The result is a "package" that contains all application files and a "script" that describes the application setup process.

To "push" an application to MetaFrame XP servers equipped with the Installer, publish the script to those servers. The application will then be distributed and automatically installed onto MetaFrame XP servers across the enterprise.

IM also helps to sort out uninstall issues associated with many applications. For example, with many uninstall programs, application components can be left behind on the server. With IM, the Installer component tracks every application component installed and completely uninstalls the components when the administrator elects to "unpublish" the application on a specific server. This simplifies the relocation of applications from one server to another.

Load Management

Load management is available inMetaFrame XPa and XPe versions to assist administrators in maximizing the utilization of server resources and maintaining optimum user experience. Load management is a concept familiar to many administrators of Microsoft Terminal Server Edition, but it has a special meaning in the context of MetaFrame XP server operation.

With Microsoft's NT Server 4.0 TSE, Windows 2000, and Windows Server 2003 operating systems, multiuser computing capabilities are viewed as a service, much like SQL or Exchange services. Due to this orientation, Microsoft's approach to balancing system load across multiple servers focuses less on the nature and requirements of the load itself (application sessions in the case of multiuser computing), and more on the distribution of the session load across multiple systems. In effect, clients are presented with a virtual IP address representing multiple servers with replicated resources and services. As each server reaches a load threshold, incoming client session requests are forwarded to a server with available resources.

MetaFrame XP takes load managing from the server level to the application level, adding features such as automatic session reconnection and enhanced manageability to terminal services, fine-tuning the concept of load management considerably.

With MetaFrame XP Load Management, an application can be published for execution on any or all MetaFrame servers in a server farm. When an application or desktop session that has been configured for multiple servers is launched by an ICA client, MetaFrame XP Load Management selects which server will run the application based on a set of tunable parameters. Administrators have access to load management variables via the Citrix Management Console (CMC).

How the Load Manager Works

Administrators use the CMC to set load-management parameters. Load management makes decisions based on administrator-defined rules that define lower and upper limits on a number of variables that are defined by load evaluators tracked on each server. Load evaluators are numbers between 0 (free) and 10,000 (fully utilized). The zone data collectors are responsible for keeping track of each server's load evaluators and directing users to the least-busy servers. When more than one rule is applied to a load evaluator, the evaluator with the highest load value defines the load of the server.

Load evaluators can have up to 12 rules. These rules can be broken into four categories: moving average, moving average compared to high threshold, incremental, and Boolean. These categories are explained in more detail next.

Moving average uses rules based on percentage values to calculate load values. The administrator defines a low threshold where the load manager reports no load and a high threshold that the load manager reports a full load. When the moving average is between the low and high thresholds, the load is determined as the percentage multiplied by 10,000. Two-rule types operate with the moving average: CPU utilization, constituting the average usage of CPUs; and memory usage, which is the average of the physical and virtual memory in the server.

The moving average compared to the high threshold reports no load when the moving average is below the low threshold. When the moving average is at or above the high threshold, the load manager reports a full load. When the moving average is between the low and high thresholds, the load manager reports a load value based on the upper threshold value and 0. The lower threshold value is not used in calculating the load. There are five rules that use moving average compared to the high threshold. Context Switches calculate load based on CPU context switches, meaning the OS switches between processes. Disk Data I/O calculates load based on all I/O throughput in kilobytes of disks. Disk Operations calculates load based on disk operations per second for all disks. Page Faults calculates load based on the number of page faults per second, which is the number of pages that the Operating System accesses that have been flushed to disk. Page Swap calculates load based on the number of page swaps per second, which happens when the OS swaps physical memory to virtual memory on disk.

The incremental rules are user friendly and do not require performance monitor or calculations between upper and lower thresholds. All calculations are based on a full load maximum value specified by the MetaFrame XP administrator. When the maximum number specified is reached, the load manager reports full load. Otherwise, the load manager reports a percentage based on the maximum. The load value is calculated by dividing 10,000 by the rule value, then multiplying that value by the current counter. Three rules are in this classification; Application User Load calculates the load based on the number of users connected to an application. Server User Load calculates the load based on the number of users connected to a server. License Threshold calculates load based on the number of assigned connection license counts in use on the server.

Boolean rules are based on conditions being either true or false. If the conditions are met, or found to be "true," access is allowed. Otherwise, it is denied. These rules can be used in conjunction with other load evaluator rules, because they have no associated load values. If no other rules are applied in conjunction with a Boolean rule, all connections are directed to the same server. When one of these rules takes effect, it does not enforce the rule on users already connected. For instance, if the Scheduling rule disables an application at a certain hour, users employing the application can stay connected. However, if the users log off, they cannot reconnect to the application during the hours it is disabled. Boolean rules have two evaluators. IP Range enables or disables access to a server or published application based on source IP address. IP Range rules do not function in mixed mode. Scheduling enables or disables access to a server or published application during specific time periods. Scheduling, like all load evaluators, is checked only during login/application launch.

Load Management in a Mixed Citrix Environment

The MetaFrame XP farm needs to be kept in mixed mode to allow the use of load management when MetaFrame 1.8 or MetaFrame for UNIX servers are to coexist with MetaFrame XP servers. When operating in mixed mode, MetaFrame XP servers communicate with MetaFrame 1.8 servers through the ICA Browser and Program Neighborhood services. MetaFrame XP servers communicate with each other using IMA, but the ICA Browser service is responsible for application resolution and communication with MetaFrame 1.8 and MetaFrame for UNIX servers. For load balancing to work correctly in mixed mode, a MetaFrame XP server must be the master ICA Browser. The following differences exist between operating in native mode:

▼   In mixed mode, application load evaluators and IP Range rules are ignored.

■   qfarm reports load information from MetaFrame XP servers only. Use qserver/load to view load information in a mixed-mode environment.

■   The load monitor tool reports MetaFrame XP information only.

▲   Published applications must have the same name (case-sensitive) in both farms for load balancing to work.

APPLICATION PUBLISHING

Application publishing refers to the installation and configuration of applications on a multiuser server (or server farm), so they can be accessed readily by users. MetaFrame enhances the basic application publishing capabilities of TSE by providing a Published Application Manager to facilitate the process of fielding an application.

The objective of the Published Application Manager is not only to ease the burden of administrators, but also to shield users from the complexities of setting up applications for use on their clients. When an application is published using the Published Application Manager utility, user access is simplified in three ways:

▼ **Application addressing**   Instead of connecting to a MetaFrame server by its IP address or server name, users can connect to a specific application by whatever name has been assigned to the application itself. Connecting to applications by name eliminates the need for users to remember which servers contain which applications.

■ **Application navigation**   With applications published under MetaFrame, the user does not need to possess knowledge of the Windows NT 4.0, Windows 2000, or Windows Server 2003 desktop (Windows NT Explorer or Program Manager) to find and start applications after connecting to MetaFrame servers. Instead, published applications present the user with the desired application in an ICA session.

▲ **User authentication**   Instead of logging on and logging off multiple MetaFrame servers to access applications, Program Neighborhood allows users to authenticate themselves a single time to all servers and obtain immediate access to all applications configured for their user group or specific username. Also, publishing applications for the special Anonymous user group allows user authentication processes to be eliminated completely. This can be a useful time-saver when publishing applications for general use by all users on the network.

User Accounts

MetaFrame application publishing provides ICA session access to two types of user accounts: anonymous and explicit. Before publishing an application, it is important to first consider who the users will be, what they will be doing when they run the application, and where they will be connecting from. This will define whether the users should be anonymous or explicitly defined (named users with full authentication).

The total number of users, whether anonymous or explicit, who can be logged on to the MetaFrame server at the same time is contingent upon an organization's licensed user count and on server and bandwidth limitations. These limitations need to be clearly understood before proceeding with application publishing (Chapter 11 discusses server and farm sizing in detail).

Anonymous User Accounts

During MetaFrame installation, the Setup program creates a special user group called "Anonymous." By default, this local Windows 2003 account contains 15 user accounts with account usernames in the format Anon000 through Anon015. Anonymous users are afforded guest permissions by default.

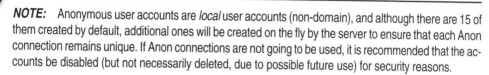

NOTE: Anonymous user accounts are *local* user accounts (non-domain), and although there are 15 of them created by default, additional ones will be created on the fly by the server to ensure that each Anon connection remains unique. If Anon connections are not going to be used, it is recommended that the accounts be disabled (but not necessarily deleted, due to possible future use) for security reasons.

If an application that is to be published on the MetaFrame server is intended to be accessed by guest-level users, the application can be configured using the Published Application Manager to allow access by anonymous users. When a user starts an anonymous application, the MetaFrame server does not require an explicit username and password to log the user on to the server, but selects a user from a pool of anonymous users who are not currently logged on. Anonymous user accounts are granted minimal ICA session permissions, including

▼   Ten-minute idle (no user activity) time-out.

■   Automatic End Session on broken connection or time-out.

■   No password requirement.

▲   Password cannot be changed by user.

Anonymous user accounts do not have a persistent identity. That is to say, no user information is retained when an anonymous user session ends. Any desktop settings, user-specific files, or other resources created or configured by the user are discarded at the end of the ICA session. Because of the inherent permission limitations of anonymous user accounts, the 15 anonymous user accounts created during MetaFrame installation usually do not require any further maintenance.

Explicit User Accounts

Explicit users, which are created and maintained via the Active Directory User Manager, have a "permanent" existence. Their desktop settings, security settings, and so on, are retained between sessions for each user in a user profile.

Explicit users can be of any user class and are generally created for a specific purpose. Their access permissions may be changed by using the Active Directory User Manager.

Identifying what groups of users will have access to an application that is about to be published will aid in server and link resource planning and may even expedite the publishing process. Administrators can capitalize on group settings and extend application access to multiple users concurrently. Conversely, using the Anonymous group is a handy way to make general-purpose applications available to the broadest possible user community in the least amount of time.

MetaFrame Password Manager

Citrix MetaFrame Password Manager (CMPM) is a single sign-on solution designed specifically for MetaFrame XP and MetaFrame Secure Access Manager. CMPM provides password security and single sign-on access to Windows, web, proprietary, and host-based applications running in the MetaFrame Access Suite environment. Users authenticate once with a single password, and MetaFrame Password Manager does the rest, automatically logging in to any password-protected information system, enforcing password policies, monitoring all password-related events, and automating end-user tasks, including password changes.

CMPM is comprised of three components:

▼ A Directory Service to centrally store the password and user information. Three choices are available: File Sync (comes native with CMPM), Microsoft Active Directory, and LDAP, which consists of Sun ONE Identity Server and Novell eDirectory.

■ The MetaFrame Presentation Server Agent—a 32-bit agent that runs on MetaFrame servers or on a local client workstation

▲ MetaFrame Password Manager Console

Once a user has logged in and authenticated to a directory service, the agent intercepts any future password requests with a query, asking if the user would like the password manager to manage this password. If the user answers yes, then the password information is stored in the central directory service store and handed back to the client workstation when the workstation queries for that password again.

MetaFrame Password Manager enhances security by centralizing security policies, providing an encrypted file for each user's credentials, and allowing IT administrators to automatically generate passwords that are more difficult to crack and to change them more frequently, if needed.

CMPM can either be purchased with the Access Suite Bundle or individually.

Application Publishing Security

In addition to considering the user population for an application, administrators also need to consider the security requirements of the applications they are planning to publish. MetaFrame XP provides additional methods, beyond those of Microsoft operating systems, for securing access to applications published on the MetaFrame server.

Limiting Users to Published Applications

Users of a specific connection type (dial-up, for example) can be restricted to running published applications only. By allowing users to solely access predefined applications, unauthorized users are prevented from obtaining access to the Windows desktop or a command prompt as their initial application unless published by an administrator. This type of security may be obtained by using the Advanced Connection Settings dialog box in the Connection Configuration utility.

It is important to note however that many applications and utilities have major security holes (for example, some applications permit a user to launch other applications [explorer.exe or cmd.exe] from within them). Thus a significant amount of time must be spent putting in place policies, profiles, and registry changes to more securely lock down the operating system and applications. Enterprise environments should consider a lockdown application (two popular lockdown application companies that are certified to work in an SBC environment are triCerat RES and AppSense, covered in more depth in Chapters 11, 13 and 15) to specifically automate the lockdown tasks.

Limiting Applications

The Citrix Management Console allows an administrator to restrict an application to specified users or groups of users, assuming they have been given explicit user access.

Firewall Security and Limited Access
from Non-Authorized External Users

With security at the forefront of most enterprise activities, the Internet firewall has become non-optional for every enterprise to protect their resources from non-authorized Internet intrusion. But, since the Internet is such a necessary access method for many users, the firewall often poses a very difficult trade-off—full security versus easy access. MetaFrame Secure Gateway solves this trade-off by providing both easy access and industry recognized security. MetaFrame Secure Gateway is covered in much more depth later in this chapter, as well as in Chapter 16.

Usernames and Passwords

As long as explicit user accounts are specified, MetaFrame XP supports a large number of authentication approaches. For starters, strong password authentication is essential for security (see Chapter 8 for a more detailed password discussion). Even better, consider a second factor authentication approach (using not only something a user knows, but a second authentication method such as something unique that only a specific user has), such as a smart card, token, or biometric). MetaFrame XP FR-3 is fully integrated with RSA and Secure Computing's second factor authentication, as well as a large variety of authentication tools (biometric, smart card, and so on) that integrate with RSA and Secure Computing's authentication software. Additionally, companies like Secure Computing provide a method to integrate the second factor authentication with MetaFrame Web Integration access, Program Neighborhood access, and Windows 2000 Active Directory access, to make authentication seamless to the user community. See Chapter 8 for more detail and discussion on security.

ACLcheck Utility

An ACLcheck utility supplied with MetaFrame examines the security ACLs associated with MetaFrame XP files and directories. This utility can be used to report on any potential security breaches.

Application Execution Shell

The Application Execution Shell (App) in MetaFrame allows administrators to write application execution scripts that perform actions before and after application execution. These scripts can be used in connection with other security utilities to check the security of MetaFrame servers and clients.

METAFRAME AS A WEB APPLICATION ACCESS CENTER

In these days of electronic business and the Internet, companies are also porting applications to intranets, extranets, and to the Internet, where they can be used by business partners and even consumers. MetaFrame XP facilitates this objective with MetaFrame Web Interface, Web Interface Extensions, and MetaFrame Secure Access Manager. One thing common to all versions of Web Interface is the ability to use pass-through or single sign-on for multiple applications.

MetaFrame Secure Gateway

In our view, one of the most significant new features developed by Citrix in the past three years is MetaFrame Secure Gateway, which is included in all editions of MetaFrame XP. Although Citrix has long provided access via the Internet, enterprise organizations often struggled with providing Internet access to SBC environments due to security concerns. Although both Citrix's ICA and Microsoft's RDP support 128-bit encryption, both protocols also require that firewall ports be opened, at both the client and data-center sides of the Internet. This firewall change creates both logistical and security challenges for companies, especially in instances where the far-side firewall may not be influenced. One example of this is when a company's employees are housed on other company's campuses (either temporarily or for the duration of a longer project), and, as such, often cannot affect the firewall rules at their location.

Secure Gateway solves this problem by converting ICA traffic from port 1494 to port 443 (SSL) in the data-center DMZ. Since SSL is a widely supported standard and utilized for many other web purposes, it provides a very standard and accepted transmission method for traffic traversing firewalls and the Internet. Secure Gateway requires several additional server hardware components. See Figure 3-4 for a diagram of a Secure Gateway implementation.

Web Interface for MetaFrame

MetaFrame XP includes MetaFrame Web Interface for (formerly NFuse Classic) with the XPs and XPa editions. This product enables users to integrate applications and data that are published into customized web portals for the end user, who then can access applications via a web browser.

In addition to publishing applications to the familiar web browser interface, another popular use of MetaFrame Web Interface foris to deploy the ICA client itself. MetaFrame Web Interface provides for automatic download and updates of the ICA client, largely transparent to the user, upon user login. This provides a very fast and clean deployment and update mechanism for first-time Citrix users and remote users.

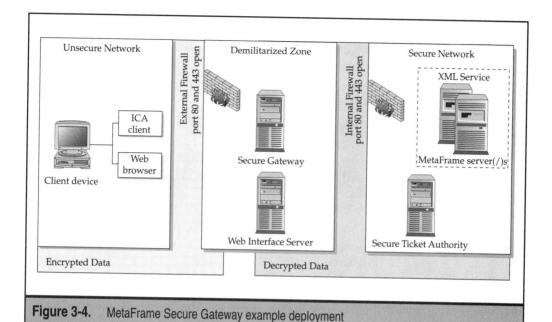

Figure 3-4.   MetaFrame Secure Gateway example deployment

Using MetaFrame Web Interface, the presentation layer elements of multiple applications can be combined on a single page for exposure to the end user as a single, unified application. A simple wizard is provided to aid the administrator in defining the portal contents, which may include applications hosted on MetaFrame XP and MetaFrame for UNIX servers. Support for MetaFrame for UNIX enables the Web Interface for MetaFrame portal to be used to integrate both Windows and UNIX-based applications and data.

Web Interface for MetaFrame access centers can be customized to meet the needs of individual users, who access their applications in accordance with a user or group account login, or general, purpose access centers that can be fielded for access by anonymous users. Either way, the access centers, like other MetaFrame applications, are managed via the same set of MetaFrame utilities used to manage and control other applications published through MetaFrame.

MetaFrame Web Interface Extensions

MetaFrame Web Interface Extension (formerly Citrix Enterprise Services for NFuse (ESN)) is included with XPe and performs the same tasks as Web Interface for MetaFrame XP with the additional feature of multiple farm aggregation.

Web Interface Extension for MetaFrame XP enables highly scaled application provisioning from MetaFrame by aggregating application sets from multiple farms. When combined with MetaFrame Secure Gateway, it provides a simple, secure, single point to access business-critical applications.

MetaFrame Web Interface Extension provides the following solutions:

▼ Multiple farms operating in the enterprise can be used more efficiently and managed more easily.

■ Administrators don't have to rely on web programming skills to control the operation of Web Interface for MetaFrame XP.

■ Users only have to provide credentials once, not for each application accessed via MetaFrame XP.

▲ Administrators and users can set values for each MetaFrame XP application instead of being restricted to single global values for all users and all applications.

MetaFrame Secure Access Manager

MetaFrame Secure Access Manager (MSAM) is a stand-alone application that, while able to enhance MetaFrame, does not require MetaFrame. MSAM is a member of the MetaFrame Access Suite, and can be purchased individually or bundled with the suite. It is not included with MetaFrame XP. MSAM is a full-blown Access Solution, comparable to portal products like Microsoft SharePoint Portal Server or Plumtree Corporate Portal. MSAM differs from MetaFrame Web Interface in that it is designed to be a common interface for the aggregation of many different types of corporate data and applications rather than just thin deployment of Windows and UNIX applications. MSAM differentiates itself from Portal products by providing a wizard-based tool with content delivery agents (CDAs) that automate such tasks as placing MetaFrame ICA icons within the web access page, or grabbing Microsoft Exchange content and placing it within the web page.

MSAM can quickly, and through a wizard-based tool, create a single, secured web interface that has a portion of the window showing a message from the president of the company, another portion of the window showing the number of customers in a call queue for support, another portion of the window that is a customer information lookup for pertinent data, a portion of the window showing applications available (both ICA and web based), and a final tag across the top that shows the corporate stock price. All of these sections are dynamically controlled based on the role of the user. Figure 3-5 shows a screenshot of a simple MSAM portal page.

SHADOWING

In addition to providing tools for managing application publishing, MetaFrame delivers a utility targeted at reducing administrative costs by enabling the remote support of users of published applications. *Session Shadowing* enables the administrator (or help-desk personnel) to remotely join, or take control, of another user's ICA session. When activated, Session Shadowing displays the user's screen on the administrator's console. Optionally,

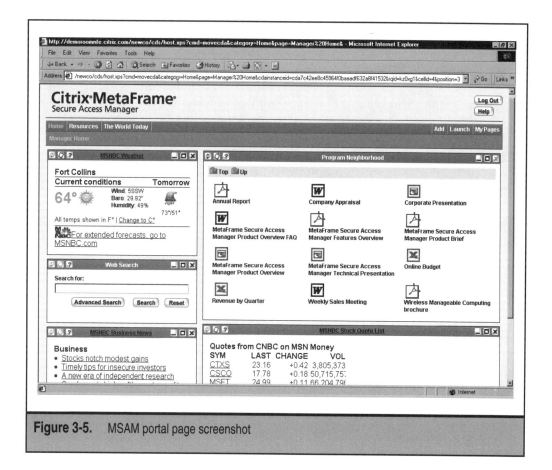

Figure 3-5. MSAM portal page screenshot

the administrator can assume control of the remote user's mouse and keyboard, which enables demonstrations.

In addition to facilitating help desk and troubleshooting processes, Session Shadowing can also be used in online interactive teaching and call-center applications.

Additional security has been added to MetaFrame XP to limit or disable shadowing during installation that cannot be reversed. Administrators can disable shadowing of ICA sessions on all servers in a server farm if legal privacy requirements prohibit the shadowing of users' sessions. Alternatively, it may be necessary to disable shadowing on servers that host sensitive applications, such as personnel or payroll applications, in order to protect confidential data. MetaFrame XP Setup provides options on the Shadowing

Setup page for an administrator to limit or disable shadowing at installation time. When shadowing is enabled, an administrator has the option to select the following restrictions:

▼ **Prohibit remote control of ICA sessions**.   By default, MetaFrame XP gives administrators the ability to input keystroke and mouse control during session shadowing. Select this option if you want administrators to be able to shadow without input. In some cases, shadowing without input hides administrator presence.

■ **Prohibit shadow connections without notification**.   By default, MetaFrame XP notifies users with a prompt when an administrator is attempting to shadow their sessions. Select this option to deny administrators the ability to shadow sessions without sending this notification.

■ **Prohibit shadow connections without logging**.   Events such as shadowing attempts, successes, and failures can be logged in the Windows event log and examined using Event Viewer. Select this option to enable logging.

▲ **Do not allow shadowing of ICA sessions on this server**.   This option permanently disables shadowing by anyone of all ICA sessions on the server.

Configuring Session Shadowing

Session Shadowing is configured at the time of connection configuration. The shadowing settings in the Advanced Connection Settings dialog box control the behavior of shadowing for all sessions on the connection. Setting options include

▼ **Enabled**   Specifies that sessions on the connection can be shadowed.

■ **Disabled**   Specifies that sessions on the connection cannot be shadowed.

■ **Input On**   Allows the shadower to input keyboard and mouse actions to the shadowed session.

▲ **Notify On**   Specifies that the shadowed user gets a message asking if it is OK for the shadowing to occur.

Session Shadowing Initiation

The initiation of Session Shadowing can be accomplished via the Shadow taskbar, the Citrix Management Console, or from a command line. Each interface is well documented and reasonably self-explanatory.

Citrix MetaFrame Conferencing Manager

Citrix MetaFrame Conferencing Manager adds intuitive application conferencing to MetaFrame XP. This application is a new member of the MetaFrame Access Suite and can be purchased as an individual package or bundled with the Suite. Conferencing Manager integrates three components: a Microsoft Exchange/Outlook calendar form; a new Conferencing Manager interface that initiates, cancels, and manages the users and applications of the conferences; and MetaFrame XP's session shadowing features. These three components create an intuitive interface by which users create and join a collaborative conference session among multiple people. Because shadowing cannot occur across multiple MetaFrame XP servers, each conference is limited to the number of sessions that one server can support (typically about 100 people on a four-processor MetaFrame XP server running Microsoft PowerPoint).

Conferencing Manager eliminates the geographical distance between team members, increases the productivity of meetings, and allows easy collaboration. Teams can utilize Conferencing Manager to share application sessions, work together on document editing, and conduct online training, regardless of the location of individual team members or the access devices or network connections they're using.

METAFRAME LICENSING

The MetaFrame license is more than an agreement describing the cost to the user and revenue to the vendor. It is a technical licensing implementation in which licenses are pooled by the MetaFrame servers themselves and used to calculate authorized use of the product (see Tables 3-3 and 3-4). In short, if the license provides for 20 users to connect to a MetaFrame server, user number 21 will be locked out by the server.

	Connection Licenses	
	With Subscription Advantage	*Without Subscription Advantage*
MetaFrame XPs	$290	$250
MetaFrame XPa	$345	$300
MetaFrame Xpe	$400	$350

Table 3-3.   List Pricing (New Customer)

		Connection Licenses	
Upgrading From	Upgrading To	*With Subscription Advantage*	*Without Subscription Advantage*
MetaFrame XPs	MetaFrame XPa	$100	$55
MetaFrame XPa	MetaFrame XPe	$105	$55
MetaFrame XPs	MetaFrame XPe	$160	$110

Table 3-4.   List Pricing (Upgrades)

Citrix delivers MetaFrame licenses in three ways: the shrink wrap method, corporate licensing, and ASP licensing.

The Shrink-Wrap Method

Administrators can purchase the base product and licenses for 20 concurrent users.

As configurations expand, bulk user packs can be purchased to meet changing needs. Additional MetaFrame XP user licenses can be added in increments of 5, 10, 20, or 50 concurrent users.

Easy Licensing

Easy Licensing is designed for customers with up to 500 concurrent licenses that wish to take advantage of electronic licensing. On-demand licensing allows administrators to purchase what is needed when it is needed. This licensing also allows for auto activation for rapid deployment. Another advantage to Easy Licensing is that it does not have a complex paper contract, but rather uses a "click to accept" online agreement (similar to opening packaged products).

Corporate Licensing

Corporate licensing programs are available for large license quantities. This program uses a point-based system with four discount levels for corporations and a special education discount level. In addition, special pricing is available for corporate customers who adopt a "long-term strategic use" posture. In this case, cumulative purchases drive discounts. This program is designed for customers with 500 to 5000 concurrent seats.

Flex Licensing

Flex licensing is designed for companies with more than 5000 concurrent seats. Flex Licensing requires a custom contract, called a Global 2000 agreement, reserved for enterprise customers. The advantage of Flex licensing, in addition to a very significant discount, is that Citrix provides additional license automation to make it easier to install and activate MetaFrame licensing across a large quantity of servers.

Subscription Advantage

Subscription Advantage provides customers with a convenient way to keep their Citrix software current and maximize their server-based computing investments. Customers receive software upgrades, enhancements, and maintenance releases that become available during the term of your subscription. Subscription Advantage is for a one-year term and can be renewed each year.

METAFRAME PRESENTATION CENTER FOR UNIX

Although this book is primarily focused on MetaFrame XP for Windows 2003, UNIX-based applications continue to be a mainstay of many large enterprise environments, and Windows and UNIX users alike can benefit from seamless, single point, webified access to these applications. Because of the overall value of server-based computing in providing web-based seamless access to all applications from any device, for all users, the authors felt strongly that MetaFrame for UNIX should be covered in this book. A large majority of the features and infrastructure discussed in these pages will apply equally to MetaFrame Presentation Server for UNIX and MetaFrame XP for Windows 2003. Features and tools such as MetaFrame Web Interface, MetaFrame Secure Gateway, load management, and any-device access are further promoted by bringing the UNIX applications to the Citrix SBC infrastructure fold.

Although some long-time UNIX administrators argue that UNIX has supported multiuser functionality for years through X-Window, and thus MetaFrame for UNIX is not needed, they are missing out. Due to the feature-rich GUI environments of most UNIX desktops and applications, X-Windows (even compressed X) is very network-intensive. Because of this nature, costly WAN topologies need to be implemented, and low bandwidth connections are almost non-supportable due to performance issues. Additionally, X-Windows does not support such MetaFrame features as shadowing, copy and paste of both text and graphics between the local client and remote server environments, auto-creation of local printers and client drive mapping, and most importantly, Web Interface integration with Windows and web applications.

Based in part on the success and popularity of MetaFrame XP in the Windows application hosting environment, Citrix recently announced the latest version of the MetaFrame product suite aimed at the hosting of UNIX, X-Window, and Java applications: MetaFrame for UNIX Version 1.2. The product, which at present supports IBM AIX, Sun Solaris, and HP-UX platforms, as well as virtually any custom or commercially packaged UNIX applications, offers the same value as MetaFrame XP, but with a UNIX/Java twist: low-bandwidth, universal client access over any network connection to any UNIX or Java application.

At the core of the MetaFrame for UNIX product is a modified X11R6.3 server. This does not replace the X11 server supplied with most UNIX operating systems but is specifically used to enable ICA-connected sessions running on MetaFrame for UNIX. MetaFrame for UNIX runs all standard X11 applications using the modified X server rather than the native X11 server.

In operation, the modified X11 server talks to a UNIX-ported ICA stack (Winstation Driver, Protocol Driver, and Transport Driver), which performs an X-to-ICA conversion. This is key to delivering applications seamlessly to clients from all MetaFrame platforms.

In addition to the modified X11 server and ported ICA stack, MetaFrame for UNIX also provides an ICA browser for use in load balancing and client browsing, a "listener" to intercept incoming ICA connections, and a "Frame Manager," which manages all the sessions currently running on the server.

The same core functionality used by MetaFrame for UNIX to deploy X11 and other applications hosted on UNIX servers can also be applied to Java applications. At first, this capability may seem redundant: in theory, Java applications are already portable to any device. In reality, however, Java client-side application deployments still confront numerous challenges.

Downloading Java applications entails the use of the available client-server network protocol, which is often not optimized for low-bandwidth connections. This results in the major complaint about Java applications—that they are sometimes incredibly slow to download for operation. Operating the Java application, which is executed locally on a server, over a bandwidth-optimized ICA connection provides a higher performance solution to this issue.

Java applications also fall prey to peculiarities in the Java Virtual Machine that runs on the client system. Not all JVMs are the same, and it is often the case that a Java application that runs perfectly in one JVM behaves very differently in another. MetaFrame for UNIX solves this problem by executing Java applications within the server's JVM environment.

Utilizing a single, server-based JVM also saves time and money when developing and testing Java applications developed in-house. Once the application is working in the server JVM, it can be deployed instantly to any ICA client device.

It should also be noted that the Java Virtual Machine is typically a large piece of software. While the development of an embedded JVM is under way, ultra-thin client devices lack the capacity to run a JVM that offers sufficient features or performance. This issue is removed through the use of the MetaFrame for UNIX solution.

In summary, MetaFrame for UNIX Operating Systems can be an important adjunct to Windows-based MetaFrame servers in heterogeneous server environments. MetaFrame for UNIX can be included in server farm and load-balancing schemes, and applications hosted on MetaFrame for UNIX systems may be published individually or as part of integrated Web Interface Access Centers for integrated access by end users.

PART II

Designing an Enterprise SBC Solution

CHAPTER 4

Preparing Your Organization for an On-Demand Enterprise Implementation

Constructing an on-demand enterprise requires extensive planning and resources. In addition to the technical challenges, political and cultural factors inevitably play a part in a server-based computing implementation. This chapter covers the steps involved in building an on-demand enterprise infrastructure. We start the process with a small proof-of-concept pilot program to ensure application compatibility with Terminal Services. We then look at putting together a feasibility committee to define the project's scope and objectives as well as to seek executive sponsorship and determine financial justification. A guide to performing an infrastructure assessment is followed by a project-planning outline. The steps involved in planning an enterprise SBC environment are as follows:

1. Establish a non-production proof-of-concept pilot program.

2. Establish a production proof-of-concept pilot program.

3. Assemble a feasibility committee.

4. Recruit an executive sponsor.

5. Justify the project financially.

6. Assemble a project planning team.

7. Create a project definition document.

8. Perform an infrastructure assessment.

9. Generate a project design plan.

10. Expand the pilot to beta stage.

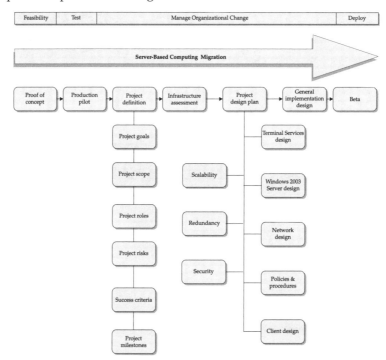

THE PROOF-OF-CONCEPT PILOT PROGRAM

Applications are the driving force behind server-based computing, and it makes little sense to go through the expense and trouble of planning for an enterprise implementation until you know that your organization's applications will run adequately within this environment. An inexpensive proof-of-concept pilot program enables you to test application compatibility both individually and when running on Terminal Services. It also enables you to measure performance and to more accurately gauge the server resources required to implement an enterprise server-based computing environment.

Starting with a Non-Production Pilot Program

Although you may ultimately wish to run all of your organization's applications under SBC, the decision to implement server-based computing generally depends upon successfully running a small number of critical applications. These are the applications that should first be loaded on a server running Terminal Services and MetaFrame XP Presentation Server offline. If the results are not acceptable, adjustments to the applications or operating system may be required. Once the crucial applications are running well on MetaFrame XP Presentation Server, other less-crucial applications can be added, if desired. If SBC users will be using foreign-language versions of Terminal Services and MetaFrame XP Presentation Server, a separate proof-of-concept pilot program should be set up for each language since different hotfixes and patches are often required.

Expanding to a Production Pilot Program

Once the offline pilot program is stable, you can expand it to include a small number of pilot users. Great care, though, should go into the selection of these participants. A natural inclination of IT people is to choose from two types of users. The first type is a user who has an immediate computing need that the pilot program will solve, such as a requirement for an upgraded PC. The second type of user is someone who is known to be difficult because he is particularly demanding or requires constant help. The thinking here is that if server-based computing can make a difficult user happy, it can make anyone happy. Using these selection criteria, though, is toying with disaster. A pilot program is likely to have some bugs that need to be worked out. The wrong participant may loudly complain about the problems of working with Terminal Services. If the complaint reaches the ears of an executive, the whole on-demand enterprise (ODE) initiative could be killed. The organization might then lose the opportunity to reap the benefits and savings of server-based computing simply because of poor selection of participants.

Pilot users should be a representative sample of those who will ultimately use Terminal Services, but they should be friendly to the concept and understanding about the likelihood of encountering initial problems until IT works them out. Avoid choosing people for any reason other than testing the server-based computing concept.

Goals of the production pilot include measuring the time it takes for loading the various applications, reviewing methods for performance tuning, and focusing on user issues such as usability and functionality.

Capacity Planning

Most organizations do not convert their entire infrastructure to an on-demand enterprise at once. Almost inevitably, though, SBC becomes increasingly utilized once implemented and as the benefits of the on-demand enterprise begin to manifest themselves. It is important, therefore, to adequately plan for growth and to implement a system that is scalable. A pilot deployment is a great opportunity to gather capacity metrics in a controlled environment with actual users. It also allows administrators to monitor all components of the implementation such as server capacity, bandwidth utilizations, Directory Services integrations, peripherals, and file storage. A good practice is to build a pilot environment that contains 30 to 40 percent more capacity than the expected user load for the pilot. The extra capacity gives the administrator an adequate buffer for unexpected bottlenecks that may arise during testing. When the pilot is converted to a beta, the additional resources will undoubtedly be used. Therefore, resources are not wasted.

Hybrids or Pure Thin Clients

Operating in a hybrid mode occurs when a user continues to run one or more applications on his or her local PC. If pilot participants will be operating in hybrid mode, make sure their desktops are configured so that they know whether they are in a local session or in a MetaFrame session. This can be accomplished using application publishing (as explained in Chapter 13).

Even if Windows terminals are not in your organization's on-demand enterprise plans, we recommend securing one for the pilot program. Since a Windows terminal is completely dependent upon server-based computing to operate, installing one contributes to a deeper understanding of the new ODE. You may find that the Windows terminal "brick" has uses that you hadn't previously considered, such as serving as an employee's home "PC."

CAUTION: If you are going to have pilot users run legacy PCs, make sure the PCs are high-quality, reliable models (though they do not need to be powerful machines). In one of the authors' projects, a teacher became frustrated because her extremely cheap PC's keyboard broke when she was made a pilot MetaFrame user. Unfortunately, she had grown attached to her low-end keyboard, and despite our best efforts, we could not convince her that her keyboard's failure had nothing to do with Terminal Services. She ended up poisoning the entire project by warning the other teachers not to let Citrix into their classrooms "because it breaks keyboards."

Headquarters and/or Remote Office Users

If you have hybrid pilot users in a remote office who are connected by limited bandwidth, it is essential that you instruct them in proper usage. You do not want them, for instance, to back up files from their local hard drives to the MetaFrame server at headquarters. This will chew up bandwidth and may cause performance degradation for other users in the remote office. As discussed in Chapters 6 and 17, you might also consider setting up bandwidth management as part of your pilot program in order to ensure adequate WAN performance.

TIP: Even if you have no intention of putting headquarters users onto Terminal Services, you should consider setting up at least one corporate IT person as part of the pilot program. Again, this will help to foster understanding of the server-based computing concept and enable your IT staff to experience it firsthand.

Change Control

Many organizations really struggle with how to keep up with change control. It is important for the success of the pilot that a focus is made on maintaining a stable environment, on consolidating and scheduling updates, on obtaining sign-off authority for changes, on proper regression testing, and on maintaining a detailed rollback plan in the event that new applications disrupt the pilot. Implementation support is extremely difficult when too many people or teams have their hands in the pot. It is also very difficult to monitor the systems when servers are frequently down for maintenance.

If you don't have change control procedures in place for IT infrastructure changes, we recommend creating a simple Excel spreadsheet with a tab for each server. On that tab you can have columns for date, change, changed by, and approved by. Another option is to create a mail-enabled public folder in Exchange. Allowing administrators to e-mail any change to an address, such as citrixchanges@company.com, would then make the changes easily available for review.

Documenting Performance

Document your expectations of the pilot program before you begin. Decide up-front what success will look like and how it will be measured, and after the pilot program, create a report on whether the success metrics were met. Document any problems encountered along with their solutions. Document any open issues along with the actions being taken to resolve them.

Pilot Server(s)

Ideally, two load-balanced servers will be utilized for the production pilot program in order to provide redundancy. In most cases, though, organizations will probably use only one server in order to keep expenses lower during the proof-of-concept phase. Organizations can generally use a single server for testing load balancing by utilizing a product such as VMWare or Microsoft Virtual Server. The server should still be close enough to your expected production rollout model to make the results meaningful. For instance, using a Hewlett-Packard server with only two CPUs and half the RAM of your ultimate intended Hewlett-Packard MetaFrame server is probably OK. Using a different brand with different CPU and memory configurations is not a good idea.

Applications

If you are running anything other than 32-bit applications, be prepared for less than optimal performance. Make users aware of what they can expect from various applications. Use products such as the resource manager (RM) component of MetaFrame Presentation Server to test application performance results under simulated greater usage and for providing an audit trail in case of application failure. If performance is less than expected, try removing questionable applications to see if a particular product is causing problems.

THE FEASIBILITY COMMITTEE

Once the proof-of-concept pilot program has proven that the necessary applications run together acceptably within Terminal Services, it is time to determine whether an enterprise server-based computing deployment makes sense for the organization. The decision process of whether to implement an on-demand enterprise should include an evaluation of the proposed project's impact on the organization from operational, financial, cultural, and political perspectives.

A feasibility committee made up of IT personnel and employees from other appropriate departments should assess the merits of migrating to server-based computing. The first task of the feasibility committee will be to broadly define the project's scope along with its benefits. The committee must then evaluate the strategic fit of an on-demand enterprise model within the organization. The next steps include finding an executive sponsor and preparing a financial justification for the project. The committee's resulting report can then be utilized to help guide the planning team's work should the SBC project move forward.

Project Scope

Server-based computing might be limited to deployment of a single application, or it may encompass the entire desktop. It might be utilized only in certain departments or regions, or it may be implemented as the new corporate standard. In general, the more extensively an organization implements an SBC, the more money it will save compared with using PC-based computing. (In Chapter 1, we covered the composition of these savings as well as many other benefits of an on-demand enterprise.) The feasibility committee must determine whether a complete enterprise rollout is practical, or a scaled-back implementation is more appropriate.

Corporate Culture Considerations

The economies achieved from implementing server-based computing inevitably make it much less expensive than decentralized PC-based computing. A hidden potential cost, though, is the turmoil that may result from introducing such huge changes into the computing environment without identifying the problem areas and properly preparing the organization for the changes.

Centralized Standards

The nature of PC-based computing makes it difficult for organizations to enforce IT standards. Typically, corporate IT is unaware of many applications that users run locally or departmentally. Although SBC offers IT the flexibility to allow users to run local applications, it also makes it easy to lock down desktops. Since greater lockdown equates to less administration, IT will tend to exploit this advantage. Even if IT decides to host only a few critical corporate applications, these particular programs now will be outside the direct control of users.

In many organizations, greater IT control is taken for granted as an advantage. Banks, for instance, typically have a tradition of mainframe hosting and readily embrace computing standards for PC users. A software development firm, on the other hand, may decide that the creative benefits of unbridled individual computing outweigh the lower costs obtained from enforcing centralized standards.

The feasibility committee needs to evaluate whether standardization is an acceptable condition within their organizational environment.

Understanding User Perceptions of the Network Infrastructure and IT

The distribution of economic and IT resources mandated by distributed processing often results in a network infrastructure that is plagued with performance and reliability problems. In these environments, users will be reluctant to give up control of their desktops to IT.

NOTE: The feasibility committee must call attention to a networking infrastructure that suffers from performance or reliability problems, but this does not mean that the SBC project should be abandoned. On the contrary. As long as IT can fix the existing problems, an uncompromising first review presents an opportunity to drive rapid project acceptance. IT should initially implement smaller Terminal Services beta projects that deliver better reliability and performance to thin-client users than to their fat-client peers. This strategy can quickly build enthusiasm for the new technology and, in turn, help enable IT to plan an enterprise-wide implementation of server-based computing.

Political Considerations

In many organizations, the disparate nature of distributed processing has led to control of IT budgets by different departments or divisions. Creating an on-demand enterprise is a costly endeavor that affects users throughout the organization. The feasibility committee needs to determine whether the organization will be able to marshal the resources to implement such an encompassing project.

Reduced IT Staff

Gartner Group reported that the staffing required to support a fat-client environment is five times greater than the staffing required to support a thin-client environment. An on-demand enterprise utilizing server-based computing can eliminate the need for remote office IT personnel or even for entire regional IT departments. It is the job of the feasibility committee to evaluate whether the corporate culture will permit elimination of unnecessary network administration, help desk personnel, and PC technician positions.

IT Staff Salaries

Since the majority of organizational processing under SBC takes place at central data centers, the network administrators must be quite skilled. They may require higher salaries than their peers in many distributed processing environments, perhaps even higher than their managers. The feasibility committee must assess whether these types of administrators are already on staff and, if not, whether the organization's salary structure will allow for hiring them.

TIP: Access infrastructure is too encompassing, and too vital to efficiency (and eventual savings), to allow for skimping on anything in the data center—including the people who run it. If higher wages for a select network administrator would wreak havoc on the IT department's existing salary structure, consider alternative solutions, such as outsourcing the position.

Finding an Executive Sponsor

Gaining an executive sponsor and executive support is, without question, the single most important thing I did for this project. The challenges that followed during the next nine months would have been difficult, if not impossible, to overcome without the complete backing of the most senior folks in our company.

—Anthony Lackey, Vice President of MIS, Chief Technology Officer, ABM Industries

Many people simply resist change, particularly if they feel they are giving something up. A server-based computing paradigm is very different from traditional PC-based computing and is bound to cause some disharmony. Executive sponsorship is essential for successfully transforming into an on-demand enterprise. Upper management must make it absolutely clear that the server-based computing initiative is something that will happen and that everyone is expected to make work. Ideally, the CIO and other selected executives should switch from PCs to Windows terminals in order to show their complete support for the project.

Justifying SBC Financially

As the feasibility committee members discuss the scope and organizational ramifications of building an on-demand enterprise, they are likely to become more aware of the enormous savings and compelling benefits it will provide. In order for the project to move forward, they need to convey this information to management. Most corporate decision makers will require an in-depth financial analysis of the specific impacts of migrating to server-based computing. They will primarily be interested in the estimated cost of the project and the return on the required investment. A reasonable time frame over which to calculate these figures usually ranges from three to five years.

Although it may seem both very difficult and impractical to estimate project costs without first doing a detailed infrastructure assessment and in-depth planning, this is not the case. The components of an enterprise SBC environment are not difficult to estimate on a "big picture" basis. And since the resulting savings over PC-based computing are likely to be very high, broad estimates are all that is required for a revealing financial analysis.

We recommend taking a three-pronged approach to building a financial analysis, and we give examples in Appendix B. First, present the hard cost savings. This can be done by comparing the estimated costs of staying with PC-based computing over a period of three to five years versus the estimated costs of implementing SBC. Hard costs include easily identified expenditures such as hardware purchases and help desk personnel salaries. In most cases, the hard savings alone will more than justify the entire project. This will isolate the feasibility committee from detractors who might try to take shots at the financial analysis.

Next, present the estimated soft cost savings. These are real savings, but their quantification may be harder to agree upon. For instance, how much does it really cost the organization when users suffer downtime as their PCs are upgraded? The model presented in Appendix B shows how these types of savings can be estimated. Presenting them as part of the financial analysis gives management a better idea of the ultimate economic impact of migrating to an on-demand enterprise.

The third component is a list of the expected benefits from SBC. These benefits can sometimes be quantified, but often have just as big an impact if they are listed without specific numbers. As described in Chapter 1, the business benefits of building an on-demand enterprise often have more strategic importance to the organization than the hard and soft savings combined.

The last element is a qualitative high-level description of the specific benefits an on-demand enterprise can provide in terms of enhanced security and the much greater disaster/recovery and business continuity potential. This can also include the ability to more easily comply with regulations such as Sarbanes-Oxley and HIPAA while lowering the cost of discovery and the risk of litigation.

THE PROJECT PLANNING TEAM

Once an executive sponsor has been identified and management has accepted the feasibility committee's financial analysis of implementing ODE, a planning team can be assembled.

The project planning team will be primarily comprised of IT staff, including hands-on technical people. It should also include some members from the feasibility committee and possibly representatives from multiple departments or divisions. This will help ensure that the organization's enterprise goals are met with this enterprise deployment. Each member's role and expected contributions should be defined. Accountability should be established.

Consultants

Since the ODE rides on top of Windows Server technology, many organizations are inclined to plan the entire process internally and use only existing staff. This is probably not an optimal utilization of resources. We recommend seeking out Citrix specialists who have designed and implemented multiple large-scale server-based computing migrations. The experience they bring to the table should pay for their fees many times over.

Depending upon the size of the project and organization, it may also be worthwhile to consider using a change management consultant who is very experienced in helping implement organization-wide change. As with all consultants, we recommend requesting and checking references.

NOTE: Citrix has stratified its reseller channel into three categories: silver, gold, and platinum. Platinum resellers represent approximately the top one percent of all Citrix resellers. They must have a minimum of six Citrix certified engineers on staff, and they are the most likely to have the resources and experience to successfully implement an enterprise server-based computing project. Of course, you should carefully check the references and ascertain the capabilities of any consultants you engage.

The Project Definition Document

The first task of the planning committee is to prepare a document defining project goals, scope, roles, and risks along with success criteria and milestones. This will be a living document that will guide the planning team through the infrastructure assessment, design, and implementation stages. As expectations, requirements, and conditions change, the planning definition document will serve as a touchstone for keeping the project on track.

Project Goals

While saving money is likely to be an important objective, the strategic advantages and other benefits described in Chapter 1 may be even more important considerations. Clearly defined project goals serve as a benchmark as the server-based computing project rolls out.

Project Scope

The preliminary work done by the feasibility committee combined with management's reaction to the financial analysis enable the planning committee to identify the parameters of the SBC project. In particular, the committee must select the applications to be run via SBC along with expectations for stability and for upgrades during the implementation process. Adding a new application, for example, requires extensive testing as well as the creation of a new server image. What's known as *scope creep* is inevitable, and guidelines need to be established for an approval process when requests for additional applications or features are made. Allowances must also be made for delays caused by these changes.

Project Roles

Keeping the project's executive sponsor closely informed of progress will help garner upper management support when needed. The project also requires both an IT owner and a high-level business owner who can intercede to work through any problems that may arise. A project manager needs to be assigned along with a backup project manager who can make decisions in the event the project manager is unavailable. Outlining escalation procedures for contacting the appropriate decision maker in the event that the project manager is unable or unwilling to solve a problem helps to keep things on track. If the rollout is large enough, both a quality assurance person and a training coordinator should be assigned to the project as well.

Project Risks

Identifying risks such as scope creep, unavailability of resources, and lack of user acceptance helps the committee include strategies for reducing the risk of problems with the project. Contingency plans should also be included.

The Criteria for Success

Identifying the criteria by which the project will be judged a success enables the planning and implementation teams to better focus their energies. If user satisfaction is a requirement for success, for example, user surveys should be designed along with a mechanism for their distribution, collection, and tabulation. We recommend simple electronic forms allowing users to grade the SBC project on items such as performance, functionality, and reliability. Figure 4-1 shows a sample of the Lotus Notes–based survey forms that ABM e-mailed to their users.

Project Milestones

The infrastructure assessment and upgrade, design document, beta implementation, enterprise rollout, and administrator and user training are examples of project milestones.

Change Management

> *Organizations are first and foremost social systems. Without people, there can be no organization . . . Organizations are hotly and intensely political.*
>
> —Fred Nickols, Change Management Expert

The analysis prepared by the feasibility committee regarding corporate culture and politics should be incorporated into a plan for successful organizational change. Potential implementation of new application standards, user perceptions of IT, reductions in IT staff and IT salaries, and other political considerations need to be addressed and solutions for them found. For instance, one of our customers created an organizational change plan that began with a meeting of the presidents of all the business units. By explaining the benefits of an on-demand enterprise, he turned the presidents into allies that helped smooth

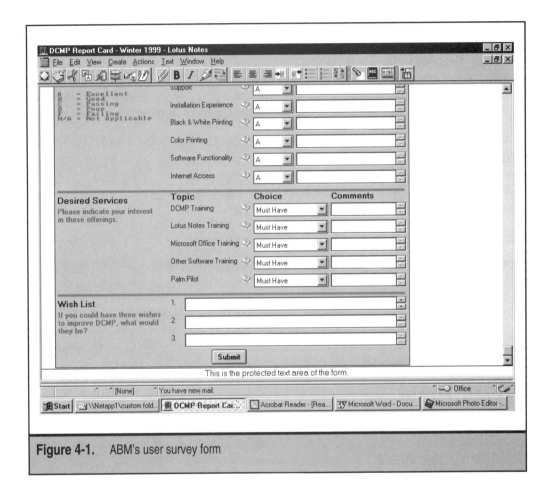

Figure 4-1.   ABM's user survey form

the process of organizational change. Preparing for organizational change is covered more thoroughly in Chapter 10.

INFRASTRUCTURE ASSESSMENT

To produce a meaningful SBC planning document, a detailed infrastructure assessment must first be completed. This assessment includes identifying the appropriate contacts for each category and conducting meetings with them.

Another purpose behind the infrastructure assessment is to discover and remedy any infrastructure problems prior to a server-based computing rollout. In a PC-based computing environment, employees are often used to things being sloppy. Although the network might have some performance or downtime problems, users tend to be somewhat understanding because they commonly save files to their local hard drives anyway.

When users destroy their PC configurations by adding a software utility or deleting an INI file, they often ask a peer for help rather than making an embarrassing support call to IT. Since users work on *their* personal computers and departments run *their* own servers, they are less likely to complain to IT staff or management even when problems arise that are not of their own making.

In a server-based computing environment, employees' *personal* computers become *corporate* computers. While vastly more efficient from an organizational standpoint, users lose the status conferred by having ever more powerful PCs. They are more likely to complain about problems that they would never have mentioned in a PC-based computing environment. Since users are completely dependent upon a central server farm for most or all of their applications, any instability or performance problems in the network infrastructure will instantly be amplified. The new technology will often be blamed for the existing infrastructure problems. Back-end file servers, the data center server backbone, and wide area connectivity all need to be running flawlessly or the enterprise deployment of server-based computing will be in jeopardy of failing.

The Application Environment

Server-based computing is about the delivery of applications. It is therefore crucial that all relevant information about the hosted applications be identified.

Application Database Sources

List the source of any database information utilized by applications, including the database application, the host system, and its geographical location.

Operating Under Terminal Services

Describe whether manufacturer support exists for running each application under Windows Server 2003 Terminal Services. List any manufacturer requirements for this environment as well as any caveats.

Application Composition

Describe the language of each application as well as whether it is client, server, or Telnet.

Application Architecture

Determine whether or not the application is built for a multiuser environment.

TIP: Custom applications can be particularly tricky. You will want to make sure that the applications use Microsoft multiple-user architecture that utilizes roaming profiles. This means that the applications are user-specific, that users have their own separate settings and will not be sharing them (HKEY_CURRENT_USER versus HKEY_LOCAL_MACHINE). The applications should also have subordinate files, such as log files or temp files, that can be redirected to the user's Windows directory and/or Temp directory. A program that is not user-specific but has global settings means that a user making setting switches will affect all users on that server. If the application is not written as user-specific, you will need to lock those keys in the registry to prevent users from changing them.

Manufacturer Support Contracts

If manufacturer support contracts exist for any of the applications, include the relevant information along with phone numbers and the appropriate identification authorization.

Application Requirements

List specific operating conditions for each application, including

- ▼ Memory requirements
- ■ Disk space requirements
- ■ Sound requirements
- ■ Drive mapping requirements
- ■ Any patches or service packs
- ▲ Location of the install files

Application Issues

List any application issues that could affect performance within an ODE environment. For instance, if an application tends to cause blue screens when running in a PC-based computing environment, the planning committee must be aware that similar problems are likely to occur under server-based computing.

Application Packaging

Describe how the application is distributed to users within the existing PC-based computing environment. How often is the application revised? How is it packaged? For instance, can users install updates with a single mouse-click?

Internal Application Support

Identify any internal support contacts for all internal and line-of-business applications. Identify any internal application owners who are responsible for deploying new versions of applications.

The Hardware Environment

The planning process will be based upon knowledge about the existing hardware environment for servers and host systems. Because SBC users will likely require far more central storage for their data, existing storage subsystems are a particularly important element to consider.

The Data Center Environment

Evaluating existing data center sites for power, cooling, and physical security will let the project planning team assess whether they are adequate for hosting the SBC data center(s).

The System Management Environment (SME)

Evaluating the existing SME enables the planning committee to incorporate it into the server-based computing design. This includes identifying any existing tools for measuring metrics, such as HP OpenView.

The Support Structure and Processes

Determining the different levels of support resources available will help the planning team arrive at a strategy for providing support during the implementation. Also define the way support calls are placed and relayed. What help desk package is in use, if any? How is a PC call handled versus an operating system issue? Are any service level agreements (SLAs) currently defined? How is support localized in remote offices?

The Testing Environment

Creating a testing environment is crucial to implementing and successfully maintaining an on-demand enterprise. The planning team needs to know if a current formalized testing environment exists and if testing labs are available.

Change Control Procedures

What change control policies and procedures are in place today? What kind of approval process is required for making changes? Does a database application exist for recording all changes to critical systems? Is there a quality assurance group?

 TIP: In many organizations, the IT administrators learned their trade on a PC rather than in a host systems environment. They may be used to making changes on-the-fly and not recording the changes they make. This approach will cause SBC to fail. A mainframe shop mentality with rigorous change control is essential for success.

The Training Environment

Is there a formalized training group? Are classrooms available? What kind of training is commonly used for IT people? For end users?

The Windows Server Environment

Identifying components such as protocols used, the existing domain structure, naming conventions, and partitioning is essential information for planning a Terminal Services infrastructure.

Network Architecture

Defining the existing network architecture is crucial to designing a solid SBC infrastructure, including routers, switches, protocols, policy servers, bandwidth allocation policies, remote office servers, existing redundancy options, and remote access capabilities. Any existing network reliability or performance problems such as client latency issues need to be identified and ultimately resolved prior to the server-based computing rollout.

The Security Environment

In order for the planning committee to design the proper secure Terminal Services environment, they need to know the following: What firewalls are in place? How is dial-up security currently handled? What internal policies are in place on NT servers? How is lockdown of NTFS partitions handled? Is there a security group?

The Backup Environment

Increased data consolidation within SBC will likely require increased storage systems and, therefore, new backup systems. The planning committee needs to know what kind of data backup mechanisms and backup policies exist today.

The Printing Environment

Printing is a big issue under Terminal Services, and the existing environment needs to be defined. Does printing take place through locally attached printers or only on the network? What network protocols are used? What are the types and number of printers? What print drivers are required? Are print servers used in remote offices today?

The Client Environment

Define the client environment of the SBC participants. This includes categories of users, their location, and whether they have access to a local server. Also describe the details of the specific clients, such as device (PC, laptop, UNIX workstation, handheld), model, local O/S, and any existing performance or reliability issues.

THE PROJECT DESIGN PLAN

The project plan incorporates all aspects of the SBC design. This plan includes both the project definition document and results of the infrastructure assessment. The financial analysis performed by the feasibility committee should be fine-tuned throughout the planning process until the final planning document includes a solid estimate for project costs.

The planning document should clearly convey the organization's server-based computing migration strategy and be suitable for presentation to both executives and auditors. It discusses the various options that the planning team considered for each major component of the project, along with the rationale behind the team's ultimate decision.

Incorporated as part of the plan should be the considerations given to capacity planning, redundancy, and security. The tremendous advantages accruing from the centralization that

SBC enables can become huge liabilities if scalability is not easily incorporated, a crucial data center component without a redundant part should fail, or the system's security is compromised.

The project plan also serves as a roadmap for the project managers and implementation team as they work to institute an enterprise SBC environment. Detailed explanations of the design plan are discussed in the remaining chapters in this part of the book. An overview of the design plan follows.

Terminal Services Design

Designing the Terminal Services environment will be difficult for organizations unfamiliar with the basics of server-based computing. We recommend that the appropriate IT personnel take courses in Terminal Services, MetaFrame XP Presentation Server, and Advanced MetaFrame XP Presentation Server before beginning the design process. Since SBC consolidates processing into a central data center(s), it is important to plan for redundancy of all key components. The MetaFrame XP Presentation Server server farm with load-balancing has built-in redundancy, but special awareness should be given to implementing it for other servers such as Windows Server 2003, SQL, e-mail, and web services. Redundancy should also be included for other critical components such as network switches, load-balancers, routers, storage units, and bandwidth management devices.

Application Architecture Design

Define the strategy both for deploying the on-demand enterprise environment and for handling legacy applications that will not be supported. Users may be allowed, for instance, to run legacy applications locally as long as they want. Alternatively, they may be given a deadline for transitioning to corporate-approved and -supported applications. (Application strategies are covered in more detail in Chapter 13.)

Data Center Architecture Design

The planning team needs to determine the number of data centers, based upon demographic, geographic, disaster recovery, and business requirements. They must evaluate site considerations, including power, cooling, fire suppression, and physical security. They also must evaluate options for either hosting the centers internally or using co-location centers, such as AT&T or Verio. (Data center architecture is discussed more thoroughly in Chapter 5.)

Disaster Recovery/Business Continuity Design

Since users are completely dependent upon SBC for all of their hosted application processing, disaster recovery is an extremely important component. Fortunately, server-based computing makes a real-time disaster recovery solution far more practical and affordable than in a PC-based computing environment. (A variety of disaster recovery options are discussed in Chapter 19.)

Network Backbone Design

Each data center requires a high-speed backbone connecting the MetaFrame server farm with other servers in the data center. Small organizations may be able to get by with 100-Mbps switched Ethernet. Large firms will likely require ATM or switched gigabit. Redundant network interface cards (NICs) and switches should be incorporated as part of the design. (The network backbone is discussed more thoroughly in Chapter 6.)

Server Farm Architecture Design

The findings from the proof-of-concept pilot program will enable the planning committee to select server quantity, type, sizing, and configuration for the Terminal Services implementation. The Citrix resource manager component and Windows Performance Monitor can help determine server scalability. Other tools can simulate server loads. If DOS or 16-bit applications will be run, extra servers may be required for a multitiered server farm. Likewise, support for multiple languages will necessitate additional servers for each language. (Server farm architecture is discussed more thoroughly in Chapter 12.)

File Services Design

When users store all of their data at corporate data centers, unique problems arise in handling file services efficiently. The project team should evaluate the different options, including server clustering of general-purpose file servers, storage area networks (SANs), and network attached storage (NAS). Archive systems and backup software and services must also be selected. (File services are covered in detail in Chapter 6 and in Appendix A.)

Print Server Architecture Design

Printing tends to be one of the most difficult and time-consuming parts of an enterprise server-based computing implementation. Decisions must be made about the configuration of one or more central print servers at each data center as well as the type and quantity of print servers in remote offices. Just a few of the other printer-related decisions the team will have to make include integration of host system printing, local PC printing, printer auto-creation to create temporary printer assignments for mobile users, trusted print sources, lockdown of registries, and control over printer access. (Printing is discussed in detail in Chapter 18.)

User Profiles Design

Most Terminal Services implementations utilize either mandatory or roaming profiles, but we recommend that organizations use scripting to enable desktop lockdown while allowing users the flexibility to select default drives and printers. (We present our scripting techniques in Chapter 15.)

Login Script Design

To minimize administration, there should be one script that works for both fat and thin clients. Additionally, login scripts should be designed to run very quickly and efficiently.

Automation Design

You will want to automate application installation and updates, server imaging processes, and client installations using products such as Citrix Installation Manager (IM) and Norton Ghost. (Automation design is covered exhaustively in Part III of this book.)

Windows Server Design

Designing a Windows server infrastructure to support Terminal Services is a key part of the planning process. The following components are included.

Domain Model Design

When designing large enterprise infrastructures, it is easy to design a domain that entails frequent and inefficient replication. For a server-based computing environment, we generally recommend a single master domain model to separate authentication of users and groups from authentication of resources. (Domains are explained in more detail in Chapter 8.)

Active Directory Design

Active Directory planning and configuration tends to be much simpler in an enterprise ODE environment. This is because there is generally no need to worry about intersite replication since all domain controllers are in the data center. Another concern that is eliminated is the need to accommodate authentication over the WAN by users in small offices without local domain controllers. (Active Directory Design is covered in Chapter 6.)

WINS Architecture Design

Under server-based computing, WINS is less likely to be required. (In Chapter 6, we discuss when and how to use WINS.)

Backup Architecture Design

If the infrastructure assessment reveals inadequate backup systems to handle the demands of centralized data storage, the archive systems and backup software and services require selection. (Backup systems are covered in Appendix A.)

Back-End Database Design

The size and configuration of a back-end database in a server-based computing environment, where all users will be hitting one database at one time, will often be different from a distributed database model, where several database servers are located across the enterprise. The distributed servers would handle a relatively small number of users and have replicated data backed up and stored at a central point. The server-based computing model might require far more powerful database server(s) or clustered servers at the data center, depending on usage, as well as middleware application changes.

Network Design

A sound network infrastructure is vital to supporting an ODE environment. In addition to remedying any shortfalls discovered during the infrastructure assessment, the following issues should be addressed.

Topologies

Because the MetaFrame ICA Client uses such little bandwidth, the composition of the topology to the desktop is generally not of great importance as long as it is reliable. In most cases, 4-Mbps Token Ring will deliver the same performance as switched 100 Mbps.

WAN Architecture

An ODE environment requires a robust, scalable, and highly reliable WAN design because remote office users are completely dependent upon the MetaFrame servers at the corporate data centers. The planning team must evaluate the different connectivity options, including the Internet and redundancy options. During the transition from PC-based to server-based computing, residual traffic will chew up an inordinate amount of bandwidth. The project plan must allow for this temporary increased bandwidth requirement during the migration process. (Bandwidth management, including packet prioritization, is often essential in order to ensure adequate performance in a Terminal Services wide area network.)

Alternative bandwidth capabilities should also be designed into the system. For instance, if the primary connectivity to remote offices is frame relay, alternative DSL connections to the Internet should be available for backup. Even a dial-up line can keep people in business in the event of a major catastrophe. The ultimate redundancy is to utilize the unique capabilities of the ODE to build a disaster recovery solution with multiple fail-over data centers. (Wide area connectivity is discussed more thoroughly in Chapter 5.)

Remote Access Design

The project planning team needs to choose the appropriate remote access strategy, whether using leased lines, frame relay, dial-up lines, or the Internet. (Remote access design considerations, including connection and redundancy strategies, profiles, and gateway routing, are detailed in Chapter 6.)

The Systems Management Environment

If the infrastructure assessment indicates that a network management package is already utilized as part of the existing PC-based computing environment, the planning team should extend it to encompass the SBC architecture. The team should also decide on how the existing network management package, or a new one, can best be configured to work with server-based computing packages such as Citrix resource manager. (Network management environments are covered in detail in Chapter 9.)

Metrics Design   As part of the systems management environment, the planning team should determine which metrics are to be collected and analyzed in order to develop strategies for expansion and for limiting bottlenecks. Citrix resource manager is a good tool to use in this capacity, though it may overlap with existing utilities such as HP OpenView.

Policies and Procedures Design

As is the case with the mainframe model of computing, clearly defined policies and procedures are essential for enterprise SBC success. Adding an application or making a small change to a central router can have severe consequences for hundreds or thousands of SBC users. Although we continue to emphasize the numerous advantages of an enterprise server-based computing environment, it does require that the days of the network cowboy come to an end.

> *Having been raised, from an MIS perspective, in the midrange and micro eras of computing, my staff had a hard time rethinking the way they do things. For example, while "maintenance windows" were commonplace in the days of the mainframe, they've seemingly disappeared in the PC era. My network technicians were used to shutting a system down minutes after announcing it. We all had to relearn what the MIS personnel we replaced 10 to 15 years ago knew as second nature.*
>
> —Anthony Lackey, Vice President of MIS,
> Chief Technology Officer, ABM Industries

Data Center Policies and Procedures Design

The planning document should include the organization's strategy for managing environmental changes.

TIP: Depending upon the current policies and procedures as revealed in the infrastructure assessment, new requirements may be necessary. For example, a workflow-enabled database should track all changes by administrators and implementers to the Terminal Services infrastructure.

User Policies and Procedures Design

Decisions must be made about data access, device access, and adding new devices. For example, will users be allowed to access local devices from a Citrix ICA session? If so, this policy can have unanticipated ramifications, such as security concerns. (Policies and procedures are discussed more thoroughly in Chapter 15.)

Client Design

The planning committee should identify the different client categories and the levels to which they are expected to utilize SBC services. They must further decide how to specifically set up the clients, and how to configure user desktops. Choices must be made regarding policies for local browsing, emulation, drive mappings, PC local operating systems, local hardware peripherals, and integration with handheld devices such as Palm Pilots. If Windows terminals will be used, the planning team must evaluate the different options and choose the brand and models most appropriate for their organization. (Client implementation is discussed more thoroughly in Chapter 7.)

Client Operating Systems

A primary benefit of centralized computing is the standardization of applications. While standard client equipment and operating systems make administration easier, one of the most compelling strengths of server-based computing is its ability to effectively manage a heterogeneous environment. Still, different operating systems do have different ramifications for functionality under Terminal Services.

User Interface Design

Users can launch entire MetaFrame XP Presentation Server desktops, or simply click icons generated through Citrix Program Neighborhood. The Citrix web interface component enables application publishing to a browser. Citrix MetaFrame Secure Access Manager allows access to all features of the web interface component of MetaFrame Presentation Server as well as the ability to aggregate information from across the enterprise, the Internet, and other data sources and to present it to users in a secure, personalized manner.

Integration with Local Devices

Design strategies must be included for client integration with local printers, handheld units, scanners, bar code readers, and cash drawers.

Non-Windows Client Design

MetaFrame XP Presentation Server enables UNIX workstations, as well as Linux and Macintosh users, to run Windows applications without requiring a separate PC. MetaFrame XP Presentation Server for UNIX (UX/AIX/Solaris) adds the functionality of the X-Window protocol. Users can subsequently launch either Windows or UNIX applications from the same screen.

Data Organization Design

When users migrate to Terminal Services, policies will need to be set about where their data will be stored for different applications (central server storage versus local storage). Creating broad policies that extend across all access infrastructure users will greatly facilitate the ability of help desk personnel to provide prompt support.

Client Application Design

Different application strategies may be appropriate for different categories of users. For instance, mobile users will likely have some local applications, while office users may have none.

Other Client Design Considerations

Groups, drive mappings, and login script strategies must be designed for the different categories of users.

Security Design

Although security should permeate all aspects of the project design plan, a specific security strategy should be identified. Firewall integration, account management, auditing, and the Terminal Services registry should all be included. (Security is discussed more thoroughly in Chapter 9.)

General Implementation Design

The implementation plan should cover training, user communications, data migration, project management, change management, and customer care.

Training Plan

A training plan needs to be designed for support personnel, system administrators, and end users.

TIP: Once end users are set up to access their desktop through Citrix, you can coordinate a more formal introductory training class by using the MetaFrame XP Presentation Server shadowing capabilities. The trainer can have several users simultaneously shadow her PC. Setting up a concurrent conference call provides the audio to describe the visual orientation.

Support Personnel   The low administrative requirements of server-based computing combined with features such as shadowing will enable help desk personnel to support many more users once the on-demand enterprise migration is complete. During the transition, however, increased staff and training will likely be necessary to handle the demands of the new architecture while supporting users on the old PC-based computing platform.

End Users   Distribution of rainbow packets for general information and at-a-glance documents for frequently asked questions are an expedient way to provide quick user orientation to server-based computing. A *rainbow* document is modeled after the colorful organizational wall charts found in many hospitals for quick reference to services and locations. The rainbow document literally contains a rainbow of colored sheets, each a bit narrower than the other, providing easy reference to the topics on the exposed edge. Some relevant topics might be "Getting Help," "Finding Your Files," "Glossary of Terms," and "Your Thin-Client Desktop."

Project Management

The planning team should incorporate the essentials of project management as part of the plan. Implementation teams must have well-defined tasks, and required resources must be identified. An estimated timeline for the project beta testing and rollout should be included as part of the planning document.

An enterprise server-based computing migration requires project manager authority, stakeholder buy-in, project reporting and tracking, task assignment, project change control, scope creep control, organizational change management, and timeline management. (Project management is discussed in detail in Chapter 10.)

Change Management

The planning document should include the organization's strategy for managing environmental changes in order to enhance management and end-user benefits. Administrator and end-user training, user reference guides, asset tracking, and a frequently asked questions (FAQs) database should all be incorporated as part of the project. The planning team should include survey forms for gathering information prior to implementation and for measuring user satisfaction as the rollout takes place.

A method for communicating migration plans to users is a very important component of change management. While an on-demand enterprise will provide users with enhanced capabilities and support, it still involves change. Advanced orientation and education will make the process go much more smoothly. (Strategies for internal marketing are discussed in Chapter 10.)

Customer Care

The help desk department will be able to handle many more users once the migration to server-based computing is complete. During the transition, however, increased staff may be necessary to handle the glitches of the new architecture while supporting users on the old PC-based computing platform. (Customer care is given further consideration in Chapter 10.)

Migrating to Server-Based Computing

The planning document should include a roadmap for migrating from fat client to thin client. Also clearly documented should be strategies for consolidating data from both PCs and remote office servers, thus minimizing downtime, and creating a "virtual call center" based upon skill sets.

Expanding the Pilot Test to a Beta

The planning team must decide at what point the proof-of-concept pilot test will be expanded to a beta implementation, and they must decide the parameters of the beta. Objectives should be defined and results measured in order to allow adjustments to the team's migration strategy if required. A scope variance process needs to define who has authority to sign off on out-of-scope items, for example, including a new application as part of the beta. (The beta implementation is discussed in more detail in Chapter 10.)

CHAPTER 5

Server-Based Computing Data Center Architecture

In this chapter, we discuss the importance of building and running a server-based computing environment in a secure, reliable data center facility. The need for this approach may be obvious to IT personnel with a background in host systems, but we will define the data center in the context of building a server-based computing environment. This centralized computing model often entails a new paradigm for network administrators whose IT experience is limited to running distributed networks based on traditional PC technology. The data center plays a far more important role with server-based computing than it does in a distributed network environment, especially in a post-9/11 business world of zero acceptable downtime, and the expectation of anytime, anywhere business continuity. The Citrix concepts of on-demand and in-control computing start at the data center—if the data center is not built right, the entire project will be compromised.

This chapter will discuss several key considerations—including the environment, network, and deployment—for the data center architecture. Chapters 17 and 19 will carry the concepts of this chapter forward, detailing a redundant data center solution that solves the business continuity and disaster recovery concerns of all businesses today.

WHAT IS A DATA CENTER?

An SBC *data center* in this context is a central site or location that houses the server-based computing resources for a company. This site is characterized by limited physical access, superior network capacity, power capacity, power quality, and a degree of internal redundancy for these computing resources. Using Windows Terminal Services and Citrix MetaFrame Access Suite in a data center can now provide a familiar PC desktop environment for users, no matter where they are located. Users take their desktop, and any other necessary resources with them wherever they go.

The data center was traditionally the realm of the mainframe, but Terminal Services and MetaFrame are changing this paradigm. Although the centralized mainframe environment is comparatively easy to support, companies will continue migrating to easy-to-use PC applications. Organizations are desperate for a technology that combines the desirable elements of the centralized computing model with the ability to deliver the desired application services to the end user. This is the basis for the server-based computing model utilizing Windows Terminal Services and Citrix MetaFrame Access Suite presented in this book. In the following sections, we present some important considerations in designing, building, and running a centralized data center environment with server-based computing technology.

DESIGNING AN SBC DATA CENTER: OVERALL CONSIDERATIONS

Several seemingly disparate factors come into play when designing a server-based computing data center that, when considered together, provide the overall solution of a secure, reliable, and cost-effective environment. Some of these factors, such as disaster recovery, are traditional concerns of the mainframe world, but they take on additional facets when considered as part of a computing environment using MetaFrame and Terminal Services. We will examine disaster recovery and business continuity at length in Chapter 19, but touch on it briefly here due to the high level of importance placed on this topic in today's world.

Disaster Recovery and Business Continuity

When initially considering the consolidation of distributed corporate servers, an organization may be concerned about "putting all its eggs in one basket." In most distributed computing environments, a single failed server probably affects only a small group of people. When everyone is connected to the same server (even a "virtual" one), however, its failure could be disastrous. Fortunately, an SBC environment running Terminal Services with Citrix MetaFrame Access Suite provides a very flexible and cost-effective approach to building redundancy across multiple geographies, power grids, data access grids, and user access points. Chapter 19 will provide greater detail on why we strongly recommend organizations utilize two data centers (one main data center and one geographically separate backup data center) and how to technically configure this solution. For the purposes of this chapter though, we will focus on the requirements of the first data center, with the assumption that additional data centers will be similar, if not identical.

NOTE: The SBC computing model is a high-availability solution, not a fail-over solution, as data that is residing in memory within a session that has not been written to disk will be lost when a user is moved to another server due to hardware failure, a server reboot, or a server blue-screen.

Outsourcing

Once a company performs an assessment of its ability to host a data center using some of the criteria presented in this chapter, they may find that they do not have adequate facilities or infrastructure in place. It may be too costly to create the proper infrastructure, or it may be undesirable to take on the task for a variety of reasons. In this case, the organization may consider taking on a partner to build and run its data center. Many companies find that even if they can build and run a data center internally, outsourcing is still attractive due to cost, staffing, location, or built-in resiliency. Let's look more closely at the advantages and limitations of outsourcing a data center.

The potential advantages of outsourcing include

▼   Facilities built specifically for data center hosting already exist, and in fact, most data hosting facilities currently have significant excess capacity. Thus, new construction is rarely necessary.

■   Redundant power, cooling systems, raised floor, and fire suppression are often already in place.

- Physical security is usually better than the individual companies' internal security. Guards on duty, biometric authentication, escorted access, and other measures are typical.

- Hosting facilities are often built very close to the points of presence (POPs) of a local exchange carrier (LEC). In some cases, they are built into the same location as a LEC, which can dramatically decrease WAN communication costs.

- Managed services that can supplement a company's existing staff are usually available. These services are invariably less expensive than hiring someone to perform routine operations such as exchanging tapes or rebooting frozen servers.

- Hosting facilities carry their own liability insurance, which could have a significant impact on the cost of business continuity insurance.

- Many facilities can customize the service level agreement they offer or bundle hosting services with network telecommunication services.

The limitations of outsourcing include

- A company's access to its equipment is usually restricted or monitored. Outsourcing puts further demands on the design to create an operation that can run unattended.

- WAN connectivity is limited to what the hosting center has available. It can be more difficult to get upgraded bandwidth because the hosting center has to filter such requests through the plans in place for the entire facility.

- It may be more difficult to get internal approval to outsource the expense because the hosting services appear as a bottom-line cost, whereas many information technology costs are buried in other areas such as facilities and telecommunications.

- If unmanaged space is obtained, it may be difficult or impractical for a company to have one of its own staff onsite at the hosting facility for extended periods of time.

CASE STUDY:
Home State Bank Builds Their Own SBC Data Center

Home State Bank (HSB), a regional bank headquartered in Colorado with 180 employees, seven branch banking centers, and assets of $370 million, decided to build a data center to host their server-based computing environment following a consolidation with American Bank, another mid-sized regional bank.

Jim Hansen, Chief Information Officer of HSB, commented on the decision to build a new data center: "Consolidation of the two locally owned and independent community banks forced us to bring two distinct network environments into one. The consolidation also brought about a change in the means of providing end-user connectivity and access to their applications and services. The bank decided to move to publishing applications where applicable through Citrix MetaFrame Presentation Server via Web Interface to help minimize end-user support and keep upgrades to a minimum. We knew we needed to centralize everything from both banks, and there were no large data centers in our region to outsource to, so we decided we needed to build our own."

HSB built their first data center in March of 2003 for $130,000, with plans to replicate their data center to an off-site data center within one year. HSB's data center currently houses ten Terminal servers, 15 application servers, the routers and telecommunication equipment for the branch bank WAN, firewalls, Internet banking equipment, and a large tape jukebox backup system.

Some additional details of the data center include

▼   The data center was built in a bank clearing house basement next to a bank vault—thus, it was protected on three sides by a bank vault and on the fourth side by ground.

■   500 square feet of data center space, with 1500 square feet of accompanying office space.

■   A Liebert 16KVA uninterruptible power supply, expandable to 20KVA, capable of maintaining power in the data center for 15 minutes.

■   Water, moisture, fire, and physical security alarm systems.

■   Ceiling-mounted data cable and power racks.

▲   HVAC environmental control (ten tons of air-conditioning).

CASE STUDY:
ABM Chooses AT&T to House Their Main Data Center

ABM Industries is a Fortune 1000 Company that provides outsourced facilities services. ABM has 63,000 employees worldwide. Their SBC infrastructure required a data center that would support over 50 servers and 2500 concurrent users.

Anthony Lackey, Vice President of MIS, and Chief Technology Officer, for ABM Industries, commented on the decision to outsource the data center in 1999: "The decision to co-locate the data center was a simple one. First, the single biggest vulnerability point for a thin-client solution is the network portal into the data center. Second, the physical connection from one's office to the network provider's central office is typically the most likely failure point. By co-locating our data center facilities with our network provider, we significantly reduced our vulnerability. Besides eliminating the risk of the last mile, we also eliminate a great deal of expense."

ABM saved approximately $25,000 per month on their ATM circuit by locating their data center inside a POP where AT&T maintained a hosting facility. In this case, there was no local exchange carrier (LEC) involved, and the customer could connect directly to the national carrier's backbone on a different floor of the same building. Key features of the AT&T facility that were important to ABM in the evaluation process were the following:

▼ Uninterruptible power: four (expandable to six) 375kVA UPS systems (N+1), dual (N+1) solar turbine generators 750kW (with an 8000-gallon fuel capacity).

■ Dual power feeds to each cabinet from two different power systems.

■ HVAC environmental control from central plant (150 tons of air-conditioning equipment cooling 60 watts per square foot).

■ Switched and diverse paths for WAN links; redundant OC-3/OC-12/OC-48 connections to multiple network access points.

■ Fully staffed network operations center with trained systems administrators, data center technicians, and network engineers on duty 24 hours a day, seven days a week.

■ Secured cabinets or caged environment with customized space allocation.

■ State-of-the-art VESDA fire detection system (100 times more sensitive than conventional fire detection systems) backed up by a cross-zoned conventional system to prevent emergency power-off due to early detection.

▲ State-of-the-art Inergen fire suppression system.

Outage Mitigation Strategies

Having a good Disaster Recovery plan in place is small comfort to users if they are experiencing regular interruptions in service. Centralizing computing resources makes it all the more important to incorporate a high degree of resiliency into a design. This goes far beyond just making sure the hard drives in the file server are in a RAID configuration. Companies must take a global view of the entire infrastructure and assess the following:

▼ *Identify single points of failure.* Even if the file server is clustered, what happens if the WAN connection fails?

■ *Implement redundancy in critical system components.* If one server is good, two are better. If possible, they should carry balanced loads or, at the very least, have an identical backup server to put online in case one fails.

■ *Establish a regular testing schedule for all redundant systems.* Many organizations have backup plans that fail when called upon. Thus it is important to document and test the backup systems until you are comfortable that they can be relied upon in a time of crises.

■ *Establish support escalation procedures for all systems* before *there is an outage.* Document the support phone numbers, customer account information, and what needs to be said to get past the first tier of support.

■ *Review the vendor service levels for critical components, and assess where they may need to supplement them or have spare parts on hand.* Is the vendor capable of meeting their established service level? What is the recourse if they fail to perform as promised? Is support available somewhere else? Is the cost of having an extra, preconfigured unit on hand in case of failure justified?

■ *Establish a process for management approval of any significant change to the systems.* Two heads are always better than one when it comes to managing change. Companies should ensure that both peers and management know about, and approve of, what is happening at the data center.

■ *Document* any *change made to* any *system.* For routine changes, approval may not be necessary, but companies should make sure there is a process to capture what happened anyway. The audit trail can be invaluable for troubleshooting.

■ *Develop a healthy intolerance for error.* An organization should never let itself say, "Well, it just works that way." They should obtain regular feedback from the user community by establishing a Customer Survey around items like perceived downtime, system speed, and so on, and should give feedback to their vendors and manufacturers. They must keep pushing until things work the way they want them to work.

▲ *Build some extra capacity into the solution.* Being able to try a new version of an application or service pack or hot fix without risking downtime of the production system is extremely important.

Chapter 10 has more information on establishing service levels and operational procedures as well as samples for documenting various processes at the data center and throughout your organization.

Organizational Issues

Whether an organization decides to outsource the data center or run it themselves, it is crucial they not underestimate the organizational impact of moving toward this sort of unattended operation. Unless such a center is already running, the following needs to be done:

▼ Come up with a three-shift staffing plan (or at least three-shift coverage).

■ Decide whether current staff has sufficient training and experience to manage the new environment.

■ Determine whether current staff is culturally ready to deal with the "mainframe mind-set" required to make the server-based computing environment reliable and stable. In other words, can they manage the systems using rigorous change control and testing procedures?

■ Decide which of the existing staff needs to be on-site and when.

■ If outsourcing, determine which services the vendor will be providing and which will be handled internally.

▲ If outsourcing, make sure there is a clean division and escalation procedure between internal and external support resources.

ENVIRONMENTAL CONSIDERATIONS

When a network and server farm is set up in the data center, environmental factors such as power, cooling, and potential disasters must be considered. If outsourcing, the vendor should be able to provide details on the physical setup of the facility.

Power

The utilization of an emergency or standby generator is essential when considering power outages that may affect a data center. Outages caused by the local utility that last no longer than 15 minutes will typically be supported by an uninterruptible power supply (UPS). However, a standby emergency generator is necessary to support longer outages.

Each component has a power rating, usually in watts, that it requires for continuous use. At best, inadequate power will strain the power supply of the component. At worst, it will cause production failure. If the facility has a UPS, it must have adequate capacity now as well as the ability to handle future growth plans. Another consideration is how long can the UPS keep the systems running in the event of a sustained power failure?

Is there a generator backup? If so, how many gallons of fuel does it have, and how many hours of operation will that yield? During a power failure, it may be difficult to gracefully shut down all of the servers and equipment. Liebert, Tripp Lite, American Power Conversion (APC), and other vendors provide good data center solutions, including software and hardware components for power backup, generator switchover, and server shutdown.

Assessing Your Power Requirements

The first step in assessing the actual power requirements and the resulting UPS need is to estimate the load. This is done in slightly different ways for different equipment, but it comes down to estimating the operating voltage, the load (in watts), and a factor for how often the unit is in operation at this voltage and load—sometimes called a *power factor*. An example for a high-end server might be: operating voltage = 120 volts, load = 400 watts, and power factor = .75 (since it is in continuous operation at nearly peak utilization). This information should be readily available from the manufacturer either in printed documentation or from their web site. A company should collect and total this information for all of their equipment. Using this example, 15 servers would require 4500 watts ($400 \times .75 \times 15$) plus a "fudge factor" in case multiple servers suddenly run at peak loads—5000 to 5200 watts would be wise.

Next, the site voltage should be determined. Data center facilities can often handle multiple voltages, but 230V/400V is common. An organization needs to consider how much room for growth they will need, and make sure there are adequate connections to support future equipment.

NOTE: Facilities at an LEC might also supply 48VDC.

Uninterruptible Power Supply

Organizations selecting an uninterruptible power supply (UPS) need to determine how long they need their equipment to remain functional after power fails. A UPS vendor will be able to provide you an estimate of run time after power failure based on the total number of watts for your equipment. UPS systems are usually rated in volt-amps. The conversion from watts to volt-amps is $V \times A = W / 0.8$. Using the earlier example, 5200 watts would require ($5200 / .8$) = 6500 volt-amps.

HVAC Units for Cooling and Humidity Control

We have been called in to many organizations to resolve unstable software and server problems, only to discover that the temperature where the servers were running was well over 90 degrees Fahrenheit. Servers and Telco equipment generate a great deal of heat, and will function inconsistently and often sustain permanent damage if their environment has significant temperature variations or remains consistently warm (typically, 66–70 degrees Fahrenheit is considered optimal, with temperature variations of no more than +/−5 degrees per day). The less the variation and the cooler the temperature (but not below 65 degrees), the longer the equipment will operate optimally. Cooling should not only be sufficient for normal operation, but should have adequate backup. The ideal situation is to have a redundant cooling system with sufficient power backup to support it.

The cooling system utilized must not add excess moisture to the environment. Industrial evaporators are available to avoid this potential problem. Many higher-end cooling systems have built-in moisture suppression. Detectors should be installed to provide an alert when moisture exceeds recommended levels. Keep in mind that a dry environment means that people working in the data center should drink adequate amounts of water, thus water fountains should be placed at convenient locations.

HVAC Evaluation

When evaluating HVAC units, the following factors should be considered:

▼ The temperature and humidity tolerances of equipment

■ The amount of space to be cooled (in cubic feet)

■ The period of operation (evenings? weekends?)

■ Seasonal needs (are some months much hotter than others?)

▲ Whether people will be working for prolonged periods in close proximity to the equipment

Fire Suppression

Data center certified fire suppression systems are extremely important in any operational facility. The systems use some type of mechanism to help extinguish fires without damaging hardware or facilities. Today's fire suppression systems must comply with environmental concerns regarding ozone depletion and human safety. This is an important consideration if the data center will be staffed and there is a potential for the fire suppression system to be activated while people are present.

Fire Suppression System Types

Many types of systems are available that comply with environmental requirements and use different agents to suppress fires. We recommend comparing the quality of the different types of fire suppression systems to determine which one best fits the data center setup. Table 5-1 lists the advantages and disadvantages of some of the different systems currently available.

Seismic and Other Environmental Activity

For data centers in California or other seismically active areas, adequate facility bracing is a must. Facilities should meet or exceed the earthquake regulations for the area. In addition, computer hardware racks and cabinets, and other equipment should have their own

Type of System	Chemical Agent	Advantages	Disadvantages
Precharge sprinkler	Water	Provides the best suppression of all fires and protection for structures. No water sits above sensitive equipment.	Extra plumbing is required, including lines and routing of pipes to avoid the data center and sensitive equipment. Major water damage is likely when discharged.
Wet sprinkler	Water	Provides the best suppression of all fires and protection for structures.	Accidental discharge from human or environmental factors can set it off. Major water damage is likely when discharged.
FM-200	Heptaflouropropane	Doesn't displace oxygen, so it is safe when people are present.	High cost.
Inergen	Argon, nitrogen, and CO_2 (stands for *Iner*t gas and nitro*gen*)	Allows storage or flow over data center room. Inergen leaves enough oxygen for people to breathe.	High cost, large storage space.

Table 5-1.   Comparison of Commercial Fire Suppression Systems

bracing and be able to pass inspection. Other geographical areas have different environmental concerns that should be planned for; for example, possible hurricanes in Florida, or major snow storm–based power outages in some northern states.

Physical Security

If most, or all, of an organization's computing infrastructure will be housed at a data center, it is imperative that physical access be restricted and monitored. Many outsourced hosting facilities have security guards, card-key access, motion sensors, and silent alarms. Despite tremendous amounts of time and money spent protecting a network with hardware and software security, data can still be at considerable risk if physical security is not considered. We discuss security in more detail in Chapter 8.

NETWORK CONSIDERATIONS

In the next sections, we discuss some important factors to consider when planning the data network connections into a data center. Chapter 6 is dedicated to network design and provides much more detail on these and other topics.

User Geography and Location of the Data Center

The geographic dispersion of the user community plays a major role in the site selection for a data center. Whether a company has only domestic or domestic and international offices has a profound influence on data center aspects such as availability for WAN bandwidth and hot sites. Ideally, the chosen site should yield the lowest overall network cost from the national exchange carriers while meeting all the other requirements mentioned in this chapter. One of the single largest cost items in building your data center will be the data network. Anyone who has ever ordered a data line from a local or national carrier knows that the distance from their office (demarcation point or *demark*) to the carrier's point of presence (POP) can translate into hundreds or thousands of dollars per month. A data center is no exception. If installing high-bandwidth connections such as ATM, an organization could be looking at thousands of dollars in cost for a very short distance to the local POP.

Time Zones

Both Windows 2003 and Citrix MetaFrame XP support time-zone translation—meaning that the client machine will display the time based on its local time zone rather than the time zone of the server. This is a critical feature for organizations whose users may be in physically disparate time zones relative to where the servers are physically located.

Bandwidth Availability

Another consideration in planning network connections is bandwidth availability in the area where the data center is located. The required circuits may be easily ordered now, but what about in six months or a year? It is vital that a company understands the capacity available, usually from the LEC, and its growth plans. We have seen many customers experience delays in their entire data center build-outs because there were no additional circuits available from the LEC, and no one thought to check in advance (or they were over-promised by the LEC when they did enquire).

TIP: It has been our experience over many years that telecommunication carriers are often overly optimistic when estimating the time required to install a circuit. They are similarly overly optimistic about the time required to make an installed circuit work smoothly. It is important to build extra time into the schedule for getting the circuit in and working.

Bandwidth Management

Due to the nature of IP, any amount of network bandwidth can be swallowed up by a variety of both important and unimportant applications, with no respect to priority. Thus, having the tools in place to manage, understand, report, and prioritize bandwidth is critical. A discussion of tools for managing and prioritizing bandwidth is included in Chapter 6.

Reliability

An unreliable network can kill a project. It is crucial that an organization ensure that its bandwidth carrier can provide detailed reliability statistics of the circuits to be used. Especially in the case of newer topologies like ATM, incorrect assumptions of flawless performance may lead to project failure. It is wise to get customer references, and ask those companies how the carrier's product is working for them. Organizations should also allow adequate time for their own testing to make sure the circuits are sufficiently reliable to meet their needs.

Network Redundancy

It makes little sense to design all of the components of a data center with fail-over capability if the network represents a single point of failure. This is especially important with a server-based computing design. Users will rely on the network to reach one or a few data centers; it must be resistant to production outages. Buying a redundant circuit can be expensive, but carriers are often able to sell access to a circuit to more than one company for far less than the circuit itself would cost. In case the primary circuit fails, they can switch customers to this backup so they can continue operation. If a secondary live circuit is not practical or affordable, another option is putting a second type of lower-bandwidth circuit in place. These backups will not provide as much bandwidth of course, but some access would at least be available.

Using the Internet as a Redundant Network

Since most businesses and many households today have Internet access, the Internet makes an obvious choice (assuming it can be secured) for access into the data center or as a backup network access path into the data center if private line access is lost. With the release of MetaFrame Secure Gateway, Citrix made it very easy for organizations to utilize the Internet as an access point into the data center. With Secure Gateway, all ICA data traversing from the Internet to the data center (and back to the Internet) is encrypted using SSL encryption (port 443), and no additional firewall portholes or client-side software is required.

Virtual private network (VPN) technology may also be utilized for this same purpose (encryption of ICA traffic going over the Internet). In the case of VPN technology, we strongly recommend the use of hardware encryption devices at the data center rather than software termination. Additionally, we have found that VPNs tend to require a significant amount of administrative overhead due to the complexity and update requirements of the client-side VPN software. Both Secure Gateway and VPN technology are discussed in detail in Chapter 6.

Cable Management

Just as managing the data center requires more meticulous methods than in a distributed environment, setting up the cabling requires careful organization. Cable management systems with easy-to-understand labeling and adequate capacity for growth should be used. Color-coding can contribute significantly to finding the right cable quickly. Red could be used for critical LAN and WAN ports, for example. Green could be used for mission-critical servers, and so on.

Just as important, power cables should not be a pile of spaghetti. Cable trays and ties will keep cables out of the way and help to organize them. Equipment power cables should plug neatly into racks and cabinets, and the large power cables from the racks should plug into the under-floor power grid with only enough slack to allow for moving the floor panels.

OTHER CONSIDERATIONS IN DATA CENTER DESIGN

There are a number of issues that may apply to a company when considering the centralization of its MetaFrame servers. It is not possible to anticipate every conceivable issue of designing a data center, but the following topics cover some issues we have run into in the past that may help in planning.

Legacy Hosting

Determine if applications will run on MetaFrame servers that need to access data or programs on legacy systems (enterprise resource planning (ERP), database query and reporting tools, and terminal emulation are all examples of such applications). If this is the case, the legacy systems and MetaFrame servers should be co-located to optimize the network bandwidth required between these systems, as shown in Figure 5-1.

Offsite Data Storage

Even with a secure and reliable data center, data backups should be taken off-site to a *hardened* location or copied to an off-site location daily. A hardened location is one in which proper fire and moisture protection has been ensured, as well as physical security for data storage media. During a production failure or disaster involving a loss of site, such backups can mean the difference between a quick recovery and no recovery at all. Many national and regional firms specialize in data storage. Other firms will use a frame relay connection or the Internet to back up data to a secure offsite location. If a company is outsourcing its data center, they must make sure they have tape exchange or electronic vaulting as part of the service level agreement (SLA) with their vendor. Otherwise, one of their own people will have to travel to the data center daily to change tapes.

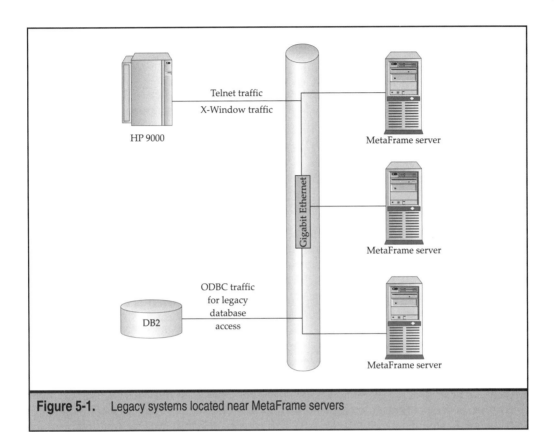

Figure 5-1.   Legacy systems located near MetaFrame servers

Unusual Connectivity

An organization needs to consider if they have systems with network topologies or connection requirements different from those of their MetaFrame servers. Any different topologies, such as SNA, token ring, serial lines, and telephony, will need to be incorporated into the network and facilities design. Bridging or conversion technologies may be required, and they may not work the same way in a MetaFrame and Terminal Services environment as they do in a standard Windows environment. For example, if there is a Computer Telephony Integration (CTI) application that allows users to retrieve their voice mail through a PC Windows interface utilizing individual IP addresses, it will probably not work on a MetaFrame XP server without modification since a MetaFrame XP server will use the same IP address for all users.

Nonstandard Systems

Card readers, document scanners, time-card systems, or other automated systems with dependent applications must be taken into account when building a MetaFrame server farm. Depending on the exact nature of these automated systems, one may not be able to incorporate them as part of the server-based computing architecture. Here are some guidelines for making sure these systems will work in a new environment:

▼ If the system has associated software that runs in DOS, see whether there is a Windows 32-bit version. Even better, look for a version that has been tested and certified with Terminal Services. Windows 2000 and Windows 2003 no longer support DOS applications running on Terminal Services (although some DOS applications still work).

■ If the system has code that already runs on a server (such as NetWare or Windows 2000), see whether you can keep the server in place and run the client software on the MetaFrame server.

■ If the system runs at the user's desktop, make sure any services it needs, such as printing or use of serial ports, will work with Windows Server 2003 or MetaFrame XP's port redirection capabilities.

▲ Test these systems sooner rather than later in the deployment cycle so that there is time to respond if an upgrade or complete revision of the design is needed to find a new solution.

Rogue Servers and Applications

An organization should ask itself if its group or project team is in control of all the servers in the enterprise that may be affected by a project. Especially in a large enterprise, it is likely that some servers and applications have been set up regionally without their knowledge. Unless it actively investigates beforehand, the first time a company hears of such systems may be when they disable a network circuit or otherwise cut off the regional users from the rest of the network. It is wise to develop a plan to have a *sunset period* in which these locations are given a certain amount of time to phase out these systems and begin to access their applications from the new data center.

CHAPTER 6

Designing Your Network for Server-Based Computing

While network design considerations for server-based computing share many common design criteria with traditional distributed fat-client networks, the server-based computing paradigm adds several unique considerations to the design process. With minimal changes, the same networks that support classic Windows-based computing environments can be optimized to support a server-based computing scenario. The goal of this chapter is to recap common design fundamentals, introduce characteristics unique to server-based computing, and give insights on how to apply them to networking projects. A successful design project requires extensive knowledge of network services, technologies, media, protocols, security, and concepts. These areas, in varying levels of detail, are addressed in this chapter; however, less experienced network administrators should review Appendix A to brush up on the ISO/OSI model and specific local area network (LAN) and wide area network (WAN) hardware technologies. Designers are assumed to have a detailed knowledge of the software (applications) environment and the user community (types, numbers, locations, and applications requirements) they must support.

Network design is both a structured process in that it requires a logical (top-down) approach, and an iterative process that requires decisions resolved at each stage to be re-evaluated in subsequent stages as a sanity check. The top-down view starts with defining high-level goals and objectives that the target architecture must support. Once these goals are understood, proven design principles can be applied to define the problem as a set of smaller, segmented design efforts. These modular component design efforts produce functional baseline configurations for common sets of network needs, analogous to programmers creating "reusable code." Next, the process quantifies and defines the services needed to interconnect these network building blocks into a cohesive infrastructure. Given that these modular building blocks are primarily hardware based and have few recurring costs, interconnectivity in the enterprise, and its high recurring cost, can be the most contentious element of the design. To counter the cost and impact of enterprise bandwidth requirements, bandwidth management capabilities are discussed to allow inclusion where appropriate.

The last section of this chapter provides notional logical diagrams of typical modular building blocks designers may need, as well as a selection of composite network designs for common server-based computing architectures.

How is a network that is designed for server-based computing different from one designed for traditional distributed computing? Sun Microsystems' marketing slogan sums it up: "The Network is the Computer." In a network composed of thin clients connected to a data center, every single user has almost constant communication between the desktop device and the MetaFrame servers. Clients establish a connection that uses from 20 Kbps to 30 Kbps of bandwidth. This connection links the client to the server that does the application serving. In a traditional distributed computing network, the client does its own processing for the most part and makes file requests over the network that are highly variable with regard to the bandwidth used. If a distributed application server is used, the application code resides on the server and is loaded over the network into the client's memory when the program is executed. This is in addition to the file I/O already mentioned. Figure 6-1 shows how these three scenarios compare.

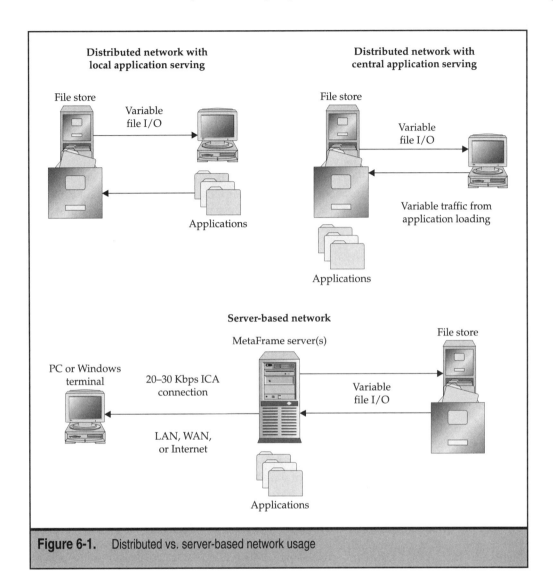

Figure 6-1.   Distributed vs. server-based network usage

HIGH-LEVEL DESIGN GOALS

In a perfect world, network administrators would be allowed the luxury of designing a server-based computing infrastructure from the ground up. As this is seldom the case, some fundamental design goals are necessary. The design goals used to successfully baseline an infrastructure to support server-based computing are speed, scalability, resiliency, manageability, auditability, and cost-effectiveness.

Speed

Initially, the concept of "speed" as a critical design criterion may seem contrary to one of the thin-client mantras: reduced bandwidth. Speed in this case refers to speed within the network core, not to clients on the network edge. Server-to-server communications within the network core must be as fast (in terms of raw speed) and as clean (in terms of controlling broadcast and superfluous traffic) as economically possible. In a load-balanced multiserver environment, users must still log on to the network, and roaming profiles are essential in providing users with a consistent, seamless experience, independent of which server actually services their application needs. These profiles must be retrieved from a central location at logon, before the user's application is available. Any delay in the initial logon and profile download process will be perceived as poor application performance. Application server to backend server (database server, file server, mail server) calls need the same rapid response for file opens, database queries, mail messages, and the like. Again, any delay in moving data from server to server is perceived by the user as an application performance problem, when in reality it may be a network core bandwidth bottleneck. Finally, insulating the servers from superfluous network traffic (broadcasts, routing protocols, and so on) improves server performance by eliminating network-driven CPU interrupts. Every Layer 2 broadcast frame (ff-ff-ff-ff-ff-ff) forces a network-driven interrupt for every server that "hears" the frame. Common sources of this event are older AppleTalk protocols, Microsoft networking with improper NetBIOS name resolution, and Novell Server Advertisement Protocol (SAP) broadcasts.

Scalability

It is important not to underestimate network growth requirements. Capacity planning of network infrastructure is often overlooked or sacrificed to budgetary constraints. Adding an additional server to an existing server farm can be relatively simple (from a technical standpoint) and easy to justify (in terms of hardware and software budgets). Adding additional servers clearly ties to increases in company requirements or users' demands (new applications, more offices, and more users). Justifying infrastructure hardware (LAN switches, routers, and so on) upgrades or purchases often proves more difficult. From a budgetary view, infrastructure tends to be less visible and perceived as a "one-time" cost. A decentralized environment migrating to a server-based environment will necessarily require increased resources in terms of servers, LAN capacity, and potentially WAN bandwidth. This chapter provides guidelines for estimating the various parts of the network, but every organization must gauge for itself how much its IT requirements will increase, and how much corresponding capacity should be designed into the network. There are two financially equivalent methods for incorporating expandability into the network. A company either can purchase components that are scalable, or it can choose vendors that provide generous trade-in policies on old equipment.

Resiliency

Resiliency is the ability to easily recover from and adjust to misfortune or change. This is certainly a desirable end state for an enterprise network. Each component should have its own ability to recover from failure or should be part of a larger system of failure recovery. Network resiliency incorporates concepts of both outage mitigation and disaster recovery. Determining just what level of resiliency must be incorporated into the network design requires a careful process of balancing three factors: level of cost (how much will it cost to build in resiliency versus how much could be lost without it?); level of effort (how much effort is required to implement and manage the resilient network versus how much effort to recover from a failure in a non-resilient network?); and level of risk (what is the probability that a specific type of failure will occur versus level of cost and level of effort to include failure mitigation in the network design?). As a general rule, unacceptably high risks are usually mollified by outage mitigation (designed-in redundancy, survivability, or fault tolerance). When risk does not warrant building in redundancy (that is, planning a hardware solution to mitigate damage from a 500-year flood), disaster recovery planning is usually required. Chapter 19 discusses disaster recovery and business continuity planning in detail.

Outage Mitigation

Outage mitigation is really just a fancy term for fault tolerance. When looking at server hardware, system administrators usually assume RAID for hard drives to make them fault tolerant. Similar features can be designed into network hardware, connectivity, and services. The end goal is to eliminate the potential for failures that impact the production environment. For hardware, consider redundant power sources and supplies, redundant Layer 2 connectivity (dual network cards and switch ports), and redundant network hardware (Layer 2 and Layer 3 processors). In terms of connectivity, consider redundant or self-healing WAN connectivity as well as redundant Layer 2 paths. For services, critical services such as directory services, name resolution, and authentication must be fault tolerant so that a single server failure does not cripple the production environment.

Disaster Recovery

A catastrophe or even a serious mishap that could include losing access to the data center calls for disaster recovery. In such cases, data moved offsite is prepared and put into production at another site. Engineering this capability into the network design at an early stage can save time and prevent you from having to ask for a budget increase later. An example of this type of technology is offsite data replication. If the storage system is replicating some or all of your corporate data to a recovery facility, the loss of your main data center is not likely to be catastrophic for the company. You can use this data along with spare hardware and software to get users back online in a timely manner.

Manageability

The extensive work that network equipment vendors have done during the last few years to simplify their equipment's administration requirements makes this design goal almost a given, but it still bears mentioning. Can the IT staff easily access the component's settings? How does this work—through a Web-enabled GUI or perhaps as a Microsoft Management

Console plug-in? Is management of the component self-contained or does it fit into an overall management architecture, such as HP OpenView or CA UniCenter? The component should make it easy to do the following tasks:

▼ Check and back up the current settings or configurations to disk.

■ Copy and make changes to the current settings without altering them, then later activate the changes either manually or on a schedule.

■ Provide real-time reporting on important system metrics—for example, bandwidth utilization and port statistics such as error rates, retransmissions, and packet loss. Ideally, this information is provided through SNMP, RMON, or some other well-known management protocol.

▲ If using multiple units of the same type, provide a method to create a standard configuration for each and a method to address and manage all of them centrally. For example, if using Windows terminals, they should allow the downloading of firmware images and settings from a central location.

Auditability

Even components that are well designed for both resiliency and manageability are not impervious to occasional unexpected crashes. The components should provide enough detailed system and transaction information to make troubleshooting relatively simple. On many systems, such as routers and switches, troubleshooting is facilitated by detailed logging information. The log should include

▼ Security validations and violations (access denials)

■ Detailed error information

■ Detailed transaction information

▲ Crash dump of the operating system kernel (or the equivalent) to aid in troubleshooting

Cost-Effectiveness

An organization may decide it needs the latest, cutting-edge network technology to make its system "really fly." However, unless they have unusual or very business-specific needs for this technology, they may find that the added expense of acquiring it is not justified. Just a short while ago, Gigabit Ethernet switches were prohibitively expensive. Could every organization benefit from the extra speed? Possibly, but is the benefit worth the price? The average company that runs word processors and spreadsheets, and accesses data from legacy databases would not realize the same benefit as a special-effects company that needs to move digital film files through the network. When comparing components that are similar in nearly every way, it may come down to answering the question, "Which gives the most bang for the buck?"

DESIGN PRINCIPLES

Translating high-level goals into a specific design can be a daunting task. Even if design services are outsourced to a consultant, the network administrator must have a clear understanding of the process to ensure any proposed design will meet requirements. The design process must meet goals in four major areas:

▼ **Infrastructure** The LAN/WAN connectivity.

■ **Services** Both network services (directory services, DNS, and so on) and applications services provided by the server-based computing paradigm.

■ **Access** The ways and means employed to actually connect users to applications consistently, reliably, and securely.

▲ **Security** Designs must protect servers and resources from attack and exploitation, enforce methods to positively identify authorized users and restrict access to only appropriate services and applications, and protect data from disclosure or tampering during transport.

Infrastructure Design

Numerous models exist to aide in planning a network infrastructure, but Cisco Systems' hierarchical enterprise design methodology is the most logical and produces the most consistent results. This approach breaks the design process into manageable blocks so that networks are designed to function within the performance and scale limits of applications, protocols, and network services. The three key elements are Structure (designing to control failure domains); Hierarchy (designing based on a functional approach); and Modularity (designing for incremental expansion and growth).

Hierarchy

Designing around Cisco's three-tier hierarchical structure defines three "layers" of the hierarchy: the core layer, the distribution layer, and the access layer. Access layers typically provide the OSI Layer 2 and Layer 3 connectivity for local LAN segment (clients), remote LAN/WAN segments, and the data center server farm. The access layer enforces locally significant policies such as security, Quality of Service (QoS), and addressing. Access layer "modules" usually share common addressing (subnets and gateways) and local LAN segments, common local architectures (all Ethernet or all Token Ring), and common communities of interest (site based or business-unit based). The distribution layer provides concentration points for multiple access layer connections either as routed connections or Layer 3 switched connections. The distribution layer enforces security boundaries (firewalls, access lists) and network policies (rate control, QoS, and so on). In a typical enterprise network, the distribution layer insulates access layer blocks and the core from the overall complexity of the network. In the server-based computing world, the distribution layer aggregates multiple access modes and methods and delivers connections to the network core for consistent performance. For WAN connectivity, the distribution layer is the key to resiliency. Although the core layer can be a WAN or MAN (metropolitan area network) core, this text is primarily concerned with the campus or corporate core that provides connectivity to the server farm. In theory, the server farm would connect to the core via its own access layer and the common distribution layer. In practice for a data center–centric approach, the access and distribution layers are often collapsed directly onto an OSI Layer 3 core switch. The sample network design topologies later in this chapter assign network components to one of these three layers.

Modularity

Modularity in design depends on a functional building block approach. Modular network designs provide several key benefits throughout their life cycle: scalability to ease growth, cost effectiveness by buying blocks of capability as demand grows, streamlined training, simplified troubleshooting, and the capability to distribute network management if required. Treating components as functional building blocks helps define interconnection and interoperability standards. For example, at the top level, a modular design defines a "standard" medium-sized remote office as an access router running OSPF and a 10/100/1000 Ethernet switch. Additional requirements may be specified, but avoid defining end equipment or specific vendors.

Structure

Factoring structure into your network design involves logically dividing the network to control failure domains and both Layer 2 and Layer 3. The term *failure domain* means engineering the network design such that failures or adverse conditions in a network segment are not propagated to other segments. For example, uncontrolled broadcast storms from a single node in a Layer 2 Ethernet LAN can bring the entire LAN to its knees. Structurally, Virtual LANs bounded by Layer 3 switches or routers can be employed to control the size of the broadcast domain. Similarly, Spanning Tree Protocol (STP) convergence in a large Layer 2 segment can disrupt traffic flow for an unacceptable duration. Since STP is essential in a loop-free redundant Layer 2 design, the size (and hence convergence time) of the STP domain needs to be controlled, and Virtual LANs (VLANs) control this behavior. Other structural elements include multicast domains, the distribution of redundant connections among separate platforms, and IP subnet size. IP subnetting can be critical when trying to control Layer 3 convergence: efficient designs use a hierarchical IP addressing scheme that supports route summarization, reducing individual routing updates and even eliminating the need to update some routes when a failure occurs.

Services Design

From the perspective of an application server in a server farm, critical services provided by the network must be available to "serve" applications to users. These include Directory Services (in a directory-service–enabled environment), name resolution to include Domain Name System (DNS) and Windows Internet Name Service (WINS), and authentication services (logon services, certificate validation, RADIUS, and token or smart cards).

Directory Services

Directory Services are integrated into most modern network operating systems. The two major offerings relevant to server-based computing are Novell's eDirectory (an updated, portable version of Novell Directory Services (NDS)) and Microsoft's Active Directory (also updated in Windows Server 2003). Both offerings are loosely based on the original x.500 directory services standard, both offer Lightweight Directory Access Protocol (LDAP) support at varying levels, and both are capable of some "directory integrated application" support. All directory services implementations organize data based on a hierarchical data structure to define types of network resources (users, services, applications, and computers) and their respective properties or attributes. The directory contains both the structure and the unique values assigned to each entity. From a management standpoint, directory services allow data about network entities to be stored as a single instance that is globally accessible. In a directory-enabled network, the directory services must be constantly available to allow normal network activities (file access, logon, application use, and so forth). They must also be extensible, robust, and redundant.

Active Directory is Microsoft's directory services component rolled out in conjunction with Windows 2000. The original implementation was traceable to the directory services functions in Microsoft Exchange. The Windows Server 2003 iteration includes improved LDAP compliance, additional security functionality (cross-Forest authentication and authorization through Forest-level trust relationships), administrative capabilities (most notably, new Group Policy management specific to Terminal Servers and Group Policy modeling), as well as the ability to edit multiple directory objects at once. Active Directory provides very limited integration with other directory services and can only manage Windows 2000 and later platforms.

eDirectory is Novell's directory services module. Built on the basic functions of NDS, eDirectory is more standards compliant than Active Directory, is ported to other operating systems, and allows management of data in other directories from a common interface. eDirectory authentication uses Public Key Infrastructure (PKI) standards while Microsoft employs a modified version of Kerberos.

Metadirectory Services, a "directory of directories," are partially built into eDirectory. Active Directory has no built-in equivalent, so Microsoft offers Microsoft Metadirectory Services (MMS) as an add-on. MMS provides multidirectory integration via "agents" that provide connectivity to network operating systems and directory systems (Microsoft Windows NT, Active Directory, Novell NDS and Bindery, iPlanet Directory, X.500 systems, and Banyan VINES), e-mail systems (Novell GroupWise, Lotus Notes, Domino, cc:Mail, and Microsoft Exchange), applications (PeopleSoft, SAP, ERP, and XML/DSML-based systems), and common database and file-based systems (Microsoft SQL Server, Oracle, LDIF, and so forth).

In a pure Windows environment (Windows 2000/XP/2003), Active Directory meets the needs of server-based computing, and at no additional cost. If a true "enterprise" directory service is required, consider eDirectory or Microsoft's add-on products.

Name Resolution

Both Domain DNS and WINS are essential in most SBC networks. Microsoft's Active Directory relies on viable DNS to locate directory servers and other network service providers (Domain Controllers, LDAP servers, and Global Catalog servers). In a Terminal Services server farm, inability to locate and access DNS results in logon failures and inability to access resources (such as resolving ODBC connections by Fully Qualified Domain Name (FQDN)), and forces administrators to manipulate IP address registrations on multiple machines rather than changing DNS pointers. WINS also remains critical. Even in a "native mode," a Windows network as NetBIOS is still used for down-level clients, and many legacy applications require NT-type NetBIOS-based syntax (\\SERVERNAME\SHARENAME) to locate and connect to resources. Improperly configured or unavailable WINS can lead to inaccessible resources and excessive broadcast traffic from broadcast name resolution.

Authentication Services

Secondary or even tertiary authentication (above and beyond basic Windows authentication) has become commonplace, but designers still tend to overlook the need for redundancy in authentication services. Many network environments (the Department of Defense, health care providers, and R&D activities) require multilevel authentication (two- or three-factor authentication). This may involve SSL certificates, biometrics, smart cards, retina scanners, and RADIUS or other extensible authentication methods. In these cases, the Terminal Server often provides the supplicant, but a valid authentication server must be available to authorize access to the network or application. For example, failure of a single RADIUS server should not deny all users access to production services.

Access Design

The need for users to access the SBC resources from a variety of locations using different access methods, media, and possibly protocols, must be factored in to any design. Logically, designing to meet access requirements consists of two processes: Protocol Selection and Access Method definition. Subsequent sections of this chapter map specific Access Methods to modular, hierarchical Access Layer building blocks.

Protocol Selection

Aside from a multitude of other technical advantages discussed in Chapter 2, the ICA client supports NetBEUI, IPX/SPX, and TCP/IP for MetaFrame, while the RDP client still only supports TCP/IP for Terminal Services. Appendix A contains a more detailed discussion of each protocol, along with advantages and limitations.

From an architectural standpoint, TCP/IP is the preferred protocol. Aside from its technical advantage (the entire Internet is based on TCP/IP), IPX/SPX and NetBEUI should only be considered as integrating technologies to bring legacy systems into your new network, and then only until they can be migrated to TCP/IP. As a general rule, multiprotocol bindings to support a legacy LAN (IPX/SP and NetBEUI) should be eliminated as rapidly as possible.

Access Method

Defining required access methods is really an exercise in identifying the user community and the locations or environments from which they need to connect. In all cases, bandwidth requirements per method must be evaluated to "close the loop" and ensure that every required means of access (local, remote, dedicated media, dial-up, virtual private network (VPN), and so on) is afforded adequate bandwidth to support the number of concurrent connections expected. In most cases, enumerating the applications available to a user may be via direct client connection (Program Neighborhood) or Web-based front end (Citrix NFuse Classic). The following are common access methods based on user environments and locations:

▼ **Traditional LAN access**   Local user community with direct high-speed deterministic bandwidth and little need for encryption.

■ **Wireless LAN (WLAN) access**   Similar to a traditional LAN, but with a greater need for security due to the lack of defined physical boundaries. Usually requires secondary authentication (like a dial-up user) as well as some level of encryption.

■ **Branch office, dedicated media**   The classic distributed branch office environment. Connection to the SBC core is via dedicated, deterministic WAN media (T1, Frame Relay, ATM, and so on) and supports both SBC connectivity and other network services. Dedicated access for remote branch offices is essential when Quality of Service (QoS) for packetized voice or video is required.

■ **Branch office, VPN access**   Similar to the dedicated media paradigm, but site-to-site bandwidth is non-deterministic. The branch office is connected to the SBC core network via a branch-to-branch VPN and all site-to-site traffic traverses the VPN. Typically used for smaller branch offices or to international sites or offices where dedicated access is cost prohibitive. Traffic inside the VPN tunnel can be controlled and managed, but the tunnel itself traverses the Internet and no QoS guarantees are possible.

■ **Remote user Internet access (applications only)**   Connection is via non-deterministic bandwidth over the public Internet. Usually requires some level of encryption and may require multifactor authentication. Users access only SBC resources, no direct LAN access. This method may include wireless data over mobile phones (second (2G) or third (3G)) technologies.

■ **Remote user Internet access (applications and LAN)**   Connection uses a VPN over non-deterministic bandwidth via the public Internet. Usually requires increased levels of encryption and multifactor authentication to protect the LAN environment. Users access SBC resources and directly access the local LAN for drive mapping, printing, or "fat client" applications. The most common example is roaming executives or sales staff that need SBC applications and the ability to synchronize handheld devices with corporate mail servers (for example, Palm Pilot users). This may also include IT Staff that need to access and manage LAN resources and servers.

▲ **Direct dial access**   Used for direct connection to the SBC core via any of several remote access methods. May be either via direct dial to an SBC member server as an asynchronous serial connection or through a remote access concentrator (RAS services on a server or hardware concentrator). Dial-up media may be either analog (typical modem) or digital (ISDN, BRI, or PRI). Analog access is limited to 33.6 Kbps while digital access can provide up to 56 Kbps for analog modem users and multiples of 64 Kbps (64, 128, 192, 256, and so on) for ISDN users. Direct dial access usually does not require strong encryption but does require multilevel or multifactor authentication.

Security Design

An SBC network differs little from a traditional network when it comes to security considerations; basic network security mechanisms must be in place.

▼ **Network security**   Designs should include firewalls, access lists on routers and Layer 3 switches, and intrusion detection systems (IDSs).

■ **User security**   Authentication, authorization, and access (AAA) mechanisms must be tailored to the environment and access method. Internal "wired" users are generally considered trusted and are subject to normal security policies and principles. Remote or non-wired users must be positively identified before being granted access to SBC or other network resources. Beyond normal logon (username and password) authentication, common methods include Remote Access Dial-in User Service (RADIUS), tokens or smart cards (RSA's SecurID, Secure Computing's Safeword), and biometric authenticators (fingerprint or retina scanners).

▲ **Data security**   Although the actual data for a thin-client connection is a stream of video data and input device data (pointing device and keyboard), the data must still be protected from intercept and exploitation. This is particularly true of credentials used to access the session. There are two common methods of protecting this data. The first method is Secure Sockets Layer (SSL) or Transport Layer Security (TLS) encryption based on certificates and Public Key Infrastructure (PKI). The second method is IP Security (IPSec) using the Digital Encryption Standard (DES) or Advanced Encryption Standard (AES). Other mechanisms may be used in specialized cases, for example, NSA's FORTEZZA (SKIPJACK) encryption cards or Wireless Equivalent Privacy (WEP) for WLANs.

INFRASTRUCTURE DESIGN—MODULAR BUILDING BLOCKS

Designing the network infrastructure for server-based computing involves selecting the right modular components to meet requirements and then connecting them together in a cost-effective and efficient manner. This three-tiered infrastructure (core, distribution, and access) can be developed one layer at a time, as long as standards-based components are used and the access methods are known. Figure 6-2 shows common symbols used for network design diagrams.

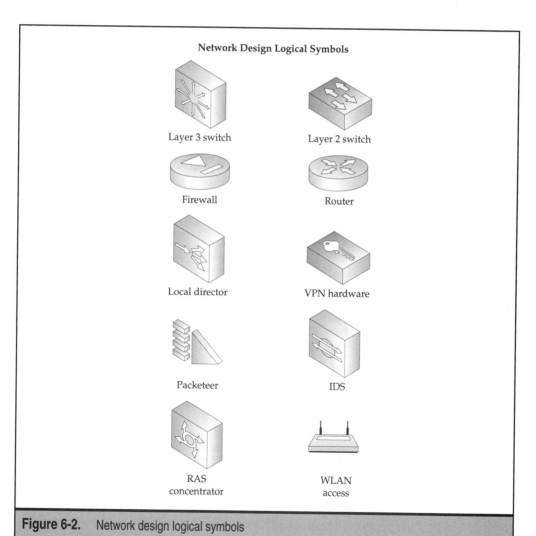

Figure 6-2. Network design logical symbols

Core Layer

The network core for an SBC network is typically a collapsed backbone that aggregates true "core" components (high-speed switching) and the access and distribution layer elements supporting the SBC farm into a single platform or several similar platforms. The core should be a Layer 3–switched backbone designed to be redundant, expandable, and fast. The core can be either Layer 2 or Layer 3, with Layer 3 preferred due to faster convergence in response to failures (Layer 3 cores rely on routing table convergence, which takes only seconds, while Layer 2 cores rely on STP, which can take 30–40 seconds or longer).

High-end Layer 3 core devices are chassis-based Layer 3 switches with redundant Layer 2 (switching) and Layer 3 (routing) components. For smaller networks, similar non-redundant fixed-configuration devices are widely available. Specifically, the network core should provide

▼ Layer 3 TCP/IP switching. The ability to transport IP packets across the core at "wire" (gigabit) speeds by rewriting packet headers, as opposed to routing packets individually. Some switches support a limited (slower) ability to handle IPX/SPX packets at Layer 3. NetBEUI is not supported at Layer 3 and must be bridged at Layer 2.

■ Layer 2 "cut-through" switching. The ability to transport Layer 2 frames across the core without excessive buffering or processing. Low-end and older switches use slower switching methods such as store-and-forward and are unsuitable as core devices.

■ Support for virtual LANs (VLANs) to segment traffic and separate groups of servers, Layer 2 server and user segments, and connections to other access or distribution layer devices.

■ Support for Fast Ethernet and Gigabit Ethernet.

■ Built-in support for network performance monitoring and management.

■ Support for link aggregation using fast ether channel (FEC) or gigabit ether channel (GEC) technology via Port Aggregation Protocol (PAgP) or 802.3ad Link Aggregation Control Protocol (LACP).

■ Support for advanced routing protocols (EIGRP, OSPF, IS-IS, BGP).

■ Support for router redundancy protocols (HSRP, VRRP) at Layer 3 and path redundancy at Layer 2 paths (Spanning Tree Protocol (STP)) with fast convergence.

■ Incremental growth capacity via additional modules or additional devices.

▲ High-capacity non-blocking backplane. Typical high-end chassis-based solutions offer 64-Gbps or higher capacity, while fixed configuration low-end solutions provide 10–20 Gbps.

Because of the complexity and variability, network diagrams of "core" layer topologies are included only in the complete network diagrams in the final section of this chapter.

Distribution Layer

The distribution layer provides aggregation of connections to groups of users and is generally categorized as either a LAN distribution point (connected to client access layer switches or media) or a WAN distribution layer (connecting to remote sites and services, to include the Internet). Distribution layer hardware is usually Layer 3 switches for large corporate or campus LANs and routers for WAN aggregation. In smaller networks, the core and distribution layers can be collapsed onto a single Layer 3 device. Distribution layer topologies are included only in the complete network diagrams in the final section of this chapter.

The distribution layer may include QoS, bandwidth management, and limited security enforcement (firewall, packet inspection, or access list filtering). Specific distribution layer hardware and media should be determined by the type and number of access layer connections required.

Connections between the distribution layer and the core should be Layer 3 to allow for policy and security enforcement and to isolate broadcast traffic. Connectivity between distribution aggregation points and the core typically employs multiple VLANs using Fast Ethernet or Gigabit Ethernet.

Access Layer

Access layer building blocks are the most variable modular building blocks. The typical campus or corporate network requires multiple types to meet specific media connectivity and access method needs. The complement of access layer modules will determine the size and nature of most distribution layer devices. For remote sites and Internet connectivity, the access layer also provides the real security perimeter (firewall, proxy servers, and so on).

LAN Access Module

LAN access components are usually Layer 2 Fast Ethernet switches in campus wiring closets. These switches may have redundant Layer 2 uplinks to a Layer 3 distribution switch (large networks) or uplink directly to the Layer 3 core (smaller networks). Modern designs use single or multigigabit aggregated uplinks configured as 802.1q VLAN trunks (see Figure 6-3). Each trunk consists of one or more Gigabit Ethernet connections, each carrying multiple virtual LANs (one for marketing, one for sales, one for engineering, and so on). Access layer switches share many of the common characteristics of distribution and core switches including management, cut-through switching, Layer 2 aggregation, 802.1p Class of Service (CoS) tagging, and so forth.

WLAN Access Module

Despite security concerns, wireless local area networks (WLANs) have become ubiquitous throughout organizations today, and as such are a critical part of most networks.

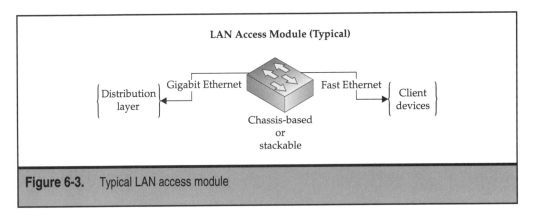

Figure 6-3.   Typical LAN access module

NOTE: Adding to the wireless discussion, Sprint, Verizon, and other mobile wireless providers have released G3 wireless Internet access (wWLAN) with up to 144K of bandwidth that is quickly gaining popularity as a server-based computing access choice. For the purposes of this book, wireless Internet access options will be handled as simply another external Internet connection option, not to be confused with WLAN.

We will explore WLAN security in detail in Chapter 8, but for the purposes of a network discussion, WLAN access components are Layer 2, even though they are shared rather than switched Ethernet. This increases the impact of broadcast traffic on each client and also means the aggregate bandwidth is shared by all users of a given WLAN segment. Current WLAN 802.11-series standards provide aggregate bandwidth ranging from 11 Mbps (802.11b) to 54 Mbps (802.11a). WLAN access modules should include necessary AAA support (AAA is also discussed in depth in Chapter 8) in the network core in the form of RADIUS servers (see Figure 6-4). In smaller networks, low-end WLAN hardware can provide basic services with limited security (128-bit WEP, not secondary authentication), while large or more sensitive networks need high-end hardware that provides dynamic encryption keys, built-in protection from "man-in-the-middle" or bit-flipping attacks, and support for secondary authentication as well as 802.1Q virtual LANs and QoS support. It is essential that WLAN segments be isolated from the core by Layer 3 devices.

WAN Access Module, Branch Office—Dedicated Media

A typical remote branch office WAN access module consists of standard Layer 2 Ethernet switches and an access router (see Figure 6-5). These offices are usually connected to the data center by dedicated media (frame relay, ISDN, ATM, T1, or similar media) and do not require extensive security such as firewalls. Security is usually in the form of access list filters to control either traffic flow or route distribution (or both). WAN access routers may support Layer 3 QoS if warranted by corporate applications. Where connecting bandwidth is limited, bandwidth managers such as Packeteer PacketShapers may also be included as an optional component.

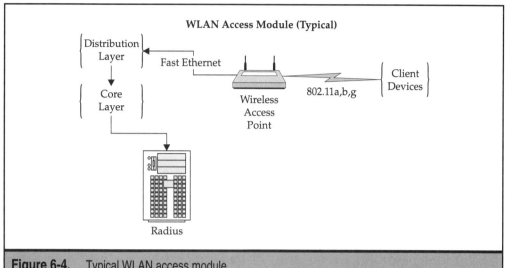

Figure 6-4.   Typical WLAN access module

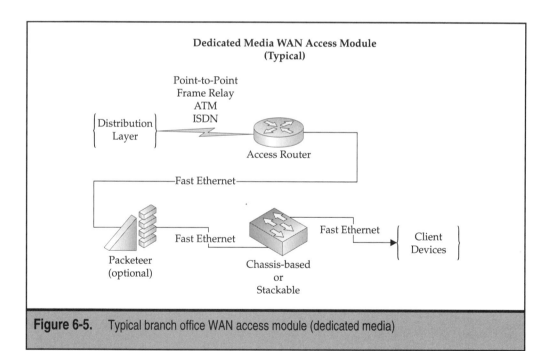

Figure 6-5.   Typical branch office WAN access module (dedicated media)

WAN Access Module, Branch Office—VPN Access

Remote offices, which use an office-to-office VPN to tunnel from the branch network to the core network, require compatible VPN hardware at the branch and at the data center. The branch office configuration is similar to the dedicated media branch office with a firewall/VPN device added between the LAN switch and the WAN media (see Figures 6-6 through 6-8). This may be in the form of a VPN/firewall feature incorporated into the WAN access router, or a separate device in line between the switch and the router. In either case, all traffic from the remote site to the data center is encrypted and transported through the VPN tunnel. Internet connectivity may be via any media subject to bandwidth requirements. One key consideration is the added overhead that VPN connectivity requires. IPSec encapsulation adds 10–25 percent additional overhead to the data stream, as well as an additional processing workload on the VPN device. When designing VPN connectivity, ensure Internet bandwidth allows for concurrent thin-client sessions plus IPSec overhead.

WAN Access Module, Data Center VPN Termination

When either remote user VPN access or remote office VPN access is required, a VPN termination suite is required at the data center end. If only office-to-office connections and a limited number of user connections are to be supported, corporate firewalls or VPN routers can terminate all required connections. If the capability to terminate connections from multiple branch offices with substantially different VPN needs and/or a large number of users with differing VPN access constraints is needed, consider a purpose-built VPN

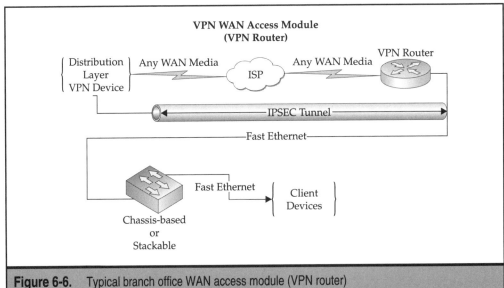

Figure 6-6. Typical branch office WAN access module (VPN router)

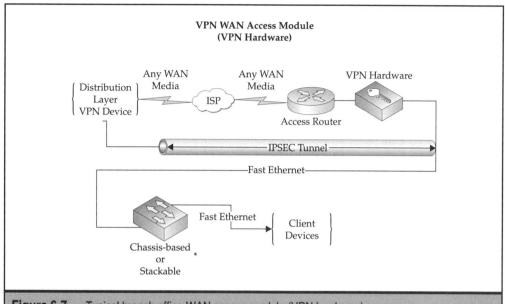

Figure 6-7. Typical branch office WAN access module (VPN hardware)

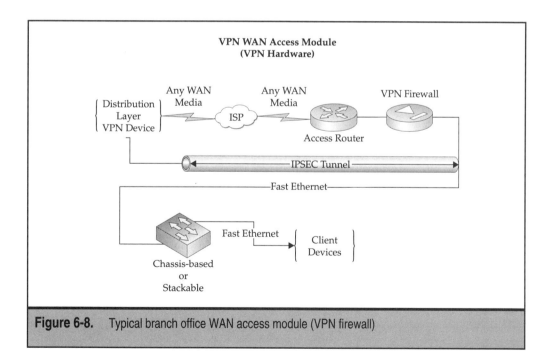

Figure 6-8. Typical branch office WAN access module (VPN firewall)

concentrator. Depending on security requirements, the VPN connections may be routed directly to the corporate LAN or they may be forced through the corporate firewall to apply additional security restrictions.

Data center Internet bandwidth must meet the same capacity requirements as remote branches, and may require a separate Internet connection to support VPN terminations (and insulate the VPN Internet connection from the variable bandwidth demands of users surfing the Internet. Optionally, a bandwidth manager (PacketShaper) at the data center access layer can give preferential treatment to IPSec traffic.

Offices that use an office-to-office VPN to tunnel from the branch network to the core network require compatible VPN hardware at the branch and at the data center. The branch office configuration is similar to the dedicated media branch office with a firewall/ VPN device added between the LAN switch and the WAN media (see Figure 6-9). This may be in the form of a VPN/firewall feature incorporated into the WAN access router, or a separate device in line between the switch and the router. In either case, all traffic from the remote site to the data center is encrypted and transported through the VPN tunnel. Internet connectivity may be via any media subject to bandwidth requirements.

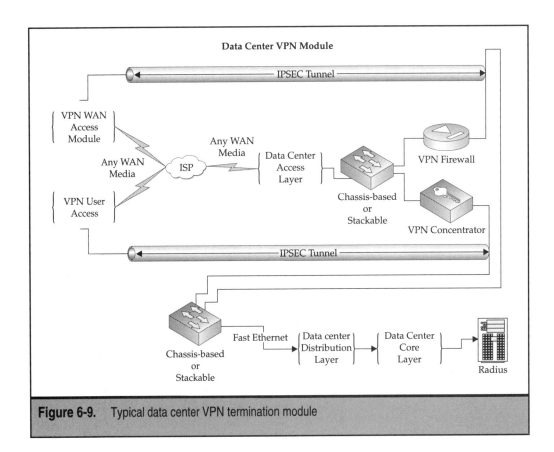

Figure 6-9.   Typical data center VPN termination module

WAN Access Module, Remote User Internet Access

The infrastructure suite needed to provide individual remote users with thin-client applications over the Internet exists only at the data center (see Figure 6-10). Actual components of this module are dependent upon the criticality of the remote user access, data

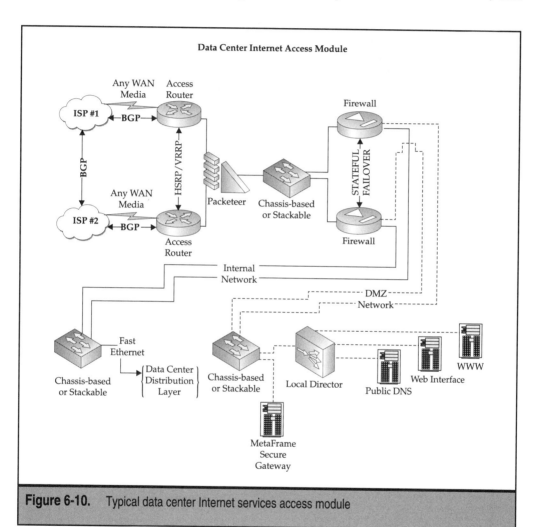

Figure 6-10. Typical data center Internet services access module

security requirements, and the number of remote users. Assuming high-level requirements for all three elements, the module would consist of a redundant Internet upstream connection backed by a redundant firewall. Although Program Neighborhood could be used to enumerate applications, MetaFrame Web Interface is the preferred method and would require redundancy in DNS servers and front-end web servers. If secure access is required, redundant MetaFrame Secure Gateway platforms would also be required. Finally, extremely heavy Internet-based user loads, typical of an application service provider, can be augmented with specialized server aggregation appliances such as Cisco's Local Director to offload DNS and HTTP load balancing.

Direct Dial Remote Access Module

Dial-up access to the SBC resources may be either direct asynchronous or PPP based. Direct access can be to either a specific server via multiport modems or modem sharing, but this approach severely limits the ability to effectively balance the client load across the server farm and constrains bandwidth to the client to a maximum of 33.6 Kbps. The preferred solution requires a Remote Access Service (RAS) server or concentrator either through a server platform (Windows Routing and Remote Access) or a concentrator such as a Cisco Universal Gateway or a Lucent Portmaster (see Figure 6-11). In either case, ISDN access, either BRI or PRI, is essential; it allows the RAS device to provide the digital termination of analog or digital calls and achieve speeds greater than 33.6 Kbps. RAS devices require the same type of core services (AAA services) as WLAN modules. In general, a single suite of AAA servers should be able to support WLAN, RAS, and VPN user authentication. As an added benefit, the same RAS device that terminates client connections can also terminate routed ISDN branch-to-branch connections to connect small or home offices to the corporate data center. Accessibility of the data center network from the public switched telephone network (PSTN) mandates strong authentication. Further, firewall filtering of these dial-up connections is highly recommended.

INFRASTRUCTURE DESIGN—CONNECTING THE MODULES

Once the component module requirements are defined, specific connecting media can be specified and accurate bandwidth calculations are possible to correctly scale that media. The need for specialized bandwidth managers can also be assessed.

Media Selection

LAN Media

In the context of server-based computing, the LAN resides in two places—inside the data center and inside the remote office. The data center LAN is potentially very complex, while the remote office LAN will be relatively simple, containing little more than a

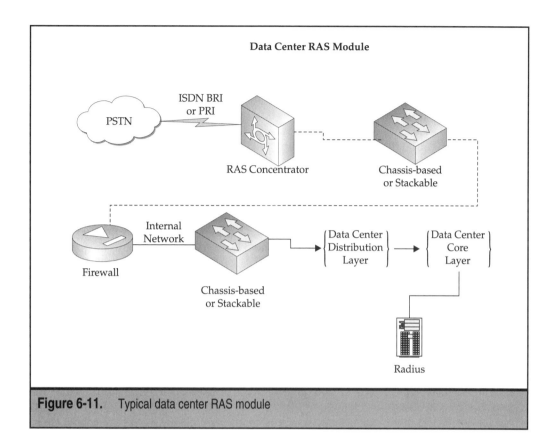

Data Center RAS Module

Figure 6-11.   Typical data center RAS module

workgroup media concentration point, client devices (PCs or thin clients), and LAN peripherals (printers, storage devices, and so on).

▼   **Ethernet**   As originally defined (10BaseT, 10Base2), Ethernet was a shared media technology using Carrier Sense Multiple Access/Collision Detection (CSMA/CD) technology and both Layer 2 repeaters and multiport repeaters (hubs). These residual shared Ethernet environments define a large collision domain and, as such, suffer from performance limitations imposed by CSMA/CD. More specifically, collisions are a normal and expected part of half-duplex shared Ethernet, but they effectively limit performance to 35 percent of rated capacity. This means a 10-Mbps Ethernet segment is saturated at 3.5-Mbps throughput. Additionally, half-duplex operations increase the latency due to interframe delays built into the Ethernet standard to minimize collisions. In a switched infrastructure, modern network cards can operate full-duplex, allowing sustained operation at near 90 percent of capacity, both for send and receive (approaching 20-Mbps throughput).

- **Fast Ethernet**   Fast Ethernet is also referred to as 100BaseT to indicate that it provides for a transmission standard of 100 Mbps across the LAN. The 100BaseT standard is backward compatible with 10-Mbps Ethernet. Many vendors tout "dual speed hubs" capable of simultaneous support for both shared Ethernet and shared Fast Ethernet; however, in a mixed speed environment, the Ethernet bus must arbitrate to the rate of the station transmitting. Multispeed hub performance can be worse than a pure 10-Mbps environment due to excessive bus arbitration. Use of dual-speed hubs is strongly discouraged. On the other hand, dual speed switched Ethernet does not incur this penalty. As of this writing, switched Fast Ethernet is the de facto standard for LAN technology with regard to client connectivity. Cabling must meet EIA/TIA Category 5 standards to guarantee reliable Fast Ethernet connectivity.

- **Gigabit Ethernet**   This transmission standard provides for sending one billion bits per second across the LAN. It has also been incorporated into the standard Ethernet specification (802.3z) and uses the same Carrier Sense Multiple Access with Collision Detection (CSMA/CD) protocol, same frame format, and same frame size as its predecessors. Gigabit Ethernet is always switched versus shared and is normally full-duplex. Generically referred to as 1000Base-X, transmission media can be fiber optic (1000BaseSX (multimode) or 1000BaseLX (single mode)), unshielded twisted pair (1000BaseT over 4-pair Category 5 cable), or shielded twisted pair (1000BaseCX over 2-pair 150 ohm shielded cable). Gigabit Ethernet is rapidly emerging as the de facto standard for data center server connectivity to the data center core, and for connecting LAN access layer aggregation points to the core or distribution layer.

- **Token Bus/Token Ring**   Token Bus is similar to Ethernet but uses a different method to avoid contention. Instead of listening to traffic and detection collisions, it attempts to control the sequence of which nodes use the network at what time. The node holds a "token" and passes it on to the next node when it is finished transmitting. Any node can receive a message but cannot transmit unless it holds a token. Token Bus networks are laid out in a serial bus fashion with many nodes daisy-chained together. Token Ring, on the other hand, is implemented in a ring topology. The main difference between the two is how the token is handled. In Token Ring, the token becomes part of the packet. With Token Bus, the packet is a separate message that is passed after a node has finished transmitting. Token Ring networks have many of the advantages of Ethernet and even started out with higher possible bandwidth (about 16 Mbps). However, Ethernet is now the unquestioned standard. Token Ring is usually part of a legacy network connecting mainframes, minicomputers, or other IBM equipment.

- **ATM for LAN**   Asynchronous Transfer Mode was once viewed as an alternative to Ethernet-based technologies in a LAN environment. Manufacturers originally touted "ATM to the desktop" as the future of high-bandwidth access. This never materialized in large-scale desktop deployments for many reasons, not the least of which is cost. ATM network cards and associated network devices are still far more expensive than their Ethernet-based counterparts, and less widely available. Two primary factors have contributed to the loss of interest in ATM in LANs: the rising speed and falling cost of Ethernet-based technologies (10-Gbps Ethernet is available now), and the extreme complexity of internetworking LAN segments using ATM LAN Emulation (LANE).

▲   **F/CDDI**   Fiber/Copper Distributed Data Interface is a 100-Mbps LAN topology designed to operate over optical cabling (FDDI) and standard copper cabling (CDDI). Both use a media access protocol similar to Token Ring (token passing) and employ a dual counter-rotating ring topology. As a Metropolitan Area Network (MAN) backbone, FDDI is very attractive and performs exceptionally under high-load conditions. Maximum ring distances for FDDI are up to 200 km for a single ring topology and 100 km for a dual ring topology. CDDI rings are limited to 100 m.

WAN Media

The wide area network (WAN) is the vehicle for transporting data across the enterprise. In a server-based computing environment, the design of the WAN infrastructure is crucial to the IT enterprise. It is essential to create a WAN design that is robust, scalable, and highly reliable in order to protect the value of the data that must flow across the WAN. Interconnecting media types for WAN services include

▼   **Frame relay**   Frame relay service is available virtually worldwide. It employs virtual circuits (usually permanent virtual circuits (PVC)) mapped at Layer 2 over T3, T1, FT1, or 56K connections. Multiple PVCs can be carried over a single physical (for example, T1) access facility and aggregate bandwidth of all PVCs can exceed the physical media bandwidth (oversubscription). For example, four 512-Kbps PVCs can be provisioned over a single T1 access line. Individual PVCs can be provisioned with a guaranteed transmission rate called the Committed Information Rate (CIR) and the ability to burst above this rate, on demand, if frame relay network bandwidth is available. Burst traffic is not guaranteed and can be ruthlessly discarded. For WAN connectivity, the combination of all thin-client (RDP, ICA) traffic and packetized voice or video traffic must be less than the CIR to ensure reliable performance. Further, QoS restriction cannot be applied to traffic rates above CIR. If physical media is significantly oversubscribed (greater than 1.5:1), thin-client performance may be degraded.

■   **Point-to-point serial**   Point-to-point serial service is available in many formats including 56 Kbps, fractional T1 service (FT1) in multiples of 64 Kbps from 64–1472 Kbps, and full T1 (1.544 Mbps, 1.536 Mbps usable). Dedicated point-to-point circuits have been around for a long time and are often the most cost-effective means when short distances are involved. These circuits can either be leased from a service provider or local telephone company (TelCo), or be completely private if the company owns the copper cable facilities. (See Figure 6-12.)

■ **ATM**   Asynchronous transfer mode combines the best features of the older packet-switched networks and the newer frame-switched networks. ATM's small (53-byte) cell-based protocol data unit and advanced inherent management features make ATM the most flexible and predictable technology currently available. Data rates for tariffed ATM services are based on a T1, T3, or Synchronous Optical Network (SONET) physical media with ATM virtual circuit equivalents provisioned much like frame relay. SONET optical carrier levels range from OC1 (51.840 Mbps) through OC48 (2.48832 Gbps). ATM delivers variable bandwidth and allows direct integration with other WAN services such as frame relay and xDSL. ATM is also the defined multiplex layer standard for SONET and the basis for future technologies such as broadband ISDN (B-ISDN). (See Figure 6-13.)

■ **Integrated Services Digital Network (ISDN)**   ISDN was announced in the late 1970s as a way to provide simultaneous voice and data over the same line. ISDN uses the same basic copper wiring as Plain Old Telephone Service (POTS), but its Basic Rate Interface (BRI) offers two 56-Kbps or 64-Kbps bearer channels and one 16-Kbps data channel (2B+D). B-channels carry the data payload (digital data or digitized voice) while the D-channel executes call control and management. For higher demand environments, the ISDN Primary Rate Interface (PRI), offers 23 standard B-channels and one 64-Kbps D-channel over a single T1 facility.

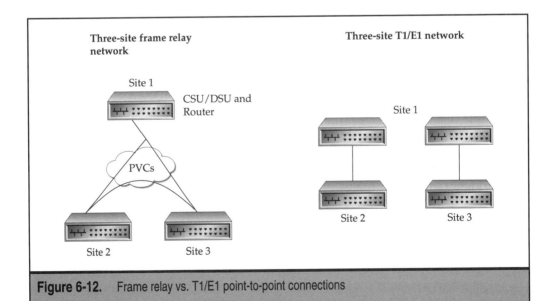

Figure 6-12.   Frame relay vs. T1/E1 point-to-point connections

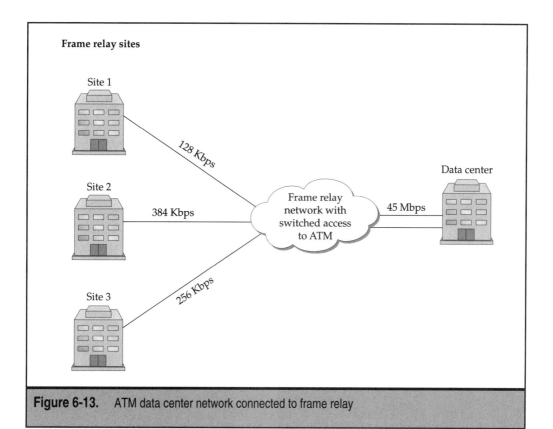

Frame relay sites

Site 1

128 Kbps

Site 2

384 Kbps

Frame relay network with switched access to ATM

45 Mbps

Data center

Site 3

256 Kbps

Figure 6-13.   ATM data center network connected to frame relay

B-channels can be used individually or bonded together. ISDN is a point-to-point technology and provides deterministic, but expensive, bandwidth. ISDN BRI is commonly used as a dial-on-demand backup for dedicated frame relay circuits. (See Figure 6-14.)

■ **Digital Subscriber Line (DSL)**   Various flavors of DSL are available in most areas, but without ATM to the data center or a value-added Internet service provider (ISP), the DSL circuits must terminate at a service provider for Internet access only. TelCos provide Asymmetric DSL (ADSL) at various rates based on physical loop distances from their Central Office (CO) to the customer premises. ADSL is low cost and, as the name implies, has asymmetric bandwidth, meaning less upstream capacity than downstream capacity. Symmetric DSL (SDSL) is normally provided by specialized service providers with their equipment co-located at the TelCo CO. SDSL can reach greater distances and often higher speeds than ADSL, but at three to six times the monthly cost. IDSL, a form of "unswitched" ISDN in which the connection is permanent between the customer premises and the CO, provides speeds equivalent to ISDN BRI, but

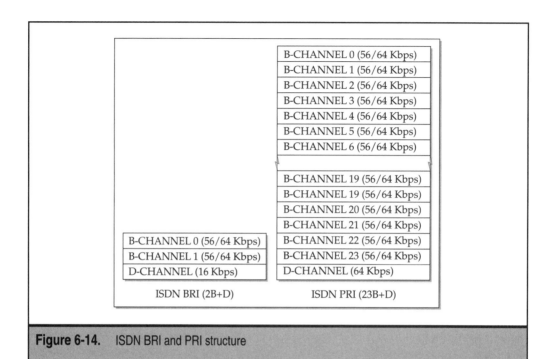

Figure 6-14.   ISDN BRI and PRI structure

without the high usage–based billing. The downside of ISDL is that you have an ISDN line that can't call anywhere. Like frame relay, DSL providers charge based on bandwidth, but seldom provide guaranteed performance like frame relay's CIR. More recent TelCo offerings (at a higher price) include ADSL with business-class service level agreements for throughput and availability. DSL is very low cost compared to other options, but is generally only usable as Internet access—unless you have ATM to the data center or work with a value-added ISP. Value-added ISPs can terminate multiple circuit types (ADSL, ISDL, and so on) from remote offices and provide consistent bandwidth via any circuit type to the data center, in effect becoming an offsite WAN access and distribution layer.

- **Cable modem**   Cable modems connect to the existing cable TV (CATV) coaxial network to provide new services such as Internet access to subscribers. Speeds can reach a theoretical 36 Mbps, but end-node technology (such as a network interface card) does not yet exist to take advantage of this speed. Speeds of 2 Mbps to 10 Mbps are more common. The service is asymmetrical in its current implementation with download speeds that are far faster than upload speeds, and raw bandwidth that's shared among a large number of users. No service level agreement is available, nor are repair times guaranteed for failed services. Cable modems are only suitable for very small offices or home offices, or where no cost-effective competing technology is available and VPN or Internet-based access to the SBC resources is appropriate.

▲ **Internet/VPN**   Though not a "media" in the same sense as the other technologies discussed here, it does provide an alternative connectivity option. A virtual private network (VPN) uses the Internet as a valid network infrastructure option for connecting small or remote offices and telecommuters.

Planning Network Bandwidth

Planning network bandwidth may seem like an obvious need, but it is often skipped because it is difficult to predict the normal bandwidth utilization of a given device or user on the network. However, by using modeling based on nominal predicted values, bandwidth requirements can be accurately projected. When planning network bandwidth, keep the following guidelines in mind:

▼ Point-to-point WAN links are saturated when they reach 70–80 percent of rated capacity; in other words, do not plan to push more than 1.2 Mbps of traffic over a point-to-point T1.

■ Frame relay and ATM connections are saturated when they reach 90 percent of rated capacity per virtual circuit. Additionally, exceeding the CIR means transport is not guaranteed.

■ Allow 25 percent additional bandwidth for any VPN link.

■ Always calculate required voice or video bandwidth first, add thin-client session bandwidth, and then add bandwidth for all remaining services that must use the link (routing protocols, time service, Internet browsing, mail services, Windows domain traffic, printing, and so on). On links that are never primary access for Internet services (Web, FTP, mail, streaming media, and so on), 30 percent additional bandwidth above and beyond voice/video and thin-client requirements is a good starting figure.

■ WAN bandwidth per thin-client user is nominally 30 Kbps, depending on application usages and graphics. Plan based on *concurrent* connections, not total user population.

■ Printing inside the thin-client session will add up to an additional 20-Kbps concurrent printing connection. Concurrent printing usually equals less than 20 percent of all concurrent sessions.

▲ On links that provide primary access to Internet services, all available bandwidth can be consumed by Internet service traffic. Plan baseline thin-client bandwidth as mentioned previously in this list, adding at least 50 percent for Internet service access, and plan for bandwidth management to protect thin-client bandwidth allocations. (Use Table 6-1 as a reference.)

Concurrent Users	Bandwidth per User	Base Citrix Bandwidth	ICA Printing?	ICA Printing Bandwidth	Total Citrix Bandwidth	Primary Internet?	Excess Bandwidth	Required Bandwidth	WAN Media Type	Load Factor	Service
30	30 Kbps	900 Kbps	Yes	180 Kbps	1080 Kbps	No	30% (324 Kbps)	1424 Kbps	Pt-Pt	70%	E1 (2.048MB)
25	30 Kbps	750 Kbps	No	0 Kbps	900 Kbps	No	30% (300 Kbps)	1050 Kbps	Pt-Pt	70%	T1 (1.544MB)
30	30 Kbps	900 Kbps	Yes	180 Kbps	1080 Kbps	No	30% (324 Kbps)	1424 Kbps	VPN	75%	2MB ATM VC
30	30 Kbps	900 Kbps	Yes	180 Kbps	1080 Kbps	No	30% (324 Kbps)	1424 Kbps	Frame relay	90%	1.6 MB CIR
30	30 Kbps	900 Kbps	No	0 Kbps	900 Kbps	No	30% (300 Kbps)	1200 Kbps	Frame relay	90%	1344K CIR
30	30 Kbps	900 Kbps	No	0 Kbps	900 Kbps	Yes	50% (450 Kbps)	1350 Kbps	Frame relay	90%	1536K CIR

Table 6-1. Sample WAN Bandwidth Calculation Worksheet

Bandwidth Management

In most thin-client WAN environments, "calculated" bandwidth should provide optimal performance, but seldom does. Even strict corporate policies on acceptable use of bandwidth cannot protect thin-client bandwidth when the network administrator downloads a large file or a user finds a new way to access music and media sharing sites. These unpredictable behaviors can degrade SBC services to remote users due to bandwidth starvation or excessive latency. There are several technologies available to more tightly control bandwidth utilization and assure responsive service environments: Layer 2 CoS and queuing, Layer 3 QoS and queuing, router-based bandwidth managers (Cisco's NBAR), and appliance-based bandwidth managers (Packeteer). Each of these has its respective strengths and weaknesses and all share several common characteristics. In addition, all of these technologies must have a mechanism for differentiating more important traffic from less important traffic, a process called *classification*. Traffic may or may not be "marked" and tagged with its particular priority, but subsequent network devices must be able to recognize the classifications and apply policies or rules to prioritize or constrain specific traffic types. All must have a means for identifying traffic as more important or less important than other traffic.

When applying bandwidth management technologies to WAN traffic flows, the following general rules apply:

▼   Do not prioritize any traffic above network management traffic. This usually is a factor only on Layer 2 CoS implementations where data (digitized voice and application frames) are incorrectly tagged as priority 7. Management and control information (STP, VLAN status messages) must not compete with user traffic.

■   Digitized voice and video have a very high priority. They must have instantaneous bandwidth and the lowest possible latency through Layer 2 and 3 devices (priority queuing).

■   Thin-client user access has a high priority. ICA/RDP traffic has the same priority as character-interactive terminal emulation traffic. Although far more graphical than "green screen" applications, performance is perceived the same by users. If a user presses ENTER and doesn't get a timely application response (as fast as a local session), thin-client performance is deemed unacceptable.

■   Mission-critical applications such as ERP packages should receive a higher priority than personal productivity applications or web applications such as browsers and FTP.

■   Average utilization of network resources should be high, thus saving money by avoiding unnecessary upgrades.

▲   Rules for bandwidth utilization or bandwidth blocking should be by application, user, and group.

TIP: More bandwidth, not less, is needed when migrating users to a new network. It is likely that the old and new network will have to run on some of the same network segments while users are moved from the old network to the new data center network. Tasks such as user data migration, interim file server reassignment, and "backhauling" user data to legacy systems not yet on the new network can all add up to an increased bandwidth need. Some of this is unavoidable, but some of the need can be mitigated with careful planning and staging of which systems will be migrated in which order. When an organization does not underestimate bandwidth needs, it enjoys a lower risk of having unhappy users before projects get started.

Layer 2 CoS and Queuing   Applying Layer 2 CoS prioritization to LAN traffic has several weaknesses: It is only locally significant (CoS tags are frame based and not transported across Layer 3 boundaries); granular control, by application or service, is not widely supported; and most applications are incapable of originating traffic with and tagging frames with CoS values. Several vendors provide network interface cards capable of applying CoS and QoS tags to frames or packets, but this feature is on or off and cannot differentiate application layer traffic. Microsoft's Generic Quality of Service (GQoS) API allows software developers to access CoS and QoS features through the Windows 2003 server operating system. However, the API is not widely supported and only a limited number of Microsoft multimedia applications currently use the GQoS API. Most Layer 2 network devices have one or two input queues per port and up to four output queues. Out of the box, all traffic is routed through the default queue (low priority) on a first-in/first-out basis. CoS can be applied to frames at the source or upon entry to the switch to redirect the output to use a higher priority queue. Higher priority queues are always serviced (emptied) first, reducing latency. In a server-based computing paradigm, there is little to be gained from accelerating frames through the network at Layer 2.

Layer 3 QoS and Queuing   Quality of Service at Layer 3 encompasses classifying traffic (via a standard or extended access list), protocol (such as URLs, stateful protocols, or Layer 4 protocol), input port, IP Precedence or DSCP, or Ethernet 802.1p class of service (CoS). Traffic classification using access lists is processor intensive and should be avoided. Once traffic is classified it must be marked with the appropriate value to ensure end-to- end QoS treatment is enforced. Marking methods are three IP Precedence bits in the IP Type of Service (ToS) byte; six Differentiated Services Code Point (DSCP) bits in the IP ToS byte; three MPLS Experimental (EXP) bits; three Ethernet 802.1p CoS bits; and one ATM cell loss probability (CLP) bit. In most IP networks, marking is accomplished by IP Precedence or DSCP. Finally, different queuing strategies are applied to each marked class. Fair queuing (FQ) assigns an equal share of network bandwidth to each application. An application is usually defined by a standard TCP service port (for example, port 80 is HTTP). Weighted fair queuing (WFQ) allows an administrator to prioritize specific traffic by setting the IP Precedence or DSCP value, but the Layer 3 device automatically assigns the corresponding queue. WFQ is the default for Cisco routers on links below 2 Mbps. Priority Queuing (PQ) classifies traffic into one of the predefined queues: high, medium, normal, and low priority queues. The high priority traffic is serviced first, then medium priority traffic, followed by normal and low priority traffic. PQ can starve low priority queues if high priority traffic flows are always present. Class-based weighted fair queuing (CBWFQ) is similar to WFQ but with more advanced differentiation of output queues. No guaranteed priority queue is allowed. Finally, low latency queuing (LLQ) is the preferred method for prioritizing thin-client traffic at Layer 3. LLQ can assign a strict priority queue with static guaranteed bandwidth to digitized voice or video, assign multiple resource queues with assured bandwidth and preferential treatment, and allow a default queue for "all other" traffic. Queuing works well in a network with only occasional and transitory congestion. If each and every aspect of a network is precisely designed and it never varies from the design baseline, queuing will provide all of the bandwidth management thin clients require. Absent a perfect network, queuing has the following characteristics and limitations:

▼ Queuing requires no special software on client devices.

■ Packets delayed beyond a timeout period in queues get dropped and require retransmission, causing more traffic and more queue depth.

■ Queuing manages only outbound traffic, assuming the inbound traffic has already come in over the congested inbound link. To be effective, queuing methods must match at both ends of the link. When dealing with Internet connections, queuing is generally ineffective.

▲ Queuing has no flow-by-flow QoS mechanism.

Router-Based Bandwidth Management   Cisco's Network Based Application Recognition (NBAR) provides intelligent network classification coupled with automation of queuing processes. NBAR is a Cisco IOS classification engine that can recognize a wide variety of applications, including Citrix, Web-based applications, and client/server applications. Additional features allow user-specified application definitions (by port and protocol). Once the application is recognized, NBAR can invoke the full range of QoS classification, marking, and queuing features, as well as selectively drop packets from the network. Although it is "application aware," NBAR relies on concurring devices to collectively implement QoS policies, and remains an "outbound" technology.

Appliance-Based Bandwidth Managers (TCP Rate Control)   TCP rate control provides a method to manage both inbound and outbound traffic by manipulating the internal parameters in the TCP sliding window. TCP rate control evenly distributes packet transmissions by controlling TCP acknowledgments to the sender. This causes the sender to throttle back, avoiding packet tossing when there is insufficient bandwidth. As packet bursts are eliminated in favor of a smoothed traffic flow, overall network utilization is driven up as high as 80 percent. In a network without rate control, typical average utilization is around 40 percent. TCP rate control operates at Layer 4, performing TCP packet and flow analysis, and above Layer 4, analyzing application-specific data. TCP rate control has the following advantages:

▼ Works whether applications are aware of it or not.

■ Reduces packet loss and retransmissions.

- Drives network utilization up as high as 80 percent.
- Provides bandwidth management to a specific rate (rate-based QoS).
- Provides flow-by-flow QoS.
- Provides both inbound and outbound control.
- ▲ Prevents congestion *before* it occurs.

On the other hand, TCP rate control has the following limitations:

- ▼ Not built into any routers yet.
- Only works on TCP/IP; all other protocols get queued.
- ▲ Currently available from only a few vendors.

Packet prioritization using TCP rate control is a method of ensuring that general WAN traffic does not interfere with critical or preferred data. Using packet prioritization, thin-client traffic can be given guaranteed bandwidth, which results in low perceived latency and speedy application performance, and contributes to a high level of user satisfaction in the server-based computing environment.

Packeteer created the category of hardware-based TCP rate control appliances with its PacketShaper product. Other manufacturers including Sitara and NetReality offer competing technologies, but Packeteer products were selected for an in-depth discussion.

In a simple deployment, a PacketShaper (shown in Figure 6-15) is an access layer device that sits between the router or firewall and the LAN infrastructure, and proactively manages WAN traffic to ensure that critical applications receive the bandwidth they require. For SBC environments, the bandwidth manager resides at remote sites with large enough bandwidth requirements to justify the expense. A PacketShaper is always placed inside the site router so it can manage the traffic flow before routing. In a large network, there is also value in placing a PacketShaper at the data center to control Internet services bandwidth and protect Internet-based remote users from being degraded by main site users surfing the Web. In this configuration, individual traffic flows cannot be managed, however, good traffic (thin clients, IPSec) can be given somewhat preferential treatment, and less-critical traffic flows can be throttled to ensure bandwidth remains available for thin-client flows. Though it is not possible to manage individual sessions this way, it is possible to create partitions for particular types of traffic. The flow-by-flow management happens in the PacketShapers at the edge of the network. There are several PacketShaper models available, and they are priced by the amount of bandwidth they are capable of managing. Packeteer has recently added new features, including the ability to manage enterprisewide devices from a central policy center.

- ▼ **Bandwidth per session**　With the PacketShaper it is possible to set a policy that will guarantee 20 Kbps of bandwidth for each ICA session. This has a few important effects. First, each session is protected from every other session. A user browsing animated web pages over ICA still only gets 20 Kbps and

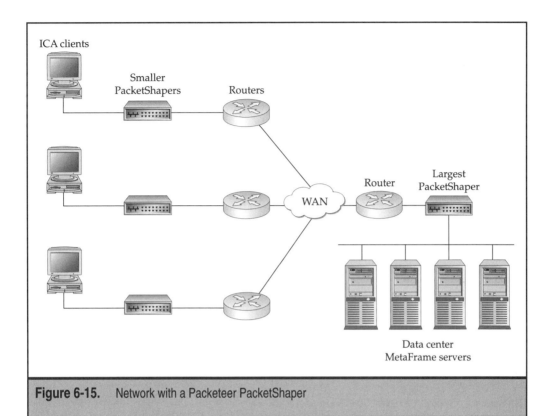

ICA clients

Smaller
PacketShapers   Routers

Largest
PacketShaper

Router

WAN

Data center
MetaFrame servers

Figure 6-15.   Network with a Packeteer PacketShaper

perceives decreased performance. Another user accessing office applications or e-mail would notice no difference, and their sessions would seem responsive. Second, no user would ever get a session with less than 20 Kbps. In the cases where the network was near saturation and insufficient WAN bandwidth was available, the PacketShaper would have stopped the session from being created rather than allow creation in a degraded environment (see Figure 6-16).

■ **Partitioning**   Partitions allow the administrator to logically "carve up" the available bandwidth and assign portions to each application or type of traffic, as shown in Figure 6-17. For example, in a frame relay circuit with a port speed of 1.544 Mbps, you might assign 80 percent of bandwidth to ICA traffic, 10 percent to HTTP, and 10 percent to LPR/LPD for printing. If any portion is not being fully utilized, the PacketShaper can allow the other partitions to share its available bandwidth.

▲ **Prioritization**   Prioritization is the simplest of the three options. Prioritization allows you to assign a number between 1 and 7 to a traffic flow, 1 being the highest. In this case, as utilization of the available bandwidth increases, the

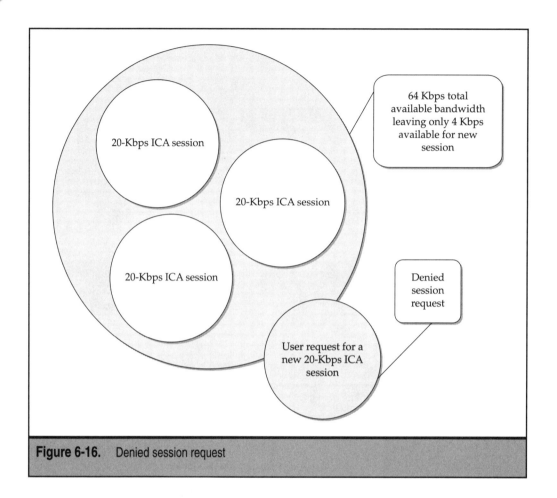

Figure 6-16. Denied session request

PacketShaper uses its own algorithms to make sure Priority 1 traffic gets more "slices" of bandwidth than Priority 3, as shown in Figure 6-18.

Of the three methods discussed in this section, session-based policies and partitions are recommended for ICA traffic. A session-based policy that guarantees 20 Kbps but allows bursts of up to 50 Kbps is ideal for ICA. However, such a policy can only be implemented when the PacketShaper can control the inbound and outbound traffic, which means it cannot be done over the Internet. In such a case, a partition policy can be used. Depending on the size of the network pipe, it could, for example, be guaranteed that 50 percent of the bandwidth is available to ICA. The remaining bandwidth could be left "unmanaged" or partitions could be defined for the most common, known protocols such as HTTP and Telnet. Priority-based packet shaping with ICA should be avoided simply because it makes it harder to predict the behavior of a PacketShaper. This is because a priority is not absolute and relies on some fairly complex algorithms to shape the

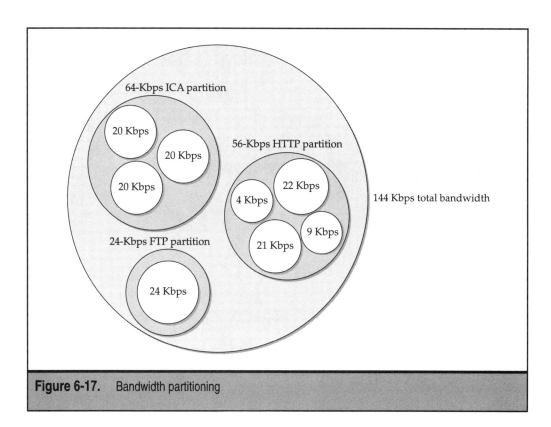

Figure 6-17. Bandwidth partitioning

traffic. Partitions and session policies are more rigid, and therefore more predictable and easier to administer.

A limitation of packet prioritization is that print traffic (and resulting print output speed) may be reduced because bandwidth is guaranteed to ICA traffic. Users may find this delay unsatisfactory. If so, one may choose to increase WAN bandwidth to allow more room for print traffic. Printing is a complex issue in this environment and is discussed in more detail in Chapter 18. Another potential problem with packet prioritization is that Internet browsing speed may be reduced because of the guaranteed bandwidth reserved for ICA traffic. Our experience has shown that Internet browsing that includes rapid screen refresh rates appears to substantially increase ICA packet bandwidth requirements—sometimes to as much as 50 Kbps—although Citrix has made great strides in fixing this with Feature Release 3. Disabling Java, ActiveMovie, or other plug-in technology can mitigate this problem that causes the screen to refresh more than a static page. Few companies consider Web browsing to be mission critical (quite the opposite it seems), so this might not be a problem.

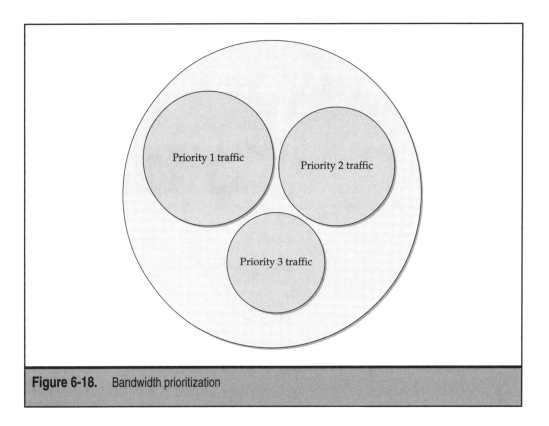

Figure 6-18. Bandwidth prioritization

Packeteer in Action Figure 6-19 shows a sample report output from a Packeteer unit configured to monitor a small business Internet link. The customer relies on Citrix to provide applications to remote branch offices via the Internet. The main site (data center) has a 1.5-Mbps SDSL circuit to a local Internet service provider (ISP). The first graph shows poor response time for the customer's ERP/financial application (NAVISION) deployed over Citrix. Although server response times are somewhat suspect, network latency drives the total response time well above the recommended threshold of 500ms. The second graph shows that "bursty" HTTP traffic is consuming virtually all of the available WAN bandwidth, and that the bursts coincide with delays in Citrix response times. Graph three shows total (link) bandwidth consumption, and the final chart shows that HTTP consumes 48 percent of all available bandwidth, with HTTP and WinMedia accounting for nearly two-thirds of all bandwidth. The Packeteer's TCP rate control can "partition" the Internet pipe to ensure HTTP cannot deny Citrix access to needed bandwidth. As an added benefit, the Packeteer analysis proved that the ISP was only providing 1 Mbps of available bandwidth, not the 1.5-Mbps circuit the customer paid for. The ISP agreed to rebate $2500.00 in fees for substandard services.

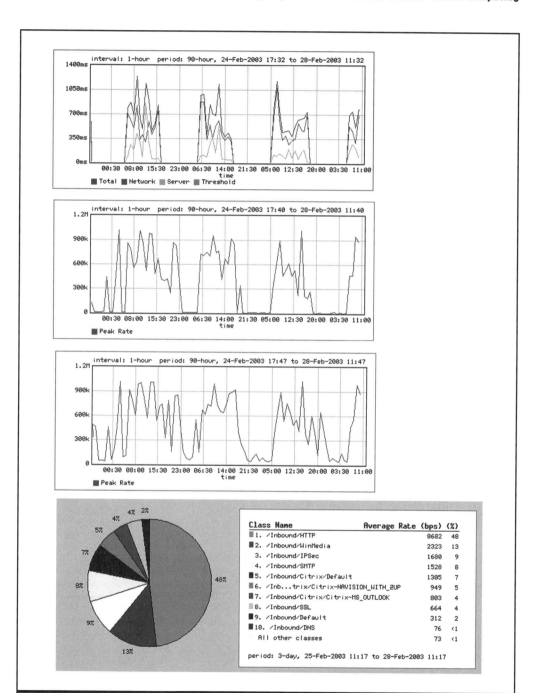

Figure 6-19. Packeteer analysis report

PUTTING IT ALL TOGETHER—SAMPLE NETWORKS

The following diagrams illustrate notional networks supporting various levels of SBC activity. Due to size constraints, none of the diagrams are intended to be complete in every detail or completely accurate in depicting physical connectivity. Chapter 17 will delve into greater detail regarding each aspect of a sample network. When documenting your network design (a necessity), three major documents are needed. First, a physical diagram similar to those that follow. Second, a logical diagram to document the relationship between Layer 2 boundaries (VLANs) and Layer 3 boundaries (routed networks) for each protocol (TCP/IP, IPX/SPX, and so on) you must support. Finally, a documented naming and addressing scheme, to address both protocol address and naming convention (NetBIOS Name, DNS Host Name), is essential.

As examples, three business scopes (small businesses, medium-sized businesses, and large businesses) are addressed. Additionally, the medium-sized business shows two possible scenarios, branches connected via private WAN media and an Internet-centric and VPN approach.

The Small Business Network

The small business model (see Figure 6-20) uses the same basic equipment as larger scale deployments, but separation between hierarchical layers is limited. The local distribution, core, and server access layers are collapsed and exist on the same Layer 3 switch. Multiple protocols are isolated by separate Layer 2 VLANs connected to the Layer 3 core; this concept is implied, but not illustrated, in subsequent diagrams.

The Medium-Sized Business Network

The medium-sized business network shares component parts with its small business counterpart, but employs more specialized distribution and core layer hardware to isolate local users, DMZ networks, and branch offices from the production server environment in the core.

Figure 6-21 depicts a typical mid-sized business with large branch offices connected via dedicated media. The distribution layer switch serves to aggregate traffic from LAN, WAN, and Internet sources, and to insulate the core switch and server farm from this traffic.

Figure 6-22 depicts a model more suited to a medium-sized business with many small branches (such as point of sale (POS) sites) where dedicated WAN media is cost-prohibitive. A combination of Internet access to the Web Interface site, VPN access, and secure access via MetaFrame Secure Gateway provides a flexible, secure WAN without dedicated links. In both cases, branch-to-Internet or LAN user-to-Internet traffic flows never traverse the core, and are kept in check by the Packeteer (to protect Internet-based users and VPN traffic).

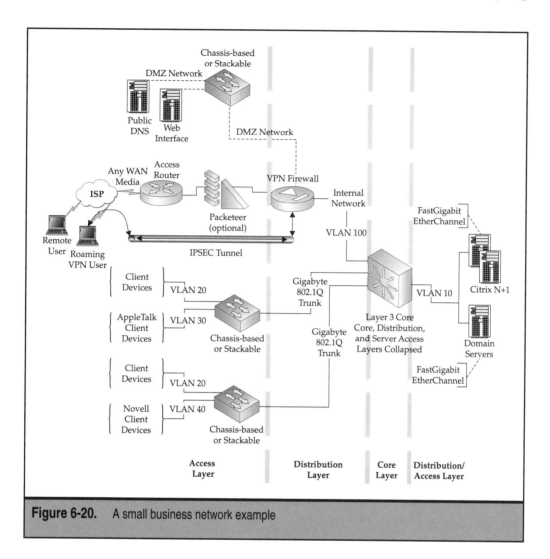

Figure 6-20.   A small business network example

Again, like the small business model, the "server-specific" access and distribution layers are collapsed onto the core switch (see Figure 6-23). Redundant connectivity is added between the core and the distribution layer switch for reliability and survivability. All aspects of the local server farm, particularly the Citrix MetaFrame farm, are more robust and more redundant.

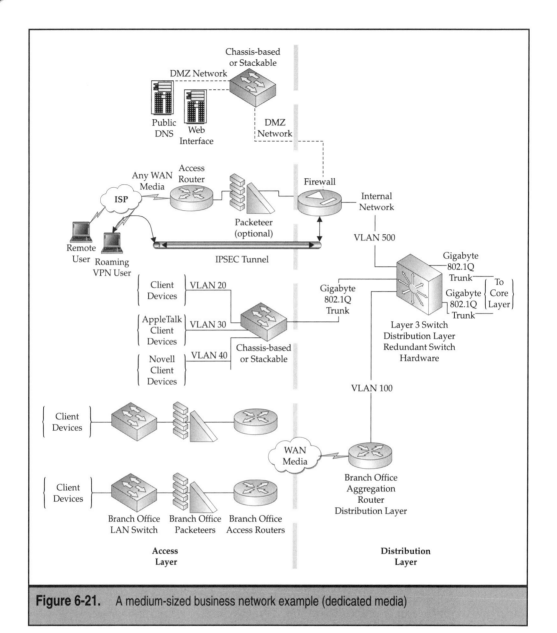

Figure 6-21. A medium-sized business network example (dedicated media)

The Large Business Network

The large business model (the beginnings of a true enterprise model) moves away from a collapsed structure to a hierarchical network design where each layer is purpose-built.

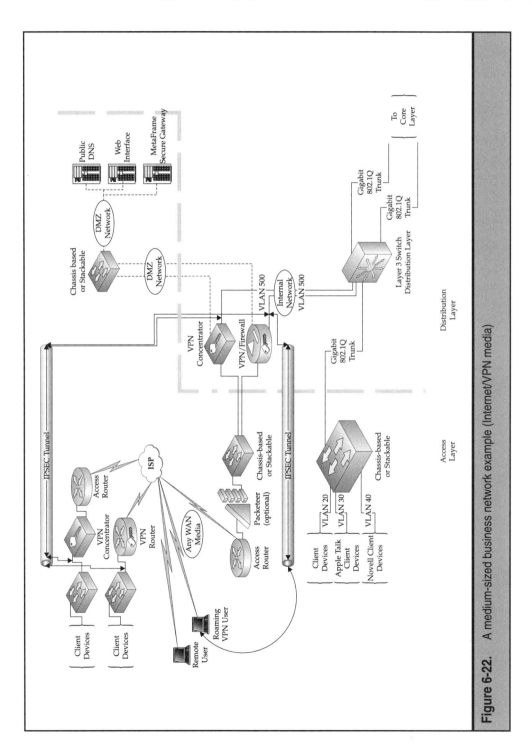

Figure 6-22. A medium-sized business network example (Internet/VPN media)

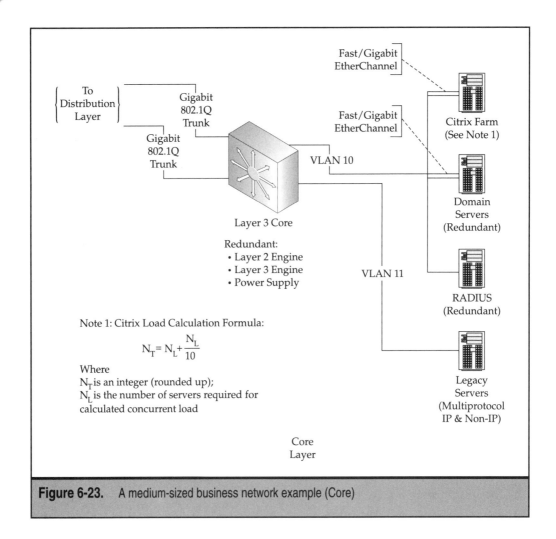

Figure 6-23. A medium-sized business network example (Core)

Layer 2 connectivity becomes far less prevalent, with redundant Layer 3 links being the norm.

Figure 6-24 illustrates the more robust access layer structure expected in a large business model. Note the redundant Internet, multiple VPN methods, and access aggregation for specific groups of services (WAN aggregation router).

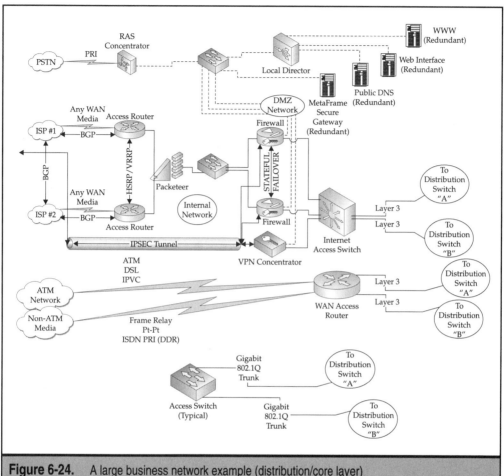

Figure 6-24. A large business network example (distribution/core layer)

Typical large business distribution and core components are shown in Figure 6-25. Virtually every aspect of the distribution and core layers are redundant and "self-healing" by either Layer 3 route convergence or Layer 2 (STP) convergence. For additional resiliency, the Citrix Metaframe server farm itself has been split into two physical farms. Both physical farms still function as a single logical load-balanced farm, even on different subnets. The implication is that if an organization requires on-campus survivability and has adequate (gigabit) connectivity, it can distribute the farm across multiple buildings with no loss of functionality.

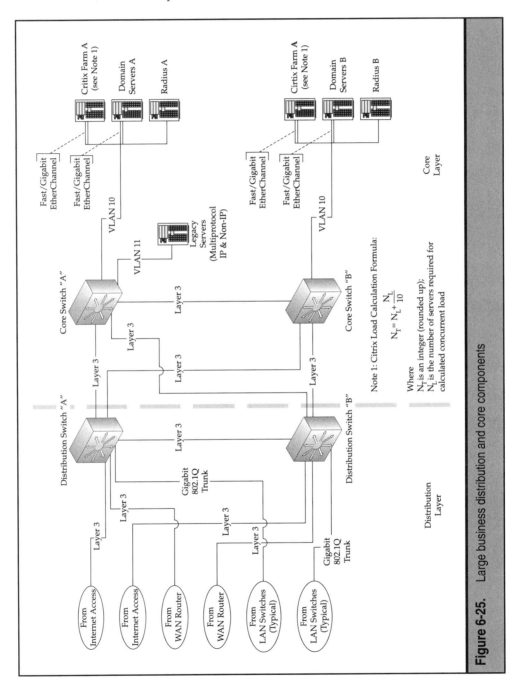

Figure 6-25.   Large business distribution and core components

CHAPTER 7

The Client Environment

In this chapter, we will introduce and discuss four categories of desktop devices used to access the server-based computing (SBC) applications: thin client (a Windows Terminal or fully locked down PC dedicated to running only a web browser and/or ICA client), mobile (laptop), simple hybrid (a device running both server-based applications and local applications, with no local peripheral support), and complex hybrid (a device with a local hard drive running both local and server-based applications and supporting local peripherals). We will also discuss deployment strategies and installation tips not covered by the standard documentation from the manufacturers. Finally, we will introduce the concept of the *client decision matrix* to help you establish standards for determining the appropriate client for a given user or group.

In general, use the simplest (or "thinnest") client device available to take full advantage of the cost savings derived from lower up-front costs, lower setup costs, significantly reduced software maintenance, reduced hardware maintenance, and fewer repairs. Although the concept and approach of thin clients has not changed since the inception of server-based computing, price and performance have both improved dramatically. It is now possible to procure a high-performance Windows Terminal thin-client device for $290 (monitor is extra) from several manufacturers, including Wyse, Neoware, Maxspeed, and others. Although we have had many people argue that they procure PCs for about this same cost, we have never discovered that to be true. Although most consumer-based retail outlets advertise a $500 PC, corporations today are often spending over $1000 per PC in order to get a fully configured PC with Windows XP Professional operating system, networking, and a three-year warranty. Table 7-1 provides a comparison between the costs of a PC and a Windows terminal thin client.

The numbers from Table 7-1 are very conservative by most industry standards. Gartner Group estimates that most enterprise organizations spend closer to $7000 per PC per year, because the number of non-automated reconfigurations and software installations are much greater than the numbers used here. Additionally, the $50 per hour for internal billable rate is lower than most enterprise organizations experience for a fully loaded cost. Regardless though, we wanted to use conservative numbers to make it inarguable. Notice that for an organization considering technology-refreshing 100 PCs per year, even if all "soft costs" are ignored, the up-front savings for just the initial procurement and setup costs will be $64,750 per year. If soft costs are included, and a three-year cost outlay is looked at for an enterprise organization, these savings are very significant.

Although the advantages and up-front costs of a Windows Terminal are compelling, some organizations may not be able to fully convert to Windows Terminals, or may need to run a mix of Windows Terminals and PCs. Organizations that may not be able to replace all PCs with Windows Terminals include

▼ Organizations that have large numbers of newer PCs (less than two years old) that cannot be easily discarded (some organizations are leasing their desktop PCs, which will dictate whether it is advantageous or impossible to get rid of the PCs).

■ Organizations still supporting 16-bit or DOS applications that won't run effectively in an SBC environment, and thus must be run using the processing power and operating system of a "local" PC.

▲ Organizations that will only be supporting a portion of their users or applications on the SBC environment.

Task	Hybrid PC—Dell Optiplex with Windows XP Pro, Three-Year Warranty	Windows Terminal—Wyse Winterm 1200LE (Thin Client)
Initial procurement cost	$799	$289
Initial configuration and installation time (assume Ghost imaging for the PC, but include ghost image setup and maintenance time)	3 hours @ $50/hour internal billable rate = $150	15 minutes @ $50/hour internal billable rate = $12.50
Operating system upgrade price (assume one new revision of Windows operating system over three-year period)	$200 + 2 hours @ $50/hour internal billable rate for a total price of $300	$0—Wyse 1200LE is Linux-based and firmware updates are pushed from management software
Software upgrade time (assume one new revision of MS Office and one new revision of other desktop applications per year must be installed and configured)	6 hours @ $50/hour internal billable rate = $300	$5—software updates will be done once at the server for all clients; assuming hundreds of clients, the cost per client is very small
Assume one local workstation touch per quarter required for maintenance and security patching of operating systems and web browsers; assume management software will be used to push out patches (SMS for PCs, Wyse Rapport for Winterms)	8 hours per year, 24 hours over three-year period @ $50/hour internal billable rate for a total cost of $1200 to configure and manage the management software	2 hours per year, 6 hours over three-year period @ $50/hour internal billable rate for a total cost of $300 to configure and manage the management software
Hardware repair—assume one warranty repair is required over the three-year period, necessitating reload and reconfiguration	3 hours @ $50/hour internal billable rate = $150	15 minutes @ $50/hour internal billable rate = $12.50
Total three-year cost	$2599	$619

Table 7-1. Three-Year Price Comparison—PC vs. Windows Terminals

A large number of organizations end up running a mix of clients and client devices, at least for a period of time, for these reasons. As such, it is necessary to explore complementary technologies to make hybrid and mobile users take on as many of the desirable characteristics of the thin client as possible. The most significant gain of the thin client—that of not having to install, manage, update, or repair local applications—can be realized from any client device, with the correct configuration and management tools. In discussing these hybrids, we will describe the available technology and techniques needed to accomplish this.

CLIENT CLASSIFICATIONS

The categories of client devices are shown in Table 7-2.

Although client devices tend to be compared more commonly than client types, it is important to note that there is a great deal of overlap today with client devices. That is, both software and hardware exist today to lock down a PC such that it fits the description of a thin client. Conversely, many new Windows terminals have local web browsers and support for client peripherals (via USB, parallel ports, and/or serial ports). Thus, these thin clients can be categorized as simple or even complex hybrid clients. Additionally, with the large number of new device types on the scene, like Tablet PCs, handheld devices, Linux devices, and Windows CE tablets, it saves time to discuss client types (and include client devices which can fulfill that role) rather than to discuss only devices.

The matrix of client types in Table 7-2 is meant to provide an idea of total cost of ownership (TCO) of the client type. For example, a Windows terminal that supports a local web browser, peripheral devices, and a complex local OS (like Windows XP Embedded), and thus fits into the complex hybrid type, will be more expensive to procure, configure,

Client Category	Remote Applications	Supports Secure Access from Outside the LAN	Local Web Browser	Local Applications	Support of Local Peripherals	Local File Sharing
Thin client only	×	–	–			
Mobile user	×	×	×	×	–	–
Simple hybrid	×	×	×	×		
Complex hybrid	×	×	×	×	×	×

* × indicates that the client has the requirement.

– indicates that the client *could* have the requirement.

Table 7-2.   Client Categories*

manage, and maintain than a Windows terminal that simply supports an ICA client (even though both devices may be sold as a "thin client"). For the purposes of our discussion, both devices would not be classified as a thin client. We only classify Windows terminals that support an ICA client as a thin client. It is also important to note that this client matrix does not define operating systems. If Citrix MetaFrame XP will be used, its support of hundreds of operating system variations ensures the use of Linux-based devices and Windows CE–based devices, as well as the more common assortment of Windows 95 through Windows XP-based devices. If only Windows Terminal Services will be used, the device choice becomes more limited.

Since total cost of ownership is not the only consideration when choosing which client type and client devices to support, a significant task in designing the SBC environment is to figure out which client types and devices will be procured and supported.

THE CLIENT DECISION MATRIX

The process of changing a user's desktop environment can be a traumatic experience for both the IT staff and the end user. Since PCs have long been organizational fixtures, often being used as part of a corporate rewards system (the best employees often get the best PCs), unless it is handled correctly, users will fight hard against any change toward a simpler client environment. Usually, end users will not be able to see how the change benefits themselves or their company. In order to help sell the idea (cultural change is discussed in detail in Chapter 10) and ensure non-biased decisions are made, a client decision matrix should be used. Defining such a matrix will provide the following benefits:

▼ By applying the same set of criteria to the classification of each user, you will avoid making decisions based on political or nontechnical reasons.

■ When the decision-making process is communicated to users, they will not feel they are being singled out, but rather are subject to the same rules as everyone else.

▲ Users can be classified *en masse,* relatively quickly, and decisions about the number of clients of each type, necessary upgrades, or disposition plans can then be made.

Start out with two basic evaluation questions, as described here.

Does the User Require Access to Only SBC-Based Applications?   In other words, does the user only need access to the applications already slated for hosting in the SBC environment? If so, the categorization of that user can be easily made.

Is the User's Existing Computer an SBC-Compatible Device?   Since the ICA and RDP clients are so thin, a large majority of devices in use in organizations today will work well in nearly any client role. For the purposes of this text, PC includes any common device, regardless of operating system, that is capable of running ICA and/or RDP.

NOTE: According to Citrix, version 7.00 of the ICA client for Windows (32-bit) requires

▼ Windows 95 (OSR2 or later), Windows 98, Windows Me, Windows 2000, Windows 2003, Windows XP, or Windows NT 4.0

■ 8MB RAM or greater for Windows 9x, 16MB RAM or greater for Windows NT 4.0, 32MB or greater for Windows Me and Windows 2000, and 128MB RAM for Windows XP

▲ Internet Explorer Version 5.0 or later, or Netscape Navigator or Communicator Version 5.0 or later

Table 7-3 shows the resulting decision matrix, with deployment plans for each category of user.

NOTE: All users will run an application from the SBC environment—not locally—if it is available. The exception to this rule is the mobile user who may be allowed to run applications locally if she does not have consistent access to the Internet or wireless WAN (Sprint, Verizon, AT&T, or others).

Hach will save over $50,000 in one year just on the up-front cost savings of buying $289 Wyse 1200LE terminals rather than the $1600 we previously spent on new Dell PCs.

—Sonya Freeman, Hach Company

Category	Deployment
User requires only SBC applications, and currently has a non-SBC-capable device.	User gets standard Windows terminal. Existing PC goes through disposition (disposal, donation).
User requires only SBC applications, and currently has an SBC-capable device.	User gets standard Windows terminal. Device goes into pool to be reassigned.
User requires both SBC and non-SBC applications, and currently has a non-SBC-capable device.	User gets SBC-capable device from reassignment pool or new purchase.
User requires both SBC and non-SBC applications, and currently has an SBC-capable device.	IT staff disables or uninstalls applications from PC that exists in the SBC environment.

Table 7-3. Client Decision Matrix

PC Disposition

The problem that arises when updating so many desktops is what to do with all the replaced devices. This can be a significant problem for an organization that is committed to being as thin as possible. PCs that are no longer appropriate for a given user may still have book value, and the company will need to see some kind of return on them. The following are some ideas for dealing with this, based on what we have seen at other organizations.

Reassignment Pool

As the preceding client decision matrix indicates, even if a PC is considered SBC capable, it may be removed from a user's desktop strictly based on the user's need. Why do this? When the total cost of ownership is examined for any desktop PC versus any Windows terminal, the reason becomes clear. Even a new PC with plenty of book value costs far more to support than a Windows terminal. We examined the reasons for this in detail in Chapters 1 and 4, but the gist is that a PC is far more prone to spawn a call to the help desk due to an application or operating system problem than is a Windows terminal, on which very little can go wrong.

The idea behind a reassignment pool is to create a standard for PCs to be used in your organization and assign the PCs to those users with a legitimate need. As PCs come in, they can be evaluated for reuse, rebuilt to the proper specifications, and cloned with a standard image of the operating system, web browser, and the ICA client. The standard image contains the base operating system in as locked down a state as possible, the ICA client, a recent web browser, and whatever other minimal applications are needed. The user's specific application can then be loaded. This sounds like a lot of work, and it is. But it is far less work in the long run to deliver a PC in a known state than to deal with one in an unknown state later in the field. The reassignment pool process is illustrated next:

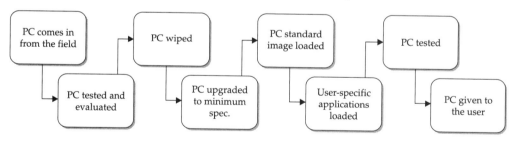

PC Disposal

Now that there is a plan to reuse PCs that have some value—either financial or technical—what do we do with PCs that have no book value, are outdated, or are broken in some way? The two obvious choices are donation and disposal.

Many non-profit organizations accept donated PCs, but quite often their minimum requirements are high since many of them aren't using SBC, and thus need reasonable computing power to run a newer operating system and applications. Nevertheless, it is worth discovering if your old gear is worth something to someone else. One nonprofit organization that helps with this process is the National Association for the Exchange of Industrial Resources (NAEIR). See their web site at http://www.naeir.com/.

The disposal option has also become more complicated, as most computer parts are considered low-level hazardous materials. Contact your local landfill for information on computer disposal.

So far in this chapter, we have talked a lot about getting rid of the PCs in an organization. This may or may not be an acceptable approach for your particular situation, but it is an optimal one in terms of TCO. For people leaning toward keeping PCs and just running applications in an SBC environment, it is important to understand that this decision will have a big impact on the overall value returned by the project. The following are some advantages and limitations to consider if you plan to keep most of the PCs in your organization.

The advantages of keeping PCs include

▼ PCs are ubiquitous. It is likely that your organization already has a large number of PCs with residual book value and would like to use them if possible.

■ The skills necessary to support PCs are already available. Supporting other types of devices may take additional training.

▲ PCs are multipurpose platforms that can perform many functions outside those required for an SBC environment.

The limitations of using PCs include

▼ Public studies show that PCs are significantly more expensive to administer than Windows Terminals.

■ PCs have many moving parts that are far more prone to failure than a solid state device.

■ PCs are prone to obsolescence, which also contributes to the high TCO. This problem is somewhat mitigated by using the PC as a thin client, but if you plan to run *any* applications locally, you still must deal with the constant hardware upgrades required when upgrading software.

▲ PCs require additional configuration and possibly additional software to approach the level of security and stability of a Windows terminal. PCs should only be delivered in your organization if first locked down in a manner that prevents users from making detrimental changes to the registry or loading unauthorized software.

HYBRID CLIENTS

Regardless of whether PCs are used in a limited or widespread manner, many organizations have a certain number of hybrid clients on their networks. Hybrid clients can be divided into three categories:

▼   **Simple**   A simple hybrid is a client device running just enough software to interact with the SBC environment. This usually means the ICA client, web browser, and possibly a client for the management software or framework in use at your company. No data is stored locally.

■   **Complex**   The complex hybrid is a client device that not only runs the ICA and management clients, but also local applications. It may also do local file sharing and have local peripherals.

▲   **Mobile**   A mobile hybrid is similar to the complex hybrid, but usually has an even greater number of local applications. Although the need for local applications used to be unavoidable, with the new ubiquitous access to Internet bandwidth (Verizon, Sprint, AT&T, Nextel, City and Airport WiFi, and Boeing's Internet access now being deployed on board airlines) many users can now utilize SBC-based applications literally any time, anywhere from their laptop devices.

Full Desktop vs. Published Applications

Citrix provides SBC administrators the option of publishing to end users a full desktop interface to the MetaFrame servers—effectively providing desktop users with a window that looks identical to a desktop PC running Windows XP Professional—or providing the user with individual applications, launching from within their local desktop or web browser environment. Which to choose depends on the overall environment, the number of applications to be deployed, and whether thin clients or hybrid clients will be used. The decision to publish individual applications or the entire desktop has many ramifications, from end-user experience and performance to security. Both of these options are available in any client type or device scenario.

Publishing Individual Applications

In the case where a MetaFrame server farm is used to deploy only one application, or a small selection of applications to end users (hybrid clients), the published application option has many benefits. A published application can be published directly to a user's Windows desktop using Citrix Program Neighborhood or directly to a web browser interface using MetaFrame Web Interface.

Published applications have the added benefit of being more secure than granting access to a full desktop because of the lack of access to common system tools, such as the Start menu and the Control Panel. Additionally, publishing only an application as opposed to the full desktop ensures that users do not have access to applications not required for their job function (as an example, non-accounting users won't see the accounting applications). In a full desktop environment, these items could allow a user to potentially harm—unintentionally or otherwise—the SBC server environment. That said, additional steps still need to be taken to secure such integrative applications as Internet Explorer and MS Office, which can still leave back doors to system utilities if not locked down with proper security policies.

Aside from security reasons, published applications also have the side benefit of consuming system resources (memory, processor, etc.) more efficiently. The reason for this lies in the fact that because the entire Windows shell is not loaded, only those resource processes required to execute the application are started (per user). Under high user loads this could mean up to 20 percent additional resources are available for either additional user connections or a better user experience for those connected.

One significant downside to published applications is that they can be confusing to end users. Users may find it difficult to distinguish between applications that are running locally and those published from the MetaFrame farm. Additionally, the fact that users cannot access some system configurations, such as printer settings, can cause challenges.

To address this issue, Citrix released Program Neighborhood Agent (PN Agent) with Feature Release 1 to provide tighter integration between locally available resources and those in the SBC environment. With PN Agent, an administrator configures the client side agent to utilize a Web Interface server. As the user authenticates, desktop objects, start menu icons, system tray utilities, and/or client side MIME type mappings are pushed down from the Web Interface server. Just as with standard published applications, the administrator has the ability to leverage existing user control mechanisms (Active Directory, etc.) by creating access objects to allow user rights to only those features they require to fulfill their job role. There are even settings to allow users to customize their own environment variables, at the discretion of the SBC administrator. The user has the benefit of the same look and feel they have always had, but with the added benefit of server centric application management and control. This is an example of a complex but elegant hybrid application deployment scenario.

Publishing the Desktop

For environments in which all or most applications will be provided to users by the SBC environment, and environments with a majority of Windows terminals, we strongly recommend publishing the full desktop as opposed to just the applications. Although publishing the full desktop requires the desktop lockdown discussed in the next section, the published desktop is simpler and more intuitive for end users. With a published desktop, end users see the full interface they are accustomed to seeing, while from a hybrid client a user will see two Start menus (if the published desktop is set up to run as a percent of screen size), making it more obvious whether they are using an application locally or from the SBC farm. Additionally, Windows terminals based on Linux do not intuitively switch between published applications, whereas if the desktop is published, the normal hotkeys and windowing controls hold true to what users are accustomed to.

When using a published desktop, the ICA client can be published to the Desktop to provide access to other applications or servers not supported on the server in which a user is logged in (this is called the ICA Passthrough feature). It is important to note though that there is a significant performance penalty associated with using the ICA Passthrough, both for the end users and in terms of server resources. If users are complaining of slow screen scroll, make sure they are not running the application through ICA Passthrough.

Desktop Lockdown

Since most organizations will utilize PCs either in full thin-client mode, or in hybrid mode, locking down the PCs is critical to keep them from continuing to be an ongoing help-desk call. Additionally, these same methods are useful for locking down the published desktop environment of the MetaFrame farm. Although the tools we recommend for locking down PCs are quite good, and will dramatically reduce the administration and maintenance required, desktop hardware failure will still generate a help desk call.

According to several studies, including one by the Gartner Group cited in Chapter 4, the PC operating system is the source of most of the support requests from users. Even though the ICA client runs on a variety of operating systems, including MacOS and Linux, this discussion will be focused on Windows client devices since they are the most common (and, therefore, most in need of being locked down).

Registry Settings

The various Zero Administration Kits (ZAK) published by Microsoft for Windows 95, 98, NT Workstation, NT 4.0 TSE, and Windows 2000 Professional, contain a wealth of information on beneficial changes to the system registry. The strategy is to make changes to *prevent* the following:

▼ **Installing applications**   Since the PC should come to users with the necessary local applications installed, along with the ICA client for running applications from the SBC, end-user application installation should be prohibited. Upgrades or requests for new applications should go through the help desk.

■ **Changing system settings**   Even more so than with applications, desktops should prohibit users from making changes to system settings. Setting appearance or screen savers seem innocuous at first, but simple changes like this can generate calls to the help desk when they conflict with the use of a given application. We recommend preventing *any* change to the system settings.

▲ **Recognizing installed hardware**   If the client operating system has the ability to recognize new hardware, it can prompt the user to install drivers. The drivers may conflict with other drivers or system libraries and, again, generate calls to the help desk. Even if users know how to install hardware, the standard operating system image should prevent them from doing it. Even plug-and-play devices have no place in the corporate desktop. It may seem simple to plug in a USB device, for example, since it will be automatically recognized, but quite often even harmless peripherals can wreak havoc on a system and prompt an all-day service repair call while the technician performs investigative work to try to determine what changed and how to fix it.

The methods for locking down Microsoft desktops have evolved over the years, although as we discuss next, there is still ample room for third-party providers to intervene and offer good solutions. For Windows 2000 Professional and Windows XP Professional, user and group policies are reasonably powerful and easy to change through the Policy

Editor. For older desktop operating systems (Windows NT 4.0, Windows 98, Windows 95, and so on) policy tools were lacking, and thus Microsoft released scripts provided in Zero Administration Kits. For example, the ZAK for NT Workstation contains command files to install NT in an unattended fashion (cmdlines.txt), make custom registry changes for applications (appcmds.cmd), and set restricted access to the file system (acls.cmd). Be warned, the settings chosen tend to be *very* restricted and may cause problems with specific or custom applications. The various client ZAKs are supplied free of charge from Microsoft's web site and should be evaluated as a way to restrict user activities on the desktop. At the very least they can provide a platform from which to build custom scripts.

NOTE: Administrators should always extract all of the contents of a ZAK and only use those parts that look applicable instead of allowing them to auto install. The auto install components may make major modification to file system permissions and other security structures that may not be the intention during the evaluation stage.

Third-Party Software for Desktop Lockdown

In the last three years, several software providers have built tools to automate the lockdown of PCs and the PC user environment. Providers of software for restricting user activities present a friendlier interface than Policy editor and Regedit32 and can track and roll back changes, as well as provide myriad management and performance optimization features. We have utilized tools from four software vendors that provide lockdown for both the server user environment and the desktop environment. Although there are many other vendors, the four that we have used and can recommend for desktop lockdown are RES, NCD ThinPath PC, triCerat, and AppSense. Applications from these providers make user profile, policy, or direct registry changes to a workstation based on either a standard image or a centralized rules database. The rules can be assigned by user, group, application, or even time schedule. Though the result of these applications' activities are to change the registry on the client device operating system—something that can be done manually—these vendors do it in a way that is easy to manage and scales across a large organization. Perhaps most important, these applications are compatible with both distributed and centralized application hosting. They can impose the same restrictions on an application hosted from a MetaFrame XP server farm as they can on one running on a local desktop.

Profiles

Although profiles will be the main topic of Chapter 15, they are worth a quick mention in this section, as they impact the overall client design. Windows Server 2000 and 2003 utilize user profiles to specify a variety of user environmental and applications settings. Important items like MAPI and ODBC settings are maintained in the user profile. Because of their importance to user functionality as well as their tendency to grow fast and large like pre-pubescent elephants, user profiles represent a difficult challenge in the design of the system. For instance, they can be configured as mandatory, roaming, or a hybrid of a mandatory and roaming profile. A great deal of industry work has gone into creating some best practices for hybrid user profiles, as well as development of best practices for roaming profiles. Even the lockdown applications discussed earlier address user profiles, and some of them claim to alleviate the need for roaming profiles all together.

We recommend using roaming user profiles, but have ourselves used the tips and tricks provided in Chapter 15 to keep a tight reign on the size and storage of the roaming profiles. For the purposes of design, be sure to follow the steps laid out in Chapter 6 for network design to ensure that sufficient network bandwidth and disk space are allocated to support roaming profiles. From a purely client device standpoint, it is nice to note that Windows terminals are not affected by user profiles, although any published applications they log into will be. On the Hybrid PC side, administrators should be careful to keep the PC profiles separated from the Terminal Services Profiles, as discussed in Chapter 15.

Software Distribution and Server-Based Computing

Since many enterprises today utilize software distribution applications like Microsoft SMS, the question arises about how these will integrate and how this function will be performed in an SBC environment. The answer is threefold:

1. One of the clear advantages of server-based computing is that we no longer need to install, configure, and maintain applications on the desktop. Thus, unless the desktops will be used in Hybrid mode, the software distribution headache and accompanying software tools will disappear at the desktop level.

2. The only exception to point 1 is the ICA client, which must be distributed, configured, and maintained on all client desktops. Although a software distribution tool can be used for this purpose, we recommend using Citrix Web Interface for MetaFrame to deploy the ICA client. When a desktop uses a web browser to navigate to the MetaFrame Web Interface site and clicks an application icon, the ICA client will download and self-configure.

3. Software distribution automation can be a significant time saver at the server level for large enterprises with a significant number of servers. In an SBC environment, the applications must be installed on all of the servers serving them, which can be a significant undertaking for organizations with 10–1000 MetaFrame servers. Citrix provides a tool for this purpose, MetaFrame Installation Manager, embedded in MetaFrame XPe, that we will cover in depth in Chapter 13.

The ICA Client for Hybrids

In Chapter 3, we presented the connectivity options of the ICA client, including Program Neighborhood, MetaFrame Web Interface, and MetaFrame Secure Gateway. In this section, we will focus on the differences between the various hybrid clients you might consider.

Significant Platform Differences

For purposes of this discussion, the 32-bit ICA client for Windows will be considered the functional base for all other client versions. Although in the past other clients typically contained fewer features or worked slightly differently, Citrix has dedicated significant resources to ensure that other devices have similar feature sets and performance.

▼ **Macintosh** The ICA client for the MacOS prior to OS X was missing many features such as support for audio, peripherals, and remapping of local ports. But with OS X, Citrix released a new, full-featured client that has nearly identical features to the Windows 32-bit client. Like all non-Windows ICA clients, the Mac client provides access to Windows key sequences through local key combinations.

■ **Linux/UNIX** The Linux/UNIX clients offer complete functionality for any non-Windows ICA client, but not all features are supported on all flavors of UNIX. Check your platform against the feature list in Chapter 14 for specific support. The Program Neighborhood is not supported, but virtually all other functions are present. Windows key sequences are provided through local key combinations designed not to conflict with the ALT key sequences normally reserved for the X-Window System, though these can be reprogrammed if desired.

▲ **Web Interface clients** MetaFrame Web Interface allows administrators to configure the web site to provide a specific ICA client or an ICA client based on client operating system, or to allow the user to choose which ICA client they want to use. The 32-bit ICA client provides the most features, but with MetaFrame XP Feature Release 3, Citrix updated the Java client to provide nearly the same functionality as the full 32-bit client. This client can be very useful when being run from kiosks or other locked down environments.

Local Peripherals

Local peripherals can be automatically mapped from the desktop to the server, but not without a price. The data stream used by the device must travel over the network from the server farm to the client device. This can cause excessive bandwidth utilization unless measures are taken to control it. Bandwidth management and control methods are discussed in Chapters 6 and 17.

NOTE: The ICA COM and LPT port redirection provides support for a variety of local peripherals to be used, but many peripheral configurations require tuning and tweaking in a SBC environment because the ports do not work exactly as they would if they were local ports. For example, we have found that excessive latency over a WAN connection can cause redirected devices to behave erratically, and, in fact, the devices can exasperate the bandwidth problem and cause other network services to fail. Additionally, COM port and LPT port redirection aren't supported through ICA Passthrough connections.

WINDOWS TERMINALS (THIN CLIENT ONLY)

Windows terminals are available from a variety of manufacturers, with many variations on the same theme. Most Windows terminals have no moving parts, except perhaps for a fan, and all the operating system and client software is stored in hardware. They typically run Windows CE, Linux, or Embedded Windows XP as the operating system, and implementations of other software, such as the network protocol stack, are proprietary to the device. This and the fact that they have different CPUs and graphics capabilities contribute to the performance differences between the devices. In no particular order, some of the devices we've tested and used in production are the Wyse Winterm, Maxspeed Maxterm, Neoware Capio and Eon, and IBM NetStation. We've tested other brands from HP, IBM, and other companies, but most are simply OEM versions of one of these other terminals. All of the Windows terminals have a very small form factor, and some are built into a CRT or flat screen monitor. Additionally, all of the devices are low-power consumption devices, a feature that can add to the savings versus PCs for large enterprises with thousands of devices. Here is what a basic Windows terminal setup looks like:

In addition to offering the necessary ICA or RDP software to connect to the SBC server farm, most thin-client models offer emulation and connectivity software such as legacy terminal emulation clients (IBM 3270 and Telnet, for example). Local browsing is also available with either proprietary browsers or OEM versions of Netscape Navigator or Microsoft Internet Explorer. There can be a significant advantage in cost and ease of use in having multiple connectivity software in the device when integrating the terminal into an environment where legacy functions as well as the new features of the SBC must be supported. This is a key differentiator among products. Figure 7-1 shows how a Windows terminal with different types of local embedded software might connect to a variety of server resources.

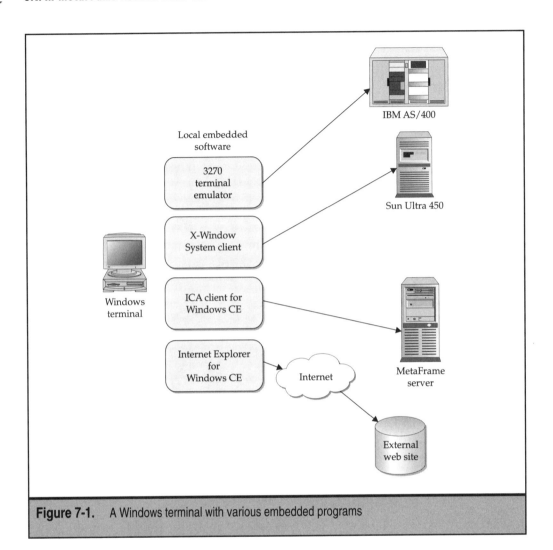

Figure 7-1. A Windows terminal with various embedded programs

Windows Terminal Management

Another key differentiator that is not always clear when evaluating different Windows terminals is how they are managed. Most manufacturers have developed or purchased their own proprietary management software that can monitor the terminals and report errors as well as provide software updates via automatic download on boot. Additionally, some manufacturers provide hooks to integrate the terminals into a management framework, such as HP OpenView. Manufacturer-supplied software can work as long as it is sufficiently scalable to handle the network infrastructure in your company. If it can't, consider a solution that integrates into a management framework. At the very least, the terminal should send SNMP messages and supply a MIB for your management software (please see Chapter 9 for more detail on SNMP management).

Although the key point of a Windows terminal is to keep the desktop simple and re-duce desktop administration costs to zero, there is still an amount of administration overhead associated with a Windows Terminal (updating the ICA client every six months, for example), and thus a Windows terminal with good management software can further reduce administration costs. Wyse, Maxspeed, and Neoware all include re-mote management software that monitor the terminals, integrate with SNMP manage-ment software, and remotely update the terminals with software updates.

Functional Differences

The ICA client for Windows CE and Embedded Windows XP supports all of the func-tions of the standard 32-bit ICA client for Windows, as does the client for Linux on Win-dows terminals. The differences between running the client on a PC versus a Windows terminal are

▼ **Client software updates**   Although most terminals now provide management software that will automate upgrades to the embedded software, these upgrades remain challenging given the newness of firmware management software applications. Upgrades are typically done via an automatic or scheduled download. Some terminals support the MetaFrame Auto Update feature, which can be a big time saver when a new version of the ICA client needs to be deployed. At the very least, look for a terminal with management software that supports a centralized method for downloading software (either operating system images or applications) and rebooting the terminal without user intervention.

■ **Local browsing**   Embedded browsers are limited with regard to storing local data and using plug-ins. They offer a limited bookmark list and, of course, do not allow plug-ins or other downloads.

■ **Java**   Stand-alone Java applications (those that do not require a browser to run) require a Java Virtual Machine (JVM) to be installed on the Windows terminal firmware. The JVM must be the correct version, and the Java application must also be loaded into firmware in order to execute.

■ **Autologin**   Similar to the Task Station function in the ZAK for Windows 95 and 98, Autologin can be used when you want to present a limited number of choices to the user when logging in. When Autologin is enabled, the user is limited to one terminal session, either a desktop or a specific, published application. If you want the user to have access to multiple published applications at login, Autologin should be disabled.

■ **Connection security**   Most terminals now support 128-bit ICA encryption as well as the SSL/TLS security required to connect to a MetaFrame Secure Gateway.

▲ **Configuration security lockout** Whatever configuration settings the terminal offers, it is important they also prevent users from changing them once established. If the configuration cannot be protected, you run the risk of configuration-related support calls driving up the TCO.

WEB INTERFACE FOR METAFRAME

Web Interface for MetaFrame (formerly called NFuse Classic) evolved from the Citrix ALE technology used to deploy applications to web browser clients. Web Interface combines the web-publishing features of the ALE client with many of the management features of Program Neighborhood, including the ability to dynamically publish a new application to a logged-on user. Users just click the Refresh button on their browser, and the new application icon appears on the desktop within the browser. Web Interface comes standard with a default web page setup that provides an administrator with a very simple and quick setup of the Web Interface. The web page can be customized with any standard HTML tool. An example of a default Web Interface session is shown next:

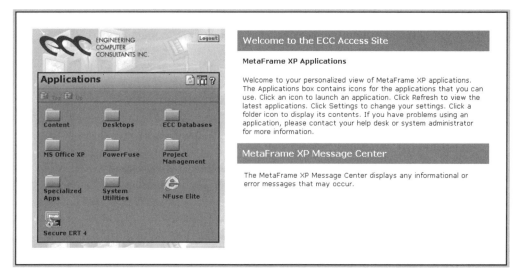

Web Interface is a three-tier solution that includes a MetaFrame server component, a web server component, and an ICA client component with the web browser. Web Interface doesn't replace the ICA client; rather, it interoperates with it to provide the capabilities native to the operating system platform. Web Interface extends the publishing capabilities of the ALE client by providing a means to integrate applications from other sources, such as MetaFrame for UNIX, and by allowing applications and access to be customized by users. Figure 7-2 shows the Web Interface application publishing architecture.

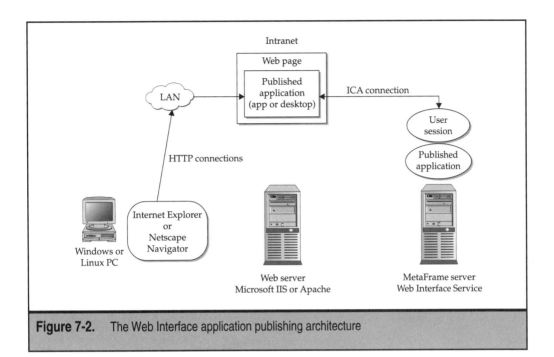

Figure 7-2. The Web Interface application publishing architecture

Web Interface supports the features of Program Neighborhood within the context of the browser. Instead of pushing an application icon to a PC's desktop using the Seamless Windows feature, the icon will appear on the desktop within the browser.

A subtle but important advance offered by Web Interface is that the web components can be configured to resolve application names to IP addresses, eliminating the need for the ICA client to use the UDP-based ICA browser. UDP access can then be eliminated from the firewall, thus enhancing overall security. Further, by utilizing MetaFrame Secure Gateway Server with Web Interface (discussed in Chapters 2, 8, and 16), no outside firewall ports have to be open at all, and the MetaFrame servers can be placed securely inside the firewall.

Finally, Web Interface offers both client and server scripting capabilities to run external programs, customize the user session, or integrate with other web technologies such as COM, Java Server Pages, or Active Server Pages.

Three components are required to run Web Interface for MetaFrame: a MetaFrame server running the Web Interface Service, a supported web server (Microsoft IIS or Apache), and an ICA client with a supported web browser.

Web Interface for MetaFrame, along with its big brother MetaFrame Secure Access Manager, which further automates the creation and integration of a full-blown access center, will be covered in depth in Chapter 16.

OTHER CLIENT DEVICES

Thus far, we have discussed PCs and Windows terminals as the most common devices used to access the MetaFrame server farm. Since the ICA protocol has been ported to Windows CE, Linux, and even some cell phones, the server farm can be accessed from a variety of client devices, as shown in Figure 7-3. We are seeing integration with devices from tablet PCs in the medical field to proprietary devices running global positioning for transportation companies. Though it is clearly not practical to run a Windows desktop on the tiny 320×260 screens of some of these devices, it can be very useful to run a small, published application. Imagine a warehouse in which each stockperson had an HP iPAQ with wireless networking and a physical inventory application that fed directly into the corporate inventory database. Perhaps your company has a large number of hourly employees who could use a Windows terminal touch screen to punch in and out of a virtual time-clock application. Using an example of sales force automation, perhaps a field salesperson could use his handheld computer to wirelessly connect to the home office and check stock before filling an order, or check and approve special bulk pricing for an important customer.

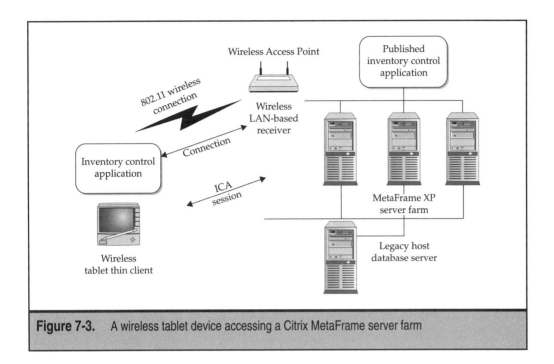

Figure 7-3.   A wireless tablet device accessing a Citrix MetaFrame server farm

Once an organization has committed to deploying server-based computing, there are innumerable ways to extend the information infrastructure to remote employees, customers, and even the public.

CHAPTER 8

Security

The meaning of "security" as it relates to information systems is often diluted to include only security related to clients and servers. This narrow view can be a fatal flaw in corporate information security. One of the early definitions of security for computer networks came from the *IBM Dictionary of Computing* published in 1994 by McGraw-Hill, Inc.:

> *Information Security: the concepts, techniques, technical measures, and administrative measures used to protect information assets from deliberate or inadvertent unauthorized acquisition, damage, disclosure, manipulation, modification, loss, or use.*

This chapter deals primarily with security concepts, components, and design elements. In that light, many of the concepts and discussions are beyond the scope of what a server-based computing (SBC) systems administrator will directly control; however, that System Administrator must be able to accurately represent security requirements to other staff members who are responsible for design and implementation. Today's enterprises require that all staff are cognizant and vigilant with security, and the on-demand and in-control enterprise requirements dictate that security be a forethought and not an afterthought to any IT solution. Detailed implementation of security in an enterprise infrastructure is addressed in Chapter 17.

THE NATURE OF SECURITY

As in a chain, the security of the whole computer system is only as strong as the weakest link. A global or systemic model is critical to the formulation of an effective approach to security in the enterprise. It is not uncommon for large companies to decide, almost arbitrarily, that a particular area of their network is open to attack and invest tens of thousands of dollars to "patch the fence" without realizing that someone could walk right through the front gate. In one case we worked with, a company invested $50,000 in an Internet firewall without setting up a system to enforce strong passwords. With the firewall in place, no one could enter the system from the Internet—that is, unless the intruder could guess that the system administrator's password was his daughter's first name and birthday.

Taking a global view of security for the enterprise can be intimidating, which may account for the woefully inadequate attention paid to the subject by many companies. It is important to realize however, that the effects of securing your infrastructure are *cumulative.* Even a few simple changes to secure certain access points to the network can make a huge difference. For example, installing an effective Internet firewall can be a strong deterrent to the casual hacker. Before deciding to install such a system, however, you need to assess the overall security posture of the infrastructure. Without such an assessment, you could be securing part of your network while leaving another part open to attack. When getting started, it is useful to ask yourself: what are you trying to protect?

What Are You Trying to Protect?

The generic answer, more often than not, is "corporate data." Corporate data must be protected from

▼ **Data access**   Access must be limited only to appropriate users without impacting authorized access to data or application performance when manipulating data. Figure 8-1 shows the correlation between the level of security and its impact on a user's ability to work. The three security paradigms, Open, Restricted, and Closed, are discussed later in this chapter. The common criteria linked to data access are Authentication, Authorization, and Accounting (AAA), and are described as follows:

■ *Authentication*   The ability to positively identify the authorized user, often via two or more factors (username and password, plus biometric, one-time security code tokens).

■ *Authorization*   The determination of which resources an authenticated user may access, and what rights or permissions they have for each resource. This can be very broad as in file and directory permissions, or very granular as in record-level access controls within a structured database.

■ *Accounting*   The ability to track what a user did or attempted to do. This is particularly critical with regard to audit trails required in most regulated industries.

■ **Data integrity**   Data must not be modified or altered except by authorized individuals or processes. AAA rules determine which individuals have the right to perform these operations on the data, and can record what modifications were actually made. Data integrity during transport becomes a serious problem when classic client-server applications are deployed over non-secure (unencrypted) media. A "man-in-the-middle" attack may compromise data integrity yet remain undetected. In an SBC environment, transaction information remains within the local network, and screen updates and data input (mouse clicks and keystrokes) are contained within the RDP or ICA data stream. The nature of an ICA session makes "man-in-the-middle" or session hijacking attacks extremely difficult to complete since attackers cannot easily synchronize with the video stream.

■ **Network resources**   Both processing capability and network capacity must be protected to ensure business continuity. Inappropriate or unauthorized use of processing power may deny service to legitimate applications or processes. Improper control of data storage may allow unauthorized data to consume storage capacity. Network bandwidth and access must be protected from intentional and inadvertent disruption. Denial of service (DoS) events may be intentional (directed at corporate servers, firewalls, and so on), or unintentional (a side effect of unauthorized use of resources). As an example, a customer uses

Citrix to deploy Geographic Information Systems (GIS) data to a large remote customer. Overall performance of Internet access and Citrix access slowed to a crawl. The cause was isolated to saturation of the customer's Internet T1 by FTP downloads from an internal web server. The server had been hacked, hidden directories created for bootleg copies of a non-English version of Windows 2000, and the download instructions circulated through a European chat room. A single incident deprived the company of processing power (the hacked server), application services (Citrix access was unstable), storage capacity (drive space), and network access bandwidth. Further, it created a potential for liability as their FTP site hosted bootleg software.

▲ **Liability, reputation, business continuity**   These categories are included because companies may actually have to close their doors if certain data becomes public. Engineering designs, business merger and acquisition plans, or other data that constitutes a competitive advantage, if exposed, could have a crippling effect on operations. If it can be proven that a company's officers knew about the lack of security and were negligent in correcting it, they could be liable for damages to the stockholders. A company that allowed its security weaknesses to be used to exploit another company or network could be liable for damages. Corporate image and reputation are extremely sensitive for some businesses. For instance, who would keep their money in a bank with a history of security problems? Worse yet, what if security weaknesses allowed a business's web site to host child pornography, and the business's servers and data were seized as part of a criminal investigation?

The key to securing the corporate infrastructure is a comprehensive security policy. Although addressing all aspects of information security is well beyond the scope of this book, a basic understanding of the breadth of security issues and the security measures necessary in a corporate SBC environment is essential knowledge. Most governmental entities, "regulated" industries (banking, stock trading, healthcare services), and many large businesses mandate certification and accreditation processes, with a concise written security policy as a prerequisite for certification or accreditation. Examples of these mandates include

▼ Department of Defense Information Technology Security Certification and Accreditation Process (DITSCAP)

■ Health Insurance Portability and Accountability Act (HIPAA)

▲ Gramm-Leach-Bliley (GLB) Act of 1999 (Financial Services Modernization Bill)

Toward that end, a number of leading vendors and industry groups have produced methodologies and guidance for developing and implementing a corporate security policy. Among the leaders are

▼ BS 7799-1/ISO-I7799 Standard for Information Security Management Systems (ISMS) (complex and detailed, analogous to ISO 9000 for security)

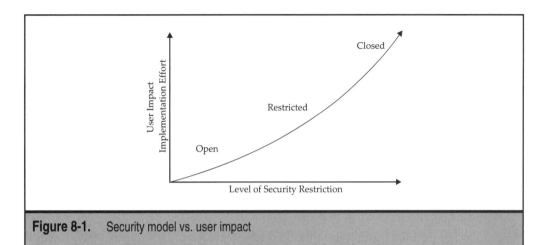

Figure 8-1. Security model vs. user impact

- Internet Security Systems' ADDME (Assess, Design, Deploy, Manage, Educate) Security Lifecycle Methodology (based on ISO 17799) (www.iss.net)
- Cisco System's SAFE: A Security Blueprint for Enterprise Networks (www.cisco.com/safe)
- ▲ The SANS Institute (www.sans.org)

All of these methodologies vary in complexity and depth, but maintain the same two-part theme: policy and process. The policy component must provide a comprehensive security policy that includes a combination of physical security measures, technical security measures, and administrative security measures to protect the information system. The process component must provide an iterative process to monitor and maintain the policy and associated measures. Cisco Systems' Security Wheel (Figure 8-2) provides a superb illustration of the iterative security management process.

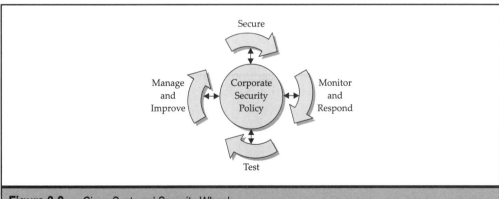

Figure 8-2. Cisco Systems' Security Wheel

DEVELOPING A SECURITY POLICY

For a business with no pre-existing security policy, establishing and implementing a viable security policy is a daunting task. When server-based computing is a key part of the business model, some aspects of overall security are greatly simplified (security of individual desktop PCs), while others become far more critical (access to applications servers). Further, the manner in which server-based services are delivered to remote users (Internet, VPN, MetaFrame Secure Gateway, and Wireless LAN/WAN) becomes a significant factor in selecting which measures are used to enforce the security policy. In any case, the tasks required to develop a corporate security policy are similar.

▼ Assess the security posture (baselining).

■ Define written policy requirements and goals.

■ Design technical, administrative, and physical security measures.

▲ Implement and test.

Security Posture Assessment

A security posture assessment establishes the baseline for "what is." Posture assessments are typically very granular evaluations of all aspects of the network, and include

▼ Current documented policies and procedures (administrative measures).

■ Physical security of resources (servers, network hardware, tape and software libraries).

■ Network access and exposure points.

■ Mapping of Hosts (devices), operating systems and versioning, and services (HTTP, ICA, and so on).

■ Definition of protection requirements. For example: Is data on disk to be stored clear-text or encrypted? Will Terminal Services applications allow anonymous access?

■ Efficacy of antivirus software.

■ A multiperspective simulated attack on network resources. This typically includes internal and external penetration and exploit attempts as well as denial of service attacks on ingress points.

▲ Risk assessment.

Risk Assessment

Risk assessment is the process of evaluating each security weakness or threat and determining both the potential impact and the probability or likelihood that the weakness can be exploited. Clearly identifying risks and their potential business impact helps determine whether a specific security measure is ultimately cost effective. Figure 8-3 shows the correlation between security risk or exposure and the cost to mitigate the risk.

Weaknesses stem from one of three common sources:

▼   **Technology weaknesses**   Inherent limitations in network and computing technology; for example, the predictable TCP sequence numbers generated by the Microsoft IP protocol stack. Technology weaknesses are usually mitigated by a technical security measure.

■   **Configuration weaknesses**   Improper configuration of any network service can create an easy avenue of attack. Configuration weaknesses are usually mitigated by a combination of administrative security measures, including configuration control and configuration audits.

▲   **Policy weaknesses**   Inappropriate, poorly defined, or improperly implemented and managed policies. For example, a policy that allows weak passwords. Policy weaknesses also include internal politics that circumvent or subvert necessary security measures.

Threats are broadly categorized by source: internal (from within the organization) or external (from outside the organization); and by type: reconnaissance, unauthorized access or use, denial of service, or data manipulation.

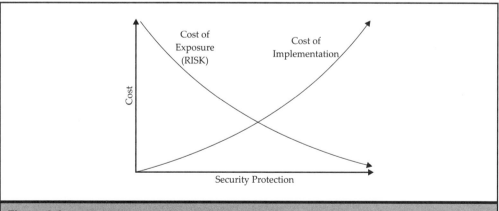

Figure 8-3.   Implementation cost vs. risk

Policy Definition

There are three broad concepts for security paradigms:

▼ **Open**   Common in academia and other bastions of anarchy

■ **Restricted**   The most common balance of security needs versus business requirements and cost

▲ **Closed**   Often seen in DoD and some financial environments

In most corporate enterprise networks, the Restricted paradigm is preferred.

At the top level, the Security Policy should address the security needs and manner by which security is managed and controlled. Specific security measures (physical, administrative, and technical) should be identified in the overall security policy.

Physical Security Measures

Physical security may not seem complex, but critical resources (server rooms, network equipment closets, and data and software storage) are often left open to unrestricted access. Security consultants and auditors are often able to walk directly into server rooms, and even remove equipment without being challenged. Any resource that can be physically accessed (server, firewall, router, and so forth) can be compromised. Depending on the sensitivity of the data, measures may range from simple lock-and-key security measures to electronically monitored and controlled access (badges, retina scanners, and other devices).

Administrative Security Measures

Written, enforceable administrative policies and practices are essential elements of the overall security policy. Administrative security measures can become an end unto themselves if not approached with common sense. Businesses often focus too much on documenting and delineating every aspect of security and end up with a one-time written policy that is both unenforceable and not enforced. To be viable, security policy documents must be clear, concise, and specific in scope, applicability, and responsibility. Standards and procedures must be supported and enforced from the top down. If violating a security policy has no consequences, the policy itself is inconsequential. Common policy requirements include

▼ Acceptable encryption

■ Acceptable use of information systems

■ Modem connections

■ Antivirus

■ Security audits

■ Database credentials

■ Firewall configuration control and management

- ■ DMZ system security
- ■ Password management and control
- ■ Remote access
- ■ Risk assessment
- ■ Router security
- ■ Server security
- ■ Third-party network connections
- ■ Virtual private network
- ■ Wireless network connectivity
- ▲ Facility access controls

Technical Security Measures

Technical security measures constitute the most significant and costly portion of the overall security plan. Technical measures are implemented end-to-end to enforce security without relying on human intervention. These measures include capabilities such as firewalls, proxies, encryption, multifactor authentication, operating system hardening, and user environment control.

Security Design Technical Considerations

In a typical distributed network, computing resources are dispersed throughout the enterprise, as shown in Figure 8-4. This means that sensitive information resides on the hard drives of employees' personal computers and on work group servers at several locations. If physical access to data is one area of concern for securing that data, it can be said that such a distributed model is less secure than a centralized model.

In the centralized model, shown in Figure 8-5, the bulk of computing resources are concentrated in one or just a few data centers. As a result, physical access to that data is much more restricted. Does this mean that server-based computing is inherently more secure than distributed computing? It may seem so, but there are numerous areas of concern in server-based computing that make such a blanket assertion shortsighted.

Areas of Exposure

Like the network design considerations discussed in Chapter 6, security in an SBC network shares many commonalities with a traditional network, as well as a number of unique exposures. The common exposure areas parallel the hierarchical design modules (building blocks) from Chapter 6.

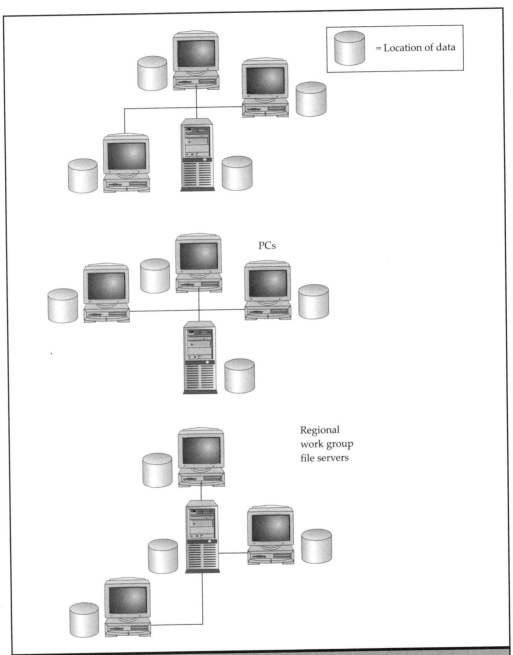

= Location of data

PCs

Regional
work group
file servers

Figure 8-4. A distributed network in which each regional work site has its own resident file server

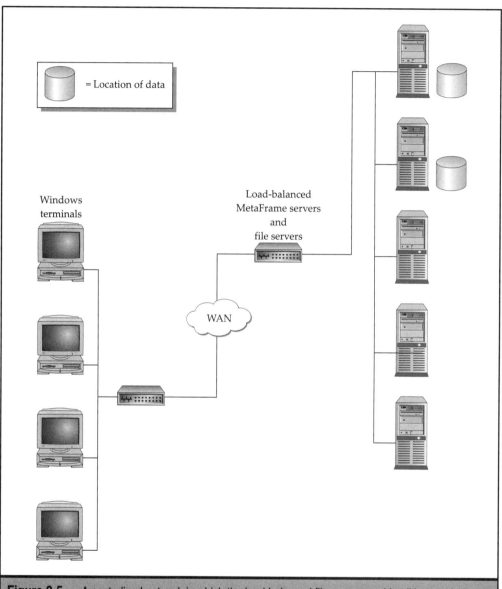

Figure 8-5.   A centralized network in which the load-balanced file servers reside all in one place

Access Layer Exposures

The point where clients first access the SBC infrastructure is the most critical line of defense. Proper security enforcement at the edge reduces the complexity of security measures that must be implemented in the core on the servers.

▼ **LAN access**   Internal LAN users are generally the most trusted group of users because their environment and behavior can be seen and easily monitored. Minimal security measures must still be in place to protect the network hardware, network bandwidth, and other LAN access segments. Port-based security on Layer 2 switches can effectively lock out unauthorized client devices and notify an administrator of any unauthorized event. Access lists at Layer 2-to-Layer 3 boundaries can enforce and restrict traffic flows to only authorized address ranges. Virus protection and control, although often overlooked when all the critical applications and data are server-based, is an absolute must. Even if client devices cannot propagate malicious logic to the applications servers or network data stores, client-to-client propagation of the infection (Code Red, Nimda, and so on) can saturate network bandwidth or server resources and result in denial of service.

■ **wLAN access**   Wireless LAN segments (not to be confused with wireless access via public networks) present additional risks to any network. Above and beyond the security exposure of wired LAN segments, wLANs can allow surreptitious connection without need of physical access to the network. wLAN identification features such as the Service Set Identifier (SSID) are often misconstrued as security features. The SSID is simply a network name and allows visibility of the network much the same as a browse list in Windows networking. The SSID is clear-text and can be sniffed by any client. Effective wLAN security in a corporate environment requires three components. First, extensible authentication methods (EAP) should be used so that users must authenticate before being granted *any* access to the network. Second, the wireless LAN segment should be isolated from the rest of the enterprise by strict firewall rules. In a traditional distributed computing network, this is extremely complex and often ends with rules that allow any wireless source to pass through the firewall. In a server-based computing network, security is far easier—only the client transport protocol must be allowed through (ICA, RDP, and SSL). Finally, the wLAN segment must use a combination of advanced security techniques to overcome weaknesses in Wireless Equivalency Privacy (WEP). Cisco Systems' wireless technology supports a long list of security enhancements that all wLAN segments should use:

  ■ 128-bit WEP

  ■ Extensible authentication via RADIUS or other means

  ■ Dynamic WEP keys (the initial key is valid only for authentication, then dynamic per-session keys are generated)

- Key hashing and key aging (time-based or traffic-based) with automatic rekeying. If the encryption key changes often enough, eavesdropping attacks cannot compile enough raw data from the same key sequence to allow a key-cracking program to decrypt the data.

- Message Integrity Check (MIC) to prevent man-in-the-middle attacks.

- **WAN access (private networks)** Remote branch offices connected over dedicated media are secured much the same as local LAN access segments, but primary filtering should be done at the remote site to avoid data transmission over expensive WAN links. Virus protection remains essential at remote branches.

- **WAN access (virtual private networks)** VPN-connected remote branch offices are like dedicated media connected offices, with the exception of the site-to-site transport. All data transported between the sites is by definition "trusted," but traverses the untrusted Internet and must be encrypted for transmission. VPN connections should always use IPSec and ESP mode.

- **Internet access/Internet remote access** Internet access exposures are the most threatening and most exploited. All Internet access should be protected by a reliable firewall, monitored by intrusion detection capabilities, and authenticated to positively identify inbound access requests as legitimate. At minimum, the logon process should be encrypted to protect usernames and passwords from compromise. Highly secure access to the server-based computing resources requires full encryption via IPSec VPN or SSL/TLS. If SSL/TLS is selected, connections should traverse an application proxy to prevent direct access to the internal servers. In terms of security boundaries, the emerging technologies associated with wireless cellular (wWAN) access are really just another Internet user with limited bandwidth.

- ▲ **Direct-dial access** Security measures associated with direct dial-up access are similar to those employed for wLAN segments. Remote Access Service (RAS) users can be given essentially open access to the Internet and external resources, but should be limited to RDP/ICA/SSL access.

Distribution Layer Exposure

The network distribution layer is an ideal enforcement point to control data flow from segment to segment as well as to implement intrusion detection systems (IDS). Although we normally think of the firewall as an Internet firewall, the DMZ portions of the firewall that support remote RAS and wLAN segments are really part of the network distribution layer. For additional protection, remote WAN and Layer 3 LAN aggregation points can provide firewall functionality through router-based firewall features.

Core Layer Exposure

The core layer requires special attention in the server-based computing model. The core hardware (switch) requires only the normal protection afforded network hardware, but the connected servers that provide application services (Citrix), data storage (file servers and database servers), and network services (authentication, name resolution, and so on) must be secured to a greater degree than in the traditional distributed environment. Remember, the user's applications and environment exists on the application server—the user is already inside all of the filters, firewalls, and access lists provided by the network infrastructure. Security within these core servers falls into two general categories: server hardening—the measures taken to implement server-side security through access controls, software configuration, and policies; and user environment control—measures to contain and restrict the users to their approved applications and access capabilities.

Technical Measures

This section will provide more detail on suggested technical measures to ensure enterprise security. Measures addressed are the most commonly needed and employed technologies, but the list is not all-inclusive.

Firewalls

Network firewalls are the primary line of defense against external security threats; however, a firewall is not a panacea of network security. A firewall is a system or group of systems that enforce a boundary between two or more networks. In the classic implementation (shown in Figure 8-6), the firewall system is comprised of a packet-filtering perimeter router, an isolation LAN (screened subnet) with a dual-homed bastion host, and an interior packet-filtering router.

Commercially developed firewalls are available in two primary form factors: appliances and computers. Appliances are preconfigured with an operating system and necessary network connections, while computer-based products provide software only and allow the user to determine what hardware is employed. Firewall software can be either a purpose-built hardened OS or application software that executes firewall functions on a general purpose (GP) operating system (Windows, UNIX variations, and so on). Application software that rides on a GP OS should be avoided. In addition to the processing overhead (GUI interface, "user" features), the firewall is subject to the inherent weaknesses in the GP OS design, which are publicly available as application interface specifications. A quick look at reports of hacking and intrusions will show every GP OS has a long list of vulnerabilities.

Most firewalls perform a number of different functions, but the following are common capabilities:

▼ **Protection of internal resources**   Hides internal addressing schemes and hosts from external detection.

■ **Authentication**   Uses strong authentication techniques to verify a user's identity before granting access to corporate information.

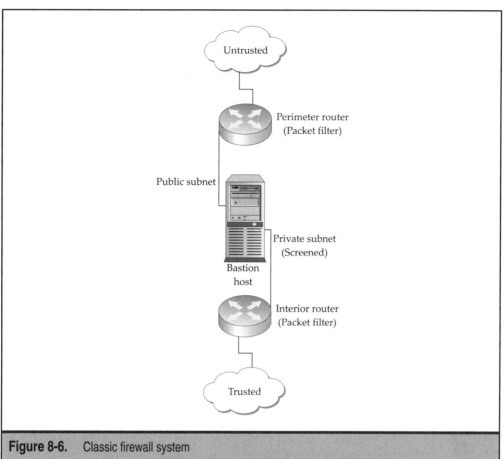

Figure 8-6.   Classic firewall system

- ■ **Privacy**   Protects, via encryption, sessions, and data streams destined for a remote network segment over untrusted networks (VPNs).

- ▲ **Auditing**   Provides detailed logging and accounting of communication attempts and other relevant metrics.

In addition to these common features, firewall solutions should offer

- ▼ **Attack and intrusion detection**   The ability to detect common attacks and intrusion attempts such as denial of service and spoofing.

- ■ **Content security**   A firewall should be "application aware" for a minimal set of common Internet applications (FTP, SMTP, and so on). It should be possible to define access rules based on the application that is attempting to pass through the firewall.

■ **High availability**   The firewall systems should be hardened enough to protect themselves from being brought down by an attack or simple mishap. More critical, firewall implementations should be redundant, with automatic fail-over.

▲ **Electronic countermeasures**   The ability to mitigate common attacks and intrusion attempts such as denial of service and spoofing, as well as the ability to protect the firewall from direct attack.

Types of Firewalls   There are four general types of Internet firewalls, or, to be more accurate, three types plus a hybrid.

▼ **Packet filtering firewalls**   Filtering firewalls screen packets based on addresses and packet options. They operate at the IP packet level (Layer 3) and make simple security decisions (drop or forward) based on data in the packet header. Packet filtering firewalls may be one of three subtypes:

■ **Static filtering**   This is used on most routers. Filter rules must be manually changed and are comprised of source and destination pairs as well as protocol and port values. No logic is used to determine session state or packet sequence.

■ **Dynamic filtering**   In this subtype, an outside process changes the filtering rules dynamically, based on router-observed events (for example, one might allow FTP packets in from the outside, if someone on the inside requested an FTP session).

■ **Stateful inspection**   A technology that is similar to dynamic filtering, with the addition of more granular examination of data contained in the IP packet.

Dynamic filtering and stateful inspection firewalls keep a dynamic state table to make changes to the filtering rules based on events.

■ **Circuit gateways**   Circuit gateways operate at the network transport layer. Again, connections are authorized based on address pairs. Circuit gateways usually cannot look at data traffic flowing between one network and another, but they do prevent direct connections between one network and another. Sessions from outside are terminated on the gateway and a new session from the gateway to the internal protected host is generated. Circuit gateways may introduce latency and jitter into RDP or ICA sessions under heavy loads.

■ **Application gateways**   Application gateways (or proxy-based firewalls) operate at the application level (Layer 7) and can examine information at that level. Decisions are made based on address pairs, application content (for instance, URLs), and application data, such as commands passed within FTP or SMTP command channels. Few vendors provide application-aware firewalls capable of managing RDP or ICA traffic, and enhancements to RDP or ICA require a revision of the firewall source code. One notable exception is Secure Computing's *Sidewinder G_2* firewall (actually a hybrid firewall), which includes a Citrix-certified application proxy for ICA traffic.

▲   **Hybrid firewalls**   As the name implies, hybrid firewalls use elements of more than one type of firewall. Most modern firewalls combine stateful inspection and application gateway services to manage the security boundary.

Firewalls for Server-Based Computing   Hybrid firewall systems are strongly recommended for server-based computing. Industry leaders in firewall technology include Cisco Systems (PIX), Nokia (Checkpoint), and Secure Computing (Sidewinder). The firewall system, as shown in Figure 8-7, should include a perimeter router capable of static or dynamic packet filtering (to offload simple filtering and protect the firewall from direct attack), a hybrid firewall element using stateful inspection and either a cut-through

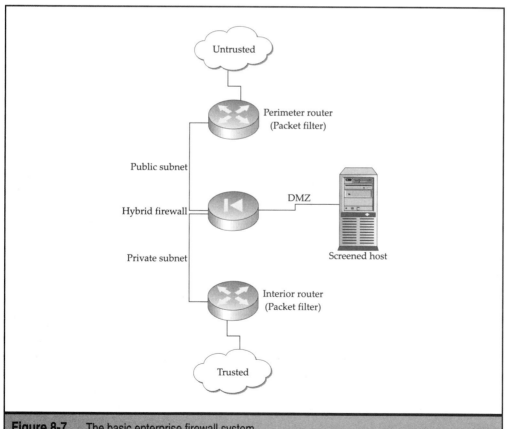

Figure 8-7.   The basic enterprise firewall system

proxy or an ICA application proxy, and an interior router capable of static or dynamic packet filtering.

Enhancements to ICA since the early MetaFrame versions eliminate the need for firewalls to support UDP Passthrough for ICA browser services (UDP port 1604). Stateful inspection firewalls must "approximate" a session state for UDP by using timers, since UDP is a stateless protocol. MetaFrame now supports TCP-based XML services in lieu of ICA browser services.

Encryption

Using the Internet as part of the corporate WAN infrastructure has obvious security implications. The Internet is a public network, and as such, exposes an enterprise's private information to unauthorized individuals by its very nature. The Internet is often an integral part of delivering applications to remote users in a server-based computing network, however. Internet delivery provides virtually universal access to clients, built-in resiliency, and dramatic cost reductions as compared to dedicated media. There are two basic encrypted transport methodologies used for SBC network connectivity: virtual private networks (VPNs) and Public Key Infrastructure (PKI) encryption via Secure Sockets Layer (SSL) or Transport Layer Security (TLS).

Encryption Standards   Encryption standards define both the mechanics of the encryption process and the complexity of the key. For all at-risk data transmissions (anything traversing the Internet), strong encryption should always be used. For SSL/TLS, use a minimum 128-bit key (RC4 with 128-bit encryption and MD5 message authentication, yielding 3.4×10^{38} possible key values). If security is paramount, consider Triple-DES (3DES with 168-bit key and SHA-1 message authentication yields 3.7×10^{50} possible key values). When SSL is used, avoid SSL 2.0 implementations, and instead use SSL 3.0 or TLS.

There are two basic types of encryption algorithms: symmetric (or private key) and public key. Private key encryption requires that the same key used to encrypt the data be used to decrypt the data and is most commonly seen in VPN configurations. The advantage is speed, since less computation is involved than in other methods. The main disadvantage is that the key must be distributed to the intended recipient through some secure mechanism; the symmetric algorithm itself provides no way to distribute the key. The second type of algorithm, the public key, calculates a list of keys, some of which can only encrypt the data and some of which can only decrypt the data. The encryption key is the public key, and the decryption key is the private key. A message encrypted with the former can only be decrypted by the latter. A major advantage of this scheme is that the encryption key can travel in the open without compromising security. Having the public key will not allow someone to decrypt the data.

NOTE: In some applications, such as Secure Socket Layer (SSL), the public key is made freely available to any client requesting it. The client machine uses the public key to encrypt the data before sending it over the unprotected network. Only the possessor of the private key will be able to decrypt it. This is how e-commerce sites can function: any customer who comes to the site can obtain the public key without any special arrangement or mechanism.

Several encryption algorithm and transport standards have arisen that have been adopted by Microsoft, Citrix, and others. Understanding them will allow an administrator to judge for themselves whether a specific standard is appropriate for their server-based computing project. By implementing an encryption algorithm and transport method in the network backbone, the task of authenticating and securing the network session is made further transparent to the end user. Cisco, Lucent, Nortel, and other vendors facilitate this seamless authentication by their adoption of one or more security standards.

▼ **Microsoft Point-to-Point Encryption (MPPE)**   MPPE uses preshared keys for authentication. This method uses a shared, secret key that is previously agreed upon by two systems. MPPE can be used as the authentication method for PPTP or L2TP. Both are supported in Windows 2000 Server and Windows Server 2003.

■ **Internet Protocol Security (IPSec)**   IPSec is the de facto standard for point-to-point VPN encryption. The great advantage of IPSec is that it is end-to-end at the network layer. Application security protocols like SSL require the application to change, while data link protocols like PPTP only protect a user on that specific link; the packets travel over other links in the clear. IPSec provides two choices of security service: Authentication Header (AH), which essentially allows authentication of the sender of data and is not considered highly secure, and Encapsulating Security Payload (ESP), which supports both authentication of the sender and encryption of data. The specific information associated with each of these services is inserted into the packet in a header that follows the IP packet header. Separate key protocols can be selected, such as the ISAKMP/ Oakley protocol. Since it is implemented at the protocol layer, IPSec is an excellent choice for server-based computing. It does not interfere with higher-level protocols like ICA and therefore is nearly transparent to the end user.

■ **Point-to-Point-Tunneling Protocol (PPTP)**   PPTP is an extension of the Point-to-Point Protocol (PPP) and has two functions. First, it establishes a control channel between the client and the server. Second, it builds a "tunnel" for passing data between the client and the server. The tunnel is constructed using an encryption algorithm (PPTP can support many) so that the client and server exchange keys. PPTP supports multiple tunnels with a single control channel and can multiplex between them. PPTP currently enjoys the widest support in network backbone equipment such as routers and switches.

▲ **Layer 2 Tunneling Protocol (L2TP)**   L2TP is an alternative to PPTP proposed by Cisco Systems. Like PPTP, L2TP is an extension of PPP and attempts to include the best features of PPTP. Like PPTP, it can encapsulate other protocols besides TCP/IP. L2TP provides flexibility in the assignment of IP addresses when TCP/IP is used. Dynamic, static, and privately managed IP addresses are supported. It uses a similar keyed encryption scheme to establish a tunnel. Both L2TP and PPTP are proposed IETF standards. Both are also supported as standards in all Cisco routers.

Encryption for Server-Based Computing   Both ICA and RDP support basic encryption services through their respective client and server configurations. RDP requires a "non-standard" port (TCP 3389) to be open through the firewall, and does not support authentication prior to connecting to the target server (secure application proxy). ICA has variable levels of security, and can be reconfigured to operate on a "standard" port that is usually permitted through enterprise firewalls—TCP 443 (HTTPS). By default, the ICA protocol adds little to the security already existing in Terminal Services. ICA uses a very basic method to encrypt, or more accurately scramble, the data stream by using a key. It is really meant to help ensure that clear-text is not visible in the data stream. By invoking the 128-bit encryption option for ICA connections, the ICA session is encrypted with a 128-bit key RC5 encryption algorithm from RSA Data Security. RC5 uses a combination of symmetric and public-private key algorithms. The MetaFrame XP client and server use the Diffie-Hellman key agreement algorithm with a 1024-bit key to generate RC5 keys. Citrix bills this client as being safe enough to run sessions over the Internet, and indeed, many companies use or base their products on the RC5 encryption algorithm. Windows Server 2003 RDC services use 128-bit, bi-directional RC4 encryption. Both Windows 2003 (with the encryption module) and Citrix MetaFrame XP Feature Release 3 are now certified as FIPS 140–compliant for use in Federal Government information systems. In either case, the direct connection from client to target server creates additional concerns, even when passing through most stateful inspection firewalls. Citrix remedies this problem through its MetaFrame Secure Gateway product as shown in Figure 8-8. MetaFrame Secure Gateway is a specialized SSL application proxy, which supports integration with web-based application access (MetaFrame Web Interface), multifactor authentication technologies like RADIUS or Secure Computing's SecureID, application layer isolation of internal and external hosts (internal Citrix servers are not exposed to the public Internet), and session management via ticketing.

Authentication, Authorization, and Accounting Services

Authentication, authorization, and accounting (AAA) services provide the means to identify a user, grant access to specific resources, and document what the user did and when they did it. The vast majority of AAA services in a Windows Server 2003 server environment are provided by the Windows security model with authentication in the form of user account/password settings, authorization provided by discretionary Access Control Lists (on files, shares, and other OS-controlled resources like print services), and accounting provided through event logs and event auditing policies. Windows Server 2003 Terminal Services and Citrix MetaFrame XP both support two-factor authentication (smart card). More robust authentication such as three-factor authentication requires third-party software.

TIP: In Windows Server 2003, you can add users and groups directly to the Remote Desktop Users group to allow RDP or ICA access. Remote Desktop for Administration (equivalent to Windows 2000 Terminal Services—Remote Administration Mode) is now completely separate from Terminal Services (Windows 2000 Terminal Services—Application Server Mode).

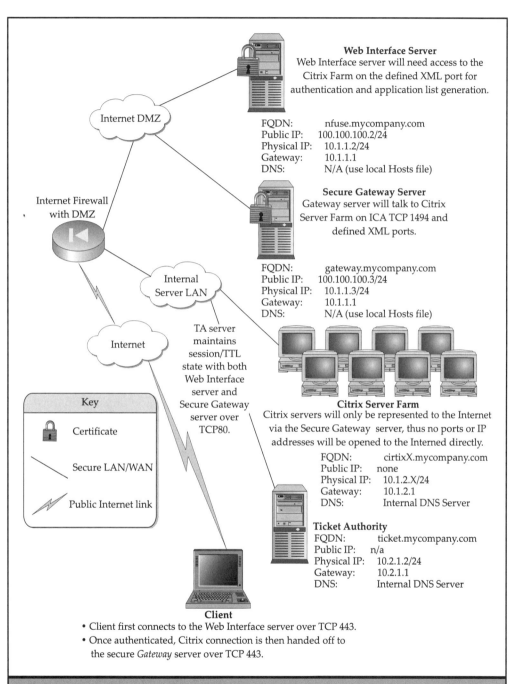

Web Interface Server
Web Interface server will need access to the
Citrix Farm on the defined XML port for
authentication and application list generation.

FQDN: nfuse.mycompany.com
Public IP: 100.100.100.2/24
Physical IP: 10.1.1.2/24
Gateway: 10.1.1.1
DNS: N/A (use local Hosts file)

Secure Gateway Server
Gateway server will talk to Citrix
Server Farm on ICA TCP 1494 and
defined XML ports.

FQDN: gateway.mycompany.com
Public IP: 100.100.100.3/24
Physical IP: 10.1.1.3/24
Gateway: 10.1.1.1
DNS: N/A (use local Hosts file)

Internet DMZ

Internet Firewall
with DMZ

Internal
Server LAN

Internet

TA server
maintains
session/TTL
state with both
Web Interface
server and
Secure Gateway
server over
TCP80.

Key

🔒 Certificate

／ Secure LAN/WAN

⚡ Public Internet link

Citrix Server Farm
Citrix servers will only be represented to the Internet
via the Secure Gateway server, thus no ports or IP
addresses will be opened to the Interned directly.

FQDN: cirtixX.mycompany.com
Public IP: none
Physical IP: 10.1.2.X/24
Gateway: 10.1.2.1
DNS: Internal DNS Server

Ticket Authority
FQDN: ticket.mycompany.com
Public IP: n/a
Physical IP: 10.2.1.2/24
Gateway: 10.2.1.1
DNS: Internal DNS Server

Client
• Client first connects to the Web Interface server over TCP 443.
• Once authenticated, Citrix connection is then handed off to
   the secure *Gateway* server over TCP 443.

Figure 8-8.   MetaFrame Secure Gateway

Auditing

Basic auditing should always be provided by server event logs and system logs from firewalls and routers. Most database applications can support record-level auditing and transaction logging. Auditing by itself is a nice feature for 20/20 hindsight, but is of little use unless audit events are configured to generate administrative alert and notification messages.

Windows Server 2003 adds additional auditing capabilities to meet common government requirements and supplement intrusion detection mechanisms. Notable changes include operation-based auditing (analogous to accounting in AAA services) and per-user selective auditing (by name); and enhanced logon/logoff and account management auditing–logon/logoff events now contain IP address and caller information.

The Microsoft Audit Collection System (MACS), a client-server application to be released in support of Windows Server 2003, provides real-time security event collection, and stores event data in a SQL database for ready analysis. MACS can create a security boundary so that event-log data can be independently audited without the possibility of users or administrators tampering with the event data. This type of independent collection and audit are becoming the norm for regulated industries.

Intrusion Detection Systems

Intrusion detection systems (IDS) are now built in to many firewall products. A fully evolved IDS system should encompass both Network IDS (NIDS) implemented on firewalls, routers, or appliances, and Host IDS (HIDS) implemented via software services on vulnerable servers. Enterprise NIDS services go well beyond the built-in capabilities of most firewalls. For example, Cisco's PIX firewall recognizes less than 100 attack profiles (natively), has only limited autonomous response capability, and attack signatures are not regularly updated. When coupled with Cisco's IDS appliances, hundreds of attacks are recognized, signatures are updated much like antivirus software, and the IDS appliance can dynamically issue configuration change commands to the firewall to block attacks as they occur. HIDS on the other hand function much like a firewall at the OS kernel level—any API or kernel call that is not specifically preapproved by the administrator requires explicit authorization. Calls that are not "authorized" are blocked by default, which means HIDS can block and log as yet "undefined" attacks.

Content Filtering

Although not a technical security measure per se, filtering and management of Internet content, more specifically, filtering of user access to web content, and electronic mail content filtering and management are used to address two of the biggest liability and reputation issues in business today. Uncontrolled employee access to inappropriate (as determined by the corporate acceptable use policy) Internet sites not only can damage the corporate image and risk civil and legal prosecution, but can be a precursor to internal attacks on network security and resources. Case in point: an employee who surfs hacker web sites may be looking for tools to use, or they may be technologically illiterate and download malicious logic that compromises the network. With regard to electronic mail, businesses may be concerned about unacceptable mail content originated or received under the corporate identity, spam that consumes storage resources, or originated content that divulges sensitive information. E-mail filtering is usually accomplished both on a bastion host in an Internet DMZ (ingress filtering of objectionable content and spam), and on the corporate mail server itself to control employee-to-employee and employee-to-external content. An additional "filtering" capability can be provided by the Packeteer bandwidth manager discussed in Chapter 6. Since the Packeteer recognizes applications, to include chat and instant messaging programs and protocols (MS-Chat, AIM, MSN Messenger), peer-to-peer sharing applications (Napster, Gnutella, Bear Share, Lime Wire), and commonly abused Internet bandwidth hogs (Windows Media, QuickTime, Real Media), these applications can be assigned a policy of zero bits per second or "never admit" to block access by application. Chat programs are of particular concern as they often use dynamic ports and are one of the most active vectors for malicious logic ("bots"). Few business users can substantiate a legitimate need for chat, instant messaging, Internet file sharing, or streaming media.

Virus Protection

Enterprise virus protection is a "must have" in any computing environment. A single uncontrolled outbreak can cost tens of thousand of dollars in PC disinfection costs alone. Heavily infected networks must often be isolated from the Internet and taken out of service to allow IT staff to get ahead of rampant infections. Although most enterprise antivirus solutions offer similar capabilities, the solutions' effectiveness is determined more by implementation and maintenance ease than actual protection. The system must be universally installed, employ a locked configuration to prevent software from being disabled, and support centralized real-time reporting and alerting. In an SBC environment, the most common differentiator is the behavior of the scanner software in a multiuser environment. Initially, only Trend Micro's Server Protect product would consistently run correctly in a multiuser environment—most products created a new instance of the scanner for every instance of a user application or session; Server Protect generated a single instance in the system's context to monitor all writes to the server. Virus protection products must work seamlessly on all of the enterprise computer systems. Other enterprise vendors have since improved their products' support for Windows Terminal Services and Citrix MetaFrame.

Server Hardening

Server hardening measures are specific to the server OS and applications. In the Windows NT Terminal Server/Citrix MetaFrame XP environment, extensive modifications to the registry, directory and file permissions, and registry permissions were required to "secure" the server. Beginning with Windows 2000 and continuing in Windows Server 2003, the vast majority of these changes are made dynamically when Terminal Services mode is invoked. Server hardening in general can be risky—although standard security lockdowns may work with Terminal Servers and well-behaved applications, the vast majority of legacy applications do not fully comply with Microsoft's Terminal Services API and will experience problems.

   To fully harden a Terminal Server (as in the DoD C2 Trusted Computer System Criteria), some changes are still required. Microsoft and Citrix have online databases and security sites that detail changes in server configuration from file and directory permissions, to password and authentication methods, to configuration of server-side protocol stacks. Additional changes to baseline security configurations can be implemented with Microsoft's Security Configuration Editor. For those who want government-type security restrictions, configuration guides (including Windows 2000 Terminal Services) and preconfigured *.inf files for the Security Configuration Editor may be downloaded from the National Security Agency's (NSA) System and Network Attack Center (SNAC) at www.nsa.gov/snac/win2k/.

CAUTION: Never run the automated lockdown tools like the Security Configuration Editor on production servers. Always test first.

Patching known vulnerabilities and exploits with hotfixes and service packs is really fundamental software maintenance, and yet is often overlooked. Built-in features like Windows Update are more robust in Windows Server 2003. Supplemental tools such as the Baseline Security Analyzer, which includes a command-line hotfix checker (HFNetCheck), can help verify the state of the server.

Service management has historically been a manual process. Microsoft designed Windows NT and Windows 2000 with a rather extensive list of services that were installed by default. Windows Server 2003 has eliminated 19 major services from the default installation sequence.

The following is a short summary list of important security changes in Windows Server 2003:

▼ Stronger ACL to stop access to the root directory (c:\).

■ Changed default share ACL from Everyone:F to Everyone:R.

■ Changed DLL search order to start in system directory.

■ Hardened Internet Explorer.

■ Increased restrictions on Anonymous users and changed group membership: Anonymous users are no longer members of "Everyone" by default.

■ Put limits on blank passwords. Changed account permissions; local accounts that have blank passwords cannot be used to remotely connect to a machine.

■ Set LanManCompatibilityLevel=2 on Servers\Domain Controllers, by default. Windows Server 2003 will not emit insecure LanMan responses, without being set to do so.

■ Restricted remote execution of console applications to administrators only.

■ Created two new accounts to run services with lower privileges.

■ IIS not installed by default.

▲ Some services changed to disabled by default, including

  ■ Alerter

  ■ Clipbook

- Distributed link tracking server
- License logging
- Messenger
- NetMeeting remote desktop sharing
- Routing and remote access
- Themes

Microsoft supplies a wide variety of built-in tools to help secure the Terminal Server. In Windows 2003, policy-based enforcement (group policies) is expanded to include Terminal Services–specific policies.

One interesting feature provided by PowerFuse, a third-party environment lockdown utility designed for Terminal Services, is the ability to protect the Terminal Server from "rogue" applications (accidental or intentional). Administrators can define resource consumption limits for applications and the PowerFuse CPUShield will police the application to prevent denial of service.

User Environment Management

Because the user environment and experience in an SBC environment exist on the server, lockdown can be easier than in a distributed computing environment. Conversely, there is a far greater need for such security measures.

In relatively simple (from a security standpoint) Windows networks, Windows' group policies are an effective means of controlling the user environment. In Windows Server 2003, the cumbersome Windows AppSec tool for locking down application availability has been replaced with built-in Software Restriction Polices.

In a Citrix MetaFrame XP server environment, many lockdown tasks are mitigated by Citrix's ability to publish applications and content directly, without the complexities and security problems associated with a full Windows "shell." When possible, running only Published Applications obviates the need to lock down many settings associated with desktops and menus—applications run in a seamless window with no exposure of the underlying Windows shell (explorer.exe).

As the number of users, different policies, and nested policies grow, the viability of group policies diminishes rapidly. Not only are complex nested policies hard to understand and decipher, excessive nesting can slow logon times substantially. Even the Citrix Published Applications are not suitable for all environments. Users may need, or legacy applications may demand, access to Windows shell components. In the worst-case scenarios, applications may be dependent upon "desktop" functionality, but incapable of running correctly when standard group polices are applied. In complex situations, third-party lockdown products like PowerFuse greatly simplify administration. Users and applications can be provided a dynamic locked desktop, complete with an alternative (more secure) Windows shell component. PowerFuse adds a number of essential features, like the ability to control the spawning of child processes and executables. For example, the ability to block calls to launch Internet Explorer from an embedded URL in an e-mail message.

CHAPTER 9

Network Management

In the old days of small work group LANs, it was relatively easy for a system administrator to keep tabs on the status of desktop PCs, servers, and the network simply by looking at the lights on the front of the equipment. As these networks grew in complexity and scope, it became more than any person, or group of people, could do to know the status of all parts of the network at all times. This problem provided the challenge for the first network management system (NMS). The early NMS software was little more than a log reader, similar to the Event Viewer in Windows Server 2003 today. Next, the ability to read status and alert messages in a standard format was added. This standard format became the Simple Network Management Protocol (SNMP). Manufacturers quickly added the ability to format and send SNMP messages to all of their equipment. Today, virtually all network infrastructure devices such as routers, switches, bridges, and CSU/DSUs, as well as servers and operating systems, can report their status using SNMP. It is this capability that makes modern NMS packages like Microsoft Systems Management Server (SMS) and Microsoft Operations Manager (MOM), Citrix Resource Manager (RM), and HP OpenView possible. The ability to receive and collate SNMP messages is only the tip of the iceberg of what an NMS can do and what your organization should use it for.

Although server-based computing is, by nature, more centralized and architecturally simpler than distributed computing, this does not mitigate the need for a strong system management environment (SME). It is even more critical to establish service level agreements for services delivered and to use tools, such as an NMS, to manage them. This chapter discusses general SME messaging standards, SME characteristics including monitoring and reporting for server-based computing, and concepts for SME implementation using tools from Microsoft, Citrix, Hewlett-Packard, and others.

PEOPLE, PROCESSES, AND PRODUCT

Utilizing an NMS is only part of an organization's overall SME. An SME consists of the people, processes, and product ("three Ps") within an organization that effectively manage the computing resources of that organization. "Product" is more accurately "technology," but "two Ps and a T" doesn't have the same punch as "three Ps." We find the simplest way to think of the interrelationship between the three Ps is in terms of service level agreements (SLAs).

SERVICE LEVEL AGREEMENTS

An SLA in this context is an agreement between the IT staff and the user community about the services being provided, the manner in which they are delivered, the responsibilities of the IT support staff, and the responsibilities of the users. An SLA serves many important functions, including setting the expectations of the users about the scope of services being delivered and providing accountability and a baseline of measurement for the IT staff. The established SLAs in your organization also provide the framework for the SME. After all, if you don't first figure out what you are managing and how you will manage it, what good will a tool do you? In addition to incorporating the three Ps, a service level agreement should address the following three areas of responsibility:

▼ **Availability**   This section should explain when the services are provided, the frequency (if appropriate), and the nature of the services.

■ **Performance**   This section describes how the service is to be performed and any underlying processes related to the delivery of the service.

▲ **Usability**   This section should show how to measure whether the service is being used effectively. For example, a measure of success could be infrequent help desk calls.

Table 9-1 shows a sample SLA for an enterprise backup service.

Ideally, the SLA is an extension of the overall business goals. Defining a group of SLAs for an organization that has never used them can be a daunting task. The following tips will help you with the effort:

▼ Start by deciding which parts of your infrastructure go directly to supporting your business goals, and define exactly how that happens.

■ Do not define an SLA in terms of your current support capability. Think "outside the box" regarding how a particular service *should* be delivered. The result will be your goal for the SLA. Now work backward and figure out what has to be done to reach the ideal SLA.

▲ Rather than starting at the ground level with individual SLAs for particular services, try laying down some universal rules for a so-called Master SLA. After all, some things will apply to nearly every service you deliver. A good place to start is with the help desk, where all user calls are taken. Decide how the help desk will handle, prioritize, and assign calls. The problem response time, for example, will be a standard time for all nonpriority calls. Once that is established, you can think about whether different services may need different handling for priority calls. Decide what the mission and goals are of the IT staff overall and how they support the business. Work backward from that to how the service management function must be defined to align with those goals.

Establishing a viable SLA for the user community (whether corporate users or fee-for-service (ASP) users) mandates equivalent SLAs with your providers. For example, most WAN providers (Qwest, Sprint, AT&T) will guarantee various parameters (availability, bandwidth, latency) that impact your ability to deliver service to users. Ensure internal SLAs do not invoke more stringent quality and reliability guarantees than external SLAs.

The subject of defining and working with SLAs is adequate material for a book all its own. Our intention here is to get you started in framing your network management services in terms of SLAs. You will find them to be not only a great help in sorting through the "noise" of information collected, but also an invaluable communication tool for users, IT staff, and management alike.

Volumes to Be Backed Up	Availability	Performance	Usability
Palo Alto data center, Network appliance filer cluster (400GB), HP 9000 Oracle database (120GB), Denver data center, Network appliance filer cluster (800GB), and HP 9000 Oracle database (220GB). Backup device is a Spectra Logic tape library with eight drives using AIT tapes at each data center.	Daily incremental backups of all volumes. Weekly full backups. Monthly full backups. Quarterly full backups. Three months of daily tapes are used, then rotated. Online backups: a snapshot is taken every 4 hours for the NetApp. The last 12 snapshots are available, covering 48 hours. Archive/grooming backup every two weeks.	Backups are scheduled and designed not to affect production system performance. Five weeks of tapes per month are used. Daily log report is generated noting which tapes are in what backup set. Full backups are taken offsite the following Wednesday and are returned according to a three-month cycle. Sample files are restored and verified three times per week. Archive/grooming backup: files not touched in 14 months are written to tape every two weeks and are deleted from production storage after three backups.	Problem response according to standard help desk SLA. Nonpriority requests for restorations and archive turnaround is three days. Service performance reports are published weekly to users via an intranet site.

Table 9-1. SLA for Enterprise Backup

MESSAGING STANDARDS

You will need to be familiar with current messaging standards for network management and understand the basics of how they work in order to effectively plan an SME.

TCP/IP and UDP

We defined TCP/IP and UDP in Chapter 6, but we mention them again here in the context of network management in order to show the different philosophies under which some of the standards were created. To put things in perspective, there are two major components in an SNMP-based management system: the management station and the SNMP agent. The management station polls agents on a cyclic basis to assess status and health. The agent responds to these queries with formatted information. Additionally, the agent can send an unsolicited SNMP "trap" asynchronously when it detects a health- or status-related event. The normal SNMP transport protocol is UDP, which uses a "best effort" delivery mechanism. There is no guarantee the packet will ever arrive at its destination. The advantage is that UDP packets are small and of a similar size, lacking the complexity of a TCP/IP packet.

NOTE: UDP packets are not of fixed size; they are variable up to 65,536 bytes—the largest datagram IP can support. Generally, UDP frames will be 576 bytes or less, because IP requires all network links to support an MTU of 576 bytes. Sending a UDP datagram larger than this risks fragmentation.

Given the limitations of UDP, it may seem that TCP is more appropriate for delivery of management information. This is not necessarily true; it depends on the application. All TCP really does is automatically retransmit if it doesn't receive an acknowledgment (ACK). When running with UDP, the SNMP manager is responsible for detecting the lack of response and retransmitting. Consider the case in which a response packet is lost, and the network remains down for five seconds. With a TCP-based SNMP, TCP will retransmit several times and will eventually deliver the response. The response it delivers will be at least five seconds out-of-date. With UDP, the management console will reissue the request, and when the network is finally operational again, the response will be the most up-to-date possible.

NOTE: A trap, however, can be lost. Generally, administrators don't depend on SNMP traps as the only notification of failures because traps work poorly in a lot of NMS implementations. Instead, the management console periodically polls for status.

TCP/IP also lacks a guaranteed delivery mechanism, but it at least supports packet resequencing and destination routing, making it less prone to delivery failure. This is important when considering which protocol would provide a better transport option for system status and alert messages.

Simple Network Management Protocol

Simple Network Management Protocol (SNMP) is an application layer protocol that uses the underlying transport services of the protocol stack. SNMP version 1 (SNMPv1) uses UDP and IP. The inclusion of SNMPv1 in networking equipment is widespread and you are likely to encounter it. SNMPv2 has been enhanced in a number of ways to make it more robust than its predecessor and is the most common implementation today. Ironically, SNMPv2 fell far short of the vision set forth in its specification, particularly in the area of security. SNMPv3 is the implementation designed to address the security issue as well as the other shortcomings of its predecessors. The current specifications, RFCs, and a supported hardware list can be found at www.snmp.org.

NOTE: SNMPv1 and SNMPv2 have significant security weaknesses. Microsoft implementations rely on these versions and default to one community string (public) and "Accept Packets from all hosts." Immediately upon installation of the SNMP service, these values should be changed to a unique community string and "Accept Packets from these hosts" with a list of valid host addresses. Virtually every LAN/WAN hardware vendor's default implementation of SNMP suffers from these same weaknesses, with community strings of "public," "private," or a documented string, and no trap or manager restrictions. Thus, it is important to always change default SNMP settings.

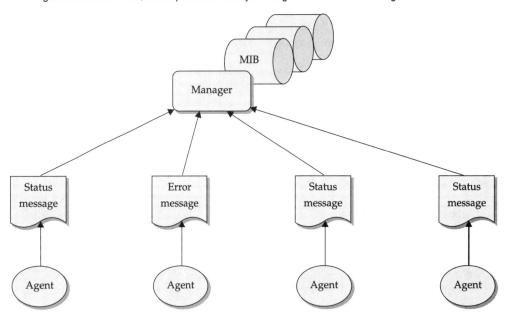

The data exchanged between managers and agents follows a standard hierarchical format described as the management information base (MIB). The manager is responsible for taking the MIB data sent by the agents, interpreting the format, aggregating, collating, and correlating it to higher-level events. The manager's task is also to make this information available for queries or reports. The structure of the MIBs is defined by the IETF in several requests for comments (RFCs), and new MIBs are being created all the time. MIBs for various categories of devices store their information in a standard place on the tree hierarchy. Thus, all routers are in the same branch of the tree, all hubs are in the same branch, and all CSU/DSU devices are in the same branch, as shown in Figure 9-1—a simplified view of a network equipment MIB.

SNMP's *community* is similar to a domain in NT networking. An SNMP community defines a set of agents that are related in some way. A community could define a company division, a geographic location (such as a data center), or even a similar class of equipment, such as all routers. A manager can typically receive and process messages from multiple communities and provide views into the messages separated by those communities, as shown in Figure 9-2.

SNMP is being improved and extended continuously, but the current widespread standard is SNMPv2. Though any implementation must provide the basic features of the manager and agent, vendors are free to add functionality as they see fit based on the needs of the platform. SNMP has the following advantages and limitations.

Some advantages of SNMP include

▼   It works well in its limited scope and is easy to extend.

■   Agents are ubiquitous on network equipment and operating systems.

■   The specifications are simple and easy to implement.

■   The performance overhead of an agent is minimal.

▲   A polling approach to collecting data is good for managed objects on a LAN.

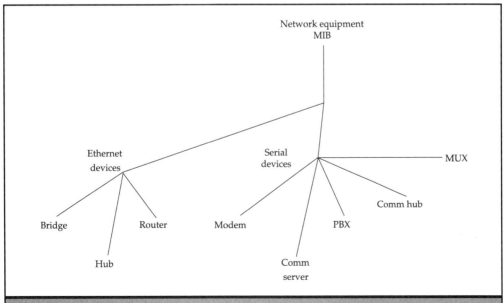

Figure 9-1.   The MIB hierarchy

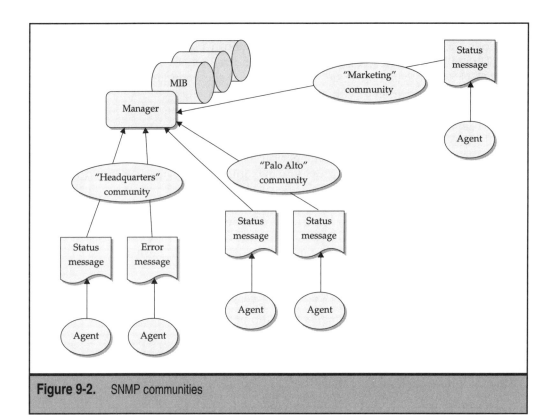

Figure 9-2. SNMP communities

Limitations include

▼ Weak security!

■ It is very limited in scope and does not scale well in large implementations.

■ Its unique messaging structure makes it hard to integrate with other management tools.

■ Polling can cause a large bandwidth overhead in large networks.

▲ It has many vendor-specific extensions to each standard MIB.

NOTE: SNMPv1 and SNMPv2 can coexist by implementing a so-called SNMP Proxy to convert message formats. Many manufacturers of monitoring tools, such as Hewlett-Packard, include such a proxy with their standard offerings.

Remote Monitoring Agent

Defined in RFC 1757, Remote Monitoring Agent (RMON) is an extension of the most current SNMP MIB structure (MIB II) and attempts to address many of its limitations. RMON collects nine types of information:

▼ Host table of all addresses

■ Host statistics

■ Historical data

■ Alarm thresholds

■ Configurable statistics

■ Traffic matrix with all nodes

■ "Host top N" tables

■ Packet capture/protocol analysis

▲ Distributed logging of events

RMON represents the next generation in network monitoring and addresses the need for network planning, fault troubleshooting, and performance tuning better than any other current monitoring implementation. The additional capabilities of RMON change the agent-manager paradigm somewhat. Since sending richer data packets over the network would increase the SNMP demand for bandwidth significantly, implementations of RMON agents are typically "smarter" than their SNMP counterparts. That is, more processing is done on the agent platform, and only aggregated information is sent over the network. The trade-off is that more processing power is needed on the agent platform.

CMIP

Similar to RMON, the complexity required of a Common Management Information Protocol (CMIP) agent and the potential amount of information the agent sends over the network are high. It is a common feature in telecommunications equipment specifications, but it is rarely used in practice. It was probably included due to the fact that messages can be sent over an alternate channel from those used by data.

NOTE: SNMP is common in telecommunications equipment, even though the ISO standards say it shouldn't be. For example, the Sonet D1+D2+D3 bytes are an out-of-band communications channel used to communicate control and management information between Sonet equipment. According to the Sonet specifications, CMIP is used over this channel. If you look at actual Sonet networks, the D1+D2+D3 channel is actually carrying either Bellcore's old ASCII command language, or SNMP.

CMIP functions similarly to SNMP in that it sends an alert if certain thresholds are reached or a fault is detected.

Some advantages of CMIP are

▼ Its object-oriented approach is very ordered, making extensions relatively easy to accomplish and manage.

■ It supports communication between managers as well as managers and agents.

▲ It supplies a standard framework for automation.

Limitations include

▼ It is not widely supported in the data-networking world.

■ It is the most complex protocol and puts high demands on the agent platform.

■ Its sheer complexity also means that CMIP implementations from different vendors frequently cannot communicate.

▲ Its extensible messaging architecture can cause high network bandwidth utilization.

SYSTEM MANAGEMENT ENVIRONMENT FOR SERVER-BASED COMPUTING

In a server-based computing environment, where information resources are centralized, the need for tools and procedures that serve to decrease the frequency of unscheduled downtime is more important than ever. The organizational mandate for on-demand computing and full, secure control of the environment dictates that the operations necessary to support an SBC environment have more in common with the Network Operation Center (NOC) of an Internet service provider (ISP) or commercial hosting service than with a traditional, distributed corporate network. It is no longer acceptable for IT staff to discover problems after they occur, as an audit function. They must have tools and procedures in place to perform predictive analysis on potential problems and to isolate and contain problems during the troubleshooting process. An effective systems management environment will address these needs through measurement of the various systems and through the enforcement of service level agreements. The data collected during measurement can be used in troubleshooting and making corrections. For example, if a MetaFrame server crashes due to an application fault, the Citrix RM package will have recorded which applications were running at the time of the crash. Without this information, it would be challenging to find the crash's exact cause. An effective SME has the following objectives:

▼ Improving the availability and performance of the SBC resources.

■ Lowering the cost of IT maintenance and support services.

▲ Providing a service-level view of SBC resources.

The "people" part of the three Ps is made up not only of users and IT staff, but also any group affected by the services being delivered. For many organizations, this means external customers, business partners, and even competitors. The SLAs associated with the services being delivered, and the associated reports, are the "process" part of the three Ps and are, collectively, the tool that shows whether the preceding objectives are being met. The "product" consists of all the hardware and software necessary to deliver the information needed to measure the SLAs. Any technology utilized in the SME should meet the following basic requirements:

▼ **Provide a central point of control for managing heterogeneous systems**
A "central point" refers to one tool or collection mechanism used to gather information from all sources. The actual data repository could be distributed to multiple locations where administrative activity takes place.

■ **Allow event management across heterogeneous systems and network devices**   The toolset should support all the common operating system and network hardware platforms and provide enough extensibility for custom interfaces to be configured, if necessary.

▲ **Provide service-level views of any portion of the infrastructure**   A "service-level view" is an aggregation of lower-level events that correlate to show the impact of various failures in terms of an established SLA. A message stating "Server 110 has crashed with an unknown error" has far less meaning than "Application service capacity has decreased by 10 percent" and "Application services for users in the San Antonio region have been interrupted."

To further refine these requirements, more detail on the exact duties to be incorporated in the SME is needed. Defining in specific terms what will be measured and how it will be measured will greatly aid in the selection of the proper technology. We will discuss SME tools later in the chapter.

Configuration Management

Arguably, the most common problem in managing distributed computer systems is configuration management. Even companies with very organized IT staffs can have complete chaos on the desktop with regard to which application or application versions are installed and which changes to the operating system are allowed. In an SBC environment, the chaos, so to speak, is limited to the data centers, but the need for configuration management is even greater. If a user changes a setting on his PC that causes it to crash, that user experiences unscheduled downtime. If an administrator makes a change to a MetaFrame server that causes it to crash, every user currently logged on to that server experiences unscheduled downtime. An effective SME must have in place controls to restrict and audit changes within the data center. A configuration management system should have the following characteristics:

▼ **A clearly defined operational baseline**   The baseline defines the starting point for the management process.

■ **A change tracking system**   A process for requesting, submitting, prioritizing, approving, and testing changes to the operational baseline. Once a change has completed the process, it becomes part of the baseline.

■ **Defined categories and priorities for changes**   For example, some changes need to be tracked, such as changes to group membership and administrative rights, but can be safely implemented as an extension of the current baseline. Others must be implemented very quickly and may disrupt user activity, such as critical security patches. From a software management perspective, most organization configuration management systems differentiate between patches, enhancements, and major revisions, and often employ a "release" process where any or all of these must be tested and certified in a development/test environment before implementation in production systems.

▲ **Implementation procedures**   Necessary steps that must be taken before implementation, such as how to save the current state before a change, how to decide if a change is not working, how to back out of a change, and how to use collected information to modify the original change request and resubmit it.

Modern computing environments are far too complex for an automated tool to check and restrict any change. A combination of an effective automated tool and "best practice" procedures for change management is the key to a successful configuration management function.

Security Management

Security management serves to ensure that users only have access to the applications, servers, and other computing resources they are authorized to use. Again, a combination of automated tools and employee policies are called for. The implementation of an Internet firewall to prevent unauthorized external access will do nothing to prevent a disgruntled employee from accessing and publishing confidential information. Only the combination of automated internal system limitations, effective monitoring, published "acceptable use" policies, and committed enforcement of those policies can serve to deter such unforeseen incidents.

Alerting

As we discussed in Chapter 8, it is not enough simply to log attempts to bypass security within the SBC environment. An effective SME should include a network management tool that will actively alert the appropriate personnel if a security breach of sufficient severity is detected. For example, say an employee discovers the registry settings where his group information is stored and figures out how to change that value to Admin without using the management console. First, the registry should not allow the change to be made by that user because it has been locked against changes by anyone not currently in the Admin group. However, if the change is somehow made, the system should log an event in the event log (auditing). The management agent program on that system should watch the event log, detect the event, and send a page to the security administrator. Alternatively, the offending user's account could be locked, as shown in Figure 9-3.

IP Address and Host Name Management

In a large enterprise network, managing the identity of each node on the network can be a daunting task. Many network management tools will "autodiscover" nodes on the network, but this task can be laborious and chew up processing and network bandwidth

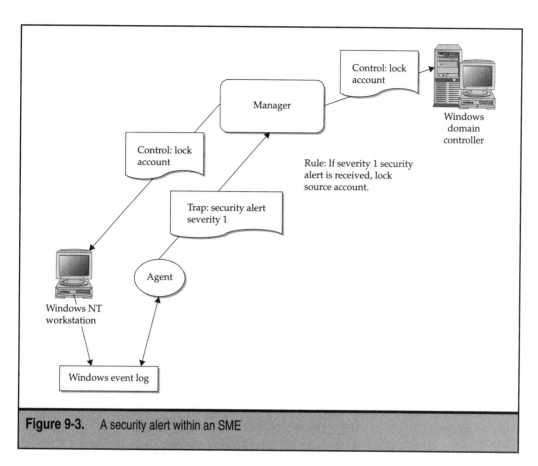

Figure 9-3. A security alert within an SME

unless the addressing and naming schemes are well ordered. An effective SME will include policies for standard naming practices as well as an efficient IP addressing scheme. There are several common attributes for host naming that must be considered:

▼ The namespace must be self-documenting. If you need to refer to a cross-reference chart to decode the host name, the namespace is not administratively usable. As a minimum, the namespace should self-document the server, client, and peripheral (printer) pieces of the network infrastructure.

■ For Windows environments that use Active Directory and DNS:

   ■ Ensure only valid characters are used (no underscores).

   ■ Keep it short. DNS, and hence Active Directory, namespace prepend data. A fully qualified host named CitrixServer01-Win-Seattle.Child Domain.ParentDomain.com may be self-documenting, but it is unmanageable (and nearly un-typeable). A host name of CTX01W-SEA.ChildDomain.ParentDomain.com is far more usable.

▲ For Windows environments that also use WINS:

  ■ NETBIOS host names are limited to 15 characters (a Microsoft specification).

  ■ Observe the limitations on allowable characters (\ * + = | : ; " ? < > , are prohibited). Some "allowable" NETBIOS name characters (@ # $ % ^ & ( ) _ ' { } . ~ !) are incompatible with the DNS character set and should not be used.

  ■ Try to match the NETBIOS name to the DNS host name.

Some ideas we have seen effectively used are

▼ Create host names based on department and geographic location, followed by a numerical value. For example, a user's Windows terminal in the Seattle accounting division might have SEAWBT-ACC16 as a host name.

■ Create host names incorporating the type of device. (To extend the preceding example, an LPR printer might be named SEALPR-ACC4 or SEAP-ACCHP8100.)

▲ Using octets within an IP address to map a host identity should be avoided. Although some limited identity can be established, this invariably leads to an IP address scheme that is neither hierarchical nor extensible.

NOTE: Many large organizations use Dynamic Host Control Protocol (DHCP) and Dynamic Domain Name Service (DDNS) to dynamically assign IP addresses and host names, respectively, to network nodes. These services have several advantages, including automated host name standardization and reduction of the number of IP addresses in use at one time by assigning temporary ones from a pool. If you utilize these services in your organization, be aware that it may complicate the SME if the NMS you choose is not compatible with, or not aware of, these services. An NMS must be able to discover and manage dynamically assigned hosts, or you will have the problem of all of these nodes going unmanaged.

Using Service Level Agreements

As we mentioned earlier, a service level agreement defines the policies and procedures that will be used within the SME. The execution of those policies and procedures will rely in equal parts on automated tools and "acceptable use" policies that the employees within the organization must abide by. Employing SLAs within the SME will have the following effects:

▼ **User expectations will be much closer to the reality of how a particular service is delivered.** Many users see the network as a public utility that has 100-percent uptime. This is a good goal but often is not realistic. Publishing an SLA will show the users what *is* realistic and what their options are if the service delivery doesn't conform to the SLA. After all, very few public utilities can show a track record of sustained 100-percent uptime.

■ **IT staff growth will slow.** IT organizations without SLAs tend to spend an inordinate amount of time "fighting fires" because service personnel don't know where the boundaries are for the service they are providing. Users don't know where those boundaries are either. The cumulative effect is that users will inevitably try to get as much service as they can, and the service staff will try to satisfy the users by delivering as much as they can. This serves to increase the number of service personnel needed.

▲ **IT service quality will increase.** When the service is well defined and understood by users and service personnel alike, the delivery of that service will be more consistent. This happens for a couple of reasons. First, the people trained to administer the systems have more time to pay attention to their effective management since they spend less time fighting fires. Second, the users' expectations of the service will be more in line with its delivery, which will reduce the number of complaints. A relatively new concept, Application Quality-of-Service (Application QoS), is a measure of how effectively applications are delivered to the user and thus can be one measure of IT service quality in an SBC environment. Application QoS service level views can be found in some of the network management tools we will discuss later in the chapter.

System Management Environment Architecture

With what has been defined so far, we can now look in detail at some specific duties covered by an effective SME for the data center. The overall architecture should include, at a minimum, the functions described in the following sections for the entire SBC infrastructure.

Network Discovery

It would be incredibly tedious if you had to enter information about each node before it could be managed. Fortunately, nearly every modern NMS tool provides the ability to actively discover information about nodes on the network. Though most polling is TCP/IP-based, an effective NMS uses a variety of other methods to discover nodes, including NetBIOS and SAP broadcasts. The basic philosophy is "anything that will work." The majority of nodes will respond *somehow*, and those that don't can be handled as an exception and entered manually. Network discovery is a function shared by both the agent and the manager, and is shown in Figure 9-4.

Hardware and Software Inventory

This function is similar to node discovery in design but is much more detailed. Once a node is discovered and is identified, the discovery process will interrogate the device to find out about the software and hardware configuration. If fat clients must be used, this can be an invaluable tool to "meter" software—that is, to find out if the number of licenses

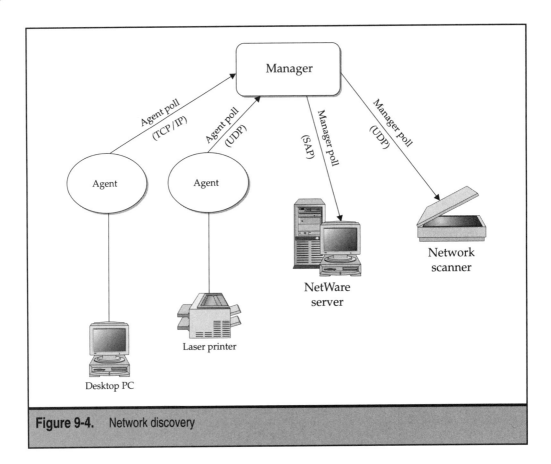

Figure 9-4. Network discovery

purchased matches the number of licenses in use. It can also aid in creating inventories of hardware that need to be upgraded for a particular project. Similar functionality is available for peripheral and network devices. Hardware and software inventory data is usually rolled into the overall configuration management process.

Monitoring and Messaging

The most common agent function is to "watch" the system and look for problems as defined in a rule base. Ideally, this rule base is administered centrally and shared by all similar agents. The agent's job is to send an appropriate message whenever an item in the rule base is triggered, as illustrated in Figure 9-5. These items can consist of both errors, or traps, and collections of information such as traffic thresholds, disk utilization, and log sizes.

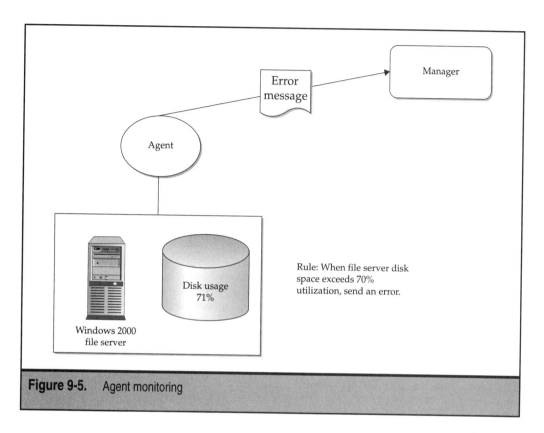

Figure 9-5. Agent monitoring

With SNMP-based systems, the agent processes events and sends messages with little to no filtering or processing on the local system. This is acceptable because SNMP messages are typically small and not likely to flood the network. In systems with more intelligent agents, where much more detailed information can be collected, the agent has the added task of collating or summarizing the data before sending it to the manager. Otherwise, the added traffic caused by unsummarized messages could cause a bandwidth utilization problem.

NOTE: SNMP uses standard UDP ports 161 and 162. Port 162 is reserved for traps only. As a result, it can be made subject to bandwidth utilization rules in a router (queuing) or in a device such as the Packeteer Packetshaper. Similarly, CMIP reserves UDP and TCP ports 163 for the agent and 164 for the manager. These ports are common, but your platform may use different ones.

Management by Exception or Negative Monitoring   This can be a function of an agent or a manager. Sometimes *not* receiving a piece of information from a system is just as critical as receiving one. A system may become unresponsive without ever sending a trap. In cases like this, it is useful to have a periodic "heartbeat"—a small message that says nothing more than, "I'm here." If the agent or manager does not receive this heartbeat, an alert is generated for follow-up. We have found this type of monitoring to be a crucial part of the SME since not all platforms send alerts when they are supposed to.

Network Monitoring and Tracking   The NETMON program, which ships with versions of Windows, can track network traffic at a very detailed level, but its scope is limited to the data streams coming into and going out of the server it is running on, or the similar nodes it can recognize. An SME must measure network traffic and problems between any two arbitrary points. It should follow established rules to do detailed monitoring on critical paths, such as between data centers, an Internet router, or between MetaFrame servers and back-end database servers. Thresholds can be established that serve to guarantee acceptable performance and send alerts if those thresholds are reached. In many ways, an SBC environment's heavy reliance on network performance makes this one of the most crucial monitoring functions. Effective monitoring in the SME can provide critical data for predictive analysis about when the network is approaching saturation before it ever happens. Figure 9-6 shows how agents at multiple sites can feed data to a centralized manager.

Remote Diagnostics   By using the MetaFrame shadowing function, administrators can attach to and run a user's session anywhere on the network from a central location. Similarly, an SME should offer the ability to attach to network equipment and perform basic operations, such as uploading and downloading configurations and rebooting. If a particular node cannot be reached, the SME should provide enough data from surrounding nodes to determine what is wrong with the unresponsive equipment.

Data Collection
While monitoring is the primary duty of the agent, data collection is the primary responsibility of the manager. The manager must record all incoming information without filtering, or auditing could be compromised. Relevant information can be easily extracted from the manager's database using query and reporting tools.

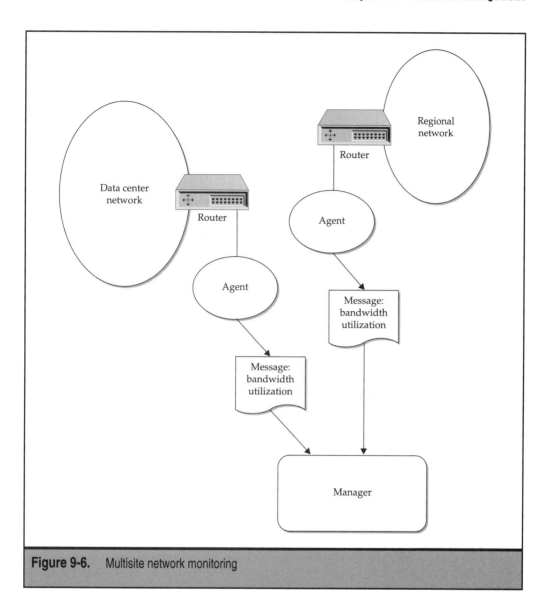

Figure 9-6.   Multisite network monitoring

Data Collation and Event Correlation

There should be a function above the level of the manager or managers (see Figure 9-7) that collates data from all sources and compares this data with established patterns and

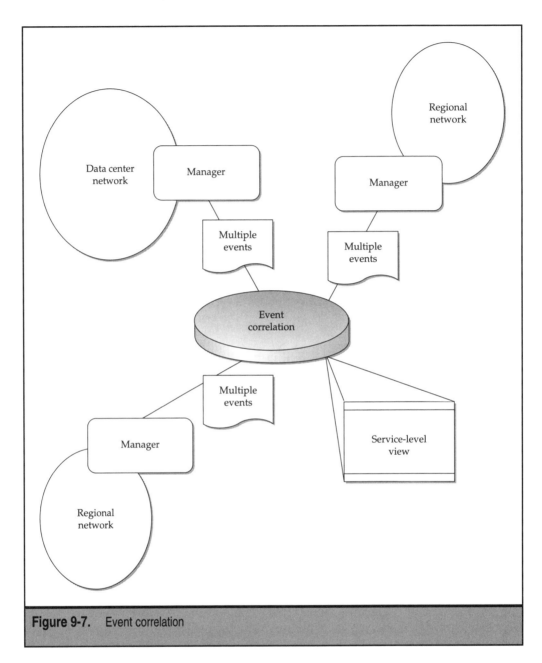

Figure 9-7. Event correlation

rules. This type of collation is called *event correlation*. When the events have been correlated, the result can be expressed in terms of an SLA.

For example, a large enterprise network has a router failure between a large regional office and the main data center. The router sends a trap saying that the memory stack has been corrupted. Immediately after the router goes down, several other traps indicating that the regional office cannot be reached are sent from surrounding nodes at the data center. The manager in the data center collects several hundred messages in only a few minutes. At the point the first critical message is received by the manager, an automatic page is sent to the system administrator on duty. When the system administrator logs on and begins investigating the problem, he sees the hundreds of messages in the database. Fortunately, the event correlation function has categorized the different messages for him. He checks the display of service level views and sees that the SLAs for network connectivity and application services to the regional office are not being met. His reaction to these issues is defined in the SLA for the associated service. Now he can use filtered queries to examine the detailed messages from across the network in order to solve the problem.

NOTE: Though having service level views into problems is extremely useful, sometimes getting the information as soon as it is sent by an agent is more desirable. It is perfectly acceptable to define certain key events from key agents so that they travel the entire escalation path directly to an administrator for follow-up. It is even possible to define some agents so that they send a page at the same time that a trap is sent across the network. (Sometimes bad news needs to travel faster than good news for an SLA to be met.)

Other SME Functions

A few additional functions common to an SME take on slightly different roles when applied to the SBC infrastructure. We discuss these next.

Software Distribution/Unattended Install   When thinking in terms of a thin client, MetaFrame performs the function of software distribution. There is no reason to distribute an application any further than the server farm when nothing is running on the desktop except the ICA Client. Thus, the need for unattended installation of desktop software loses its importance (security updates and core OS updates remain important). Even with a server farm containing 50 servers, it is not that difficult to install applications manually if necessary. This would be a far different proposition with 5000 desktops.

NOTE: Fortunately, it is not necessary to install applications manually on your server farm. We will discuss methods for streamlining this process in Chapters 12 and 13.

If you don't have the luxury of taking the entire enterprise to thin-client devices, software distribution and installation are more important and should be considered a critical part of the SME. We will discuss this function as part of the tools discussion later in the chapter. Figure 9-8 shows software distribution in a thin-client network, while Figure 9-9 shows the same function in a traditional distributed, or fat-client, network. For Enterprises that need remote security and core OS updates, Microsoft provides a new service, the Software Update Service (SUS), that links to Windows update and allows administrators to apply a subset of Microsoft's Systems Management Server (SMS) capabilities to Windows 2000 clients and servers, Windows Server 2003, and Windows XP.

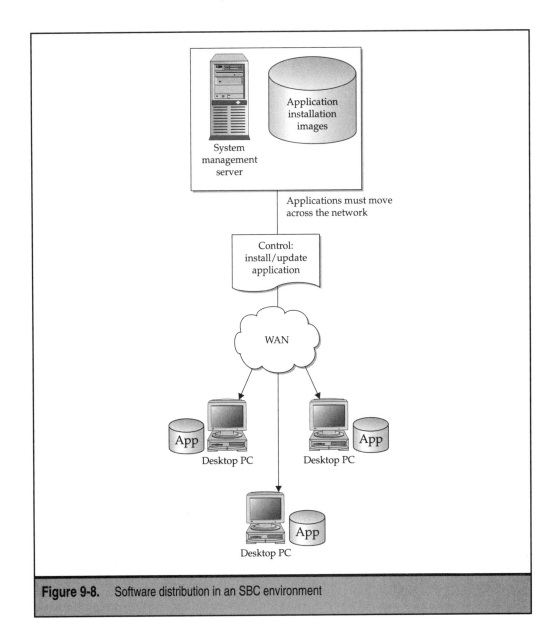

Figure 9-8.   Software distribution in an SBC environment

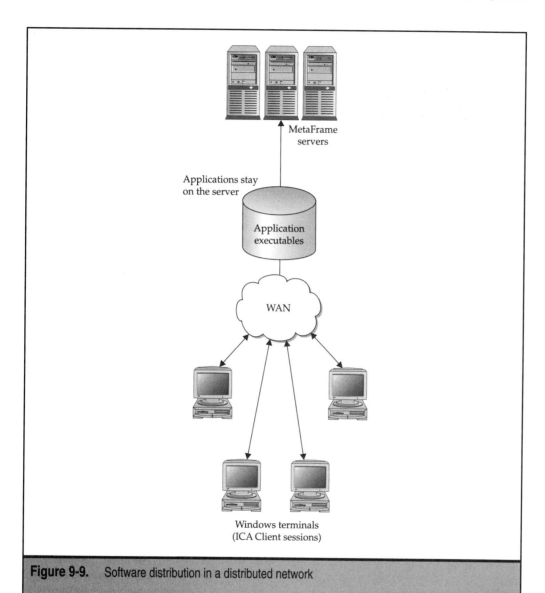

Figure 9-9.   Software distribution in a distributed network

Software Metering   Similarly, software metering becomes far simpler in a server-based computing environment. All the applications are running on the server farm, and administrators can use Citrix RM to determine which users are running which applications. Furthermore, scripting techniques can be used to assign application access to user groups and to lock down the desktop to the point where users cannot run unauthorized applications. PowerFuse, one of the "security" tools mentioned in Chapter 8, has an added benefit of allowing an application to be published to a large number of users while restricting concurrency to stay within licensing limitations. We will discuss these methods in Chapters 12, 13, 15, and 20.

In a distributed client network, software metering becomes much more complex and difficult to manage. Typically, an agent running locally on the desktop takes on the task of conversing with a manager and determining whether a user is authorized to run a particular application. The agent also takes any punitive measures necessary.

Desktop Lockdown   A common function of SME tools has historically been to lock down the desktop so that users cannot install unauthorized applications or make changes to the local operating system that would make it unstable or affect performance. Chapter 15 discusses desktop lockdown of the MetaFrame XP servers using Group Policies and profiles as well as third-party applications like RES PowerFuse, AppSense, and triCerat. In a distributed environment, these same tools, in addition to other major SME tools from Microsoft and HP, provide this functionality for each desktop.

Desktop Remote Diagnostics   In the past, remote control tools such as PCAnywhere from Symantec were used to connect to a user's desktop and allow an administrator to see what the user sees. With MetaFrame, the session shadowing feature built into the ICA session protocol provides this functionality from a central location in an efficient manner.

Management Reporting

The parts of the SME architecture presented so far have dealt mainly with collecting information and controlling the environment. Publishing and sharing the collected information and the results of those efforts for control are just as important. The value of management information increases the more it is shared. The IT staff should adopt a policy of "no secrets" and share information in terms of measured SLAs with users and management. That being said, it is also important to present the information formatted appropriately for the audience. Management typically is most interested in bottom-line information and would not find a detailed network performance graph very useful. A one- or two-page report listing each service level and the key metrics used to show whether that service level is being met would likely be more appropriate. Users make up a diverse group in most large organizations, making it prudent to err on the side of showing too much information. We have found that publishing the user SLA reports on a corporate intranet is a convenient method since it provides a central location for the information. If a more proactive method for distributing the information is desired, the URL for the intranet page can be e-mailed to the users.

NOTE: The format of your reports should *not* be determined by the capabilities of the measurement and reporting tools. The report should reflect the results of business-driven service level agreements in order to be useful to their recipients. If your SME tools can produce the reports using this format, so much the better. If they cannot, don't be afraid to process some of the reporting data manually until an automated system can be worked out.

Communication Plan Part of effective reporting is establishing a communication plan. A communication plan can also be thought of in this context as a "reporting SLA." You must decide who is to receive the reports, at what frequency, and at what level of detail. If interaction between individuals or groups for review or approval is needed, define how this is going to happen and document it as part of the plan. One very effective approach that is gaining popularity is to use the MetaFrame Secure Access Manager (MSAM) access product (discussed in detail in Chapter 16) to dynamically publish these reports to users, based on their role login, via a web interface that also contains other useful content for their job function.

On the subject of what to publish, we have found the following reports to be very useful.

Daily Reports The idea behind a daily report is to provide users and management with a concise view of performance against SLAs. The report should show only key indicators for each SLA. Sometimes called a *hot sheet*, this report should only be one or two pages in length. Figure 9-10 shows an example of such a report. The ideal delivery mechanism for such a report is on an intranet site (such as an MSAM site, as discussed earlier) or through e-mail. Enterprises often combine the hot sheet with other pertinent information that may effect user service over the next 24 to 72 hours, such as downtime or approved configuration changes from the configuration management process.

Periodic Reporting Periodic reports should have more detail than daily reports. At whatever interval is defined in the communication plan, detailed performance information should be published to users and management. This type of report should show *all* indicators used to measure SLA performance. The data used to generate this type of report is

Daily Report									
Network Connectivity	Target	Mon	Tues	Wed	Thurs	Fri	WTD	MTD	YTD
*Availability		Fri-Sun	Mon	Tues	Wed	Thurs	WTD	MTD	YTD
Lost User Hours	5hrs per yr.								
Core Hours (9AM-8PM)	per user	0	3				3	23	23
All Hours (except maint.)		0	3				3	23	23
Servers-Lost User Hours	15min/week								
Core Hours (9AM-8PM)	in hours	0	0				0	0	5
All Other Hours (except maint.)		0	0				0	0	5
Perfect Days (0 Lost Hours)		1	0				1	29	135
*Usability									
Total 911 Calls	1 per week	0	0				0	0	45
*Performance									
# User sessions monitored	564								
Hours 'Slow'	0	0	0				0	3	7

Figure 9-10. A daily report or hot sheet

also used for predictive analysis or *trending*. For example, periodic views of disk space utilization will show how fast new disk space is consumed and when new storage should be put online. Trend reports allow you to stay ahead of demand and avoid resource-based outages.

ENTERPRISE SME TOOLS

We consider two classifications of tools in this discussion: system management tools and framework tools. Framework tools are designed to manage virtually all components in the enterprise, including servers, routers, backplanes, and anything with a local management agent. Framework tools can integrate with other tools such as those for help desk call tracking. They are designed to be extensible and often come with a built-in scripting capability to allow them to manage equipment that otherwise wouldn't be. Examples of such tools include HP OpenView, Tivoli Netview, and CA UniCenter TNG. Framework tools can include targeted component programs for doing specific functions, and they often overlap with system management tools. However, they are really intended for large enterprise networks.

NOTE: The Citrix MetaFrame Network Manager integrates into enterprise framework tools. Currently, Network Manager requires Citrix MetaFrame XPe (not XPa or XPs) with Feature Release 3 (recommended), Microsoft base SNMP service, and compilation of the Citrix MIBs into the framework manager's MIB database. Network Manager support is limited to Windows-based versions of the framework management platforms.

System management tools are far more targeted in scope and typically focus on only part of the infrastructure. Examples of such tools are MetaFrame Resource Management (RM), CiscoWorks 2000, Microsoft Operations Manager (MOM), and Microsoft System Management Server (SMS). System management tools fit well within a large management framework. Since framework tools often sacrifice deep functionality for broad coverage, the combination of the two is often required. This paradigm of cooperative management tools is covered in depth in the white paper entitled "Complementing Enterprise Management Platforms with Microsoft SMS," available from D. H. Brown Associates (www.dhbrown.com). Since this book's focus is on MetaFrame and Terminal Services, we will provide a detailed look at RM, MOM, and SMS and leave the evaluation of framework tools to the reader.

MetaFrame Resource Management

RM is the only management product specifically designed for MetaFrame and Terminal Services. It is an invaluable tool for collecting information in a session-based format on applications in use and system resources consumed. Its key features include audit trail capability, system monitoring, and billing reports.

RM can be used with most ODBC-compliant databases such as Microsoft SQL Server and Oracle. A wide range of data is captured, including applications used and the time they are in use, as well as logs of connections, disconnections, and duration.

TIP: We recommend creating a file Data Source Name (DSN) (as opposed to a system DSN) because it saves time when setting up multiple servers. The DSN definition file can be placed on a file server and loaded on each MetaFrame server as needed. We also recommend setting the database to purge data automatically every few weeks or so if billing is not being used. If billing is being used, it will purge the data as part of its process.

Many graphs can be created from various system metrics, such as application ranking and system utilization over time. The following shows some of the report types that are available:

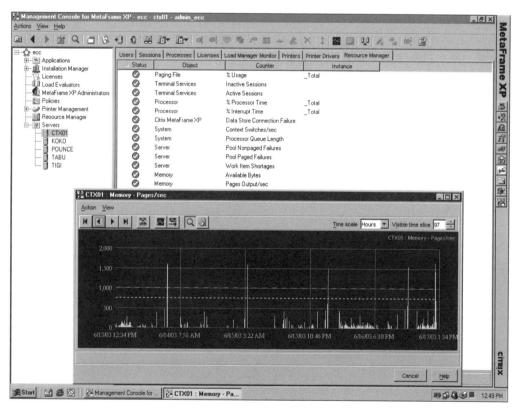

RM tracks over 30 real-time performance metrics and displays them with green, yellow, or red status indicators. One or multiple servers can be monitored from the same screen. Event thresholds can be defined, and when reached, RM can send out an SNMP message, page, or e-mail.

CAUTION: The default alarm profile was designed for a small server with a light load. A new profile needs to be created after collecting a baseline of information for a few days or weeks. The period should be long enough to get a representative sample of usage. The problem is that certain counters fluctuate wildly, and unless the alarm profile thresholds are set high enough, RM will generate alarms too frequently.

If your organization wishes to use a charge-back model, the RM billing services can be used. Fees can be tracked for connection time and various types of system utilization. Users can be grouped into cost centers for reporting.

When RM is used in a server farm, the data collection service runs in the background of each MetaFrame server, as shown in Figure 9-11.

Microsoft System Management Server

SMS 2.0, the current version of System Management Server, provides its services through interaction with the underlying Windows Management Instrumentation (WMI), though it does have limited ability to receive and read SNMP and CMIP messages. SMS 2.0 adds significant features for Enterprise users, to include Active Directory integration and services optimization for low-bandwidth remote users.

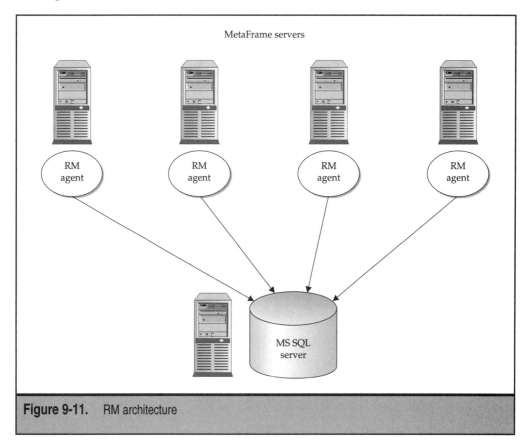

Figure 9-11. RM architecture

Windows Management Instrumentation

WMI is an implementation of the Desktop Management Task Force's (DMTF) Web-Based Enterprise Management (WBEM) initiative. It utilizes the Common Information model (CIM), also defined by the DMTF, to represent network nodes in an object-oriented fashion. SMS creates a global view of information resources using information gleaned from the network. It works very well for status reporting and does provide some downstream management in the form of remote control and diagnostics, software inventory, distribution and metering, and hardware inventory.

SMS is part of the Microsoft BackOffice suite of products. It can provide detailed monitoring functions for other members of the BackOffice family and store its accumulated information in a SQL Server database. A small client program acts as the SMS agent and provides the server with relevant statistical and error information.

SMS version 2.0 has been enhanced to support thousands of client nodes on a single server instance, though for purposes of practical deployment you will at least want to run a cluster of two servers.

SMS version 2.0 has been enhanced to include a wide range of support features, including

▼ The Software Update Services Feature Pack. This is specifically designed to quickly and effectively apply critical security updates for Windows and Office. This Feature Pack provides the following tools:

■ Security Update Inventory Tool

■ Microsoft Office Inventory Tool for Updates

■ Distribute Software Updates Wizard

■ SMS Web Reporting Tool with Web Reports Add-in for Software Updates

▲ Management of most Microsoft OS platforms. The native Microsoft SUS cannot manage patch deployment for Win9x of WinNT systems; SMS can.

Microsoft Windows 2000, together with the Active Directory service, makes it possible to use Group Policy to manage desktops. Group Policy is designed primarily to give organizations better control over user and computer settings, and thus make it easier to standardize desktop operating environments. Group Policy can also be used to install software on certain machines. Although Group Policy can scale to meet the needs of organizations of any size, its software distribution features are very limited in their functionality, and are intended primarily for smaller organizations. Medium-sized and large organizations will find the advanced software distribution features of SMS meet their needs far better than Group Policy, providing benefits such as

▼ Complete hardware and software inventory for effective planning of software rollouts

■ Rich targeting based upon this inventory to ensure the right software pieces get to the right users and machines

■ A complete status system for tracking success and failure of distributions

- ■ A full scheduling system for determining when and how the software should be installed

- ■ A simple, web-based reporting tool for extracting all of this information

- ▲ Automated, WAN-aware distribution components for ensuring that software can flow easily throughout your enterprise without adversely affecting your network

The functionality provided by these tools is completely integrated with Systems Management Server inventory and software distribution to offer a simplified, largely automated solution for the deployment of security and Microsoft Office software updates.

Windows 2000 Server and Windows Server 2003 Management

With Windows 2000 Server and Windows Server 2003, the WMI programs are built into the operating system. Active Directory provides a global view of resources and abstracts the resources available from one server to be equally available to all users in a domain, or across domains.

Microsoft Operations Manager

Microsoft Operations Manager (MOM) is Microsoft's latest effort to migrate Windows platforms to Enterprise management platform status. It provides the first true Microsoft "Enterprise" event management and reporting capabilities by integrating event management and alerting from multiple servers into a single entity. MOM works as a snap-in to the Microsoft Management Console for a consistent look and feel and supports virtually every Microsoft server environment, from multiple SMS servers to Exchange 2000, to Terminal Services. To extend the functionality of MOM, Citrix has released the Citrix MetaFrame XP Management Pack for the Microsoft Operations Manager (MOM) 2000 and Citrix MetaFrame XP Provider for Microsoft Windows Management Instrumentation (WMI). These products integrate monitoring of MetaFrame XP servers and server farms into Microsoft Operations Manager and give Citrix customers greater flexibility in managing MetaFrame XP server farms. MOM provides an extensible management interface for interoperability with UNIX systems. Most importantly for the IT staffer: MOM is essentially ready to run (and generate reports and manage events) out of the box. Specific key features include

- ▼ **Distributed event management**   MOM 2000 captures a wide variety of system and applications events from Windows systems distributed across an Enterprise environment and aggregates them into a central event repository. These events can be consolidated to provide administrators with a high-level view of server and service availability, while also allowing an operator to drill down easily into the detailed event stream, all from a single console view at their desk.

- **Rules**   Administrator-created rules in Microsoft Operations Manager 2000 allow the system to react automatically to incoming message streams, either to respond to a specific fault scenario with a predefined action, or to consolidate the messages into a more meaningful or significant event. Such rules allow MOM 2000 to react intelligently to anticipated event patterns, triggering actions or administrative alerts. Rules can also link an event sequence to Citrix KnowledgeBase articles, instantly providing operators with guidance on probable causes, the approved response to a specific problem scenario and links to additional information.

- **Alerts**   Any MOM 2000 rule can be configured to generate specific alerts with associated severity levels. An alert can represent a single event or multiple events from many sources. At any time, an administrator can drill down on an alert to trace its history, the events associated with it and any related Citrix KnowledgeBase articles. In addition, alerts can optionally trigger e-mails, pages, SNMP traps, and scripts to notify specific system operators and other management systems of emerging issues.

- **Reporting**   MOM 2000 provides access to a broad range of pre-configured reports and charts. The reports generated allow administrators to review, at a glance, the status of systems and services on the network and to plan changes to the infrastructure based on performance and availability data. MOM 2000 can generate HTML snapshots of all generated reports. These can then be exported to a web server for access from web browsers, meeting the requirement to make performance data visible to the user and management communities.

MOM and Citrix MetaFrame

The Citrix MetaFrame XP Management Pack is a plug-in to Microsoft Operations Manager that enables system administrators to monitor the health and availability of MetaFrame XPe servers and server farms, and anticipate and react quickly to many problems that may occur. The Citrix MetaFrame XP Management Pack interprets and reports on information supplied by the Citrix MetaFrame XP Provider software that runs on MetaFrame XPe servers, and also on system events generated on XPe servers. The Citrix MetaFrame XP Management Pack provides system administrators with real-time event and performance monitoring of MetaFrame XPe servers and server farms, from the MOM Administrator console. The Citrix MetaFrame XP Management Pack also includes an extensive knowledge base, with links to Citrix KnowledgeBase articles and other sources of information, which administrators can use to interpret events and troubleshoot problems.

Figure 9-12 shows a typical MOM Administrator Console display of open alerts from Citrix MetaFrame servers.

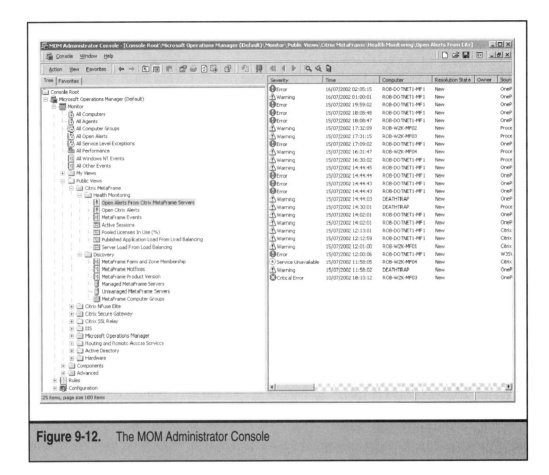

Figure 9-12. The MOM Administrator Console

The following key features are provided when MOM and the Citrix MetaFrame XP Management Pack are integrated into an SBC environment:

▼ **Event management** The Citrix MetaFrame XP Management Pack captures a variety of events from MetaFrame servers and server farms. These events are collated and then presented to the administrator via the MOM Administrator Console, allowing an overall view of MetaFrame server operation.

■ **Performance monitoring** You can use the Citrix MetaFrame XP Management Pack to monitor MetaFrame server performance. Rules can be customized and new rules created to set thresholds for key performance attributes in the server farm.

■ **Extensive knowledge base** The Citrix MetaFrame XP Management Pack includes an extensive product support knowledge base, including links to relevant Citrix KnowledgeBase articles. Centralized access to information about managing MetaFrame servers enables administrators to quickly interpret events and troubleshoot problems.

■ **Customizable rules and alerts**   You can configure the Citrix MetaFrame XP Management Pack to alter how it responds to an event. You do this by modifying and extending the rules to best suit your environment. For example, you can configure the rule for the ICA session disconnection rate so that the alert that is triggered is meaningful and appropriate to your site. Citrix KnowledgeBase documentation is available to help you with this customization.

■ **Citrix MetaFrame views**   Citrix MetaFrame views are available in the Public Views folder. These views allow you to monitor events and alerts raised for MetaFrame XPe servers and server farms, and to identify trends and performance issues occurring on MetaFrame servers and published applications.

■ **The Citrix notification group**   The Citrix MetaFrame XP Management Pack includes a notification group, called the Citrix MetaFrame Administrators group. You can configure this group to ensure that the appropriate people are notified about problems with MetaFrame servers and server farms.

▲ **Easy installation**   The Citrix MetaFrame XP Management Pack consists of a single file that is available from the Citrix web site. To install the Citrix MetaFrame XP Management Pack, simply import this file into MOM using the MOM Administrator Console.

Citrix MetaFrame Views in MOM   The Citrix MetaFrame XP Management Pack includes a number of Citrix MetaFrame views that are available in the Public Views folder in the MOM Administrator Console. These views allow an administrator to monitor events and alerts raised for MetaFrame XPe servers and server farms, and to identify trends and performance issues occurring on MetaFrame servers and published applications.

NOTE: In the Citrix MetaFrame XP Management Pack, a managed MetaFrame server is a MetaFrame XPe server that is running both Feature Release 2 or later, and the Citrix MetaFrame XP Provider (discussed later), and that has a Feature Release 2 or later license installed and activated. Note that after installing and activating a Feature Release 2 or 3 license, it may take until the next computer scan before MetaFrame servers are recognized as managed. An unmanaged MetaFrame server is a server running MetaFrame 1.8, XPa, XPs, or XPe without the Citrix MetaFrame XP Provider or a Feature Release 2 license.

There are two main types of Citrix MetaFrame views: Health Monitoring views and Discovery views. Health Monitoring views provide system administrators with real-time event and alert information, together with performance monitoring details about MetaFrame XPe servers and server farms. Discovery views provide an overview of the structure of your MetaFrame installation, together with information about individual MetaFrame servers. Table 9-2 provides a summary of the views.

View Type	View Name	View Description
Health	MetaFrame Events	Displays all the events raised by MetaFrame components on managed MetaFrame servers.
Health	Open Alerts From Citrix MetaFrame Servers	Displays all unresolved alerts raised against managed MetaFrame servers by all management packs (not only the Citrix MetaFrame XP Management Pack).
Health	Open Citrix Alerts	Displays all unresolved alerts raised by the Citrix MetaFrame XP Management Pack.
Health	Active Sessions	Displays the number of active sessions on each managed MetaFrame server.
Health	Published Application Load From Load Balancing	Displays the published application load from the MetaFrame Load Manager component. Note that this information is available only if you are using Citrix Load Manager in your server farm and you have configured the application load level in the Citrix Management Console.
Health	Server Load From Load Balancing	Displays the server load from the MetaFrame Load Manager component. Note that this information is available only if you are using Citrix Load Manager in your server farm.
Health	Pooled Licenses In Use	Displays the number of pooled licenses in use in each server farm, as a percentage of the total number of pooled licenses in the farm. After you install the Citrix MetaFrame XP Management Pack, this view is empty until 3:55 A.M. the next day.

Table 9-2.   Citrix MetaFrame Views

View Type	View Name	View Description
Discovery	Managed MetaFrame Servers	Displays all managed Citrix MetaFrame XPe servers in the Citrix MetaFrame Managed Servers computer group.
Discovery	Unmanaged MetaFrame Servers	Displays all unmanaged Citrix MetaFrame servers in the Citrix MetaFrame Unmanaged Servers computer group.
Discovery	MetaFrame Product Version	Displays information about the MetaFrame software versions on each managed MetaFrame server. After you install the Citrix MetaFrame XP Management Pack, this view is empty until 3:55 A.M. the next day.
Discovery	MetaFrame Hotfixes	Displays information about the MetaFrame hotfixes installed on each managed MetaFrame server. After you install the Citrix MetaFrame XP Management Pack, this view is empty until 3:55 A.M. the next day.
Discovery	MetaFrame Computer Groups	Displays all MetaFrame server farm and zone computer groups configured by the administrator.

Table 9-2.   Citrix MetaFrame Views *(continued)*

With MOM, the Citrix MetaFrame XP Management Pack can collect and analyze data from multiple farms, zones, and servers, and distill critical management information for the Administrator. Additionally, the Management Pack includes a number of predefined Citrix rules and scripts for generating alerts.

The Citrix MetaFrame XP Provider   As mentioned in the preceding Note, MOM requires access to the Citrix MetaFrame XP Provider for WMI to function. The Citrix WMI provider integrates with the Windows Management Instrumentation (WMI), a standard management infrastructure included as part of Microsoft Windows 2000 and XP. WMI is designed to help system administrators manage large, complex enterprise systems, applications, and networks. WMI is a standard for accessing and sharing management information from a variety of underlying technologies in an enterprise environment. It provides system administrators with a single, consistent object-oriented interface to monitor and control system components locally or remotely.

The Citrix MetaFrame XP WMI Provider acts as an intermediary between the CIM (Common Information Model) Object Manager and the system being managed. The purpose of a WMI provider is to extract management information from the underlying system and present this to a WMI consumer (MOM). The Citrix MetaFrame XP Provider supplies information that includes

▼ **Farm data**   A Citrix server farm is a group of Citrix servers managed as a single entity. Details about servers in the farm, zones in the farm, published applications, and pooled licenses are provided.

■ **Zone data**   A zone is a grouping of Citrix servers that share a common data collector, which is a MetaFrame XP server that receives information from all the servers in the zone. The name of the zone in which the MetaFrame server operates is provided, together with details about the master and the other servers in the zone

■ **Server data**   Information about the MetaFrame server on which the Citrix MetaFrame XP Provider is installed is supplied—for example, details about the licenses assigned and in use, sessions, and applications running.

■ **Session data**   Information about the ICA sessions running on the server is provided, such as session ID and name, together with information about the processes running within a session.

■ **Citrix license data**   Citrix license details, such as the status of licenses and the grace period, are provided, together with information about license groups. For example, details about the licenses in the group and the number of pooled connection licenses available and in use.

■ **Load balancing data**   If you are using MetaFrame Load Manager, information is provided about the server load level and the application load level on the local MetaFrame server. Note that you must configure the application load level in the Citrix Management Console.

■ **Management Console**   The server load level is configured by default. For more information about Citrix Load Manager, see the Load Manager Getting Started guide and the online help.

■ **Application data**   Published application details, such as the name, type, and version number of applications are provided. Information about applications published on a particular MetaFrame server is also supplied.

■ **User data**   User details, such as username and account information are provided, together with information about user groups and membership.

■ **Static instances**   The date and time of static instances such as zone elections and disconnected sessions is recorded. This data is useful in monitoring whether or not these events are occurring too frequently.

▲ **Events**   Information about events that occur, such as when an application is published, deleted, moved, or updated is provided. Also included are details about the creation, maintenance, and deletion of published application folders, servers, server folders, and sessions, together with many more events.

The Citrix MetaFrame XP Provider allows you to

▼ **Log off a session**   Logging off a session terminates the connection and all running programs. The user cannot reconnect to the session.

■ **Disconnect a session**   Disconnecting a session terminates the connection between the server and the client. However, the user is not logged off and all running programs remain active. The user can later reconnect to the disconnected session.

▲ **Send messages to users**   You can send messages to particular sessions.

PART III

Implementing an On-Demand Server-Based Computing Environment

As part of transitioning from design to implementation, organizations must be able to translate the theoretical values and concepts discussed in Part II of this book into actions. Simply put: Transition from concept to concrete. The authors felt that a more "real-world" set of circumstances and requirements was essential for managers, engineers, administrators, and technicians to focus on design principles and relate them to specific outcomes relevant to their own environments. To ensure a consistent approach, an "actual" set of parameters was needed, and the following enterprise customer was created as a case study. As a disclaimer, readers are reminded that no implementation was ever as easy as one envisioned in a textbook case, nor were the textbook cases "all inclusive." This study is no different; however, the authors intentionally designed a complex paradigm to showcase as many design elements and considerations as possible. Throughout Part III of this book, all references are in the context of this case study. Readers are strongly encouraged to take their time reviewing the description of our theoretical customer and keep that image in mind as they read the next 11 chapters.

CASE STUDY: CLINICAL MEDICAL EQUIPMENT

Clinical Medical Equipment Corporation (CME) is a fictitious company that designs, manufactures, sells, and supports a proprietary diagnostic and treatment module for the health care industry worldwide.

The CME Global Structure

Figure 10-1 shows the top-level wide-area-networking schematic of CME. CME maintains a data center at its five-building campus headquarters in Chicago, Illinois (Figure 10-2) supporting 1500 local users and another 1500 remote users at remote offices. The CME global structure consists of:

▼ CME-CORP

    ■ Provides services to two regional offices (CME-WEST and CME-EUR) and the Manufacturing Plant (CME-MEX)

    ■ Provides services to all mobile users and the beta test site

    ■ Provides services to 50 directly connected Sales Offices with 15–20 employees, each under the administrative control of their respective region

        ■ WEST region: 10 Offices

        ■ EUR region: 10 offices

        ■ CORP region: 30 offices

■ CME-WEST located in Seattle with 200 users, responsible for the Asia-Pacific region

■ CME-WEST will be the disaster recovery site for CME-CORP

■ CME-EUR located in Frankfurt with 200 users, responsible for the EU, Middle East, and Africa

■ CME-MEX located in Mexico City with 300 users

▲ CME-TEST, also located in Chicago, but on the university campus

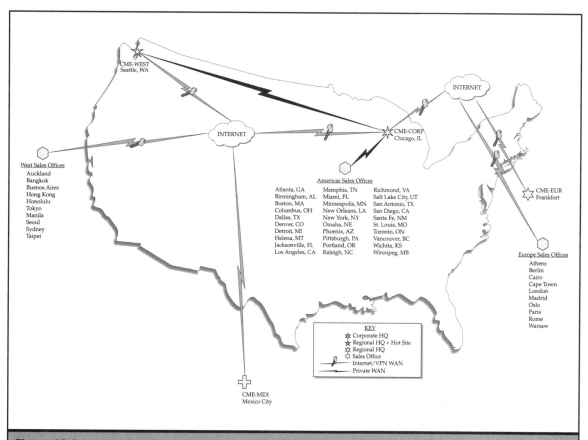

Figure 10-1. The Clinical Medical Equipment (CME) network schematic

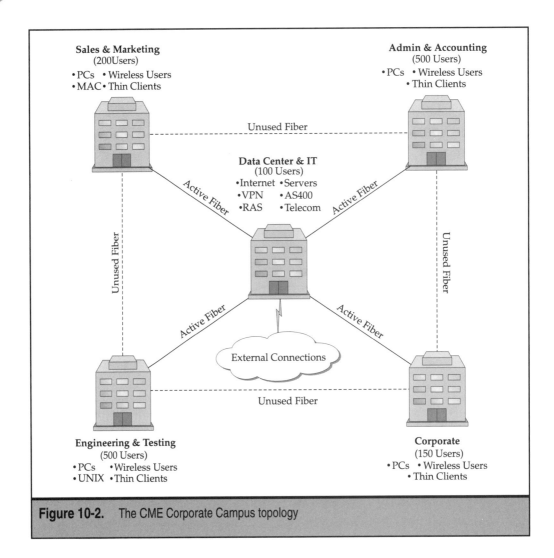

Figure 10-2. The CME Corporate Campus topology

The CME Computing Paradigm

Systems and capabilities required/planned at CME-Corporate include

▼ Windows-based network for server services and applications, file and print services, database applications (SQL, Oracle), web services, and e-mail services

■ Macintosh clients for graphic arts and marketing

■ AS400 for legacy manufacturing data

■ Citrix MetaFrame XPe for user access to most corporate applications

■ Unix hosts for CAD applications and engineering

- Citrix MetaFrame for UNIX, allowing non-UNIX hosts to access UNIX applications, and providing UNIX application access to remote users and users over slower WAN links

- VPN access for remote offices and roaming users (50 concurrent users)

- Web-based access to Citrix MetaFrame services (up to 200 concurrent users)

- A test pilot of remote sales people using Sprint PCS cards with Internet Access

- Wireless LAN access to Citrix for conference rooms, meeting rooms, and roaming users; wireless access (restricted to Internet access) may be required for visitors

- Dial-up access for roaming users who are unable to access an ISP (up to 20 concurrent users)

- Applications: Internally developed manufacturing applications utilizing an Oracle database, Microsoft Dynamics (with MS SQL DB back-end), Microsoft Office XP (other versions are used throughout the company, but standardization on the XP version is desired), Microsoft CRM, Microsoft Exchange, Parametric Technologies Pro/Engineer (and associated data management tools using an Oracle Database), AutoCAD, Microsoft Visual Studio.NET, Adobe InDesign and Illustrator, and a legacy, custom developed AS400 manufacturing tracking application

- "Portal" access to limited CME applications for key customers and suppliers via Citrix MetaFrame Secure Access Manager

- ▲ Interactive collaboration within applications via Citrix MetaFrame Conferencing Manager

The CME Business Model

The CME product integrates hardware, software, and logic, and as such, the next-generation product contains individually identifiable patient information as defined by HIPPA, thus requiring a network that can be adjusted to support HIPPA security standards when the next-generation product is deployed.

The CME Corporate headquarters campus consolidates the CME "brain trust." Virtually all product development, design, and business strategy efforts are conducted there. Seamless interoperability with dispersed sales and regional offices, as well as the ability to share services and resources with the manufacturing plant are essential. Senior staff members frequently travel from site to site and must have a consistent computing environment with access to necessary data and resources.

The CME regional offices are primarily tasked with sales-support coordination and ensuring acceptance (technical and political/legal) of the CME product in their respective region.

Sales and support offices provide direct site survey, installation, and on-going support for the CME medical module product. Per-site design and engineering is accomplished by the staff at CME-CORP.

CME learned from effective marketing strategies of other high-tech vendors and has deployed a "beta" test facility at the local university's medical college. The test facility is staffed by rotating groups of CME employees who provide real-world testing in a clinical environment, and who are also integrated with faculty, students, and clinicians. CME's strategy is to leverage their product into the academic side of the medical industry so that it becomes an essential tool in the industry at large—what students and clinicians learn in school they will demand in the workplace.

Corporate, regional, and sales office staff frequently travel to perspective customer and supplier sites and must have full access to corporate data and resources to do their jobs. Additionally, many employees require full home-based access to corporate applications to facilitate off-hours work, flexible schedules, and continuity for employees on temporary leave.

The CME SBC Business Case

CME managers determined their current IT structure was both expensive and virtually unmanageable, given the large number of sites, time zones, and applications. SBC was selected as the new paradigm and must solve current problems. At the top level, CME's goals for their SBC implementation are:

▼ *Reduce IT costs.* Staff and hardware/software costs are skyrocketing as more sites are brought online. Most sales offices do not have "full time" IT staff and have resorted to hiring temporary workers to try and keep systems up-to-date. Data distributed throughout the enterprise cannot be accessed easily and sites are demanding increased bandwidth to support moving information from site to site. A prime target for hard cost reduction is the PC replacement budget. The ongoing cost of CME's five-year PC replacement cycle of 600 PCs per year is over $720,000 per year.

■ *Standardize applications and application deployment.* Regional and sales offices are seldom on the same version (or even the same applications) when it comes to office automation software. Regional versions of office automation products are purchased locally, deployed inconsistently, and incorrectly licensed. English versions of office automation products perform inconsistently on non-English OS platforms. New software versions are deployed at each site and often the first site is already deploying the next new version before the last site even has the current version installed.

■ *Provide consistent service irrespective of location.* Employees who travel or work from home lack real-time access to most of the information they need. Staffs have resorted to everything from Instant Messaging to remote control software to keep in touch and gain access to corporate information.

■ *Provide the ability to rapidly activate new sites.* CME projects a 50-percent increase in sales offices over the next three years. In many overseas locations, dedicated WAN access may be unavailable, take up to a year to install, or be cost-prohibitive.

▲ *Provide a secure infrastructure that is extensible to meet U.S. (HIPPA, DoD) and foreign-nation security requirements.* Additionally, CME's technology is considered extremely proprietary and a likely target for industrial espionage.

CHAPTER 10

Project Managing and Deploying an Enterprise SBC Environment

After the project plan design is complete, the implementation begins. Project management is a key element in successful execution. This chapter, while not attempting an in-depth discussion of such a large topic, covers certain elements crucial to an SBC implementation, including preparing for organizational change, executive sponsorship, project manager authority, stakeholder buy-in, project reporting and tracking, task assignment, project change control, scope creep, and timeline management. We show examples of how tools such as service-level agreements and help desk software help manage changes to the environment to enhance benefits to management and end users. We also talk about the needs for the support environment both during and after the implementation.

This chapter also covers the methodologies for migrating from a PC-based to a server-based computing environment. First, we'll review the process of setting up a proof-of-concept pilot program. We next talk about expanding the pilot to a beta in order to identify and resolve any issues that arise in a small-scale production environment. We then cover expanding the beta to an enterprisewide rollout of Terminal Services. Finally, we discuss postproduction processes of ongoing measurement and reporting, change control, upgrades, and changes to the environment.

PREPARING FOR ORGANIZATIONAL CHANGE

When word of the [server-based computing] project started to spread across the company, a flood of requests for new PCs came in. The requests for new systems were threefold higher than the previous year. Some folks figured we wouldn't ask them to discard a brand new system. A letter from our CFO to all controllers in all divisions reminded them that this project was not optional and that all PC purchases would be subject to heightened scrutiny.

—Anthony Lackey, Vice President of MIS,
Chief Technology Officer, ABM Industries

In most organizations, it is difficult to successfully migrate to a server-based computing environment through mandate alone. An edict from top management is essential, but the planning team needs to supplement it with a strategy for internally selling the project as part of their overall change management plan. IT will probably have ultimate project ownership, and an IT member will probably have to take the initiative in promoting server-based computing throughout the organization. For purposes of this chapter, we will assume that the IT person leading the initiative is the CIO.

TIP: IT people often underestimate the resistance that a paradigm shift to an enterprise SBC nearly always generates.

Implementing an enterprise SBC environment does not involve a major alteration in an organization's mission statement or culture. It does, however, change to some extent the way in which employees accomplish their daily work. Planning for organizational change can address these concerns and help minimize project roadblocks. The steps for managing the change process are

1. Establish a need and sense of urgency for implementing SBC.
2. Create a compelling vision of the SBC environment.
3. Recruit executive support.
4. Carefully plan the process.
5. Communicate to all stakeholders.
6. Build SBC momentum and remove obstacles.
7. Monitor the progress.
8. Publicize early successes.
9. Expand the SBC environment.
10. Prepare for future SBC-enabled capabilities.

Establishing a Need for Implementing SBC

The Project Definition Document discussed in Chapter 4 should include the justifications for SBC. A sense of urgency should now be included in order to generate support. A letter from the CEO, for example, can explain the financial benefits that will accrue from SBC and consequently make it clear that this is a course of action the organization is undertaking.

Creating a Compelling Vision of the SBC Environment

While the CIO may have a vision for an organizational-wide SBC deployment, the actual implementation often unfolds over various stages. It is important to develop a vision that can be shared with management and users alike in an on-demand enterprise. The pilot and beta can be very useful in this regard. A particularly attractive advantage that can be demonstrated to both users and management is the ability to work seamlessly from home through the Internet. Users tend to get very excited by this capability because of the vastly increased flexibility it affords them. They no longer need to be constrained by physical location. Management is naturally enthusiastic as well because the productivity of their employees can significantly rise since they are no longer unable to work due to a cold or car troubles.

Recruiting Executive Support

In Chapter 4, we discussed the importance of obtaining executive sponsorship for the project. Inevitably, conflicts will arise in terms of resource availability, and even outright opposition to the project can surface. The executive sponsor must be able to step in and resolve these issues in order to keep the project on track.

In order to better facilitate organizational change, promotion of the project should be expanded to enlist the support of other top managers. The CIO should meet with the appropriate executives either in a group or individually. She should take the time to explain the server-based computing philosophy to them along with the financial and other benefits that they can expect. She should also be realistic about the challenges they can expect to face during the project implementation and the results they will see upon its completion. Her team should customize an appropriate excerpt from the project plan to hand out to these executives.

If a subscription model for SBC billing will be adopted, the CIO should explain to the executives how the program works and how it will impact their departmental budgets. She can emphasize that the IT department will utilize this model to break even but do so in a manner that enables departments to operate far more efficiently and with greater accountability than under a PC-based computing environment. The subscription-billing model for an enterprise SBC environment is discussed in Appendix D.

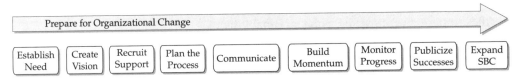

Carefully Planning the Process

Chapter 4 explores the intricate technical planning recommended for an enterprise SBC deployment. It is also important to plan for handling the organizational issues identified by the feasibility committee during the organizational assessment.

IT Staff Assessment

Is the IT staff ready for server-based computing? They should be early users of the technology during the pilot phase and be convinced enough about the benefits that they are advocates themselves.

If the IT staff is used to operate in the ad hoc manner normally associated with network administration, they need to understand that server-based computing requires the rigors of mainframe shop methodology, including limited access, change control, and planning and procedures. Controls must be put into place to ensure that the IT staff will help, not hinder, the SBC implementation. If certain staff members are unwilling or unable to support the project, they should be reassigned to another support area.

Skill Levels   Does the IT staff have the necessary skills to install and manage an enterprise SBC environment? They must have Windows 2003 Server expertise and experience, including the ability to do registry edits. Scripting capabilities are also a requirement for large implementations. A router expert must be available to manage large wide area networks. A skills assessment should be part of the initial project planning, and training or additional personnel obtained in order to cover the skill areas that are lacking.

IT Training   What training is appropriate for the IT staff prior to implementation? A Windows Terminal Services class and MetaFrame XP class are strongly recommended. If most of the work will eventually be done internally, an advanced MetaFrame XP course is recommended as well.

Cultural Assessment

How will server-based computing be received in the organization? The design plan should be modified, where necessary, in order to ensure that the organization's cultural norms will not be a roadblock to success.

Working Environment   In an environment where users commonly run similar applications and work as part of a unit, such as a bank, SBC is likely to be very well accepted. Users will immediately appreciate the higher reliability and increased flexibility that SBC enables. An engineering firm, on the other hand, with independent users accustomed to purchasing and loading their own software, will likely run into severe resistance if they try to force employees to operate only in the thin-client mode.

Remote Users   Remote users tend to be very enthusiastic toward SBC because they receive access to the corporate databases and networking services they need in order to do their jobs more productively. It is crucial to provide both adequate and redundant bandwidth to prevent problems with reliability and performance that can quickly turn remote users against server-based computing.

Managers   Managers, in general, tend to resist the idea of SBC until they actually use one; then they quickly become converts. They are usually impressed by the increased productivity they witness among their employees, as well as the capability for their employees to work from home. The project management team can help foster enthusiasm among the managers for SBC by showing them when the reduced corporate IT costs should be reflected on departmental bottom lines.

Political Assessment

Politics usually comes down to allocation of resources, money, power, or all three. How will the SBC project impact the profit-and-loss statements of the different departments involved? What happens to a regional IT division when the computing model switches to a centralized SBC architecture? It is important to be aware of these issues in order to take actions to minimize potential disruption to the project. Some scenarios and resolutions are described in the next section in this chapter, "Communicating to All Stakeholders."

Communicating to All Stakeholders

Communication is perhaps the biggest key to successfully managing organizational change. In addition to the executive communications mentioned previously, it is also important to educate and inform both internal IT staff and middle management as well as PC users.

IT Staff

Migrating to SBC invokes a fear on the part of IT that often significantly supersedes that of end users. PC fix-it technicians, for example, will likely see SBC as a threat to their job security. Regional IT staff will also be wary since the need for remote office support personnel usually is eliminated. The CIO must come up with a strategy that presents the project's advantages, including fewer user complaints, elimination of the majority of help desk calls, much more efficient troubleshooting, and more time for IT staff to learn new and challenging technologies to help the organization move forward.

Middle Management and PC Users

Videos can be more effective internal marketing tools than white papers. A video that presents the technology from the user's perspective can be prepared for all PC users in the company. The CEO can add legitimacy by starting the video off with a supportive introduction. The video can help with the orientation process by including footage of the Windows terminal that will be utilized and how the new desktops will look, the applications that will be available via SBC, and the process for migrating users' existing data.

Large companies may wish to create a separate video targeted specifically toward middle management. This video can focus on the high-level benefits of server-based computing. It should emphasize how removing the frustrations of PC-based computing leaves employees with more time to concentrate on their business.

Other techniques to help market the concept can include rainbow packets, at-a-glance documents for frequently asked questions, e-mail messages, and phone calls.

CAUTION: Do not oversell the enterprise SBC environment. Set realistic expectations. Make sure users know the benefits, but also let them know about any problems or limitations they can expect to encounter, particularly in terms of performance and reliability, during the implementation period. Remember the rule of effective selling: underpromise and over deliver.

Building SBC Momentum and Removing Obstacles

The ultimate goal of IT should be to create a buzz about the project. This can be accomplished by keeping the pilot program small and controlled, and by making sure the beta is a resounding success. Including capabilities that are either not possible, or much more difficult to accomplish, in the fat-client environment (such as effective logon from home, document collaboration, and single sign-on) helps make server-based computing particularly attractive. Improved help desk support is another SBC attribute often highly valued by users. It is important to limit the size and scope of the beta not only to ensure control, but also to help create an atmosphere of scarcity and exclusivity. The objective is to have users clamoring to be included as part of the SBC project. Limiting PC purchases before an enterprise rollout also makes users more eager to get on the server-based computing bandwagon.

Users and department heads must buy into the goals of the SBC project and understand its powerful positive implications for the organization.

Management Meetings

Hold group meetings with managers from different departments or divisions. Give them a chance to air their concerns and perspectives. Emphasize the benefits to the entire organization of implementing server-based computing. Stress that, although they may perceive that their employees have less control over their environment within SBC, managers actually now can devote time to their business rather than to managing their computing infrastructure.

While the goal for these meetings should be to provide a forum for managers to ask questions and air concerns, it should be clear that the project is going to take place. It is important to emphasize the positive benefits and develop a spirit of cooperation and enthusiasm.

Entitlement Issues

Department staff may feel that, because the money for the new system is coming out of their budget, they are entitled to their own servers. Employees, meanwhile, may feel they are entitled to their own PCs to run in fat-client mode. These perceptions need to be changed. Users need to understand the benefits that server-based computing provides to the organization as a whole. Some former capabilities, such as the ability to operate CD-ROMs, might be limited if they run in pure thin-client mode. On the other hand, users will gain computing advantages such as the ability to see their desktop from any PC or Windows terminal. Another powerful user incentive is the potential for telecommuting. Many users discover that they prefer a server-based computing environment because they experience increased reliability and performance. They also do not have to worry about causing problems by inadvertently changing their desktop. A properly configured SBC environment will limit their ability to delete icons or INI files or create other mischief.

Problems with Perception of Central IT

If the corporate network has a history of performance or reliability problems, department managers are going to be very reluctant to put all of their eggs in the corporate data center basket. To reassure them, explain the elaborate steps that are being taken to upgrade the network infrastructure and describe the policies and procedures that will result in a far more reliable network environment. Explaining the redundancy and disaster recovery capabilities of the SBC environment can help further mitigate any fears.

It is often productive to define an SLA in cooperation with the department managers in order to clarify expectations. If IT fails to meet the SLAs, the managers should have some recourse, such as credits in a bill-back situation.

Budgetary Concerns

Server-based computing, by definition, means centralized computing. Individual computing fiefdoms will disappear. You may wish to implement a billing model that charges departments for actual system usage in order to alleviate fears of arbitrary budgetary impacts. An example of such a subscription-billing model is presented in Appendix C.

Disposition Issues

If the project design plan calls for replacing certain PCs with Windows terminals, department heads may not be happy about the impact on their budgets. During this preliminary stage, discuss disposition issues and how they will impact book value. If possible, incorporate charitable deductions in order to lower the burden.

Monitoring the Progress

Constantly solicit and measure user feedback. IT can then make any adjustments necessary in order to ensure user satisfaction. This will add a great deal to the process of building a very successful enterprise SBC environment.

Publicizing Early Successes

Internal success stories should be generated about the attributes of the on-demand enterprise. The idea is to create a buzz around the organization where people are excited about, rather than resistant to, the upcoming changes. At the VA Medical Center, for example, we had a doctor thank our implementation team for making his life better because he could now access so much more of the data he needed, and he could do it much more quickly and far more easily than he could in the previous distributed PC environment.

Expanding the SBC Environment

Most organizations choose to roll out to enterprise SBC in phases. The original scope of the project is often less than a complete enterprise deployment. As the SBC phases are successfully implemented, and the user surveys show improved satisfaction with IT, the scope of the SBC environment can be expanded. Providing feedback to management about the existing and expected financial savings can help to further promote SBC expansion.

Preparing for Future SBC-Enabled Opportunities

Once the SBC environment has been expanded throughout the enterprise, the organization's IT department should run exceptionally well. Employees will have more computing capabilities than before, at a much lower IT budget, and with fewer IT personnel. The organization will also have opportunities that go beyond those that are realistic in a distributed PC environment. We discuss some of those opportunities in this book, such as business continuance, more efficient centralized storage devices, and greatly enhanced security and virus protection. But, other possibilities are now potentially available as well. For instance, a large janitorial organization might decide to have a Windows terminal manufacturer make their terminals look like time clocks in order to enable janitors to enter data right into the ERP application. A construction company might outfit foreman and inspectors with wireless tablet devices in order to have real-time information flow back and forth from the job sites. An organization concerned about ramifications from the Sarbanes-Oxley Act might introduce third-party products such as KVS, which will enable them to track and categorize all e-mail documents for quick and simple discovery.

CAUSES OF PROJECT FAILURE

Examples of server-based computing failures are, unfortunately, not in short supply. They often occur when an organization implements a server-based computing pilot or beta with a goal toward enterprise expansion, but then forgoes the rollout. Many organizations approach a Terminal Services implementation from a PC networking perspective. Although it is sometimes possible to deploy a successful Windows 2003 Server or Novell network without extensive planning and piloting, this will rarely work in an enterprise server-based computing deployment. Think of installing an enterprise SBC environment as replacing employees' PCs with a mainframe. Both cultural and political aspects are added to the technical challenges to make unplanned deployment nearly a guarantee of failure.

Inadequate Preparation for Organizational Change

IT often underestimates the impact of SBC on the various cultural and political aspects of the organization. Preparing for the organizational change as described earlier in this chapter is a key component to a successful enterprise deployment.

Skipping Project Planning Steps

Many organizations skip the pilot, project definition, and infrastructure assessment steps and go straight to project planning, or even a beta. This is bound to be troublesome if not an outright failure.

Lack of a Proof-of-Concept Pilot

The proof-of-concept pilot is essential for testing all applications under server-based computing before implementation. Proceeding immediately to a production pilot or beta can leave users frustrated with application performance or reliability or both. Even a small number of frustrated users can provide the type of negative feedback that will quell any further server-based computing expansion.

Lack of a Project Definition Document

Some internal evangelists might be sold on the idea of enterprise SBC and persuade management to implement one without enough thought to the objectives, scope, roles, risks, and success criteria. Without a project definition document, the planning, project management, and implementation teams have no touchstone with which to keep the project on track.

Lack of an Infrastructure Assessment

Project design committees often like to skip the infrastructure assessment step and jump straight to planning. This tends to be the most enjoyable part of the project, when participants contribute their knowledge to build a solution. Unfortunately, it is virtually impossible to create an optimally effective plan without a detailed infrastructure assessment. Additionally, infrastructure flaws that are tolerated under distributed computing are likely to be amplified in a server-based computing environment. When users become completely dependent upon a central server farm for executing their applications, the infrastructure has to be extremely solid.

Inadequate Planning

Sometimes, even large server-based computing implementations are performed without knowledge of basic tools and methodologies that can dramatically facilitate deployment. We once had lunch with the architects of a 5000-seat MetaFrame project who were complaining about bandwidth issues. It turned out that they had never even heard of the bandwidth management tools discussed in Chapter 6. Using bandwidth management from the start would have prevented their problems.

PROJECT MANAGEMENT

Astute project management is key to a successful SBC conversion. Here are the major steps in project managing an enterprise SBC implementation:

1. Identify a project manager.
2. Put together a project management team.
3. Create a project implementation plan.
4. Prepare for implementation.
5. Start the project.
6. Provide user support.
7. Measure success.

Identifying a Project Manager

A dedicated and competent project manager is essential to a successful implementation. There should be only one manager for the overall project, and that person should have both the responsibility and the authority to keep it on track. Communication is key. The project manager needs to make sure that both good and bad news travel fast.

> **_CAUTION:_** According to a four-year study by The Standish Group International of 23,000 IT projects, only 24 percent of the projects are successful (*ComputerWorld: Online News*, 06/18/98). The larger the project, the less chance it has for success. Migrating to a server-based computing environment is a major IT project. Give this project the full attention of your IT staff, and do not run it in parallel with other IT projects.

Putting Together a Project Management Team

Although one project manager should have overall authority, it is often a good idea to appoint a team to assist with the project implementation plan. An IT manager and business manager are two key positions that help resolve problems and keep the project on track. Someone from procurement should be on the team along with experts in the various technologies that will be utilized. The executive sponsor should at least be associated with the team in order to lend his or her authority. It is important to include employees who are involved in the areas of the company that will be affected by the project. This provides two benefits: first, the team benefits from their expertise in the area in question; and second, the employees get to be involved in the change, with the hope that they will be less resistant to it.

Controlling Project Change

Scope creep is highly likely in a large SBC deployment. Users will often insist on accessing applications that were never included in the plan. They may insist that the project's viability in terms of meeting established performance and uptime SLAs as well as projected ROI targets hinges on these additions. The ability to rapidly deploy an application in a server-based computing environment is one of its strongest selling features, yet the application implementation is a detailed process requiring extensive preliminary testing. A change control process is essential for keeping the SBC project on track.

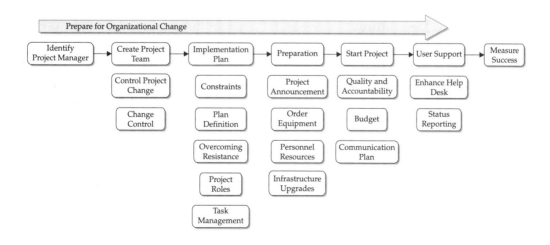

Change Control Process

Change requests in server-based computing range from minor, such as a user's request to continue accessing his local C drive, to major, such as a demand to host a DOS application that is known to have problems running under Windows 2003 Server. Because you are implementing a central processing environment, all changes to the design plan should be approved by the project manager and recorded. Changes that will affect the project budget or schedule may require additional approval.

Consider, for example, a request to add an application to the Terminal Services environment during the server farm rollout phase. This requires that the rollout be postponed while the new application is thoroughly tested in conjunction with the other hosted applications. All affected parties and stakeholders require notification of the rollout postponement. Once the new configuration proves stable, a new server image disk needs to be created, and the server rollout begins again. Since this seemingly innocuous change can have broad implications, not only for the project time and budget but also for many users, it is probably appropriate to have the business manager and IT manager sign off on the change along with the project manager.

Change Control Guidelines

Changes should only be made when required by stakeholders or when circumstances cause a significant deviation from the project design plan. The reasons for all changes should be documented along with any changes to the schedule or budget that result.

Conflict Resolution

Conflicts are inevitable in a large project. An enterprise SBC environment will demand IT resources that are already likely to be in short supply. Some users will be frustrated at a perceived loss of personal flexibility. Many users consider themselves IT experts and will disagree with the technology or the way it is deployed. Conflicts should be quickly referred to the project manager for resolution. Approaches to solving the problem include

▼ **Ignoring the conflict**   Sometimes it is better for the project manager to simply ignore the conflict if it is not likely to have a big impact on the project or is likely to resolve itself.

■ **Breaking up the fight**   This approach is useful if both parties are stuck in an argument. The project manager can interfere in order to take the energy out of the argument.

■ **Compromising**   Compromise may be required at times, such as allowing a user who was scheduled to be entirely thin client to run in hybrid mode. Keep in mind, though, that any nonstandard implementations detract from overall project efficiency and organizational computing effectiveness.

■ **Confronting**   This approach involves getting all parties together to work out their problem in an environment promoting conflict resolution.

▲   **Forcing a resolution**   Sometimes the project manager must use his or her authority, or the authority of the IT manager or the business manager, to mandate a resolution. This method should be used as a last resort.

Creating a Project Implementation Plan

An enterprise SBC project starts with a project definition document that states the goals, scope, roles, risks, success criteria, and project milestones. The project design plan then lays out the specifics of the major SBC components. A project implementation plan is the third step in this process. While the project planning document provides a roadmap for implementation, the project implementation document covers the project management aspects of migrating to an SBC environment.

Project Constraints

The project implementation plan must be created with regard to time, money, and people resources. Identifying these constraints will help determine how to apply corporate resources to the project. The following table indicates that management has decreed the SBC implementation be done quickly:

	Most Constrained	Moderately Constrained	Least Constrained
Time	X		
Budget		X	
People			X

Time is the most important element, while human resources are less constrained. Since time has the least flexibility, internal resources need to be diverted to the SBC project, while funds also should be used to bring in outside consultants and perhaps implementers.

Another constraint, often inevitable in a server-based computing implementation, is user satisfaction. Users can make or break an SBC implementation, and they are likely to resist the change if no preparatory work is done. It is therefore essential for the project manager to keep the users in mind when designing the project plan. The objective should be both to minimize disruption in user operations and to generate enthusiasm among users for the new server-based computing paradigm.

Defining Your Plan

Your plan will take shape as you define the major elements of implementation. Consider timing, key milestones, and budget, and communicate the plan to everyone involved.

Project Timing   Time is invariably the most constrained resource, and it is often not the most visible to participants. Clearly communicating the timing of the project's phases will help to convey the appropriate level of urgency.

Key Milestones   Identifying key milestones enables participants to easily measure progress. Stakeholders should be involved in defining milestones. The milestones can provide a chance for the team to pause and ask, "Where are we and how far do we have to go?" They can also provide an opportunity for positive communication to the stakeholders and the company at large when they are reached on time and on budget.

Estimated Project Costs and Cash Flows   Defining the broad budget for the project conveys the significance of the resources being expended. It also enables appropriate stakeholders to measure expenditures against it.

Implementation Strategy   There are certainly many different ways to implement SBC. Providing a summary of your strategic approach will help eliminate confusion and uncertainty.

Upside and Downside Potentials   Any new IT project has risks as well as potential rewards. Upside potential in this environment can include many unexpected results such as increased sharing of best practices among previously isolated corporate divisions.

Likely Points of Resistance with Strategies for Overcoming Them

Potential technical, financial, and political roadblocks should be listed along with approaches for resolving them. For instance, if employees in a particular remote office are determined to keep their own file server and LAN, a strategy for a phased implementation in their case might be appropriate.

Technical Challenges   Terminal Services is an evolving technology. Technical challenges will be present in every large enterprise rollout. Identify any problem areas that could jeopardize customer satisfaction with the project. Set action plans for resolving technical challenges. For instance, if a 16-bit application is quirky on Windows 2003 Server, it should either not be hosted, or it should be isolated on a separate server or server farm and accessed from the main production farm via Passthrough.

Identifying Unresolved Design Issues   Some design parameters will remain vague prior to the project implementation. These questionable areas should be referred to experts to help eliminate any confusion or uncertainty. For instance, when designing a Network-Attached Storage solution, we bring in the manufacturer in order to size the unit appropriately.

Defining Project Roles

Define the roles and responsibilities of staff members during the project implementation. Some of the roles you might need to define include project management assistance, teams for implementing server-based computing migration, procurement, wide area network implementation, bandwidth management facilitation, and storage consolidation. If using an integrator or consultants, define their roles, responsibilities, and tasks as well. These may be limited to consulting, or they may include project management or hands-on implementation.

Managing the Tasks

Projects are broken down by tasks that can be defined as a unit of work that is important to the project completion. Tasks can also include related subtasks. Assign managers to each task and set performance SLAs. For instance, one task may be to order an ATM link to the data center by a certain date. The SLA may be to order all data lines and equipment on or before the due date.

Developing a Work Breakdown Structure Tasks need to be organized into logical milestones, sequenced, assigned, associated with necessary resources for their completion, and communicated to team members. The work breakdown structure (WBS) is a standard method of organizing project tasks in one of two formats: either an organizational chart with each box listing tasks, as shown in Figure 10-3, or an outline WBS, as shown in Figure 10-4. The outline form tends to work better for projects with many layers of tasks. Both techniques show the different levels required and include subprojects or milestones, major tasks, subtasks, and minor tasks.

Developing a Project Schedule The key is to find ways to schedule parallel activities in order to complete the project within the allotted time frame. Building an enterprise SBC architecture is somewhat akin to a construction project. The most common scheduling technique in this case is the critical path method (CPM), which uses historical data to estimate task durations.

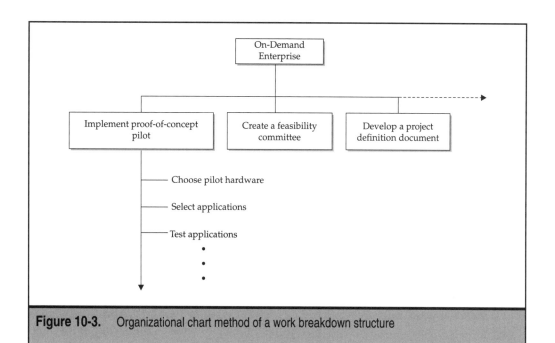

Figure 10-3. Organizational chart method of a work breakdown structure

Implement a proof-of-concept pilot

1. Choose pilot platform
    1.1 Configure MetaFrame XP server
    1.2 Identify back-end file server and network backbone
    1.3 Configure MetaFrame XP server on network backbone
    1.4 Set up Windows terminal

2. Select applications
    2.1 Select representative samples
    2.2 Eliminate duplications
    2.3 Develop selection criteria

3. Test applications
    3.1 Create test lists
    3.2 Test components
    3.3 Test functions
        3.3.1 Test specific functions
        3.3.2 Test generic functions

Figure 10-4. Outline method of a work breakdown structure

Coordinating Tasks In a large enterprise project, different elements of the organization will require coordination between them. Assign specific managers, as necessary, to ensure this coordination takes place. For each task it should be clear who has ultimate responsibility for its completion. Though several people may contribute, only one person can be responsible. This is the person whom the project manager will rely on for communication on the status of that task.

Defining Project Documentation Detail how the project will be documented for IT staff, managers, and end users. This documentation should conform to the communication plan described later in this chapter. It should include documentation about the data center configuration as well as about equipment and data lines at each remote office.

Establishing an Internal Marketing Plan Formulate an internal marketing plan, as described in Chapter 1. Identify points of resistance in the organization and establish action plans for overcoming them.

Preparing for Implementation

Organizational preparation for the project implementation should start with a word from the executive sponsor. Surveys can then be distributed in order to more precisely define the project tasks. Ordering lines and equipment is the next step in preparing for deployment of implementation teams.

Announcing the Project to the Organization

Announcement of the project should incorporate sponsorship statements from key corporate executives and give all employees a clear vision of what is coming, what it will look like, what to expect, how it will benefit them and the organization, and how it will affect their daily work. At ABM Industries, the vice president of MIS created a "Back to Business" video that emphasized SBC's ability to eliminate much of the futzing that PCs tend to foster. By mixing humor with a description of benefits, ABM created an extremely effective marketing tool.

Executive Mandate

Although we put a lot of emphasis on selling the project to users, an executive mandate is still required. A formal letter should go out from a high-ranking executive, preferably the CEO, telling all managers and users that SBC will be taking place. It should emphasize that this is an organizational initiative and that everyone is expected to make it work.

Surveys

The distributed nature of a PC-based computing environment means that many organizations, particularly larger ones, do not have a good grasp of the exact equipment and applications run by users. This is especially the case with remote offices or where managers have had the authority to purchase their own hardware and software. Creating surveys for both users and remote offices will enable the project manager to assess the true environmental condition and make appropriate ordering decisions. Even organizations with an existing network management system (NMS) in place often find that the inventory capabilities are not accurate enough to rely upon. In such cases, the inventory report from the NMS can be used as a basis for the survey, and then the user representative for the site can be asked to correct the report.

WAN Survey   If the existing WAN infrastructure does not provide adequate connectivity to all remote offices under Terminal Services, a site survey should be completed at least 60 days before the installation in order to allow for bandwidth upgrades. This timing is crucial due to the inevitable delays caused by the local and national exchange carriers. A user count and printer count (including types of printers) will help determine the type and size of bandwidth connection to each site. Including the address and ZIP code helps the WAN team decide whether certain technologies, such as a DSL connection, are viable options.

LAN Survey   Make sure the LANs in the selected remote offices are ready for a transition to server-based computing. For example, daisy-chained hubs that might have worked in a PC-based computing environment can kill server-based computing sessions. This is because users often have at least one more Ethernet hop to the data center server backbone that may be enough to exceed the IEEE Ethernet standard. Another example is a poorly performing server that may have problems when the implementation team tries to copy data from it. Such problems can also give the field deployment teams a "heads up" for what equipment they might need in order to migrate local desktops and servers. For example, if the LAN backbone has problems, the field technician might plan on bringing his own hub to connect the server to the deployment PC with a CD-RW drive to pull the data from the server.

Application Survey   Despite the best efforts of the planning committee and despite any company policies that are created regarding the SBC implementation, some users in remote offices will nearly always have local applications that they insist are required for them to do their job. It is far better to learn about these applications ahead of time in order to make appropriate accommodations for them as part of the implementation design process.

> **NOTE:**   In the infrastructure assessment phase described in Chapter 4, we discussed the importance of learning everything about an application before hosting it via server-based computing. This rule must still be followed even in the sometimes-unwieldy arena of remote office migration. We learned this the hard way. In one implementation, we came across many custom-written applications utilized in remote offices. Most were written in Microsoft Access and easily migrated to server-based computing. At one site, however, we migrated an application to the corporate data center and were told it no longer worked. After extensive debugging, we asked the user for more information. The user replied, "The application never really worked, but I thought that it might work once you moved it."

Printer Survey   An accurate count of the number and type of printers and print servers will help determine the type and size of connection required to each remote site. It is also important to determine any printers required apart from users' default printers. Printers that are not going to be supported as part of the SBC environment should be eliminated. Otherwise, they are bound to cause problems and may even lead to Terminal Services blue screens. The implementation team can bring new printers with them to replace the nonsupported units.

IP Address Survey   It is important that the IP addresses are managed across the enterprise. Whether this is done manually or by using management software, the point is that the lack of a workable scheme can cause a lot of system administration overhead and confusion. If such a system is not in place before the SBC project, consider using the project as an excuse to put one in place.

PC Survey   Determining the condition of each user's PC may aid a decision about whether to replace it with a Windows terminal. Create criteria for determining whether a PC is compatible with the SBC environment. This might include having an existing network interface card (NIC), having an existing desired local operating system, or being within a certain number of years old.

User Survey   Complete a user survey at least two weeks before installation to allow enough time to order and ship required equipment as well as to set up the user accounts. This survey should cover all relevant information about each user, including whether the user requires access to only SBC-approved applications and whether the user's existing machine meets SBC standards. The survey should also measure users' satisfaction with the existing computing environment in order to establish a baseline for judging the success of the SBC environment once implemented.

Order Equipment

Equipment must be ordered for the SBC implementation as well as for any upgrades to the existing infrastructure.

Equipment Purchase Lead Time   The surveys will show the existing type and condition of the equipment at headquarters and at remote offices. Order new equipment required for the installation a minimum of two weeks beforehand. This is necessary in order to stage the equipment prior to a large rollout. If you are rolling out 2500 Windows terminals to remote offices, for example, the logistics become daunting in terms of delivery confirmation, asset tracking, and shipping.

Asset Tracking System   It is important to have some type of asset tracking system in place in order to record the equipment ordered and where it is deployed. If your organization does not yet utilize one, the SBC project is a good time to start. Ideally, the system would be accessible by the field deployment technicians so that as they deploy each user, they can enter that user's equipment information directly into the system.

Remote Office LANs   Remote offices may have inadequate hubs, or even lack a network altogether. Order any hubs, switches, network interface cards, print servers, and cabling to be put in place ahead of the migration team. If you are ordering for many remote offices, order four weeks ahead of time to allow for staging and shipping.

Personnel Resources

Necessary personnel must be identified for both the upgrades and for the actual project implementation. For instance, later in this chapter we describe the composition of the implementation teams. Decisions need to be made about the number of technicians required to migrate users at headquarters and at all remote offices. While the actual migration time for a user in a remote office can often be kept down to about an hour, travel and logistics make a four-hour average estimate more realistic. The time, money, and resource constraints will determine how many technicians are assigned to the project.

Infrastructure Upgrades

In Chapter 4, we discussed the importance of doing an in-depth infrastructure assessment. The project management team needs to review that assessment again, factoring in the results from the surveys. Deficiencies in the network infrastructure that were tolerated in a PC-based computing environment are likely to be disastrous once users depend upon the corporate data center for all of their processing. Any infrastructure deficiencies must be resolved prior to the SBC migration. Both equipment and human resources must be secured for the upgrades and for the project implementation.

Data Center Upgrade   The data center often requires upgrades such as implementing a gigabit switching solution or a new firewall to enable secure Internet access. These projects require planning and implementation before the enterprise rollout.

Network Backbone Upgrade   One way to think of the MetaFrame XP server farm is as if it were actually hundreds or thousands of PCs. The backbone infrastructure, therefore, needs to be both very fast and reliable. Examine the existing backbone carefully using a network analysis tool, if necessary, in order to spot any deficiencies. Any problems must be fixed before the beta implementation.

Network Operating System Upgrades   Some organizations take the opportunity during an SBC implementation to either upgrade or migrate their network operating systems. This should be treated as a separate subproject, and the migration or upgrade should be completed before the server-based computing enterprise rollout—ideally, before the beta. Attempting to do this project concurrently with an enterprise SBC implementation leaves far too many variables to troubleshoot in the event of problems. It can have another undesirable side effect: users who experience problems related to the change in operating system or infrastructure may think that the Terminal Services or MetaFrame XP software is responsible.

Data Center Storage   The project design planning document will include the selected storage medium at the data center, whether NAS, SAN, or general-purpose file servers. The surveys will show the amount of hard drive storage currently required by users and by remote office servers, enabling ordering of the appropriate storage for the data center. Of course, user and remote office storage requirements for SBC-hosted applications can be ignored. Significant economies of scale are obtained by centralizing all data storage instead of requiring a surplus for each user. As a result, the requirement for central storage will be less than the cumulative totals of existing distributed hard drives.

Wide Area Network Upgrades   The surveys will show the number of users per remote office, enabling decisions about how much bandwidth to supply. Some organizations will install their first WAN as part of the SBC architecture. Others will upgrade their existing

We found that Citrix can easily become a lightning rod for blame. If, during a thin-client migration, users suffer from infrastructure or other problems completely unrelated to Citrix, they still are likely to think it is the cause. Perhaps this is just a case of transference, but the remedy is clearly to minimize potential problems by not trying to do other IT projects concurrent with a Citrix implementation.

—Sean Finley, Assistant Vice President and
Deputy Director of Electronic Services,
ABM Industries

system, while still other organizations will add redundancy. In an ideal world, this implementation should be completed well before the SBC rollout, but in practice it is often not possible. Allow 60 days for ordering and installing data connectivity lines or upgrades whether using a frame relay connection, a leased line, DSL, cable, or ISDN. Do not rely on your telecommunications company; follow up to make sure they are staying on schedule. Test the lines once they are in place before sending an implementation team to a remote office. Also test redundancy, even if this is just a dial-up to the data center.

Starting the Project

Establish a regular meeting schedule to review milestones and budgets. Work on the exception principle. Focus on what is not going according to plan. Fix it fast. Be prepared to add resources in order to meet the schedule. Issue a weekly list of targets and key troubleshooting assignments.

Maintaining Quality and Accountability

Make careful and informed decisions about key equipment purchases or leases. System reliability should be a prime consideration in any SBC project. Unreliable system elements can jeopardize overall system performance. Monitor all subcontractors and vendors to ensure that they are staying on target with their assigned tasks. Move quickly to correct targets that aren't being met.

Project Budget

It will be difficult to accurately estimate the budget required for a large SBC deployment because of the tremendous number of variables involved. Fortunately, server-based computing tends to save organizations so much money that even significant budget overruns would compare favorably with the PC-based computing alternative. Appendix B shows how to prepare a financial analysis of server-based computing versus PC-based computing.

Budget Contingencies   Management will want to see a budget and expect the project manager to hold to it. This is why it is important to build in contingencies for travel, cost overruns, and unexpected problems. It will sometimes be necessary to spend more than planned in order to achieve the desired results. It is also wiser to deviate from the budget in order to circumvent a problem before it becomes a crisis. Again, the vast savings enabled by the overall project should make this the wise alternative.

Budget Monitoring   Tying the budget to the project milestones is a good method for monitoring progress and keeping expenditures on track. It also can provide stakeholders with a clearer example of benefits. For instance, a project milestone might be replacing 500 old PCs with new Windows terminals. The Windows terminals cost $400 each, while purchasing 500 new PCs would cost $1000 each (including the extra installation PCs require). Offset the project budget at this point against the cost of purchasing new PCs and the cost of upgrading those new PCs in two or three years.

Communication Plan

It is essential to communicate about the project with users. We recommend over-communicating about the project migration parameters and expectations. Regular e-mails are certainly valuable. Prepare a list of frequently asked questions (FAQs) to help inform users about their new environment.

Issue Regular Project Updates   Relay the key achievements since the last update. Talk about the project status and where the project is going in the next period. Discuss what is required to ensure success. Part of the established communication plan should be to report on the project's progress to key stakeholders.

Handling Complaints   Enhance the help desk department as explained later in the chapter. Enlist the aid of regional managers, if necessary, to help set user expectations during the implementation. Managing user expectations is something that should be done continuously during the process. This will decrease the number of calls to the help desk.

Publishing Deployment News   Use e-mail or an intranet to publish ongoing news about the migration. Let users know of potential bottlenecks or other problems before they take place. Share the wins as well. Publish user testimonials about the migration.

Deployment Guide   Creating a deployment guide for implementation teams is discussed later in this chapter. In some organizations, users will be doing their own client setup. In these cases, the deployment guide can be of great assistance to them as well.

Customer Care

Providing adequate user support is essential to a successful enterprise SBC implementation. Even though users may experience initial problems, they will have much better attitudes if they can receive prompt and competent help.

Enhancing the Current Support Structure

Part of the infrastructure assessment described in Chapter 4 is an analysis of the organization's help desk methodology and escalation procedures. Once the enterprise SBC environment is in place and stabilized, help desk requirements will fall. Not only does Citrix MetaFrame XP enable superior troubleshooting through shadowing capabilities, but also the number of problems will fall because the processing takes place centrally. During the implementation phase, however, the frequency of support requests will increase. In addition to the confusion and problems of implementing a new computing infrastructure, the help desk will, in effect, be supporting two environments during the transition. Be prepared to supplement the help desk with additional personnel during this period.

Establishing Service Level Agreements Establish and manage service level agreements (SLAs) for the help desk during project implementation. Ensure that users receive the help they need to get them through the transition without frustration.

Support Processes Tech support should cover every shift and every time zone. A process should be in place, and the appropriate personnel identified, for escalating problems that are not resolved by the first-line support people in an acceptable time frame.

Virtual Call Center Create a virtual call center where any member of the implementation team can assist if required. Use help desk software to enable this collaboration among different individuals from different areas working on the same user problem. ABM Industries, for instance, wrote custom software in Lotus Notes that tracks every help desk request from initiation of the call to ticket closing. Any implementation team member can sort by user or by problem in order to more quickly troubleshoot and resolve the issue.

Triage Process Have a swat team available to go onsite to handle particularly tricky problems that surface during the implementation. Consider using outside experts for the SWAT team that have a high level of experience with MetaFrame XP, Windows, and networking.

Status Reporting

The help desk should work in conjunction with the purchasing department and the project management team to give continuous status updates. These updates can take place through phone calls, e-mail, and an intranet. They should reflect user attitudes about the migration process in order for adjustments to be made.

Measuring Success

Establish success metrics ahead of time and measure results against them. For instance, an SLA might be to enable users in remote offices to access their data within 24 hours of migrating to server-based computing. Measure and report the actual results of how long it takes users to gain access.

Using Measurement Tools at Milestones

Survey users at project milestones to measure their perceptions versus expectations. For instance, a project milestone might be to have all small remote offices online as SBC users. Surveying users can reveal any problems with performance or reliability, which will enable adjustments to the design plan before proceeding to the next milestone.

Project Success on a Macro Level

On a macro level, metrics should include project performance against budgeted costs, estimated timelines, and user satisfaction. Measuring success is discussed further in this chapter under the section "Postproduction Management of the SBC Environment."

PROOF-OF-CONCEPT PILOT PROGRAM

In Chapter 4, we discussed setting up a proof-of-concept pilot program as an important element in the design of an enterprise SBC environment. The pilot is also the first step in an enterprise rollout. It serves as a basic test of application performance using Terminal Services.

At first, the pilot program should be a nonproduction system designed to ensure that the desired applications perform together adequately over MetaFrame and Terminal Services. The next step is to expand the nonproduction pilot to a small production pilot with carefully selected participants running specific applications.

Pilot Platform

The pilot hardware should be representative of the hardware that will eventually be used in the data center to support the enterprise rollout. The pilot program should not be constrained by any difficulties or limitations in the existing network infrastructure. For instance, if the network backbone is causing latency issues, the pilot should be set up on a separate backbone. If a data line to a remote office frequently fails, then the remote office should not be part of the pilot program.

Application Selection

The objective is to load all applications to be hosted under SBC as part of the proof-of-concept, nonproduction pilot program. That being said, most organizations have far too many applications to reasonably host together in a MetaFrame environment. During the infrastructure assessment and project plan design process, the appropriate applications are studied in great detail and are carefully selected for server-based computing. Since the pilot takes place before this assessment begins, you can pare down the applications to be hosted in this environment by following a few rules of thumb:

▼ *Use representative samples.* Applications should be a representative sample of the production suite.

■ *Eliminate duplications.* Look over the list of all applications to eliminate obvious duplications. For instance, if 90 percent of projected SBC users run Microsoft Office and 10 percent run Corel WordPerfect Office, you can reasonably assume that MS Office will win out as the new corporate standard under server-based computing.

▲ *Develop selection criteria.* Create a list with "must-have" and "should-have" features to help pare down the applications in the pilot program. For instance, a must-have feature would be that an application is stable under standard NT workstation. A should-have feature would be that the application is 32 bit.

Testing

The performance, stability, and interaction of the various applications individually and collectively under Terminal Services must be tested and evaluated. One way to do this is by using test lists.

The application information gathered during the infrastructure assessment can be used to prepare the test lists. The lists should include the attributes to be tested along with the expected outcomes. Record the actual outcome for each test and whether it passed or failed. In Chapter 15, we discuss application testing in some detail.

Expanding to a Production Pilot Program

Start with a prepilot survey geared to recording the current state of user performance, reliability, and satisfaction in a fat-client environment. Use the survey results to set expectations for the users about the performance under MetaFrame XP. Be sure they are prepared for the inevitable problems that the new environment will precipitate, as well as for any differences they are likely to encounter by running their applications in a server-based computing environment.

It is acceptable to ask "leading" questions in the survey to set expectations, but they should strive for quantifiable answers where practical. For example, instead of asking, "Does your PC crash on a daily basis?" you can ask, "How many times per day does your PC need to be rebooted?" The results should be tabulated and published to the users who participated. If an intranet site is available, consider doing the survey online rather than with paper forms.

Selecting Applications

The objective of the pilot program is to prove the value of server-based computing by running crucial applications successfully in this environment. Misbehaving, but noncrucial, applications should not be included as part of the production pilot. They can be tested further for inclusion as part of the beta if their problems can be solved or isolated using a two-tier server farm, as discussed in Chapter 12.

> **TIP:**   You can use batch files or WSH (Windows Scripting Host) to remove or move icons from SBC applications that are currently run locally on a user's PC. This allows for a quick rollback in the event that the pilot program does not succeed.

The following are some minimum requirements for running an application in a production pilot program. These are suggestions to help get you started on your own list.

▼   The application is stable in the current distributed environment.

■   If it is a DOS application, it does not extensively poll the keyboard. This can cause huge CPU utilization on the MetaFrame XP server. You should seriously consider replacing any DOS application with a 32-bit Windows version if possible.

■ If it is an older or custom application, make sure it doesn't use hard-coded pathnames for files. Since most paths need to be user specific in a multiuser environment, this can cause major headaches.

■ The application represents the most users possible. Using our previous example, we would want to test MS Office and not WordPerfect Office because the former represents 90 percent of the users.

▲ Applications with back-end integration requirements (such as database or terminal session connectivity) have upgraded to the latest version. We have found that many applications that fit this description, such as IBM Client Access or various reporting packages, work fine in a multiuser environment but *only* if you use the latest version.

Testing and Evaluation

Start with the test lists defined in the pilot program for component and system testing, and layer in tests aimed at the production environment. Such tests would include a larger number of users running the applications, competing network traffic, reconnection to a user session, use of shadowing to support an application, and the effect on applications of backing up and restoring data.

Determine what performance data needs to be collected and how to collect it. System management tools such as Citrix RM can be useful here, as well as user surveys. One of the best testing methods at this stage is simply saturation: let the users pound away at the applications, and see what they come up with.

Selecting the Participants

The production pilot program should include a larger sample of users than the nonproduction pilot, but the number should remain relatively small. The exact number will be based on the size of your organization and the complexity of your application environment. Ideally, the users selected should be representative of the users who will participate in the SBC environment, but they should also be friendly to the project. We have found that keeping the number of participants in the production pilot between five and ten users, and no more than 50 for large companies, seems to work best.

Choose which categories of users will participate in the pilot, keeping in mind that you are looking for a representative mix of the ultimate SBC participants. A small pilot, therefore, might still include thin-client only, mobile, and hybrid users. We recommend including at least one Windows terminal as part of the pilot, if possible, in order to get across the point that this is a new way of delivering applications. Of course, a Windows terminal can only be used when all required applications for a user or group are accessible over MetaFrame XP.

Location of users is also important. If users in remote offices will be part of the pilot program, the network's wide-area infrastructure needs to be very sound. As discussed in Chapter 4, remote office users should be trained ahead of time not to engage in excessive bandwidth utilization practices such as copying data from a local hard drive back to the data center server, or downloading MP3 files from the Internet connection via the MetaFrame XP server farm. Alternatively, you should have a method to limit the bandwidth available to users. We've already discussed TCP rate control and custom queuing as two common methods. We've summarized these and other requirements as follows:

▼ Choose a small but representative mix of users. The users selected should access different groups of applications from different types of clients.

■ Use this opportunity to test key parts of your infrastructure with server-based computing. Choose users in major regional offices, telecommuters, and VPN users.

■ Choose users who are open to the thin-client concept. Demanding users are fine as long as the demands are reasonable, but avoid high-maintenance users.

▲ At this stage, choose users who are computer literate and can make the "paradigm shift" necessary to participate fully. We are not saying they have to be programmers or system administrators, just experienced users who have some command of their current desktop.

Customer Care During the Pilot

We discussed customer care in detail earlier in this chapter. It is crucial to alert the help desk and to put special mechanisms in place for expediting any problems users encounter. A sour experience during the pilot program, even among friendly users, could end up poisoning the entire SBC project. On the other hand, if users receive fast and competent responses to issues that arise, they are more likely to start an early, strong, favorable buzz about the new technology. A good technique is to have a "triage" process in which the help desk can quickly categorize a pilot call from a normal production call and route it appropriately. After a call is identified and routed to the first tier of support, it should go directly to the pilot implementation team. This is an excellent method for keeping the team in tune with the users and making continuous, incremental improvements to the pilot environment.

Training Techniques

It is important for the ultimate success of the project to formulate a training plan for all employees involved, including users, help desk technicians (all levels), and administrators. Some suggestions are provided here:

▼ **Users**   If your organization, like many, is already using a Windows desktop environment, moving to SBC will not represent a large functional difference to users. Training a large number of users is also very expensive. We recommend integrating a short orientation, perhaps 15 to 30 minutes, into the user migration process. The user should be oriented, the data migrated, the client installed, and the client device configured all during the same visit by a deployment technician.

■ **Help desk** The people fielding technical support and administrative requests must not only understand the basics of server-based computing, but they must also be trained in how to do whatever they do now in the new environment. Creating users, adding them to groups, and giving them access to file storage and applications are different tasks in MetaFrame XP and must be the subject of training. The deployment team is a good source of targeted information on these operations, so build time into the schedule to allow them input into the training plan.

▲ **System administrators** These individuals usually represent the smallest group and need the most training. They will eventually receive calls from other groups and are responsible for solving problems in production. You should build money into the budget for the training programs offered by Citrix and Microsoft. Specifically, the Citrix Certified Administrator (CCA) and Microsoft Certified System Engineer (MCSE) should be considered for administrators.

Controlling the Pilot Program

A carefully implemented pilot program is likely to be successful, but this very success leads to quick requests for enhancements. It is important not to cave into pressure from users to introduce new variables, such as additional applications, as part of the pilot. Do not stray from your pilot plan until after the initial testing is complete. If adjustments such as adding applications must be made before a beta implementation, the initial proof-of-concept testing offline should be repeated and then the new server image introduced to the users. Don't assume that since the production pilot worked with ten applications that it is acceptable to add an 11th. Everything must be tested before being deployed. Also realize that your deployment team is limited. If you are forced to spend a lot of time testing new applications or features at the last minute, it is likely to have an impact on the schedule.

Creating a Variance Process Define a variance process before the pilot that defines the handling of scope creep. You can publish this process as part of the user survey or other communication given to the pilot users. Decide who needs to approve requests for additional applications or pilot participants, and have a mechanism ready to handle this process. We've found such requests often come from management members who outrank the deployment team. If you *must* implement a change, be ready to clearly and concisely communicate the impact it will have on the deployment schedule, resources, and cost.

Handling Objections to Server-Based Computing Despite careful pilot participant selection, some users may still object to the concept. Be prepared to do a quick sales job that shows them both the personal and corporate benefits of migrating to an SBC environment. If you run into unreasonable or unfounded objections, be ready to pass them to the proper management members. The executive sponsor for the pilot is an excellent choice to help handle objections. Another important tool is to have the facts at hand regarding any objection.

We've found that users sometimes couch objections in terms sympathetic to their case that do not always reflect the facts. For example, a user may go to his manager and say, "The pilot team says I can't have the printer on my desk anymore." In reality, the pilot team published a list of compatible printers, and this user's printer wasn't on it. Be ready to tell this user and his manager how they can get a compatible printer or what to do as a work-around.

Assessing Performance

Document your expectations of the pilot program before you begin. Decide up-front upon the success metrics for the pilot. Take measurements of application performance in the current distributed environment, and compare these to performance under server-based computing. For example, the time it takes to launch Microsoft Word can be measured in both environments. (It should be faster under server-based computing.) Other examples include the time it takes to print a certain document or to open a specific file.

In addition to the user-oriented metrics mentioned, include *system* and *cost* metrics. An example of a system metric is the time it currently takes to support a regional file server when it fails as compared to the time it takes to fix a file server in the data center. An example of a cost metric would be the cost of flying a technician to the site where a problem is occurring as opposed to having a technician handle the problem at the data center.

After the pilot, create a report on whether success metrics were met. Document any problems encountered along with their solutions. Document any open issues or new questions raised by the pilot, along with the actions being taken to resolve them.

EXPANDING THE PILOT PROGRAM TO A BETA

A beta deployment, while conceptually still a pilot, should represent users and environments that will be part of the enterprise rollout. The beta will be invaluable as a mechanism for discovering and resolving major performance issues before going to enterprise production. It should not be implemented until after the design for the enterprise rollout is well underway and the funds for the entire project have been justified. Even so, a poorly performing beta could end up killing the project; therefore, it is essential the beta be implemented with the same high level of diligence used in the pilot phases. You should also try to make the beta implementation as nondisruptive to the current production environment as possible by running as many services in parallel as allowable. For example, if you intend to run a new network backplane and a new enterprise-class file server for the SBC implementation, leave the old systems online as you bring up the new systems. Users can then move from the old to the new system incrementally. This also serves the purpose of "leaving yourself an out." The smooth running of your business is more important than this project. If something doesn't go right, be able to go back to a known, reliable state.

Customer Care During Beta

As with the pilot program, responsiveness to users' problems will greatly influence their opinions about the project. Enhance the help desk and call center staff for quicker turnaround.

In the spirit of having no secrets from the user community, a published outage log should be created for users via an intranet web site or through an internal electronic forms application such as Microsoft Exchange or Lotus Notes. Encourage users to let IT know about any system outages or problems. Also provide a forum for beta participants to offer feedback unrelated to problems. This can help increase user satisfaction.

Now is the time to refine the support process and be ready for production. Help desk personnel, along with system administrators, should be trained and ready for the demand. If you intend to deploy system management servers or a network management framework tool that integrates with your help desk system, they should go through final implementation at this point.

Maintenance Window

As with a mainframe environment, a maintenance window should be scheduled once a production server–based computing environment is in place. During this time, the deployment team and system administrators will perform tasks that require a significant portion of the infrastructure to be offline. Such activities include hardware and software upgrades, switching over network connections or carrier lines, or troubleshooting and correcting problems before they cause a production outage.

The maintenance window should be scheduled during the least disruptive time. If an organization is international in scope or works 24/7, it may be difficult to set aside a regular time slot, but it should be done if possible. During the implementation process of both the beta and the enterprise deployment, the maintenance window will likely need to occur more frequently than after project completion. It is important to user acceptance to avoid unscheduled downtime whenever possible. Since SBC users are completely dependent on the network for their processing, unscheduled downtime will create unhappiness and loss of productivity.

Unscheduled Nonemergency Maintenance

Some organizations might not be able to, or may not wish to, have a regularly scheduled maintenance window. In these situations, carefully created procedures should still be utilized to ensure minimal disruption to the organization. For instance, the policy may be to give users at least three days notice before nonemergency maintenance will be performed. Scripting can be created to send out initial e-mails to the affected parties explaining the nature of the maintenance, the likely effects, and the projected duration. A reminder e-mail might be sent again a few hours before the maintenance begins.

Emergency Maintenance

Sometimes, with or without regular maintenance windows, emergency maintenance procedures will need to take place. Again, policies should be developed ahead of time to let affected users know about the maintenance with as much time as possible in order to minimize work disruption. Keep in mind that the maintenance can potentially affect the work of hundreds or thousands of SBC users.

The rigorous testing done in the pilot and beta phases is intended to keep unscheduled downtime to an absolute minimum. In cases where it does happen, make sure the help desk has emergency response procedures in place. One option is to include a recorded message explaining the situation, the expected resolution, and the projected service restoration time. The idea is to avoid burdening the help desk or technicians with a lot of user calls reporting the same, known problem when they should be concentrating their efforts on restoring service.

Infrastructure Assessment

The beta should utilize the same hardware slated to be part of the enterprise rollout. The network infrastructure now plays a crucial role. A network problem that goes unnoticed or is tolerated under a PC-based computing environment is likely to be amplified many times under a server-based computing environment. For example, one organization we worked with had Novell servers with malfunctioning routing. Users did not notice it when running in fat-client mode. When they became completely dependent upon MetaFrame servers, the routing problems quickly became intolerable.

One intended outcome of the infrastructure assessment is to identify any network or infrastructure issues and resolve them before a beta rollout. Some problems, though, are likely to be missed. IT should be prepared to resolve them quickly as they show up. Users should understand that a beta is still an expanded pilot and that bugs will have to be worked out.

Adequate Bandwidth

Ensure that bandwidth will be adequate to remote offices where users will be part of the beta. User counts should be verified. Bandwidth management tools that actually shape WAN traffic such as Packeteer PacketShapers should be utilized, if possible. Take into consideration any additional traffic required during the transition period, and order the bandwidth accordingly.

Local Legacy System Access

In an enterprise server–based computing rollout, we recommend putting databases adjacent to the MetaFrame XP server farm. During the beta, though, this may not always be possible. Remote users may require access to local servers or host systems, but their sessions are now running on the MetaFrame XP server farm at headquarters. As Figure 10-5 shows, this means that users are accessing local servers across the WAN. Depending

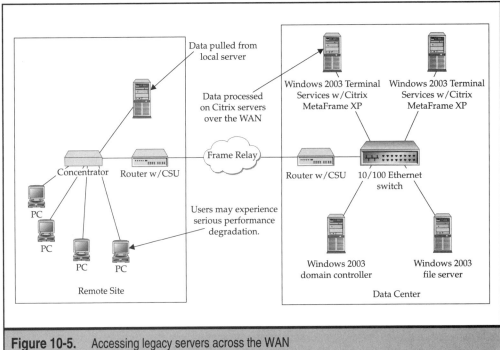

Figure 10-5. Accessing legacy servers across the WAN

upon the databases and WAN bandwidth, they may experience much slower performance than they are used to. The beta participants should have their expectations set accordingly, along with the knowledge that it is a temporary problem that will be eliminated once the enterprise rollout takes place.

The other reason that legacy systems need focused attention is that they tend to be expensive or special purpose and cannot easily be run in parallel as the server-based computing project plan may dictate. These systems usually need to be "cut over" rather abruptly as they move from the old to the new environment. A separate, detailed project plan to accomplish this is required, as is a separate project team to address the special needs of these systems.

Local File Sharing

During the beta, remote users may still be allowed to share files locally. During the enterprise rollout, this practice should be eliminated wherever possible. The beta is the perfect time to start making the transition.

CD-ROM Sharing

If users at a site need to share CD-ROMs, this can be done using a small CD-ROM server or even a PC with sharing enabled. We recommend against this if it can be avoided because it is difficult to support centrally. If CD-ROMs must be shared, place a CD-ROM server at the data center nearest the user, and use groups and scripting to give the user access to the volumes as part of the login process.

Application Considerations During Beta

Make sure that all of the applications to be run via server-based computing are part of the beta. Some selection criteria include

- ▼ The total number of people who need to run the application
- ■ How often the users require access to the application
- ▲ How many users would have to remain on PCs instead of Windows terminals if you do not migrate the application

Some applications may have exhibited troublesome signs during the pilot, but it might take a beta to see how they really perform under a production environment. In this case, the problematic applications should be layered into the beta one at a time in order to minimize disruption to other applications and to users' perceptions of the SBC environment's reliability.

Apply the same rigor for testing these new applications before deploying them as part of the beta as you would if deploying them in your enterprise production environment. The beta is your last chance to work the kinks out of the testing and deployment process before going live.

User Selection During Beta

The beta should be a microcosm of the ultimate enterprise SBC environment. As with the pilot phases, users should be friendly to the concept of server-based computing. Users can be layered into the beta until all categories and groups of users are represented.

Also, be sure to get an accurate count for the number of users in remote offices. If the number is too low, the bandwidth ordered will not be sufficient. As with the production pilot, users should also be aware that they will be participating in a beta and are likely to have some performance and reliability issues come up.

> *Properly documenting and testing key procedures during the beta process is one of the fundamental elements to a successful large-scale SBC deployment. The documents Westaff developed were an indispensable tool, which allowed us to efficiently create over 1100 user accounts for over 260 locations. It also enabled us to maintain consistency among all accounts and helped us complete our rollout one month ahead of schedule.*
>
> —Rob Hutter,
> Systems Engineering Manager, Westaff

Testing During Beta

The test lists prepared for the pilot program should be updated for the beta and utilized again. In addition, appropriate infrastructure tests for bandwidth and redundancy should be performed, and their results evaluated. The beta period is the time to hone a healthy intolerance for error. If a system is not performing as expected, it should be fixed immediately. After all, garbage doesn't smell better with age.

Service Level Agreements

Earlier in this chapter, we introduced the concept of a service level agreement (SLA) and how to use SLAs for the enterprise SBC environment. You can also apply SLAs effectively to the deployment process. They can be used to provide the pilot and beta users with the proper expectations for system stability, performance, and help desk response times, for example. It is important both to set service level agreements and to manage them. For instance, a beta user may have a problem with her newly installed ICA client. This affects her ability to participate in the beta, but it does not affect her ability to do work. The associated SLA for help desk response should reflect this by allowing enough time for overburdened technicians to respond to more critical problems first.

Incorporating What You Learned from the Pilot Program

Now is the time to review the information collected during the pilot. Help desk call logs, user requests and comments, performance metrics, application changes performed, and system administration logs all provide a wealth of information and a platform for improvement during the beta phase.

Beta Assessment

IT must honestly assess whether the beta environment meets the production scope requirements. If not, adjustments must be made either to the technology or to the scope. Sometimes, the beta will have outcomes exceeding expectations that might also lead to scope reevaluations. For example, an organization originally intending to deploy only a couple of applications may determine that users are eager to run all of their applications in the new way. If this is the case, the beta should reflect any changes before the enterprise rollout occurs.

ENTERPRISE ROLLOUT

All contingencies must be completed before the start of the enterprise rollout. Data centers and network upgrades should be complete. Equipment staging should be ready. Rollout teams should be ready to be deployed.

User Training During Rollout

Ensure high attendance for training sessions through management e-mails and user incentives. Be creative. Include project marketing along with the training sessions in order to reinforce initial project acceptance. Use rainbow packets, desk-side orientation, and videos. If your help desk charges users per incident, establish a grace period for free support during the conversion. As discussed previously, the amount of training necessary is likely to be limited to a short orientation to the new environment. Of much greater importance is effective marketing to get the users to embrace the change as something positive.

Expanding Service Level Agreements

Beta SLAs should be expanded to fit the conditions appropriate to a production rollout. For example, you may want to intentionally set the help desk response to a short period—say, one hour—for newly converted users, to make sure any initial problems are solved quickly.

Creating a Deployment Guide

For a large enterprise conversion to server-based computing, creating a deployment guide can be very helpful in making the process go smoothly. This is particularly important if you have a large number of remote offices requiring multiple implementation teams. Though the audience for such a guide is technically proficient, it is important to have a guide for reasons of consistency. If deployment technicians are allowed to carry out the migration their own way, it will be that much more difficult to troubleshoot problems as they arise. The deployment guide should include the following sections:

▼ **User communication FAQ** Arm the deployment technician with answers to common questions encountered during the pilot and beta stages. This type of FAQ will help tremendously with conflict resolution and will help maintain a professional image for the technician.

■ **Contact information** List the appropriate contacts and phone extensions for IT staff to support specific issues, including desktop migration, printer setups, wide area network problems, and Windows terminals. The escalation paths for different types of problems should be clear.

■ **Data migration procedure** Spell out the specific steps for migrating data. Figure 10-6 shows a copy of the data migration procedure that ABM Industries used for their remote offices.

▲ **Client installations** The deployment guide should include detailed instructions for installing each type of ICA client you intend to deploy. Each installation method should include a checklist and any relevant screenshots to make the procedure clear.

TIP: Using Web Interface for MetaFrame to deploy applications or a published desktop will automatically deploy the ICA client and keep it current with the latest release.

■ **Desktop device configuration** Include a table showing all categories of users and their associated devices, such as hybrid PCs, laptops, and Windows terminals. Include a list of the appropriate equipment for each category of user, such as a monitor or network card. Include IP and DNS setup as well as things like how to set up LPD printing on Windows terminals.

■ **Shadowing users** Support personnel can use shadowing to take control of users' PCs or Windows terminals for troubleshooting purposes. Show how to set up shadowing, including screen prints for each step.

■ **VPN or Internet dial-up connectivity** If remote users are connecting to the data center through a WAN or VPN, explain how to set up the VPN client software on a PC, configure the Windows terminal's SecureICA functions, or whatever is appropriate to your environment.

■ **Printing** Recap which printers are supported and which ones will work with bandwidth management devices, if appropriate. If printers are not supported, include instructions about the proper procedures to take when such a printer is encountered during deployment.

■ **IP address scheme** A workable IP addressing scheme needs to be implemented if it hasn't been already. If DHCP is to be used, explain how to configure the client to take advantage of it.

▲ **General migration issues** Include answers to problems that the implementation team may encounter, such as what to do if a user scheduled for migration is absent or if a user's PC is not operating properly under MetaFrame.

Checklist and Procedures

Data Migration Procedure (all desktops)

1. Determine if total amount of data to be copied from all sources is less than 20MB (C:\ & H:\). If so, skip to WAN-Based File Copy Procedure below.

2. Determine the file system type of the PC. DOS/Windows 3.x should be FAT16. Windows 9x should be FAT32 and Windows NT should be NTFS. Choose the appropriate boot disk for the PC.

3. Determine the number of hard drives and the number of partitions on each hard drive. The easiest way to do this is with the DOS FDISK program.

4. Attach Jaz drive to user's PC and insert the floppy chosen in step 2 in drive A:. Reboot the PC.

5. After boot scandisk will run on the C: drive. When the A:\ prompt appears run scandisk.

Figure 10-6. ABM's data migration procedure guidelines

Creating Migration Databases

A huge migration involves a large number of employees, all requiring current information. Developing databases to sort and track this information will significantly enhance the process. Making this database available in some ubiquitous fashion, such as web publishing, will help assure its adoption and currency. The following are some ideas for different aspects of the deployment process that you should consider tracking in this way.

Locations Database

List every location and pertinent information, including current status, data connectivity status, number of users, type of users, and the implementation team assigned. The implementation, WAN, and procurement teams should update this database as part of their normal process. For example, after a user is installed, the deployment team member can connect to the locations database from the user's new client and enter the information that the user has been installed and any asset information on the equipment assigned to that user.

Change-Management Database

Track everything that changes at the data center, including new applications, printer drivers, and all unscheduled downtime. This enables much better troubleshooting of modifications causing problems. Significant changes in the field, such as large bandwidth increases, premise router changes, and the like, can also be entered here for all to see.

Survey Databases

User surveys taken at the various deployment stages can be entered and the results tracked here.

Migrating Headquarters

Converting users at headquarters to a server-based computing environment is much easier than migrating remote offices. The planning design document should cover most of the contingencies you are likely to run up against when migrating headquarters. The close proximity of these users to IT and the lack of bandwidth variables make it relatively easy to identify and remedy problems. For these reasons, it is generally advisable to migrate headquarters before migrating users at remote offices, even though the latter may have the greater need. As always, new users should be added to the SBC environment in layers in order to minimize disruptions caused by unexpected problems.

User Training for Headquarters Migration

If IT is unable to bring users to headquarters for training before migration, they will have to rely on videos and other media such as documentation for much of the server-based computing orientation. A quick training procedure should be developed for the implementation team to use when they are at the site doing the conversion.

Client Operating System Upgrades

Although the MetaFrame XP client will operate with nearly any client, from DOS to Windows XP to LINUX, some organizations prefer to standardize on one operating system platform to make administration easier. In this case, the operating system can be migrated as part of the implementation process. Since the result will be users accessing their applications from the corporate data center, individual PC issues are a minor concern in terms of project success.

User Data Migration

It is possible to write scripts to migrate data off users' local PCs and transfer it to a centralized file server. This can be accomplished through batch files or with WSH (Windows Scripting Host).

Desktop Application Migration

In the pilot program, we recommended leaving local applications in place and moving, or removing, icons. In a production environment, we recommend eliminating SBC applications from local PCs altogether in order to ensure that users operate only in the intended server-based computing environment. There are many methods for uninstalling applications. Microsoft SMS has this capability, or you can "roll your own," using scripting tools such as WSH and ADSI, as mentioned in Chapter 15.

Planning for Remote Office Migration

The project design document will almost certainly focus on the corporate data center and users at headquarters. Although remote offices and their users can be categorized in broad terms, the project plan is not likely to encompass specific implementation details if a large number of remote facilities are part of the project. In these cases, we recommend creating a separate implementation plan for the actual server-based computing rollout.

Assess Remote Office Infrastructure

Completing a detailed assessment of the remote office networks and environments enables much better planning and, consequently, a much smoother implementation. A good tool for this is a site survey. You can assess the infrastructure, the number of users, equipment, and any other special needs in the survey. As we will discuss later in the chapter, you will have several teams available for doing field deployments. During the inevitable periods when the team members are not in the field due to scheduling, have them perform the surveys.

NOTE: You may already have a tool in place, such as Microsoft SMS, that is capable of doing hardware inventory across the WAN. This is useful but is not a substitute for a site survey. Use the polling results from SMS during the survey as part of the discussion with the people onsite, but don't treat it as gospel. Not all hardware you are interested in will respond to a poll, and you need to be as accurate as possible.

Determining Time Constraints

Since implementing SBC is usually very economically advantageous, time is often the biggest project constraint. Establish guidelines to ensure that project timelines are met. Communicate these time limits to users before the implementation in order to help gain their support in making the migration successful. Make the time limits part of the SLA for the implementation team, and manage them. This means accurate collection of the data and publishing the results to the team. Then discuss what can be done to improve problem times.

Implementation Team Follow-Up   Create a way for the implementation teams to check on the status of each time-critical item remotely. One method to accomplish this follow-up is to create an intranet site that can be accessed once the user is online.

System Implementation Time Limit   Set a maximum amount of time that an implementation team member can spend on any single system to ensure that an office can be migrated in a reasonable amount of time. For instance, you may determine that converting a user to server-based computing should take no more than an hour. If a conversion runs over an hour, the user is given a Windows terminal, and her existing data is not migrated to the data center. Though this is obviously not ideal, it will keep the project on track and only inconvenience the user in question.

PC Preparation Time Limit   Set a limit, tied to the conversion time limit, on how much time to spend preparing a PC for migration. For instance, if the conversion time limit for a PC is an hour, you may wish to set a 30-minute time limit on preparing the PC.

Communication Lines   If a new or upgraded WAN was put into place, confirm that the line was installed, and test connectivity before the implementation team's arrival at a remote office. Do not, under any circumstances, rely on the telecommunication provider's word that the line is in and working. Test it yourself.

User Accounts   Set up user accounts in NT a minimum of one day before the installation. The help desk, in cooperation with the field deployment teams, should do the setup.

Remote Office Data Migration

In a typical conversion from PC-based to server-based computing, data will be migrated from PCs and remote office servers back to the corporate data center. Remember that the migration process can take longer than planned due to unexpected problems such as delays in the WAN implementations, conflicts in employee work schedules, and delayed shipments of hardware.

User Training for Remote Office Migration

Users should first be exposed to preliminary marketing materials and videos so that they know what to expect. The implementation team's responsibilities should include a brief user training session. Users should sign forms indicating that they have received training prior to the implementation team's departure.

In some organizations, the ability of SBC to deliver computing capabilities inexpensively means that it will sometimes be a user's first experience with networking services, or even with using a computer. In these cases, extra thought needs to go into the training of using the PC, applications, and network in order to save the help desk from a deluge of calls.

Desktop Data Migration

There are many techniques for migrating data from PCs back to the data center, depending upon the infrastructure and service level agreements. It is important to come up with a universal method where possible. In a local area network environment, the bandwidth should be sufficient to copy the data directly to the servers. If a wide area network has sufficient bandwidth to copy files to the data center, this methodology will be the easiest to use. Your first impulse might be to copy the user data over the network to the data center. In a large, distributed organization with many offices, this could quickly cripple the network. Sometimes simple methods are the best ones. After trying many sophisticated methods, we've found the following works well:

1. Tell the users that they will have access to their current working files immediately, and the rest of the data on their hard disks in 48 hours, as part of the deployment SLA.
2. Make sure the users' accounts and login environment are ready.
3. From the users' desktops, copy their working files across the network to the data center. The data allowance for this copy should be small—perhaps 5MB to 10MB maximum. Most users will have far less data than this.
4. Using a prepared boot disk and a parallel-attached backup device, reboot the PC and copy the contents to the removable media.

NOTE: There are many options when deciding what to copy to the media in such an operation. If users have been using Windows for a while, most of their data is probably in the My Documents folder. Rather than guess, it is better to copy all data except the Windows directory. Program files, of course, should not be copied.

5. Send the removable media via overnight shipping to the data center.
6. Provide a brief orientation. When users log in, they should immediately have access to their working files and new applications.
7. Within 48 hours, load the removable media at the data center and copy the files into the users' directories.

NOTE: If minimal filtering was carried out when copying the data from the client, filtering should be done when restoring the media at the data center. Consider a simple script that copies files by extension (*.xls, *.doc, *.wri, and so on) to the users' new home directories. It will catch most of the data they need. If anything is missed, you still have the removable media to refer to. Store this media long enough to be sure users won't be likely to need another restore.

At ABM Industries, our engineers worked in conjunction with personnel to form six migration teams. We used Jaz drives to back up data from PCs, and tape drives to back up data from servers. We sent the drives and tapes back to the data center by overnight delivery, where they were restored to ABM's Network Appliance Filer. We had an SLA in place that guaranteed users access to their information within 48 hours of conversion to the new environment.

Migration of Server Data   Data can be moved to the data center before the rollout via backup tapes. Anything that changes after that date can be moved over the WAN. Any modern backup program can do backups based on the "archive bit" of the file that is set each time a file is written to tape. A full backup of the server can be done and sent to the data center before the deployment team arrives. After all the users at that site have been converted, a differential backup (only changed files) is run and sent via overnight delivery to the data center. Those files are then restored as soon as possible. This scheme works because any file the user is currently working on is copied to the data center over the WAN for immediate access as part of that user's migration process.

Rogue Applications

Even the best planning often does not prepare implementation teams for what they face in the field. When unexpected applications are discovered, the project manager should be immediately notified, particularly if the users are scheduled to be converted to run in thin-client mode only. A decision can then be made about whether to allow access to the applications locally, or to halt the rollout and do the preparatory testing required to host the applications over SBC. One technique is to migrate what you can at that office but leave one or two PCs and the local file server just for running the problem application. Establish a "sunset period" in which the equipment will be removed and the application will no longer be available or supported.

Remote Office Migration Teams

A project with many remote offices will likely require several teams to ensure a successful migration within a reasonable time period. These might include one or more implementation teams, a WAN team, and a procurement team.

Implementation Teams

Enough implementation teams should be chosen to meet the timelines for data migration. An implementation team completes the appropriate remote site surveys and submits them (online preferably) to the WAN team. The WAN team can then make sure that adequate communication lines are ordered and installed before the field team's arrival.

Choosing Team Members   Desirable qualities for team members include both technical skills and training capabilities. Personality and training skills generally outweigh technical skills. Making the implementation process very simple can compensate for the lack of technical skills in implementers. On the other hand, superior technical skills do not compensate for the lack of interpersonal skills. When implementers do a good job explaining the server-based computing system, the users are more understanding when inevitable problems occur. The individual team member should be armed with skills for conflict resolution and must be familiar with the support and escalation process. Team members must also be people that the users will trust and want to work with.

Consultant/IT Staff Mix   If using a consulting company to help with your migration, we recommend using a mix of internal and external consultants on each team. This provides expertise and objectivity combined with internal IT and organizational knowledge. It also provides a good, informal method of transferring knowledge from external experts to internal staff.

Facilitating Effective Teamwork   It is important that the implementation teams work together and share their experiences in order to avoid making the same mistake twice. Facilitate this practice by giving each team member a cell phone and two-way radio, by giving each member access to the corporate e-mail system, and by having members of the project management team join each implementation team for part of their trips. Scheduling weekly teleconferences for all members can be particularly useful in helping to avoid making repetitive mistakes and for sharing ways to improve the implementation process among all teams and members. These conferences can also be a forum for sharing good news and quickly improving methods when problems occur.

The Road Kit   The material that each deployment team member will carry makes up the *road kit*. It should be well stocked, and the procedures for replenishing it should be simple and understood by team members before they visit the first site. Using our example methods described in the chapter, a road kit might contain a boot disk, CD-RW drive, laptop, overnight courier materials, Ethernet cables, cross-over cables, and an extra floppy drive.

WAN Team

The WAN team orders data connections and bandwidth upgrades. They confirm the installation of these lines. They order and ship any required routers or bandwidth management devices to remote sites before the implementation, or make sure the telecommunication provider does so.

Procurement Team

Responsible for the overall logistics of the project, the procurement team orders and ships the equipment. They should check to ensure receipt of the equipment at least one week before installation. The procurement team also updates the remote office surveys to reflect the new equipment and properly tracks the asset on the company's books after it has been installed. They should also process equipment returns and have the ability to quickly respond to mistakes and make sure the deployment team and the site have the equipment they need.

Deployment Challenges

Every server-based computing implementation will face unique challenges depending upon the existing environment, project scope, and technology utilized. Some issues will be impossible to anticipate. Others are fairly common and include travel, printing, local file sharing, CD-ROM sharing, and access to legacy systems from remote locations.

TIP: Do not make assumptions. When replacing a user's PC with a Windows terminal for one of our clients, the implementation team encountered a particularly irate user. The implementation team member could not get the new terminal to communicate with the existing monitor despite hours of trouble-shooting. After a second day of lost productivity, the team leader finally discovered that the monitor had never worked. The user neglected to tell the installer because he wanted to see if the new Windows terminal could fix it.

Travel

Extensive remote office implementations require dealing with issues such as travel arrangements and scheduling. Covering large geographical regions may necessitate a great deal of travel, which may in turn limit the number of willing participants on implementation teams. In addition, last-minute scheduling changes can quickly eat up the travel budget. Careful planning and control are essential in managing this project cost.

Bad Tapes or Backups

It is best not to rely on existing backup tapes. The safest procedure is not to wipe out any hard drives or recycle existing PCs until you are sure that all required data is off the PCs, on the new servers, and the users have had the opportunity to confirm this and sign off on the operation.

Printing

Printing is such a major challenge that we devoted Chapter 17 to it. In general, try to standardize as much as possible on the printers used. In particular, try to limit the print drivers to those supported natively by Windows Server 2003. Some older printers simply will not run well under Terminal Services. Replacing these printers before the migration will eliminate the added pressure on the implementation teams of ordering new ones onsite.

Data Line Procurement

Anticipate problems in getting WAN connectivity completed according to installation promises. Plan to do more work up front in order to ensure that the data connectivity is complete before installation. Even when a local exchange carrier (LEC) confirms that a data connection is complete, take the time to test it yourself. We've seen miscommunication between an LEC and a national telecommunication carrier cost a project weeks of time and thousands of dollars.

PCs

Using Web Interface for MetaFrame automatically deploys and keeps the ICA client current. Otherwise, even the easy task of installing the Citrix MetaFrame XP client can become arduous when migrating thousands of users. In this case, the easier migration may be to simply give users a Windows terminal.

Inaccurate Site Surveys

Most organizations depend on user surveys to determine the type and state of equipment in remote offices. Impress upon the survey respondents how crucial it is for them to report this information accurately in order to avoid costly implementation delays and potential downtime. If your organization already has a tool in place that does hardware inventories, such as Microsoft SMS or HP OpenView, make sure the data is current. If possible, confirm critical items shown in the inventory, such as site routers or servers, with a phone call.

POSTPRODUCTION MANAGEMENT OF THE SBC ENVIRONMENT

SBC is now rolled out across the enterprise. Your users are happy, and your IT staff has joined the swelling ranks of server-based computing evangelists. Performance should be compared with both expectations and established success metrics. The results should be reported to both management and users.

Measuring User Satisfaction

One method for measuring user satisfaction is to send out surveys asking users to grade the project on various criteria, including performance, reliability, how well it meets expectations, ease of use, training, and implementation. Compare the user satisfaction results with those obtained in surveys taken before the SBC deployment. You can also use the surveys to find out what other attributes users would like.

Rate Project Milestones

Were project milestones reached on time? For instance, one milestone may have been to migrate all headquarters users within 60 days of the project start. Record and publish the results.

Updating the Budget

Measure actual expenditures against the budget. Update the financial feasibility model with the project costs as well as with costs as they accrue going forward. This will enable a return on investment (ROI) to be calculated for the project over a three-to-five-year period.

Measuring SBC Benefits

During the beta and the production deployment, you established service levels for your SBC environment. These service levels represent an agreement between the IT staff and the user community. Part of the agreement is that the IT staff will manage the system to meet certain established metrics and goals. The data needed to establish whether these goals are being met needs to be collected diligently and continuously. For example, if part of the SLA is 99.99 percent system uptime, every blue screen or other server outage needs to be recorded, as well as major network disruptions for a given region or data center.

Publishing Results

The collected data does no good unless the appropriate people review it. There should be a policy of no secrets between the IT staff and the user community. Establish a reporting cycle as part of the SLA. It may not be critical for a user to see daily status, but it may be appropriate to display quarterly or monthly SLA results. This will depend on your corporate culture and what your internal reporting capabilities are.

Establishing an SBC Steering Committee

A technique for keeping IT staff and the user community focused on continuous improvement is to create a committee made up of both groups. The user representatives should be as diverse as the reach of the server-based computing project. If the SBC environment is multinational, a representative from each major region or country should participate. The exact scope and responsibility of the committee will depend on your corporate culture, but it should at least evaluate and recommend changes to the server-based computing environment.

Providing a Forum for Feedback "Outside the Box"

The help desk will record user problems and outages. In addition, you should provide a way for any employee of the company to give suggestions or constructive criticism. This input should be reviewed and evaluated by the steering committee. We've found that brilliant suggestions sometimes come from the most unlikely places.

Making Fact-Based Decisions on the Future Direction of Your SBC Environment

Collecting and reporting on established SLAs and keeping the users involved results in invaluable information for making decisions about the future of your company's server-based computing initiative. Even after a successful rollout, there may be factions within the company that remain unconvinced as to the value of server-based computing. Having facts to back up a recommendation to expand the infrastructure or add applications can mean the difference between an environment's success or its failure.

Establishing a Server-Based Computing Lab

To maintain a high quality of service, it is necessary to maintain a lab environment where new versions of software and hardware can be evaluated and tested. This lab does not need to be onsite. In fact, manufacturers often allow their facilities to be used for this purpose, as long as you agree to share the results. Regularly check the web sites of Microsoft and Citrix for the latest information on changes and upgrades. The Citrix knowledge base, in particular, is an excellent place to find this kind of information. Since your SBC environment is now tested and stable, any change must be rigorously evaluated and tested before deployment.

Sharing Your Experiences

After getting the proper clearance from management, seek out other companies that have undergone similar server-based computing deployments, and offer to share information. Even if a nondisclosure agreement is necessary, the result will be an enrichment of the server-based computing environment at each company. Participate in server-based computing-related forums and events from Citrix and Microsoft to keep up on the latest developments and share your experiences. Finally, seek out peers on the Internet, in discussion groups, chat rooms, e-forums, or other areas.

Server-based computing on an enterprise level is an emerging technology. Manufacturers of server-based computing hardware and software are eager to help you publicize your success by writing and publishing success stories. In this way, you can help contribute to the growing momentum behind this new and tremendously exciting industry.

CHAPTER 11

Server Configuration: Windows Terminal Services

As we've established thus far in this book, it takes far more to build a server-based computing environment than just following the installation manuals for the software. In this chapter, we will discuss the installation and configuration tips, tricks, and techniques we have developed over the last five years of working with the server-based computing products from Citrix and Microsoft. Clearly, the majority of the work required to build an SBC environment is in building and configuring the servers and applications, and thus this chapter covers the many nuances and tricks to sizing and building a stable Terminal Services Farm based on Windows 2000/2003. The next chapter, Chapter 12, will cover the installation and configuration of Citrix MetaFrame, and Chapter 13 will cover the installation of the applications. All three chapters will provide installation steps in the form of checklists. Our checklists will include not only the steps to installing and configuring the software, but also explanations of pertinent options and their effects, indications where additional configuration may be required, information on hotfixes and service packs, and general information we think is necessary in order to deploy the technology effectively.

We will assume, for the purposes of this chapter, that the reader is familiar with the basics of installing and configuring, and with administering Windows 2000 Server.

Although we provide detailed, step-by-step instructions, we are not advocating that every server be built from scratch. Rather, we will also discuss how to use various tools to effectively create additional servers from a standard image. This standard image will be accessed from an application deployment server or CD-ROM to automatically build additional servers in the server farm.

CAUTION: Many of the suggestions and recommendations in this chapter involve making changes directly to the registry.

We recommend that readers adhere to the following safety guidelines before making any of these changes to the registry:

▼   Become familiar with REGEDT32 and REGEDIT (REGEDIT is fully functional in Windows 2003, but REGEDT32 is required in some instances in Windows 2000 due to deficiencies with REGEDIT).

■   *Always* make backups to the key being changed with the REGEDT32 "save key" feature. This will allow you to go back to a previous state and possibly save hours of rebuilding as you create your first "gold image."

▲   Never change the registry on a production server or on a server you can't otherwise afford to lose.

We have tested these changes on several production systems, but it isn't possible to test them on all hardware platforms and configuration settings. As such, we recommend strongly that you follow the pilot and beta methodology and thoroughly test these changes before relying on them in a production SBC environment.

PLANNING THE TERMINAL SERVER HARDWARE PLATFORM

Prior to purchasing the servers and installing the operating system, the first question that must be answered is how many servers are needed. The art of determining how many and what size servers are required for a server-based computing infrastructure has long been argued and discussed with more disagreement than agreement. The disagreement surrounds the fact that both applications and end users vary greatly from organization to organization in terms of required resources, how they use the resources, how often they use them, and how well behaved they are (that is, do the applications or users have memory leaks, large bandwidth requirements, crashing problems, or other difficulties). Chapter 10 detailed how to build a pilot environment and the need for testing prior to implementation. Testing is absolutely essential to providing an organization with the basics of whether applications will perform in an SBC environment, and whether they will scale to multiple users. However, the problem with a simple test in a small pilot environment is that most applications, networks, and servers do not scale linearly indefinitely (due to the large number of variables just listed), making it unreliable to simply extrapolate based on a small testing environment. Thus, if an organization plans to scale an SBC to the enterprise with 500 users or more, we strongly recommend simulating a larger number of users. A good test plan is to build a test environment to simulate at least 10 percent of the eventual expected number of concurrent users to understand and estimate how many servers are needed. Using our case study as an example, Clinical Medical Equipment Corporation (CME) (introduced in Chapter 10), with 3000 total users and 2500 concurrent users, we will need to test 250 concurrent users. Prior to detailing how to perform large-scale simulations, a discussion on server hardware and operating system installation is worthwhile.

The following section discusses server hardware in more depth and provides some examples of what size servers to start with and what server components to consider.

Server Hardware

Since an SBC environment puts all users at the mercy of the servers, server hardware has always been a major point of discussion. Four years ago, there was a dramatic performance, reliability, and support difference between "white box" servers and servers sold by the top three server players (then HP, Compaq, and IBM). Ever since, major industry changes in the form of dramatic cost reduction of the hardware, Intel hardware standardization, and the globalization of third-party support, have all come together to dramatically level the playing field of server hardware manufacturers. Today, Dell consistently competes head-to-head with HP (which now incorporates Compaq) and IBM, and we have found that many white-box vendors produce reliable hardware with almost identical components to HP, Dell, and IBM. Although the risk of destroying an SBC project by choosing the wrong server hardware platform is now lower than it was four years ago, we still highly recommend choosing a provider that is Windows Server 2003 certified by Microsoft, and that has proven priority onsite, 24/7 support.

NOTE: It is important to keep each server in the farm as similar as possible, because variations in hardware can lead to the need for additional images or scripting work. Thus, when purchasing servers, buy sufficient quantities to account for items like future growth (plan at least one year out), redundancy requirements, and test systems.

Central Processing Units

The number of processors, the amount of memory, and I/O speed will all influence the number of users that can run applications on a server. Since enterprises will be running servers in a load-balanced farm, the number of users per server must be balanced against the number of servers in the farm. Additionally, because of the shared DLL environment of Windows 2000 and 2003, some applications may have conflicts with other applications, memory leaks, or other programmatical deficiencies, thus requiring additional servers to house separate applications. Consequently, a greater number of low-scale servers will provide more fault-tolerance and application flexibility (and if they crash, fewer users will be affected), while a smaller number of highly scaleable servers (say, 4-, 16-, or 32-processor servers) will be simpler to manage and will take less space, HVAC, and power in the data center. For all but the largest environments, we have found a good compromise, both based on cost and functionality, to be two-processor servers with 2–4GB of RAM in a 2U rack-based form factor running Windows Server 2003, Standard Edition. A two-processor server (P4 Zeon) or better will provide excellent performance for 20–60 users, depending on the application suite (see the server-sizing discussion that follows). For larger enterprises (2500 users or more), blade servers or highly scalable servers should be considered in order to minimize the data center requirements and daily management activities. Additionally, as 16–32 processor servers become more commonplace, the use of VMware Server or Microsoft Connectix Virtual Server products to virtualize 4–16 Windows Server 2003 servers on one hardware machine may become economically advantageous. The determining factor will be in how HP, IBM, and other high-end server manufacturers price these highly scalable hardware platforms. Regarding our case study, CME Corp., the decision is not obvious, as the 2500 concurrent user count can go either way, depending on how many users we can fit on a server, available data center space, and current cost of the hardware options. Since the most significant variable is the number of users per server, the discussion later in this chapter on how to perform a more precise server sizing test is critical.

Memory

Nearly all servers today come with ECC (Error-Correcting Code) memory, and most have a maximum capacity of 4–6GB in a basic configuration. Windows Server 2003 Standard Edition will accept 4GB of memory, and the 32-bit Enterprise and Datacenter Editions support 32GB and 64GB respectively. As stated earlier, we only recommend the use of highly scalable servers (four processors or more, 32GB or more of memory) in SBC environments with over 2500 users in conjunction with a Virtualization product (for example, VMware Server or Microsoft Connectix Virtual Server), as the Virtualization reduces the risk of having hundreds of users impacted by one blue-screen or fatal software error.

Network Interface Cards

Most servers today come with Gigabit networking built-in, and in most cases, dual Gigabit networking. If a network card needs to be added to a server, we recommend only using the "server" type—that is, those NICs that have their own processor and can offload the job of handling network traffic from the CPU. We also recommend using two NICs in a *teaming* configuration to provide additional bandwidth to the server as well as redundancy (if one network card fails, the server remains live since it can run off of the remaining live card).

NOTE: Most 10/100 NICs have the ability to autonegotiate between speeds and full- and half-duplex settings. We have experienced significant problems with this in production, especially when mixing NICs and network backbone equipment from different vendors. Thus, we strongly recommend nailing the cards to 100Mbit full-duplex (assuming that the server NICs plug into a 100Mbit switch), and standardizing it on all equipment. See Chapter 6 for a more detailed discussion of network design and requirements.

Server Hard Drives

The hard drive system plays a different role with terminal servers than it does for standard file servers. In general, no user data is stored or written on a terminal server, and a server image will be available for rebuild, so the main goal when designing and building the hard drive system for a terminal server is read speed and uptime. We have found hardware RAID 5 to be a cost-effective approach to gaining both read speed and uptime (if any one of the drives fails, the server will remain up). RAID 5 requires a minimum of three drives and a hardware RAID controller. We recommend the use of the smallest, fastest drives available (18GB, 15K RPM at the time of this writing.)

Another option that is becoming affordably priced and offers even greater speed and reliability is solid state drive systems. Because solid state drives do not have moving parts, they can be up to 800 percent faster and dramatically more reliable than EIDE or SCSI drives. We suspect that as vendors increase reliability and the cost of solid state systems decrease, they will become common place in SBC environments.

Other Hardware Factors

The following are related recommendations for an SBC hardware environment:

▼ **Power supplies**   Server power supplies should be redundant and fail over automatically if the primary unit fails.

■ **Racking**   All server farms should be racked for safety, scalability, and ease of access. Never put servers on unsecured shelves within a rack.

- ■ **Cable management** Clearly label or color code (or both) all cables traveling between servers and the network patch panel or network backbone. It will save a tremendous amount of time later when troubleshooting a connection.

- ▲ **Multiconsole** Use a multiconsole switch instead of installing a monitor or keyboard for each server. It saves space, power, and HVAC.

PRE-INSTALLATION CONSIDERATIONS

Before getting started with loading and configuring Windows Server 2000 or 2003, there are some important considerations to think about.

- ▼ *Review the Microsoft hardware compatibility list.* Microsoft publishes this list at http://www.microsoft.com/hwdq/hcl/, but does not guarantee that the hardware listed will work flawlessly with Terminal Services, nor that hardware not listed will not work. It does certify that the hardware listed has been tested and provides a good starting point for evaluation. Only consider hardware not on the list if it is known to work with Terminal Services and MetaFrame.

- ■ *Make sure your existing file server, domain controllers, and Active Directory infrastructure are installed and functioning properly.* You will be storing scripts, Group Policy objects, and templates centrally, not on each MetaFrame server. In addition, a file server will need to be installed and be accessible when your servers go online.

- ■ *Make sure all required drivers and startup disks are available.* Even with the maturity of the Windows Server platform, hardware is constantly changing, and special drivers may be required for RAID controllers, NICs, the BIOS, or other server components when loading Windows Server 2000/2003. Make sure these are available and on the appropriate media before you begin.

- ■ *Review information on platform-specific issues.* The respective web-based knowledge bases from Citrix and Microsoft have a wealth of information on different server hardware. It is prudent to review this information and circumvent potential problems before they occur. This review may even serve to change your mind about which hardware to purchase.

- ■ *Prepare hardware.* Thoroughly prepare and test your hardware before attempting to load any software. Make sure all shipping protection has been removed. Open the case and make sure all components are securely seated and installed correctly. Power-on the server and run the vendor's diagnostics on the entire system. If your vendor hasn't "burned in" the server, let the diagnostics run at least overnight, if not for a few days, to eliminate any "lemons" before you begin to rely on the system.

- ▲ *Double-check the data center environment.* Don't assume power, cooling, or moisture levels are adequate. Check them out with the data center staff and compare them to published tolerances from the hardware manufacturer.

OPERATING SYSTEM INSTALLATION PROCEDURES

The following step-by-step instructions are meant to provide a quick reference for installing Windows 2000 Server and Windows Server 2003 with Terminal Services. Included in these instructions are the post-installation changes we recommend to address limitations in the operating system itself. These limitations are often due to insufficient default values, but they can also be settings to work around bugs, or simply changes we think are necessary to the "health and well-being" of an SBC environment. After each recommended change, we provide the setting value or instructions, as well as the reason. Where possible, we have also provided a URL reference with more information on why that change may be necessary.

For the first server build in the farm, document every step in order to create installation procedure documentation. This documentation will be the blue print for all future server builds and serve as a portion of a disaster recovery plan.

The following is an example of the installation procedures needed for Windows 2000 Server:

Step	Description
1.	Install and configure server hardware: –Unpackage and prep hardware –Update the firmware to the latest versions
2.	If hardware like Compaq/Dell servers will be used, run the appropriate configuration software—for example, Smart Start.
3.	Press F6 to install third-party SCSI or RAID driver(s) that are not currently on the Windows 2000 CD-ROM, if needed.
4.	Press ENTER to continue with the installation.
5.	Press F8 to agree with the license agreement.
6.	Follow on screen prompts to create the appropriate partitions.
7.	Select to format the partition using the NTFS file system. Setup will format the partition and copy installation files. When completed, it will reboot the system and continue to the GUI setup.
8.	Click Next to continue.
9.	Select the regional settings and click Next.
10.	Enter a name and company name and click Next.
11.	Select the appropriate license settings and click Next.
12.	Select a computer name, enter the administrator password, and click Next.

NOTE   that Windows 2000 allows passwords of up to 127 characters. We recommend that the Administrator account password be at minimum nine characters long and that it includes at least one punctuation mark or non-printing ASCII character in the first seven characters.

Step   Description

13.   The installer will now be prompted to select the Windows 2000 components to be installed. We recommend selecting only what is needed, and to remove the following:

–Accessories and Utilities   Multimedia, games, and chat. In Communications, we remove Chat and Phone Dialer as well as the accessibility wizards.

–Indexing Service

–Internet Information Services (IIS)   In addition to increasing security risks on a MetaFrame server, if IIS is left checked, the installer will have the option of installing NFuse during the install of MetaFrame, which is not recommended, as NFuse should be separated from the application servers.

–Script Debugger

In addition, mark the Terminal Services check box to enable Terminal Services.

14.   Select the Date and Time settings and click Next.

15.   Select Application Server Mode and click Next.

16.   Select the default permissions for application compatibility.

–Permissions compatible with Windows 2000 users   This setting gives default Terminal Services users the same permissions as a member of the users group and could cause issues with some legacy applications.

–Permissions compatible with Terminal Server 4.0 users   This setting gives default Terminal Services users full access to critical registry and file system locations, thus enabling support for legacy applications while creating a possible security hole and, more important, giving the end user the ability to affect the stability of the system.

Click Next.

17.   The installer is now prompted to configure the network settings. We highly recommend configuring the network adapter cards now. Select Custom and click Next.

18.   Double-click Internet Protocol (TCP/IP) and enter the appropriate TCP/IP address information documented during the design phase.

Note: We recommend entering the FQDN for the domain the server is a part of in the DNS Suffix for this connection area of the DNS tab, located behind the Advanced button.

Click Next.

19.   The next screen will ask if you would like to join a domain or remain part of a workgroup. Select the appropriate setting and click Next.

Setup continues by copying system files and registering system components.

Step	Description
20.	Click Finish to reboot and log on for the first time.
21.	Install any necessary drivers. The system should be placed into install mode to install any hardware or hardware drivers. Refer to the "Installing and Configuring Applications" section in Chapter 13 for more information on install mode.

Choose Start | Run. In the dialog box that appears, type: **change user /install**. Then click OK.

When the install of the new hardware is completed, place the system back in Execute mode.

Choose Start | Run. In the dialog box that appears, type: **change user /execute**. Then click OK.

| 22. | If the Novell Client is required, install it at this point. |

When completed, disable the Novell System Tray Icon.

Disable the Novell System Tray icon by using this key:

[HKEY_LOCAL_MACHINE\SOFTWARE\Novell\Network Provider\ Menu Items] "Enable System Icon"=string:YES.

If slow logons are experienced, adjust the network bindings order.

| 23. | Install Microsoft Service Pack 2. It can be found at http://www .microsoft.com/windows2000/downloads/servicepacks/sp3/default.asp. |

NOTE: As of this writing, we do NOT recommend installing Service Pack 3. Be sure to test all service packs on a non-production server prior to installing them in a production environment.

| 24. | Install any Microsoft security roll-up hotfixes or patches. |

These can be downloaded from http://www.microsoft.com/windows2000/downloads/critical/q311401/ default.asp.

For more information check http://www.microsoft.com/technet/treeview/default.asp?url=/technet/ security/news/w2ksrp1.asp.

| 25. | Run Microsoft Windows Update and install all critical updates and service packs, root certificates, and Windows compatibility updates. These can be found at the following web address: http://www.microsoft.com/windowsupdate |

NOTE: Remember to use change user /install mode for any updates. For more information on change user /install mode, please refer to Chapter 13.

Step	Description
26.	Set the media type, duplex setting, and the speed that the NIC is required to use within the environment. Verify that the switch or managed switch is configured to the preferred setting. Never allow the NIC to "auto detect" the settings. Go to Start | Settings | Control Panel | Network and Dial-Up Connections. Right-click Local Area Network. Choose Properties | Configure. Then click the Advanced Tab.
27.	Disable any additional network interface cards or implement NIC teaming per the supplied vendor installation procedures. Go to Start | Settings | Control Panel | Network and Dial-Up Connections. Right-click any additional NICs and click Disable.
28.	Create and format any additional partitions.
29.	Move the page file to another faster drive or the second partition, if available, and set the PAGEFILE to 2.1 (4095MB max) times the total amount of physical RAM installed on the server. Go to Start | Settings | Control Panel. Double-click the System applet. Select the Advanced tab. Choose Performance Options, then select Change.
30.	Increase the Registry Size. 125MB should be sufficient. Go to Start | Settings | Control Panel. Double-click the System applet. Select the Advanced tab. Choose Performance Options, then select Change and change the Registry Size (the last field at the bottom of the page).

The following is an example of the installation procedures needed for Windows Server 2003:

Step	Description
1.	If hardware like Compaq/Dell servers will be used, run the appropriate configuration software—for example, Smart Start.
2.	Press F6 to install third-party SCSI or RAID driver(s) that are not currently on the Windows Server 2003 CD-ROM, if needed.
3.	Press ENTER to continue with the installation.
4.	Press F8 to agree with the license agreement.
5.	Follow onscreen prompts to create the appropriate partitions.
6.	Select to format the partition using the NTFS file system. Setup will format the partition and copy installation files. When completed, it will reboot the system and continue to the GUI setup.

Step	Description

7.   Select the regional settings and click Next.

8.   Enter a name and company name and click Next.

9.   Enter the Product Key and click Next.

10.   Select the appropriate license settings and click Next.

11.   Select a computer name, enter the administrator password, and click Next.

 NOTE: Windows Server 2003 allows passwords of up to 127 characters. We recommend that the Administrator account password be a minimum of nine characters long and that it include at least one punctuation mark or non-printing ASCII character in the first seven characters.

12.   Select the appropriate Date and Time setting and click Next.

13.   The installer is now prompted to configure the network settings. We highly recommend configuring the network adapter cards now. Select Custom and click Next.

14.   Double-click Internet Protocol (TCP/IP) and enter the appropriate TCP/IP address information documented during the design phase.

 NOTE: It is recommended to enter the FQDN for the domain the server is a part of in the DNS Suffix for this connection area of the DNS tab, which is located behind the Advanced button.
Click Next.

15.   The next screen will ask if you would like to join a domain or stay a part of a workgroup. Select the appropriate setting and click Next.
Setup continues by copying system files and registering system components.

16.   Click Finish to reboot and log on for the first time.

17.   The server will display the Manage Server GUI after the initial logon.
Click the Add or Remove a Role link.

18.   Click Next to continue.

19.   Select Terminal Server and click Next.

20.   Click Next to install Terminal Server.

21.   Close all programs and click OK.

22.   The server will reboot and you will need to log on again.

23.   Click Finish in the Configure Your Server Wizard.

Step	Description
24.	For Windows Server 2003, you have to assign the groups that will be allowed to access the terminal server through Terminal Services
	Go to Start	All Programs	Administrative Tools	Computer Management. Click Local Users and Groups to expand it. Then click Groups. Double-click Remote Desktop Users, and add the users or groups that are appropriate.
25.	We recommend removing any unnecessary components from Windows.
	Go to Start	Control Panel	Add/Remove Programs. Select Add/Remove Windows Components.
	We recommend always removing the Accessibility Wizard and Communication Folder from the Accessories and Utilities.
26.	Install any necessary drivers. To do so, the system should be placed in install mode. Refer to the "Installing and Configuring Applications" section in Chapter 13 for more information on install mode.
	Choose Start	Run. In the dialog box that appears, type **change user /install**. Then click OK.
	When the install of the new hardware is completed, place the system back in Execute mode.
	Choose Start	Run. In the dialog box that appears, type **change user /execute**. Then click OK.
27.	If the Novell Client is required, install it at this point.
	When completed, disable the Novell System Tray icon.
	To disable the Novell System Tray icon, use the following key:
	[HKEY_LOCAL_MACHINE\SOFTWARE\Novell\Network Provider\ Menu Items] "Enable System Icon"=string:YES.
	If slow logons are experienced, adjust the network bindings order.
28.	Run Microsoft Windows Update and install all critical updates and service packs, root certificates, and Windows compatibility updates.
	These can be downloaded from the following web address: http:// www.microsoft.com/windowsupdate.
	Note: Remember to use change user /install mode for any updates. For more information on change user /install mode, please refer to Chapter 13.
29.	Set the media type, duplex setting, and the speed that the NIC is required to use within the environment. Verify that the switch or managed switch is configured to the preferred setting. Never allow the NIC to "auto detect" the settings.
	Go to Start	Control Panel	Network Connections. Right-click Local Area Network. Choose Properties	Configure. Then click the Advanced Tab.

Step	Description
30.	Disable any additional Network Interface Cards or implement NIC Teaming per the supplied vendor installation procedures.
	Go to Start | Control Panel | Network Connections. Right-click any additional NICs and click Disable.
31.	Create and format any additional partitions.
32.	Move the page file to another faster drive or the second partition if available and set the PAGEFILE to 2.1 (4095MB max) times the total amount of physical RAM installed on the server.
	Go to Start | Control Panel. Double-click the System applet. Click the Advanced tab. Click Settings under Performance, then select the Advanced tab and choose Change.

Service Packs and Hotfixes

The Golden Rule for loading post-release service packs and hotfixes is "Don't Unless You Have To." Unfortunately, critical applications or hardware issues often require service packs or hotfixes to correct critical problems or install the latest releases. Microsoft periodically releases service packs that are the culmination of fixes to problems discovered by customers and Microsoft technical support. Customers with an urgent need for a fix that was created after a service pack can often receive it in the form of a hotfix from Microsoft technical support. Citrix also releases periodic service packs in order to reduce the number of interim hotfixes.

The following list shows the current recommended service packs as of this writing:

▼ **Windows NT Server 4.0, Terminal Server Edition**   Service Pack 6 and security roll up, found at http://www.microsoft.com/ntserver/ terminalserver/downloads/critical/q317636/default.asp.

■ **Windows 2000 Server Service Pack 3**

▲ **Windows Server 2003**   No service packs as of this writing, only post-release hotfixes.

We strongly recommend checking the Citrix and Microsoft web sites for the current level of service packs and related issues to evaluate whether they apply.

NOTE: Windows 2000 and 2003 use a "Windows Update" feature similar to Windows 98 that allows hotfixes to be automatically downloaded from the Internet. We strongly recommend against allowing automatic update on production servers. It does not provide the level of testing rigor that is required to maintain a stable and robust server farm.

PERFORMANCE OPTIMIZATION

Performance Optimization of Terminal Servers is quickly evolving from a mystic art to a tested science. There are now many useful resources and tools to aid in performance optimization, and the quest toward more efficient use of hardware and better performance for end users is certainly a noble use of time. One notable web resource is http://www.tweakcitrix.com.

In addition to resources like the tweakcitrix web site, there are a variety of add-on tools to Citrix that provide performance enhancement and application control. Four products that we have used and recommend are

▼ **RES PowerFuse**   PowerFuse is a software tool that reduces server pauses caused by misbehaving applications by intercepting an application that is using more resources than allowed (for example, if the threshold is set to 90 percent, and any application passes that percentage, it is relegated to a lower priority). PowerFuse also provides user and application lockdown, software metering, printer control, and other useful SBC tools. A demonstration copy can be found at http://www.powerfuse.com.

■ **AppSense**   AppSense has created an all-encompassing suite of tools for server-based computing that does everything from desktop lockdown and GUI policy configuration, to performance Process Management (IPM) technology, which dynamically manages the level of processor and memory utilization allocated to each user. More information and evaluation software can be found at http://www.appsense.com.

■ **triCerat**   tricerat has a similar printer, profile, and lockdown solution set to PowerFuse and AppSense. Although these solutions do not specifically map to performance enhancement, we have found that the user performance perception can be dramatically impacted by efficient profile deployment, application lockdown, and printer control. More information and evaluation software can be found at http://www.tricerate.com.

■ **RTO Software (formerly Kevsoft)**   TScale (also offered by Wyse as Expedian) improves server performance 30–40 percent by optimizing virtual memory use on the server. An evaluation copy can be found at http://www.wyse.com/ products/ software/expedian.htm or at http://www.rtosoft.com/evaluate_ts.html.

▲ **Tigi**   Tigi drives, as discussed earlier in this chapter, are solid state drives that replace the standard hard drive or RAID sybsystem of a MetaFrame server. Due to the amount of processing and I/O bottleneck that is reduced by the use of a solid state drive, some MetaFrame servers may support up to twice as many users with a Tigi drive than with a standard drive bottleneck subsystem.

AUTOMATED SERVER CREATION

Since much of the work needed to create and maintain a user's desktop is mitigated by moving to server-based computing, the main job of building IT infrastructure becomes that of server and network configuration. Although many organizations intend to standardize the server build process, few can accomplish this goal by merely writing install instructions. The server build process, including the application installation, typically will incorporate hundreds of manual steps and is thus prone to installation errors and omissions. As the number and frequency of new servers and applications increases, the task of building and maintaining the servers becomes quite onerous. The other problem is one of change control and consistency. Unless there is a standard method for building a server, a myriad of problems are bound to crop up. These can include DLL library conflicts, application version differences, application optional component differences, and driver conflicts. In this section, we will introduce two methods to address this task: server *imaging* (also referred to as cloning) and unattended scripted installs. Though they are not mutually exclusive, they do have a different focus.

Imaging is the process by which a standard collection of software components is defined, tested, and certified. This collection includes the operating system, the applications, utilities, and any system configuration changes necessary to make the system work, as shown in Figure 11-1. A system image is often created using a third-party utility such as Symantec Ghost Corporate Edition and PowerQuest's DeployCenter software. These programs allow great flexibility in how the image gets loaded on a target system. Options include creating a self-loading image on a media set like a bootable floppy disk

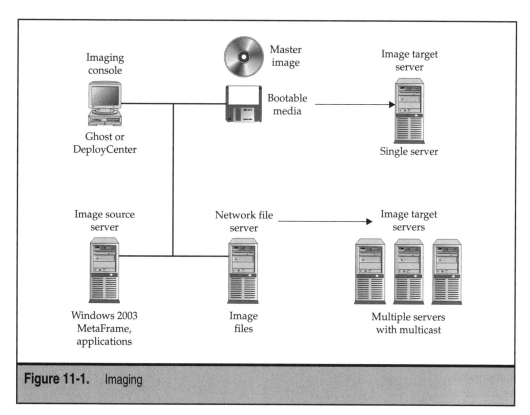

Figure 11-1.   Imaging

and CD-ROM, or creating a software distribution server in which the same image can be "multicasted" to multiple target servers. Using such products can speed up the loading process by orders of magnitude. The imaging method for bulk server creation has the following advantages:

▼ The imaging process requires no programming or scripting knowledge.

■ Multicasting an image to multiple target servers saves time and is a standard feature of most server imaging products.

▲ Imaging can save on backup space, backup window time, and server restore time. By saving the images from the critical servers each night, there is no longer a need to include the server OS and applications in the backup job, although it is important to back up the imaging server on a regular schedule (for instance, once per week).

Limitations of imaging include

▼ An image is specific to each hardware type. Differences in NICs, video cards, array controllers, and manufacturers are difficult or impossible to handle within a simple image. Thus multiple images are often required and can be timely to maintain.

■ It is difficult to track all the components and configuration changes that go into an image. For example, many large enterprise applications have several options that can be chosen during installation that affect how the application will run. Unless all of these options are recorded, there is no way to be sure which were chosen when the image was created.

▲ After the image is successfully installed on a target computer, information that is unique to the computer must be changed. This information includes the system identifier (SID), IP address, and so on.

Scripting the bulk server creation process involves the creation of recorded software packages that can be replayed on target servers, as shown in Figure 11-2. A package can simply be the standard application software setup program that runs unattended with a predefined answer file, or it can be a proprietary set of software components and system configuration changes created with a commercial software packaging program such as Citrix Installation Manager (IM). One server acts as a deployment host and contains the software packages. Windows Scripting Host can be used to replay the packages and make any needed configuration changes the same way on all servers. Optionally, a tool such as IM from Citrix can be used to create application packages. IM has its own facility for distributing these packages. The scripting method of bulk server creation has the following advantages:

▼ One build can support different hardware types.

■ Microsoft supports scripting.

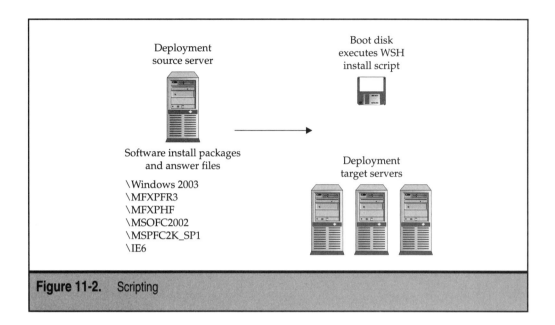

Figure 11-2.   Scripting

- A high degree of flexibility for loading applications, service packs, utilities, and making configuration changes is possible with scripting.
- A single application can be changed and deployed without significantly affecting the actual deployment script.
- ▲ It provides consistency at the OS level across all configured builds. This consistency helps provide stability for the entire environment.

Limitations include

- ▼ If anything other than a commercial package such as IM or Microsoft System Management Server (SMS) is used, knowledge of scripting is required. Though we feel the effort is justified, learning VBScript or JScript requires a higher level of commitment than simple batch programming.
- ▲ Areas of the operating system, such as the %systemroot% directory, must be granted read/write access for all users in order for the scripts to run. Though these security holes can be closed later, this must be taken into account during the server build process.

The two methods for building servers, using an imaging product and scripting, are not mutually exclusive. In fact, they can be used together quite effectively. We will discuss an example of this later in the chapter.

Imaging Products

Both Symantec Ghost and PowerQuest DeployCenter imaging programs include free trial versions with a built-in expiration feature. DeployCenter can be found at http://www.powerquest.com/ downloads/eval-corp.cfm. Symantec Ghost can be found at http://www.symantec.com/ sabu/ghost/indexB.html.

Both products have unique features. However, a simple, generalized procedure for creating a disk image can be abstracted. First, to create a disk image, follow these steps:

1. Boot to the network with the boot CD-ROM or floppy. This floppy is created manually or with utilities from Symantec or PowerQuest. The boot disk will map a network drive for storing images.

2. Once booted, run the imaging client program from the floppy or from the mapped network drive.

3. Select Disk to Image from the client interface.

4. Choose a location on the network to store the file and proceed.

To load a disk image, follow these steps:

1. Boot to the network with the boot floppy from the target computer.

2. Once booted, run the imaging client program from the floppy or from the mapped network drive.

3. Choose Image to Disk from the client interface.

4. Choose the correct image file from the network drive and proceed.

5. Remove the boot CD-ROM while the target computer is being imaged so that it will reboot from the local hard drive once imaged.

Microsoft Support

To overcome some of the postinstallation configuration problems that can crop up, Microsoft created a System Preparation Utility (SPU) for Windows NT, and Microsoft continues to support system cloning with Windows 2000 and 2003 with Sysprep version 1.1. The release of these tools coincides with Microsoft's public endorsement of cloning technology. The Windows SPU provides each cloned PC with a unique system identifier (SID). It provides a registry entry that Microsoft technical support can use to determine whether a system has been cloned. Refer to the Microsoft web site at http://www.microsoft.com/windows2000/techinfo/planning/default.asp to download this utility. We have used these products many times with no trouble for server cloning. We also know firsthand of at least two major PC hardware manufacturers that use cloning products internally.

PowerQuest DeployCenter Version 5.5

PowerQuest DeployCenter software allows users to image and deploy Windows Server 2003, Windows 2000 Server, Windows 2000 Advanced Server, and Windows NT Server machines, as well as Windows 98, Millennium, and 2000 Professional. DeployCenter automatically converts a PDC (primary domain controller) to a BDC (backup domain controller) when an image file is restored. An image can be created directly to a SCSI or ATAPI CD-R or CD-R/W drive. DeployCenter supports multicast and unicast deployment, and has a custom script builder that streamlines the process of preparing a system for cloning and deployment by providing a simple interface for creating, editing, and testing Microsoft SysPrep answer files. DeployCenter also has a feature that will reassign a new unique SID.

Symantec Ghost Corporate Edition Version 7.5

Ghost is the most mature of the imaging software products and is still arguably the best and most reliable utility for cloning computers. Version 7.5 now includes a multicast feature as well as native support for Windows 2000 Remote Installation Server. Ghost can be used to roll out Windows 2000, Windows XP, and PXE-Compliant (PC98) computers. The program includes some excellent utilities such as Ghost Walker, which can assign a compatible SID, and Ghost Explorer, which allows the selection of individual files and directories within an image file.

TIP: There is a potential problem with user profile corruption when the profile is dynamically loaded on a newly built server with time stamps newer than the profile. This same problem occurs on servers that were cloned or built manually. The work-around is to set the server's clock back to well before the profile was created, perhaps one year. After the first login as the Administrator, set the clock to the current date and time.

FURTHER STANDARD IMAGE DEFINITION

Obviously the best use of imaging and scripting (scripting is covered in Chapter 22) occurs after the server is completely configured. Chapters 12 and 13 will finish the building process by covering the Citrix installation and configuration, and the application's installation and configuration. Chapter 13 will also discuss software installation and version management automation using Citrix Installation Manager software. With all these things in place, the final cloning can be performed.

Server Sizing and Capacity Planning

With the maturation of server-based computing, a variety of software tools have emerged to provide SBC server capacity planning and testing. Mercury Interactive's LoadRunner (http://www.mercuryinteractive.com) and Scapa Technologies' StressTest (http://www.scapatech.com) have both developed an extensive set of planning, testing, and monitoring software tools that provide very sophisticated analysis and results for large enterprise environments attempting to determine how many servers will be required for a given user load and performance expectation. Both of these tools are relatively simple to use and will test the aggregate effects of all variables on a Terminal Server Farm, including server load, network bandwidth, encryption, compression, and so on. These tools make it very easy to run all-encompassing tests, and measure the results effectively.

But, with inexpensive, high-powered, small form-factor rack servers now readily available on every street corner, the tradeoff between an inexact estimate of the number of required servers and the time and money required to work with an enterprise tool must be weighed. Since neither tool is inexpensive (StressTest lists for $25,000 and LoadRunner lists for $50,000) it is our opinion that environments with less than 2500 users may benefit from a less expensive (albeit less automated) approach. We will detail an approach in this section that provides reasonably accurate server-sizing data points for small to mid-sized environments. Note that as an environment reaches 2500 users or more, this approach is very tedious and time-consuming, thus necessitating the use of one of the enterprise tools mentioned earlier.

User and Application Simulation

The goal of simulation is to determine with relative accuracy, the number of servers required to support a given amount of users at a given acceptable performance level.

NOTE: The number of terminal servers is not the only concern when considering the capacity and scalability of an environment. As an environment grows, other services such as network bandwidth, file servers, license servers, web servers, security servers, and others, will also require additional resources.

In order to build an effective simulation, it is important to define two variables:

1. The major applications that the environment will support.
2. The performance speed or response time required (typically defined in wait time) for a function to occur (for example, an acceptable wait time for Word to start after a user has clicked the icon might be 1.5 seconds, based on a typical wait time for users' current fat-client environment).

Once these variables are defined, there are three steps to complete the simulation and gather the data:

1. Create a script or automated process to simulate a user running an application or performing a task.
2. Prepare to monitor the server farm.
3. Execute the scripts simulating multiple users, across multiple sessions (and preferably across multiple servers in a load-balanced test farm).

These three steps warrant additional discussion.

Create a Script or Automated Process   Although the option of rounding up a large herd of test users and asking them to run their applications for several days in the test environment may sound appealing, in most cases it will be desirable to automate the process by creating a script or automated procedure to closely simulate the way users perform their jobs and tasks in the environment. The challenge with creating the script or process to run the simulation is that the users' use of applications and processes must be understood in order to obtain accurate results. This can only be accomplished by interviewing and observing live users prior to creating the script.

Once the approach is understood, the next step is to choose a scripting tool. Three potential scripting tools are WinTask, WinBatch, and AutoIT. These tools range in price from free to $100, and provide a macro-type recording feature, which creates a recording file that can be launched from a command prompt.

Preparing to Monitor the Server Farm   Prior to actually executing the scripts, it is important to put a monitoring tool in place to gather results while the simulation is running. Two obvious monitoring and reporting tools are Citrix Resource Manager (RM) and Windows Performance Monitor. Since RM will be covered in Chapter 21, and Performance Monitor tends to be simple and quick to configure for this purpose, we will cover it briefly here:

1. Configure Performance Monitor (perfmon.exe) to create a new log file.

2. We recommend logging, at a minimum, the following counters on all servers in the test environment:

   ■ Terminal Services: Active Sessions

   ■ Physical Disk: % Disk Time

   ■ Memory: Pages/sec

   ■ Processor: % Processor Time:_Total

   ■ Network Interface: Bytes Total/sec

3. Keep in mind that there are also specific counters for Citrix and Terminal Services (under Citrix and ICA and Terminal Services) that may be very helpful, especially for larger simulations where counters like Zone Collections, IMA traffic, and IMA data store communications need to be understood in order for background components and servers to be scaled appropriately.

Execute the Scripts   Once the Performance Monitor logging is configured, we are ready to begin the simulation. Since connecting hundreds of client desktops and running from workstation to workstation to invoke the script is not on most folks' fun-to-do list, we recommend utilizing the Citrix Server Test Kit (CSTK) and a group of specialized client machines to automate the simulation of a large number of users and sessions. The CSTK is free, and can be downloaded from http://www.citrix.com/cdn.

A CSTK environment has four main components:

▼ **The CSTK Console**   This is the interface that runs on the server farm and is used to start and stop the tests, apply simulation scripts, and configure test-user accounts.

- ■ **The user simulation scripts**   These are the scripts created in the previous section. The CSTK tool also includes some useful scripts for more generic tasks such as Internet Explorer and Microsoft Office 2000.

- ■ **The CSTK client**   The client tool runs on every ICA test session and employs the user simulation scripts.

- ▲ **The client launcher utility**   This is the secret ingredient. It can be used to automatically launch multiple ICA clients from one PC or virtual machine environment. It also saves gobs of time over having to manually log on and launch 100 different sessions.

As we stated earlier in this chapter, we recommend simulating at least 10 percent of the final number of concurrent users. The CSTK supports running multiple test sessions from one client machine, although the number of sessions will be limited by the memory of the client machine (about 12MB of memory per client session is required). Thus, for small test environments, a group of thin clients or low-end PCs may provide sufficient capacity. In the case of a larger environment though—take our case study CME Corp., for example—a 10 percent test will require 250 concurrent client sessions. Clearly, a more creative approach will be necessary for larger environments in order to keep the test environment from becoming overly expensive and space consuming.

One approach that dramatically reduces the size of the client test environment is to utilize powerful client PC workstations running virtual machine software like VMware Workstation or Microsoft Connectix Virtual PC to create multiple client operating system environments that will each run multiple client sessions. Powerful PC workstations for this purpose can be procured for well under $1000 and can support up to 48 client sessions per workstation. The minimum specifications for the client test workstation are

- ▼ Intel P4 1.6 GHz

- ■ 1GB of memory

- ■ 40GB hard drive

- ■ 100MBit network interface

- ■ VMware Workstation version 4 or Microsoft Connectix Virtual PC for Windows version 5

- ▲ Windows 95, Windows 98, Windows ME, Linux, Windows 2000 Professional, or Windows XP—If the production environment will contain a mixture of these clients, then run a mixture on a test workstation. VMWare and Connectix both support hosting all of these running virtually as guest operating systems simultaneously from Windows Server 2003 or Linux.

Once the client test workstations are configured, load the CSTK environment and configure up to eight client sessions on each of six virtual machines within the server. Once the test is completed, turn off the performance monitor logging and go back to performance monitor to study the logs. Depending on the results, additional users can be added and tested, or fewer users tested to determine the maximum number of users supported at a specific performance expectation.

Brian S. Madden's well-written book *Citrix MetaFrame XP Advanced Technical Design Guide, Second Edition* gives the following step-by-step guide to using the CSTK (used by permission):

From this section, it is obvious that capacity planning is a multiphased, complex project, but it is an absolutely necessary project, in all but the smallest environments, to ensure success of a Terminal Services deployment.

Detailed Steps to Use CSTK to Conduct the User-Load Simulation

In order to understand how the CSTK works, let's review step-by-step how it's used:

1. The first thing you need to do is prepare your environment. Ideally, you'll be able to run your tests on an isolated test network. Gather your MetaFrame server and the necessary ICA client devices. (You'll probably want to activate the Citrix licenses on your test server so that an annoying pop-up window does not break your scripts every ten minutes.) Just remember that "officially" Citrix advises against activating your server until it is finalized. It's your call.

2. If you haven't done so already, install the CSTK on your server. (Remember to put your server into install mode first.) After the CSTK is installed, you'll notice that the "CSTK Client" is automatically launched whenever a user logs on. For now, you can just ignore that.

3. Launch the CSTK administrative console. (Go to Start | Programs | Citrix Server Test Kit 2.1 | CSTK Console.) You will use this console to configure your testing environment and run your tests.

4. Import the application simulation scripts created earlier into the CSTK environment. This process will make these scripts available to the CSTK. To do this, choose Tools | Add Application Scripts. You can specify anything you want for the Script Name. Use the "Browse" button to browse to the path of the executable of your script. You can specify any necessary command-line parameters in the Parameters box. For example, if you used AutoIt to create your script, you might need to specify AutoIt.exe in the Program Name box, and yoursrcriptname.txt in the Parameters box. Specify whether your application applies to "Normal Users" or "Power Users." Normal users will only run one script at a time, and power users will run multiple scripts simultaneously.

5. After you've added the Application Test Scripts application scripts, you need to configure groups of test users that will use your scripts (go to User Group | Add, or click the plus (+) button on the toolbar). When you specify users, you're essentially indicating which application scripts run for which users when they log on. When adding a user group, the first question you're asked is whether you want to add a group of Normal Users or Power Users. Make your selection and click OK.

6. Next, you need to specify a range of usernames that will run an application script (or scripts) when they log on. Specify the usernames by entering the basename and the number of users. For example, to apply a script to users "brian1" through "brian 5," you would enter "brian" as the basename and "5" as the number of users. If this is the first time that you're using the CSTK and you don't have any test user accounts created, you can click the Create Users button. This will create the test user accounts based on the baseline name and number of users. These user accounts are created with blank passwords.

7. Before you click OK, highlight the script or scripts you want this user group to run and click the Add button. If you elected to create normal users, selecting multiple scripts will cause the users to run them one by one and the list of available scripts will only show those that you've designated for normal users. If you elected to create power users, selecting multiple scripts will cause the users to execute them all at the same time, and the list of available scripts will only show those that you've designated for power users. In a sense, normal users execute their application scripts in a "serial" fashion, and power users execute them in a "parallel" fashion.

8. Once you add a group of users and click OK, you'll see them listed on the main CSTK console screen. You can add as many groups of users as you want (as long as the basenames are not the same in two different groups).

9. At this point, the CSTK is fully configured and you should save your testing environment configuration. You can save the entire configuration, including user groups and applications, by choosing File | Save Configuration File. Your settings are then saved as an INI file with a .CST file extension. You can load your settings into the CSTK so that you don't have to manually set up everything from scratch in the future. When you save a configuration file, it does not include the application script information. When adding application scripts to the CSTK, they are available until deleted. If you delete one, loading a configuration file where it was used will not bring it back.

10. In order to begin the testing process, choose Test | Start Test or click the lightning bolt button on the toolbar. You'll notice that starting the test doesn't actually do anything. You have to log users on in order for the scripts to execute. This is also a good time to start your performance monitor logging process as described back in step 6.

11. From one of your ICA client devices, log on as one of your test users. This should be a user that is configured in one of the user groups in the CSTK console. Since a shortcut to the CSTK Client was added to the All Users\Startup folder when the CSTK was installed, it will launch after logon and the appropriate application script or scripts will start to run.

12. In order to easily launch multiple ICA sessions from a single 32-bit Windows client device, you can use the CSTK Client Launcher. Log on to a client workstation and run CSTKlaun.exeCSTKlaun.exe from the "ClntLaun" folder of the CSTK directory. When you run it, it will detect the path of the ICA client executable (wfcrun.exe). Verify that this path is correct and enter the usernames that you want the sessions to be run from. The username entries follow the same baseline syntax as the groups within the CSTK. For example, if you have ten test workstations that you plan to use for ten sessions each, you would configure your CSTK for usernames "test1" through "test100." Then, you would configure the CSTK Client Launcher to use "test1" through "test10" on the first workstation, "test11" through "test20" on the second workstation, and so on.

13. After you specify the users that will run on a workstation, you need to click the Create Entries button in the CSTK Client Launcher to create custom ICA connections for each user in the workstation's Program Neighborhood. Clicking this button brings up a screen that allows you to specify the default options used for each connection (such as the name of the server to connect to, protocols, and so on) Configure your options as needed and click OK.

14. Before you run your test, click the Advanced Delay button to specify the delay between sessions. This allows you to choose how much time passes between launching sessions. One of the nice features is that it permits you to specify progressively more time as more sessions are launched, allowing you to anticipate slower responses as the server gets more loaded.

15. After you've configured the delay, click the Run button on the Launcher's main screen. ICA user sessions will begin to be launched, and they will run the scripts that you specified for the user groups in the CSTK console.

As you add users to your testing environment, you should add them in small groups. For example, if you're testing 100 users, you might want to add ten users every five minutes for the first hour or so, and then add users one-by-one. By doing this, you'll be able to figure out how each user affects the overall system.

Don't forget to stop your performance monitor recording log once your testing is complete. Once it's stopped, you can examine it to determine the results of your test.

CHAPTER 12

Server Configuration:
Citrix MetaFrame
Presentation Server

Chapter 11 covered in depth Terminal Services installation, including server sizing and server imaging, and detailed Terminal Services optimization. The next step in the process of an SBC environment creation is the installation and configuration of MetaFrame XP Presentation Server software (MetaFrame XP) and its components.

CITRIX METAFRAME XP PRESENTATION SERVER INSTALLATION AND CONFIGURATION

Chapter 3 discussed MetaFrame, its functions, and its purposes in detail, but for the purposes of quick review, here are several reasons to add MetaFrame XP to a Terminal Services–based SBC environment:

▼ **Secure, encrypted access without having to open firewall holes**   MetaFrame Secure Gateway provides a secure infrastructure by which users can access the SBC environment literally anywhere, anytime, and anyplace, regardless of the firewall configurations, assuming the environment allows SSL (port 443) traffic. Although Terminal Services RDP traffic is encrypted, it requires that port 3389 be open on both the data-center firewall and the user's location. Full installation and configuration details for MetaFrame Secure Gateway will be provided in Chapter 16.

■ **True application load management**   Microsoft's built-in Network Load Balancing can be effective for environments with 100 users or less, but enterprise environments absolutely require a more robust and flexible approach in determining which users and applications are placed on which servers under what circumstances.

■ **The Citrix Web Interface wizard–based deployment tool**   Not only does this tool provide an automated approach to deploying access to the SBC environment, but just as handy, it provides an automated approach to deploying the ICA Client itself. Full installation and configuration details for MetaFrame Web Interface will be provided in Chapter 16.

■ **Universal Access to applications from any client device**   Although Microsoft now supports client access from Macintosh OS X and Windows clients, Citrix not only provides support for Mac and Windows, but also for over 100 client operating systems, including most varieties of UNIX and Linux, DOS, and embedded devices.

■ **Enterprise management tools**   Citrix offers Resource Manager, Installation Manager, and Network Manager, as well as a host of embedded management tools that provide administrators with critical information and the automation of enterprise SBC server environments.

▲ **Citrix Password Manager and Conferencing Manager**   Password Manager and Conferencing Manager are the newest brothers to MetaFrame XP in the Citrix MetaFrame Access Suite family. Password Manager provides a simple and elegant single sign-on solution for MetaFrame XP environments (although it also works in non-Metaframe environments), and Conferencing Manager provides an all-inclusive collaborative conference interface that leverages the shadow features of MetaFrame XP. These two products further enhance the user experience of the server-based computing environment.

METAFRAME XP PRESENTATION SERVER (METAFRAME XP)

MetaFrame XP is available for Windows NT 4.0 Terminal Services Edition (although support from Microsoft and Citrix is no longer widely available), Windows 2000 Server (all editions), and Windows Server 2003 (Standard, Enterprise, and Datacenter editions). At the time of this writing, MetaFrame XP Feature Release 3 (FR-3) is the latest release. Citrix introduces new feature releases on a six-month schedule, so plan to install or update feature releases as needed. Feature releases and other Citrix hotfixes and evaluation software can be downloaded from http://www.citrix.com/download.

Preparing the Citrix Data Store Environment

As discussed in Chapter 3, Citrix provides four choices for database storage of the Data Store, including MS Jet (based on MS Access), MS SQL Server (and its run-time cousin MSDE, officially supported with Feature Release 3), Oracle, and IBM DB2. Since this text focuses on enterprise environments, we will look at Microsoft SQL Server. Although Oracle and DB2 are also excellent enterprise database choices, SQL Server, according to Citrix customer information, has been the most deployed database of enterprises for the purpose of Citrix Data Store collection. SQL supports all current Citrix Features, including Database replication, direct-mode access, and the Resource Manager Summary Database feature that came with FR-2. MSDE also supports these features, without the need for a SQL client access license, although it is limited in database size. For readers interested in running the Citrix Data Store on Oracle, we highly recommend referencing the MetaFrame XP Advanced Concepts guide.

Installation and Preparation of Microsoft SQL Server

If your enterprise already has a SQL Server 2000 with available capacity, simply connect to it according to the following MetaFrame installation instructions. If a SQL server with capacity is not readily available, it will need to be installed and configured on a dedicated Windows 2000 or 2003 Server hardware box. Obviously, the management of a SQL server is a full-time activity all to itself, but for the purposes of a Citrix Data Store, a general default installation (with some minor adjustments) running on a dedicated hardware box will suffice. For security, stability, and functionality reasons it is imperative to keep current with the latest service pack level.

To download the latest service pack for Microsoft SQL Server 2000, visit http://www.microsoft.com/sql/downloads/default.asp.

NOTE: If you installed Microsoft SQL Server 2000 using the *Typical* installation option or via unattended installation procedures (sqlins.iss file), then you will need to set the default SQL authentication mode. By default, Windows Authentication is the default security model. Therefore, when you try to connect a MetaFrame server to the newly created Data Store by using a standard SQL login like system administrator (SA), you will receive the following error message:
Unable to connect to server SERVER_NAME:

Server: Msg 18452, Level 16, State 1[Microsoft][ODBC SQL Server Driver][SQL Server]
Login failed for user 'sa'. Reason: Not associated with a trusted SQL Server connection.

To prevent this behavior, change the authentication mode to Mixed from the SQL Enterprise Manager on the SQL server (located on the Security tab of the server properties).

Creating the MetaFrame XP Data Store with SQL Server 2000

Once the SQL server is running, the Data Store can be created on the SQL Server. The following instructions provide step-by-step instructions for creating the Data Store:

1. Choose Start | Programs | Microsoft SQL Server | Enterprise Manager.

2. In the Enterprise Manager's left pane, expand the tree until you reach the folder level:

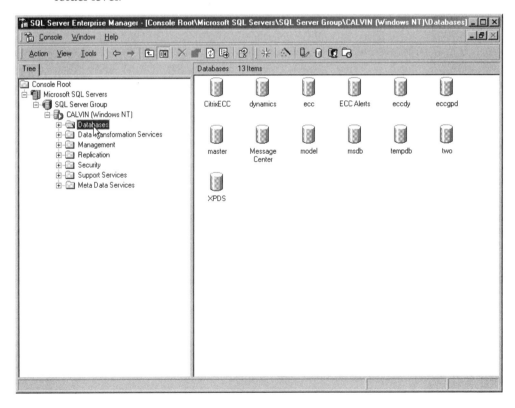

3. Right-click the Databases folder and choose New Database.

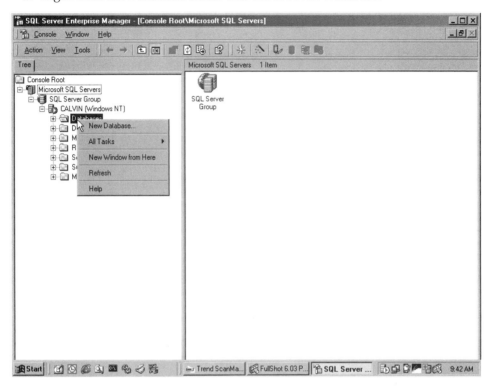

4. A dialog box appears. In the Name box, enter a name and click OK.

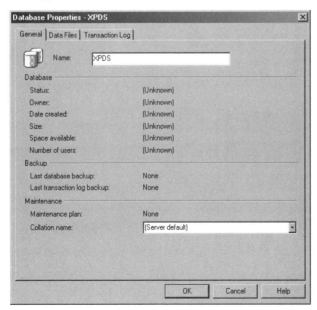

5. Expand the Security folder.

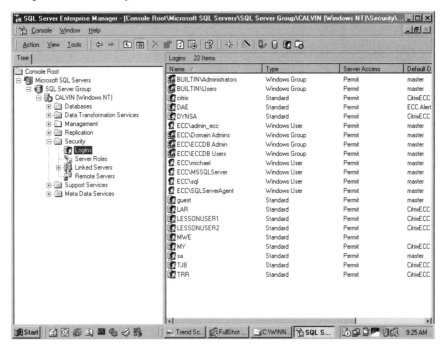

6. Right-click Logins and choose New Login.

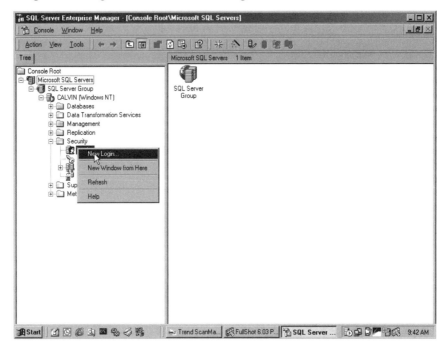

7. A dialog box appears with the General tab displayed. In the Name box, enter a name. Make note of the name because you will need to enter it during the MetaFrame XP installation.

8. In the Authentication section of the General tab, click SQL Server Authentication and enter a password. Remember the password; you must enter it during the MetaFrame XP installation.

9. In the Defaults area of the General tab, change the Database to the name you specified in Step 4.

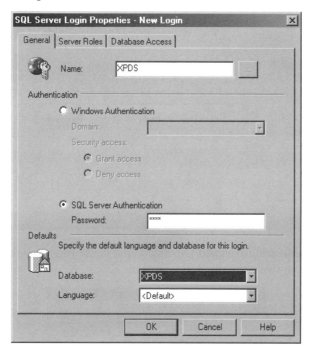

10. Click the Database Access tab. In the Database list, select the database name specified in Step 4.

11. In the Database Roles list, select DB_Owner. Leave other selected roles checked.

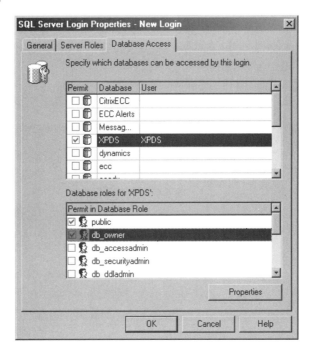

12. Click OK. You are prompted to confirm the password you created in Step 5. Doing so completes the database creation.

Citrix MetaFrame XP Installation Requirements

For a new Citrix MetaFrame XP Server installation or upgrade, the following is required:

▼ 1GB of free disk space

- MS Windows 2000 Server with Service Pack 2 or Windows Server 2003
- ▲ Installer 2.0 (Windows 2003 comes native with MS Installer 2.0) or Windows 2000 SP3

Preinstallation Tasks

Prior to installation, you should do the following:

- ▼ Choose the server farm name to be used.
- Configure the Data Store per the instructions given previously in this chapter.
- Obtain FR-3 products and connection licenses from http://www.mycitrix.com.
- Record alternative server addresses.
- ▲ Verify Citrix XML port settings following the install.

Installation Instructions for Citrix MetaFrame XP with Feature Release 3 (FR-3)

These step-by-step instructions for installing MetaFrame with FR-3 are not intended to be all-inclusive, but will provide a good basis for installation in most organizations.

Installing Microsoft Windows Installer Service 2.0

If using Windows 2003, the Windows installer is already updated, but in Windows 2000, the first task in installing MetaFrame XP is to install Windows Installer version 2.0.
   The following details how to install Microsoft Windows Installer Service 2.0:

1. Browse to the \support\msi20\ folder on the MetaFrame XP Feature Release 3 server CD-ROM and double-click instmsiw.exe.
2. Setup will update the Windows Installer Service and prompt you to click OK to continue.
3. Click Yes to reboot the server.

Step-by-Step Installation Instructions for MetaFrame XP Feature Release 3

To install MetaFrame XP FR-3, do the following:

1. Place the Metaframe XP FR3 CD-ROM into the CD-ROM drive and let it autorun.

2. Click the button next to Install or Update Metaframe.

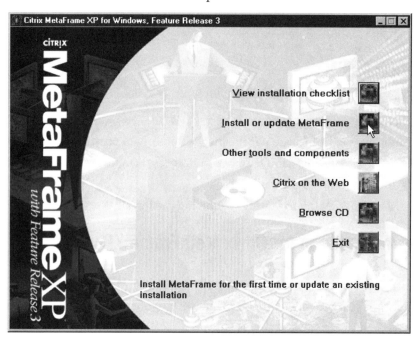

3. Click the button next to Metaframe XP Feature Release 3.

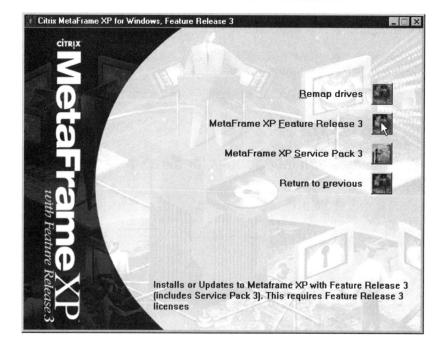

4. Click Next on the Welcome to the Citrix Metaframe XP for Windows Installation Wizard.

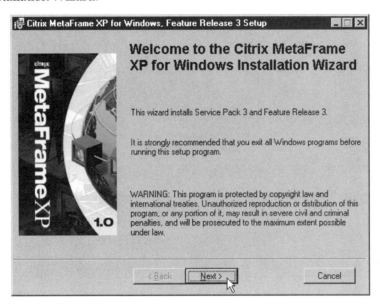

5. Select the radio button for I Accept The License Agreement and click Next.

6. Select the radio button for the version of Metaframe that was purchased and click Next.

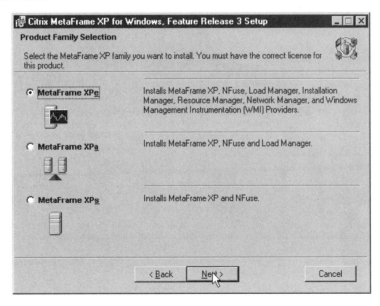

7. Select the appropriate Product Code and click Next.

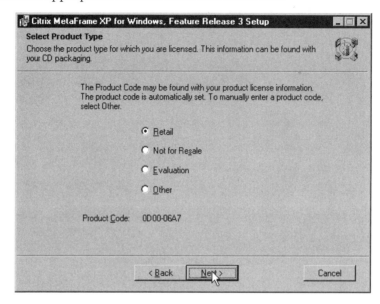

8. Make sure you select the appropriate installation options and click Next.

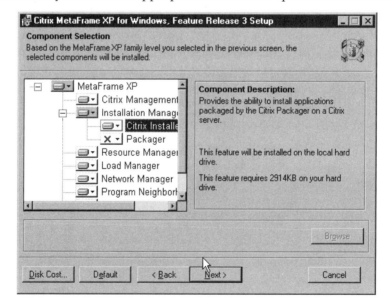

NOTE: Do not install Web Interface for MetaFrame on a Citrix MetaFrame XP/Windows 2003 Terminal Server. Although Web Interface for MetaFrame can be installed on the MetaFrame XP server for pilot or small test environments, it is not recommended for production environments due to inherent insecurity and potential performance bottlenecks. Additionally, if using Installation Manager, only install the Installation Manager packager service on the packager server.

9. Choose to create a new farm if it is a new farm installation, or choose to join a farm if it is an additional server, then click Next.

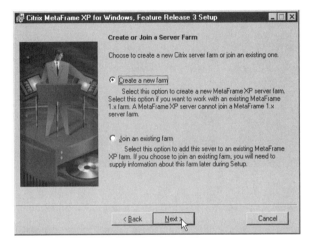

10. Enter the farm name as well as the appropriate Data Store type (we will be using Microsoft SQL server for this example) and click Next. The default zone name will be the subnet address (192.168.250.0 shown in the example). Users can change this to Houston Zone or something that is more explanatory than the subnet address, but all future server builds will have to join that zone when they are built.

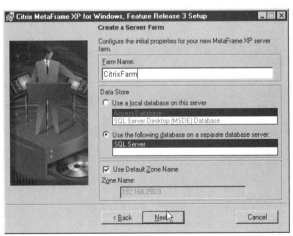

11. Enter an appropriate description for the ODBC data source and choose the appropriate database server, then click Next.

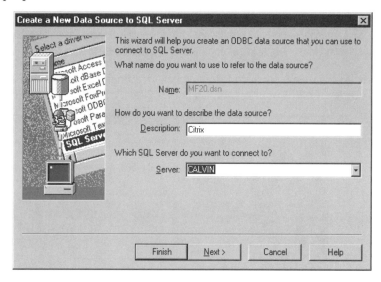

12. Select SQL server authentication and enter the login ID and password that was created in the SQL portion of the install, then click Next.

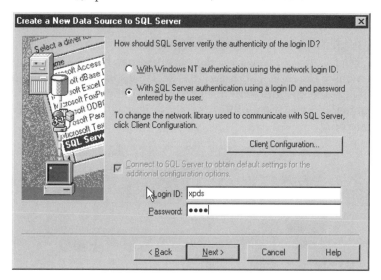

13. Make sure the default database is the one you created for the Citrix Data Store and click Next.

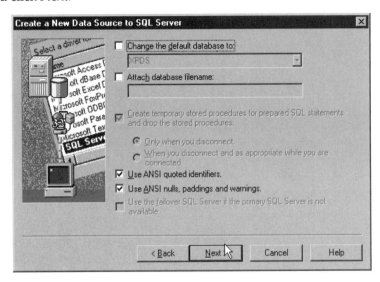

14. Click Finish to complete the data source creation and it will bring up an ODBC Microsoft SQL Server Setup screen:

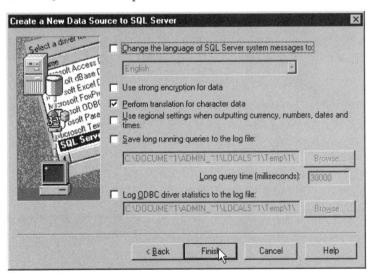

15. Click the Test Data Source button.

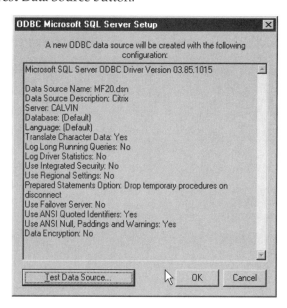

16. Make sure the test was successful and click OK for the Test Results, then click OK again when you go back to the ODBC Microsoft SQL Server Setup screen.

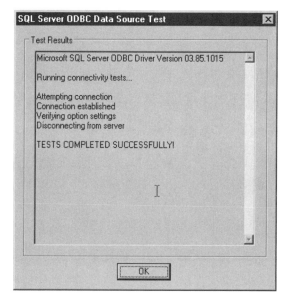

17. Enter the appropriate account for the initial Citrix Farm administrator and click Next.

NOTE: It is important to use a domain administrator account, and to create several local administrator accounts following installation. If this is not done and the domain settings are changed, the CMC will become inaccessible, requiring a full rebuild of the server.

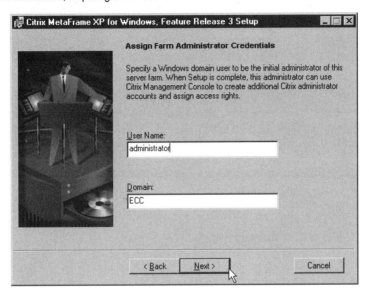

18. Select the appropriate shadow permissions and click Next.

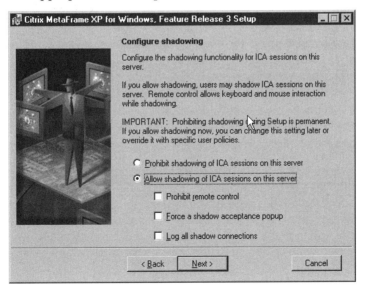

NOTE: If you choose the option to prohibit shadowing of the ICA sessions on this server, a full reinstall of MetaFrame XP will have to be performed to reverse this decision. On the other hand, if shadowing is enabled during installation, it can later be disabled using the Citrix Connection Configuration Utility without a reinstall.

19. Configure the XML service port (it is frequently changed from 80 to 8080 or 8081 to support the Web Interface for MetaFrame and MetaFrame Secure Gateway installation discussed in Chapter 16), document the port chosen, and click Next.

20. Click Finish to accept the installation options and to install the product.

21. After installation is complete, select the option to Launch The Client Distribution Wizard and click Finish.

22. Click Next on the Welcome screen.

23. Select the appropriate source location and click Next.

24. Click Next to choose a Typical install.

25. After the installation of the ICA clients, click Finish.

26. Click Yes to restart the server.

CITRIX METAFRAME FOR UNIX

Although this book is primarily focused on MetaFrame XP for Windows 2003, UNIX-based applications continue to be a mainstay of many large enterprise environments, and Windows and UNIX users alike can benefit from seamless, single-point, webified access to these applications. Because of the overall value of server-based computing in providing web-based seamless access to all applications from any device, for all users, the authors felt strongly that MetaFrame for UNIX should be featured in this book. A large majority of the features and infrastructure discussed throughout this book will apply equally to MetaFrame for UNIX and MetaFrame XP for Windows 2003. Features and tools such as Web Interface for MetaFrame, MetaFrame Secure Gateway, Load Management, and any-device access are further promoted by bringing the UNIX applications to the Citrix SBC infrastructure fold.

MetaFrame for UNIX version 1.2 offers the same value as MetaFrame for Windows, but with a UNIX/Java twist: low-bandwidth, universal client access over any network connection to any UNIX or Java application. MetaFrame for UNIX provides web-based access to these applications from any of Citrix's over 200 client platform choices, at a lower cost per seat than many X-Window client applications. An additional benefit is a dramatically lower bandwidth use, allowing remote deployment of applications that have rarely seen their way past the local area network. MetaFrame for UNIX supports a large majority of Citrix usability features across platforms. An example is the copy and paste feature–a user from any type of client device can copy and paste between any ICA applications, regardless of whether the application is running from a UNIX server, Windows 2003 Server, or Windows 2000 Server.

Integrating MetaFrame for UNIX with Other Citrix Servers

MetaFrame for UNIX will coexist with other Citrix servers (for example, MetaFrame XP) on a network by sharing master browser information. License pooling only works though if the XP servers are in mixed mode for interoperability.

Although MetaFrame for UNIX Operating Systems servers cannot be added to MetaFrame XP server farms, an ICA Passthrough client can be utilized to access applications on MetaFrame for UNIX using Program Neighborhood. Using ICA passthrough technology will allow non-Win32 ICA Clients to take advantage of the Citrix Program Neighborhood features. This is done by publishing the ICA Client on a MetaFrame for Windows server and having clients "pass through" the server's Citrix Program Neighborhood client to access a server farm. Alternatively, Citrix XML Service with Web Interface for MetaFrame can be used to provide users with access to Windows and UNIX applications from one location.

NOTE: Cross-server administration between Windows and UNIX versions of MetaFrame is not possible with this release.

System Requirements

This section lists the minimum machine specifications and operating system requirements for MetaFrame for UNIX.

Minimum Machine Specifications

The minimum machine specifications depend upon how many connections are to be supported. As a general rule, we recommend each server have between 16 and 24MB of RAM per ICA connection. However, the memory may need to increase depending upon the type of applications being hosted and the session properties, such as color depth and size. Table 12-1 lists the minimum hardware specifications and are intended as guidelines only. Note that these requirements are much lower than the typical hardware requirements for a Windows MetaFrame XP environment, largely due to the assumption that most UNIX applications and operating systems make more efficient use of the hardware.

Platform	Requirement for 1–3 Connections	Requirement for More Than Three Connections
Sun Solaris SPARC	Sparcstation 20 128MB RAM	Ultra-30 UltraSPARC-II 248 MHz
Sun Solaris Intel	P133 128MB RAM	PII 300 256MB RAM
HP-UX	C110 120 MHz PA-RISC 128MB RAM	A400 440 MHz PA-RISC 256MB RAM
IBM AIX	43P Model 150 128MB RAM	44P Model 270 256MB RAM

Table 12-1.   MetaFrame for UNIX Hardware Requirements

UNIX Operating System Requirements

This section provides information about the operating system requirements for MetaFrame for UNIX on each of the platforms.

Table 12-2 shows the operating system requirements for MetaFrame for UNIX.

NOTE: On Solaris versions 7, 8, and 9, the SUNWxwoft X-Window System optional fonts and SUNWuiu8 Iconv modules for UTF-8 Locale packages are installed when you do an end-user install. On Solaris 2.6, the packages are not installed in an end-user install.

Operating System Patches   For information about the operating system patches that are required, see document CTX222222 in the Solution KnowledgeBase on the Citrix web site at http://knowledgebase.citrix.com/. The information in the Solution KnowledgeBase is updated regularly.

Euro Currency Symbol Support

MetaFrame for UNIX supports the ISO 8859-15 Euro-currency symbol, if the underlying UNIX operating system supports it. To ensure this support, you may need to install patches recommended by your operating system and hardware vendor. See the web site for your operating system manufacturer or contact your hardware vendor for details of the appropriate patches and for instructions for ensuring Euro symbol support.

Platform	Supported Operating Systems	Required Operating System Software/Packages
Sun Solaris SPARC	- Solaris 2.6 (also known as SunOS 5.6) - Solaris 7 (also known as Solaris 2.7 and SunOS 5.7) - Solaris 8, SPARC version - Solaris 9, SPARC version	- X-Window System with the appropriate window manager for the platform—for example, CDE - SUNWxwoft X-Window System optional fonts - SUNWuiu8 Iconv modules for UTF-8 Locale (Check if these packages are installed using the **pkginfo** command, see note following this table). - The Iconv libraries must be installed—check that the following files exist in the /usr/lib/iconv folder: UCS-2*.so UTF-8*.so 8859-1*.so
Sun Solaris Intel	Solaris 8 Intel version	Same as earlier entry for Sun Solaris SPARC
HP-UX	HP-UX version 11.x (including 11i)	- X-Window System with the appropriate window manager for the platform—for example, CDE
IBM AIX	AIX version 4.3.3, 5.1, and 5.2	- X-Window System with the appropriate window manager for the platform—for example, CDE

Table 12-2.   Operating System Requirements for MetaFrame for UNIX

Installing MetaFrame Version 1.2

This section explains how to

▼   Create the Citrix server administrator user and group

▲   Install MetaFrame for UNIX for the first time

Installation Overview

Perform the following steps to install MetaFrame:

1. For first-time installations of MetaFrame, create the Citrix server administrator user and group accounts.

2. Install MetaFrame from the CD-ROM.

3. For first-time installations of MetaFrame, add the MetaFrame path(s) to all users' paths, so that the MetaFrame commands can be executed.

4. Start the MetaFrame processes on the server.

Creating the Citrix Server Administrator User and Group   For first-time installations of MetaFrame for UNIX, create the Citrix server administrator group account and a user in this group before installing MetaFrame. This account is required by some MetaFrame commands that demand special administration rights for MetaFrame, but do not require root access to the UNIX system.

NOTE: You must set up the Citrix server administrator group and user account before installing MetaFrame. The installation will fail if the ctxadm group and ctxsrvr user have not been created. Do not use the Citrix server administrator user or group for any purposes other than MetaFrame system administration.

Create the Citrix server administrator's group using the group name **ctxadm** and create a Citrix server administrator using the username **ctxsrvr**. Make sure the ctxsrvr user is added to the ctxadm group, and that the ctxadm group is its primary group.

Installing MetaFrame for UNIX on Solaris

Although the installation of MetaFrame for UNIX varies slightly for all supported versions of UNIX, we will cover the installation on Solaris, as this offers a good example of the steps and procedures required.

This section describes how to install MetaFrame for UNIX version 1.2 for the first time.

1. Log on as root at the server on which MetaFrame for UNIX will be installed.

2. Mount the MetaFrame CD-ROM.

3. Change to the directory for the version of MetaFrame to be installed. For example, type: **cd /cdrom/mfunix/solaris_version (cd /cdrom/mfu_fr2/solaris)** where *solaris_version* is the name of the directory on the CD-ROM for the platform architecture (SPARC or Intel) of Solaris being used. The path is usually /cdrom/ mfunix/... but it may change depending on how the specific system mounts the CD-ROM.

4. To install the MetaFrame package, type **pkgadd –d /cdrom/mfunix/ pkgfile_name pkg**. This starts the package installation script. For example, **pkgadd –d /cdrom/mfunix/solaris/CTXSmf**.

NOTE: Use the command in Step 4 rather than the command syntax listed in the MetaFrame for UNIX administration guide from Citrix—the Citrix guide is incorrect.

5. At the prompt for the startup/shutdown script installation, type **y** to start MetaFrame when the machine is booted and stop it when the machine is shut down. If answered yes, the script S99ctxsrv is installed in the /etc/rc2.d directory.

6. At the prompt for the man page installation, type **y** to install the MetaFrame man pages.

7. At the prompt for anonymous users, type **y** to create 15 anonymous user accounts to enable guest access (this is optional, and generally not recommended for security reasons).

8. At the prompt about security settings for setuid/setgid, type **y** to set the correct file permissions for the MetaFrame files and processes (a yes answer to this question is required, or MetaFrame will not operate correctly).

9. At the next prompt, type **y** to continue installing MetaFrame. When complete, a message states that the installation was successful and the command prompt is displayed.

NOTE: Do not attempt to share via NFS or copy the MetaFrame for UNIX installation files between servers. The configuration database cannot be duplicated.

Setting the Paths to MetaFrame for UNIX Commands   There are two types of MetaFrame commands: user and system administrating commands. Any user can run the user commands, which include the MetaFrame commands for logging off and disconnecting from a server. User commands are installed in /opt/CTXSmf/bin/ for Solaris and HP-UX, and in /usr/lpp/ CTXSmf/bin for AIX.

System administration commands can only be run by the ctxsrvr user (or members of the ctxadm group). Commands in this group include server, published application, and ICA Browser configuration tools. Administration commands are installed in /opt/ CTXSmf/sbin for Solaris and HP-UX, and /usr/lpp/CTXSmf/sbin for AIX.

Generally, nothing has to be done to allow users to run user commands from their sessions. The path to these commands is added to each user's path upon connection to the server, so any user can access MetaFrame user commands from an ICA session. However, configuration may have to be performed for users to access MetaFrame commands if the user's shell script startup file (for example, .profile or .login) overrides the path. For instance, on HP-UX, the default system profile (/etc/profile) sets the PATH environment variable explicitly.

To configure user access to MetaFrame commands if C shell is being used, use a .login file for the user, and add the path to the user commands. For example:

▼ For HP-UX and Solaris: setenv PATH ${PATH}:/opt/CTXSmf/bin

▲ For AIX: setenv PATH ${PATH}:/usr/lpp/CTXSmf/bin

If a Bourne or similar shell is being used, employ a .profile file for the user, and add the path to the user commands. For example:

▼ For HP-UX and Solaris: PATH=${PATH}:/opt/CTXSmf/binexport PATH

▲ For AIX: PATH=${PATH}:/usr/lpp/CTXSmf/binexport PATH

In addition to the user commands, a Citrix server administrator should be able to run the system administration commands. After a first-time installation of MetaFrame, the system needs to be configured so that the ctxsrvr user can run all the commands from the MetaFrame server console, and also from an ICA session.

To configure ctxsrvr access to MetaFrame commands when using a C shell, use a .login file for the ctxsrvr user, and add the path to the user and administrator commands. For example:

▼ For HP-UX and Solaris: setenv PATH {PATH}:/opt/CTXSmf/sbin:/opt/CTXSmf/sbin

▲ For AIX: setenv PATH ${PATH}:/usr/lpp/CTXSmf/sbin:/usr/lpp/CTXSmf/sbin

If a Bourne or similar shell will be used, use a .profile file for the ctxsrvr user, and add the path to the user and administrator commands. For example:

▼ For HP-UX and Solaris: PATH=${PATH}:/opt/CTXSmf/sbin:/opt/CTXSmf/sbinexport PATH

▲ For AIX: PATH=${PATH}:/usr/lpp/CTXSmf/sbin:/usr/lpp/CTXSmf/sbinexport PATH

Setting the Path to the Man Pages   Generally, nothing needs to be done to allow users to display man pages for MetaFrame for UNIX commands from a session. The path to these files is added to every user's MANPATH environment variable upon connection to the server. However, access may need to be configured to the MetaFrame man pages if the user's shell script startup file (for example, .profile or .login) overrides the path.

To display the MetaFrame man pages from the server console when logging on as ctxsrvr, the MANPATH environment variable must be set to point to the location of the installed man pages. This is only required if this is the first install of MetaFrame on the server.

To set the MANPATH environment variable…

If using a C shell:

▼ For HP-UX and Solaris: setenv MANPATH ${MANPATH}:/opt/CTXSmf/man

▲   For AIX: setenv MANPATH ${MANPATH}:/usr/lpp/CTXSmf/man

If using a Bourne shell:

▼   For HP-UX and Solaris: MANPATH=${MANPATH}:/opt/CTXSmf/man

▲   For AIX: export MANPATH

Starting and Stopping MetaFrame for UNIX

When installation is complete, start the MetaFrame process on each server using the **ctxsrv** command.

To start MetaFrame:

1.   Log on at the MetaFrame server as a Citrix server administrator (for example, log in with the default user **ctxsrvr**).

2.   At the command prompt, type **ctxsrv start**.

NOTE: If during installation you chose to add the startup/shutdown script, MetaFrame will automatically start when the machine is booted.

To stop the MetaFrame process on a server, use the **ctxshutdown** command. With **ctxshutdown**, the time can be specified for when the shutdown process will begin, and users can be notified that the server is about to shut down.

When the shutdown process begins, applications will terminate, except for those that have registered window hints. These applications will attempt to interactively log users off by displaying a series of prompts. With **ctxshutdown**, the maximum duration that users have to respond to these prompts can be specified. Any sessions that are still active when this period expires are terminated and the users are automatically logged off. The server prevents users from logging on during the shutdown process.

To stop MetaFrame:

1.   Log on to the MetaFrame server as a Citrix server administrator.

2.   At the command prompt: use the **ctxshutdown** command to shut down the server using the defaults. By default, the server shutdown process begins after 60 seconds; the message "Server shutting down. Auto logoff in 60 seconds" is sent to all users logged on to the server. Applications that have registered window hints (the WM_DELETE_WINDOW attribute) have a further 30 seconds to interactively log users off before terminating. To specify other parameters with the **ctxshutdown** command, see Table 12-3 for a list of parameters and descriptions of what they do.

Publishing a MetaFrame for UNIX Application

Once MetaFrame and any desired UNIX applications are installed on the UNIX server, the next step is to publish the application. Once the application is published, it will be

To Perform the Following:	Use This Command:
Shut down the server using the defaults. By default, the server shutdown process begins after 60 seconds; the message "Server shutting down. Auto logoff in 60 seconds" is sent to all users logged on to the server. Applications that have registered window hints (the WM_DELETE_WINDOW attribute) have a further 30 seconds to interactively log users off before terminating.	**ctxshutdown**
Operate in quiet mode. This reduces the amount of information displayed to the administrator by the **ctxshutdown** command.	**ctxshutdown -q**
Specify when the shutdown process will begin, and how long the message will be displayed, in seconds. The default is 60 seconds. When this period expires and the shutdown process begins, applications that have registered window hints (the WM_DELETE_WINDOW attribute) will attempt to interactively log the user off. Applications that have not registered window hints will terminate immediately.	**ctxshutdown -m seconds**
Specify how much time applications with registered window hints (the WM_DELETE_WINDOW attribute) have in seconds to interactively log users off. The default is 30 seconds. When this period expires, any remaining sessions are automatically terminated, users are automatically logged off, and the MetaFrame process stops.	**ctxshutdown -l seconds**
Specify the message displayed to all users logged on to the server. If you do not specify a message, the default message "Server shutting down. Auto logoff in x seconds" is displayed, where x = the number of seconds specified in the -m option (or the default of 60 seconds, if this is not specified).	**ctxshutdown message**

Table 12-3. ctxshutdown Command Parameters

available to any ICA client (version 6.0 and later) and can be published via Web Interface for MetaFrame (see Chapter 16).

Use the **ctxappcfg** command to publish an application. The command prompts the administrator for the information required to publish the application. Application installation is not part of the application publishing process. Before an application can be published, both MetaFrame for UNIX and the application must be installed. The order in which the application and MetaFrame are installed does not matter. Once an application is installed, it can be published at any time.

To publish an application:

1. Log on to the MetaFrame for UNIX server as a Citrix server administrator.

2. At the command prompt, type **ctxappcfg**.

3. You will see the following prompt: App Config>. Type **add**. When you add a new application, the program requests each item of information required. Table 12-4 lists the syntax and parameters for the App Config Add program.

   The published application is automatically enabled. It can now be accessed from an ICA Client by setting up a connection to this published application from the client, or by configuring Web Interface for MetaFrame.

4. At the App Config prompt, type **exit**.

NOTE: A user cannot use the root account (su) to log on or connect to a MetaFrame for UNIX application, even though MetaFrame XP allows connecting to MetaFrame XP published applications as the administrator user.

About ICA Client Keyboard Support

This section describes how to use ICA Client devices with non-English keyboards with MetaFrame for UNIX servers. MetaFrame for UNIX supports ICA Client devices that use the following keyboards:

▼ US English 409

■ UK English 809

■ French 40c

■ German 407

■ Swedish 41d

■ Spanish 40a

▲ Italian 410

Configuring Non-English Keyboard Support   To configure non-English keyboard support:

1. Ensure you start the server in the country locale of the ICA Client keyboard that your users are using. For example, if your users have German keyboards, start the server in a German locale. This ensures that the session runs in an appropriate locale where fonts containing the required keyboard symbols are in the font path and keyboard symbols appear correctly on the screen.

At the Prompt:	Type:
Name:	The user selects this name when setting up an ICA connection to this published application. The name does not need to be the same as the name of the executable file for a particular program.
Command line:	The command line required to run the application or script file—for example: /usr/bin/diary.bin.
Working directory:	The default working directory. This directory must exist. Leave blank to specify the user's home directory. Note that ~/*sub-dir* is supported; ~*otheruser* is not.
Anonymous [yes | no]	**y** if the application is for anonymous use only, or **n** if it is only for users with explicit accounts.

Table 12-4.   Syntax and Parameters for the App Config Add Program

2. Make sure your users select the appropriate keyboard in the Settings dialog box on the client device. For further information about selecting keyboards, refer to the *Client Administrator's Guides* for the clients you are deploying.

NOTE: You can alter the locale for an individual user by setting environment variables in their startup files.

Troubleshooting Non-English Keyboard Support   If users experience problems obtaining accent symbols, such as the circumflex accent (^), it may be that the application they are using does not support *dead keys*. A dead key is a key that does not produce a character when pressed—instead, it modifies the character produced by the next key press. For example, on a generic French PC keyboard the ^ (circumflex) key is a dead key. When this key is pressed, and then the A key is pressed, "â" is generated.

Configuring MetaFrame for UNIX Event Logging

Following an initial install of MetaFrame for UNIX, events are not configured to be sent to the system log (syslog).

MetaFrame uses the following event log levels:

▼   user.notice

■   user.info

■   user.warning

- ■   user.err
- ▲   user.debug

To record MetaFrame events, add a line to the /etc/syslog.conf file and specify the event log levels to be recorded. You must be logged in as root to edit syslog.conf.

NOTE: The event log level names that MetaFrame uses may also be used by other programs. You may see messages from other software in the event log.

For example, adding the following line to the end of syslog.conf (separated with a tab, not a space) causes all event log messages from MetaFrame for UNIX to be put in the file /var/adm/messages:

- ▼   For Solaris and AIX: user.notice;user.info /var/adm/messages
- ▲   For HP-UX: user.notice;user.info /var/adm/syslog/syslog.log

NOTE: The file you use (for example, /var/adm/messages) must exist. If it does not, then create it. You may also want to send certain types of MetaFrame event details to the console. For example, to ensure that all MetaFrame for UNIX error messages appear on the console, add this line to the file /etc/syslog.conf: user.err /dev/console. For details about configuring system event logging, see the syslog.conf man page.

Configuration Requirements to Run Version 1.2 Features

Generally, after installing or upgrading to MetaFrame for UNIX version 1.2, the following is required in order to fully utilize the latest features of this release. Some items to consider:

- ▼   Ensure that your ICA Client users are running Version 6.3 or later ICA Clients. Without Version 6.3 or later ICA Clients, users will be unable to take advantage of some of the new features, including:
  - ■   Greater ICA session size and color depth
  - ■   Multimonitor display
  - ■   Greater bandwidth efficiency
  - ■   HTTP browsing
  - ■   SSL security

  The latest ICA Clients are available for download at http://www.citrix.com/download/.

- ▲   Ensure that version 1.6 of the Citrix XML Service or later is installed on all MetaFrame for UNIX servers. Version 1.7 of the Citrix XML Service is available as an optional package that can be chosen during the installation of version 1.2. If the latest version of the XML Service is not used, the new features will not be available to users who connect to applications via Web Interface for MetaFrame.

NOTE: If you are installing the XML Service on a machine for the first time (in other words, the XML Service is not installed on the machine already) publishing is disabled by default. Therefore, before the XML Service will respond to Web Interface or client HTTP browsing requests, publishing must be enabled.

CITRIX LICENSING

The next section provides detailed information and instructions on MetaFrame XP and MetaFrame for UNIX licensing, as well as the new mlicense utility.

MetaFrame XP FR-3 Licensing

Software licensing, just like software, continues to evolve. Both Microsoft and Citrix licensing is required for all Citrix MetaFrame XP environments. As discussed in Chapter 2, Microsoft licensing with Windows 2003 offers both a per-user and per-seat (per computer) implementation. Citrix licensing is offered on a concurrent user basis. With both Microsoft and Citrix licensing, the license is not only an agreement describing the cost to the user and revenue to the vendor, it is also a technical implementation in which licenses are managed by the servers, and user access is disallowed if insufficient licenses are available. Although most companies today look at software licensing as purely an ethical and legal concern, for many applications, including Citrix and Microsoft, it is also a technical concern. On more than one occasion we have received calls from customers in a panic because users couldn't get logged in as a result of too few licenses, or a configuration mistake with the licensing.

The technical implementation of Citrix MetaFrame XP licensing requires that one license be available for each concurrent user ICA connection to a MetaFrame XP server farm. The ICA Client software is essentially free, as it can be installed on any device at no cost. Of course, when it is used to connect to a server, it will use up a concurrent license on the server farm. The MetaFrame XP licensing is sufficiently intelligent enough to recognize when a single user is running more than one session into the farm, and thus only take one license for that user. Because MetaFrame XP connection licenses are version specific (that is, they understand the difference between an XPs server and an XPe server), we highly recommend that all server farms use the same MetaFrame XP version. This will avoid the problem of MetaFrame checking out two licenses to a single user because that user is connecting to both a MetaFrame XPs server and secondly to a MetaFrame XPe server.

Once the first MetaFrame XP starter pack is purchased, the server software and license can be installed on as many servers as desired. The license code provides for concurrent connections, regardless of how many servers those connections are spread across, as long as all the servers are in the same farm. Obviously, each additional server does require a new license of Windows 2003 Server, but from a Citrix standpoint, the number of servers has little bearing on the number of concurrent licenses. This provides a great deal of flexibility for SBC administrators, allowing them to add servers as more power or flexibility is needed within the farm, without having to purchase more Citrix licensing.

> **TIP:** Possibly the most significant gain from this new licensing paradigm is that it allows an administrator to build non-production test servers within his farm without having to purchase additional Citrix licenses.

How Citrix MetaFrame XP Licenses Are Purchased

Citrix sells its software licenses through a worldwide group of resellers who purchase the licenses through several large distributors or, in the case of the Global 2000 program, the resellers purchase the Flex licenses from Citrix directly. Chapter 3 covers the various licensing program options. It is important to note from a technical standpoint that the program the licenses are purchased under will affect the technical implementation of how they are input and activated.

Citrix Retail and Flex Software Licensing   Any standard purchase of less than 375 licenses will be provided through resellers in the form of standard retail license packs or Easy Licensing electronic licensing packs. There are two main differences between Easy Licensing and standard retail licensing:

▼   With Easy Licensing, all ordering and delivery is done from http://www.MyCitrix.com, in conjunction with a reseller. Since no physical paper is shipped, the time between order and install is dramatically reduced.

▲   Easy Licensing does not require activation—simply key in the license codes and you are ready to go. In contrast, standard retail license packs require a two-step procedure of keying in the licensing, and then going to the Citrix site to activate the licenses.

Retail and Easy License packs of Citrix XPs, XPa, or XPe come in two varieties:

▼   A 20-user starter pack

▲   A concurrent license pack (in increments of 5, 10, 20, 50, and 100 concurrent user licenses)

The main difference between the starter pack and the concurrent license pack is that the starter pack comes with media and documentation (an obvious requirement for first-time Citrix buyers). It is important to note, however, that a starter pack also comes with a starter license, which must be installed prior to installing any connection packs.

Corporate and Educational License Agreement Purchases   Corporations purchasing more than 375 concurrent user licenses at a time may choose to buy licenses under Citrix's Corporate License Program (CLP) through the reseller channel. CLP licenses (referred to as open licenses) require a purchase up-front, but offer a significant discount. Open licenses come in the same 5, 10, 20, 50, and 100 concurrent license packs, but rather than requiring a starter pack, the open licenses come with a product code and a media kit (purchased separately). The media kit and product codes again can be installed on as many servers in the farm as desired. The license codes are installed and activated in the same way as all other Citrix codes. Since most open licenses involve a large number of installations, administrators will benefit from the new mlicense tool detailed next. This tool provides an automated method to install and activate a large number of licenses.

Technical Aspects of How MetaFrame XP Licensing Works

MetaFrame XP licensing is all stored and managed at the server level. There is never any licensing installed, managed, gathered, or stored on any client device. The MetaFrame XP license keys are installed and activated through the Citrix Management Console or by using the mlicense utility (see the mlicense section that follows). Once the license keys are installed, Citrix then stores the license keys in the Citrix farm's IMA Data Store. Each server in the farm contains a local host cache database of the IMA licensing data to ensure users are not denied access to the farm if one server is down. If a server loses connectivity to the farm for more than 96 hours, the licensing component of the IMA service stops, and users are no longer able to log on to that particular server.

The zone data collectors for the IMA Data Store track the license usage within the server farm. The IMA communication within the farm keeps all of the servers constantly up-to-date regarding total number of licenses available and in use.

When a user initiates an ICA connection with a MetaFrame XP server, a license is checked out from the IMA Data Store pool. When the user logs off, the connection license is checked back in to the pool of available licenses in the Data Store.

Adding, Activating, and Backing Up Licenses with the mlicense Utility   The following processes do not work if the licenses have already been manually added to the Citrix Management Console.

Use the mlicense utility to add multiple licenses, activate multiple licenses, and back up licenses in a MetaFrame XP server farm. mlicense can be used in a MetaFrame XP server farm with servers running MetaFrame XP Feature Release 1, 2, or 3. MetaFrame XP Feature Release 3 includes the mlicense utility. For the purposes of this utility, the term *serial number* refers to license numbers before they are added to the farm and the term *license number* is synonymous with license string and license key.

Perform the following tasks before running mlicense:

1.   Create a filename.txt file and input all of the license serial numbers to be added to the MetaFrame XP server farm. You can add other text to the filename.txt file, such as section headings. The mlicense utility reads the license serial numbers in the file and then adds them to the Data Store.

NOTE: Use all uppercase letters when adding license serial numbers to the filename.txt file.

2. For MetaFrame XP Feature Release 2 server farms, download and install Hotfix XE102W064 on each of the servers. This hotfix must be present on the MetaFrame XP Feature Release 2 servers before running mlicense in the farm.

3. For MetaFrame XP Feature Release 1 and 2 server farms, download the mlicense utility from ftp://ftp.citrix.com/etaXP/Utils/mlicense.exe and copy Mlicense.exe to the %system Root%\System32 directory on one of the servers in the farm.

Directions for Using mlicense   Full administrative rights or delegated administrative rights are required to execute this command.

1. From a command prompt, run the command parameters listed in Table 12-5. For example: C:\Documents and Settings\Administrator>**mlicense add /I C:\Temp\filename.txt /O C:\Temp\filename.xml.**

NOTE: You can save the filename.xml file to a directory of your choice by specifying the directory path. mlicense outputs the filename.xml file, which includes the license numbers to be used for activation.

2. Open the web browser and navigate to the Multiple Activation page on the Citrix Activation (CAS) web site. Upload the filename.xml file. The web site processes the filename.xml file and returns a filename_processed.xml file. Save the filename_processed.xml file on the server.

NOTE: Detailed directions for using the CAS web site are on the CAS Multiple License Activation web page.

3. Run the **mlicense activate** command, using the filename_processed.xml file. Use the command parameters listed next as an example:

   C:\Program Files\Citrix\System32>**mlicense activate /I filename_processed.xml**

   The licenses are now activated in the MetaFrame farm.

4. After activating the licenses, use the backup feature of mlicense to create a backup file of the licenses; for example:

   C:\Documents and Settings\Administrator>**mlicense backup /O**

   C:\Temp\backupfilename.txtMLicense

5. Use this command-line utility to add groups of licenses to a MetaFrame XP Feature Release 1 or Feature Release 2 farm. Executing mlicense with no parameters displays help for the utility.

done

Table 12-5 lists the syntax and parameters for the mlicense command line utility. Use this command-line utility with the parameters and syntax listed in Table 12-5 to add groups of licenses

Command Syntax	Parameters	Parameter Options
mlicense /?	/? — Displays the syntax for the utility and information about the utility's options.	
mlicense [activate /I filename_processed.xml]	filename_processed .xml — The filename of the license number and activation codes output file from the CAS Multiple License Activation CAS web site to be used.	/activate filename_processed.xml — Activates the filename_processed.xml licenses in the MetaFrame farm. When this command is successfully completed, mlicense displays the message, "Successfully activated all the licenses." /I — Input command.
mLicense [/L number] [/Q]	number — The maximum number of license numbers that each filename.XML file will contain. The maximum number that can be specified is 2000.	/L — Allows you to list the number of licenses to be put in the filename.xml file by mlicense. This is optional. /Q — This command runs after mlicense /L.
mlicense [backup /O backupfilename.txt]	backupfilename.txt — The filename containing a backup of the license serial numbers.	/Backup — Saves the serial number strings from the MetaFrame farm in the backupfilename.txt file for backup and disaster recovery purposes. /O — Output

Table 12-5.   mlicense Command-Line Utility Syntax and Parameters

Command Syntax	Parameters	Parameter Options
mlicense [add /I filename.txt] [/O filename.xml]	filename.txt — The name of the text file listing all of the license serial numbers to be added. filename.xml — The name of the output .XML file specified when using the <mlicense add /I filename.txt /O filename.xml> syntax. This file is uploaded to the CAS Multiple License Activation web site.	/add filename.txt — Adds the license serial numbers from the filename.txt file to the mlicense tool. When this command is successfully completed, mlicense displays the message, "Successfully added all the serial numbers." mlicense does not add autoactivated licenses to the filename.xml file. When creating the filename.txt file, be sure to use all uppercase letters.

Table 12-5.   mlicense Command-Line Utility Syntax and Parameters *(continued)*

Example: **mlicense add /I C:\Temp\filename.txt /O C:\Temp\filename.xml /L 10**
The preceding example puts ten license numbers in each of the filename.xml files. The first file is named filename.xml, the second file is named filename_1.xml, then filename_2.xml, and so on. If you do not use the /L option and the filename.txt file has more than 2000 license numbers, mlicense creates filename.xml with the initial 2000 license numbers and filename_1.xml with any license numbers over and above the initial 2000.

For example, if filename.txt contains 2100 license numbers, mlicense creates filename.xml that contains 2000 license numbers and filename_1.xml that contains the additional 100 license numbers.

Example: **<mlicense add /I C:\Temp\filename.txt /O C:\Temp\filename.xml /L 10 /Q>**

This allows the output file naming convention to restart. In this example, it overwrites the existing files such as filename.xml, filename_1.xml, and filename._2.xml in the directory. If you do not use the /Q option, the files are created using the next number available in the naming convention, such as filename_3.xml, filename_4.xml, and filename_5.xml.

Citrix MetaFrame for UNIX Version 1.2 Licensing

Citrix MetaFrame for UNIX licensing is different from Citrix MetaFrame XP licensing in four significant ways:

1. MetaFrame for UNIX is licensed per server and per concurrent user. For instance, a 15-user license can only be put on one server—if additional server power is required, even though the first server is only supporting five users, a second 15-user license is required. Although server licenses can be pooled as the farm grows (using Citrix load balancing), more thought and planning need to go into determining how many servers will be needed to support the number of expected concurrent users.

NOTE: Citrix sells MetaFrame for UNIX in base packs as small as three users to alleviate the pain of having to buy MetaFrame for UNIX for 20 users for a small server that may only be capable of supporting three users.

2. MetaFrame for UNIX is sold in a base license (as opposed to a Starter Kit like MetaFrame XP) of 3 or 15 users, and additional bump packs of 5, 10, 20, 50, and 100 concurrent connection licenses. The bump packs are not interchangeable with MetaFrame XP bump packs (and the pricing is different as well).

3. MetaFrame for UNIX does not have different versions like MetaFrame XPs, XPa, or XPe. Instead, the additional features of Citrix Load balancing are sold and licensed as separate products.

4. Microsoft licensing is not required.

Because of these differences, as of version 1.2, licensing cannot be shared between MetaFrame XP server farms and MetaFrame for UNIX server farms unless the MetaFrame XP servers are in mixed mode. Additionally, mlicense will not work with MetaFrame for UNIX. Citrix is currently considering using the same licensing management for both MetaFrame for UNIX and MetaFrame XP, so common management and more seamless license pooling between products may be available with future releases.

Although the MetaFrame for UNIX licensing is not as consumer friendly, it is cheaper per concurrent connection license. Additionally, MetaFrame for UNIX deals with multiple concurrent licensing similarly to MetaFrame XP in that it generally is efficient enough to use only one license for one user, even if they have multiple sessions open to multiple MetaFrame for UNIX servers. MetaFrame for UNIX's client device licensing allows users to start multiple sessions on the same server or on different servers, while using only a single Citrix user count, assuming the following conditions exist:

1. All connections must be from the same client device.

2. When a user starts a second session on the same Citrix server as the first session, the new session does not consume a second user count. When a user

starts a second session on a different Citrix server, the new session does not consume a second user count if all the following conditions are true:

- The first session consumed a pooled user count.
- The user makes all connections from the same client device.
- All servers are on the same subnet (using the same master ICA Browser).

Citrix servers exhaust all local (unpooled) user counts before consuming pooled user counts. Therefore, a user assigned a local user count uses a second user count when starting a second session on a different Citrix server.

Installing MetaFrame for UNIX Licenses   To install the licenses on a Citrix for MetaFrame server, install the software, enter the serial numbers, and activate the licenses through the activation tool using the following steps:

1. Add the supplied serial number using the **ctxlicense** command. At the command prompt, type **ctxlicense -add serial-number**. Type the serial number exactly as it appears (it is case sensitive). A message will state that the Citrix license has been successfully added. MetaFrame generates and displays a unique 35-character license number, based on the serial number entered. The serial number is the 25-character number that can be found in three places:

   - On the sticker on the back of the CD-ROM booklet, in version 1.1
   - On the sealed inside flap of the CD-ROM pack, in Feature Release 1
   - On a web site, if you have been given a URL through an electronic licensing program

2. Get an activation code from Citrix for the license from the Citrix product activation web site http://www.citrix.com/activate/ and follow the instructions on the screen. You will need to supply the 35-character license number generated in Step 1.

3. Activate the Citrix license using **ctxlicense**. At the command prompt, type **ctxlicense -activate license-number activation-code**. Paste in the license number from the Clipboard, or type it in, and type in the activation code supplied by Citrix. A message stating that the Citrix license has been successfully activated appears. The software is now ready for use.

MetaFrame for UNIX License Pooling   By default, all user licenses are pooled across Citrix servers. You can reserve licenses for use only on a local Citrix server by lowering the number of pooled licenses. Unpooled local licenses are not available to other Citrix servers and cannot be used for client device licensing.

To change the pooled user count, the 35-character license number must be supplied. To display all Citrix licensing information for a specific server or server pool, use **ctxlicense -list** from a command prompt (logged in as a Citrix administrator). A description of each license, the license number, user count and pooled user count, and an indication of whether it is activated or not, is provided.

To change the pooled user count across MetaFrame for UNIX servers:

1. Log on to the MetaFrame server as a Citrix server administrator.

2. At the command prompt, type **ctxlicense -pool license-number pooled-count**

The pooled count must be between zero and the total number of user counts installed with this license number. Any remaining user counts become local to this server only.

Since MetaFrame for UNIX does not have an IMA Data Store like MetaFrame XP, the licenses are all stored on the first installed server, and a backup copy is stored on the second installed server. If the license server should fail, the backup server will continue to license users for 48 hours, after which all licensing will be lost.

NOTE: The default settings for pooled licenses will generally reduce the number of licenses a company needs, and as such, the pooled count shouldn't be changed without a lot of thought about how it may change the license count available.

CHAPTER 13

Application Installation and Configuration

The purpose of the infrastructure discussed so far in this book is to provide software applications to users. Whether these applications automate the organization (say, using ERP, MRP, or CAD/CAM), provide recordkeeping and documentation for them (with such things as accounting applications, word processors, spread sheets, document management, and so on), or allow the organization to communicate effectively (through e-mail, printing, file sharing, or presentation software), applications have become critical to a vast majority of organizations and their users. Without applications, there is no need for IT infrastructure of any kind.

Since all enterprise organizations (as well as a large majority of small- and mid-sized businesses) today have applications that fill these needs, the debate comes down to how to most effectively and cost-efficiently build an IT infrastructure that provides these applications to users that need them. Additionally, many organizations, as they have grown and become more diverse, desire to deploy these applications to a wider set of users with fewer constraints.

At the core of the on-demand computing (ODC) value statement is providing these applications to users anytime, anyplace, from any device. Of course it goes without saying that the users must be able to run the applications without delay, slowness, or problems, and with the latest base of available features. We have made the argument throughout this book that server-based computing (SBC) succeeds at all of these far more efficiently than standard client-server computing. There is one large caveat though—the applications have to work in the SBC environment. If the applications don't run as well, or better, in an SBC environment as they do from a desktop PC, then the SBC project will fail. With this said, it is obvious that application installation and configuration is the fulcrum upon which any server-based computing project will swing from success to failure.

Chapters 10 and 11 both discussed building a pilot or test environment prior to making any significant investment in SBC infrastructure. The most significant reason for the test environment is to ensure that an organization's applications run effectively in an SBC setting. Although chances are good that most, if not all, of your applications will run in an SBC environment because of Microsoft's push to make application developers want the Windows 2000 and 2003 certifications, there are still older applications, or poorly written ones, that remain at the core of many organizations. The success of any SBC project depends largely on whether these applications can be fixed, upgraded or replaced, run in hybrid mode (run locally on some users' machines while all other applications are run from the server) for a period of time, or relegated to a kiosk where users access it as needed. If none of these are an option, the project simply can't go forward.

This chapter will focus on how applications are installed in an SBC environment, the applications' requirements, some tricks to making non-conforming applications work, application optimization, specific tips and checklists for common applications, and application testing methodology.

The installation and testing methodology presented in this chapter is not only critical at implementation, but throughout the life of the server-based environment. All application installation and updates, even minor hotfixes, must be subjected to a strict systematic installation and testing methodology.

APPLICATION STRATEGIES

The idea behind building an SBC environment in the first place is to provide a means of distributing common applications to users that is low in cost and complexity, but high in functionality and performance. It is important to keep this "end state" in mind when selecting or writing applications to be run in an SBC environment. An application that is not stable in a traditional distributed computing network isn't likely to work any better under server-based computing. In fact, it may exhibit new problems. It is also critical to take the client environment into account. If both PCs and Windows terminals are being evaluated, the capabilities and user experience of each are quite different and will affect application functionality.

All application installation and updates, even minor hotfixes, must be subjected to a strict systematic installation and testing methodology. From a high level, we suggest the following methodology:

1. Identify and confirm the requirement for the installation, update, or hotfix.

2. Research the manufacturer instructions and warnings for the software to be installed.

3. If the fix is simply a hotfix or software update, utilize MetaFrame Installation Manager (IM) to unpublish (uninstall) the current version of the software from the test environment. Reinstall the original application using IM. Although this process may seem unnecessary, it is critical, as it ensures a common starting point when the update is propagated to other servers.

4. Install the application in the test environment.

    ■ Run any postinstallation scripts or application compatibility tests.

    ■ Configure the application.

5. Perform the testing algorithm recommended in the "Application Testing Procedure" section of this chapter.

    ■ Make any necessary fixes, registry changes, or optimizations.

6. Following full testing, use IM to publish the application to one production server. If it is an update or hotfix, utilize the IM image that includes the full uninstallation and reinstallation as recommended in Step 3.

7. Re-perform the testing algorithm.

8. Publish to the remaining required production servers.

Application Features and Requirements

We have created the following list of features and requirements to aid you in the application selection process:

▼ Applications should be stable and perform well in a traditional, distributed computing environment.

■ The application should have stated support from the manufacturer. In the early days of server-based computing technology, application support was hit or miss (more miss than hit). With Windows 2000 Server, and now Windows Server 2003, however, in order for a software package to gain the Microsoft Windows Certification, the application must also support execution under Terminal Services. As such, multiuser support has become the norm rather than the exception.

■ Ideally, an application should execute in multithreaded fashion and make efficient use of memory and CPU resources when running in a multiuser environment. Note that this precludes DOS and all 16-bit applications, although there are tricks we will discuss later in this chapter that may allow them to limp by.

■ The use of multimedia in applications should be kept to an absolute minimum. Sound, graphics, or video should be limited to mission-critical features only, because the complexity and cost of the extra network bandwidth consumed by these features must be justified.

▲ The application should make the most use of the Windows printing system and be as efficient as possible in the creation and distribution of print jobs. Here again, we issue a warning regarding graphic-intensive programs: they typically generate enormous print files that then travel over the LAN or WAN to the printer. This must be taken into account when planning for the management of the available bandwidth.

Application Optimization

We discuss the process of installing and configuring applications in later sections. But first, it is necessary to address some specific optimization issues for the following categories of applications.

DOS and 16-Bit Applications

In order for a DOS or 16-bit application to run under Windows NT 4.0, a separate resource pool must be created for that program. This is due to the fact that such applications cannot share memory in the same way as 32-bit programs that were created specifically to run on Windows NT. This resource pooling program is called "ntvdm" for "NT Virtual Dos Machine." It uses the partitioning capability of the Intel architecture to create a virtual 8086 environment in which each DOS program can run. When running a DOS or 16-bit Windows program on Windows NT, ntvdm will show up as the executable in the task manager, rather than the program executable itself.

NOTE: Windows 2000 Server and Windows Server 2003 do not effectively support ntvdm, so if DOS or 16-bit applications are required, plan to build a Windows NT 4.0 TSE/MetaFrame XP server environment and dedicate it to running these applications.

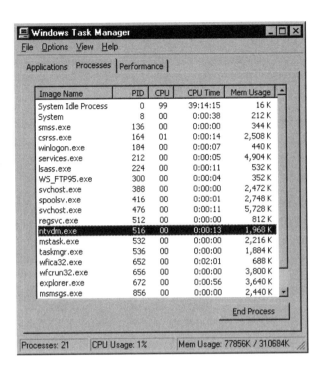

Because these older programs cannot share resources, they do not scale well. We have seen environments in which an application was being migrated from an older 16-bit version to a newer 32-bit version. The 16-bit program took two to three times the resources of its newer 32-bit cousin. We realize these older programs may still be required, particularly as part of a migration effort, but every effort should be made to phase them out completely.

DOS Program Keyboard Polling   Another feature to look out for with DOS programs is keyboard polling. Most DOS programs were written to run in a single-user environment, and data entry screens typically do nothing until the user presses a key. In order to respond as quickly as possible, the program polls the keyboard, sometimes hundreds or thousands of times per second. In a multiuser environment this can wreak havoc with system performance. Even though Windows NT runs ntvdm to give such a program its own resource pool, it must still grant access to hardware components such as the keyboard, mouse, and video. In some cases, the keyboard polling can be adjusted to more reasonable levels by using a standard command like **DOSKBD** or a third-party utility such as Clip2F or Tame. If the DOS program will not respond to limiting the keyboard polling, it should not be used in an SBC environment. A problematic DOS application will often consume 100 percent of the available resources on a MetaFrame XP server. Again, DOS keyboard utilities are not available under Windows 2000 Server or Windows Server 2003, so Windows NT 4.0 TSE must be used to run a DOS application.

TIP: The DOSKBD (or other similar utility) can be run from the autoexec.nt file that is accessed for each DOS session. The autoexec.nt file is specified with the PIF editor. Issuing the following command at the command prompt can collect initial statistics on the DOS application:
DOSKBD /StartMonitor SOMEPROG.EXE

32-Bit Applications and the Registry

Just because an application is written to be 32-bit does not mean it makes effective use of the registry. It is important that such an application use the registry to store its settings for a variety of reasons.

▼ Application packaging is much simpler when all changes made by the installation process are stored in a particular group of registry keys.

▲ The application installation process in Terminal Services (**change user /install**) makes a copy of the registry changes that an install program generates for each user (HKEY_CURRENT_USER). If an application uses an INI file or incorrectly writes user-specific information to the HKEY_LOCAL_MACHINE key, it is problematic to get that application functioning in a multiuser environment.

Custom Applications

Many custom applications work quite well in an SBC environment. Such applications should be 32-bit and avoid hard-coded values for elements such as network paths or data sources. Keep in mind any library dependencies such as those required by Visual Basic, too, since these libraries will have to be installed with the applications on each Terminal Server in the farm.

An application should write all user-specific information to the HKEY_ CURRENT_USER registry key and all global system information to the HKEY_LOCAL_ MACHINE key.

INSTALLING AND CONFIGURING APPLICATIONS

Since the operating system needs to allow multiple users to run and access applications (and thus application registry settings) simultaneously, a program must be installed in such a fashion that the registry changes are replicated for all users. There are two basic methods for installing an application on a MetaFrame XP server to cause this replication to take place. The recommended method is to use the Control Panel and run the Add/Remove Programs application. The other is to run the **change user /install** and **change user /execute** commands from a command prompt.

Using Add/Remove Programs

The advantage to installing an application using Add/Remove Programs from the Control Panel is that it creates the "shadow key" properly in all cases. The Add/Remove Programs application monitors changes to the HKEY_CURRENT_USER key and saves them in the shadow key. This key is then propagated to each user, as shown in Figure 13-1, so that they may have unique settings for that application.

NOTE: Do not allow the system to reboot until after you click Finish in the Add/Remove Programs application to ensure that the shadow key information is safely written.

Using Change User /Install

Using the **change user/install** command works well most of the time, but we have seen that in some cases shadow key information is missed. For example, there is a known problem installing Internet Explorer in this manner, but it works perfectly well using the Add/Remove Programs application. This method involves opening a command prompt, typing **change user /install**, installing the application, then typing **change user /execute**.

NOTE: If you use this method, make sure you do not allow the system to reboot without first issuing the **change user /execute** command. If you do not issue the command, the system may not properly record the changes to the registry.

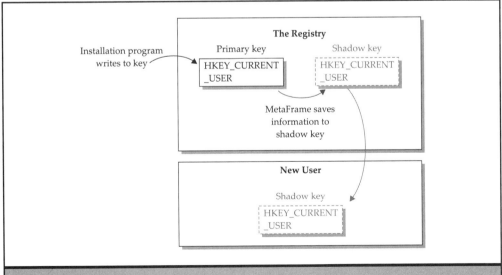

Figure 13-1. Shadow key propagation

The Application Installation Checklist

The basic procedure for installing applications on a Windows 2000 Server or Windows Server 2003 running MetaFrame XP is as follows:

1. Make sure you are logged onto the test server console as a member of the local Administrators group.

2. Reset any remote sessions with the Citrix Management Console.

3. Disable logons to the server using the Citrix Management Console (select Server | Properties | MetaFrame XP settings, then uncheck the Enable Logons to this Server check box) to prevent users from logging in during the application installation.

4. Run the Add/Remove Programs application and select the application's setup program to begin installation.

5. Click Finish after the application has completed installation and before the server reboots.

6. If an application compatibility script exists, run it. Review the notes in the script and any "read me" notes on application compatibility, then perform any other necessary steps.

7. At this point, the application is installed, and testing can begin.

NOTE: Though you can uninstall an application with Add/Remove Programs, we don't recommend it. We recommend using the imaging process outlined in Chapter 11 or Installation Manager (discussed later in this chapter) to create standard server images including packaged applications. If an application needs to be removed, simply restore the image that was current before the application package was installed or unpublish the application within Installation Manager. Other methods can leave remnants of the application in the form of leftover registry changes or library files that can cause problems with the system or with other applications.

Postinstallation Changes

Although a large majority of current applications run without a hitch in a Windows 2000 Server and Windows Server 2003 Terminal Services environment, there remain some older and more rogue applications that simply aren't designed appropriately. For the older applications, a bit of tweaking may be needed after installation on the MetaFrame XP server using the Add/Remove Programs application or the command-line method. Most postinstallation changes provide necessary changes to user-specific program settings, or library file locations.

As multiuser environments have grown increasingly popular, some application vendors have created fixes to make their applications work in a Terminal Services environment. An *application compatibility script* is a batch file that makes any changes to the operating system that are necessary for a specific application to function in a multiuser environment. There are two types of Application Compatibility Scripts: Install and Logon.

Install Scripts

The two main functions of the Install Script are to remove any inappropriate changes to the HKEY_LOCAL_MACHINE registry key, and to verify that the logon scripts are correct. An Install Script will first verify that the root drive has been properly specified. If it has not, the script will open the ROOTDRV2.CMD file so it can be specified. If the root drive has been specified, it proceeds to correct inappropriate writes to HKEY_LOCAL_MACHINE as well as perform any other necessary cleanup work to make the application run correctly. Finally, it adds a call to the USRLOGN2.CMD file that will call the appropriate Logon Script for the application.

Logon Scripts

As the name implies, these scripts are designed to correct problems with the user logon environment, either with the HKEY_CURRENT_USER key, the user's home directory, or user-specific application settings. The USRLOGN2.CMD batch file calls the application Logon Scripts. This script is called by the main logon file, USRLOGON.CMD. USRLOGON.CMD is responsible for creating the RootDrive variable used by all logon scripts to identify the user's home directory.

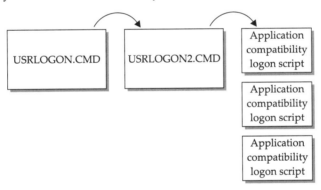

The RootDrive variable defines both the user's home drive and the home path and can be used instead of the UNC path defined in the user properties of the Computer Management utility. Use of the drive letter is preferable because the user will not have access to directories above the directory where the home drive is mapped.

Softricity SoftGrid for Terminal Servers

It is important to note that a useful third-party tool is available to resolve some of the typical application installation problems with application compatibility, DLL conflicts, and Windows registry conflicts. Softricity (www.softricity.com/products/) offers a product called SoftGrid for Terminal Servers that dramatically changes the application installation and deployment approach. With the SoftGrid solution, applications are never installed on the Terminal Servers. Instead, applications run inside Softricity's SystemGuard virtual environment, which protects the computer's operating system from any alterations and enables the application to run intact.

SystemGuard is a virtual run-time environment within which an application executes. It maintains the integrity and reliability of the operating system by shielding it from change that is normally created by the application as it is installed and run. However, since the applications execute locally, access is still available to all local services including cut and paste, OLE, printing and network drives.

We recommend that enterprise environments with 1000 or more users consider Softricity or other similar solutions to reduce the complexity and testing required on Terminal Servers providing large numbers of applications.

Installation Tips

Though it is impossible to provide installation tips for all common applications, we thought it would be appropriate to include a few to set expectations. There is a wealth of information about application configurations on the Citrix web site (http://support.citrix.com). We have found the online knowledge center (Citrix's knowledge base and user forums) to be particularly useful, as it contains many technical notes from other users on application difficulties and the methods used to fix or work around them.

The following examples show the format for application installation and configuration checklists. They are provided both as an example of the process of installing an application under MetaFrame XP and as a suggestion for recordkeeping purposes.

Example Installation Instructions—Installing Microsoft Office XP on Windows Server 2003 for Use in a Terminal Services/MetaFrame Environment

For the purposes of providing an example of a common application installation in a Terminal Services environment, we will utilize our fictional case study, CME Corp introduced in Chapter 10, as an example. CME Corp, a medical device manufacturer with 3000 employees worldwide, will be deploying Microsoft Office XP. In order to install Office XP in the Terminal Services environment, a Microsoft Transform file (MST) will be used for installation. The MST file allows for full customization of the install, including configuration of the Outlook profile with a user-specific profile.

NOTE: Unlike Office 2000, Office XP does not require a special transform to install Office on a Terminal Services–enabled computer. Office XP Setup detects that it is being run under Terminal Services and it preconfigures all the proper options. Because a transform file allows a custom configuration, including Outlook Profile configuration, we will cover the custom transform file setup in this section.

To install Office, do the following:

1. Create an administrative installation of Office XP.

2. Install the Microsoft Office XP Resource Kit. The ORK can be downloaded from www.microsoft.com/office/ork/xp/appndx/appa04.htm.

3. Create a custom Microsoft Transform file.

4. Execute the Microsoft Office XP installation program to install Microsoft Office XP. (CME Corp will use Installation Manager as described later in this chapter, and thus will need to add the package to the CMC.)

NOTE: Installation of Office XP on a Terminal Services–enabled system requires the use of the Application Server mode configuration. A computer configured for Remote Administration mode is not recognized by Office XP Setup and installs Office XP as if it were being installed to a generic workstation.

Creating an Administrative Installation of Office XP   To create an administrative installation of Office XP, run the setup program with a /a switch and choose an installation directory on an easily accessible network share. For example, from the desktop of any Windows 2000 Server machine in the environment, click Start | Run, and then type **setup.exe /a path\name SHORTFILENAMES=TRUE /qb /L* path\name of log file**.

The following are various command-line options available:

▼   **/a**   Enables Windows Installer to perform an administrative installation of a product on a network share.

■   **SHORTFILENAMES=TRUE**   Directs Windows Installer to create all filenames and folders with MS-DOS-compatible filenames. Required when you run Windows Installer from the command line.

■   **/qb**   Sets the user interface to the basic level (simple progress and error handling).

■   **/L***   Turns on logging and sets a path for the log file. The * flag causes the switch to log all information.

▲   **path\name of log file**   Path and filename of the Windows Installer log file.

Installing the Office XP Resource Kit   The Office XP resource kit can be downloaded from www.microsoft.com/office/ork/xp/appndx/appa04.htm. Install it accepting all of the defaults.

Creating a Custom Office XP Terminal Services Transform File   After installing the Office XP Resource Kit, we are ready to create a custom Microsoft Terminal Server Transform (MST) file with the Custom Installation Wizard for CME's environment. We will later use this file with Installation Manager to deploy Office XP to all current and future MetaFrame Servers.

To create and configure a custom Microsoft Office XP Terminal Services Transform file:

1. Click Start | Programs | Microsoft Office Tools | Microsoft Office XP Resource Kit Tools | Custom Installation Wizard. Click Next to go forward with the installation.

2. Click the Browse button.

3. Browse to the PROPLUS.MSI file (this filename will be different for the Premium or Standard versions of Office XP) located on the administrative installation share and click OK, then click Next.

4. Select Create a new MST file and click Next.

5. Select a location and name the file TERMSRVR.MST to save the new MST and click Next.

6. Specify the Default installation path and the Organization name and click Next.

7. Specify if you want to uninstall any previous Office versions as part of the Office XP install and click Next.

8. Select the features that you do not want to install and click Next. (Set the installation state of the selected feature to Not Available, Hidden, or Locked. Select the Do Not Migrate Previous Installation State check box.)

NOTE: The Do Not Migrate Previous Installation States check box must be selected for each feature that is set to Not Available, Hidden, or Locked. Carefully choose which features to install. Features like animation and the office assistant should *not* be installed, since they can cause unnecessary strain on the server.

9. Click Next on the following screens, making any customizations appropriate.

10. On the Outlook Screen: customize the Default Profile page, choose New Profile, and name the profile **%username%**, then click Next.

11. Select Configure an Exchange Server connection and enter an Exchange Server name, then click Next.

12. Click Customize Additional Outlook Profile and Account Information.

13. Click Add and choose Outlook Address Book, then click Next and Finish on the Add Account Wizard.

14. Click Next.

15. Continue to click Next while making any appropriate changes until the wizard is complete.

Executing the Microsoft Office XP Installation Program   For basic installation to one server, use the Add/Remove Programs or change user /install as described earlier in this chapter and click Start | Run, then type **setup.exe TRANSFORMS=C:\TERMSRVR.MST /qb**. Click OK.

To install this application to multiple servers, please see the "MetaFrame Installation Manager" section later in this chapter.

Managing the Application List

Before launching into the application test process, it is important to have a controllable list of applications targeted for production. The list should be as small as possible but still have representative applications in any category that your company needs to use. What must be avoided is a lack of standardization within a category. For example, a large organization may be using both Microsoft Office 2000 and Office XP. Make every effort to choose one application (or suite, in this case) for deployment in the SBC environment. It will reduce complexity, ease support, and cause less confusion to the user community.

Application Testing Procedure

Each application should go through two phases of testing—component testing and system testing—in order to assess how it functions running by itself and as part of a fully configured server. The strategy is to have as much breadth and depth of testing coverage as is practical, given the realities of most fast-paced corporate IT departments. The effort of creating and refining an application testing process is worthwhile. Over time, the IT staff will become fast, proficient, and confident at running the tests.

Component Testing

This phase of testing is designed to exercise an application running by itself in a multiuser environment. This can be especially important with applications that were not written specifically for this environment, do not have application-compatibility scripts, or are older DOS or 16-bit applications.

Generic Functions   The generic functions of the component test phase are functions that are common to most applications. Examples of generic functions are Execute (run the program), Exit, File-Print, File-Open, and Cut and Paste. Coverage of generic functions is important to ensure the application works as expected in a multiuser environment. One test list can be created that will cover every application slated for deployment, or at least broad categories of applications. Not every test on the list will apply, but running the test list is important nonetheless.

Specific Functions   As the name implies, these are functions that are specific to each application. At least one test list should be created for each application to cover specific functions. Examples are running a custom macro in Microsoft Excel, creating a new project in Visual J++, and changing the color saturation in Adobe Photoshop.

System Testing

The system-testing phase is designed to ensure that an application behaves predictably on a server loaded with other applications. This is also typically the phase that includes some load testing for performance. A system test involves running the following steps:

▼   Run the component tests again on a fully configured server. Such a server has all the applications slated for production deployment loaded, the network connected, and is participating in a domain, a server farm, and load balancing. The idea is to set up an environment that is as close to the production environment as possible.

■ Test necessary application integration functions—for example, database access through Microsoft Excel, cutting and pasting between applications, running a mail-merge macro in Microsoft Word, or running a custom client application that provides a front-end user interface to a legacy system.

■ Load test the application. Establish as many user sessions as are likely to be used in production. This can either be done literally, or through scripting or a commercial testing application covered in Chapter 11. Have several people run test lists on the application simultaneously.

▲ Test the application using all targeted client environments. This includes not only desktop PCs, laptops, and Windows terminals, but also different points in the enterprise network and other different types of network connections.

Anecdotal Testing

We have found that a period of "beating on the application" after all other formal testing has been done is often very useful. This type of undirected testing allows the testers to think "outside the box" and exercise functions that the test-list creators may not have thought of. Anecdotal testing is no substitute for formal testing and should never be used as the sole testing method.

Test Lists

There is no secret to creating good test lists, but there is an art to it that can only be mastered with practice. The most important thing to remember is not to let "best get in the way of better." In other words, it is better to start with a basic test list and make it better over time than to delay the test process until the perfect test list is completed. The perfect test list will never be realized without experience in the process.

We have provided an example test list as a starting point. Feel free to adapt it to other programs or even modify its structure to fit your needs. Table 13-1 shows a test list of generic functions that can be applied to most applications. In addition to this generic list, a more specific list should also be developed to ensure that a particular application's functionality has been fully tested.

NOTE: Substitute the generic information in the tables with information specific to the application being tested.

Pass or Fail Status

Once a test list has been run, a report of the application, test lists, tests run, and the status can be generated. It is not unreasonable to expect an application to pass all tests before being considered for production deployment.

Step	Test (Generic)	Description	Expected Result	Result	Pass/ Fail	Notes
1	Launch Method #1	Click the Application icon on the desktop.	The application executes.	Application is executed.	P	
2	Launch Method #2	Click Start | Programs, the program group, and the application name.	The application executes.	Application is executed.	P	
3	Open a document	Choose File | Open from the menu.	The default or last data directory is displayed.	The default directory was displayed.	P	Might want to run this test two more times to see which directory is displayed.
4	Print a document	Choose File | Print from the menu.	Current document prints in full.	Document printed.	P	
...						
24	Exit Method #1	Choose File | Exit from the menu.	The application exits.	Application is exited	P	
25	Exit Method #2	Click the X in the upper-right corner of the main application window.	The application exits.	Application is exited	P	This method is faster.

Table 13-1.   Generic Functions Test List 1

Test Cycles

All test lists run on a particular application are considered one *test cycle*. Keep in mind, all tests may not pass. Following the test cycle, and after any fixes or corrections have been made, all test lists with failed tests should be run again. Once all the failed tests have passed, a final run of the entire suite of test lists is advisable to make sure nothing new was "broken" during this phase. This is often referred to as *regression testing*. The cycle repeats until all tests pass or until the pass percentage meets a predetermined acceptance level. Once all tests have passed or met the goal, the application can be considered a candidate for production deployment.

THE PRODUCTION DEPLOYMENT PROCESS

Once an application has completed the testing process, it is time to manage its deployment into the production environment. Unless extensive load testing was done before deployment, we recommend putting the application on one or just a few servers to begin with and using the ICA Passthrough capability to direct users to the new application, as shown in Figure 13-2. You should also consider having an "early adopter" user group that can begin employing the application before it is deployed throughout the enterprise. A week or two of running the application in this manner can reveal any last-minute issues not discovered in testing, without unduly burdening the user community with problems.

Sample Process Checklist for Application Deployment

The following checklist provides a guideline for an application deployment process. Modify it to fit your organization and established procedures.

1. A qualified request for application support is made to IT.
2. Verification that management has approved the application is completed.

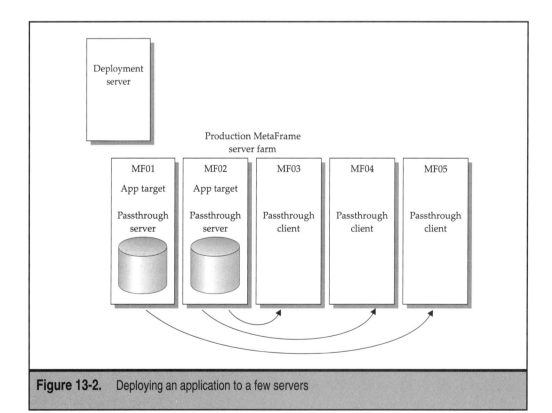

Figure 13-2.   Deploying an application to a few servers

3. A contact person for the application has been identified. This person will be the point of contact for communicating the application's status.

4. Review of the application's specifications and requirements is done.

   ■ Is the software 32-bit?

   ■ Are there registry entries?

   ■ If internally developed, are network paths hard-coded?

   ■ Are there any system library dependencies?

5. Install the application on the test server. Document all steps of the install.

6. Perform any necessary software configurations for operation in a Terminal Services environment—for example, registry changes, INI file settings, file or directory modifications.

7. Create specific function test lists. Determine the suitability of generic function test lists and modify as appropriate. Create test lists for both component and system test phases.

8. Begin Test Cycle 1. Perform component testing.

9. Repeat component testing until all tests have passed, or the pass percentage is acceptable.

10. Begin system testing. Add the application to the last good server image that includes other production applications and operating system modifications. Rerun component tests and add system tests.

11. As part of system testing, load-test the application. Test with a single user, (usually the contact specified in Step 3).

12. Get five test users from the contact to run selected system test lists. Determine whether further load testing is necessary or if results can be extrapolated from the five-user test.

13. Repeat the test cycle until all system tests have passed.

14. Turn over testing documentation and certification to production IT staff for installation.

15. Install the application on one or two production servers. Set up ICA Passthrough to make the application available to the appropriate users. Monitor the server's performance to ensure that there are no utilization spikes or any other irregularities.

16. Survey users to see if the application is performing properly.

17. Schedule production deployment using a chosen distribution method (for instance, imaging or Installation Manager—covered later in this chapter).

18. Deploy the application.

19. After one week of production, survey a sample of users to see if the application is performing properly.

Mass Deployment

Once an application has gone through the preceding installation and testing procedure, Step 17 calls for production deployment across the farm to all users who need the application. Obviously, in smaller organizations, the installation of an application on two or three servers is often less time-consuming than the time it would take to automate and implement the process. But, in larger enterprises, such as our case study, CME Corp, the installation of an application across 100 servers can be a daunting task. In this case, the investment in developing the automation and deploying it pays off very quickly. We have seen large enterprises deploy full suites of applications overnight across thousands of servers to thousands of users by utilizing one of the automation procedures we will detail here.

Imaging Software

As detailed in Chapter 11, Ghost and DeployCenter can be utilized to build a standard server installation image and clone that image to multiple other servers. This process is extremely useful for the initial builds of the servers, and for major rebuilds, but can be tedious for minor application upgrades and maintenance (such as hotfixes and patches). For the purposes of server and application maintenance and singular application installs, we recommend the use of MetaFrame Installation Manager.

METAFRAME INSTALLATION MANAGER

Installation Manager (IM) is designed to automate the application installation process and facilitate application replication across MetaFrame XP servers throughout the enterprise. Although IM does not facilitate the initial server building and configuration process, it is quite handy for software installation and maintenance. Through the use of IM, applications can be distributed across multiple servers in minutes rather than days or weeks. MetaFrame Installation Manager is bundled with MetaFrame XPe and cannot be purchased separately. IM is fully integrated into the CMC.

MetaFrame Installation Manager creates a central repository for software application packaging and distribution. Having a central repository that packages, distributes, and inventories applications aids administrators by

▼ Allowing all software to be managed in a single location

■ Allowing scheduling of application deployment/distribution during low server load times

▲ Allowing retention/tracking of all applications/versions contained in each server in the server farm

If the farm is configured using an application load-balanced architecture, IM allows for the rapid tuning and placement of applications onto the server groups, as well as ensuring consistency across all server types.

IM Components

This section provides details regarding the IM components.

Packager

IM Packager monitors application installation routines and records changes as installation commands in a script. The script file and application files are used to install the application on target servers in the MetaFrame server farm.

Since the Packager is primarily responsible for recording application installations, it is recommended that Packager run in an environment that closely approximates the environment of the target servers.

Installer Service

Installer Service interprets the ADF or MSI File in the package and installs the software on the target servers. In order for the package to execute on a server, the Installer Service must be installed and running.

File Server

A file server is required to store application packages that have been created by the Packager. A network share must be created on the file server with read-write permissions and be accessible to all servers using IM to install applications. Once a package is created and stored, the administrator can deploy the package referencing the network share point to the target servers in the server farm.

Citrix Installation Manager Plug-In

Citrix Installation Manager Plug-In is a plug-in that works with the Citrix Management Console (CMC). Using the Citrix Installation Manager Plug-In, an administrator can

▼   Schedule install and uninstall jobs

■   View a job's status

■   View packages

■   Change package properties

▲   Create server groups

The Application Packaging Process   In creating an application package, the administrator is granted three options:

▼   **Package Installation Recording**   Packager captures the procedures to install an application.

■ **Package an Unattended Program**   Packager prompts for the application and associated command-line parameters. This is for applications that can be installed without a user interface.

▲ **Package Selected Files**   Packager prompts for files and/or folders.

If the option Package Installation Recording is selected, the Packager prompts for the choice of adding Application Compatibility Scripts and/or Additional Files. It then records the installation of an application and builds the package, which is stored in the network file share.

If the option A Package for an Unattended Program is selected, the Packager requests the application executable, optional command-line parameters, and any additional files. The executable, command-line parameters, and additional files are then compiled into a package and stored in the network file share.

If the option Package Selected Files is selected, the Packager prompts for the files and/or folders. These files and/or folders are collected and created as a package that is stored in the network file share.

Figure 13-3 provides a conceptual design of the package-building process.

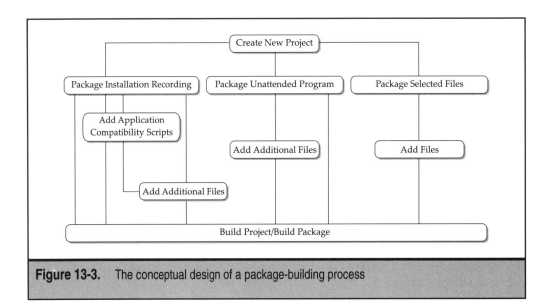

Figure 13-3.   The conceptual design of a package-building process

The Job Process

A job is a package that has been scheduled for installation or uninstallation on target servers. The process to create a job is displayed in Figure 13-4. To create a job, the administrator selects a package to be installed or uninstalled. The Job window prompts for the target

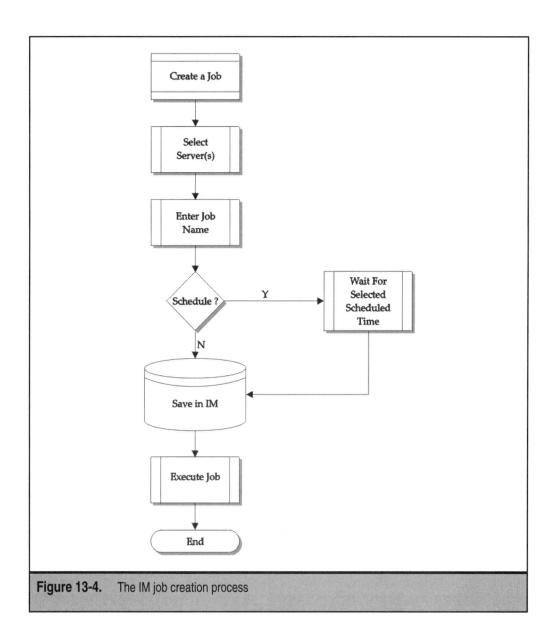

Figure 13-4.   The IM job creation process

servers to process the job, the name of the job, and a schedule for the job. If the administrator chooses to execute the job immediately, the job is saved to IM and then immediately executed. If the administrator chooses to schedule the job later, the job is saved to IM and executed at the scheduled time.

IM Installation and Configuration

For our case study of CME Corp, we will plan to install Office XP across the entire server farm of 100 Windows Server 2003 Terminal Servers running Citrix MetaFrame XP FR-3.

The following tasks were completed prior to the installation of other components.

▼ Windows Server 2003 with MetaFrame XP FR-3 was installed and fully tested on the test server farm.

▲ All server fully qualified domain names were registered in DNS.

Since IM is part of MetaFrame XPe, XPe was selected as the type of product version to install. The MetaFrame installation was performed according to the instructions listed in Chapter 12.

The environment setup shown in Figure 13-5 involves four servers. The configurations of the servers in Figure 13-5 are listed in Table 13-2.

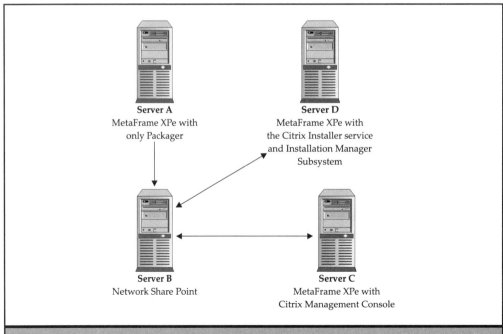

Server A
MetaFrame XPe with
only Packager

Server D
MetaFrame XPe with
the Citrix Installer service
and Installation Manager
Subsystem

Server B
Network Share Point

Server C
MetaFrame XPe with
Citrix Management Console

Figure 13-5. Installation Manager server configurations

Server Name	Operating System (OS)	Application and Function
Server A	Windows Server 2003 with MetaFrame XP FR-3	IM Packager software packaging server
Server B	Any accessible network file share	Network share point
Server C	Windows Server 2003 with MetaFrame XPe FR-3	Management Console
Server D	Windows Server 2003 with MetaFrame XPe FR-3	IM installer service and IM subsystem

Table 13-2. Server Configurations for Installation Manager

This environment operates by creating and storing packages on a network server file share (Server B). After the packages are created, the packages can be deployed to Servers A, C, and D, although in a large environment like CME Corp, the machines serving these roles should be dedicated to provide the flexibility and bandwidth necessary.

Packaging Office XP for IM Deployment

Microsoft Office XP uses a Microsoft Installer package (MSI) for unattended installation. The MSI file for MS Office XP is PROPLUS.msi. We will utilize the custom transform file we created earlier in the chapter.

To create a MetaFrame Installation Manager Package for Office XP, the following steps must be performed.

1. Create a folder for Office XP on the IM network share server (Server B).

2. Insert the MS Office XP CD or connect to a network share with Office XP.

3. Open a command prompt on Server A.

4. Change drives to either the CD-ROM drive or the network share with MS Office 2000.

5. Type the following: **msiexec /a PROPLUS.msi**.

6. Enter the product code.

7. Enter the IM network share path (**Server B\Office XP share**)—the Office XP administrator installation files will be copied.

8. Copy the Termsrvr.mst file created earlier in the chapter to the IM network share path (\\Server B\Office XP share) on Server B.

Creating the Office XP Package   The following steps should be performed in order to add the Office XP MSI package (or any other MSI package) to the CMC.

1. Open the CMC.
2. Expand the Installation Manager node.
3. Right-click the Packages node.
4. Select Add Package.
5. Enter the package name.
6. Choose Yes to add transforms or command-line parameters.
7. Add the Termsrvr.mst file.

Scheduling MS Office XP Package for Target Servers   The following steps detail the procedures required for scheduling and installing the MS Office XP Package on target servers.

1. Open the CMC.
2. Expand the Installation Manager node.
3. Expand the Packages node.
4. Right-click the Office XP package.
5. Select Install Package.
6. Select the target servers on which the package will be installed.
7. Click Next.
8. Schedule a time to execute the package or execute the package immediately.

CAUTION: Executing a package is bandwidth intensive. Start by testing a small package targeted to a limited number of servers to get a feel for the load that will be put on the network. For larger server farms, schedule the execution for off-hours, and spread the executions over time to ensure the network can support the additional load. Executions over a WAN will require even greater planning and testing to ensure that the package will be fully executed prior to users resuming use of the WAN.

9. Click Finish.
10. Click OK.

After these steps are completed, the CMC displays a Job entry for the Office XP package. The Job entry states the job name, status, and scheduled time.

APPLICATION LICENSING

One of the most common questions we hear when discussing server-based computing is this: How will it change the licensing requirements of an organization's applications? The answer is simple: It won't—but it will make it easier to manage, track, and add/delete licenses. Most application manufacturers license their applications either on a concurrent user basis, a per-computer basis, or a per-user basis. By having the applications and any application metering software centralized, managing and reporting of application software is dramatically simplified. Although neither Windows Server 2003 nor Citrix MetaFrame XP inherently track application usage or access, MetaFrame Resource Manager (included with MetaFrame XPe) provides a variety of tools and reports regarding user and application usage. Additionally, tools from RES, Softricity, triCerat, and AppSense provide robust application usage, metering, and reporting.

APPLICATION ACCESS AND SECURITY

Following the installation of applications, the security should be configured to only allow specific group access to applications. Some applications (for example, Office XP) will be provided to a large majority of users, whereas other applications, like accounting and payroll software, should be tightly locked down. Locking down file permissions based on group access is an obvious way to lockdown an application, but this method is usually time-consuming, as most applications have multiple components like registry entries, shared DLLs, and executable files. Additionally, many applications can be accessed through operating system holes or other applications such as web browsers. For larger environments, like our case study CME Corp, we highly recommend the use of RES, triCerat, Softricity, or AppSense utilities to provide a cleaner and more automated approach to locking down applications and their usage, while logging any non-authorized attempts at accessing the application.

CHAPTER 14

Client Configuration and Deployment

A s discussed throughout this text, server-based computing focuses the vast majority of IT work and expertise on the server environment, and simplifies the client environment to the thinnest form possible. Delivery of on-demand computing requires that the client software install and configuration be instant and invisible to end users. The advances made by both Microsoft and Citrix over the last three years continue the trend of reducing desktop configuration, in many cases to nothing. Chapter 7 detailed the client choices; this chapter, building on Chapter 7, discusses the configuration and installation of the clients.

ICA CLIENT OPTIONS FOR APPLICATION ACCESS

Windows Terminal Server with MetaFrame XP accepts connections from the following types of clients:

▼ A device running a web browser (I.E. 5.0 or Netscape 3.7 or later)

■ A thin client running ICA or RDP clients

■ A PC running any Windows operating system with an ICA or RDP client installed

■ A PowerPC Macintosh or 68K Macintosh (ICA only) or a Macintosh running OS X with an ICA or RDP client installed

■ A PC running a Linux operating system with a windowing system and an ICA client installed

■ An IBM, HP, or SUN UNIX desktop running a windowing system with an ICA client installed

■ Any number of tablet and handheld devices running Windows CE, Pocket PC, or CE.NET with an RDP or ICA client installed

▲ A Java-enabled device (anything from a cell phone to a Linux appliance) running the ICA Java client

The decision as to which of these client types an organization will use is dependant on their current network, client environment, security requirements, and whether or not an organization will be running all or just a few applications from the server-based environment (the Hybrid environment is discussed in Chapter 7). Table 14-1 compares the features of the ICA client option choices.

Our case study company CME has approximately 1500 users on the five-building campus network, and another 1500 users at remote locations throughout the world, and it supports over 600 traveling and home users. The local users have historically received a new PC every five years. In order to reduce ongoing PC costs, CME has decided to provide all applications to users utilizing server-based computing. With all applications provided through SBC, a majority of users will be able to use a thin client. Since the lease on 600 of these PCs is up this year, CME has decided to replace the PCs with thin clients, creating a mix of thin clients and PCs throughout the organization. As discussed in

Feature	Win32 7.00	CE WBT 7.00	PckPC 7.00	Java (applet only) 7.00	Mac OS X 6.30	Linux X86 7.00	Solaris SPARC 6.30	HP, AIX 6.30	SGI 6.00	Mac OS 6.20
Display + Graphics										
16/256 colors	x	x	x	256	x	x	x	x	x	x
16/24-bit color	x	x	x	x	x	x	x	x	x	x
Greater than 1280x1024	x	x	x	x	x	x	x	x	x	x
Memory cache	x	x	x	x	x	x	x	x	x	x
Persistent cache	x	x	x	x	x	x	x	x	x	x
Compression	x	x	x	x	x	x	x	x	x	x
Seamless windows	x (16)			x						
Text entry prediction	x	x	x	x	x	x	x	x	x	x
Panning	x	x	x		x	x	x	x	x	x
Scaling	x		x	x		x				
Client Devices										
Local files	x	x	x	x	x	x	x	x	x	x
Local printers	x	x	x	x	x	x	x	x	x	x
Printer detect	auto	manual	manual	manual	manual	manual	manual	manual	manual	manual
Universal Printer Driver	x				x	x				
Universal Printer Driver 2	x					x				
Serial ports	x	x	x	x (3)	x	x	x	x		x
Audio (server to client)	x	x	x	Medium	x	x	x	x	x	x
Text clipboard	x	x	x	x	x	x	x	x	x	x
RTF clipboard	x	x	x		x	x	x	x	x	x
Graphics clipboard	x	x	x		x	x	x	x	x	x
Middle button emulation	x	x	x	x	x	x (11)	x (11)	x (11)	x (11)	x
Connections										
Custom connections	x	x	x		x	x	x	x	x	x
NFuse (ALE)	x	x (6)	x (6)		x (7)	x	x (2)	x (2)	x (2)	x (7)
"Native" PN	x		x			x				
PN Lite	x	x	x			x	x	x	x	x
PN Agent	x	x	x		x	x	x	x	x	x
TCP/HTTP browsing	x	x	x	x	x	x	x	x	x	x
Disconnect/reconnect	x	x	x	x	x	x	x	x	x	x
Auto client reconnect	x (10)	x	x	x		x	x	x	x	x
Roaming user reconnect	x	x	x	n/a	x	x	x	x		x
Auto client update	x		x	x	x	x	x	x	x	x
NDS credentials	x	x	x	x	x	x	x	x		x
Ext. parameter passing	x	x	x	x	x	x	x	x		x
Content publishing	PN Agt.	manual	manual		manual	manual	manual	manual		manual
Content redir. client-svr	x					x	x	x		
Content redir. svr-client						x	x	x		
CDE integration (UNIX)						x				
Speed browse	x	x	x	x						
Packaging										
Web-install version	x (1)									
Componentized	x (15)	x		x						
ActiveX/Plug-in/applet	x			applet						
Client object (ICO)	x									
Signed packages	x		x	x						

Table 14-1.   MetaFrame XP Feature Release 3 ICA Client Comparison

	Win32 7.00	CE WBT 7.00	PcktPC 7.00	Java (applet only) 7.00	Mac OS X 6.30	Linux X86 7.00	Solaris SPARC 6.30	HP, AIX 6.30	SGI 6.00	Mac OS 6.20
Security										
Basic encryption	x	x	x	x	x	x	x	x	x	x
128-bit encryption	x	x	x	x	x	x	x	x	x	x
SOCKS 4 and 5	x	x	x	x	x	x	x	x	x	x
SSL (inc DNS resolution)	x	x	x	x	x	x	x	x		x
TLS	x	x	x	x	x	x	x	x		
Auto Proxy Discovery	x	n/a	n/a	x	x	x	x	x		
Secure Proxy	x	x	x	x	x	x	x	x		
NTLM Proxy Authentication	x	x	x							
Smart Card	x	x	x		x	x	x	x		x
International										
Time Zone support	x	x	x	x	x	x	x	x	x	x
International keyboards	x	x	x	x	x	x	x	x	x	x
Fr, Ger, Sp versions	x	x	x	x		x (12)	x (4)	x (4)	x	
Japanese version	x	x	x	x		x (12)	x (12)	x (12)	x (5)	x
Unicode Keyboard Support		x	x							
SDKs										
OEM SDK	x	x	x			x	x (13)	x (13)		
VC SDK	x	x	x			x (13)	x (13)			

1 A white paper is available explaining how to remove modules from the Win32 web client.
2 Not with Netscape 6
3 Windows and Solaris only, using third-party software
4 Fr, Ger, Sp versions of Solaris/Sparc, HP-UX and AIX clients at 3.0 functionality.
5 Fr, Sp versions of SCO, SGI, Sol x86, SunOS, and Tru64 clients have less than 3.0 level functionality. Ger version at 3.0 functionality.
6 Requires Internet and Pocket Explorer fixes from MS
7 Automated MIME registration for IE
8 Medium only, and limited sound quality due to EPOC OS constraints
9 Applet mode only
10 Not when embedded in web page, since Auto Reconnect is not supported by ICA Client Object
11 Provided by local UNIX OS, where necessary
12 Linux x86 Fr, Sp versions at 6.0 functionality
13 Available by request, comes with minimal documentation
14 Just adds parameters to "InitialProgram" string, doesn't use Control VC
15 The download-and-run zero-install ActiveX control will be updated for version 7.0. There will be a full version and a minimal version.
16 Win32 7.0 client has support for .NET "rounded" corners.

Table 14-1.   MetaFrame XP Feature Release 3 ICA Client Comparison *(continued)*

Chapter 7, purchasing thin clients rather than PCs creates significant savings (CME will save $600,000 on the first set of thin clients compared with buying PCs).

The thin clients that CME has chosen are Linux-based thin clients, with a basic ICA and RDP client, and no web browser. Additionally, these thin clients have a remote management tool that pushes the latest ICA client and ICA client configurations directly to the thin client upon boot.

Thus, for the first 600 users, the client configuration is now set. For the other 2400 users though, the client options need to be analyzed and a decision made on which ones to run where. The remaining sections of this chapter will complete this analysis and provide answers to the client choices.

The Push or Pull Client Debate

Although the device choice to run the ICA client is nearly limitless, the way in which we provide visibility of the applications to these devices is limited to four choices:

▼ MetaFrame Web Interface client

■ MetaFrame Program Neighborhood and Program Neighborhood Agent client

■ A Microsoft Terminal Server Advanced Client web interface client

▲ A manually configured ICA or RDP client connection

The first three of these choices are "push based," meaning they provide a user with the icon, configuration, client software, and updates to the client software without the user having to understand the configuration, perform it, or step through an installation. The last choice requires that a user (or administrator) perform an installation, configure the client software, and then configure a connection. In this chapter, we will focus on these four methods of client deployment and what is required for the client-side configuration. The server-side configurations, security configurations, and customization are discussed at length in Chapter 16.

All the latest Citrix ICA clients are available from Citrix's web site (www .citrix.com/downloads). There are three types of Citrix ICA Win32 client software: Program Neighborhood, Program Neighborhood Agent, and Web Client. And three varieties of client software packages: an executable (ica32.exe), a cab file (wfica.cab), and a Microsoft Installer Package (ica32.msi). All three packages have identical contents.

In order to make sense of these choices and reduce the complexity to answer the simple question of which client to use at what times, we will focus our attention back on our reference case study company, CME Corporation. CME has a very wide assortment of client devices, network configurations, application requirements, and end-user skill sets.

MetaFrame Web Interface Clients

When applications (or full desktops) are published through MetaFrame Web Interface, users access them via a web browser. This method is very easy for end users, as they only have to know a URL address (or have it bookmarked or linked to) to connect and run a MetaFrame Published application. Users only see the applications that have been published to them by the administrator (using the Citrix Management Console and users and groups from Active Directory, Novell NDS, or Novell eDir). No client configuration is required by the end user. Web Interface supports Macintosh, UNIX, and Windows client types, as well as Netscape Navigator and Windows Explorer web browsers. Figure 14-1 shows a typical MetaFrame Web Interface access site.

Our case study organization, CME, has over 400 home-based and traveling users who need remote access support, and must also support up to 200 concurrent remote users from all departments who need to work from home on nights and weekends. About 300 of these remote users are road-warrior sales people, and company executives. The home users have a large variety of client and operating system configurations, including Macintosh, Windows 98, Windows 2000, and Windows XP machines. All the remote

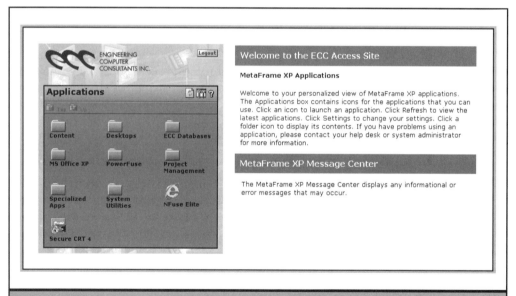

Figure 14-1. The MetaFrame Web Interface site

users need access to Outlook e-mail and their Microsoft Office applications and files. In addition to these applications, the sales group needs access to their Customer Relationship Management software package, Microsoft CRM, and the executives need access to their financial reporting and analysis tools (Microsoft Excel spreadsheets, FRx, and Crystal Reports applications, with links to the SQL server accounting databases). In Chapter 17, we will discuss the network configuration to support and secure these users, but for the purposes of this chapter, we will discuss what client they should use and how to deploy it in the simplest, lowest-cost model, with the smallest amount of ongoing support. For these CME users, we recommend using the MetaFrame Web Interface client.

Configuring the MetaFrame Web Client for Silent User Installation

To configure the ICA Win32 Web Client for silent user installation:

1. Extract the ICA client files from ica32t.exe using your preferred compression utility. This installer package is located in the following directory (substitute language with the language of the ICA client software) of the Components CD-ROM included in the MetaFrame XP media pack: Icaweb\language\ica32. Languages to choose from include

   ■ En (English)

   ■ Fr (French)

   ■ De (German)

   ■ Ja (Japanese)

   ■ Es (Spanish)

2. Locate and open the Ctxsetup.ini file in any text editor.

3. To suppress the initial user prompt, locate the InitialPrompt parameter. Change the value of the setting from 1 to **0**.

4. To suppress the Citrix License Agreement dialog box, locate the DisplayLicenseDlg parameter. Change the value of the setting from 1 to **0**.

5. Save the file and exit the text editor.

6. Repackage the client files for distribution to your users and install the ICA Win32 Web Client. The ICA Win32 Web Client self-extracting executable, ica32t.exe, is located in the directory (substitute language with the language of the ICA client software) of the Components CD-ROM included in your MetaFrame XP media pack: Icaweb\language\ica32.

Installing the ICA Win32 Web Client

To Install the ICA Win32 Web Client:

1. Run ica32t.exe.

2. The initial prompt informs you the Citrix ICA Win32 Web Client is about to be installed. Click Yes to continue setup.

3. The Citrix License Agreement appears. Click Yes to accept the agreement.

4. A window appears stating Setup is copying files to the client device. The default file location for the ICA Win32 Web Client is Program Files\ Citrix\icaweb32.

5. Citrix ICA Web Client notifies you once the install completes successfully. Click OK to clear the message.

6. If you are running Netscape Navigator, you must restart the browser.

Deploying the MetaFrame Web Interface Client

MetaFrame Web Interface provides users with four choices of client software that will be pushed to the user. The administrator can either force the use of a given client software choice, or leave it to the user to choose which one to use.

▼ **The universal Win32 web client** This client software is identical to the Program Neighborhood Win32 client except that it does not include the Program Neighborhood files and does not install an icon on the desktop or in the Start menu. The full Web Client is available as a self-extracting executable and as a .cab file. At approximately 1.8MB in size, this package is significantly smaller than the other ICA Win32 clients. The smaller size allows users to more quickly download and install the client software. You can configure the ICA Win32 Web Client for silent user installation. There is also a minimal installation choice for this client that has a significantly smaller footprint (about 1.01MB) and thus takes about half the time to download. Table 14-2 shows the feature differences between the minimal and regular Win32 web client installation.

■ **The Java ICA client** The Java ICA client was updated significantly with Feature Release 3 to include more features and run faster. The Java client enhancements include

   ■ Support for SSL communication

   ■ Unpackaged code, which allows the administrator to select which features to not install, allowing administrators to potentially decrease the download time

   ■ New connection center that supports multiple published application processing

   ■ Seamless application look and feel

   ■ Improved screen rendering (cuts down on screen flashing)

   ■ The Java client is the smallest and most non-obtrusive of the ICA clients, intended for use on machines that are heavily locked down or that don't allow

Feature	ICA Win32 Web Client	Minimal Installation
User-to-user shadowing	X	
Smart card support	X	X
Content redirection	X	
Enhanced content publishing support	X	X
Roaming User Reconnect	X	
Support for SSL/TLS encryption of ICA session data	X	X
Support for Web Interface for MetaFrame XP, NFuse Classic, and the Web Interface Extension for MetaFrame XPe	X	X
Support for MetaFrame Secure Gateway	X	X
Enhanced Internet proxy support	X	
Auto Client Reconnect	X	X
Novel Directory Services support	X	
Extended parameter passing	X	
Seamless windows	X	
Client device mapping	X	
Client drive mapping	X	X
Client printer mapping	X	X
Sound support	X	
TCP/IP + HTTP server location	X	X
Wheel mouse support	X	
Multiple monitor support	X	
Panning and scaling	X	
Per-user time-zone support	X	
Windows Clipboard integration	X	
Low bandwidth requirements	X	X
SpeedScreen latency reduction	X	
Disk caching and data compression	X	

Table 14-2. Feature Comparison of the ICA Win32 Web Client and ICA Win32 Web Client Minimal Installation

software installation (such as a Kiosk). The ICA Java client will run on any operating system that has a Java Virtual Machine (JVM) installed. The Java client is not as speed-optimized as the other ICA clients for high latency or highly graphical environments, so although it is much improved, it is still generally relegated to situations where it is the only choice that will work.

- ■ **The Macintosh client**   Citrix has ICA client software for both the older Macintosh clients (MAC OS) and the latest MAC OS X operating systems.

- ▲ **The UNIX ICA client**   UNIX users who connect to the MetaFrame Web Interface site must use the appropriate UNIX ICA or Java client. Administrators may configure MetaFrame Web Interface to automatically detect and download the appropriate UNIX client.

Since most of CME's remote users are on Windows laptops and home PCs, we recommend that CME configure Web Interface to detect and push to the users the appropriate ICA client (or ICA client update) for their machine. In order to support users from hotels, trade shows, and airport Kiosks, we recommend that CME allow users to customize their Web Interface login session to select the Java client and only those modules required to improve load speeds. We will use the full installation of the Win32 Web Client (ica32t) in order to take advantage of the additional features and performance.

The Web Interface client does not require any user or client-side configuration for CME users. There is a fair amount of server-side configuration and optimization for Web Interface though, which will be covered step by step in Chapter 16. ICA client-side optimization settings are covered later in this chapter.

A larger question should be raised at this point—why not use this client for all 3000 users at CME? Although the Web Interface client is simple and sufficiently powerful for use throughout the organization, for cases where the client machine type is fully known and controlled, there are some advantages to fully integrating the Program Neighborhood Agent client discussed next—for instance, it needs fewer clicks from the user since it doesn't require opening a web browser and going to a URL—meanwhile, it allows for more user configuration. A more obvious point for thin-client users though is that, as discussed in Chapter 7, many thin clients do not have a web browser.

Microsoft Terminal Server Advanced Client

Terminal Server Advanced Client (TSAC) was released in October of 2000 and as of this writing is essentially unchanged. TSAC is a Win32-based ActiveX control (COM object) that can be used to run Terminal Services sessions within Microsoft Internet Explorer 4.0 and later. This tool is similar in form and function to MetaFrame Web Interface, but TSAC only supports Win32-based clients running Internet Explorer. Additionally, TSAC is limited to one application or server connection per URL. Figure 14-2 shows a basic TSAC site.

The TSAC web package is downloadable from Microsoft's web site at www.microsoft .com/windows2000/server/evaluation/news/bulletins/tsac.asp and includes the downloadable ActiveX control and sample web pages that can be used as a starting point for delivering Terminal Server applications through Internet Explorer. Developers can also use

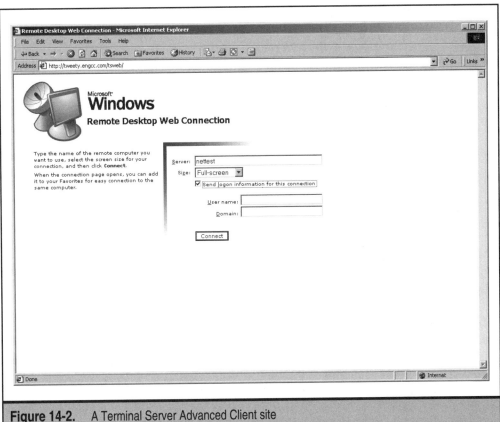

Figure 14-2. A Terminal Server Advanced Client site

the TSAC to develop client-side applications that interact with applications running on a Terminal Server. TSAC is a great tool for smaller organizations, or for smaller deployments of one or Two applications where MetaFrame XP is not being used, since it is the only RDP client that does not require desktop setup, configuration, and manual updates.

Although the RDP clients have improved dramatically over the last three years, they are still missing some critical features necessary for enterprise deployments. Chapter 3 went into more detail, but as a quick example, here are several reasons why our case study, CME Corp, will be using the ICA client rather than the RDP client:

▼ ICA supports non-Windows machines with full-featured, full-color client connections. Since CME has over 400 UNIX, Linux, and Mac machines, this support is critical.

- ICA supports enterprise application load balancing rather than just the round-robin approach utilized by RDP. This feature is critical when supporting thousands of users across nearly 100 servers.

- ICA is a non-streaming protocol. When compared with the streaming nature of RDP, ICA will support 30 to 50 percent more users on a given WAN link. Since CME has many WAN links worldwide, optimal use of these expensive links is critical.

▲ The MetaFrame Web Interface and integration with Secure Gateway provide a powerful secured access method without firewall reconfiguration or port opening. This solution is not available with RDP. The RDP solution requires opening ports on the firewall. The RDP web deployment solution is only useful with a very limited number of applications, since a user can only see one application from each URL.

MetaFrame Program Neighborhood Agent Client

With MetaFrame Feature Release 1, Citrix introduced a new Win32 client choice called Program Neighborhood Agent (PN Agent). PN Agent is a Windows 32 Desktop client that utilizes a Web Interface Server for its configuration. For local PCs, this ICA client provides a best-of-both-worlds solution, including a robust set of desktop integrated features, yet requires little to no client-side configuration.

PN Agent supports Client-to-Server Content Redirection, which utilizes the MetaFrame Web Interface Server to recognize applications and automatically update a user's MIME type associations to call ICA applications rather than local applications. For example, if a user clicks on a Microsoft Word File in Windows Explorer, the Microsoft Word Published Application from the MetaFrame XP farm will be called rather than a local copy of Microsoft Word. When a user disconnects from the MetaFrame XP farm, the MIME types are returned to their original associations.

Program Neighborhood Agent employs a simplified user interface (compared with the Full PN client), which removes complexity and features. For example, because all connection information is pushed down from a Web Interface site, the Program Neighborhood Agent does not require (or allow) a user to specify a farm to connect to, or to create a custom ICA connection.

Program Neighborhood Agent is a separate Win32 client downloadable from the Citrix web site, and is only available for Windows 32-bit clients. It is installed using the ica32a.exe or ica32a.msi files.

Program Neighborhood Agent icons can be accessed from icons placed directly on the user's Windows desktop, Start menu, or System Tray by the user, or done remotely by the administrator.

Of the 1200 local campus users at CME who won't be receiving a new thin client, about 900 are on Windows-based machines (the other 300 are on Macintosh and UNIX/Linux PCs). The Program Neighborhood Agent client makes an excellent client choice for these 900 users.

An example of how a MetaFrame-based Microsoft Great Plains installation appears to a user running from a Windows 2000 client with Program Neighborhood Agent installed is shown here. Notice that it looks identical to the user, as if it was installed locally.

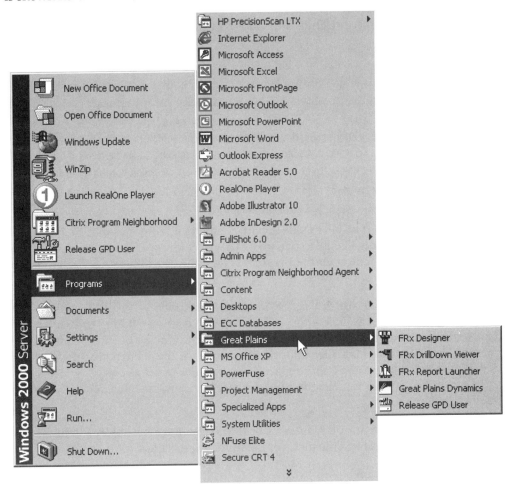

Installing the ICA Win32 Program Neighborhood Agent

The ICA Win32 PN Agent can be installed using one of the following packages:

▼ ica32a.msi   A Windows Installer package for use with Windows 2000 Active Directory Services or Microsoft Systems Management Server; approximately 1.9MB in size

▲ ica32a.exe   A self-extracting executable; approximately 2.75MB in size

Installing the ICA Win32 Program Neighborhood Agent with the Windows Installer Package   The PN Agent Windows Installer package (ica32a.msi) can be distributed with Microsoft Systems Management Server or Windows 2000 Active Directory Services. This package is located in one of the directories (substitute language with the language of the ICA client software) of the Components CD-ROM included in your MetaFrame XP media pack:

    Icaweb\language\ica32

    Icainst\language\ica32\pnagent

> **NOTE:** To install the ICA client software using the Windows Installer package, the Windows Installer Service must be installed on the client device. This service is present by default on Windows 2000 and Windows XP systems. To install ICA clients on client devices running earlier versions of the Windows operating system, you must use the self-extracting executable or install the Windows Installer 2.0 Redistributable for Windows, available at www.microsoft.com.

Since our case study, CME, has over 900 local campus PCs and another 1500 PCs at remote campus locations to install the PN Agent Client on, it is obvious that an automated choice for this installation is required. Since CME will be using Web Interface to provide the configuration information for the PN Agent client, CME will leverage Web Interface to also distribute this client software to all 2400 users.

Configuring the Windows Installer Package for Silent User Installation   The PN Agent Windows Installer package can be configured for "silent" user installation to ensure users don't see the installation options or attempt to interrupt or make the wrong installation option choices. Windows Installer informs the user when the client software is successfully installed. The user must clear the Windows Installer message box.

To configure the Program Neighborhood Agent Windows Installer package for silent user installation:

1. At a command prompt, type **msiexec /I** *MSI_Package* **/qn+ [Key=Value]…** where *MSI_Package* is the name of the installer package.

The following keys can be set:

▼   PROGRAM_FOLDER_NAME=<Start Menu Program Folder Name>, where <Start Menu Program Folder Name> is the name of the Programs folder on the Start menu containing the shortcut to the Program Neighborhood Agent software. The default value is Citrix Program Neighborhood Agent. This function is not supported during client upgrades.

■   ENABLE_DYNAMIC_CLIENT_NAME={Yes | No}. To enable dynamic client name support during silent installation, the value of the property ENABLE_DYNAMIC_CLIENT_NAME in the installer file must be Yes. To disable dynamic client name support, set this property to No.

- `CLIENT_ALLOW_DOWNGRADE={Yes | No}`. By default, this property is set to No. This prevents an installation of an earlier version of the client.

- `ENABLE_SSON={Yes | No}`. The default value is No. If you enable the SSON (Passthrough authentication) property, set the `ALLOW_REBOOT` property to No to avoid automatic rebooting of the client system.

- `SERVER_LOCATION=<Server_URL>`. The default value is PNAgent. Enter the URL of the Web Interface that hosts the configuration file. The format must be in the format http://*<servername>* or https://*<servername>*.

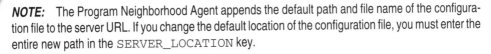

NOTE: The Program Neighborhood Agent appends the default path and file name of the configuration file to the server URL. If you change the default location of the configuration file, you must enter the entire new path in the `SERVER_LOCATION` key.

- `ALLOW_REBOOT={Yes | No}`. The default value is Yes.

- `DEFAULT_NDSCONTEXT=<Context1 [,...]>`. Include this parameter to set a default context for Novell Directory Services (NDS). If you are including more than one context, place the entire value in quotation marks and separate the contexts by a comma. The following are examples of correct parameters:

```
DEFAULT_NDSCONTEXT=Context1
DEFAULT_NDSCONTEXT="Context1,Context2"
```

The following represents an incorrect parameter:

```
DEFAULT_NDSCONTEXT=Context1,Context2
```

Central Configuration of the Program Neighborhood Agent Client

The advantage of PN Agent over the other ICA clients (other than the web client) is that it is configured centrally via the Program Neighborhood Agent Admin tool (which changes an XML file on the Web Interface server) rather than via configuration files on the local devices.

To access the Program Neighborhood Agent Admin tool, connect to http:// servername/Citrix/PNAgentAdmin/ with an administrator account on the server running MetaFrame Web Interface.

The custom options for all users running the Program Neighborhood Agent on a network are defined in a configuration file stored on the server running the MetaFrame

Web Interface. The client reads the configuration data from the server when a user launches the PN Agent, and updates at specified intervals. This allows the client to dynamically display the options the administrator wants the users to see based on the data received. The settings configured using the Admin tool affect all users who read from this configuration file.

A default configuration file, config.xml, is installed with default settings and is ready for use without modification in most network environments. However, this file can be edited, or multiple configuration files created, using the Program Neighborhood Agent Admin tool. This allows an administrator to add or remove a particular option for users quickly and to easily manage and control users' displays from a single location.

The config.xml file is placed in the \Inetpub\wwwroot\Citrix\PNAgent directory on the Web Interface server during the installation process. New and backup configuration files created using the PN Agent Admin tool are stored in the same folder as the default configuration file. The data configuration files serve two purposes:

▼ To point clients to the servers that run users' published resources

▲ To control the properties on users' local desktops, thereby defining what tabs and options users can customize

A configuration file controls the range of parameters that appear as options in the user's Properties dialog box. Users can choose from available options to set preferences for their ICA sessions, including logon mode, screen size, audio quality, and the locations of links to published resources.

Multiple configuration files can be created to fill all of an organization's needs using the Program Neighborhood Agent Admin tool. After creating a configuration file and saving it on the server running the new Web Interface, users will need to be given the new server URL that points to the new file.

NOTE: SSL/TLS-secured communications between the client, server, Web Interface, and smart card logon are not enabled by default. These features can be activated in the Server Settings section of the Program Neighborhood Agent Admin tool. In addition, SSL must be enabled on the MetaFrame server to utilize SSL/TLS-secured communications.

As discussed at length in Chapter 10, it is important to test all enterprise-wide applications in the test environment prior to full deployment. The PN Agent deployment should be tested by installing a copy of the client on a single client device, then on five devices (preferably with different Windows operating systems and environments). The test installations will allow a full evaluation of the default settings and determine whether or not adjustments are required to fit your particular network needs. Comparing between the configuration file and the client, you can monitor the effects of your changes on the client behavior.

CAUTION: The settings in the configuration file are global, thus affecting all users connecting to that instance of the file. The Program Neighborhood Agent Admin tool automatically creates a backup file (with the extension .bak) when a configuration file is loaded into the tool.

Configuring Farmwide Settings   The Program Neighborhood Agent Admin tool is divided into several sections, allowing control and definition of different aspects of the user experience. These sections include

▼   Client Tab Control

■   Server Settings

■   Logon Methods

■   Application Display

■   Application Refresh

▲   Session Options

Administrators can define whether users see any tabs in the Properties dialog box of the Program Neighborhood Agent, and also what options they can and cannot customize. Each tab, and the settings that can be customized, are detailed next.

By default, users can access the Program Neighborhood Agent Properties dialog box from the Windows System Tray. Administrators may choose to hide or display tabs in the Client Tab Control section of the Program Neighborhood Agent Admin tool, including the Server, Application Display, Application Refresh, and Session Options tabs.

NOTE: Changing these parameters directly affects the contents of the Properties dialog box for all users affected by the configuration file you are modifying. If you remove a tab from the Client view, users cannot customize any options on that tab.

Enabling and Disabling User-Customizable Options   This section contains an overview of the options available in the Properties dialog box. The instructions are presented in the order of the tabs on which each option appears.

▼   **Server Tab Options**   The Server tab options can be modified using the Program Neighborhood Agent Admin tool, located on the options pages for Server Settings and Logon Methods.

■   **Server Settings**   This allows you to configure server connection and configuration refresh settings. Other options allow you to define when users are redirected to a different server—at connection time or at a scheduled client refresh. Enable SSL/TLS communication here as well, changing URLs to use the HTTPS protocol automatically.

- **Logon Methods**   Providing a choice of multiple logon modes may be necessary in environments where multiple users employ the same client device but use different logon modes. This allows you to determine what logon methods are available to users, to force a default logon method, and to allow a user to save his password. The definable logon methods include Anonymous, Smart card, Smart card with Passthrough authentication, User prompt, and Passthrough authentication. If multiple logon methods are selected, users can choose their preferred logon method from a drop-down list. NDS credentials from the specified tree can be required from users who are prompted for a logon or who select Passthrough authentication. If you do not want users to have access to any of these options, use the Client Tab Control section of the Program Neighborhood Agent Admin tool to hide the Server tab altogether. You can show or hide the tab at any time.

NOTE: By default, users who are prompted for credentials can save their password. To disable this function, clear the **Allow user to save password** check box in the Logon Methods section of the Program Neighborhood Agent Admin tool. If you did not enable the Passthrough authentication feature when you first installed the Program Neighborhood Agent, you must reinstall the client software before you can use the Passthrough authentication logon mode.

- **Application Display Tab Options**   The options available on the Application Display tab let users place links to published resources in various locations of the client device, including the Windows desktop, the Start menu, the Windows System Tray, and any combination thereof. Using the Application Display options in the Program Neighborhood Agent Admin tool, you can define which settings users are allowed to customize. The client queries the configuration file at connection time to validate each user preference against its controlling element in the file. If you do not want users to have access to any of these options, you can use the Client Tab Control section of the Program Neighborhood Agent Admin tool to hide the Application Display tab altogether. You can show or hide the tab at any time.

- **Session Options Tab Options**   The options available on the Session Options tab let users set preferences for the window size, color depth, and sound quality of ICA sessions. Using the Session Options section of the Program Neighborhood Agent Admin tool, you can define what settings are available to the user. Users can choose each available option from a list. The preferences users set for color depth and sound quality affect the amount of bandwidth the ICA session consumes. To limit bandwidth consumption, you can force the server default for some or all of the options on this tab. Forcing the server default removes all settings for the corresponding option, other than Default, from the interface. The settings configured on the Web Interface server apply. If you do not want users to have access to any of these options, you can use the Client Tab Control section of the Program Neighborhood Agent Admin tool to hide the Session Options tab altogether. You can show or hide the tab at any time.

▲ **Application Refresh Tab Options**   The options available on the Application Refresh tab let users customize the rate at which the ICA client queries the Web Interface server to obtain an up-to-date list of their published resources. The Application Refresh tab is hidden from the Properties dialog box by default. If you want to give users control over the refresh rate, you need to enable the tab first. Enabling the Application Refresh tab makes all options on it user-customizable, unless you modify each option in the Application Refresh section of the PN Agent Admin tool.

Customizing the ICA Win32 Program Neighborhood Agent   This section presents general information about customizing user preferences on the client device running the Program Neighborhood Agent. To customize user preferences for the Program Neighborhood Agent:

1. In the Windows System Tray, right-click the Program Neighborhood Agent icon and choose Properties from the menu that appears.

2. Select the Session Options tab.

3. Make the desired configuration changes.

4. Click OK to save your changes.

For more detailed information, see the online Help for the Program Neighborhood Agent.

Configuring the Server URL   The Program Neighborhood Agent client requires input of the URL pointing to a configuration file (config.xml is the default configuration file) on the server running MetaFrame Web Interface.

Should the Web Interface server address need to be changed, the PN Agent client will also have to be updated with the new address. To change the URL of the Web Interface server from the PN Agent Client:

1. In the Windows System Tray, right-click the Program Neighborhood Agent icon and choose Properties from the menu that appears.

2. The Server tab displays the currently configured URL. Click Change and enter the server URL as directed in the dialog box that appears. Enter the URL in the format http://<servername>, or https://<servername>, to encrypt the configuration data using SSL.

3. Click Update to apply the change and return to the Server tab, or click Cancel to cancel the operation.

4. Click OK to close the Properties dialog box.

To delete memorized server URLs:

1. In the Windows System Tray, right-click the Program Neighborhood Agent icon and choose Properties from the menu that appears.

2. Select the Server tab.

3. Click Change.

4. Click the down arrow to view the entire list of memorized server URLs.

5. Right-click the URL to be deleted and select Delete from the menu that appears.

6. Click Update.

7. Click OK.

MetaFrame Program Neighborhood Client

The big brother to the Program Neighborhood Agent client is the Win32 Program Neighborhood (PN) client, which provides users access to server farms, application sets, and published applications. The primary benefit of Program Neighborhood over the Web client or the PN Agent client is that the user has a nearly infinite number of settings that can be changed to customize the client. The disadvantage is that it is more complex, must be configured at the client (rather than through the Web Interface server), and does not automatically change the MIME types on the client. Similar to PN Agent, PN allows an administrator to push the ICA application icons and configurations (that a user has been granted permission to) to the end-users' desktops (and Start menu) as soon as they start the Citrix PN client.

Program Neighborhood icons can be accessed from the PN client, or the icons can be placed directly on the user's Windows desktop or Start menu by the user, or be done remotely by the administrator.

Program Neighborhood with some custom ICA connection folders is shown next.

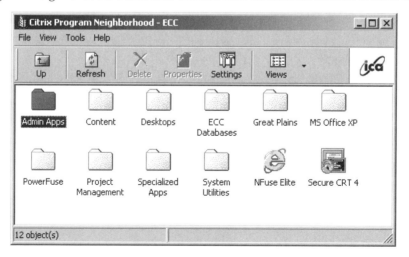

Program Neighborhood vs. Program Neighborhood Agent

Because the configuration options must be configured (either remotely or locally) via the configuration files of Program Neighborhood, rather than centrally via the Web Interface server, Program Neighborhood is more client-configuration intensive. There are a few instances in which the Full Program Neighborhood Client should be used rather than PN Agent:

▼   When there is no Web Interface server in the environment

■   When the users require detailed configuration of the client

▲   In disparate user environments, where each user has very different client settings requirements, thus making the central administration and configuration of the client software of little value

In our case study, CME, none of these instances exist, so CME will use the PN Agent client for all LAN campus PC users.

UNIX and Linux ICA Clients

Table 14-1 shows how the UNIX and Linux ICA clients stack up to the Win32 ICA clients. The Linux 7.0 client is comparable in its features and speed to the Win32 clients. The only significant missing feature of the Linux 7.0 client is the Program Neighborhood feature set, which isn't applicable to Linux. The UNIX clients remain one version behind the Linux and Win32 clients, but are still mature, fast, and feature-rich.

Although the normal deployment methods used in a Windows environment are not applicable (for instance, Active Directory, SMS, and so on), a MetaFrame Web Interface site can still be utilized to deploy the UNIX/Linux ICA client. Another option is a centrally run, and stored, script. Many UNIX and Linux environments utilize centrally stored and executed scripts for most applications in the environment, and the ICA client will deploy effectively using this method.

Our case study, CME, has 200 local and remote UNIX desktops used by engineers for Computer Aided Design and Manufacturing, as well as 100 Linux desktops utilized by the software development teams. CME utilizes both a MetaFrame Web Interface site and several c-shell scripts stored on the main file server, pathed from the UNIX and Linux machines, to run a full desktop published application. The published desktop provides Microsoft Office applications, Microsoft Outlook, MathCAD, and other PC-based engineering and mathematical applications to the engineers and developers.

Macintosh Clients

ICA and RDP clients are available for Macintosh OS X users, both of which are fast and full-featured. For users running older Macintoshes, the ICA client is the only choice available, although it is a full revision behind the Win32, Linux, and Mac OS X clients. The legacy Mac client is supported for both PowerPC and 68K versions. The ICA

Macintosh clients come in .HQX and .DMG (for OS X) formats. The configuration is very similar to the Win32 configuration (without the Program Neighborhood features). As Table 14-1 showed, features such as local drive and printer mapping are fully supported on the Macintosh ICA clients.

PERFORMANCE OPTIMIZATION OF THE ICA CLIENTS

Many optimization settings can be set to improve the ICA client user experience. Although most of these settings only make a difference (and are only necessary) with slow or highly latent connections, one of these features—SpeedScreen Browser Acceleration improves the user experience even when bandwidth is not limited.

SpeedScreen Browser Acceleration

This feature was first introduced with Feature Release 3 and ICA client version 7.0. It is available to users running Internet Explorer 5.5 or later, and enhances the speed at which images are downloaded and displayed within the ICA client.

SpeedScreen Browser Acceleration is enabled on the server by default when FR-3 is installed. To configure or enable/disable SpeedScreen Browser Acceleration on the server, from the Citrix Management Console, right-click the top level farm and choose Properties. From the Properties menu, choose the SpeedScreen Browser Acceleration property. Figure 14-3 shows the SpeedScreen Browser Acceleration properties page.

If SpeedScreen browser acceleration is enabled on the client, but not the server, SpeedScreen browser acceleration is disabled.

Optimization of ICA Connections for Wireless Wide Area Networks and Other Highly Latent Connections

Millions of MetaFrame users today access their applications over a local area network (LAN). Thanks to the low latency and high bandwidth afforded by the LAN, the user's experience is normally indistinguishable from having the applications running locally on a PC.

As we move outside of the LAN though, the connection choices for users to connect to their SBC applications in many geographies are slim, and the relatively new solutions offered by wireless WAN (wWAN) carriers like DirecPC satellite and mobile wireless carriers like Sprint, T-Mobile, Verizon, AT&T, Nextel, and others offer a tremendous solution in the SBC environment. By providing truly anytime-anywhere access to the SBC environment, these solutions enable even traveling laptop carriers to stay connected everywhere, sans the airplane itself (although Boeing is working to provide satellite connectivity on planes as well).

Wireless WANs, however, present the challenge of lower bandwidth and higher latency, as well as jitter (variable latency).

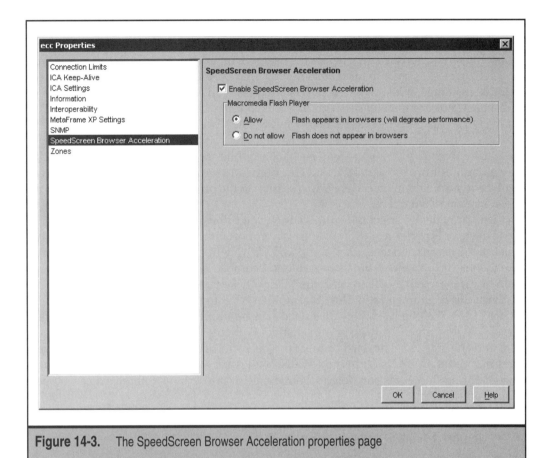

Figure 14-3. The SpeedScreen Browser Acceleration properties page

These issues can be so pronounced in wWANs that the user experience is degraded to the point of being unacceptable.

TIP: Throughput and latency are the two elements that define the speed of a network. Throughput is the quantity of data that can pass from source to destination in a specific time. Round-trip latency is the time it takes for a single data transaction to occur (that is, the time between requesting data and receiving it). Although most literature from wWAN providers focuses on throughput, the latency is far more important to MetaFrame usability. When shopping for a wWAN carrier, check on their latency.

The underlying wireless networks are based on circuit-switched voice architectures, which do not contain efficient mechanisms for sending data-link layer acknowledgements. To improve data efficiency, the networks typically wait for multiple frames to arrive before replying with an acknowledgement. This delay is directly reflected in the packet latency.

Latency has a critical impact on the MetaFrame user experience since every user action must travel across the network from the client to the server, and the server response must return to the client before the user sees an update. On a LAN, latency is typically very low—less than 10 ms. Latencies on wired WANs, however, are typically in the 50 to 200 ms range, while wireless WANs are usually in the 300 to 3000 ms range.

Latency normally increases with a corresponding increase in the size of the TCP packet. On a LAN, this increase is barely noticeable since ample bandwidth is generally available. On a wired WAN, it typically has a minor impact. On a wWAN, for example, the latency for a 32-byte packet may be 400 ms, while the latency for a 1460-byte packet may be significantly more at 1800 ms. This high (and variable) latency on a wWAN can significantly interfere with a MetaFrame session to the point where the user may find the experience unacceptable.

Citrix provides a variety of features and settings that can be set and configured to improve the user experience with wWANs. It is important to note that these changes to not equalize the user experience when compared with a wired WAN connection, but they do take the user experience from unbearable to bearable. It is also important to note that these features are not available with the Microsoft Remote Desktop Client.

Since our recommendation for all remote users is to utilize the MetaFrame Web Interface client, the client settings discussed will be implemented on the Web Interface Server. We recommend setting up two distinct Web Interface sites, one for slow connections and the other for standard connections, as some of these settings will remove features that users on LANs and wired WANs will want to maintain. If users are using a custom-configured Program Neighborhood Client, the settings referenced can be performed on the client.

The settings and features that can be set and optimized include

▼ Enable SpeedScreen3 Latency Reduction

■ Enable Maximum Data Compression

■ Enable Mouse Movement and Keystroke Queuing

■ Enable Persistent Cache

▲ Optimize IIS to cache images and utilize the Cache-Control HTTP Header

Enabling SpeedScreen Latency Reduction

Citrix developed the SpeedScreen latency features to improve the user experience over high-latency connections. SpeedScreen improves the user experience by providing immediate mouse and keyboard feedback to the client, effectively making the connection appear real-time even when it is significantly delayed. Latency reduction is available only if a client is connecting to a server that is configured for latency reduction.

SpeedScreen is set and configured both at the server side and on the client side. The client side options are Auto, On, and Off. By default, the client connections are set to Auto. The server side is configured using the SpeedScreen Latency Reduction Manager utility (choose Start | Citrix | MetaFrame XP | Speed Screen Latency Reduction Manager). Figure 14-4 shows the SpeedScreen Latency utility running on the MetaFrame server.

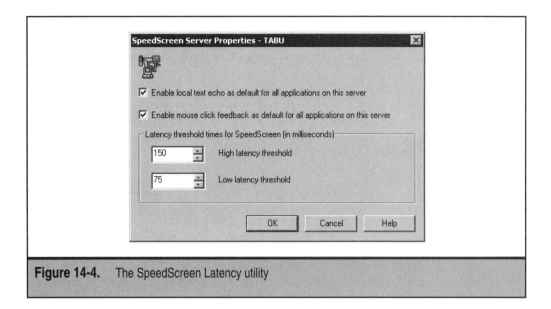

Figure 14-4.   The SpeedScreen Latency utility

There are two specific actions that the SpeedScreen Latency Protection feature will take when turned on (or when high latency is detected):

▼   **Local Text Echo**   Local Text Echo allows the ICA client software to create font characters locally on the client device without waiting for them to be sent to the MetaFrame server and then updated on the client display. When a session begins, the ICA client sends the server a list of fonts installed on the client device. As a user types a font, the local font is displayed the instant the key is depressed, giving the user immediate feedback. This feature is very useful for users over high-latency connections who do a lot of typing, as it removes the annoyance of waiting for the typing to catch up.

▲   **Mouse Click Feedback**   When Mouse Click Feedback is enabled, the cursor on the client changes from the normal select pointer (usually an arrow, depending on the mouse pointer scheme chosen) to the working-in-background pointer (usually a pointer with an hourglass). Since mouse click feedback is performed on the ICA client, the client can provide instant click feedback to the user, even if the server hasn't recognized the click yet. Anyone who has worked on a very slow PC understands how useful this feature is in reducing frustration caused from clicking multiple times on an object when it isn't clear whether the first click actually worked. When the server finally catches up with the number of clicks implemented, multiple instances are now open, and the user experience spirals downhill from there.

When the client is set to Auto, the default server settings turn these features on when the server sees latency of 500 ms or more. We recommend changing the default SpeedScreen Latency Threshold settings to 150 ms for the high-latency threshold, and 75 ms for the low-latency threshold. These settings ensure this feature is indeed activated at times when user experience is poor.

For known, slower connections (for example, if you are connecting over a wWAN or dial-in connection), set the client mode to On to force the feature on, regardless of the latency detected by the server.

To set the client mode to On via the Web Interface Server, edit the template.ica file and add the following entries:

```
ZLMouseMode  1 (0-disabled, 1-enabled, 2-auto)
ZLKeyboardMode    1
```

Enabling Data Compression

Data compression improves user experience for low-bandwidth connections. The ICA client compresses the data on the client side, and the MetaFrame server decompresses the data on the server side. This compression and decompression inflicts a processor performance penalty on both the server and the client, but with the current processor power available on both sides, this penalty is negligible. Citrix's internal test statistics show that ICA compression produces an average ratio of two to one, and higher ratios when highly graphical pages and print jobs are employed.

It is important to note that if ICA compression is enabled, a network compression tool such as Packeteer's Xpress, Expand's ACCELERATOR, or Verizon Wireless's Venturi Software Technologies will not improve performance. In fact, these tools often slow performance and cause other problems when ICA compression is enabled.

To enable maximum compression via the Web Interface Server, edit the template.ica file and add the following entries:

```
Compress    On
MaximumCompression    On
```

Queuing Mouse Movements and Keystrokes

Clicking the Queue Mouse Movements and Keystrokes check mark in the client settings causes the Program Neighborhood client to send mouse and keyboard updates less frequently to the MetaFrame server. Check this option to reduce the number of network packets sent from Program Neighborhood to the MetaFrame server. Intermediate mouse packets are discarded and the number of keystroke packets are coalesced into a single larger packet.

To set the mouse movement and keystroke queuing settings on the Web Interface server, edit the template.ica file and add the following entries:

```
MouseTimer    200
```

(This setting can be varied, but increasing this value too much could degrade interactive response.)

```
KeyboardTimer50
```

(This setting can be varied as well, but again, increasing this value too much could degrade interactive response.)

Enabling Persistent Cache

Enabling persistent cache decreases logon time and improves the performance of graphics operations during an ICA session. Since this feature requires local disk or firmware space, it is not available for some ICA clients (Windows CE thin clients, for example, as generally these devices do not have sufficient local storage space to maintain the cache files).

   To enable the persistent cache feature on the Web Interface server, edit the template.ica file and add the following entry:

```
PersistentCacheEnabled    On
```

Using the Cache-Control HTTP Header in IIS

Microsoft Internet Information Server (IIS) can be configured to improve the browsing experience of the Web Interface Web Site for wWAN users. These configurations are based on client-side caching of the Web Interface images. As IIS settings are beyond the scope of this, please refer to Microsoft IIS documentation for more information on cache settings.

SECURITY ON THE ICA CLIENT

Citrix ICA clients support integration with enterprise security standards. Some of the more typical standards supported are

▼ Connecting through a SOCKS proxy server or Secure proxy server (also known as *security proxy server*, HTTPS proxy server, or SSL tunneling proxy server)

■ Integrating the ICA Win32 Clients with the Secure Gateway or SSL Relay solutions with Secure Sockets Layer (SSL) and Transport Layer Security (TLS) protocols

▲ Connecting to a server through a firewall

Connecting to a Server Through a Proxy Server

Proxy servers are used to limit access into, and out of, a network, and to handle connections between ICA clients and MetaFrame servers. The ICA Win32 clients support SOCKS and secure proxy protocols, and can automate the detection and configuration of the ICA protocol to work with the client connection. In communicating with the MetaFrame server, the Win32 Program Neighborhood Agent and the ICA Win32 Web Client use proxy server settings that are configured remotely on the MetaFrame Web Interface server. Web Interface 2.0 is configured by default to autodetect the client web browser settings and pass these to the client's ICA session. In communicating with the web server, the ICA Win32 Program Neighborhood Agent and the ICA Win32 Web Client use the proxy server settings configured through the Internet settings of the default web browser on the client device. Obviously, the local settings of the default web browser on the client device need to be set for the appropriate proxy settings. See Chapter 16 for information about configuring proxy server settings for these ICA clients.

Using the ICA Win32 Clients with Secure Gateway for MetaFrame

For external users (and some highly secure internal users), the ICA Win32 clients can be configured to use the Secure Gateway or SSL Relay service. The clients support both SSL and TLS protocols, which are discussed at length in Chapters 8 and 16.

▼ SSL provides strong encryption to increase the privacy of ICA connections and certificate-based server authentication to ensure the server you are connecting to is a genuine server.

▲ TLS (Transport Layer Security) is the latest, standardized version of the SSL protocol. The Internet Engineering Taskforce (IETF) renamed it TLS when it took over responsibility for the development of SSL as an open standard. TLS secures data communications by providing server authentication, encryption of the data stream, and message integrity checks. Because there are only minor technical differences between SSL Version 3.0 and TLS Version 1.0, the certificates you use for SSL in your MetaFrame installation will also work with TLS. Some organizations, including those in the U.S. government, require the use of TLS to secure data communications. These organizations may also require the use of validated cryptography, such as FIPS 140. FIPS 140 (Federal Information Processing Standard) is a standard for cryptography. Security is covered in more depth in Chapters 8, 16, and 17.

System Requirements for SSL/TLS   In addition to the system requirements listed for each ICA client, the following must be met for SSL/TLS support:

▼ The client device must support 128-bit encryption.

■ The client device must have a root certificate installed that can verify the signature of the Certificate Authority on the server certificate.

▲ The ICA client must be configured to be aware of the TCP listening port number used by the SSL Relay service on the MetaFrame server.

Verifying Cipher Strength/128-Bit Encryption   Internet Explorer users can determine the encryption level of their system by doing the following:

1. Start Internet Explorer.
2. From the Help menu, click About Internet Explorer.

3. Check the Cipher Strength value. If it is less than 128 bits, you need to obtain and install a high-encryption upgrade from the Microsoft web site. Go to www.microsoft.com and search for "128-bit" or "strong encryption."

4. Download and install the upgrade. If you do not have Internet Explorer installed, or if you are not certain about the encryption level of your system, visit Microsoft's web site at www.microsoft.com to install a service pack that provides 128-bit encryption.

NOTE: The ICA Win32 clients support certificate key lengths of up to 4096 bits. Ensure that the bit lengths of your Certificate Authority root and intermediate certificates and those of your server certificates, do not exceed the bit length your ICA clients support. Otherwise, your connection may fail.

Configuring the ICA Client for Use with MetaFrame Secure Gateway   MetaFrame Secure Gateway can be configured for either *Normal* mode or *Relay* mode. With Secure Gateway in Normal mode, the only ICA Client configuration required is to enter the fully qualified domain name (FQDN) of the Secure Gateway server. If Secure Gateway is used in Relay mode, the Secure Gateway server functions as a proxy and the ICA client needs to be configured to use:

▼   The fully qualified domain name (FQDN) of the Secure Gateway server

▲   The port number of the Secure Gateway server

Configuring the ICA Win32 Program Neighborhood Agent and Web Client for MetaFrame Secure Gateway   The Win32 Program Neighborhood Agent and the Win32 Web Client use settings that are configured remotely on MetaFrame Web Interface to connect to servers running MetaFrame Secure Gateway. See Chapter 16 for information on properly setting up the Web Interface server to integrate with Secure Gateway.

Configuring the ICA Win32 Program Neighborhood Client for MetaFrame Secure Gateway   To configure the details of your Secure Gateway server:

1. Start the Program Neighborhood Client.

2. If you are configuring an application set: right-click the application set to be configured and select Application Set Settings. The Application Set dialog box appears. If you are configuring an *existing* custom ICA connection: right-click the custom ICA connection you want to configure and select Properties. The Connection Properties dialog box appears. If you are configuring *all future* custom ICA connections: right-click in a blank area of the Custom ICA Connections window and select Custom Connection Settings. The Custom ICA Connections dialog box appears.

3. If you are configuring an application set or an *existing* custom ICA connection: from the Network Protocol menu, select SSL/TLS + HTTPS. If you are configuring *all future* custom ICA connections: from the Network Protocol menu, select HTTP/HTTPS.

4. On the Connection tab, click Firewalls.

5. Enter the FQDN of the Secure Gateway server in the Secure Gateway address box.

NOTE: The FQDN must list, in sequence, the following three components:

■ Host name
■ Intermediate domain
■ Top-level domain

For example: *my_computer.my_company.com* is an FQDN, because it lists, in sequence, a host name (my_computer), an intermediate domain (my_company), and a top-level domain (com). The combination of intermediate and top-level domains (my_company.com) is generally referred to as the domain name.

6. Enter the port number in the Port box.

7. Click OK twice.

Configuring and Enabling ICA Clients for SSL and TLS

SSL and TLS are configured in the same way, use the same certificates, and are enabled simultaneously.

When SSL and TLS are enabled, each time a connection is initiated the Client attempts to use TLS first, then tries SSL. If it cannot connect with SSL, the connection fails and an error message appears.

Forcing TLS Connections for All ICA Win32 Clients   To force the ICA Win32 clients (including the ICA Win32 Web Client) to connect with TLS, the Secure Gateway server or SSL Relay service needs TLS specified in the configuration (see Chapter 16 for more details). To manually configure the ICA Win32 Program Neighborhood Client to use SSL/TLS:

1. Open the Program Neighborhood client.

2. If you are configuring an application set to use SSL/TLS: Right-click the application set you want to configure and select Application Set Settings. The Application Set dialog box appears. If you are configuring an *existing* custom ICA connection to use SSL/TLS: right-click the custom ICA connection you want to configure and select Properties. The Connection Properties dialog box appears. If you are configuring *all future* custom ICA connections to use SSL/TLS: right-click in a blank area of the Custom ICA Connections window and select Custom Connection Settings. The Custom ICA Connections dialog box appears.

3. If you are configuring an application set or an *existing* custom ICA connection: From the Network Protocol menu, select SSL/TLS + HTTPS. If you are configuring *all future* custom ICA connections: from the Network Protocol menu, select HTTP/HTTPS.

4. Add the FQDN of the SSL/TLS-enabled MetaFrame server(s) to the Address List.

5. Click OK.

To configure the ICA Win32 Program Neighborhood Agent to use SSL/TLS, do the following:

1. To use SSL/TLS to encrypt application enumeration and launch data passed between the Program Neighborhood Agent and the MetaFrame Web Interface server, configure the appropriate settings in the configuration file on the web server (see Chapter 16 for more details). The configuration file must also include the machine name of the MetaFrame server hosting the SSL certificate.

2. To use secure HTTP (HTTPS) to encrypt the configuration information passed between the Program Neighborhood Agent and the Web Interface server, enter the URL of the server hosting the configuration file in the format https://<servername> on the Server tab of the Program Neighborhood Agent Properties dialog box.

To configure the Appsrv.ini file to use TLS:

1. Exit the Program Neighborhood Agent if it is running. Make sure all Program Neighborhood components, including the Connection Center, are closed.

2. Open the individual's user-level Appsrv.ini file (default directory: %User Profile%\Application Data\ICAClient) in a text editor.

3. Locate the section named [WFClient]. Set the values of these two parameters as follows:

   - SSLCIPHERS={GOV | All}
   - SECURECHANNELPROTOCOL={TLS | Detect}. Set the value to TLS, or Detect to enable TLS. If Detect is selected, the Program Neighborhood Agent tries to connect using TLS encryption. If a connection using TLS fails, the client tries to connect using SSL.

4. Save your changes.

Certificate Revocation List Checking

New with Feature Release 3, Citrix released certificate revocation list checking. When certificate revocation list checking is enabled, the ICA Win32 clients check whether or not the server's certificate has been revoked. This feature improves the cryptographic authentication of the MetaFrame XP server and improves the overall security of the SSL/TLS connections between an ICA Win32 client and a MetaFrame XP server.

Several levels of certificate revocation list checking can be enabled. For example, the client can be configured to check only its local certificate list, or to check the local and network certificate lists. In addition, the certificate can be configured for certificate checking to allow users to log on only if all Certificate Revocation Lists are verified.

To enable certificate revocation list checking, in the Template.ica file on the Web Interface server, configure the SSLCertificateRevocationCheckPolicy setting to one of the following options:

▼ **NoCheck**   No certificate revocation list checking is performed.

■ **CheckWithNoNetworkAccess**   The local list is checked.

■ **FullAccessCheck**   The local list and any network lists are checked.

▲ **FullAccessCheckAndCRLRequired**   The local list and any network lists are checked; users can log on if all lists are verified.

Meeting FIPS 140 Security Requirements

To meet FIPS 140 security requirements, the following parameters listed in the following subsections must be included in the Template.ica file on the Web Interface server, or in the user-level Appsrv.ini file of the local client device.

Configuring the Appsrv.ini file to Meet FIPS 140 Security Requirements   To configure the Appsrv.ini file to meet FIPS 140 security requirements:

1. Exit the Program Neighborhood Agent if it is running. Make sure all Program Neighborhood components, including the Connection Center, are closed.

2. Open the individual's user-level Appsrv.ini file (default directory: %User Profile%\Application Data\ICAClient) in a text editor.

3. Locate the section named [WFClient].

4. Set the values of these three parameters as follows:

   ■ SSLENABLE=On

   ■ SSLCIPHER=GOV

   ■ SECURECHANNELPROTOCOL=TLS

5. Save your changes.

Installing Root Certificates on the ICA Win32 Clients   To use SSL/TLS to secure communications between SSL/TLS-enabled ICA clients and the MetaFrame server, a root certificate is needed on the client device that can verify the signature of the Certificate Authority on the server certificate.

The Citrix ICA Win32 clients support the Certificate Authorities supported by the Windows operating system. The root certificates for these Certificate Authorities are installed with Windows and managed using Windows utilities. They are the same root certificates used by Microsoft Internet Explorer. One exception to this is the Java client. Since this is a server-deployed client, the administrator of the Web Interface server must update the Java configuration files to include the Certificate Authority information and path.

If you use your own Certificate Authority, you must obtain a root certificate path from that Certificate Authority and install it on each client device. This root certificate path is then used and trusted by both Microsoft Internet Explorer and the Citrix ICA Win32 Client.

Depending on an organization's policies and procedures, an administrator may prefer to install the root certificate on each client device instead of directing users to install it. In most cases, if an organization is using Windows 2000 Server or Windows Server 2003 with Active Directory, the root certificate can be deployed and installed using Windows 2000 Group Profiles.

NOTE: We strongly recommend selecting a common, Internet-based, trusted Certificate Authority (such as Verisign or Thawte) to eliminate the following client-side configuration steps, regardless of whether you use Secure Gateway or SSL gateway services to make the connection.

To install a root certificate on the Win32 Client device:

1. Double-click the root certificate file. The root certificate file has the extension .cer, .crt, or .der.

2. Verify that you are installing the correct root certificate.

3. Click Install Certificate.

4. The Certificate Import Wizard starts. Click Next.

5. Choose the Place All Certificates in the Following Store option and then click Browse.

6. On the Select Certificate Store screen, select Show physical stores.

7. Expand the Trusted Root Certification Authorities store and then select Local Computer. Click OK.

8. Click Next and then click Finish. The root certificate is installed in the store you selected.

For more details about certificates, and the server-side configuration, please see Chapter 16.

Enabling Smart Card Logon

This section assumes that smart card support is enabled on the MetaFrame server, and that the client device is properly set up and configured with third-party smart card hardware and software. Refer to the documentation that came with your smart card equipment for instructions about deploying smart cards within your network.

The smart card removal policy set on the MetaFrame server determines what happens if the smart card is removed from the reader during an ICA session. The smart card removal policy is configured through, and handled by, the Windows operating system.

To enable smart card logon with Passthrough authentication requires a smart card to be present or inserted in the smart card reader at logon time. With this logon mode selected, the Program Neighborhood Agent prompts the user for a smart card personal identification number (PIN) when it starts up. Passthrough authentication then caches the PIN and passes it to the server every time the user requests a published resource. The user does not have to subsequently reenter a PIN to access published resources. If authentication based on the cached PIN fails or if a published resource itself requires user authentication, the user continues to be prompted for a PIN.

Perform the following to enable smart card logon with Passthrough authentication:

1. From the Program Neighborhood Agent Admin tool, select Logon Method from the Configuration Settings menu.

2. Click Smart Card Passthrough Authentication to select the option.

3. Save your changes.

To enable smart card logon without Passthrough authentication requires a smart card to be present or inserted in the smart card reader when the user tries to log on. With this logon mode selected, the Program Neighborhood Agent prompts the user for a smart card PIN (personal identification number) when it starts up and every time the user requests a published resource.

To enable smart card logon without Passthrough authentication, do the following:

1. From the Program Neighborhood Agent Admin tool, select Logon Method from the Configuration settings menu.

2. Click Smart Card Logon to select the option.

3. Verify that Passthrough Authentication is not selected.

4. Save your changes.

Enabling NDS Logon Support

To enable NDS Logon Support, perform the following:

1. From the Program Neighborhood Agent Admin Tool, select Logon Method from the Configuration settings menu.

2. Click Use NDS Credentials for Prompt User and Passthrough authentication to select the option.

3. Enter the default tree name.

4. Save your changes.

Connecting to a Server Through a Firewall

Network firewalls can allow or block packets based on the destination address and port.

NOTE: Additional steps beyond what is covered here may be required to connect to a MetaFrame server farm behind a firewall, depending on the firewall and server configurations. The use of a MetaFrame Web interface with Secure Gateway eliminates the requirement to perform these client-side configurations and dramatically simplifies the client setup. Please see Chapter 16 for more details.

To use the ICA Win32 Clients through a network firewall that maps the server's internal network IP address to an external Internet address, do the following:

1. Open the Program Neighborhood Client.

2. If you are configuring an application set: right-click the application set to be configured and select Application Set Settings. The Application Set dialog box appears.

3. If you are configuring a custom ICA connection: right-click the custom ICA connection you want to configure and select Custom Connection Settings. The Custom ICA Connections dialog box appears.

4. Click Add. The Add Server Location Address window appears.

5. Enter the external Internet address of the MetaFrame server.

6. Click OK. The newly added external Internet address of the MetaFrame server appears in the Address List.

7. Click Firewalls.

8. Select Use Alternate Address for Firewall Connection.

9. Click OK twice.

NOTE: All MetaFrame servers in the farm must be configured with their alternate (external) address.

Locking Down the ICA Client

As discussed in Chapters 7, 11, 13, and 15, the lockdown of the desktop device, regardless of the device, is an important aspect to maintaining a minimal maintenance client environment. If a configuration can be changed on the client machine, there is a risk that it can be broken, and of course, if the device fails, any configurations will have to be re-input. Thus, if the device can be fully locked such that user configurations and software (including client access software) cannot be changed, the environment will require significantly less support.

We introduced three applications for this purpose: RES PowerFuse, AppSense, and triCerat, all of which do a good job of efficiently and effectively locking down the desktop.

ICA and RDP Client Drive, Printer, and COM Port Mapping

Both ICA and RDP clients now support local drive, printer, and COM port mapping. Local Mapping allows the client to force the server to map a local device so that a user is able to employ a local device from within the remote server session.

Although local mapping can be very useful for remote, home, and traveling users, it is important to selectively apply local mappings in remote office and LAN environments since the data stream created from sending data back and forth from the server to the client can be very intensive, and cause other ICA/RDP sessions to fail.

All three items can be enabled or disabled from the server in the Citrix Management Console (for ICA) or the Terminal Services Configuration utility (for RDP). The server can also be configured to default to the client settings. The client local mapping settings can be configured for the RDP Client from the Local Resources tab.

Thin-Client Configuration

As discussed in Chapter 7, most thin-client vendors have management software to remotely flash updates and configurations to their thin clients. Although we prefer the simplest thin clients that just run ICA and RDP client software, we still recommend purchasing the enterprise versions of these management suites, to aid in the mass setup and configuration of thin clients. Generally, this management software requires a server running TFTP to put the management software and updated images on. Wyse, for example, provides an application called Rapport Enterprise for this purpose.

Publishing the Full Desktop vs. Seamless Windows

Prior to the advent of lockdown software it was often necessary to limit a user to a specific application or small group of applications in order to ensure that users didn't maliciously or accidentally change server settings that could cause instability (such as installing printers). By choosing to publish an application in a "desktop window," that application appears to take up the entire screen when a user logs in. The Seamless Windows feature of the Win32 ICA Client was created in order to make access to individual published applications transparent to the user. These application icons appear just as any other icons on the user's PC desktop. The user doesn't necessarily know that the application is actually running on a server. With MetaFrame XP, all applications using Seamless Windows on a user's desktop share a connection, so it is not necessary to log on again each time one of these applications is executed.

The significant downside that we have seen in using Seamless Windows with a large number of applications is that users don't understand when and where applications are coming from, and thus they struggle with understanding where their printers, files, and utilities are. In addition, if something doesn't work, they immediately blame the server farm, propagating the user community perception that the server-based solution doesn't work. Because of this user perception problem, if we are publishing more than one or two applications, we utilize a locked-down, full-desktop environment. Although it isn't as slick, when users can recognize which environment they are in, it is easier to set and meet their expectations of application access and performance.

Autoupdate

MetaFrame includes the ICA Client Update Configuration utility that allows an administrator to manage the ICA client versions in use on the network. The database of the various ICA client versions is created when MetaFrame is installed and is located in the \%*SystemRoot*%\ICA\ClientDB directory. When a new client version for a particular type of client is placed in this directory, users with that client will see a notice the next time they log on. This notice informs them that a new client is available. Depending on the settings in the Client Update Configuration utility, the user can choose to skip the update, or update at that time.

CHAPTER 15

Profiles, Policies, and Procedures

This chapter examines the different types of profiles that are available to assist in controlling and optimizing the server-based computing environment. The chapter also covers general deployment tips and guidelines for using Windows Group Policies to implement standard computing environments, and introduces the new Windows Server 2003 policy settings as well as the Group Policy Management Console (GPMC).

The last section of this chapter covers recommended best practices for using profiles and Group Policies, with the focus on SBC infrastructure as it relates to the CME case study.

USER PROFILES

A user profile is simply a registry hive in file format (NTuser.dat) and a set of profile folders (stored in *%systemdrive%*\Documents and Settings) that contain information about a specific user's environment and preference settings. Profiles include settings such as printer connections, background wallpaper, ODBC settings, MAPI settings, color schemes, shortcuts, Start menu items, desktop icons, mouse settings, folder settings, and shell folders such as My Documents. Profiles are automatically created the first time a user logs into any NT-based machine, including a Terminal Server.

NTuser.dat (the file that stores the user's registry-based preferences and configurations) is loaded by the system during logon and mapped into the registry under the subtree HKEY_CURRENT_USER. This file can be found at the root of the user's profile location, such as C:\Documents and Settings\username\NTuser.dat. The set of profile folders such as Application Data, Cookies, Desktop, and Start Menu are also located at the root of a profile location such as C:\Documents and Settings\username\Application Data. The Application Data profile folder is where applications and other system components store user data, settings, and configuration files. There are two types of profiles: local and roaming.

Local Profiles

As the name implies, a *local profile* is a user profile that exists on a single machine. By default, a user will employ a local profile and may have several local profiles on different machines. This type of profile is not very useful for the average user since it cannot traverse a load-balanced server farm. Local profiles lead to end-user confusion as applications and environment changes do not follow the users when they log in to different servers in the farm. For example, a user may change their background setting to green on one Terminal Server, log out, and then log back in to a different Terminal Server to find that the background is not green. This is caused by having two separate local profiles, with one on each server. Local profiles are useful for administrators or service accounts that do not need their settings to roam from one server to another.

Roaming Profiles

A *roaming profile* is a centrally stored version of a local profile. The profile is "roaming" in that it is copied to every computer the user logs in to as their "local" profile. There, it is utilized as a locally cached copy until the user logs out, at which point it is saved back to the central storage location for profiles. This is the primary type of profile employed in an

SBC network due to the necessity of having user settings "roam" with the user. A roaming profile can also be *mandatory*. The corresponding files have an extension specific to the type: NTuser.dat for a roaming profile and NTuser.man for mandatory roaming. Mandatory profiles are covered more in depth in the next section.

Roaming profiles allow users to make changes to their environment. These changes are then recorded in the locally stored copy of the roaming profile. Once a user logs off, the profile changes are copied back to the network share from which it was originally loaded. This profile is then used the next time the user logs in to the SBC environment. Another item to remember with roaming profiles is that the last write wins. An example of this can be seen when a user logs in to two different machines simultaneously. They may change something in their profile in one session (such as the background color to green) and proceed to log out. They then change the background color to blue in the other session and log out. As a result, the user will end up having a blue background the next time they log in to a machine. This is due to the fact that the last logout causes the profile to be written back to the profile storage location which overwrites any previous writes.

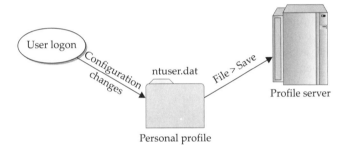

Roaming profiles have the following advantages:

▼   User-specific application settings, such as default file locations, file history, and fonts are saved to the profile.

▲   Users can customize the desktop environment. They can change colors, fonts, backgrounds, desktop icons, and the Start menu.

Default limitations of roaming profiles include

▼   Profiles have no restriction on file size, which can lead to rapidly increasing disk space and network bandwidth consumption. This becomes a problem particularly when users drag large documents onto their desktop for easy access.

▲   Users are not prevented from making changes that might render their environment unstable or unusable.

Although roaming profiles were designed to allow users to make changes, roaming profiles can be locked down to reduce the changes a user can make to their environment. A review of how to implement roaming profiles with Group Policy to achieve a balance between giving users sufficient rights to change what they need while maintaining control and manageability of the profiles is presented later in this chapter.

Mandatory Roaming Profiles

A mandatory roaming profile is a specific type of roaming profile that is preconfigured by an administer and cannot be changed by the user. This type of profile has the advantage of enforcing a common interface and a standard configuration. A user can still make modifications to the desktop, Start menu, or other elements, but the changes are lost when the user logs out, as the locally stored profile is not saved back to the network share.

Mandatory roaming profiles are created by renaming the NTuser.dat file in the roaming profile to NTuser.man. Mandatory profiles should be used for kiosk environments or where users cannot be trusted to change settings related to their profiles.

Mandatory roaming profiles have the following advantages:

▼ Profile size is fixed and typically small. This alleviates disk storage problems and potential network congestion.

■ Profile network traffic is cut in half since the locally cached profile is never copied back to the profile server.

▲ No user settings are saved. This eliminates some help-desk calls as it prevents users from inadvertently destroying their environments. If the user has made inappropriate changes to the environment, logging out and logging back in will reset them to an original configuration.

The following are disadvantages of mandatory roaming profiles:

▼ No user settings are saved. This lack of flexibility may lead to the need to create various "standard" mandatory roaming profiles to accommodate different needs.

▲ User-specific application settings, such as Microsoft Outlook profile settings, are not saved with the profile. Mailbox settings need to be set each time a user logs in to the system or be configured before the profile is changed to mandatory.

Many of the same beneficial restrictions of mandatory roaming profiles can be accomplished using a standard roaming profile without compromising flexibility. For this reason, mandatory profiles are not often utilized in the SBC environment.

Profile Mechanics

Two separate roaming profile locations can be specified in an Active Directory domain. Both are configured from within the Active Directory Users and Computers administration program.

▼ **Terminal Server Profile Path** This profile path is used when a user logs in to a server with Terminal Services running. It is configured from the Active Directory Users and Computers administration program on the Terminal Services Profile tab, as shown in Figure 15-1. This setting is strongly recommended in an SBC environment to keep users' Terminal Server profiles separate from their standard client OS profile.

NOTE: Windows Server 2003 Active Directory environments can use Group Policy to set the Terminal Server profile path.

▲ **User Profile Path** This profile path is used when a user logs into a computer without Terminal Services running (such as a local workstation or laptop) or when no specific Terminal Server profile path is specified. This profile path is configured from the Active Directory Users and Computers administration program on the Profile tab, as shown in Figure 15-2.

The importance of these two profile paths is critical in setting up an optimized SBC environment and is illustrated in the following example. Users located at the CME-EUR site log in to Windows 2000 Professional desktops before launching Citrix applications. They have a value for User Profile Path populated for their user accounts that points to a local server (\\frankfurtsrv\profiles\%*username*%). This keeps the profiles for their local workstation close to their workstation for optimal retrieval. The same users log in to MetaFrame servers that are located back at CME-CORP in Chicago, Illinois. The Terminal

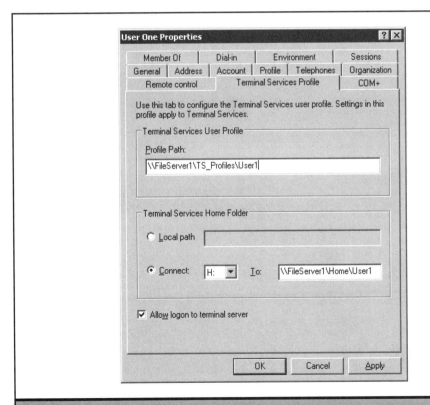

Figure 15-1. The Terminal Server profile path

Services profile path for these users points to a server located in the corporate network in Chicago (chicagosrv\profiles\%username%). This is done to avoid having profiles copied from the Frankfurt server over the WAN links to the MetaFrame XP servers and avoids user confusion that may arise from having a common profile for both their local workstation and MetaFrame XP sessions.

Profile Processing

The process that occurs when a user logs in to a Terminal Server is as follows. The Terminal Server contacts a domain controller to determine where the roaming profile is located as specified in the Terminal Services Profile text field in the user's account. If this field exists, the profile is copied down to a locally cached version of the profile. If the Terminal Services Profile field is left blank, the Terminal Server will look at the Profile Path text field and download that profile if it exists. If both fields are blank, the Terminal Server will use a local profile (if one already exists), or create one if it does not exist by copying settings from the default users profile on the machine they are logging in to. This process is illustrated in Figure 15-3.

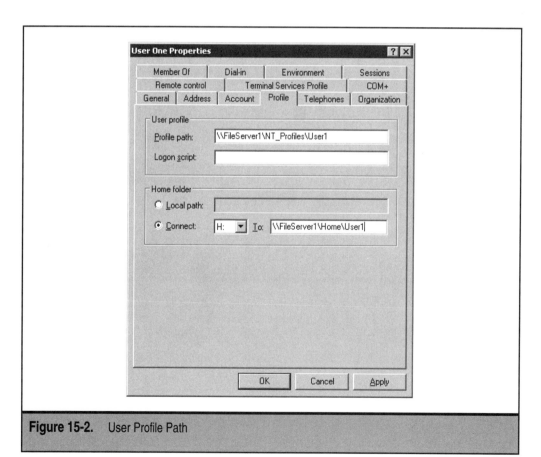

Figure 15-2. User Profile Path

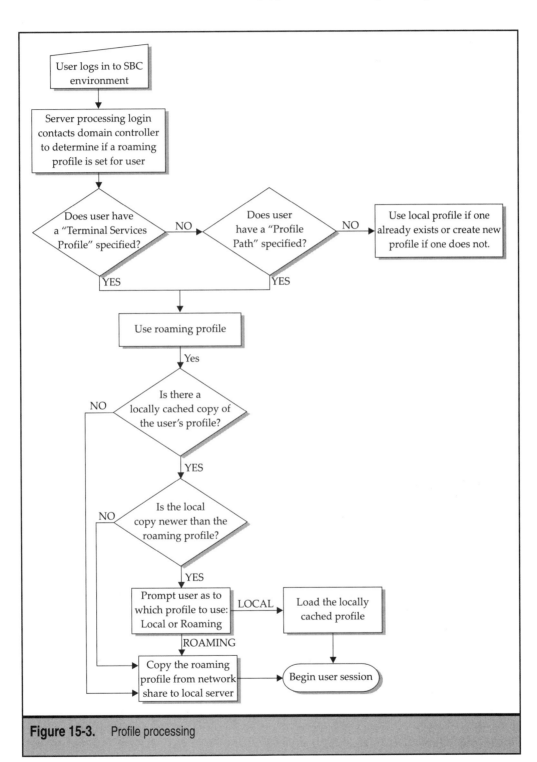

Figure 15-3. Profile processing

Home Directory

Like the profile path settings, two different home directories can be specified. Terminal Services Home Directory (shown in Figure 15-1) specifies the directory used when a user logs in to a server running Terminal Services. The Home folder (shown in Figure 15-2) specifies the user's home directory when they are not utilizing a machine with Terminal Services.

NOTE: The Terminal Services Home directory can be specified with Group Policy as described later in this chapter.

Windows 2000 and 2003 will default the home directory location to the user's profile if no other location is specified, causing a profile's size to swell as users store information at this location. Since a user's profile is copied across the network every time they log in to, or out of, another computer, the goal is to minimize the size of the profile. Home directories accomplish this by giving the users a location to store their personal information outside of the profile.

NOTE: Support for legacy applications that were not designed appropriately still may require the use of application compatibility scripts. The data from the application compatibility scripts are stored in the home directory. Chapter 13 has more information on the use of application compatibility scripts.

Home directories should be placed on network file servers that are co-located with the Terminal Servers in order to facilitate the efficient transfer of files. In relation to our case study CME Corp, we recommend creating a home directory share called "Home" on the local enterprise file server closest to the user and storing the home directories in this share.

GROUP POLICIES

Group Policies are used in Windows 2000 and Windows Server 2003 to define change and configuration management. They are used to define user and computer configurations for groups of users and computers. Configuration of Group Policy is done through the Group Policy Object Editor from within the Microsoft Management Console (MMC) snap-in. The Group Policy settings are contained in a Group Policy Object, which is associated with selected Active Directory objects such as sites, domains, and organizational units. There is also an option for local policy creation to assist in controlling specific computers.

Using Group Policy, an administrator is able to control the policy settings for the following:

▼   **Registry-based policies**   This includes Group Policy for the Windows 2000 and 2003 operating systems and their components, as well as for applications. To manage these settings, use the Administrative Templates node of the Group Policy snap-in.

- ■ **Security options**   Local computer, domain, and network security settings
- ■ **Software installation and maintenance options**   Centralized management of application installation, updates, and removal.
- ■ **Scripts options**   This includes scripts for computer startup and shutdown, as well as user logon and logoff.
- ▲ **Folder redirection options**   This allows administrators to redirect users' special folders to network storage locations.

Implementing Windows Group Policies for registry-based policies, security options, and folder redirection is essential in a well-managed SBC environment. Administrators should use Group Policy to ensure users have what they need to perform their jobs, but do not have the ability to corrupt or incorrectly configure their environment. Many common user lockdown settings are contained in the Windows Explorer component under the User Configuration section. A new Terminal Server configuration section is available in Windows Server 2003 Group Policy that did not exist in Windows 2000. The new settings are contained in the Terminal Services component under Computer Configuration. The Terminal Services component of the Computer Configuration Group Policy provides a place to set several important configurations, including

- ▼ Setting keep-alive settings
- ■ Setting the path for the Terminal Services roaming profile location
- ▲ Setting the path for the Terminal Services home directory

Machines that are a member of an Active Directory domain process Group Policies in a very systematic way. The processing order is as follows:

1. Local Group Policy Object
2. Site
3. Domain
4. Organizational unit (OU)

Exceptions to the default order are due to Group Policies being set to no override, disabled, block policy inheritance, or loopback processing. The key things to remember are the order in which policies are applied, and that a Domain setting will override a Site setting. Understanding this will help in troubleshooting problems with policy settings not being implemented. For example, if the same settings are applied at both the Site and OU levels, the OU policy will still be implemented unless special settings (such as no override) have been configured.

THE GROUP POLICY MANAGEMENT CONSOLE

Windows Server 2003 introduced a new tool to manage Group Policy called the Group Policy Management Console (GPMC). The GPMC is a separate installation and can only be used in conjunction with Windows Server 2003 machines. The installation files can be found at www.microsoft.com/windowsserver2003/gpmc. The management console can be installed on either Windows Server 2003 or Windows XP Professional with SP1.

Some of the key enhancements of the Group Policy Management Console include the following:

▼ A unified graphical interface that makes Group Policy easier to administer

■ The ability to back up and restore Group Policy Objects

■ Import/export and copy/paste of Group Policy Objects and Windows Management Instrumentation filters

■ Simplified management of Group Policy–related security and delegation

■ HTML reporting for GPO settings and the resultant set of policy data

▲ Scripting of Group Policy–related tasks exposed within this tool

The Group Policy Management Console allows an administrator to view the scope of created policies, as shown in Figure 15-4. It also enables an administrator to view the

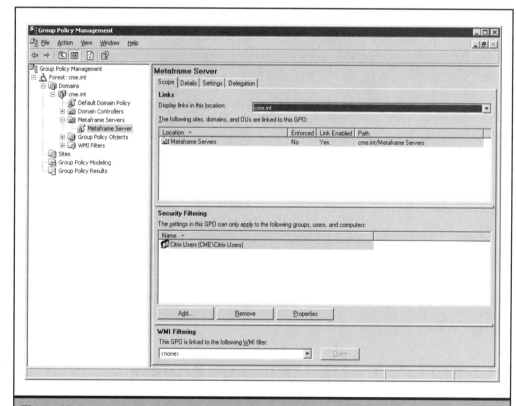

Figure 15-4. The Group Policy Management Console policy scope

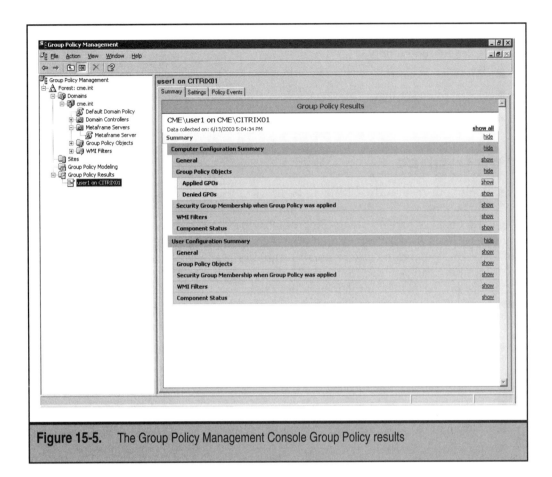

Figure 15-5. The Group Policy Management Console Group Policy results

resulting policies applied to users or computers, as you can see in Figure 15-5. This is very handy in situations where settings are not behaving as expected, as the administrator can see which policy is overriding the other and make the appropriate changes.

CITRIX POLICIES

Citrix introduced user policies in Feature Release 2 for MetaFrame XP. Citrix user policies are similar in nature to Group Policies but are restricted to controlling only MetaFrame XP–related settings. They are configured from within the CMC and can be applied to groups or specific users. They are particularly useful in configuring settings such as locking down the number of sessions a user or group of users can have, or in setting shadowing permissions. Citrix polices allow an administrator to turn on and off the following options per group or user:

▼ Local drive/printer/port mapping

■ Shadowing options and permissions

- Concurrent login sessions
- Content redirection
- Time zone controls
- Encryption settings
- ▲ Auto-client update

BEST PRACTICES

In relation to our case study, CME will be using roaming profiles for all standard users due to the fact that users will need the ability to configure application settings and have them roam between servers. Roaming profiles will exist in two locations: a roaming profile for their local workstation located on a file server at the same office, and a roaming profile for the MetaFrame environment located on a file server where the MetaFrame servers reside. CME will use local profiles for the administrators and service accounts. Mandatory profiles will be implemented for the kiosk stations that are used as job application terminals at the manufacturing sites. Some of the major challenges of a mix of local, roaming, and mandatory roaming profiles are

- ▼ Implementing different group policies for users when they log in to a Terminal Server
- Limiting the profile file size
- Locking down the desktop
- Eliminating inappropriate application features
- Limiting access to local resources
- ▲ Controlling application availability

In order to overcome these challenges, CME will use Group Policy to redirect appropriate folders to minimize profile size, lock down the desktop environment, and eliminate inappropriate application features. Citrix user policies and published applications will be used to limit access to local resources, define shadow permissions, and control application availability.

Implementing Different Group Policies for Users When They Log in to a Terminal Server

Since the Terminal Servers are special-use computers within the environment, users should have different settings and configurations applied to their environment when they log in to the MetaFrame XP servers versus logging in to a local workstation or laptop. The processes for achieving this are listed next.

1. Create a separate OU in Active Directory for the MetaFrame XP servers.

2. Move the MetaFrame XP servers to the newly created OU.

3. Create and apply a new Group Policy to the MetaFrame XP server OU.

4. Assign appropriate permissions to the Group Policy.

5. Enable loopback processing within the Group Policy Object.

Creating a Separate OU in Active Directory for the MetaFrame XP Servers

Follow these steps, as illustrated in Figure 15-6, to create a separate OU in Active Directory:

1. Choose Start I Programs I Administrative Tools I Active Directory Users and Computers.

2. Select Action I New I Organizational Unit.

3. Enter the name for the OU that will house the MetaFrame XP servers. Click OK.

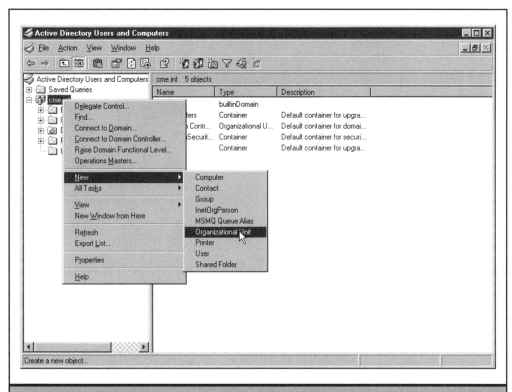

Figure 15-6.   Creating a separate OU for MetaFrame servers

Moving the MetaFrame XP Servers to the Newly Created OU

Perform the following steps to move the MetaFrame XP servers to the newly created OU:

1. Locate the MetaFrame server (found in the Servers or Computers OU), right-click it, and choose Move.

2. Select the newly created OU dedicated for MetaFrame servers and click OK.

3. Repeat this process for all MetaFrame XP servers.

Creating and Applying a New Group Policy to the MetaFrame XP Server OU

Figure 15-7 shows the creation of a new Group Policy. Follow these steps to create a new Group Policy:

1. Right-click the OU and select Properties.

2. Choose the Group Policy tab.

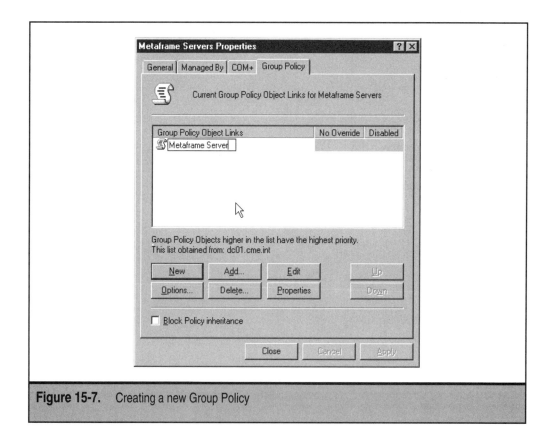

Figure 15-7. Creating a new Group Policy

3. Click New.

4. Enter an appropriate name for the Group Policy.

Assigning Appropriate Permissions to the Group Policy

Figures 15-8 and 15-9 show the application and denial of Group Policies by group. The steps to apply or remove a Group Policy are

1. Select the Group Policy Object and click Properties.

2. Select the Security tab.

3. Add and remove appropriate users and groups (deny the Apply Group Policy attribute to any user or group to which the Group Policies should not apply).

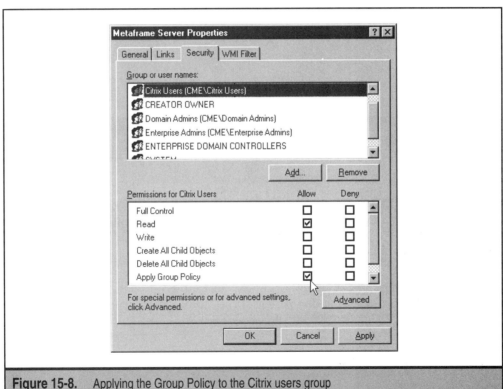

Figure 15-8.   Applying the Group Policy to the Citrix users group

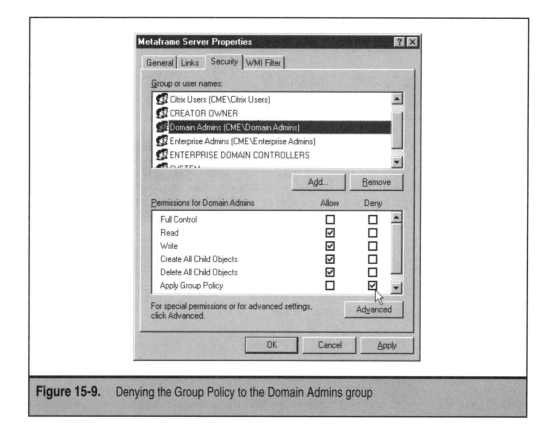

Figure 15-9.   Denying the Group Policy to the Domain Admins group

Enabling Loopback Processing Within the Group Policy Object

Figures 15-10 and 15-11 show the Group Policy Enabling process and how to change the loopback mode setting to Replace. The steps are as follows:

1. Select the Group Policy Object and click Edit.

2. Choose Computer Configuration I Administrative Templates I System I Group Policy folder and double-click to select the User Group Policy loopback processing mode.

3. Check the radio button next to Enabled.

4. Set the mode to Replace or Merge based on the user environment.

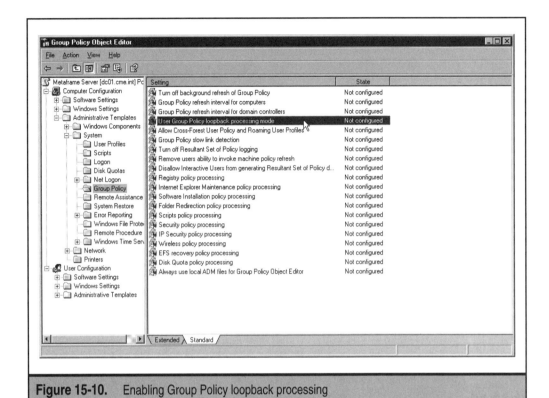

Figure 15-10. Enabling Group Policy loopback processing

NOTE: "Replace" means that the user settings defined in the computer's Group Policy Objects replace the user settings normally applied to the user through Group Policy. "Merge," on the other hand, means that the user settings defined in the computer's Group Policy Objects and the user settings normally applied to the user are combined. If the settings conflict, the user settings in the computer's Group Policy Objects take precedence over the user's normal settings.

Limiting the Profile File Size

Profiles tend to grow in size over time. This is largely due to users saving documents in their My Documents folder, dragging items onto their desktop, or saving information into the Application Data folders contained in the profile. To keep the profile sizes minimized for our case study, CME will configure network shares to store profiles, and configure the

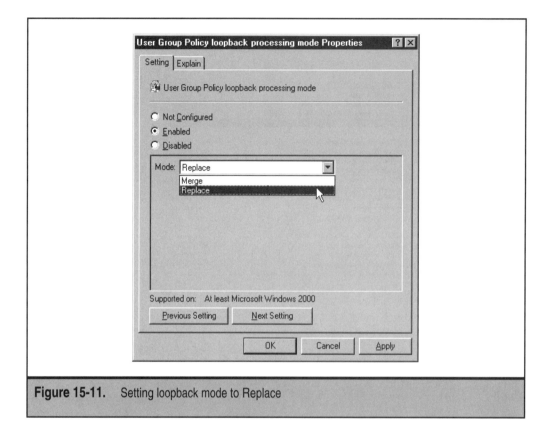

Figure 15-11. Setting loopback mode to Replace

preceding folders for redirection to the user's home directory using Group Policy. CME will store Terminal Server profiles in a share called TS_Profiles. This helps to distinguish them from normal profiles used on client operating systems. These normal profiles will be stored in a share called NT_Profiles.

The redirection of Application Data, Desktop, and My Document folders is configured within the existing Group Policy assigned to the MetaFrame server's OU as shown in Figure 15-12. To configure redirection, follow these steps:

1. Edit the existing MetaFrame Servers policy from within the Group Policy Object Editor.

2. Open User Configuration | Windows Settings | Folder Redirection.

3. Right-click Application Data and select Properties.

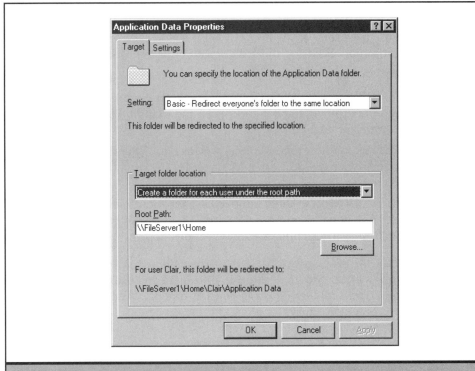

Figure 15-12. Settings for Application Data redirection

4. The setting field option should be set to Basic – Redirect everyone's folder to the same location.

5. The Target Folder Location option should be set to Create A Folder For Each User Under The Root Path.

6. Set the root path to the location of the user's home directory (\\FileServer\Home).

7. Follow steps 3 through 6 for Desktop and My Documents.

NOTE: Folder redirection through Group Policy is only available with Active Directory domains.

Locking Down the Desktop

The amount of control that users are given over their desktop environments varies from organization to organization. Securing the desktop can be accomplished in many ways, including

▼   Using Group Policy to redirect the Desktop and Start menu folders to a common read-only folder on a network share and to limit the functionality of the Windows Explorer shell.

■   Using a third-party utility such as RES Powerfuse, triCerat's Simplify Lockdown, or AppSense Application Manager for desktop lockdown and folder redirection.

▲   Using Group Policy to completely remove Desktop, Start menu, and Windows Explorer shell functionality and use the Citrix Program Neighborhood Agent client executed from the MetaFrame XP server desktop.

In reference to the CME case study, CME will use one of the third-party utilities to assist with implementing a locked-down desktop environment and use Group Policy to assist with redirecting critical folders (such as My Documents, Application Data, and Desktop) to the user's home directory.

Eliminating Inappropriate Application Features

Many common applications, such as the Microsoft Office XP Suite, have features that are not appropriate for an SBC environment. An example of this type of feature is the Office Assistant that represents the help interface in the Office XP product line. The Office Assistant utilizes unnecessary resources and, because of the animated graphic, does not perform well in a MetaFrame XP environment. Many common applications have compatible template files for Group Policy. The Office XP template file is office10.adm and the Office 2003 template file is office11.adm. These template files can be added to the Group Policy by right-clicking one of the Administrative Template areas in the Group Policy Management Console and clicking Add/Remove Templates. By clicking the Add button, an administrator can browse to the appropriate template file and add it to the Group Policy Management Console. The template files are located in the *%systemroot%*\inf directory if the application has been installed on that server; otherwise, they can be copied from the product media.

Another common area of concern is applications that display splash screens at initialization. Many of these, such as Net Meeting and Internet Explorer, can be controlled via Group Policies. Several other applications have command-line switches that enable an administrator to publish the application to users with these graphics suppressed.

Custom .adm files can be created to add additional policies as well as custom registry settings through the Group Policy interface. For more information on writing custom .adm files, please refer to Microsoft support article number 323639.

Limiting Access to Local Resources

Local resource access can be controlled through two methods. The first method is through the use of the Citrix Connection Configuration console, accessed by editing the properties of the ica-tcp or ica-ipx connection. The problem with this tool is that it has to be configured on each server individually and applies to all users logging in to the server. The better method is to use Citrix User Policies. An example of allowing access to local drives follows. A policy is configured for denying drive access as well as any other custom settings that are needed for different local LPT or COM port access. The following steps are required to set up different local drive access rules per user or group:

1. Open the Citrix Management Console and log in as a full Citrix administrator.

2. Right-click Policies and select Create Policy.

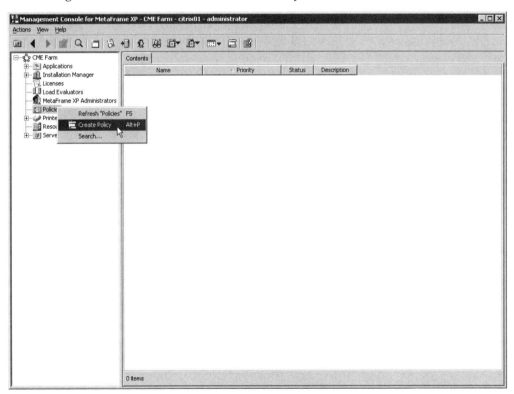

3. Enter a descriptive policy name and click OK.

4. Double-click the new policy to display the properties.

5. Open the Client Devices section.

6. Click Client Drive Mapping.

7. Click the radio button for Rule Enabled.

8. Click the selection box next to the drives that should not be available to the user or group.

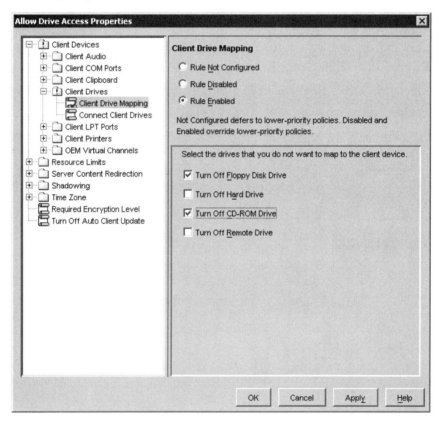

9. Click Connect Client Drives.

10. Click the radio button for Rule Enabled.

11. Click the radio button for Connect Client Drives at Logon.

12. Go back to the Client Devices section and enable access to other local resources such as COM and LPT ports and printers.

13. Click OK to close the Allow Drive Access Properties dialog box.

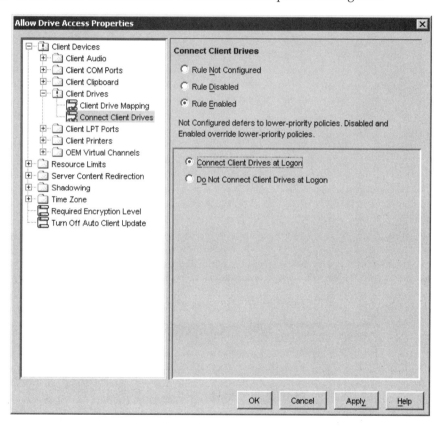

14. Right-click the policy and click Assign Users.

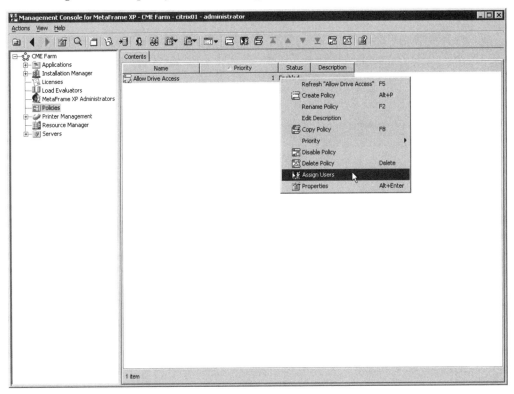

15. Add the users and groups to which you would like this policy to apply.

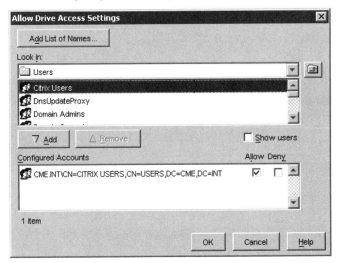

16. Click OK to close the dialog box and apply the policy to those users.

Controlling Application Availability

Application availability is controlled using Citrix published applications. When published applications are created via the Citrix Management Console (CMC), the administrator grants access to selected groups or users. All of the CME users will get their applications based on published application group membership.

Change Control

We recommend testing all changes and tracking any modifications to policies and profiles through a revision control system. This can be as simple as keeping a written change log or as complex as using revision control software such as Component Software, Inc.'s CS-RCS (www.componentsoftware.com/products/rcs/) or Merant's PVCS (www.merant.com/Products/ECM/tracker/home.asp). Whatever the case, the important thing is that all personnel involved with administering the system or making changes follow the same change control procedure and have easy access to tracking systems.

CHAPTER 16

Securing Client Access

A s discussed in Chapter 14, there are many ways to provide on-demand access to the server-based environment. Choosing which method depends on many factors, the most important of which is the location of the end users. For internal LAN/WAN users, securing access to the servers is not needed, and thus a simple deployment of MetaFrame Web Interface with Program Neighborhood Agent provides a full solution. For home-based or traveling users though (external users accessing the network via the public Internet), Citrix has developed a client access method that provides secure, simple access via a familiar web interface. A *secure access center,* for the purpose of this book, can refer to both methods available for creating a web-based access solution: *MetaFrame Secure Gateway* (the combination of MetaFrame Web Interface, Secure Ticket Authority, and MetaFrame Secure Gateway) and *MetaFrame Secure Access Manager* (a combination of Web Extensions, Secure Ticket Authority, and MetaFrame Secure Gateway). Secure Gateway and Web Interface are components of MetaFrame XP Presentation Server, and MetaFrame Secure Access Manager is a stand-alone product that integrates with MetaFrame XP Presentation Server.

SECURE ACCESS CENTER DEPLOYMENTS

Of all the trends leading organizations to server-based computing, one of the most significant is the dependency on IT staff to make everything easy to deploy and intuitive for end users. This dependency leads to the necessity of making any software deployment obvious, and void of any required end-user instructions. Thus, the largest cost savings of SBC is in the actual deployment of the application. Although Citrix allows a user to manually configure an ICA session, and even allows an administrator to automatically push an ICA application icon to users' desktops, the most recognized interface for users today is still a web interface. The web browser has become the ubiquitous access center—even the most nonsavvy end user has seen a web interface, and a significant number of the working population spends some portion of their day clicking web icons and blue hyperlinks, and typing URL addresses.

Although Citrix provides several automated ways to deploy an access center to end users (in addition to the nonautomated method of having a user create an ICA session from Citrix Program Neighborhood), the combination of MetaFrame Web Interface and MetaFrame Secure Gateway provides a secure, web-based deployment that continues to revolutionize server-based computing.

Web Interface and Secure Gateway are both included with all versions of MetaFrame XP. Web Interface is also supported on Solaris platforms, but the latest version of Secure Gateway is only supported on Windows 2000 Server or Windows Server 2003 platforms. Some enterprises will want to go further than just secure access to MetaFrame applications, however, and will deploy MetaFrame Secure Access Manager to further "webify" their environment.

CASE STUDY FOR A METAFRAME SECURE GATEWAY DEPLOYMENT

Our case study, CME Corp, has defined requirements for external access regarding traveling sales staff, home users, Internet kiosks, and wireless Internet WANS (Sprint, Verizon, T-Mobile, and others), supporting everything from dial-up to broadband connection speeds.

In order to support these requirements, CME has chosen to implement MetaFrame Web Interface with MetaFrame Secure Gateway to create an access center.

CME's secure access center deployment runs on Microsoft Internet Information Server version 6.0 on Windows Server 2003. Figure 16-1 diagrams the infrastructure pieces that make up the secure access center.

Notice from Figure 16-1 that a single dedicated server is used for both the Web Interface and the Secure Gateway software. The ability to place both Secure Gateway and Web Interface on a single server was introduced with Secure Gateway 2.0. In addition to reducing hardware costs, consolidating these two functions also reduces costs by only requiring one server certificate. Also note that in order to minimize the risk of hardware failure, two servers are used to provide fault tolerance in conjunction with a third-party load balancer.

The Secure Gateway deployment in the Demilitarized Zone (DMZ) is accompanied by a third-party server certificate from Verisign (other third-party certificates are also supported). The MetaFrame XP and MetaFrame for UNIX servers, as well as a Secure Ticket Authority (STA) server, are in the internal LAN. The STA server also has a server certificate issued by an internal Certificate Authority (CA) to encrypt the traffic from itself to the Web Interface/Secure Gateway server. Additional WAN/LAN CME network details are discussed and diagrammed in Chapter 17.

METAFRAME SECURE GATEWAY DEPLOYMENT

MetaFrame Secure Gateway functions as a secure Internet-ready gateway for Citrix Independent Computing Architecture (ICA) traffic between MetaFrame servers and Secure Sockets Layer (SSL)–enabled ICA Client workstations. All data traversing the Internet between the client workstation and the Secure Gateway server is encrypted, ensuring privacy and integrity of information flow. Secure Gateway provides a single point of entry and secures access to Citrix server farms. SSL technology is used for encryption, allowing secure transfer of data across public networks. Secure Gateway is also designed to make firewall traversal with MetaFrame solutions easier. It is completely transparent to both application programs and network devices, eliminating the need for any program modifications, firewall changes, or equipment upgrades.

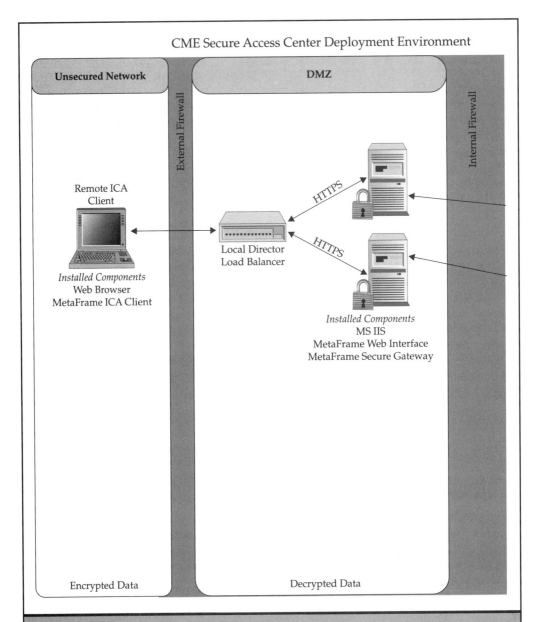

Figure 16-1. The CME secure gateway diagram

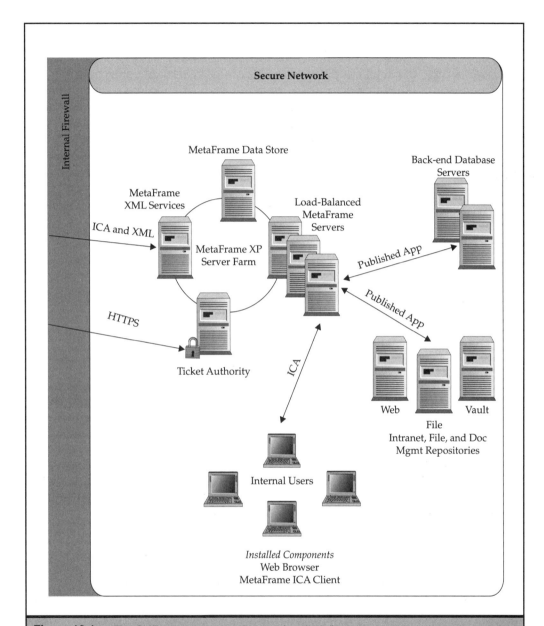

Figure 16-1. The CME secure gateway diagram *(continued)*

Benefits of a Secure Gateway Deployment

As discussed in Chapters 3 and 12, MetaFrame Secure Gateway is one of the most significant new features developed by Citrix in the past three years. Although Citrix has long provided access via the Internet, prior to Secure Gateway, organizations often struggled with providing Internet access to SBC environments due to security concerns. Although both Citrix's ICA and Microsoft's RDP protocols support 128-bit encryption, both protocols also require that firewall ports be opened at both the client and data center sides of the Internet. MetaFrame Secure Gateway solves these security issues and provides the following benefits:

▼ Strong encryption (SSL 128-bit and TLS 140-bit)

■ Authentication (achieved through Web Interface)

■ Hidden internal network addresses for Citrix servers

■ Firewall traversal through a widely accepted port (TCP port 443)

■ Simplified server certificate management (certificates are required only on the Secure Gateway server)

■ Simple support for a large number of servers

▲ No requirement for separate client software (only a Secure Gateway–enabled ICA Client is required)

This firewall change creates both logistical and security challenges for companies, especially in instances where the client-side firewall may not be modified. An example of this is when one company's employees are housed on another company's campus.

Secure Gateway solves this problem by encapsulating ICA traffic (TCP port 1494) into SSL (TCP port 443). Since SSL is a widely supported standard and utilized for many other web purposes, it provides a readily accepted transmission method for traffic traversing firewalls and the Internet.

A typical Secure Gateway deployment involves interaction of the following five Citrix components (also shown in Figure 16-2):

▼ A client device with an ICA Client, Version 6.30 or later, installed

■ The MetaFrame Web Interface server

■ The MetaFrame STA

■ The MetaFrame Secure Gateway server

▲ The Citrix MetaFrame server(s)

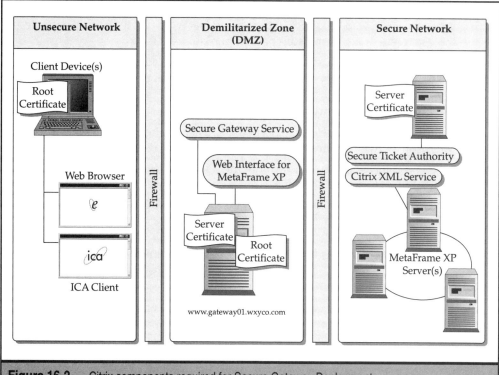

Figure 16-2.   Citrix components required for Secure Gateway Deployment

End-User Interactions When Connecting to the Secure Gateway Deployment

The following section details the interactions between the client devices and the back-end secure access center infrastructure.

The user interactions are as follows:

1. A user accesses the Web Interface URL with the web browser over port 80 (just like any other web site).

2. The IIS-based web service where Web Interface resides has a default page to redirect the user automatically to an HTTPS/SSL URL that then passes through the Secure Gateway service on the same server to secure the traffic over port 443.

3. The user is now interacting securely with the Web Interface/Secure Gateway environment and is presented with the login page.

4. The user enters their credentials and submits the authentication request, which is passed encrypted over SSL to the Secure Gateway service (thus preventing the user credentials from being passed in plain text).

5. Once the Secure Gateway service obtains the user credentials, it opens a state ticket with the STA server and then passes the credentials to the MetaFrame farm over the defined XML service port (the default is port 80 but CME will use port 8081 for security purposes).

6. The user credentials are checked via the Citrix XML service and verified by Microsoft Active Directory (or other directory services such as Novell e-Dir).

7. Based on a successful authentication, the XML service communicates back to the Web Interface service and dynamically renders an access page for the user with their application set or indicates if there are any problems, displaying them in the MetaFrame XP Message Center.

8. When a user clicks an ICA published application, the Web Interface service sends the IP address and port for the requested MetaFrame server to the STA and requests a session ticket for the user. The user-installed ICA Client then securely establishes an ICA connection over SSL/443.

9. The Secure Gateway service receives the session ticket over 443 from the client and contacts the STA for ticket validation. If the ticket is valid, the STA returns the IP address of the MetaFrame server on which the requested application resides. If the session ticket is invalid or has expired, the STA informs the Secure Gateway service and an error message appears on the client device.

10. On receipt of the IP address for the MetaFrame server, the Secure Gateway server establishes an ICA connection to the MetaFrame server over 1494 in a proxy-like manner. When the ICA connection is established, the Secure Gateway server encrypts and decrypts data flowing through the connection.

INSTALLATION OF THE SECURE GATEWAY DEPLOYMENT

The following is a list of tasks that must be completed in order to successfully install and use MetaFrame Web Interface, MetaFrame STA, and MetaFrame Secure Gateway for the CME deployment.

1. Select server(s) that meet the minimum requirements for each component (Web Interface, Secure Gateway, and STA).

2. Create DNS records for the Web Interface/Secure Gateway server and STA(s).

3. Obtain an SSL certificate for the Web Interface/Secure Gateway server using the fully qualified domain name (FQDN).

4. Optionally, obtain an SSL certificate for the STA using the FQDN.

5. Install and configure the Web Interface web server.

6. Install and configure the STA component.

7. Install and configure the Secure Gateway component.

8. Lock down the MetaFrame Secure Gateway deployment.

Secure Gateway Deployment Requirements

The following are requirements for each of the components necessary for the Secure Gateway Deployment.

Client System Requirements

▼ ICA Version 6.30 or later

▲ A web browser and operating system that support 128-bit encryption and have the appropriate root certificates installed.

Web Interface System Requirements

▼ Microsoft Windows 2000 or 2003 Server with the latest service packs and hotfixes installed. Web Interface will run on Solaris platforms as well, but since Secure Gateway does not, this total solution requires a Windows Server platform.

■ 1GB RAM.

■ Internet Information Server 5.0/6.0 (IIS) installed and configured.

▲ Citrix Secure Gateway is natively supported by Web Interface, as well as by NFuse Classic 1.6 and 1.7.

STA System Requirements

▼ Microsoft Windows 2000 or 2003 Server with the latest service packs and hotfixes installed

■ 500MB RAM

▲ Internet Information Server 5.0/6.0 (IIS) installed and configured

MetaFrame Secure Gateway System Requirements

▼ Microsoft Windows 2000 Server or Windows Server 2003 with the latest service packs and hotfixes installed

■ 1GB RAM

▲ Additional 150MB hard drive space

MetaFrame Server Farm Requirements

▼ MetaFrame XP Server for Windows with Feature Release 2 or later

and/or

■ MetaFrame Secure Access Manager, Version 2.0

and/or

▲ MetaFrame Server for UNIX Operating Systems, Version 1.1 or later

Creating DNS Records for the Web Interface/Secure Gateway Server and STA(s)

The assigned URL for the Web Interface/Secure Gateway server must be Internet resolvable. The STA only needs to be resolved by the Web Interface/Secure Gateway server. The ability to resolve FQDNs is an important security aspect required for certificate-based implementations.

Obtaining an SSL Certificate for the Web Interface/Secure Gateway Server

A Digital ID, also known as a digital certificate or SSL certificate, is the electronic equivalent of a passport or business license. It is a credential issued by a trusted authority that individuals or organizations can present electronically to prove their identity or their right to access information.

When a CA such as VeriSign issues Digital IDs, it verifies that the owner is not claiming a false identity. Just as when a government issues a passport and officially vouches for the identity of the holder, when a CA gives your business a digital certificate, it is puting its name behind your right to use your company name and web address.

This section describes the basic process for obtaining a third-party server certificate from a well-known CA such as Verisign or Thawte. The processes for obtaining a certificate may differ slightly between CAs, but the steps are basically the same. Most CAs will include a variety of services and extras with their certificate offerings. These services may include 40- or 128-bit SSL (Global Server) IDs, business authentication, and protection against economic loss resulting from the theft, corruption, impersonation, or loss of a certificate. Services may also include trials of a security analysis or security auditing service, accelerated certificate delivery, and certificate revocation and replacement periods. Be sure and check with each potential CA for details on their individual services.

CME has chosen to use a 128-bit SSL Server ID from Verisign for their Web Interface/Secure Gateway server. This will secure the traffic and packets from the Internet to the DMZ. CME uses Microsoft Certificate Services for the STA server certificate to secure the traffic and packets from the DMZ to the internal network. These certificates allow all the traffic passing from the client to the server in the Secure Gateway deployment to use port 443 through the firewalls it traverses.

Requesting the Server Certificate

In order to complete the certificate request, you must provide the following documentation to the CA:

▼ **Proof of Organization** Before a Secure Server ID can be issued, the CA will need to verify that your company or organization has the legal right to conduct business under the name you specify in your enrollment request. Documentation may include a business license, the registration of a trade name, or a Dun & Bradstreet number. If you have a Dun & Bradstreet D-U-N-S Number registered for your organization, it may help expedite the verification process and issuance of your Secure Server ID.

NOTE: Your organization's legal name must match the organization name in your enrollment request. Otherwise, the CA will be unable to authenticate your organization.

- *Proof of Domain Name*   To issue your certificate, your domain name registration must be verified against the organization name provided during enrollment. CAs can only issue a Secure Server ID to the organization that has the legal right to use the domain name. The Common Name (domain name) for the server that will use the Server ID must be the FQDN. For CME's FQDN, *"access.cme.com," cme.com* is the domain name and *access* is the host name. In *"www.cme.com," cme.com* is the domain name and *www* is the host name.

- *Generate a CSR*   Follow the instructions that came with your server software to generate a key pair and a Certificate Signing Request (CSR). Key pair generation is the creation of the server's private and public keys. A copy of the public key is included with the submitted CSR and then integrated into your Digital ID. To create the CSR, do the following:

  1. Open Internet Services Manager on the Web Interface/Secure Gateway server.

  2. Right-mouse-click on the Default Web Site link and select Properties from the context menu. On the Directory Security tab, select Server Certificate.

  3. Begin the Certificate Request Wizard.

  4. Create a new certificate. To do so, provide the following:

     a. **Name**   Pick a name that's easy for you to remember. This will correspond to the Friendly name on the summary screen. The bit length field determines the certificate's encryption strength. We recommend a setting of 1024 to provide reasonable encryption strength without sacrificing performance.

     b. **Organization and Organizational Unit**   The legal name of your organization and the name of your division or department.

     c. **The Common Name (domain name)**   This is the valid DNS name of your Web Interface site and Secure Gateway server. If you decide to change the common name of the site, you will have to obtain a new certificate. This will correspond with the Issued To: field on the summary screen.

     d. **Geographical Information**   Fill in the appropriate information.

     e. **File Name**   Name your file and place it in a location that is easy to find. The default is C:\certreq.txt; do not alter the file extension.

     f. **Request File Summary**   Confirm all the request information, and make sure the Issued To: entry matches the FQDN assigned to the Web Interface site. Also confirm that the Organization entry contains the legal name of your organization.

  5. Complete the wizard by clicking Finish.

- *Submit the CSR and Select Your Server Software*   Open a web browser on the Web Interface/Secure Gateway and enter the URL for a CA. CME used Verisign at www.verisign.com. Since each CA has their own instructions for submitting a request for a certificate, we will not document all the steps involved. However, each CA has detailed instructions on their web sites for submitting the request. Some generic answers to the required CSR information are that the request should be for a Web Server Certificate or SSL certificate, the type of server software will be Microsoft, and the encryption strength should be a minimum of 128-bit.

  When you cut and paste the request from the text file to the CA's online form, select the entire text area including the lines "-----BEGIN NEW CERTIFICATE REQUEST-----" and "-----END NEW CERTIFICATE REQUEST-----".

- *Complete and Submit the Application*   Review and confirm the information drawn from your CSR. If any of the information is incorrect, generate a new CSR with the appropriate information. Things to note for filling out the online forms include

  - **Technical contact**   This person must be authorized to run and maintain your secure web server. The technical contact receives the Secure Server ID and other notification e-mails.

  - **Organizational contact**   The organizational contact must be employed by your company. This contact must be authorized to make a binding agreement to the Secure Server Service Agreement for your organization. This should be a different person than the technical contact.

  - **Billing contact**   The billing contact receives invoices and receipts by regular mail.

- *Wait for Processing and Final Verification*   The CA now examines the information you have submitted. If everything you entered is correct, they should be able to authenticate your organization and issue your Secure Server Digital ID, usually in three to five business days. Your technical contact will usually receive an e-mail message confirming your enrollment. Final Verification is the last step of the order process and can only be completed after your organization name and domain name have been verified.

- *Install Your ID*   When your Digital ID is approved, the CA will usually e-mail it to your technical contact. When you receive your Digital ID, make a backup copy of it and store it on a floppy disk or CD-ROM, noting the date you received it. The Secure ID will look much like the request.txt file submitted earlier. Open Notepad on the server and paste in the entire certificate response including
  the lines "-----BEGIN CERTIFICATE-----" and "-----END CERTIFICATE-----". Save the file with an extension of .CER somewhere where it is easy to access. To install your Digital ID, follow these instructions:

  1. Open Internet Services Manager on the Web Interface/Secure Gateway server.

2. Right-mouse-click the Default Web Site, and from the context menu select Properties. On the Directory Security tab, select Server Certificate.

3. Complete the certificate request wizard with the following steps:

   a. Process the pending request and install the certificate.

   b. Enter the path and filename by browsing to the .CER file you saved earlier.

   c. Check the certificate summary and verify that the information contained in the response file matches the original request.

   d. Complete the wizard by clicking Finish.

The Web Interface/Secure Gateway server is now ready to continue the installation and configuration of the MetaFrame Secure Gateway.

Optional Installation of Internal STA

For maximum security, a server certificate can be installed on the STA to encrypt the traffic from the DMZ to the internal STA server using SSL encryption. An Internet-based certificate can be used, as described in the previous section, or a certificate can be obtained from your company's internal CA. For more information on configuring a nonpublic CA, such as Microsoft Certificate Services, please refer to that system's technical documentation.

Installing MetaFrame Web Interface

Although Web Interface can be installed as part of the MetaFrame XP installation, in order to take advantage of its security features for external users, we recommend installing it on a stand-alone machine in a DMZ separate from the internal domain. For LAN-based Web Interface deployments supporting Program Neighborhood Agent Clients, the Web Interface server should be installed in the LAN. If both external and internal users will be supported (which is very common), two Web Interface servers should be used—one internal and one in the DMZ.

Upgrading from Previous Versions

You can upgrade from NFuse 1.51, 1.6, or 1.7 to Web Interface using the Components CD-ROM or the Web Interface files downloaded from the Citrix web site. If you are upgrading from NFuse 1.51 (or a newer version), settings in the NFuse.properties file are migrated to the nfuse.conf file. This means that existing settings are automatically migrated to the latest version of Web Interface. If you are upgrading from a version prior to NFuse 1.51, you must first remove the old version before installation.

We recommend performing a complete reinstall of the Windows operating system and Web Interface rather than doing an upgrade from a previous version of NFuse.

When Web Interface is installed, files are installed in two main locations: the software directory and the web server's document root.

Web Interface Installation File Locations

On the Windows platform, the installation directory is located in C:\Program Files\ Citrix\NFuse. Web Interface software and configuration components are stored in the installation directory, including

▼ nfuse.properties file

■ Web Interface Java objects (.jar files)

■ nfuse.conf file

▲ ICA templates (.ica files)

NOTE: On Windows platforms, the nfuse.conf file is stored in C:\Program Files\Citrix\NFuse\conf. The Web Interface files in this location are global. Therefore, if you make changes to nfuse.conf, these settings are applied to all web pages served by this Web Interface server.

The web server's document root location depends upon where you installed your web server. On Windows, this is typically installed in the C:\Inetpub\wwwroot directory. The Web Interface presentation and layout components are stored in this location.

Required Information

When Web Interface is installed separately from MetaFrame XP using the Components CD-ROM or web download files, the installer is prompted for information during the installation that includes

▼ **MetaFrame server identity**   You must identify one or more MetaFrame servers in the farm that will act as contact points between the server farm and the Web Interface server. You can specify MetaFrame server names, IP addresses, or FQDNs. You can specify the name of any server in the farm. We highly recommend using the FQDN for ease of deployment and management.

■ **TCP/IP port**   You must specify the TCP/IP port on which the specified servers are running the Citrix XML Service. If you do not know this port number, you can determine it by checking a MetaFrame server's port information. For more information about how to do this, see the next section, "Viewing the Citrix XML Service Port Assignment." In the CME deployment, we have chosen port 8081 for the XML service running on the MetaFrame servers.

▲ **ICA Clients**   You will be prompted for the Components CD-ROM or CD image. Setup copies the contents of the CD's ICAWEB directory to a directory called /Citrix/ICAWEB that it creates off the web server's document root. All web sites created by the installation process assume that the web server contains the ICA Client files in this directory structure. If you do not want to copy the ICA Clients to the web server during Web Interface installation, you can copy them to the server later. Make sure you create the required directory structure. For example, in a typical English installation, it would be *webroot>*/Citrix/ICAWEB/ en/*<icaclientplatform>*.

Viewing the Citrix XML Service Port Assignment

The Citrix XML Service is the communication link between the MetaFrame server farm and the server running Web Interface. Since IIS shares default port 80, and it is a well-known port for hackers, an alternative port such as 8081 is recommended for the Citrix XML Service. This should have been selected during the install of MetaFrame on the first server in the farm. See Figure 16-3 for a screen shot of the configuration page for the XML port.

NOTE: To view the Citrix XML Service port assignment, open the Management Console for MetaFrame XP. In the left pane, right-click the server and select Properties. In the Properties dialog box, select the MetaFrame Settings tab to view the port assignment. If necessary, you can change the port used on the MetaFrame XP server. See Chapter 12 for more details.

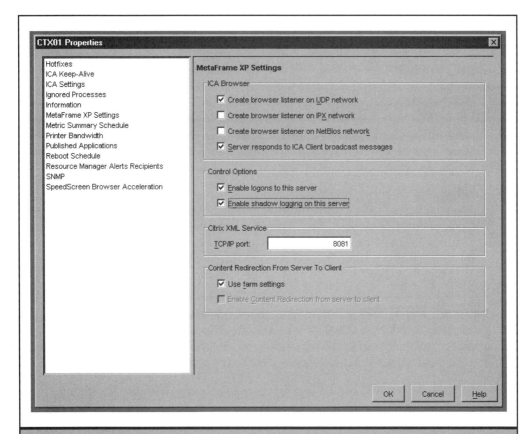

Figure 16-3. MetaFrame Management Console's XML port identification tab

Step-by-Step Installation of MetaFrame Web Interface

These steps provide a detailed installation guide for Web Interface:

1. Log in as an administrator.

2. If you are installing the Web Interface from the Components CD-ROM, insert the CD-ROM in your web server's CD drive. The Citrix MetaFrame XP Components dialog box appears. Select the Web Interface option. If you downloaded Web Interface from a download site, copy the file NFuseClassic20-IIS.msi to your web server. Double-click the file.

3. The Installation Wizard guides you through the installation process.

4. On the Welcome to Web Interface For MetaFrame XP Installation Wizard screen, click Next.

5. Read and accept the license agreement and click Next.

6. Click OK to restart IIS.

7. Click Next to accept the default location for the Web Interface files. By default, Setup will install Web Interface into the C:\Program Files\Citrix\NFuse directory. Make note of this directory as it is the directory where the NFuse.txt and nfuse .conf files reside. These will be discussed in more detail later in this chapter.

8. On the Connecting To A Citrix Server screen enter the FQDN or IP address of a Citrix server in your farm that will provide Web Interface with published application information. This will include the TCP port on which that server is running the Citrix XML service. (For CME Corp this will be 8081.) Additional servers can be added for redundancy at a later point.

9. If the port is changed from the default port of 80, a warning dialog box will appear. Click Accept to continue.

10. The next screen asks if you would like to install the ICA Clients from the Components CD to the ICAWEB directory for use in the Web Interface portal. This is highly recommended, as this is the ICA Client that will be downloaded to the users prior to starting the ICA session. This location will be the directory where all future ICA Client updates are installed. Accept the defaults and click Next.

CAUTION: Although there is an ICAWEB directory on the MetaFrame XP Presentation Server CD, installing the clients from this CD-ROM or sources other than the components CD will not create the proper directory structure under the Web Interface root web. This will cause a failure when the user attempts to install the auto-detected client due to incorrect path configurations.

11. Click Next on the Ready To Install screen to continue with the installation.

12. After installation is successful, click Finish.

13. Exit the installer screen.

14. Test the Web Interface installation by opening a web browser and in the address box type **http://localhost/citrix/metaframexp**. Enter a username, password and domain and verify that you are able to launch a published application.

Configuring Web Interface Through the Web Administration Tool

Citrix introduced a new, easy-to-use GUI administration tool to configure the MetaFrame servers, authentication settings, server-side firewall settings, client-side firewall settings, ICA Client deployment settings, and ICA customization. The Web Interface Web Administration tool is a GUI interface for making changes to the nfuse.conf file located in C:\Program Files\Citrix\NFuse\conf folder. After making changes using the Web Administration tool, simply save and apply them so the new configuration takes effect.

The Web Administration tool can only configure Windows 2000 or 2003 servers running Internet Information Server, and requires Internet Explorer version 5.0 or later. The configuration of Web Interface using the Web Administration tool will be broken into four sections:

1. General Settings
   a. Configuring User Authentication
2. Server Settings
   a. Configuring MetaFrame Farms
   b. Configuring MetaFrame Servers
   c. Configuring the Server-Side Firewall
3. Client Settings
   a. Configuring the Client-Side Firewall
   b. Controlling ICA Client Deployment
   c. Controlling ICA Customization
4. How to customize the text on the Web Interface web site
5. Introduction to Web Interface Extension Mode

General Settings

The general settings page and its configuration options provide the interface for general administration of the Web Interface site. The next section details these options and the recommended settings. To begin configuration, open a browser and enter the URL **http://localhost/citrix/metaframexp/wiadmin**. Figure 16-4 shows the Web Interface configuration page.

Configuring User Authentication   In the Authentication section, you can configure the ways in which users can authenticate to Web Interface and, subsequently, to your MetaFrame XP server farm. Authentication to Web Interface takes place when a user accesses Web Interface

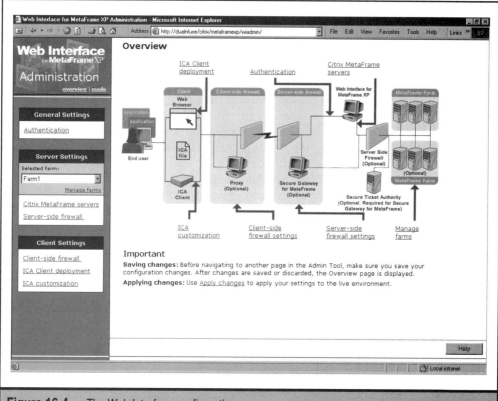

Figure 16-4. The Web Interface configuration page

using the Login dialog box. If authentication is successful, Web Interface returns the user's application set. Explicit authentication, guest logins, desktop credential passthrough (single sign-on), and smart card authentication to Web Interface can all be configured.

Methods for Authenticating to Web Interface In this section, we explore the methods Web Interface employs to authenticate users.

NOTE: The type of authentication you specify does not affect the method used for ICA Program Neighborhood Agent Clients. To change the authentication method used by the Program Neighborhood Agent Clients, edit the Config.xml file.

The following are the authentication options:

▼ **Smart card**   By selecting this check box, users can authenticate to Web Interface by inserting a smart card into a smart-card reader attached to the client device. The user is prompted for a PIN.

■ **Desktop Credential Passthrough**   By selecting this check box, users can authenticate to Web Interface using the credentials they provided when they logged in to their Windows desktop. Users do not need to reenter their credentials at the Web Interface Login page, and their application set is automatically displayed. By combining Desktop Credential Passthrough with Passthrough authentication, users are provided with single sign-on. Passthrough authentication is a feature provided by the Win32 ICA Client.

CAUTION: If the Passthrough authentication feature is enabled on the Win32 ICA Client, an attacker can send the user an ICA file that causes the user's credentials to be misrouted to an unauthorized or counterfeit MetaFrame server. Thus, we do not recommend enabling this feature.

■ **Guest login**   Selecting this check box will give guest users access through Web Interface (without requesting a username and password) to any applications published for anonymous use on the MetaFrame server(s).

▲ **Explicit authentication**   Selecting this check box requires users to supply a username and password to log in to Web Interface. You can configure User Principal Names (UPN) (*username@domain.com*, for example), Microsoft domain-based authentication, Novell Directory Service (NDS), and RSA SecurID authentication.

To configure explicit login to Web Interface:

1. Click Authentication in the left menu.
2. Select Explicitly Login.
3. Select one of the following authentication methods:

   ■ **Use UPN authentication**   This option specifies User Principle Name (UPN) authentication.

   ■ **Use NT authentication**   This option allows the specification of Microsoft domain-based authentication. To force users to log in to a specific domain, enter a domain in the Login domain field and click Add.

   ■ **Use NDS authentication**   This option allows the specification of Novell Directory Service (NDS) authentication.

   ■ **Use RSA SecurID**   This option allows the specification of an RSA SecurID authentication database for token support.

4. Under Allow User to Change Password, select Yes, On Expiry, or No. Choosing On Expiry will allow a user to change their login password only when the password has expired. When a password expires, a web page is displayed in which users can enter a new password. The expiration time is set in the operating system. On Expiry support was introduced with MetaFrame XP Feature Release 2.

Password Change Considerations   If there are differences between your MetaFrame farms, there are additional issues that should be considered before giving users the option to change their password. For example, password changing is only supported by Citrix MetaFrame XP with Feature Release 2, thus the password change request must be directed to a farm containing this version of MetaFrame XP.

CAUTION: If multiple MetaFrame XP farms utilizing different authentication domains will be supported, a password change will only affect the domain to which it is issued, potentially leading to inconsistency in the farms that can be accessed by the associated user (as the same credentials must be valid across all farms). Citrix recommends that end-user password changing be disabled in these situations.

To configure authentication to MetaFrame XP:

1. Click Authentication in the left menu.

2. To enable Passthrough authentication, select either Auto, Yes, or No under Enable ICA Client Passthrough Authentication. Auto will provide the greatest amount of compatibility with other Web Interface and MetaFrame settings. If the user logs in to the Web Interface using desktop credential Passthrough authentication, the Web Interface attempts to authenticate to MetaFrame XP using Passthrough authentication and the ICA Client passes the captured credentials to the MetaFrame server. If the user logs in to the Web Interface using a smart card, the ICA Client does not pass the captured PIN to the MetaFrame server and the user is prompted for their PIN.

3. To enable smart card authentication, select either Auto, Yes, or No. Choose No unless Smart Card support is required.

NOTE: After all the configurations have been made, click Save. The Overview page appears. Click the Apply Changes link. When the Apply Changes page appears click the Apply Changes button. Until you click this button, the configuration changes you made will not be written to the nfuse.conf file. If you exit the Administration Tool before applying the changes, all configurations will be lost.

Server Settings

This section of the Web Interface Administration page provides the hooks into the MetaFrame server farm infrastructure. It is linked from the main Web Interface admin page.

Configuring MetaFrame Farms   You can configure one or more MetaFrame farms within the same administrative domain to communicate with Web Interface. Applications from multiple MetaFrame farms are displayed in the same way as a single farm; folders are displayed first, followed by application icons. Consequently, applications with the same name from multiple farms will appear in a random position in the user's application set. We recommend you ensure application names are unique across the farms by publishing applications in folders with different names.

To create and manage the MetaFrame farms to be accessed by Web Interface, perform the following:

1. Click Manage Farms in the left menu.

2. Enter a name for the MetaFrame farm in the farm name field.

3. Click Add. The farm name appears in the Citrix MetaFrame Farms list.

4. If you specify more than one farm name, highlight a name in the list and click the up and down buttons to place these in the appropriate order. To remove a farm name, highlight it in the Citrix MetaFrame Farms list and click Remove.

NOTE: The Web Interface acquires application data from all farms before displaying applications; each farm is contacted in the order that it appears in the configuration file. As a result, a farm that is slow to respond will impact overall responsiveness when obtaining application sets.

Configuring MetaFrame Servers for Use by Web Interface   Use the Citrix MetaFrame Servers page to specify the names of one or more MetaFrame servers running the Citrix XML Service. Server settings are configured for each individual MetaFrame farm. To view and configure farm settings, select a farm from the Selected Farm drop-down list, and click the appropriate Server Settings links.

You can specify

▼ **MetaFrame servers running the XML Service**   The address of one or more MetaFrame servers running the Citrix XML Service.

■ **Fault tolerance**   This option enables fault tolerance among servers running the Citrix XML Service.

■ **Load balancing between servers**   This option enables load balancing between servers running the Citrix XML Service.

■ **XML service port**   This is the TCP/IP port used by the Citrix XML Service on the MetaFrame servers specified in the Server addresses list.

▲ **Transport type**   This is the protocol used to transport data between the server running Web Interface and the MetaFrame server.

Specifying MetaFrame Servers Running the Citrix XML Service   Specify the MetaFrame servers running the Citrix XML service in the server list box by entering the server name or IP address. By adding multiple servers from the same farm, Web Interface will detect when an error occurs while communicating with a server, and cause all further communication to be transferred to the next server in the list. The failed server is bypassed for a specific time period (by default, 60 minutes), and the bypass time period can be specified in the Bypass Any Failed Server For field in the Citrix MetaFrame Servers page. If all servers in the list fail to respond, Web Interface will retry the servers every ten seconds.

NOTE: If you are using a secure connection between the web server and the MetaFrame server (in other words, you set the Transport type to SSL Relay or HTTPS), ensure the server name you specify matches the name on the server's certificate.

Configuring Load Balancing   You can enable load balancing between servers running the Citrix XML Service by selecting the Load Balancing check box. Enabling load balancing evenly distributes all incoming session requests among the servers listed in the server address box.

Configuring the TCP/IP Port for XML Communication   To configure the MetaFrame XP farm's TCP/IP listener Port for XML Communication, enter the port number in the XML service port field. All MetaFrame servers in the farm must have the Citrix XML Service configured on the same port. For CME Corp, we used port 8081.

Configuring the Transport Protocol   To configure the transport protocol, select HTTP, HTTPS, or SSL Relay. If SSL Relay will be used, specify the TCP port of the SSL Relay in the SSL server port field. Integration with Secure Gateway eliminates the need to use anything other than the default HTTP transport type.

REMEMBER: After all the configurations have been made, perform the Save | Apply Changes | Apply Changes routine to commit the changes to the nfuse.conf file.

Configuring Server-Side Firewall   In the Server-Side Firewall section of the Web Interface Administration console, you can configure Web Interface to include the firewall IP address in the .ICA files. Depending upon how you have configured your firewall and your MetaFrame servers, you can use the Server-Side Firewall Settings page to configure Web Interface. The following types of addressing are supported within Web Interface:

▼ **Normal addressing**   The IP address given to the client is the actual address of the MetaFrame server.

■ **Network address translation**   Some firewalls use IP address translation to convert private (internal) IP addresses into public (external) IP addresses. If you are using a firewall with network address translation enabled and you have configured your MetaFrame server(s) for this feature, you need to configure the Web Interface to supply the appropriate IP address, depending upon whether clients connect from inside or outside the firewall.

▲   **Port address translation**   You can define mappings from internal MetaFrame
IP addresses to external IP addresses and ports. Using this feature, you can
route traffic to internal MetaFrame servers through a single external IP address.

From the Server-Side Firewall Settings page, the sections that can be configured by
the administrator are

▼   Default address translation setting

■   Specific address translation settings

■   MetaFrame server address translation map (for all clients using translated
address)

▲   Secure Gateway for MetaFrame (for all clients using Secure Gateway)

To help decipher these firewall interaction options, we will use our case study CME
again. CME's secure deployment places the Web Interface server in their DMZ. CME's
network administrators have chosen not to support Network Address Translation (NAT)
from their internal network into the DMZ. This dramatically simplifies the deployment
since the Citrix servers will communicate directly to the Web Interface server on their native LAN IP addresses. Additionally, since Secure Gateway will be used, there is no need
to specify alternative addresses within the configurations of the MetaFrame XP servers.
With a configuration like CME's, the only setting that requires further discussion is the
Secure Gateway for MetaFrame option. Detailed instructions for Secure Gateway configuration settings are covered later in this chapter in the "Step-by-Step Instructions for Installing and Configuring MetaFrame Secure Gateway" section.

Web Interface ICA Client Settings

The Client Settings portion of the Web Interface Administration page allows configuration of the ICA Client firewall settings, client proxy settings, client download settings,
and ICA Client customization settings.

Configuring Client-Side Firewall Settings on the Web Interface Server   If a proxy server firewall
is in place between the ICA client and the Web Interface server, you can specify whether clients must communicate with the MetaFrame server via the proxy server.
From the Client-Side Firewall Settings page, you can

▼   **Configure Default Proxy Setting**   Specify default proxy rules for clients,
or specify that proxy behavior is controlled by the ICA Client.

▲   **Configure Individual Proxy Settings**   Configure exceptions to the default
behavior by associating client addresses or partial addresses with a particular
proxy server address.

Configuring Default Proxy Settings   If a proxy server is used at the client side of your Web Interface installation, you can set default proxy rules for clients. Alternatively, you can specify that the proxy behavior is controlled by the ICA Clients. For most installations, the default value of *Auto* (Client autodetects proxy settings) provides the greatest interoperability with the variety of networks that the ICA Client runs behind, while requiring the least amount of client-side configuration. In our CME case study, their Secure Gateway deployment utilizes this Auto setting to improve the ICA client deployment choices while minimizing the need to have remote administrators make changes to their proxy server or firewall settings.

To configure the default proxy settings, click the Client-Side Firewall link. For most cases, keep the default Auto choice. The other choices are Client, None, and Use Explicit Mapping.

Configuring Individual Proxy Settings on the Web Interface Server   In the event that the default Auto setting was not chosen, the Client-Side Firewall settings page provides a place to configure exceptions to the default proxy server behavior. To do this, associate client addresses or partial addresses with a particular proxy server address.

NOTE: If web browsers connect to Web Interface through a proxy server or firewall that hides the client's IP address, the *Client address prefix* must specify the client address, as Web Interface sees it. If a web browser connects through a proxy, specify the external address of the proxy in the Client address prefix. This does not apply to Program Neighborhood Agent users.

Deploying ICA Clients with Web Interface   As discussed in previous chapters, Web Interface is an excellent tool for deploying and upgrading the ICA Client. In the ICA Client deployment page, the following actions can be accomplished in order to configure and customize the deployment of ICA Clients:

▼ **Automatically deploy the ICA Win32 Web Client**   Configure the Web Interface to automatically deploy the ICA Win32 Web Client installation file.

■ **Specify how applications are launched and embedded**   Control whether applications are launched from, or embedded into, HTML web pages.

▲ **Customize ICA Java Client deployment**   Specify the components included in the ICA Java Client deployment, or allow users to select the components that they require.

The ICA Client Deployment page of the Web Interface Administration tool provides for easy deployment and installation of the appropriate ICA Clients on client devices. Web Interface detects the user's client operating system and web browser type, then displays a link to download the appropriate ICA Client installation file. Chapter 14 identifies the differences in ICA Clients and discusses how to choose which one to use. See Table 14-1 for more information.

NOTE: To use ICA Client installation, the server running the Web Interface must contain the appropriate ICA Client installation files. Administrators should periodically (monthly) check for updates on Citrix's web site and update the Web Interface ICA Client directory (the default English directory is in %webroot%/Citrix/ICAWEB/en/).

To configure ICA Client installation, click ICA Client Deployment in the left menu. Under Client Download Setting, select either Auto, Yes, or No. The default setting is Auto, which is appropriate for most environments, as it will present to the user (via the Web Interface message center) a link to install the appropriate version of the ICA Client, based on the client operating system. If Yes is chosen, the user will always be presented with the option to install the ICA Client, which can be confusing to end users.

Also available in the Client download setting dialog box is a check box labeled Enable Automatic Download Of ICA Win32 Web Client. The advantage to enabling this feature is that, if Web Interface detects an older version of the ICA Web Client, it will allow the client to be upgraded to the latest installed version on the Web Interface server.

NOTE: To use the automatic download feature on Windows 2000 Professional clients or other locked-down workstations, users must have administrative rights on the client device, or the ActiveX control must be registered in Active Directory. See Chapter 15 for more details.

Specifying How Applications Are Launched and Embedded Web Interface allows administrators to configure how ICA published applications are launched from a web browser. The applications can either be launched as a new seamless window or embedded in the body of the web browser. The default behavior of Web Interface is to launch a new ICA seamless session window. The advantage of this behavior is that it will support multiple simultaneous ICA applications running on a user's desktop. In some instances, the web browser may be too locked down to support launching a new window (Internet Explorer in kiosk mode, for example), or an administrator may prefer to embed an application to provide users the perception of a "webified" application. In both of these scenarios, the embedded choice is appropriate.

The choice of whether applications are launched from or embedded into HTML pages is configured using the ICA Client Deployment page.

To specify how applications are launched and embedded, click on the ICA Client deployment link in the left menu. Under Embedded applications, select one of the following:

▼ **No** Choosing this option launches applications in a separate window on the local desktop. An ICA Client must be installed on the client device. If an ICA Client is not present, you can deploy ICA Clients on your users' devices using web-based ICA Client installation.

■ **Yes** This option embeds applications into web pages. Specify the ICA Client that will be used to launch the embedded application.

- **Auto** This option automatically detects the user's client device and web browser and deploys the appropriate ICA Client. If a Windows platform is detected, the ICA Win32 Web Client or Netscape plug-in is deployed, depending on the user's web browser. The Web Interface deploys the Java Client if it detects that the user is not on a Windows platform, or if it is unable to detect the user's client device and web browser.

- **Java Client** Selection of this option forces deployment of the ICA Java Client, regardless of the user's platform. The ICA Java Client can be configured to be a small download, so this option works well for users on low bandwidth connections or on devices with high levels of security that limit the install of additional software.

▲ **User decides** This selection lets users decide how to launch their applications. When this option is enabled, users can choose how their applications are launched in their Settings page. If the check box labeled By Default Launch Applications As Embedded Applications is selected, then applications are embedded into web pages by default. There will be two options to specify the ICA Client that will be used to launch the embedded application.

  - **Auto** This option automatically detects the user's client device and web browser and deploys the appropriate ICA Client.

  - **Java Client** Select this to force deployment of the ICA Java Client, regardless of the user's platform.

NOTE: If this check box is left unselected, applications will launch in a separate window on the local desktop by default.

If the Java ICA Client will be used, it can be configured in the Java Client Settings section of the ICA Client Deployment page of the Web Interface Administration site.

The size of the ICA Java Client download is determined by the packages included in the download. The fewer packages selected, the smaller the download (the download can be as small as 300K). To limit the size of the download for users on low bandwidth connections, deploy only a minimum set of components. Alternatively, administrators can enable users to control which components are required.

The following is a descriptive list of the ICA Java Client packages, which can be loaded from the Java Client Settings dialog box:

▼ **Audio** This package enables applications running on the MetaFrame server to play sounds through a sound device installed on the client computer.

■ **Clipboard** This enables users to copy text and graphics between web server applications and applications running locally on the client device.

■ **Legacy server support**   This package will allow users to connect to servers running MetaFrame XP Server for Windows with earlier Feature Releases of MetaFrame XP and MetaFrame for UNIX.

■ **Local text echo**   This option accelerates the display of the input text on the client device.

■ **SSL/TLS**   Secures communication using Secure Sockets Layer (SSL) and TLS (Transport Layer Security). SSL/TLS provides server authentication, encryption of the data stream, and message integrity checks.

■ **Encryption**   Selecting this package provides strong encryption to increase the privacy of ICA connections.

■ **Client drive mapping**   Enables users to access their local drives from within an ICA session. When a user connects to the MetaFrame server, their client drives are automatically mounted, such as floppy disks, network drives, and CD-ROM drives. Users can access their locally stored files, work with them during their ICA sessions, and save them again on a local drive or on a drive on the MetaFrame server. To enable this setting, users must also configure client drive mapping in the ICA Java Client Settings dialog box. See the *Citrix ICA Java Client Administrator's Guide* for more information.

■ **Printer mapping**   This selection enables users to print to their local or network printers from an ICA session.

▲ **Configuration UI**   This enables the ICA Java Client Settings page. This web page can be used to configure the ICA Java Client.

In addition to the preceding package options, the administrator may allow users to control which Java Client packages are enabled. To enable this feature, select the Allow User To Choose Packages check box.

The final selection in the Java Client Settings dialog box provides support for private Certificate Authorities. If you have configured Secure Gateway or the Citrix SSL Relay service with a server certificate obtained from a private CA (such as Microsoft Certificate Services), select Use Private Certificate Authority. Enter the filename for the certificate in the Root Certificate File Name field. The certificate must be located in the same directory on the web server as the Java Client packages (such as /Citrix/ICAWEB/en/icajava on IIS).

NOTE: When enabling this option, Citrix recommends that you configure the web server to use SSL/TLS connections in order to encrypt the transfer of the root certificate with the Java Client.

REMEMBER: After all the configurations have been made, perform the Save | Apply Changes | Apply Changes routine to commit the changes to the Web Interface nfuse.conf file.

Controlling ICA Customization of the Web Interface Site   The final section of the Web Interface Administration tool, ICA Customization, allows administrators to control whether users can override the default published application settings for Window size, Window color, and Audio quality.

User-configured settings are stored as cookies on the client device. These settings are remembered for all future applications launched via the Web Interface from that device. Depending on the operating system and web browser used, these cookies may be specific to each user or all users will have the same settings. Customized settings made by guest users (logged in using the Guest User option) are not saved to the client device. These settings are local to the user's machine and will not follow a user from PC to PC.

REMEMBER: After all the configurations have been made, perform the Save | Apply Changes | Apply Changes routine to commit the changes to the Web Interface nfuse.conf file.

Customizing the Text on the Web Interface Web Site

Web Interface for MetaFrame may be "branded" with custom text and graphics to customize the default web site. The following section describes how to make subtle changes that customize the site to match your organization. Figure 16-5 shows an example of a custom Web Interface application list page.

Customizing the Text on the Web Interface Default Web Site   Customization of the text found on the Web Interface web pages is done through a single file, the nfuse.txt file located in the default Web Interface directory (C:\program files\Citrix\NFuse\).

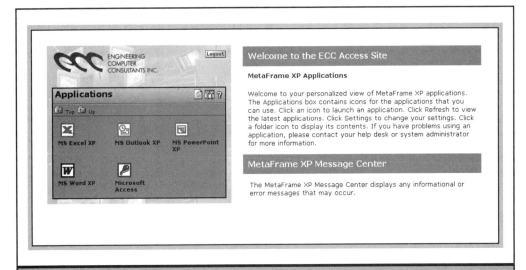

Figure 16-5.   A custom Web Interface page showing the contents of a Microsoft folder

In order to change the text on the Web Interface screens, change the text in the referenced sections (LoginTitle, Welcome, PleaseLogin, for example).

After making changes to the nfuse.txt file, restart the IIS services:

1. Click Start | Run and type **iisreset**. Click OK.
2. Verify that all the necessary services have started.

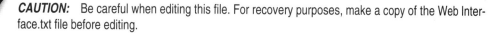

CAUTION: Be careful when editing this file. For recovery purposes, make a copy of the Web Interface.txt file before editing.

Customizing the Graphics on the Web Interface Default Web Site   Customizing graphics is more complex than customizing the text due to the nature of ASP pages. However, an administrator may substitute their own custom graphics and edit the associated .inc files to point to the new graphic files.

The graphics files are located in the \Citrix\MetaFrameXP\site\media folder under the web root of the default Web Interface web site. Two commonly modified graphics files and their associated reference files are

▼   **citrix.jpg**   This graphic is the Citrix logo found on the button on the right-hand side of the default web site. To change this logo, first place a copy of your company's logo in the aforementioned directory. Then edit the messagecenter.inc file in the Citrix\MetaFrameXP\site\include directory and replace it with the name and location of your logo.

▲   **nfusehead.gif**   This graphic is the Web Interface banner found over the login box and list of enumerated applications. To change this logo, first place a copy of your company's logo in the aforementioned directory. Then edit the layout.inc file in the Citrix\MetaFrameXP\site\include directory and replace it with the name and location of your logo.

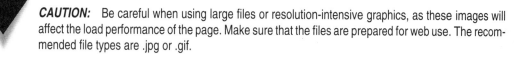

CAUTION: Be careful when using large files or resolution-intensive graphics, as these images will affect the load performance of the page. Make sure that the files are prepared for web use. The recommended file types are .jpg or .gif.

About Web Interface Extension Mode

Web Interface Extension, which is only supported in the MetaFrame XPe version, gives users the ability to access published applications from multiple MetaFrame XPe server farms located in separate administrative domains. Web Interface Extension provides users unified access to these typically disparate published application sets. This process, called *aggregation*, greatly simplifies user access to applications in organizations with multiple server farms.

NOTE: Enterprise Services for NFuse and NFuse Classic have been integrated into MetaFrame XPe. Enterprise Services for NFuse is now called Web Interface Extension for MetaFrame XP.

Configuring Web Interface Extension Mode To use Web Interface Extension, configure the Web Interface server to communicate with the MetaFrame XPe server running Web Interface Extension. This is a global setting that causes Web Interface to communicate with a server running Web Interface Extension, rather than with MetaFrame servers running the Citrix XML Service.

To configure Web Interface Extension mode, click Mode in the left menu, and select the Enable The Web Interface Extension check box. To allow desktop credential Passthrough and smart card authentication between Web Interface and the Web Interface Extension, type a password in the Password For Authenticating To The Web Interface Extension field. Web Interface Extension checks this password to authenticate the server running Web Interface.

NOTE: In addition to these basic Web Interface steps, there are myriad other configuration considerations required to support Web Interface Extension mode. Please refer to the *Web Interface Extension for MetaFrame XP Administrator's Guide* for complete details on configuring Web Interface Extension mode.

Step-by-Step Instructions for Installing *STA*

STA is an ISAPI DLL that is loaded and called by Internet Information Services (IIS) when a request for a ticket is received from Web Interface. The primary purpose of the STA is to generate and validate tickets for access to MetaFrame published applications. The recommended deployment is on a dedicated server installed in the secure network alongside the MetaFrame XP server farm. Figure 16-1, shown earlier in this chapter, depicts CME's deployment of the STA.

Installing STA

To install STA, perform the following tasks:

1. Make sure the server you are using for STA installation has IIS 5.0 or greater installed, configured, and running. If this is a Windows 2003 Web Edition server, the IIS version will be 6.0.

2. On the STA server, insert the Citrix MetaFrame XP Feature Release 3 Components CD-ROM. The Components menu will appear.

3. Click the Secure Gateway button.

4. Click Secure Ticket Authority to start the installation program. Follow the standard installation steps. During the installation folder selection screen, select an appropriate destination folder. This folder *must* be the IIS scripts folder. By default, this will be C:\inetpub\scripts. If you have altered the default location for the scripts, browse to the correct location.

Configuring STA

When installation of the software is complete, the STA Configuration tool is launched. The following information needs to be entered to configure STA:

1. Select Typical or Advanced Configuration. Our recommendation is to select the Advanced Install option to specify all the configuration values required for STA operation. Click Next.

2. Specify configuration values for STA.

   ■ **STA ID**   This is a unique identification string for the STA server. Enter a maximum of 16 alphanumeric characters, uppercase only. Spaces, punctuation, and special characters are not allowed.

   ■ **Ticket Timeout**   Specifies the lifetime (in milliseconds) of a ticket issued by the STA. A value of 0 means that the ticket will never expire. The default value for Ticket Timeout is 100000 ms (100 seconds).

   ■ **Maximum Tickets**   This option specifies the maximum number of valid tickets that an STA can be issued at any given point in time. The default value for Maximum Tickets is 100000.

3. To use the new configuration settings, the World Wide Web Publishing Service must be restarted. If you prefer to restart the service manually, clear the Restart The Service check box.

4. Click Finish to exit the configuration utility.

Changing STA's Configuration Settings

To change the configuration settings entered during the install process, run the STA Configuration tool. To run the configuration utility:

1. Click Start | Programs | Citrix | Secure Gateway | Secure Ticket Authority Configuration.

2. Make the necessary changes and click Finish to exit the utility.

NOTE: Restart the World Wide Web Publishing Service to allow configuration changes to take effect.

Step-by-Step Instructions for Installing and Configuring MetaFrame Secure Gateway

Secure Gateway acts as an SSL gateway for ICA network traffic that services requests between the ICA Client and the MetaFrame XP Server using a Windows service that must run on a Windows 2000 or 2003 server. For our case study, CME Corp, we are using a single DMZ deployment. The Secure Gateway and Web Interface components will be installed on the same machine. The following step-by-step instructions show how to implement this configuration.

Installing MetaFrame Secure Gateway

Log in as an administrator to the Web Interface/Secure Gateway server (installed in the DMZ) and perform the following tasks:

1. Insert the Citrix components CD-ROM or download the image file and select the Secure Gateway Service option.

2. For the Installation mode, select Secure Gateway Service and for the Deployment scenario choose MetaFrame XP Server Only, then proceed to the installation.

3. Install the Secure Gateway Service, Management Console, and Diagnostic tools. The default selected items are appropriate for a standard secure deployment.

Configuring the MetaFrame Secure Gateway

After installation of the Secure Gateway Service is complete, the Secure Gateway Service Configuration tool is launched. The following configuration is a typical best practices install and accommodates the needs specific to our case study, CME Corp.

1. At the configuration prompt, the administrator can choose either a Typical or Advanced configuration. We recommend an Advanced configuration to properly set Secure Gateway Service parameters such as security strengths and STA servers.

2. At the Certificate Configuration screen, select the server certificate to be used by the Secure Gateway Service. Since only one certificate can be bound to the Secure Gateway Service, ensure that the proper certificate is selected by using the View button.

3. In the Select Secure Protocol And Select Cipher Suite section, the default setting is acceptable for most commercial deployments. Check with your organization's security policy for a definitive answer.

4. An additional configuration screen allows for customization of the IP addresses and ports that the Secure Gateway server listens on for incoming client connections. The Monitor All IP Addresses check box forces the Secure Gateway to listen for client connections on all available IP addresses on this server. In the TCP port field, enter a listener port number. The Secure Gateway listens for client connections on the port specified for all available IP addresses on the server. The default TCP port, and the one we will be using, is 443.

5. Custom connection settings can be configured on the Secure Gateway server as well. These options include No Outbound Traffic Restrictions, Use The Secure Gateway Proxy, and Use An Access Control List (ACL). In a typical DMZ install, there is no need to configure these options, so the default value of No Outbound Traffic Restrictions is appropriate.

6. The (STA) configuration screen is an important component of the Secure Gateway installation. Add the FQDN of the STA and appropriately set its communication protocol. We recommend securing the communication protocol by enabling the Secured With HTTPS check box. If multiple STA servers have been deployed to support redundancy, these can be configured here but the administrator needs to ensure this matches the list of STAs configured during the Web Interface install.

7. The Connection Parameters setting allows the administrator to configure Connection Timeout (sec), Cookie Cache Timeout (sec), and Connection Limits. In most cases, the default settings are appropriate. We recommend you baseline the server during initial testing of the deployment and then modify these values to best represent your organization's deployment needs.

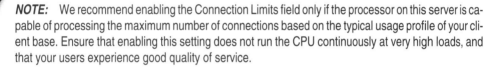

NOTE: We recommend enabling the Connection Limits field only if the processor on this server is capable of processing the maximum number of connections based on the typical usage profile of your client base. Ensure that enabling this setting does not run the CPU continuously at very high loads, and that your users experience good quality of service.

8. Logging Exclusions lists the IP addresses of network devices (load balancers, for example) that generate extraneous log information you may want to exclude from the Secure Gateway event log. Unless such devices are included in the deployment network, there is typically no need to enter any Logging Exclusions and the default of none is acceptable.

9. Under Logging Parameters, select the appropriate logging level for the environment. Since Secure Gateway writes to its own event log section, we recommend you choose the All Events Including Informational logging option during the initial deployment to help with troubleshooting and then select the Error And Fatal Events option once the deployment normalizes.

10. Under the Web Interface configuration section, enter information about the server running Web Interface and its appropriate location. For CME, we installed Web Interface on the same machine as Gateway Services. As a result, we must choose the Installed On This Computer option and input **443** in the TCP Port field to secure the communications between Web Interface and Secure Gateway.

Changing Secure Gateway Configuration Settings

To change configuration settings entered during the install process, run the Secure Gateway Service Configuration tool. Stop the Secure Gateway Service before making changes to its configuration. To run the configuration utility:

▼ Click Start | Programs | Citrix | Secure Gateway | Secure Gateway Service Configuration. Make the necessary changes. Changes made do not take effect until the service is restarted. The program restarts the service automatically; however, if you prefer to do this manually, clear the Start Secure Gateway Service check box. Click Finish to exit the utility.

Configuring the Web Interface Server to Support Secure Gateway

Now that the Secure Gateway components are configured, Web Interface must be configured to properly support the Secure Gateway installation. Web Interface provides the Web front-end that ICA Client users connect to, and supports the ticketing and authentication functions of Secure Gateway. The following list details how to configure Web Interface to utilize Citrix Secure Gateway.

1. From the Web Interface/Secure Gateway server, open the Web Interface Web Administrator (http://localhost/citrix/metaframexp/wiadmin).

2. Click the Server-Side Firewall link.

3. The Server-Side Firewall settings page is presented. Click the Secure Gateway for MetaFrame radio button in the Default Address Translation Setting section to set Secure Gateway as the default method for ICA session traffic.

4. One of the features introduced in Web Interface allows the specification of specific address translation settings per IP network. If you would like to set a specific IP network to utilize a different address translation than the default, enter the IP network number in the Client Address Prefix text box, select the Address Translation Option radio button, and click Add.

5. Scroll down to the Secure Gateway for MetaFrame section of the page.

6. Enter the FQDN address of the server running the Secure Gateway component in the Address (FQDN) text box.

7. Enter the port the Secure Gateway component is listening on in the Port text box.

8. If you have a firewall configured to perform network address translation between the Secure Gateway box and the MetaFrame server, then check the Use Alternate Addresses Of MetaFrame Servers check box.

9. In the Secure Ticket Authorities URL text box, enter the FQDN name of the server running the STA component in place of <*server*> and click the Add button.

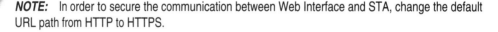

NOTE: In order to secure the communication between Web Interface and STA, change the default URL path from HTTP to HTTPS.

10. Repeat Step 9 in order to add multiple STA servers for high availability. If you will be using multiple STAs we recommend checking the Use The Secure Ticket Authority List For Load Balancing check box to enable round-robin load balancing.

11. Click Save when finished.

12. Click the Apply Changes button to commit the changes.

The Secure Gateway implementation is now complete.

New Secure Gateway Administrative Tools

Two additional tools were added to the Secure Gateway 2.0 deployment: Secure Gateway Diagnostics and Secure Gateway Management Console. After the initial install of both Web Interface and Secure Gateway is complete, run the Diagnostic tool before performing any user testing. This utility will verify that all setup and configurations are not only installed but also working properly with their back-end systems (this will test all the way down to Certificate level).

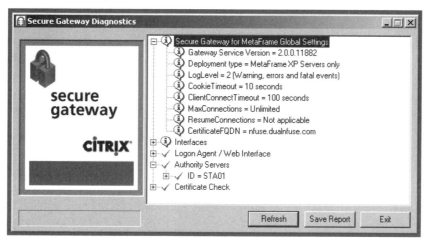

The Management Console is a useful utility to access common system administration tools (such as the event viewer). It is also useful for accessing specific information and statistics regarding the Secure Gateway services, such as number of active connections and performance.

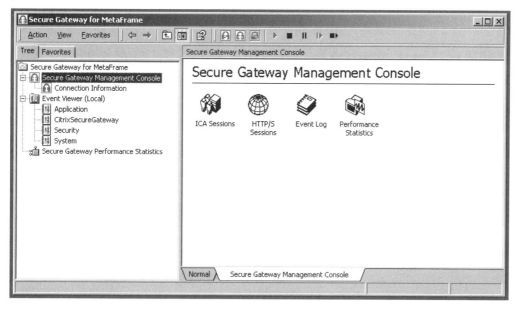

MetaFrame Secure Access Manager

As discussed earlier in this chapter, Web Interface leveraging Secure Gateway for MetaFrame provides a powerful implementation tool for user communities to securely access your Citrix MetaFrame server farm. With that said, there may be business cases or corporate mandates that dictate access to discrete applications or processes that are not necessarily available from the MetaFrame farm. Citrix developed an offering to fulfill this growing need in early 2000 by introducing their first release of a non-MetaFrame ICA server access solution: NFuse Elite.

NFuse Elite was based on Sequoia System's portal technology, which opened the door for Citrix to broaden their product offering beyond the Multi User NT/2000 architecture. After initial successful deployments of this environment and market analysis, Citrix learned from its experiences and listened to their customers/channel partners and integrated a new offering. This offering culminated in 2003 with the release of MetaFrame Secure Access Manager 2.0 (MSAM). This solution has provided many changes over the previous release, including the following noteworthy features:

▼ Secure access for remote users utilizing the same Secure Gateway for MetaFrame service described earlier.

■ Advanced indexing services, including file systems and remote web servers, via Index Server for MetaFrame.

■ Integrative support with multiple MetaFrame ICA server farms, which aggregates all access services to one easy-to-use, secure web interface.

■ Improved and updated Content Delivery Agents (CDAs) and development tools (SDKs) for wider integration with corporate data systems.

▲ International compatibility via single-byte support for non-English characters associated with Western European languages and compiled installation code for German and Spanish operating systems.

MSAM vs. MetaFrame ICA

Utilizing Citrix's years of experience in providing scalable, enterprise solutions to end-user applications, it is no surprise when examining the MSAM deployment environment that it mimics key concepts developed in the MetaFrame ICA realm. Table 16-1 shows some of the similarities between the environments.

So, with all these similarities, what makes MSAM unique? Its uniqueness resides in the concept of creating a very specific access center, which not only allows users to utilize resources from a MetaFrame server farm but also discretely provides a web-based interface into the organization's information stores. MSAM goes beyond the standard, development-intensive application of mining information from a database and providing a web look and feel to view it. Citrix has developed a standard programmatical interface tool called Content Delivery Agents (CDAs) to allow the preprogramming of connectivity between applications and a web page, and has initiated the creation of several hundred

MetaFrame ICA Environment	MetaFrame Secure Access Environment
MetaFrame XP application servers are situated in a load-balanced farm for increased scalability and data resumption of ICA user sessions.	Agent servers are arranged in a load-balanced environment to increase processing performance and data resumption of CDA data presentation.
Centralized state tracking of farm data and metrics is stored in the MetaFrame Data Store.	Agent server load information, licensing and session states are centralized to a master State Server.
MetaFrame XP provides a secure browser interface for intuitive access to Published Applications utilizing Secure Gateway and STA services, protected with SSL encryption.	Secure SSL deployment enables Internet access to the Access Center's Content Delivery Agents (CDA) utilizing Secure Gateway, Login Agent services, and STA.
MetaFrame Web Interface provides a user-customizable/administratively controlled web interface.	MSAM provides flexible user configuration and administration of the access center and available CDAs.
MetaFrame XP web and database components are simple to install and administer.	MSAM provides easy-to-install web and database components.
MetaFrame XP leverages common user group management systems (MS Active Directory, Novell E-directory, and so on) to provide access-specific Published Applications.	MSAM leverages common user group management systems (MS Active Directory, Novell E-directory, and so on) to provide access-specific CDA, and pages in the Access center.

Table 16-1. Similarities of ICA and MSAM Environments

CDAs for more popular applications and interfaces. With Content Delivery Agents, it is possible to process data on an Agent server farm and deliver an interactive experience to the end user without significant programming overhead.

The CDA becomes the focus of the MSAM deployment, just as installing and publishing applications do in the MetaFrame XP environment. One advantage is that since the administrator is centrally creating and deploying specific CDAs to access only the content (a subset of the application) a user needs to interact with, there is not the vast amount of administrative overhead required to "lock down" a Terminal Server deployment. The ability to provide data and content to a user more efficiently ultimately leads to time and money savings. An example of this is the following: Under a typical MetaFrame XP application deployment, an administrator installs the full client of the document management system and then publishes access to an end user or group. Each time a user accesses their data from within the application, it may take five to ten menu picks and a lot of user input to access the data required. Under the MSAM deployment scenario, that same administrator would instead configure a CDA and add it to the users' MSAM Access Center, which automatically drills down and pulls the data they need to interact with. Although there may be some programming required to create the interface (depending on whether a CDA already exists), the objective is to streamline user access and use of applications, content, and, ultimately, the data.

One other concept heavily emphasized by MSAM (though administratively controllable, of course) is the capability of the end user to modify the look and feel of their web-based access center. This is very similar in concept to a My Yahoo or MSN Passport–based site over the public Internet. These sites allow a user to log on to what is typically a standard public site and be presented with a personalized view of the content with the ability to customize and optimize the web experience. MSAM, unlike these public sites, does not use local cached credentials or settings to store these optimizations. This allows a user who accesses the data center from various computer resources (such as a business laptop, home machine, or Internet kiosk) to always have access to their customizations, as they are stored in the central MSAM State/Web Server located securely in the company's data center.

CME Case Study of MSAM

The CME deployment architecture requires remote Just In Time (JIT) outsourced manufacturing facilities. To effectively meet this requirement, CME's manufacturing partners require direct, secure, and easy-to-use access to a number of internal systems at CME in order to meet their manufacturing service level agreements and update their project status. For this specific case, we will look at the relationship between Nickel Plastic Parts, Inc. (NPPI) and CME.

NPPI's success has been based on its ability to provide inexpensive, high-quality injection-molded plastic parts specialized for the medical industry. NPPI key technologies involve a propriety processing method of handling raw materials before molding, as well as scrutinized methods of verifying that the parts are accurate according to engineering requirements and are sanitized for use in operating rooms. CME has experienced a long-standing relationship with NPPI, but in recent years CME's shift to JIT manufacturing processes has caused some production scheduling snags. In order to improve the success of their JIT processes, CME mandated that all its outsourced manufacturing partners, including NPPI, utilize an access solution deployed by the CME IT department to review order and forecasting data. Not only will the partner be responsible for monitoring this data and acting on it, but they will have access to overall product shipment schedules as well as the latest engineering and manufacturing requirement documents. This ensures that any late stage changes to design requirements are accounted for.

CME already has established deployments of internally developed manufacturing systems (running from Oracle Database Servers) as well as Documentum for document management and revision control of their procedures and manufacturing specification sheets. In order to provide not only real-time access, but also discrete, role-based control of these data sources, CME's IT staff has turned to Citrix's MetaFrame Secure Access Manager (MSAM) as the access center of choice for these data sources. Key features that made MSAM attractive included ease of deploying a standards-based, browser-accessible Web Interface, availability of existing MSAM Content Delivery Agents to their internal systems, as well as the security provided by MSAM's Gateway Services. Figure 16-6 shows a diagram of CME's full secure access deployment with Web Interface, Secure Gateway, and MSAM.

In this deployment, MSAM administrators are able to create an easily managed, role-based, look and feel so that when a partner accesses the MSAM web interface they are presented only with those Content Delivery Agents (CDA) that have authorization to access their portion of the manufacturing requirements and sales forecasting data from Oracle as well as process documentation from Documentum. As an added benefit, CME is also able to provide their partners with additional information on CME's general marketing, such as recent press releases, stock prices, and other pertinent information.

At the core of this deployment is the MSAM CDA. Information in each area of the access center that the user has rights to is provided by a CDA. In this case, there are one or more Oracle CDAs that connect directly to the specific information required by NPPI account managers to fulfill JIT. In addition, there is a CDA programmed to obtain process documents out of Documentum so that NPPI production teams are generating the correct parts based on the latest requirements. Both the Oracle and Documentum CDAs already exist, limiting the amount of custom programming required to build the connectivity.

In order to provide this data securely over the public Internet, without deploying an expensive and complex VPN solution, CME IT staff have opted to implement Secure Gateway services to provide SSL-encrypted data transfers over common HTTPS ports. An additional requirement was to provide the flexibility to support CME's partners' security deployments without modifications. NPPI's IT staff, for example, requires all internal users to pass through their outbound web proxies in order to gain access to Internet resources. Since Secure Gateway has no problem accepting connections from client-side proxy devices, NPPI's IT staff do not have to change their security policies in order to accommodate this solution.

Once the server-side deployment is completed by CME, NPPI users simply connect to this access center using a functional web browser supporting high encryption and the MSAM Gateway Client.

Deployment Requirements for MSAM

This section outlines the following concepts:

▼ Key services required to support the deployment

■ Minimum hardware specifications

■ Typical security requirements for an Internet deployment of MSAM

■ Scaling considerations and growth accommodation

▲ Content Delivery Agent resource sites

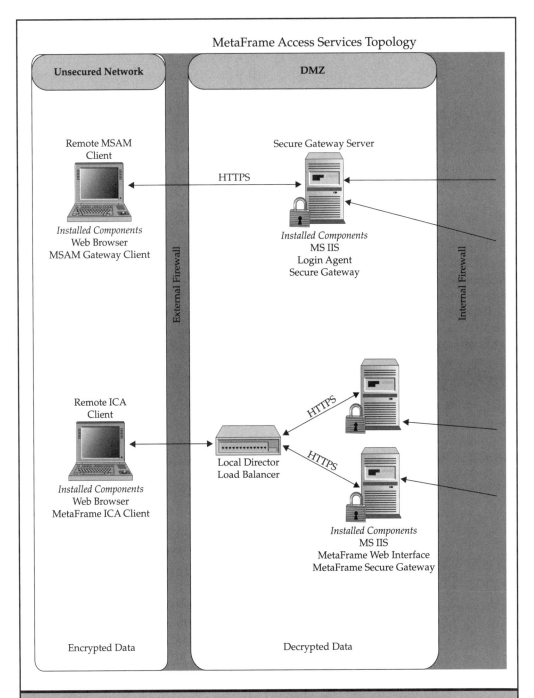

Figure 16-6. CME's full Secure Access Center deployment with Web Interface, Secure Gateway, and MSAM

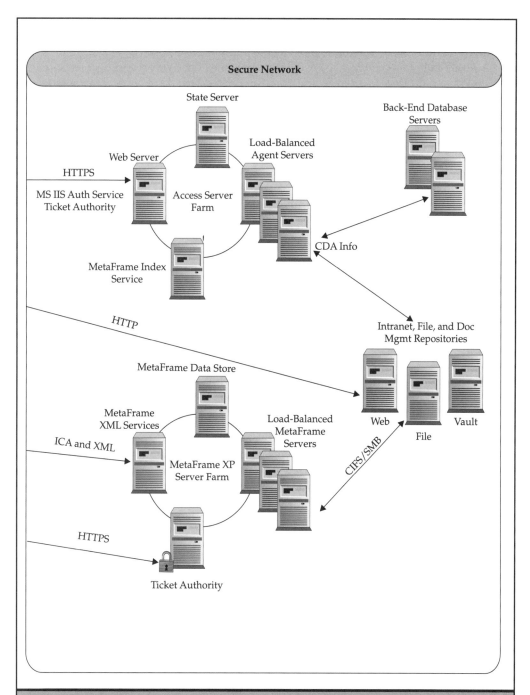

Figure 16-6. CME's full Secure Access Center deployment with Web Interface, Secure Gateway, and MSAM *(continued)*

Key MSAM Services

MSAM, in its most basic Internet-based deployment, has the following components: Secure Access Manager, Web Service extensions, STA, Agent Server, and Secure Gateway for MetaFrame and Login Agent. There are also the additional ancillary components: the user-side MSAM Gateway Client and the Index Server for MetaFrame. Table 16-2 describes the roles associated with each MSAM service.

MSAM Component Service	System Role
Secure Access Manager (SAM)	This is the core of the MSAM deployment. It maintains all information about the Access Center, CDA information, custom user information, licensing, load information, and much more. SAM also requires the existence of a database service to store information. The options are either to use the MS SQL Desktop Engine (provided on the install CD-ROM) or an enterprise Database Service such as Microsoft SQL Server.
Web Server Extensions (WSE)	These extensions are where the CDA information is presented to the user in a web format. WSE installs on MS IIS and is dynamically updated by the SAM. LAN users may access this web site directly to utilize their access center. This is also where Internet user requests are relayed by the Secure Gateway in the DMZ.
Secure Ticket Authority (STA)	The MSAM STA is installed with each Agent Server and maintains proper state information with the SAM. Secure Gateway also will utilize at least one STA for validation of secure Internet connection states.
Agent Server (AS)	Agent Server(s) are the equivalent of Citrix MetaFrame XP farm servers because they generate the bulk of the content/information for end users. In this case, the information processed is data for Content Delivery Agents instead of feature-rich GUI applications.
Secure Gateway for MetaFrame	As in a secure Web Interface deployment, Secure Gateway services enable the encryption of data into SSL packets to be relayed to the end user over HTTPS ports. This is a requirement for Internet deployments.

Table 16-2.   MSAM Services and Their Functions

MSAM Component Service	System Role
Login Agent (LA)	This is in parallel with the Secure Gateway install. LA provides the external MSAM user a web interface. It is able to log the user into the MSAM environment and install any required plug-ins (such as the Gateway Client) and can be secured for HTTPS traffic. This is a requirement for Internet deployments.
MSAM Gateway Client	The MSAM Gateway Client is key to proper Internet deployments and similar to having an ICA Client installed. Its role is to facilitate communications with the MSAM internal environments and act as a tunneling client, which will allow a remote client into LAN-based resources at the data center. For example, if there is a web site CDA that links to an internal data center URL, the Gateway Client enables the remote user to view the contents of that URL by tunneling the web browser requests to the Secure Gateway server, which then links to the internal resource. The MSAM Gateway Client is required for Internet deployments.
Index Server for MetaFrame (IS) (optional)	Index services in general can be critical to simplifying data access. Citrix has provided IS not only to index file servers and their contents, but also to hook into searchable information from any web site and other data stores. Index Server is optional to the install of MSAM but is included free with the product.

Table 16-2.   MSAM Services and Their Functions *(continued)*

NOTE: In a basic configuration, the administrator can combine MetaFrame Secure Access Manager and STA on the first server in the internal secure LAN.

Minimum MSAM Hardware Specifications   This section outlines the minimum server hardware required to deploy MSAM. In effect, as few as three servers (two internal to your data center network and one in its DMZ), can fulfill the requirements. In a later section, we discuss scaling considerations for a more robust deployment.

Component Minimum Requirements for MetaFrame Secure Access Manager

▼ 512MB of physical memory

■ Microsoft Windows 2000/2003 Server Family or later with latest service pack

■ For Windows 2000 Server, Microsoft .NET Framework 1.0 with Service Pack 2 or later

■ Microsoft Data Access Components (MDAC) Version 2.7

■ Internet Information Services (IIS) 5 or later

■ Microsoft SQL Server 2000 with Service Pack 2 or later (or)

■ Microsoft SQL Server 7 with Service Pack 3 or later (or)

■ Microsoft SQL Desktop Edition (MSDE) Service Pack 3 or later

▲ A network interface card (NIC)

Minimum Requirements for STA

▼ 256MB of physical memory.

■ 150MB additional physical memory.

■ A network interface card.

▲ To support secure communication (optional), an installed certificate and installed root path are necessary.

NOTE: The administrator can combine the Secure Gateway and the Logon Agent on the second server. This server is installed in the data center's DMZ for increased security.

Minimum Requirements for MetaFrame Secure Gateway

▼ Microsoft Windows 2000/2003 Server Family or later with latest service packs

■ 256MB RAM

■ 150MB physical memory

■ A network interface card

▲ Internet Information Services 5 or later

Minimum Requirements for Logon Agent

▼ 150MB additional physical memory

■ Installed into IIS service default root

▲ To support secure deployment an IIS-based web certificate

NOTE: Due to system resources, the index server should be installed on a separate server located on the internal LAN.

Minimum Requirements for Index Server for MetaFrame

▼ Microsoft Windows 2000/2003 Server Family or newer with latest service pack

■ Internet Information Services 5 or newer (installed by default on Windows 2000 servers)

■ Microsoft .NET Framework 1.0 with latest service pack

■ 1GB RAM

■ 10GB hard disk storage (30GB recommended)

■ 1GHz Pentium 4 dual processor

▲ A network interface card

Minimum Requirements for the Client Device

▼ Standard PC architecture

■ A network interface card

■ Internet connection

■ Compatible 32-bit Windows operating system

■ Internet Explorer 5.0 (with High Encryption Pack) or later

■ Ability to download and install browser plug-ins (the Gateway Client is deployed through browser plug-ins)

▲ Trusted root certificate path required to connect to the Secure Gateway/Login Agent server

Typical Security Requirements for an Internet Deployment of MSAM

The following security guidelines should be considered when deploying an Internet-accessible MSAM environment:

Firewall Rules

1. *Open appropriate ports.* From the Internet, TCP port 80 and 443 inbound access to the Secure Gateway/Login Agent server in the DMZ must be configured.

2. *Configure outbound and inbound access.* From the Secure Gateway /Logon Agent server in the DMZ, inbound access to STA/SAM server on port 443 and ports to any internal resource server (such as Citrix or web servers) that a CDA may call directly should be configured.

Additional Requirements

1. *Configure Address translation rules.* Proper Network Address Translation rules from internal LAN to DMZ access, and from the DMZ to the Internet, must be configured and tested.

2. *Update DNS tables.* Update forward and reverse looks for both internal and Internet DNS servers. Secure Gateway/Logon Agent server must have its FQDN registered with both internal and Internet-based DNS servers. The STA server needs only to have its FQDN registered with internal DNS servers.

3. *Install Server Certificates.* In order to properly accommodate SSL communications, a verifiable web type certificate must be bound to the Secure Gateway/Logon Agent server and a separate certificate installed on the STA. In most cases, we recommend using a standard Internet deployed certificate (for instance, Verisign, Thawte, and so on) for the Secure Gateway/Logon Agent and then using an internally generated certificate for the STA.

4. *Configure Root Certificate paths.* Users must have the root path of the Secure Gateway/Logon Agent installed on their clients (this is one of the reasons to purchase an Internet-based certificate as opposed to having to manually deploy the root CA path to each client who wishes to connect). The Secure Gateway/Logon Agent must have the root path for the certificate issued to the STA installed in its system registry in order to properly function.

Environment Scaling Considerations for MSAM

In the previous sections, we outlined what it takes to get the minimum servers implemented in order to support a functional MSAM environment. As with many minimum requirement documents, we have not accounted for "real world" enterprise deployments, where end-user performance and high availability are required. Because of the modular nature of MSAM, an administrator has the option of increasing the deployment footprint in stages or all at once depending on the initial number of users and the type of service required. The following list outlines some of the areas to consider when designing MSAM for an enterprise deployment.

1. Increase the number of Access Servers, as well as disable this responsibility on the primary Secure Access Manager machine.

   This is similar in concept to the N+1 rule of thumb in MetaFrame XP server deployments. By increasing the number of Access Servers, you not only provide more processing power to your farm, but you also increase its availability due to server redundancy.

2. Utilize an enterprise database for your state information.

   By utilizing an enterprise database service, such as MS SQL Server, instead of MS SQL Desktop Engine, performance and security are greatly improved.

For large-scale deployments, consider clustering the back-end database servers for increased availability.

3. Implement a Web/SSL load balancer for web extensions and Secure Gateway.

   This is the most reliable way of increasing availability of Internet access to the Secure Gateway/Logon Agent servers. Load Balancers have the ability to distribute the Secure Gateway process, thus eliminating a bottleneck in the event of high user loads (300–500 plus simultaneous connections).

NOTE: Do not enable any type of SSL acceleration or caching as this will degrade the end-user experience due to the dynamic nature of the data processed.

Common Content Delivery Agent Resource Sites

Since content delivery agents (CDAs) are key to a successful deployment of MSAM, it is worth noting just a few of the many available preprogrammed content delivery agent resources.

▼ **Citrix product CDs**   All CDAs available at the time of product release are included on your product CD.

■ **Citrix web site**   You can download new and updated CDAs from the Citrix web site. The main site for information about MetaFrame Secure Access Manager, including information about CDAs and software development kits (SDKs), is www.citrix.com/secureaccess.

■ **Citrix customer portal**   Registered customers can download CDAs from www.citrix.com/mycitrix.

■ **Citrix Developer Network**   The Citrix Developer Network (CDN) is an open enrollment membership program that provides access to developer toolkits, technical information, and test programs for software and hardware vendors, system integrators, licensees, and corporate developers who incorporate Citrix computing solutions into their products. For more information, go to www.citrix.com/cdn.

▲ **Microsoft web part resources**   There are a number of web part areas on the Microsoft web site, but this is a good address to get you headed in the right direction: www.microsoft.com/sharepoint/server/downloads/webparts/introduction.asp.

CAUTION: Neither Citrix nor the authors of this book have fully tested the large variety of prewritten CDA programs available. Always fully review and understand the impacts of any third-party code under consideration and always implement and thoroughly test it before using it in a production environment.

CHAPTER 17

Network Configuration

This chapter applies the design principles from Part II of the book to the process of provisioning and implementing an Enterprise network infrastructure for the case study environment (CME Corp). Specifying the detailed configuration steps for every device in the network would require a book of its own: the focus is on those components that have a direct bearing on Enterprise SBC architecture performance. Emphasis is placed on LAN/WAN transport hardware, essential security parameters to allow Citrix traffic to traverse the network, and bandwidth management relevant to Citrix traffic flows.

To keep things in perspective, network hardware manufacturers tout their products as "five 9s" for reliability (99.999 percent reliable)—but they assume power availability is a perfect 100 percent. Software vendors (including Microsoft and Citrix) cite "five 9s" for availability of their solutions, but again assume the network is 100 percent available. For CME's requirements, whether Enterprise SBC or traditional Client-Server, the network design must come as close as technically and financially possible to that perfect "100-percent" world.

To reiterate from Chapter 6, network design is interdependent on all other infrastructure components—from server services such as DNS and WINS, to IP addressing schemes, to node naming and management practices. The "implementer" must view the Enterprise implementation of server-based computing "wholistically" to ensure success.

NETWORK REQUIREMENTS DEFINITION

Defining the exact requirements (in terms of network hardware and network bandwidth) provides the key component of design and implementation. Referring to the CME case study and Figure 10-1, later in the chapter, WAN requirements are calculated first.

WAN Requirements

Based on known values (site role, location, available connectivity, use load, and so on) the CME network designers reviewed existing resources and developed WAN bandwidth and hardware requirements per site.

Current WAN Hardware

The CME infrastructure currently has a wide range of low-end, multivendor devices, many of which are somewhat antiquated. Sites are connected to CME Corp via high-cost, low-bandwidth dedicated frame relay virtual circuits carried on multiple T1 facilities. CME Corp needs to standardize devices and configurations as much as possible to ensure interoperability and simplify network management and configuration control. After analyzing the inventory, designers determined that the resources in Table 17-1 could be reused. The exact sequence of replacement and redeployment must be included on the master project timeline.

WAN Hardware	Current Site	Quantity	Projected Status	Future Use
Cisco 1760 Router	Atlanta, GA	1	Keep	Atlanta, GA
	Detroit, MI	1	Keep	Detroit, MI
	Helena, MT	1	Keep	Helena, MT
	Miami, FL	1	Keep	Miami, FL
	Minneapolis, MN	1	Keep	Minneapolis, MN
	New Orleans, LA	1	Keep	Salt Lake City, UT
	Salt Lake City, UT	1	Keep	Salt Lake City, UT
	San Antonio, TX	1	Keep	San Antonio, TX
	Winnipeg, MB	1	Keep	Winnipeg, MB
	CME Corp	2	Replace	Sales Offices
	CME-WEST	2	Replace	Sales Offices
	CME-MEX	1	Replace	Sales Offices
	CME-TNG	1	Keep	CME-TNG
Cisco PIX-515E w/FO	CME Corp	1	Replace	CME-WEST
Cisco PIX-515E	CME-WEST	1	Replace	CME-MEX
	CME-EUR	1	Keep	CME-EUR
Cisco PIX-506E	CME-TNG	1	Delete	Sales Offices
	CME-MEX	1	Replace	Sales Offices

Table 17-1. Reusable WAN Hardware

WAN Bandwidth

The bandwidth requirements fall into two basic types of service: dedicated private WAN and Internet-based VPN WAN. The three main sites have significantly different bandwidth needs than the typical Sales Office site. CME Corp must be able to handle the aggregate bandwidth of all remote sites as it hosts the enterprise core. CME-WEST needs high bandwidth to CME Corp to support replication of date and services in support of disaster recovery, as well as a reasonably robust Internet presence to allow CME-WEST to assume the role of the corporate server farm in the event of a catastrophic failure. Table 17-2 details engineering calculations for WAN bandwidth.

Required bandwidth for the CME Corp Private WAN reflects aggregated bandwidth equal to all site virtual circuits plus additional overhead. The 35MB "provisioned" capacity will in fact require ATM DS3 service.

Site	Connection Method	# Of Sites	Concurrent Citrix Users	Citrix B/W @ 30KB/User	Citrix Printing B/W	Internet B/W Overhead	Video Overhead	IPSec Overhead	Excess Bandwidth	Required Bandwidth	Service Type	Provisioned B/W per Site	VC/PVC Required
CME Corp (WAN)	Private WAN	1	1000	30000	0	0	0	0	0	30552	ATM	35000	VBR-NRT
CME Corp (Internet)	ISP	1	0	0	0	5000	n/a	1000	1000	24476	ATM	25000	UBR
CME-WEST (WAN)	Private WAN	1	100	3000	0	128	0	0	1000	4228	ATM	6000	VRB-NRT
CME-WEST (Internet)	ISP	1	0	0	0	128	1124	512	512	512	ATM	1500	UBR
CME-EUR	VPN WAN	1	100	3000	620	128	1124	512	0	4972	ATM	5000	UBR
CME-MEX	VPN WAN	1	100	3000	620	128	1124	512	512	5484	ATM	6000	UBR
CORP-Sales (Typical)	Private WAN	30	10	300	155	0	155	0	0	680	Frame relay	768	768KB CIR
WEST-Sales (Typical)	VPN WAN	10	10	300	155	0	155	155	0	680	ANY	768	n/a
EUR-Sales (Typical)	VPN WAN	10	10	300	155	0	155	155	0	680	ANY	768	n.a
CME-TNG	Private WAN	1	5	150	78	128	0	0	512	903	ATM-DSL	1000	VBR-NRT
Suplier MSAM Access	ISP	n/a	10	300	0	0	0	0	0	310	n/a	none	none
Mobile Citrix Users	ISP	n/a	50	1500	0	0	0	0	0	1850	n/a	none	none
Mobile VPN Users	ISP	n/a	20	600	0	0	216	0	0	956	n/a	none	none
Dial-Up RAS	PSTN	n/a	23	1472	n/a	n/a	n/a	n/a	n/a	1536	ISDN PRI	ISDN PRI	none

Table 17-2. WAN Bandwidth Calculation Worksheet

Required bandwidth for the CME Corp Internet reflects aggregated bandwidth equal to all inbound and outbound Internet traffic for all sites, including VPN-connected sites based on their maximum provisioned data rate, as well as Mobile VPN, Mobile Citrix, and Supplier MSAM bandwidth projections. The 25MB "provisioned" capacity will in fact require dual ATM DS3 service, with each DS3 pipe carrying a 15MB virtual circuit.

CME-WEST requirements are somewhat deceptive. Both Internet and Private WAN access are provided over ATM DS3 facilities. The WAN bandwidth is increased (well above the level justified by user access) to support on-going off-hours data replication to CME-WEST as the "hot site." Additionally, by providing service over DS3 facilities, the Sales Office site virtual circuits could be reterminated in the event of a catastrophic failure at CME Corp. Internet bandwidth is similar, the day-to-day requirement is a mere 1.5MB, but the DS3 ATM service allows the virtual circuit to change to 15MB or more to reterminate site-to-site VPNs in a disaster scenario.

For both CME-EUR and CME-MEX, bandwidth is based on availability of ATM service. Both will be sites within the Windows Server 2003 Active Directory Domain, and printing will be via network printers through the VPN (outside the Citrix ICA channel) to allow bandwidth management of VPN traffic by the Packeteer. CME-MEX bandwidth appears artificially low based on the number of users at the site, but the majority of the users are Plant Floor production workers with only occasional access to Citrix or the CME Corp services.

North American (CORP) Sales Offices will be provisioned as "interworked" circuits, reencapsulated from frame relay (site end) to ATM (CORP end).

Several peripheral bandwidth calculations are included: MSAM Access bandwidth is not "supplied" by CME, but as the remote activities terminate at CME Corp, it is included in the overall load. Dial-up RAS does not impact the raw bandwidth, but must be included in specifying the CME Corp security hardware. CME Corp will reuse their existing RAS hardware.

WAN Hardware

Basic WAN hardware suites are consistent across similar sites to ease configuration management and allow for easier network management. Again, CME Corp and CME-WEST are unique, based on their enterprise roles. As a significant segment of the corporate WAN is VPN-based, VPN termination hardware (firewalls for site-to-site connections and a VPN concentrator for client-to-site connections) are included. Table 17-3 lists the hardware the designers have selected.

The "standard" high-capacity WAN router has more than adequate horsepower for CME's WAN connections and can easily be seen as "overkill" for CME-WEST. Aside from the obvious answer, that CME-WEST may need to assume CME Corp's role, standardizing on the same model for all high-bandwidth sites ensures the redundant Internet router at CME Corp can restore service for any other router without loss of service. It is effectively a global spare that is in service to support load balancing and redundancy for CME Corp's Internet connectivity.

Purpose	Quantity	Description
Private WAN router	1	Cisco 7401ASR, 128MB Flash, 512MB DRAM, (2) FE/GE ports, T3-ATM Port Adapter, IOS IP/FW/IDS/IPSEC56
Internet router	2	Cisco 7401ASR, 128MB Flash, 512MB DRAM, (2) FE/GE ports, T3-ATM Port Adapter, IOS IP/FW/IDS/IPSEC56
Firewall/VPN	1	Cisco 535-UR and 535-FO (failover), (2) 66MHZ GE Interfaces, (2) 66MHZ 4-Port FE interfaces, 3DES License, (2) VPN Accelerator+
VPN concentrator (clients)	2	Cisco VPN 3030, redundant power supplies
Private WAN router	1	Cisco 7401ASR, 128MB Flash, 512MB DRAM, (2) FE/GE ports, T3-ATM Port Adapter, IOS IP/FW/IDS/IPSEC56
Internet router	1	Cisco 7401ASR, 128MB Flash, 512MB DRAM, (2) FE/GE ports, T3-ATM Port Adapter, IOS IP/FW/IDS/IPSEC56
Firewall/VPN	1	Cisco 515E redundant (failover) w/IPSEC 3DES, PIX-4FE Interface for DMZ support
Internet router	1	As determined by host nation and ISP; use Cisco 3725, 32MB Flash, 128MB DRAM, IOS IP/FW/IDS Plus IPSec 3DES
Firewall/VPN		Cisco 515E redundant (failover) w/IPSEC 3DES
Internet router	1	As determined by host nation and ISP; use Cisco 3725, 32MB Flash, 128MB DRAM, IOS IP/FW/IDS Plus IPSec 3DES
Firewall/VPN	1	Cisco 515E redundant (failover) w/IPSec 3DES

Table 17-3.   WAN and Security Hardware

Purpose	Quantity	Description
Private WAN router	30	Cisco 1760, 32MB Flash, 64MB DRAM, (1) FE Port, T1 CSU/DSU, IOS IP Plus Software
Internet router	10	As determined by host nation and ISP, use CME-owned 1760 with appropriate interface cards where possible
Firewall/VPN	10	PIX-506E w/IPSEC 3DES
Internet router	10	As determined by host nation and ISP, use CME-owned 1760 with appropriate interface cards where possible
Firewall/VPN	10	PIX-506E w/IPSec 3DES
Private WAN router	1	Cisco 1760, 32MB Flash, 64MB DRAM, (1) FE Port, ADSL Interface, IOS IP Plus Software

Table 17-3. WAN and Security Hardware *(continued)*

The redundant (failover) firewall with gigabit interfaces ensures low-latency throughput between the Internet router and the corporate LAN.

Although traffic load for the client access VPN is not high, redundancy is still required. As an additional benefit, the VPN Concentrator can support site-to-site tunnels with multiple authentication methods.

Primary (Internet) routers for sites outside the U.S. and Canada remain "to be determined." Hardware installed outside the U.S. usually requires both host nation approval (HNA) and acceptance by the servicing ISP. In many countries, the PSTN is a pseudo-governmental entity and protects itself from competition by restricting the hardware that can be connected. In cases where the host nation and the ISP are amenable, CME-owned routers (Cisco 3725 or Cisco 1760) would be used.

LAN Requirements

Per-site LAN requirements are based on metrics similar to the WAN calculations. The primary factor is obviously the number of hosts (Ethernet devices) at a given site, and assumes 10/100MB switched Fast Ethernet connectivity unless higher throughput (Fast Ethernet port aggregation via Fast EtherChannel (FEC), Gigabit Ethernet, or Gigabit Ethernet port aggregation via Gigabit EtherChannel (GEC)) is required. All Sales Offices and CME-TNG will use identical hardware. Regional offices and the manufacturing plant (CME-WEST,

CME-EUR, and CME-MEX) are similar but with more capacity at CME-WEST to support data center reconstitution. CME Corp is designed as a highly robust fault-tolerant infrastructure. At the four primary sites, server requirements (network cards) are identified to help calculate the number of FEC, Gigabit, and GEC ports needed.

Current LAN Hardware

The current LAN infrastructure at the four primary sites uses some Ethernet switch hardware compatible with CME's overall goals, but switches are primarily stackable units that will be replaced by faster enterprise-class, chassis-based hardware. The remaining primary site LAN hardware and all Sales Office hardware is a hodgepodge of non-manageable consumer-class devices (hubs and switches) unsuitable for CME's enterprise services. Table 17-4 lists the inventory available for reallocation.

By reallocating the switches from the main site, CME has adequate hardware to deploy manageable switches to 38 of the 50 Sales Offices, and can provide a 3508 switch

WAN Hardware	Current Site	Quantity	Projected Status	Future Use
Cisco Catalyst 3548XL-EN	CME Corp	21	Replace	Sales Offices (21)
	CME-WEST	1	Replace	Sales Offices (1)
	CME-EUR	1	Replace	Sales Offices (1)
	CME-MEX	0	n/a	
Cisco Catalyst 2950G-24-EI	CME Corp	5	Replace	Sales Offices (5)
	CME-WEST	0	n/a	
	CME-EUR	0	n/a	
	CME-MEX	3	Replace	Sales Offices (2)
				CME-EUR (1)
Cisco Catalyst 3550-48-SMI	CME Corp	12	Replace	CME-MEX (5)
				Sales Offices (7)
	CME-WEST	1	Keep	
	CME-EUR	1	Replace	Sales Offices (1)
	CME-MEX	2	Keep	
Cisco Catalyst 3508XL-EN	CME Corp	1	Replace	CME-MEX (1)
		2	Keep	Spare (2)

Table 17-4.   WAN and Security Hardware

as a wiring closet aggregation point and five 48-port switches for the manufacturing plant floor at CME-MEX.

Sales Office LAN Hardware

Sales Offices share a common set of attributes: Less than 48 users; no requirement for Gigabit Ethernet, FEC, or GEC; and a single LAN segment with no need for Layer 3 switching. Based on equipment made available by upgrading the four primary sites, CME has 75 percent of the necessary hardware for upgrading the Sales Office on-hand. LAN requirements at CME-TNG are similar to a typical sales office. CME has decided to stay with similar hardware for the remaining needs: 14 new Catalyst 2950G-24-EI switches (12 Sales Offices, one for CME-TNG, one spare).

CME-MEX LAN Hardware

CME-MEX is the first "enterprise" LAN that requires a Layer 3 switching solution. The majority of the 300 users are associated with the manufacturing floor and need only occasional LAN (or Citrix) access; hence the reallocation of switches from CME Corp meets the requirements. Host connectivity requirements are

▼ 10/100MB Ethernet (Plant Floor), 210 distributed connections, isolated from the administrative/server LAN segment by access lists (Layer 3)

■ 10/100MB Ethernet (Administrative/Servers), 135 centralized connections, isolated from the Plant Floor LAN segment by access lists (Layer 3)

■ 10/100MB Ethernet (Uplink to WAN equipment), five centralized connections, isolated by access lists (Layer 3)

▲ Gigabit Ethernet (Downlink to 3508XL-EN switch), one connection

Table 17-5 summarizes the additional LAN hardware needed for CME-MEX.

LAN Hardware	Purpose	Description
Cisco Catalyst 4507 System	LAN Core	Cisco 4507 7-slot Chassis, redundant power supplies, (2) Catalyst Supervisor 4 with Enhanced Layer 3 IOS software, (3) 48-port 10/100/100 Ethernet modules
Cisco Catalyst 3508 System	Distribution	Cisco 3508-XL-EN Chassis (Excess form CME Corp), (1) 1000BaseTX GBIC, (5) 1000BaseSX GBIC
Cisco Catalyst 3550 System	Plant Access	(5) Cisco 3550-48-SMI Chassis (Excess from CME Corp), (5) 1000BaseSX GBIC

Table 17-5.   CME-MEX LAN Hardware

CME-EUR LAN Hardware

CME-EUR is similar to CME-MEX in scope, but does not currently require a Layer 3 switching solution. To maintain consistency of hardware and position CME-EUR for future Layer 3 initiatives, the site will be built as Layer 3 from the beginning. The 200 users are associated with management and administration of the European Region sales force, as well as limited engineering functions. Host connectivity requirements are

▼ 10/100MB Ethernet (Administrative/Servers), 212 centralized connections, isolated by access lists (Layer 3)

▲ 10/100MB Ethernet (Uplink to WAN equipment), five centralized connections, isolated by access lists (Layer 3)

Table 17-6 summarizes the LAN hardware needed for CME-EUR.

CME-WEST LAN Hardware

The CME-WEST LAN is similar to CME-EUR in its day-to-day role, but the site's scope as the CME Disaster Recovery "Hot Site" requires basic additional capacity, as well as the ability to incrementally expand services. The 200 users are associated with management and administration of the West Region sales force and have limited engineering functions. Host connectivity requirements are

▼ 10/100MB Ethernet (Administrative), 217 centralized connections, isolated by access lists (Layer 3)

■ 10/100 Ethernet (Servers), four centralized connections, isolated by access lists (Layer 3) (for site support servers (domain controller, DNS, and so on))

■ Gigabit Ethernet (Servers), 16 centralized connections, isolated by access lists (Layer 3) (for stand-by servers in the Citrix farm, domain controllers, and data storage and archive subsystems needed to reconstitute CME Corp servers)

■ Gigabit Ethernet (Disaster Recovery)

    ■ Ten centralized connections for stackable switches during disaster recovery

LAN Hardware	Purpose	Description
Cisco Catalyst 4507 System	LAN Core	Cisco 4507 7-slot Chassis, redundant power supplies, (2) Supervisor 4 with Enhanced Layer 3 IOS software, (5) 48-port 10/100/100 Ethernet modules

Table 17-6.   CME-EUR LAN Hardware

■ Sixteen centralized connections for reconstituted servers during disaster recovery

■ 10/100 Ethernet (Disaster Recovery), 24 centralized connections for reconstituted servers and peripherals during disaster recover

■ 10/100 Eth10/100 Ethernet (Servers), four centralized connections, isolated by access lists (Layer 3) (for site support servers (domain controller, DNS, and so on)

▲ 10/100MB Ethernet (Uplink to WAN equipment), five centralized connections, isolated by access lists (Layer 3)

Table 17-7 summarizes the LAN hardware needed for CME-EUR.

CME Corp LAN Hardware

CME Corp, as the Enterprise core, requires significantly more resources than any other site. Requirements unique to CME Corp include the following.

Redundant Core using 1000BaseTX for servers, 1000BaseSX for infrastructure equipment such as distribution switches, and 10/100/1000BaseTX for other peripherals and low-load servers:

▼ Gigabit Ethernet (1000BaseTX)

■ Sixty-eight production Citrix MetaFrame server connection (34 per core switch)

■ Eight dual-gigabit Ethernet connections (16 ports, eight ports/four servers per core) for special purpose production Citrix MetaFrame servers (high-bandwidth applications)

■ Six test/development Citrix MetaFrame server connections (three per core) for application test and development

■ Twenty connections for infrastructure servers (domain controllers, print servers, mainframe, and so on)

LAN Hardware	Purpose	Description
Cisco Catalyst 6513 System	LAN Core	Cisco 6513 13-slot Chassis, Redundant power supplies, (2) Supervisor 720 with Enhanced Layer 3 IOS software, (6) 48-port 10/100/100 Ethernet modules, (2) 16-Port Gigabit Ethernet (TX) modules, (1) 16-port Gigabit Ethernet (GBIC) module, (10) multimode fiber-optic GBIC modules

Table 17-7.   CME-WEST LAN Hardware

- Ten dual-gigabit Ethernet connections (20 ports, ten ports/five servers per core) for special purpose high-load servers like Oracle, Microsoft Exchange, Microsoft SQL, profile/home directory file servers, and backup servers
- Gigabit Ethernet (1000BaseSX)
  - Twenty connections to Campus distribution layer concentration points (two per campus switch, two uplinks to the private WAN, and two uplinks to the VPN WAN/Internet)
- ▲ 10/100/1000BaseTX Ethernet
  - Up to 48 connections per core switch for load servers and peripherals, to include compatibility with 10MB Ethernet devices

Private WAN Interconnect Switch:

- ▼ Four 1000BaseSX connections and two 10/100/1000BaseTX connections.

VPN WAN/Internet Interconnect Switch (DMZ Distribution Switch):

- Gigabit Ethernet (1000BaseTX))
  - Four dedicated connections for firewall interconnects
- Gigabit Ethernet (1000BaseSX)
  - Eight connections for links to the ACCESS DMZ aggregation switch, routers, Core switches, and PacketShaper
- 10/100/1000BaseTX Ethernet
  - Up to 48 connections for a firewall and DMZ servers
- Intrusion Detection Module
- ▲ Content Services Module

Campus Distribution Switches (eight required):

- ▼ Up to 288 10/100/100 Ethernet connections per chassis for each of eight building concentration points
- ▲ A minimum of four gigabit fiber-optic uplinks per chassis to build backbone connectivity

Wireless LAN access switches for each campus building, as summarized in Table 17-8.

CME Corp Wireless LAN Requirements

The CME Corp Wireless LAN (WLAN) provides coverage for roaming users as well as on-demand coverage for outside events on campus (the "Courtyard"). The initial deployment will be based on the 802.11b wireless standard (11.0 MBps/2.4 GHz). The radio

LAN Hardware	Purpose	Quantity	Description
Cisco Catalyst 3550-12G System	OUTSIDE Access Switch, ACCESS DMZ, Access Switch, Spare Access Switch	3	Cisco 3550-12G, Enhanced Layer 3 IOS, (2) 1000BaseTX ports, (10) Gigabit Interface Converter (GBIC) slots; (3) 1000BaseSX Multimode fiber-optic GBIC modules
Cisco Catalyst 6506 System	DMZ Distribution Switch	1	Cisco Catalyst 6506 6-Slot Chassis; redundant power supply; (2) Supervisor2/MSFC2 with Enhanced Layer 3 IOS; (1) 16-Port Gigabit Ethernet (GBIC) module; (1) intrusion detection system (IDS) module; (1) Content Switching Module; (1) 48-Port 10/100/1000 (TX) Module; (8) 1000BaseSX Multimode fiber-optic GBIC modules, (4) 1000BaseTX GBIC modules
Cisco Catalyst 6513 System	LAN Core (A & B)	2	Cisco Catalyst 6513 13-slot Chassis; Redundant Power Supply; (2) Catalyst Supervisor 720 with Enhanced Layer 3 IOS software, 1GB DRAM, 64MB Flash; (1) 2-port 10GB dCEF720 Switching module; (5) 16-port (GBIC) Gigabit Ethernet dCEF256 Switching modules; (1) 48-port 10/100/100 CEF256 Ethernet module; (1) (65) multimode fiber-optic GBIC modules; (2) single-mode fiber-optic modules
Cisco Catalyst 4506 System	Distribution Switch (Corp-A), Distribution Switch (Admin-A), Distribution Switch (Admin-B), Distribution Switch (Sales-A), Distribution Switch (Eng-A), Distribution Switch (Eng-B), Distribution Switch (Eng-C)	1	Cisco 4506 6-Solt Chassis; redundant power supply; (1) Supervisor 4 with Enhanced Layer 3 IOS; (1) 2-GBIC/ 32-port 10/100 Ethernet module; (4) 48-port 10/100/100 Ethernet module; (3) 1000BaseSX GBIC
Cisco Catalyst 4506 System	Distribution Switch (IT-A)	1	Cisco 4506 6-Solt Chassis; redundant power supply; (1) Supervisor 4 with Enhanced Layer 3 IOS; (1) 2-GBIC/32-port 10/100 Ethernet module; (3) 48-port 10/100/100 Ethernet module; (4) 1000BaseSX GBIC

Table 17-8. CME Corp LAN Hardware

LAN Hardware	Purpose	Quantity	Description
Cisco Catalyst 3524 System	Wireless LAN Access Switches	1	(5) Cisco 3524XL-EN-PWR, 24-port 10/100 Ethernet with power injection, (6) 1000BaseSX GBIC, (1) 1000BaseTX GBIC

Table 17-8. CME Corp LAN Hardware *(continued)*

equipment can be upgraded to the 802.11a standard to provide up to 54 MBps access at 5 GHz. Table 17-9 summarizes the WLAN hardware. The combination of omni-directional and low-gain directional antennas will be installed (based on a site survey) to assure coverage throughout the campus while minimizing radiation beyond the campus boundaries.

Bandwidth Management Requirements

For most of the Private WAN network and segments of the VPN WAN network, CME designers established requirements for advanced bandwidth management, primarily to protect latency-sensitive traffic from burst, ill-behaved traffic such as NetBIOS over IP, HTTP, and printing. Per-site hardware listed in Table 17-10 is based on the site bandwidth to be "shaped."

Primary Internet Connection (CME Corp)

CME depends heavily on its Internet upstream to deliver VPN WAN connectivity (IPSec), Roaming Client Access (VPN and Citrix), MSAM Access for key suppliers, and to allow public access to the CME web site. Although these are considered the critical requirements, the majority of all outbound Internet access is provided through these same connections and competes for throughput. The upstream ISPs cannot guarantee that router-based QoS values such as IP Precedence or DSCP will be honored, so a Packeteer is essential.

LAN Hardware	Quantity	Description
Cisco Aironet 1200 Wireless Access Point	32	Cisco Aironet 1200-series Wireless Access Point configured for 802.11b
Omni Antenna	20	Indoor Omni antenna
Directional Antenna	12	Indoor/Outdoor Directional Diversity Patch antenna

Table 17-9. CME Corp WLAN Hardware

LAN Hardware	Purpose	Quantity	Description
PacketShaper 8500 System	CME Corp Private WAN	1	PacketShaper 8500 with (1) two-port 1000BaseSX fiber-optic LAN Expansion Module (LEM)
PacketShaper 6500 System	CME Corp Internet	1	PacketShaper 6500 with (1) two-port 1000BaseSX fiber-optic LEM, licensed for 45MB shaping
PacketShaper 6500 System	CME-WEST Private WAN	1	PacketShaper 6500, licensed for 45MB shaping
PacketShaper 2500 System	CME-MEX Private WAN CME-EUR Internet	2	PacketShaper 2500, licensed for 10MB shaping
PacketShaper 1550 System	Private WAN Sites	30	PacketShaper 1550, licensed for 2MB shaping

Table 17-10.   CME Bandwidth Management Hardware

Private WAN

Bandwidth management of the Private WAN encompasses both the CME Corp side and the remote site side of each virtual connection. The aggregate number of sites to be managed and monitored requires a solution that is both standardized and centrally managed.

Remote Sites   All remote sites funnel through CME Corp for all services. To ensure traffic is policed to protect Citrix and other critical traffic flows, remote sites will use low-end Packeteer units as part of a distributed bandwidth management solution.

CME-TNG   CME-TNG has far more bandwidth than the assigned staff will need. As this is not a production site, bandwidth management is desirable, not mandatory. Extensive application-level identification and control is not required, so management will be exercised via QoS features on the link routers.

CME Corp   From the network core looking out to the remote Private WAN sites, 31 separate locations must be managed. All have virtually identical parameters. A central unit capable of 30-plus individual partitions is required.

CME-WEST

CME-WEST bandwidth management is participative with the main unit on the CME Corp Private WAN connection. During normal business hours, preferential treatment is given to latency-intolerant traffic (Citrix and H.323 Video Teleconferencing (VTC)). After hours, priority is given to bulk data replication from the network core to ensure data archives at CME-WEST are current enough to reconstitute CME's business. There is no current requirement to manage bandwidth utilization over the Internet connection; however, in the event of a catastrophe at CME Corp, the CME-WEST Internet pipe would become the lifeline for CME-EUR and CME-WEST Sales Offices and would require bandwidth management.

CME-MEX and CME-EUR

Bandwidth management for both sites is somewhat limited in scope. The primary concern is to ensure the limited set of authorized outbound Internet users do not degrade performance of traffic destined for the network core via the VPN tunnel. Traffic must be managed behind the firewall.

Network Security Requirements

Security Concepts

CME's fundamental security concept is one of layered security and least-privilege. Default security levels have been assigned to ensure all firewalls offer equivalent protection, and a precise written security plan details what traffic may or may not enter (or exit) at any given level of the security model. (See Figure 17-1.)

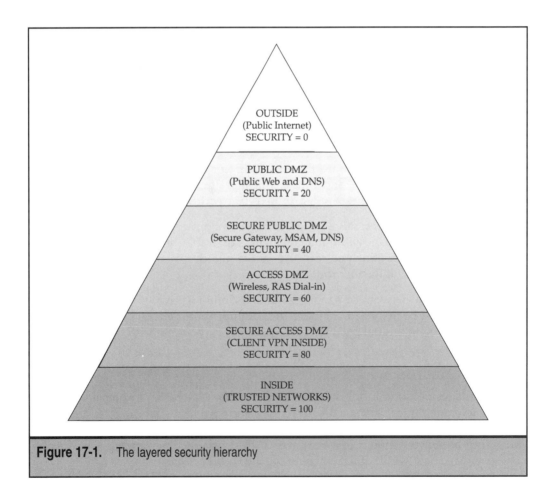

Figure 17-1. The layered security hierarchy

With the large number of security devices (firewalls, IDS, VPN Concentrator) deployed in the Enterprise, a single source management system was needed to maintain the secure environment, track configuration changes, and monitor and respond to security-related events. CME selected Cisco's CiscoWorks VPN/Security Management Solution (VMS) with additional Cisco Security Agents (CSA) for host-based IDS on exposed servers. Mirror image systems will be deployed at both locations with all configuration changes deployed from the CME Corp management suite. CiscoWorks VMS will manage all security devices, including the embedded IDS module in the DMZ Distribution switch.

Intrusion Detection for the Private WAN segment is monitored by a Cisco 4235 IDS Sensor appliance managed by the CiscoWorks VMS suite.

Finally, to ensure security on network devices, authenticate VPN and RAS user identity, and enforce security and authentication on wireless segments, CME will deploy a redundant pair of RADIUS servers using Cisco Secure Access Control Server (CSACS) at CME Corp, with a tertiary unit at CME-WEST. Table 17-11 identifies the components of the security management solution.

Network Infrastructure Management Requirements

Management of the network infrastructure encompasses a primary NMS site at CME Corp and a secondary, albeit limited, NMS capability at CME-WEST as a backup. For seamless interoperability, CME will use CiscoWorks products, specifically CiscoWorks LAN Management Solution (LMS) for the corporate campus, CiscoWorks Routed WAN Management Solution for maintaining the status and state of the Private WAN network, and CiscoWorks Wireless LAN Solutions Engine to manage the corporate WLAN segment. To control PacketShaper configurations and monitor the status of enterprise bandwidth, CME will use Packeteer's PolicyCenter and ReportCenter products. The CiscoWorks network management solution components listed in Table 17-12 share a common interface with the security management products discussed previously.

Security Software	Quantity	Description
CiscoWorks VMS	2	CiscoWorks VMS (Unrestricted)
Cisco Security Agent (Server)	1	25-Agent Bundle
Cisco Secure Access Control Server	3	CSACS, primary and redundant for CME Corp, backup for CME-WEST
Cisco IDS Sensor	1	Cisco 4235 IDS Sensor

Table 17-11. Security Management Hardware/Software

Security Software	Quantity	Description
CiscoWorks LMS	1	LAN Management Solution
CiscoWorks RWAN	2	Routed WAN Management
CiscoWorks WLSE	1	Wireless LAN Management
Packeteer PolicyCenter	1	Centralized management of Packeteer devices
Packeteer ReportCenter	1	Centralized reporting and analysis

Table 17-12.   Infrastructure Management Hardware/Software

Network Naming, Addressing, and Routing Requirements

The Host Naming Scheme

After extensive discussions and arguments, CME elected to use a host naming system that met most of their design requirements: short, self-documenting, and extensible. The most complex issue, how to easily differentiate between the 1760 router in Athens, GR, and the one in Athens, GA was resolved by basing the site name on the International Airline Travel Association (IATA) three-letter code for the major airport. Greece becomes "HEW," and Georgia becomes "AHN."

Figure 17-2 shows a partial breakdown of the naming conventions.

The Addressing Scheme

CME's Internal IP addressing scheme uses the ranges specified by RFC 1918, *Address Allocation for Private Internets*, and was designed to ensure adequate capacity for growth in terms of additional main corporate campus infrastructure and users, expansion of existing primary sites, and addition of more sales offices on demand. More importantly, the design was intended to be generally hierarchical to allow summarization of routing information at key points such as the DMZ distribution switch and the Private WAN distribution router.

The sample of the overall scheme shown in Table 17-13 does not include details on how addresses are assigned within each LAN segment subnet (DHCP ranges versus static address range or standardized ranges for specific equipment within the static range).

Public (Internet routable) IP addresses are from CME's registered block of addresses. For the purposes of the case study, CME owns 20.20.20.0/22 (20.20.20.0 to 20.20.23.254). The range 20.20.20.0/23 (20.20.20.0 to 20.20.21.254) is assigned to CME Corp, and dynamically routed via two different upstream service providers. 20.20.22.0/24 is assigned to CME-WEST for support of the disaster recovery site.

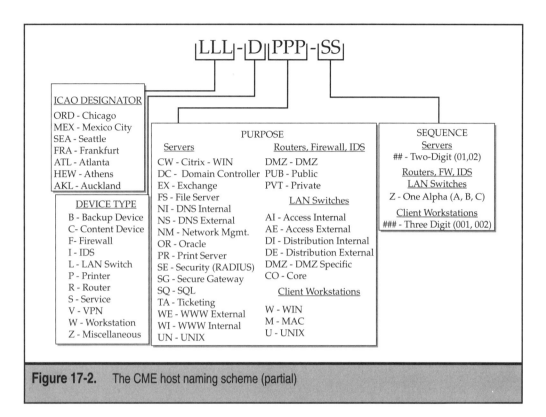

Figure 17-2.   The CME host naming scheme (partial)

Routing Protocols and Methods

The complexity of the CME network mandates careful selection of routing protocols. Given that CME's internal and external (Internet) segments will never directly exchange routing information (due to RFC 1918 addressing and security constraints), separate Interior Gateway Protocols (IGP) and Exterior Gateway Protocols (EGP) are used.

Interior Networks   Of the three logical choices for dynamic Interior Gateway Protocols (IGP), Interior Border Gateway Protocol (IBGP) was considered too complex and ill suited for the large number of small (/24 or smaller) networks. Further, the cost of resources to handle IBGP at Private WAN sites was prohibitive and redistributing IBGP routes into another IGP made little sense. Of the two remaining options, Open Shortest Path First (OSPF) and Cisco's Enhanced Interior Gateway Routing Protocol (EIGRP), EIGRP is more suited to a meshed network (like the CME Corporate Campus), and was the most appropriate choice, with one exception: the DMZ. CME will use their registered Autonomous System Number (ASN) from BGP for their EIGRP implementation, but for the sake of illustration, configurations in the case study will use Cisco Systems register ASN (109). The exception to using EIGRP as the IGP is in the DMZ: Internet routers, firewall OUTSIDE interfaces, and VPN Concentrators will all run an instance of OSPF to meet the requirement that BGP can only announce routes learned from an IGP. On the other side of the security boundary, the

SUBNET	MASK	USE	SUBNET	MASK	USE
10.0.0.0	/8	CME Master RFC 1918 Address Space	10.2.1.0	/24	Point-to-Point Links to CME-CORP LAN
10.1.0.0	/16	CME-CORP Address Space	10.2.1.0	/30	ORD-SCO-A to ORD-SCO-B
10.1.0.0	/24	CME-CORP Servers Core-A	10.2.1.4	/30	ORD-SCO-A to ORD-SDMZ-A
10.1.1.0	/24	CME-CORP Servers Core-B	10.2.1.8	/30	ORD-SCO-B to ORD-SDMZ-A
			10.2.1.12	/30	ORD-SCO-A to Future ORD-SDI-?
10.1.32.0	/24	CME-CORP LAN CORP	{------------------Sequence Continues------------------}		
10.1.33.0	/24	RESERVED LAN CORP Growth	10.2.1.28	/30	
10.1.34.0	/24	CME-CORP LAN ADM			
10.1.35.0	/24	CME-CORP LAN ADM	10.2.1.32	/30	ORD-SCO-A to ORD-SDI-A
10.1.36.0	/24	RESERVED LAN ADM Growth	10.2.1.36		ORD-SCO-A to ORD-SDI-B
{------------------Sequence Continues------------------}			10.2.1.40		ORD-SCO-A to ORD-SDI-C
10.1.44.0	/24	CME-CORP LAN IT	{------------------Sequence Continues------------------}		
10.1.45.0	/24	RESERVED LAN IT Growth	10.2.1.62	/30	ORD-SCO-A to ORD-SDI-?
10.1.46.0	/24	RESERVED LAN Growth			
10.1.47.0	/24	RESERVED LAN Growth	10.2.1.64	/30	ORD-SCO-B to ORD-SDI-A
			10.2.1.68	/30	ORD-SCO-B to ORD-SDI-B
10.2.0.0	/24	CME-CORP Point-to-Point Links	10.2.1.72	/30	ORD-SCO-B to ORD-SDI-C
10.2.0.0	/24	Point-to-Point Links to Private WAN	{------------------Sequence Continues------------------}		
10.2.0.0	/30	ORD-SCO-A to ORD-SDI-I	10.2.1.92	/30	ORD-SCO-B to ORD-SDI-?
10.2.0.4	/30	ORD-SCO-B to ORD-SDI-I			
10.2.0.8	/29	ORD-SDI-I to ORD-RPVT-A	10.101.0.0	/16	CME Private-WAN-Connected Sites LAN
10.2.0.16	/30	ORD-RPVT-A to ORD-RTNG-A	10.101.0.0	/22	CME-WEST LAN
10.2.0.20	/30	ORD-RPVT-A to Private WAN Sales Site	10.101.4.0	/22	Future Primary Site LAN
{------------------Sequence Continues------------------}			10.101.8.0	/22	Future Primary Site LAN
10.2.0.252		ORD-RPVT-A to Private WAN Sales Site	10.101.12.0	/22	Future Primary Site LAN
			10.101.32.0	/24	ORD-TNG LAN
			10.101.33.0	/24	CME Private WAN Sales Office LAN
SUBNET	**MASK**	**USE**	{------------------Sequence Continues------------------}		
10.201.0.0	/16	CME VPN-WAN-Connected Sites LAN	10.101.255.0	/24	CME Private WAN Sales Office LAN
10.201.0.0	/22	CME-EUR LAN			
10.201.4.0	/22	CME-MEX LAN			
10.201.8.0	/22	Future Primary Site LAN			
10.201.12.0	/22	Future Primary Site LAN			
10.201.32.0	/24	CME VPN WAN Sales Office LAN			
10.201.33.0	/24	CME VPN WAN Sales Office LAN			
{------------------Sequence Continues------------------}					
10.201.255.0	/24	CME VPN WAN Sales Office LAN			
10.254.0.0	/16	CME-CORP DMZ Address Space			
10.254.0.0	/24	CME-CORP PUBLIC DMZ			
10.254.1.0	/22	CME-CORP SECURE PUBLIC DMZ			
10.254.4.0	/22	CME-CORP ACCESS DMZ			
10.254.4.0	/24	CME-CORP ACCESS-DMZ Interconnect (ICF)			
10.254.5.0	/24	CME-CORP ACCESS DMZ CORP WLAN Pool			
10.254.6.0	/24	CME-CORP ACCESS DMZ ALT WLAN Pool			
10.254.7.0	/24	CME-CORP ACCESS DMZ RAS Pool			
10.254.8.0	/23	CME-CORP SECURE ACCESS DMZ			
10.254.8.0	/24	CME-CORP SECURE ACCESS DMZ ICF			
10.254.9.0	/24	CME-CORP SECURE ACCESS DMZ VPN Pools			

Table 17-13. Internal Network Addressing Scheme (Partial)

firewall, DMZ Distribution Switch (6509), and VPN Concentrator will run a separate instance of OSPF to propagate DMZ routes to the internal network. The DMZ Distribution Switch will redistribute OSPF routes into the EIGRP process.

Exterior Networks The registered ASN does dual-duty: the registration process is mandatory for use with Exterior Border Gateway Protocol (EBGP) (the Internet routing protocol) to ensure interoperability with different ISP upstream providers and allow local copies of the full Internet Routing Table to be maintained; the same ASN is used for EIGRP, even though the EIGRP ASN is never exposed outside the private network.

NETWORK CONFIGURATION

With all of the hardware, software, and concepts defined, implementation can proceed. Planners at CME developed at timeline to schedule interdependent tasks, such as site cutovers and equipment reallocations. The following configuration examples are not intended to be all-inclusive; many of the basic steps are omitted to focus on those germane to the Enterprise infrastructure and MetaFrame support.

Private WAN Sites (CORP Sales)

Private WAN Sales Offices (connected directly to CME Corp) all share common configurations. The CME-TNG configuration is similar, but with bandwidth management provided by the site router. Figures 17-3 and 17-4 depict the basic configuration for these sites.

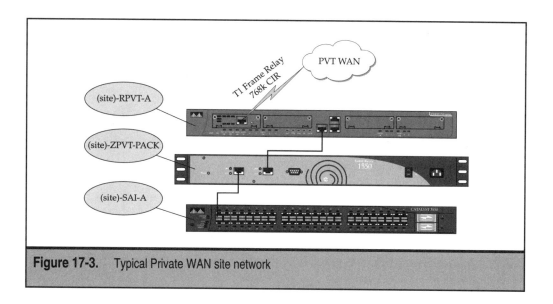

Figure 17-3. Typical Private WAN site network

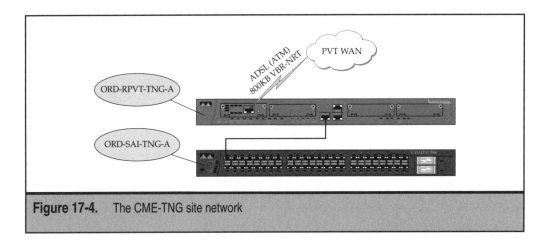

Figure 17-4. The CME-TNG site network

Router Configuration

The standard router configuration employs a single 768KB (CIR) frame relay PVC carried over a physical T1 local loop while the CME-TNG site uses an ATM VC over DSL. The two configurations are similar:

▼ Basic settings for a Private WAN frame relay connection (ATL-RPVT-A)

■ LAN settings

```
interface FastEthernet0
 description Atlanta LAN
 ip address 10.200.33.1 255.255.255.128
 speed 100
 full-duplex
```

■ WAN settings

```
interface Serial0/0
 description T1 Circuit ID 99ABGG243117
 no ip address
 encapsulation frame-relay IETF
 no fair-queue
 service-module t1 remote-alarm-enable
 frame-relay lmi-type cisco
```

■ Frame relay PVC (subinterface)

```
interface Serial0/0.16 point-to-point
 description Uplink To CME-RPVT-A
 bandwidth 768
 ip address 10.2.0.22 255.255.255.252
frame-relay interface-dlci 16
```

■ Routing

```
router eigrp 109
no auto-summary
no eigrp log-neighbor-changes
network 10.0.2.20 0.0.0.3
network 10.101.33.0 0.0.0.255
```

▲ Basic settings for a Private WAN ATM/DSL connection (ORD-RPVT-TNG-A)

■ LAN settings

```
interface FastEthernet0
description CME-TNG LAN
 ip address 10.200.32.1 255.255.255.128
 speed 100
 full-duplex
service-policy input CITRIX-LAN
```

■ WAN settings

```
interface ATM0
 description Uplink to CME-RPVT-A
 bandwidth 800
 ip address 10.2.0.18 255.255.255.252
 atm vc-per-vp 256
 no atm ilmi-keepalive
 pvc 0/32
  protocol ip 10.2.0.17
  vbr-nrt 800 800 16
  oam-pvc manage
  encapsulation aal5snap
```

■ Traffic management

```
dsl operating-mode auto
service-policy output LLQ
hold-queue 224 in
```

Bandwidth Management

The Private WAN site bandwidth management paradigm is the most simplistic: guarantee bandwidth for server-based computing and control other traffic.

Private WAN Sites (Frame Relay)   Management of traffic flows across the Private WAN network is controlled by PacketShaper units at each end of each link. A typical site configuration, shown in Figure 17-5, accomplishes the following:

▼ Guarantees essential throughput at high priority for video teleconferencing (VTC) sessions

Traffic Class Name	Class Hits	Policy Hits	Current (bps)	1 Min (bps)	Peak (bps)	Guar. Rate Failures	Pkt Exch (ms)	Partition Min-Max	Policy Type (Pri.) Guar. Limit	Top User Analysis
Inbound			0	0	0	0	NA	uncommitted - none		
Localhost	0	0	0	0	0	0	NA		Priority (6)	
H.323_VTC	0	0	0	0	0	0	NA		Rate (5) 128k-256k	
Citrix			0	0	0	0	NA			
Dynamics	0	0	0	0	0	0	NA		Rate (6) 20k	
Cerna_Epicare	0	0	0	0	0	0	NA		Rate (6) 20k	
Internet_Explorer_6	0	0	0	0	0	0	NA		Rate (4) 20k	
Microsoft_Excel	0	0	0	0	0	0	NA		Rate (4) 20k	
Microsoft_Outlook	0	0	0	0	0	0	NA		Rate (4) 20k	
Microsoft_PowerPoint	0	0	0	0	0	0	NA		Rate (4) 20k	
Microsoft_Word	0	0	0	0	0	0	NA		Rate (5) 20k	
PowerFuse_Desktop	0	0	0	0	0	0	NA		Rate (4) 30k	
Default	0	NA	0	0	0	0	NA			
Restricted Traffic			0	0	0	0	NA	0 - 64.0k		
MPEG-Audio	0	NA	0	0	0	0	NA			
QuickTime	0	NA	0	0	0	0	NA			
Real	0	NA	0	0	0	0	NA			
WinMedia	0	NA	0	0	0	0	NA			
Controlled Traffic			0	0	0	0	NA	0 - 192k		
FTP	0	0	0	0	0	0	NA		Rate (2) 0	
HTTP	0	0	0	0	0	0	NA		Rate (3) 0	
SSL	0	0	0	0	0	0	NA		Rate (3) 0	
Microsoft-ds	0	0	0	0	0	0	NA		Rate (5) 0	
NetBIOS-IP	0	0	0	0	0	0	NA		Rate (4) 0	
DNS	0	NA	0	0	0	0	NA			
Gnutella	0	0	0	0	0	0	NA		Discard	
Default	0	0	0	0	0	0	NA		Priority (3)	
Outbound			0	0	0	0	NA	uncommitted - none		

Figure 17-5. Typical private WAN Packeteer settings

■ Guarantees a minimum bandwidth to every Citrix session, with priority access to additional bandwidth. As individual applications are visible to the Packeteer, those that are known to require more initial bandwidth or that may induce user perceptions of slowness (for instance, the screen display does not keep up with keyboard input) can be given even more granular preferential treatment with regard to bandwidth.

■ A generic container for "Controlled Traffic" is created to constrain ill-behaved flows like HTTP to a reasonable amount of bandwidth. Within that container, certain applications have priority access to the constrained bandwidth. For example: FTP traffic to and from a Sales Office directly to the Internet is generally less important than HTTP from the same site.

▲ A generic container for "Restricted Traffic" is created to control applications that are not considered "essential" to business activities but are not expressly prohibited. Unacceptable traffic (Gnutella) as discarded immediately.

The Private WAN Site (ATM/DSL)   As mentioned previously, the ATM/DSL connection to the CME-TNG site does not require the expense of PacketShaper-based bandwidth management, but it still needs at least some controls to assure performance for Citrix sessions. The router (ORD-RPVT-TNG-A) is configured using Cisco's Modular Quality of Service (QoS) command-line interface (CLI) or MQC. The Traffic management command "service-policy output LLQ" shown in the basic configuration is based on the following parameters:

▼ Define Citrix traffic by protocol (TCP port)

```
access-list 101 permit tcp any any eq 1494
```

■ Classify Citrix entering from the LAN into a logical group

```
class-map match-all ICA-LAN
  match access-group 101
```

■ Mark traffic classified as "ICA-LAN" (above) for preferential treatment using IP precedence

```
policy-map CITRIX-LAN
  class ICA-LAN
   set ip precedence 5
  class class-default
   set ip precedence 0
```

■ Classify Citrix exiting to the WAN into a logical group

```
class-map match-all ICA-WAN
  match ip precedence 5
  class class-default
```

▲ Enforce preferential treatment (queuing) for up to 384KB of Citrix traffic

```
policy-map LLQ
  class ICA-WAN
   bandwidth 384
  class class-default
   fair-queue
```

VPN WAN Sites (CME-WEST Sales and CME-EUR Sales)

CME-EUR and CME-MEX Sales Office sites rely on Internet connectivity for their VPN lifeline to CME Corp. As mentioned previously, the selection of a specific Internet router may not be an option due to host nation or ISP restrictions. The relatively low bandwidth also implies that the host nation ISP or circuit provider may not guarantee service in the form of an SLA. Bandwidth management is therefore not cost effective. To ensure a limited ability to cope with failures, each site will be equipped with a dial-up modem to allow remote terminal connectivity to the firewall in the event of a failure or problem (CME Corp staff will direct connection of the modem to the firewall console and reconfigure as required). Refer to Figure 17-6 for a graphic hardware layout of a typical site.

Firewall Configuration

The standard firewall/VPN configuration for all CME-WEST and CME-EUR sites establishes a VPN tunnel but disallows outbound access to the Internet by client PCs. The IPSec tunnel settings are a mirror image of the tunnel end-point on the ORD-FPUB-A

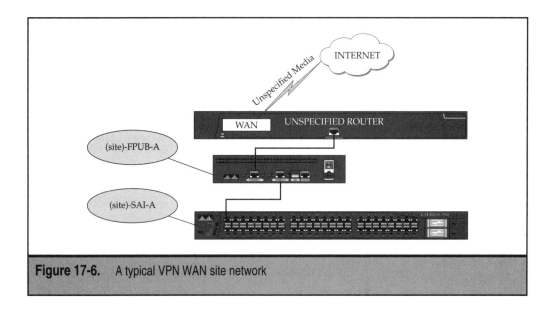

Figure 17-6. A typical VPN WAN site network

(CME Corp) firewall. IP addresses used for the public segment are as assigned by the servicing ISP.

▼ Basic settings for the HEW-FPUB-A (Athens) firewall:

```
nameif ethernet0 OUTSIDE security 0
interface ethernet0 100Full
ip address OUTSIDE 88.88.88.88 255.255.255.240
```

■ Define logical groups of objects to simplify configuration

```
object-group network CME-Servers
  object-group description CME Servers and NMS Accessible to VPN Sites
  network-object 10.1.0.0 255.255.254.0
  network-object 10.1.45.0 255.255.255.0
object-group network HEW-LAN
  object-group description CME-MEX LAN Subnets
  network-object 10.201.32.0 255.255.255.0
```

■ Define what local traffic is allowed to traverse the tunnels

```
access-list ORD-VPN permit ip object-group HEW-LAN object-group CME-Servers
access-list VPN-NO-NAT permit object-group HEW-LAN object-group CME-Servers
```

■ Exempt site-to-site VPN traffic from the Network Address Translation (NAT) process

```
nat (inside) 0 access-list VPN-NO-NAT
```

- Specify that IPSec is implicitly trusted

```
sysopt connection permit-ipsec
```

- Specify that authentication of remote side identity is by IP address

```
isakmp identity address
```

- Enable ISAKMP negotiation on the external interface

```
isakmp enable outside
```

- Define IPSec polices

```
crypto ipsec transform-set cme-set esp-3des esp-sha-hmac
crypto map cme-map 10 ipsec-isakmp
crypto map cme-map 10 set transform-set cme-set
crypto map cme-set 10 match address ORD-VPN
crypto map cme-set 10 set peer 20.20.20.4
crypto map cme-set interface OUTSIDE
```

- Define the Internet Key Exchange (IKE) policies

```
isakmp policy 10 authentication pre-share
isakmp policy 10 group 2
isakmp policy 10 encryption 3des
isakmp policy 10 hash sha
```

▼ Specify the preshared key for each tunnel

```
isakmp key h&3jN(sv5Km.(s14 address 20.20.20.4 netmask 255.255.255.255
```

CME-EUR

Like the Sales Office sites, CME-EUR relies on Internet connectivity. Unlike the sales offices, CME-EUR has a higher throughput and greater demands, including printing and Domain replication. Because of the "commercial" grade Internet requirements, CME-EUR has an SLA for their Internet service. Bandwidth management is necessary to control the traffic traversing the VPN tunnel and ensure that the relatively high number of Citrix sessions do not become "starved" for bandwidth. CME-EUR has limited onsite IT staff and will not require immediate access to a modem connection for remote reconfiguration. The CME-EUR LAN switch is a consolidated distribution and access layer module, with only limited Layer 3 requirements (isolating the internal LAN segment from the uplink to the Packeteer and firewall). The CME-EUR configuration is detailed in Figure 17-7.

Firewall Configuration

The firewall and VPN configuration for CME-EUR is similar to a Sales Office firewall configuration, but allows specific LAN hosts to access the Internet directly. The configuration example shown under CME-MEX is applicable to CME-EUR as well.

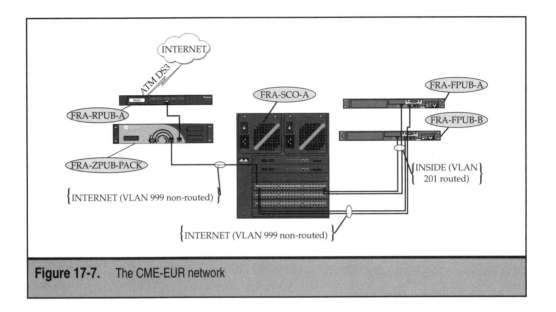

Figure 17-7.   The CME-EUR network

Bandwidth Management

Bandwidth management at CME-EUR is similar to a Private WAN site, but as almost all traffic is routed to CME Corp over the VPN tunnel, traffic must be policed *before* it enters the tunnel. Other modifications would include modified restrictions on traffic related to printing from the corporate site (NetBIOS IP, LPR), and less restrictions on Active Directory Domain replication traffic to the local domain controller.

CME-MEX

CME-MEX parallels CME-EUR, but with the additional restrictions imposed by the production environment. The manufacturing plant floor has little need for service beyond limited Citrix connectivity and no need for external Internet access through the corporate network. Again, bandwidth management is necessary to control client traffic behavior (allow reliable access to Citrix, police printing bandwidth consumption, allow management and administration staff Internet access, and restrict production subnets to corporate intranet access). Figure 17-8 shows the assembled network components.

Firewall Configuration

CME-MEX firewall and VPN parameters (conceptually identical to CME-EUR) define the subnets that traverse the VPN tunnel but allow direct outbound access for a limited number of LAN hosts, specified by a fully qualified domain name (FQDN). As these sites are domain members of the CME Active Directory domain with a local domain controller/internal DNS server, the firewall can use the internal DNS and dynamic DNS registration of DHCP-addressed LAN hosts to identify hosts granted access by FQDN. Again, the VPN parameters are a mirror image of those at CME Corp.

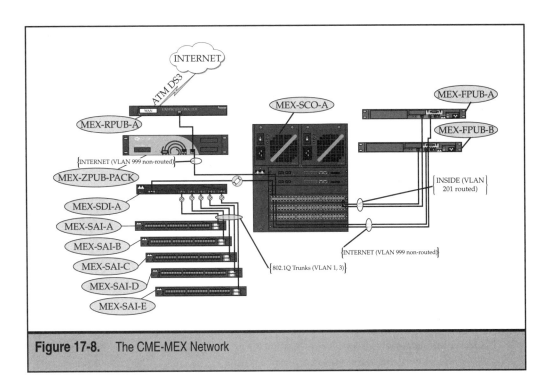

Figure 17-8. The CME-MEX Network

▼ Basic settings for MEX-FPUB-A

```
nameif ethernet0 OUTSIDE security 0
interface ethernet0 100Full
ip address OUTSIDE 66.66.66.66 255.255.255.240
```

■ Define logical groups of objects to simplify configuration

```
object-group network CME-Servers
  object-group description CME Servers and NMS Accessible to VPN Sites
  network-object 10.1.0.0 255.255.254.0
  network-object 10.1.45.0 255.255.255.0
object-group network MEX-LAN
  object-group description CME-MEX LAN Subnets
  network-object 10.201.4.0 255.255.252.0
object-group network INTERNET-ACCESS
  object-group description Local Hosts Allowed Internet Access
  network-object host mex-dc01.cme.com
```

■ Define what local traffic is allowed to traverse the tunnels

```
#notice it is a mirror of the one applied to the host PIX
access-list ORD-VPN permit ip object-group MEX-LAN object-group CME-Servers
access-list VPN-NO-NAT permit object-group MEX-LAN object-group CME-Servers
```

- Exempt site-to-site VPN traffic from the Network Address Translation process

```
nat (INSIDE) 0 access-list VPN-NO-NAT
nat (INSIDE) 1 object-group INTERNET-ACCESS
global (OUTSIDE) 1 interface
```

- Specify that IPSec is implicitly trusted

```
sysopt connection permit-ipsec
```

- Specify that authentication of remote side identity is by IP address

```
isakmp identity address
```

- Enable ISAKMP negotiation on the external interface

```
isakmp enable outside
```

- Define IPSec policies

```
crypto ipsec transform-set cme-set esp-3des esp-sha-hmacv
crypto map cme-map 10 ipsec-isakmp
crypto map cme-map 10 set transform-set cme-set
crypto map cme-set 10 match address ORD-VPN
crypto map cme-set 10 set peer 20.20.20.4
crypto map cme-set interface OUTSIDE
```

- Define Internet Key Exchange (IKE) policies

```
isakmp policy 10 authentication pre-share
isakmp policy 10 group 2
isakmp policy 10 encryption 3des
isakmp policy 10 hash sha
```

▲ Specify the preshared key for each tunnel

```
isakmp key !h^Fsn)9,Oq$z@cU address 20.20.20.4 netmask 255.255.255.255
```

Bandwidth Management

CME-MEX is a somewhat larger mirror of CME-EUR. Basic bandwidth allocations are the same, but outbound Internet access is restricted by the PacketShaper based on approved host names (manually defined in the PacketShaper rules) as compared to the host's IP address as resolved by the internal DNS on the domain controller.

Core LAN Switch Configuration

The CME-MEX core switch (MEX-SCO-A) is the first switch that requires advanced Layer 3 routing functionality with its associated VLANs. By subnetting CME-MEX's address space, the designers simplified the process of restricting access to many services from the plant floor (production) hosts. The following partial configuration shows both the Layer 2 VLAN assignments and the Layer 3 routed interfaces. Note that VLAN 1 (default) is used only for interswitch VLAN control traffic, and VLAN 999 is passed through the switch at Layer 2 for visibility, but cannot be routed to any other VLAN. Each Layer 3 VLAN interface will have access lists defined to limit accessibility from VLAN-to-VLAN. Finally, the 802.1Q trunk to the plant floor switches only transports the PLANT VLAN and the SERVER VLAN (used for management).

```
vlan 2 name SERVERS
vlan 3 name ADMIN
vlan 4 name PLANT
vlan 201 name INSIDE
vlan 999 name OUTSIDE
!
interface Vlan1
 no ip address
!
interface Vlan2
 description CME-MEX Servers
 ip address 10.201.0.129 255.255.255.128
!
interface Vlan3
 description CME-MEX ADMIN
 ip address 10.201.1.0 255.255.255.0
 ip helper-address 10.201.0.100
!
interface Vlan4
 description CME-MEX Plant Floor
 ip address 10.201.2.1 255.255.254.0
!
interface Vlan201
 description CME-MEX firewall (MEX-FPUB-A INSIDE)
 ip address 10.201.0.14 255.255.254.240
!
interface Vlan999
 no ip address
!
interface GigabitEthernet4/1
 description Uplink to PacketShaper 6500 Inside Interface
 switchport access vlan 999
 switchport mode access
 spanning-tree portfast
 speed 100
 duplex full
!
interface GigabitEthernet4/2
```

```
 description trunk to MEX-SDI-A Port Gi0/1
 switchport trunk encapsulation dot1q
 switchport trunk native vlan 2
 switchport trunk allowed vlan 1,2,4
 switchport mode trunk
!
interface GigabitEthernet4/3
 description Connected to MEX-FPUB-A OUTSIDE
 switchport access vlan 999
 switchport mode access
 spanning-tree portfast
 speed 100
 duplex full
!
interface GigabitEthernet4/4
 description Connected to MEX-FPUB-B OUTSIDE
 switchport access vlan 999
 switchport mode access
 spanning-tree portfast
 speed 100
 duplex full
!
interface GigabitEthernet4/47
 description Connected to MEX-FPUB-A INSIDE
 switchport access vlan 201
 switchport mode access
 spanning-tree portfast
 speed 100
 duplex full
!
interface GigabitEthernet4/47
 description Connected to MEX-FPUB-B INSIDE
 switchport access vlan 201
 switchport mode access
 spanning-tree portfast
 speed 100
 duplex full
!
interface GigabitEthernet5/1
 description Connected to MEX-SDC01
 switchport access vlan 2
 switchport mode access
 spanning-tree portfast
!
```

```
interface GigabitEthernet6/1
 description ADMIN Client
 switchport access vlan 3
 switchport mode access
 spanning-tree portfast
```

Access Switch Configuration (Plant Floor)

The individual access switches (MEX-SAI-A through E) on the plant floor are virtually identical. Client interfaces (fast Ethernet) are assigned to the "PLANT" VLAN, and the first gigabit Ethernet interface is configured as an 802.1Q trunk to the distribution switch (MEX-SDI-A). MEX-SDI-A interfaces are all configured as trunks, with the management address and default gateway (they are Layer 2 only) set for VLAN 2 (SERVERS).

```
vlan 2 name SERVERS
vlan 4 name PLANT
!
interface Vlan1
no ip address
interface Vlan2
 description CME-MEX Servers (Management VLAN
 ip address 10.201.0.151 255.255.255.128
!
interface GigabitEthernet0/1
 description trunk to MEX-SDI-A Port Gi0/2
 switchport trunk encapsulation dot1q
 switchport trunk native vlan 2
 switchport trunk allowed vlan 1,2,4
 switchport mode trunk
!
interface FastEthernet0/1
 description Plant Floor Access
 switchport access vlan 4
 switchport mode access
 spanning-tree portfast
!
ip default-gateway 10.201.0.129
```

CME-WEST

CME-WEST is the "backup" site for CME Corp. As shown in Figure 17-9, CME-WEST is actually an extensible subset of that infrastructure, including both Internet and Private WAN access.

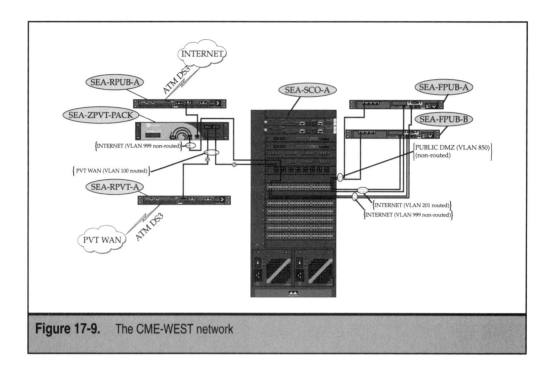

Figure 17-9. The CME-WEST network

Internet Router Configuration

The CME-WEST Internet access router (Cisco 7401) uses a single 1.5MB ATM Virtual Circuit (VC) carried over an ATM DS3 port for Internet access. The point-to-point subnet is assigned by the ISP, with CME-WEST's delegated address space routed by the ISP.

▼ Basic settings for SEA-RPUB-A

    ■ WAN interface settings

```
interface ATM1/0
 no ip address
 ip route-cache policy
 no ip mroute-cache
 atm scrambling cell-payload
 atm framing cbitplcp
 no atm ilmi-keepalive
```

    ■ ATM VC to the ISP

```
interface ATM1/0.11 point-to-point
 description Some-ISP 1.5MB Pipe
 ip address 100.100.100.102 255.255.255.252
 pvc 4/32
```

```
ubr 1500
oam-pvc manage
encapsulation aal5snap
```

■ LAN interface settings

```
interface fastethenet0/0
 description CME-WEST router-to-firewall LAN segment
 ip address 20.20.22.1 255.255.255.192
 speed 100
 duplex full
```

Firewall Configuration

The CME-WEST firewall configuration is essentially a subset of the CME Corp configuration. It allows outbound access to the Internet for selected hosts, provides a single DMZ equivalent to CME Corp's SECURE-PUBLIC DMZ for a tertiary Secure Gateway and tertiary DNS. The VPN tunnels to the remote branches are not configured, but copies of the CME Corp configuration ensure they can be rapidly created.

Private WAN Router

The CME-WEST Private WAN Cisco 7401 is virtually identical to the Internet router, with the exception of the provisioned bandwidth and service type (vbr-nrt versus ubr). Additionally, the Private WAN router participates in the dynamic routing protocol (EIGRP) common to all Private WAN sites.

▼ Basic settings for router SEA-RPVT-A

■ WAN interface settings

```
interface ATM1/0
 no ip address
 ip route-cache policy
 no ip mroute-cache
 atm scrambling cell-payload
 atm framing cbitplcp
 no atm ilmi-keepalive
```

■ ATM VC settings

```
interface ATM1/0.100 point-to-point
 description Uplink to CME Corp
 ip address 10.2.0.254 255.255.255.252
 pvc 1/10
  vbrt-nrt 6000 6000 16
  oam-pvc manage
  encapsulation aal5snap
```

- LAN interface settings

```
interface gigabitethernet0/0
 description LAN segment to CME-WEST Core (SEA-SCO-A)
 ip address 10.101.3.254 255.255.255.248
```

- Routing

```
router eigrp 109
 no auto-summary
 no eigrp log-neighbor-changes
 network 10.101.0.0 0.0.3.255
 network 10.2.0.254 0.0.0.3
```

Bandwidth Management

The PacketShaper at CME-WEST does dual-duty through the added LEM. One segment manages the 6MB connection to CME Corp while the other monitors the Internet connection. Rules for traffic management in each segment are equivalent to rules in the stand-alone counterparts at CME Corp. No IPSec rules are established for VPN termination, but should the need arise, configuration settings for the CME Corp Internet PacketShaper could be modified and imported quickly.

Core LAN Switch Configuration

The CME-WEST LAN Core is somewhat underutilized on a day-to-day basis, but the over-build is necessary to position the switch as a backup for CME Corp. The switch's Layer 3 configuration is similar to CME-MEX with VLANs defined to isolate clients from the subset of servers that are homed at CME-WEST. CME-WEST has substantially more active servers than other regional offices, including redundant domain controllers, online backup servers for network and security management, a backup Citrix server that is part of the CME Corp farm, and an array of repository and backup servers used to store images and data that are replicated from CME Corp.

A significant portion of the core switch's capacity is "preconfigured" to support drop-in LAN access switches that would be purchased and deployed as part of a disaster recovery effort. Again, configurations (including server configurations) for critical systems at CME Corp are "backed up" at CME-WEST. CME-WEST will reuse CME Corp's IP addresses and identities by re-creating the same VLANs for reconstituted servers.

CME Corp

The CME Corp infrastructure is intended to meet design objectives (fast, redundant, hierarchical, fault-tolerant, and so forth) now and in the foreseeable future. In many cases, subsystem design components for the case study, including supporting network and security management elements, are beyond what many corporate networks employ today. Conversely, many of those same networks would be redesigned and reengineered for greater capacity and survivability if the performance warranted the effort and expense.

When looking at the aggregate cost of leading edge hardware technologies, compare them to the cost of industry-leading ERP software packages and server systems—typically, infrastructure cost is a fraction of the major business application package, and the application package is considered so vital that "we lose money" when the system is down. The underlying network must be at least as reliable as the application software: based on the designer's efforts, CME's Enterprise SBC network should be up to the task.

Internet Access Module

The CME Corp high-bandwidth Internet access module consists of the Cisco 7401 routers and associated switch ports on the ORD-SDMZ-A switch. The routers operate using EBGP as a routing protocol against two upstream ISPs, and are responsible for announcing CME's primary Internet-routable subnet into the Internet routing tables. Internally, the outers use OSPF and static routes to receive routing information (routes must be learned from an IGP before being injected into the BGP process). The combination of OSPF, BGP, and redundant routers virtually eliminates the need to implement more troublesome techniques like Hot Standby Routing Protocol (HSRP) or Virtual Router Redundancy Protocol (VRRP) to ensure any combination of routes and equipment can carry critical traffic. As an added advantage, the Internet gateway routers will also maintain a full copy of the Internet routing tables for instant access.

Internet Routers   Each Internet router terminates a single 15MB ATM virtual circuit carried over a DS3 local loop. Point-to-Point subnets for each upstream ISP are provided by the ISP, and the routers run BGP, with restrictions to prevent cross-routing of ISP traffic through CME Corp. Router configurations are similar to the CME-WEST Internet router (ATM ubr service).

Firewall Configuration   The CME Corp firewall is typical of an enterprise-class firewall. It, like the regional site firewalls at CME-EUR, CME-MEX, and CME-WEST, maintains session state tracking, resulting in stateful failover to the redundant unit. Unfortunately, stateful failover cannot support IPSec tunnels since the encryption process is dynamically negotiated—all IPSec tunnels will temporarily drop during a failover. The CME Corp firewall set (ORD-FPUB-A & B) manages multiple DMZs based on the original corporate security model. Each DMZ is assigned a progressively higher (more secure) security level, with normal ingress and egress rules applied. As a footnote, isolation of the second "public" DNS in a more secure DMZ serves two purposes. First, the more secure server can be the "master" for replicating zone updates. Second, the server in the PUBLIC DMZ coexists with corporate web servers (public targets). A malicious attack on, and compromise of, a web server could expose the DNS server to a direct attack from within the same DMZ. The DNS server in the SECURE-PUBLIC DMZ shares the DMZ with servers that only allow HTTPS (SSL) traffic and are easier to secure. The ACCESS DMZ is intended to terminate inbound connections from known, unencrypted but authenticated sources (RAS, Wireless, and others), and apply inspection rules to these traffic flows. The SECURE-ACCESS DMZ is only for termination of traffic that is both encrypted during transport (with strong encryption), and authenticated (read here—VPN clients). Access lists for the CME Corp PIX are built much like lists for all other sites, but are far more complex due to the many traffic flows that must be allowed through the firewall. Even traffic originating in a "secure" segment like the SECURE-PUBLIC DMZ must be filtered by firewall rules and exposed to IDS monitoring before being allowed inside the firewall. The following subset of the firewall configuration provides the basic settings for VPN tunnels, address translation, and filtering rules.

▼ Basic settings, including failover parameters

```
nameif gb-ethernet0 OUTSIDE security 0
nameif gb-ethernet1 INSIDE security 100
nameif ethernet0 PUBLIC security 20
nameif ethernet1 SECURE-PUBLIC security 40
nameif ethernet2 ACCESS security 60
nameif ethernet3 FAILOVER security 99
nameif ethernet4 intf4 security 0
nameif ethernet5 SECURE-ACCESS security 80
interface gb-ethernet0 1000Full
interface gb-ethernet1 1000Full
interface ethernet0 100Full
interface ethernet1 100Full
interface ethernet2 100Full
interface ethernet3 100Full
interface ethernet4 100Full shutdown
interface ethernet5 100Full
ip address OUTSIDE 20.20.20.4 255.255.255.0
ip address INSIDE 10.254.10.1 255.255.255.248
ip address PUBLIC 10.254.0.1 255.255.255.0
ip address SECURE-PUBLIC 10.254.1.1 255.255.255.0
ip address ACCESS 10.254.4.1 255.255.255.248
ip address intf4 127.0.0.1 255.255.255.255
ip address FAILOVER 1.1.1.1 255.255.255.252
ip address SECURE-ACCESS 10.254.8.1 255.255.255.248
failover ip address OUTSIDE 20.20.20.5 255.255.255.0
failover ip address INSIDE 10.254.10.2 255.255.255.248
failover ip address PUBLIC 10.254.0.2 255.255.255.0
failover ip address SECURE-PUBLIC 10.254.1.2 255.255.255.0
failover ip address ACCESS 10.254.4.2 255.255.255.248
failover ip address FAILOVER 1.1.1.2 255.255.255.252
failover ip address SECURE-ACCESS 10.254.8.2 255.255.255.248
failover link FAILOVER
failover lan interface FAILOVER
failover lan enable
```

■ Enable OSPF routing processes; public routes are redistributed to the private process

```
router ospf 999
 network 20.20.20.0 255.255.255.0 area 0
router ospf 1
 network 10.254.0.0 255.255.255.0 area 20
 network 10.254.1.0 255.255.255.0 area 40
 network 10.254.4.0 255.255.255.248 area 60
 network 10.254.8.0 255.255.255.248 area 80
 network 10.254.10.0 255.255.255.248 area 100
 redistribute ospf 999
```

■ Define logical groups of objects to simplify configuration

```
object-group network CME-Servers
  object-group description CME Servers and NMS Accessible to VPN Sites
  network-object 10.1.0.0 255.255.254.0
  network-object 10.1.45.0 255.255.255.0
object-group network VPN-Sites
  object-group description LAN Subnets of Remote Sites
  group-object FRA-LAN
  group-object MEX-LAN
  group-object HEW-LAN
  group-object AKL-LAN
object-group network FRA-LAN
  object-group description CME-EUR LAN Subnets
  network-object 10.201.0.0 255.255.252.0
object-group network MEX-LAN
  object-group description CME-MEX LAN Subnets
  network-object 10.201.4.0 255.255.252.0
object-group network HEW-LAN
  object-group description Athens LAN Subnets
  network-object 10.201.32.0 255.255.255.0
object-group network AKL-LAN
  object-group description Auckland LAN Subnets
  network-object 10.201.33.0 255.255.255.0
object-group network CME-ENG
  object-group description Engineering LAN Subnets
  network-object 10.1.41.0 255.255.255.0
  network-object 10.1.42.0 255.255.255.0
  network-object 10.1.43.0 255.255.255.0
```

■ Define what local traffic is allowed to traverse the tunnels to each site

```
access-list MEX-VPN permit ip object-group CME-Servers object-group FRA-LAN
access-list FRA-VPN permit ip object-group CME-Servers object-group MEX-LAN
```

```
access-list HEW-VPN permit ip object-group CME-Servers object-group HEW-LAN
access-list AKL-VPN permit ip object-group CME-Servers object-group AKL-LAN
```

■ Exempt site-to-site VPN traffic from the Network Address Translation (NAT) process

```
access-list VPN-NO-NAT permit ip object-group CME-Servers object-group VPN-Sites
```

■ Define address translation rules for selected traffic

```
nat (inside) 0 access-list VPN-NO-NAT
nat (inside) 1 object-group CME-Servers
nat (inside) 2 object-group CME-ENG
global (outside) 1 20.20.20.192 netmask 255.255.255.255
global (outside) 2 20.20.20.193 netmask 255.255.255.255
static (inside,outside) 20.20.20.100 10.254.0.100 netmask 255.255.255.255 0 0
static (inside,outside) 20.20.20.101 10.254.1.101 netmask 255.255.255.255 0 0
static (inside,outside) 20.20.20.110 10.254.0.110 netmask 255.255.255.255 0 0
static (inside,outside) 20.20.20.111 10.254.1.111 netmask 255.255.255.255 0 0
static (inside,outside) 20.20.20.121 10.254.1.121 netmask 255.255.255.255 0 0
```

■ Specify traffic that is allowed to originate an inbound connection to web servers, secure gateway servers, DNS servers, and mail relay servers

```
access-list OUTIDE-IN permit tcp any host 20.20.20.100 eq http
access-list OUTIDE-IN permit tcp any host 20.20.20.101 eq http
access-list OUTIDE-IN permit tcp any host 20.20.20.100 eq 443
access-list OUTIDE-IN permit tcp any host 20.20.20.100 eq 443
access-list OUTIDE-IN permit udp any host 20.20.20.110 eq domain
access-list OUTIDE-IN permit udp any host 20.20.20.111 eq domain
access-list OUTIDE-IN permit tcp any host 20.20.20.121 eq smtp
access-group OUTSIDE-IN in interface OUTSIDE
```

■ Specify that IPSec is implicitly trusted

```
sysopt connection permit-ipsec
```

■ Specify that authentication of remote side identity is by IP address

```
isakmp identity address
```

■ Enable ISAKMP negotiation on the external interface

```
isakmp enable outside
```

■ Define IPSec policies

```
crypto ipsec transform-set cme-set esp-3des esp-sha-hmac
crypto map cme-map 10 ipsec-isakmp
crypto map cme-map 10 set transform-set cme-set
crypto map cme-set 10 match address MEX-VPN
```

```
crypto map cme-set 10 set peer 66.66.66.66
crypto map cme-map 11 ipsec-isakmp
crypto map cme-map 11 set transform-set cme-set
crypto map cme-set 11 match address FRA-VPN
crypto map cme-set 11 set peer 77.77.77.77
crypto map cme-map 21 ipsec-isakmp
crypto map cme-map 21 set transform-set cme-set
crypto map cme-set 21 match address HEW-VPN
crypto map cme-set 21 set peer 88.88.88.88
crypto map cme-map 22 ipsec-isakmp
crypto map cme-map 22 set transform-set cme-set
crypto map cme-set 22 match address AKL-VPN
crypto map cme-set 22 set peer 99.99.99.99
```

■ Define IKE policies

```
isakmp policy 10 authentication pre-share
isakmp policy 10 group 2
isakmp policy 10 encryption 3des
isakmp policy 10 hash sha
```

▲ Specify the per-site preshared keys

```
isakmp key !h^Fsn)9,Oq$z@cU address 66.66.66.66 netmask 255.255.255.255
isakmp key $7nA0;*45Fzq!@zQ address 77.77.77.77 netmask 255.255.255.255
isakmp key h&3jN(sv5Km.(s14 address 88.88.88.88 netmask 255.255.255.255
isakmp key @n8Ao,^674n*3bFc address 99.99.99.99 netmask 255.255.255.255
```

VPN (Client VPN)   The VPN termination for roaming clients is provided by the Cisco 3030 VPN Concentrator (redundant). Routing is a combination of static and OSPF to allow external routes to be propagated to the Internet router and PIX firewall. Individual client settings vary based on their role in the CME corporate environment—some are authenticated by the Windows 2000 Active Directory domain, some by internal accounts on the VPN concentrator, and some by RADIUS. Tunnel settings also vary, with most users locked in to "tunnel everything" for security reasons. Most tunnels use preshared keys, but the VPN concentrator is the "test-bed" for implementing certificate-based keying for future use on site-to-site PIC VPN tunnels.

Bandwidth Management   Internet bandwidth at CME Corp cannot be "shaped" in the same way internal WAN sites can, but as a minimum, certain traffic types must be protected. Figure 17-10 shows

▼ Traffic to and from the MetaFrame Secure Gateway, MSAM Access for supplier's, and public access to CME's public web presence are given preferential treatment over most inbound/outbound traffic flows.

■ IPSec, with known tunnel endpoints defined by source and destination address, is guaranteed a minimum amount of bandwidth with preferential access to

Traffic Class Name	Class Hits	Policy Hits	Current (bps)	1 Min (bps)	Peak (bps)	Guar. Rate Failures	Pkt Exch (ms)	Partition Min-Max	Policy Type (Pri.) Guar.-Limit	Top User Analysis
Inbound			0	0	0	0	NA	uncommitted - none		
Citrix MetaFrame Secure Gateway	0	0	0	0	0	0	NA		Rate (6) 30k	
Citrix MSAM	0	0	0	0	0	0	NA		Rate (5) 0-128k	
CME Public Web	0	0	0	0	0	0	NA		Rate (4) 0	
Localhost	0	0	0	0	0	0	NA		Priority (6)	
Site IPSEC Tunnels			0	0	0	0	NA			
Client VPN Tunnels	0	0	0	0	0	0	NA		Rate (6) 64k-256k	
FRA--CME-EUR VPN	0	0	0	0	0	0	NA		Rate (6) 1M-5M	
HKW--Athens VPN	0	0	0	0	0	0	NA		Rate (6) 128k-768k	
MEX--CME-MEX VPN	0	0	0	0	0	0	NA		Rate (6) 1M-6M	
Web Browsing From Citrix Server			0	0	0	0	NA	0 - 768k		
HTTP	0	0	0	0	0	0	NA		Rate (3) 0	
SSL	0	0	0	0	0	0	NA		Rate (3) 0	
HTTP	0	0	0	0	0	0	NA		Rate (3) 0	
Restricted Traffic			0	0	0	0	NA	0 - 2.0M		
SSL	0	0	0	0	0	0	NA		Rate (3) 0	
DNS	0	NA	0	0	0	0	NA			
Gnutella	0	0	0	0	0	0	NA		Discard	
Default	0	0	0	0	0	0	NA		Priority (3)	
Outbound			0	0	0	0	NA	uncommitted - none		

Figure 17-10. CME Corp Internet Packeteer settings

additional bandwidth up to the Internet access bandwidth of the remote site (after all, the Citrix traffic from the sites is inside the IPSec packets).

▲ Normal web browsing from the internal network is held as routine traffic, while web traffic sessions originated from the MetaFrame server farm are given slightly better treatment. If users see poor performance when browsing the web from Citrix, they may try to circumvent the system to cruise the web.

DMZ Distribution Switch (6509) Configuration   The DMZ distribution switch (Catalyst 6509) configuration is complex. It employs a combination of routed (Layer 3 interface) and non-routed (Layer 2 only) segments to isolate traffic flows, expose all segments to the Intrusion Detection Module (IDS), and allow management platform visibility of traffic statistics. Additionally, isolated routed subnets are created by the Content Services Module to allow it to load-balance IP traffic (HTTP and DNS) across multiple DNS and web servers. Although detailed configurations are beyond the scope of this chapter, fundamental Layer 2 and Layer 3 configurations echo those of other corporate switches with several notable exceptions:

▼ The switch runs multiple routing protocols such as

    ■ OSPF for route distribution with the PIX firewall internal interface, VPN concentrator internal interface, and the ACCESS-DMZ distribution switch (ORD-SDE-A), and RAS appliance (PortMaster)

    ■ EIGRP for route distribution with the CME Corp core switches (ORD-SCO-A and B)

    ■ Routing information is cross-distributed from OSPF to EIGRP and vice-versa

▲ Several of the isolated VLANs (isolated from the main routing processes) are visible to the Content Services Module to facilitate load-balancing of web traffic to appropriate servers.

Figure 17-11 shows the combined Internet access layer, Security and VPN modules, DMZ distribution switch, and peripheral equipment.

ACCESS-DMZ Switch Configuration   A secondary distribution switch (Cisco 3550-12G) (ORD-SDE-A) is used between the PIX firewall ACCESS DMZ interface and the separate access segments or wireless LAN (WLAN) and dial-up Remote Access Services (RAS). The 3550 enforces intersegment routing restrictions to limit the ability of wireless and RAS users to communicate directly, provides a first line of defense for the firewall against RAS or WLAN sources Denial of Service attempts, and aggregates the multiple VLAN/WLAN segments for the wireless network. Finally, to avoid exposing critical equipment and servers, the Catalyst 3550 provides DHCP server services to the WLAN segments. The switch runs OSPF on the uplink to the primary DMZ distribution switch (ORD-SDMZ-A) and on the downlink to the PortMaster. The routes to the connected Layer 3 interfaces for the wireless segments are announced up-stream, but blocked on all other interfaces by distribution lists and "passive interface" settings. The PortMaster does not need a route to the WLAN, and the WLAN devices are Layer 2 only.

The Private WAN Module

The Private WAN distribution module consists of the Cisco router, distribution aggregation switch, PacketShaper, and an IDS appliance to preinspect traffic arriving from the sites. Figure 17-12 depicts the operational configuration.

The Private WAN Router   The Cisco 7401 router is configured to use a 1000Base SX LAN interface and an ATM-DS3 WAN interface. Configuration for the routing protocol (EIGRP) is similar to the Private WAN site routers, except that it has a much larger scope of assigned subnets (10.0.2.0/24). Configuration of the ATM interface is similar to that of CME-WEST.

Bandwidth Management   The PacketShaper 8500 defines unique shaping parameters for each remote Private WAN site based on the site's assigned LAN subnet range. By controlling bandwidth at the LAN edge, the traffic destined for the Internet is "prepoliced" to appropriate values and no per-site settings are required on the Internet PacketShaper for these sites. The policies and partitions of remote sites are replicated at the main Private WAN PacketShaper. In Figure 17-13, note that the CME-TNG site (with bandwidth managed by MQC on the router) is classified as "ignore" (do not manage this traffic).

The other notable feature is the CME-WEST "HotSite Replication" rule, a time-based rule that opens up the site-to-site bandwidth after-hours and guarantees best performance to intersite data replication to support disaster recovery.

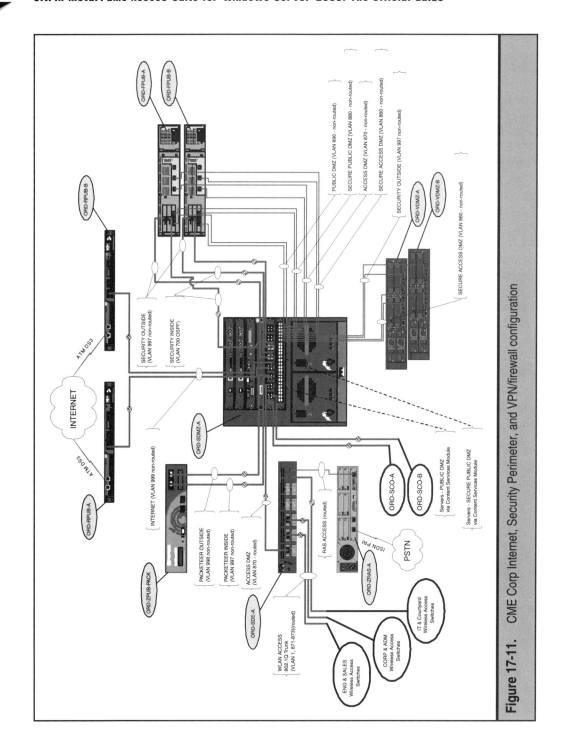

Figure 17-11. CME Corp Internet, Security Perimeter, and VPN/firewall configuration

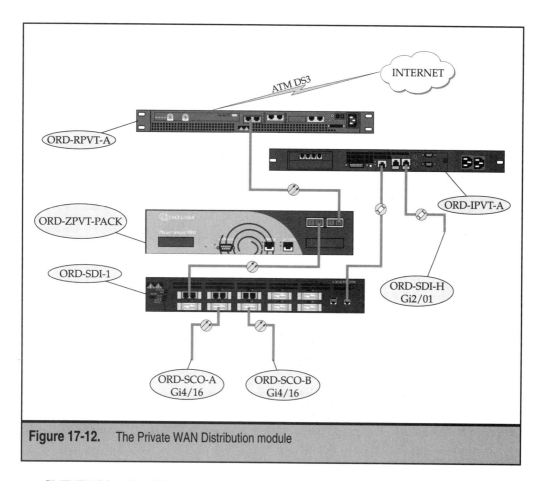

Figure 17-12.   The Private WAN Distribution module

CME-TNG bandwidth is not controlled by the PacketShaper. Instead, policing is managed by settings for the ATM Virtual Circuit (VC) on the router. To the PacketShaper, the subnets associated with CME-TNG are classified with an "Ignore" rule so that no shaping or policing of traffic flows is enabled. The same MQC parameters invoked at the CME-TNG router (ORD-RPVT-TNG-A) are used on the CME Corp's Private WAN router interface to CME-TNG. The following shows partial configurations for the CME Corp interface.

▼ WAN setting (ATM subinterface and virtual circuit. Note that the output
   queuing policy is applied to the subinterface versus the main interface at
   CME-TNG.)

```
interface ATM1/0.32 point-to-point
 description 800KB ADSL to CME-TNG
 ip address 10.2.0.17 255.255.255.252
 pvc 1/32
  vbr-nrt 800 800 16
  encapsulation aal5snap
  service-policy output CME-TNG
```

Traffic Class Name	Class Hits	Policy Hits	Current (bps)	1 Min (bps)	Peak (bps)	Guar. Rate Failures	Pkt Exch (ms)	Partition Min-Max	Policy Type (Pri.) Guar.-Limit	Top User Analysis
Inbound			0	0	0	0	NA	uncommitted - none		
Localhost	0	0	0	0	0	0	NA		Priority (6)	
ORD-TNG--CME-TNG	0	0	0	0	0	0	NA		Ignore	
ATL--Atlanta			0	0	0	0	NA	0 - 768k		
Citrix			0	0	0	0	NA			
Restricted Traffic			0	0	0	0	NA	0 - 64.0k		
Controlled Traffic			0	0	0	0	NA	0 - 192k		
Default	0	NA	0	0	0	0	NA			
SEA--CME-WEST			0	0	0	0	NA	6.0M - nonburstable		
HotSite Replication	0	0	0	0	0	0	NA		Rate (6) 2M-4M	
H.323 VTC	0	0	0	0	0	0	NA		Rate (5) 128k-256k	
Citrix			0	0	0	0	NA			
Dynamics	0	0	0	0	0	0	NA		Rate (6) 20k	
Cerna Epicare	0	0	0	0	0	0	NA		Rate (6) 20k	
Internet Explorer 6	0	0	0	0	0	0	NA		Rate (4) 20k	
Microsoft Excel	0	0	0	0	0	0	NA		Rate (4) 20k	
Microsoft Outlook	0	0	0	0	0	0	NA		Rate (4) 20k	
Microsoft PowerPoint	0	0	0	0	0	0	NA		Rate (4) 20k	
Microsoft Word	0	0	0	0	0	0	NA		Rate (5) 20k	
PowerFuse Desktop	0	0	0	0	0	0	NA		Rate (4) 30k	
Default	0	NA	0	0	0	0	NA			
Restricted Traffic			0	0	0	0	NA	0 - 192k		
MPEG-Audio	0	NA	0	0	0	0	NA			
QuickTime	0	NA	0	0	0	0	NA			
Real	0	NA	0	0	0	0	NA			
WinMedia	0	NA	0	0	0	0	NA			
Controlled Traffic			0	0	0	0	NA	0 - 1.5M		
FTP	0	0	0	0	0	0	NA		Rate (2) 0	
HTTP	0	0	0	0	0	0	NA		Rate (3) 0	
SSL	0	0	0	0	0	0	NA		Rate (3) 0	
Microsoft-ds	0	0	0	0	0	0	NA		Rate (5) 0	
NetBIOS-IP	0	0	0	0	0	0	NA		Rate (4) 0	
Default	0	NA	0	0	0	0	NA			
LAX--Los Angeles			0	0	0	0	NA	0 - 768k		
Citrix			0	0	0	0	NA			
Restricted Traffic			0	0	0	0	NA	0 - 64.0k		
Controlled Traffic			0	0	0	0	NA	0 - 192k		
Default	0	NA	0	0	0	0	NA			
DNS	0	NA	0	0	0	0	NA			
Gnutella	0	0	0	0	0	0	NA		Discard	
Default	0	0	0	0	0	0	NA		Priority (3)	
Outbound			0	0	0	0	NA	uncommitted - none		

Figure 17-13. CME Corp Private WAN PacketShaper settings

▲ Identical traffic classification and marking parameters

```
class-map match-all ICA-LAN
  match access-group 101
class-map match-all ICA-WAN
  match ip precedence 5
!
policy-map CITRIX-LAN
  class ICA-LAN
   set ip precedence 5
  class class-default
   set ip precedence 0
policy-map CME-TNG
  class ICA-WAN
   bandwidth 384
  class class-default
   fair-queue
```

```
!
access-list 101 permit tcp any any eq 1494
access-list 101 remark Identify ICA traffic by TCP Port#
```

The Campus LAN Access/Distribution Module

Access and distribution layer topology for the CME Corp campus was redesigned (based on the topology in Figure 10-2) to form a virtual "ring" (that is, in fact, a Layer 3 partial mesh) centered on the data center facility. By changing all links from individual buildings to the core to be both redundant and Layer 3 (Figure 17-14), the designers eliminated issues related to spanning tree in the campus network—spanning tree instances on each switch are only locally significant because of the Layer 3 (routed) boundary. Switch routing tables will always contain the next-best route to the core, ensuring immediate convergence in case of a link failure.

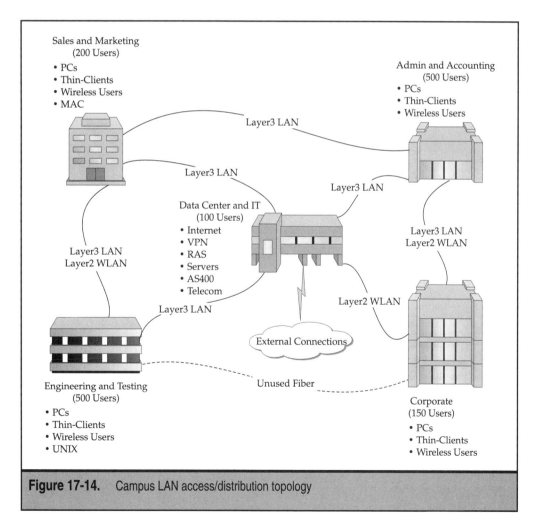

Figure 17-14. Campus LAN access/distribution topology

Typical LAN Access/Distribution Switch Configuration   The campus building switches are only partially fault-tolerant (single supervisor module), but multi-homed at Layer 3 to ensure connectivity to the core. Figure 17-15 shows the physical connectivity.

Building distribution switches in the "virtual ring" are all based on the same template: 10/100/1000 Ethernet connections for in-building hosts, with multiple fiber-optic gigabit uplinks to adjacent switches and the core switches for resiliency. Individual interfaces for switch-to-switch connectivity have no need for VLAN parameters, so they are locked in as Layer 3 routed interfaces only with the "no switchport" command.

Switch-to-switch connectivity for a typical LAN distribution switch, using ORD-SDI-C (ENG-C) as a model follows:

▼   The local LAN segment

```
vlan 2 name ENG-C-Clients
!
interface Vlan1
 no ip address
!
interface Vlan2
 description ENG-C Clients
 ip address 10.1.43.1 255.255.255.0
```

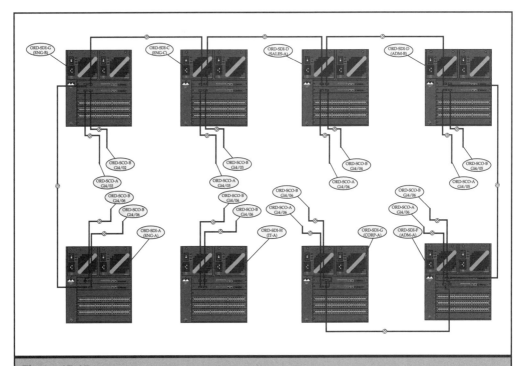

Figure 17-15.   Campus LAN access/distribution (partial)

- Switch-to-switch (distribution-to-distribution)

```
interface GigabitEthernet1/1
 description Link to ORD-SDI-B Port Gi1/2
 no switchport
 ip address 10.2.1.138 255.255.255.252
interface GigabitEthernet1/2
 description Link to ORD-SDI-D Port Gi1/1
 no switchport
 ip address 10.2.1.141 255.255.255.252
```

- Switch-to-switch (distribution-to-core)

```
interface GigabitEthernet2/1
 description Uplink to ORD-SCO-A Port Gi4/3
 no switchport
 ip address 10.2.1.42 255.255.255.252
 !
interface GigabitEthernet2/2
 description Uplink to ORD-SCO-AB Port Gi4/3
 no switchport
 ip address 10.2.1.74 255.255.255.252
```

▲ Routing

```
router eigrp 109
 no auto-summary
 no eigrp log-neighbor-changes
 network 10.1.43.0 0.0.0.255
 network 10.2.1.40 0.0.0.3
 network 10.2.1.72 0.0.0.3
 network 10.2.1.136 0.0.0.7
```

The WLAN Access Module

The WLAN Access Points (Cisco 1200 series) are configured as 802.1Q trunks on their internal (Ethernet) interfaces. VLAN 871 is used for management but is not "mapped" to an equivalent WLAN segment. VLAN 872 is mapped to the corporate WLAN on a unique non-broadcast System Security Identifier (SSID) that requires RADIUS (LEAP) authentication. By tying the WLAN segment to RADIUS, CME IT staff can force positive mutual authentication of clients, enforce session key rotation, and ensure only specifically authorized users are allowed WLAN access. VLAN 873 is mapped to a "public" WLAN that uses no encryption or authentication and assumes default SSID values (tsunami). The Layer 3 interface for VLAN 873 is filtered by multiple access lists designed to restrict WLAN clients from accessing CME Corp public servers (web servers) and the Internet. As a security measure, the Layer 3 interface on switch ORD-SDE-A is maintained in a "shutdown" state to prevent use of this segment without prior coordination. As a secondary check, access attempts (associations) are logged by the individual Access Points as an audit trail—the WLAN is "active," just not connected beyond the Access Point. Figure 17-16 shows the WLAN topology.

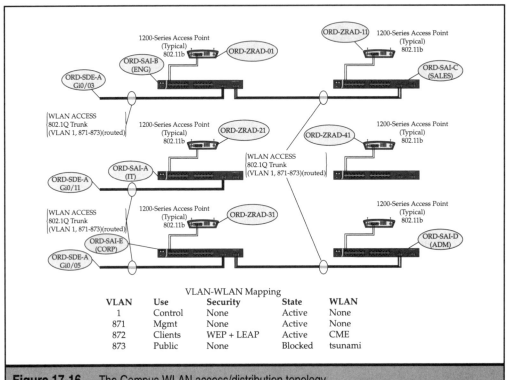

Figure 17-16. The Campus WLAN access/distribution topology

The Core Module

The dual Catalyst 6513 core (Figure 17-17) is linked by a 10GB Ethernet fiber link using single-mode fiber transceivers originally intended for far greater distance (optical attenuation is required), this allows the server farms and core switches to be physically separate in different areas of the data center without loss of throughput. Individual fiber links (Layer 3) to every campus distribution switch, the DMZ switch, and the Private WAN distribution module ensure that no single failure, or even the failure of an entire core switch, can disrupt operations. (Remember, the Citrix farm and critical servers are distributed redundantly across both switches.) Failure of the core-to-core fiber link imposes little, if any, performance penalty as the multiple links through the distribution switches will dynamically reroute and load-balance (via EIGRP) the traffic.

The Core Switch Configuration   A partial configuration from switch ORD-SCO-A illustrates the connectivity to the distribution layer and adjacent core switch. Key elements of the configuration for servers are reflected in module 9 ports 1 and 2 (Gigabit EtherChannel (GEC)), and module 12 ports 1 and 2 (Fast EtherChannel (FEC)).

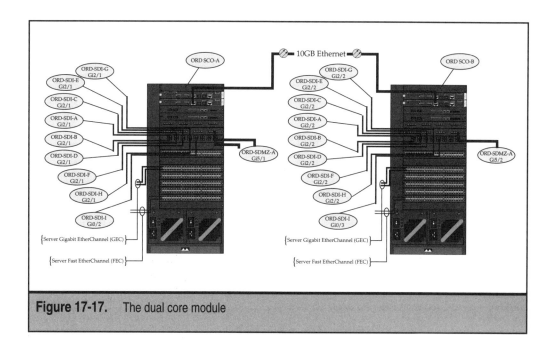

Figure 17-17. The dual core module

▼ The local LAN segment for the server farm

```
vlan 2 name ServerFarm-A
!
interface Vlan1
 no ip address
!
interface Vlan2
 description ServerFarm-A Hosts
 ip address 10.1.0.1 255.255.255.0
```

■ Switch-to-switch (core-to-core)

```
interface TenGigabitEthernet 3/0
 description Backbone link to ORD-SCO-B 3/0
 no switchport
 ip address 10.2.1.1 255.255.255.252
```

■ Switch-to-switch (ORD-SCO-A-to-distribution)

```
interface GigabitEthernet5/1
 description Link to ORD-SDI-A Port Gi2/1
 no switchport
 ip address 10.2.1.33 255.255.255.252
```

```
interface GigabitEthernet5/2
 description Link to ORD-SDI-B Port Gi2/1
 no switchport
 ip address 10.2.1.37 255.255.255.252
interface GigabitEthernet5/3
 description Link to ORD-SDI-C Port Gi2/1
 no switchport
 ip address 10.2.1.41 255.255.255.252
interface GigabitEthernet5/4
 description Link to ORD-SDI-D Port Gi2/1
 no switchport
 ip address 10.2.1.45 255.255.255.252
interface GigabitEthernet5/5
 description Link to ORD-SDI-E Port Gi2/1
 no switchport
 ip address 10.2.1.49 255.255.255.252
interface GigabitEthernet5/6
 description Link to ORD-SDI-F Port Gi2/1
 no switchport
 ip address 10.2.1.53 255.255.255.252
interface GigabitEthernet5/7
 description Link to ORD-SDI-G Port Gi2/1
 no switchport
 ip address 10.2.1.57 255.255.255.252
interface GigabitEthernet5/8
 description Link to ORD-SDI-H Port Gi2/1
 no switchport
 ip address 10.2.1.61 255.255.255.252
interface GigabitEthernet5/16
 description Link to ORD-SDMZ-A Port Gi5/1
 no switchport
 ip address 10.2.1.5 255.255.255.252
interface GigabitEthernet6/1
 description Link to ORD-SDI-I Port Gi0/3
 no switchport
 ip address 10.2.0.1 255.255.255.252
```

■ GEC for the file server

```
interface Port-channel1
 no ip address
 switchport access vlan 2
 switchport mode access
interface GigabitEthernet9/1
 description GEC-1 Primary Port (ORD-SFS-01 NIC 0)
```

```
 switchport access vlan 2
 switchport mode access
 channel-group 1 mode desirable
 spanning-tree portfast
interface GigabitEthernet9/2
 description GEC-1 Secondary Port (ORD-SFS-01 NIC 1)
 switchport access vlan 2
 switchport mode access
 channel-group 1 mode desirable
 spanning-tree portfast
```

- FEC for the RADIUS server

```
interface Port-channel101
 no ip address
 switchport access vlan 2
 switchport mode access
interface GigabitEthernet9/1
 description FEC-1 Primary Port (ORD-SSE-01 NIC 0)
 switchport access vlan 2
 switchport mode access
 channel-group 101 mode desirable
 spanning-tree portfast
 speed 100
 duplex full
interface GigabitEthernet9/2
 description FEC-1 Secondary Port (ORD-SSE-01 NIC 1)
 switchport access vlan 2
 switchport mode access
 channel-group 101 mode desirable
 spanning-tree portfast
 speed 100
 duplex full
```

▲ Routing

```
router eigrp 109
 no auto-summary
 no eigrp log-neighbor-changes
 network 10.1.0.0 0.0.0.255
 network 10.2.1.0 0.0.0.255
```

Server-Side Network Settings

Network interoperability requires correct (matching) configurations between the server-side hardware (network interface card (NIC)) and the associated switch interface.

Using Intel NIC hardware as an example, there are several critical settings that must be configured to ensure the best performance:

▼ Speed
  ■ Set manually to 100 MBps for FastEthernet
  ■ Auto-negotiate with flow control allowed for GigabitEthernet
■ Duplex
  ■ Set manually to full-duplex for FastEthernet
  ■ Auto-negotiate for GigabitEthernet
■ Power management
  ■ Disabled (no low power during standby)
▲ Load balancing
  ■ Use link aggregation (FEC or GEC)
  ■ Avoid adapter-based fault tolerance
    ■ Requires disabling spanning tree or using a hub (half-duplex)
    ■ Uses only one NIC at a time
  ■ Avoid switch-based fault tolerance
    ■ Requires spanning tree be enabled, and incurs the spanning tree listening-learning-forwarding transition delay (15 seconds) when failing over
    ■ Uses only one NIC at a time
  ■ Avoid adaptive load balancing
    ■ Only the primary NIC handles broadcast traffic
    ■ Only the primary receives traffic
    ■ Outbound NIC selection (by destination IP) is off-loaded to an operating system service

Creating an FEC/GEC   EtherChannel (Layer 2 link aggregation) is the preferred method for increasing the aggregate bandwidth available to MetaFrame or other servers. By their nature, they are fault-tolerant and can run with only one member of the team, but with two or more members active, traffic is dynamically load-balanced across a virtual "fat pipe."

Basic configuration involves creating an EtherChannel "team," and then adding members. One member must be designated as "primary" and this MAC address will register as the address of the team. Figure 17-18 shows the teamed configuration and identifies the team MAC address and IP address.

Individual member adapters must be correctly configured independently for 100MB, full-duplex. The secondary adapter is shown in Figures 17-19 through 17-21. Note that it reports the MAC address of the team/primary adapter. Finally, Figure 17-21 shows the power management settings (enabled by default) that are inappropriate for a server and may cause flapping on an FEC team.

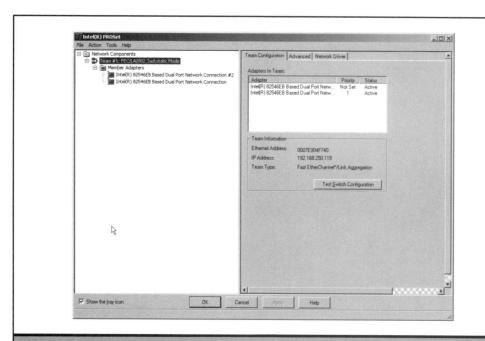

Figure 17-18. The FEC adapter team

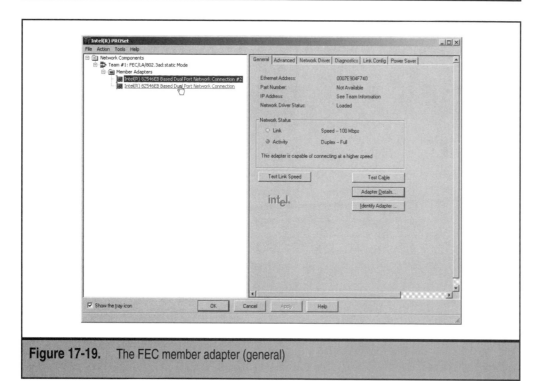

Figure 17-19. The FEC member adapter (general)

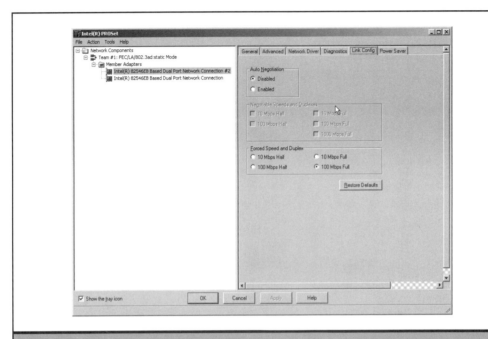

Figure 17-20.   The FEC member adapter (link settings)

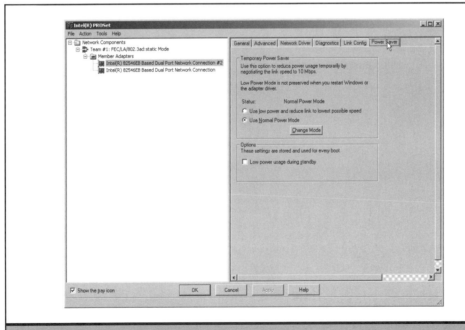

Figure 17-21.   The FEC member adapter (power management)

CHAPTER 18

Printing

Since the inception of networking, printing has been a primary concern during the design and implementation phases of building networks. Whether the issue is quality of the print job, bandwidth needs, performance requirements, paper tray demystification, or simply determining "Where did my print job go?" administrators have struggled with providing secure, fast, and simple printing solutions to their users. This chapter explains the Windows printing environment, shows the options available to administrators within MetaFrame XP, defines terminology unique to SBC printing, and provides a troubleshooting section for systematic resolution of the most common problems. Third-party print driver utilities are also discussed as alternatives for managing the SBC print environment beyond the tools inherent in MetaFrame XP.

WINDOWS PRINTING EXPLAINED

From the perspective of most users, printing is a very simple process. Type some text into an application, click the printer icon in the toolbar, and pick up the pages from the printer. Unfortunately, things aren't so simple for a system administrator. Devoting just a bit of thought to the difficulties of printing in complex environments is enough to give the average administrator a headache. In a less complex printing environment, the client computer, print server, and printer (or print device if you are fluent in Microsoft-speak) are typically all located in a single well-connected LAN environment. When printer problems occur, an administrator is able to walk to all of the devices involved in the print process to investigate and troubleshoot problems. As companies grow, expanded LANs and WANs complicate printing. The print server, client, and printer may all be on different segments of the network with some components located at different physical sites.

In an SBC environment these three key components (client, printer server, and printer) are often located across WAN links. New concepts and new terms also exist in an SBC environment, which must be understood in order to effectively design, implement, and maintain that environment. Printing problems cause end-user frustration and, in turn, cause users to reject new technology. With proper planning, testing, consideration, and a good troubleshooting methodology, however, SBC printing can be managed and work properly.

The Windows Print Process

The Windows environment effectively shields the end user from the complexities of the print process. However, to appreciate the difficulty of developing and maintaining a complex and robust print environment, an administrator must understand the fundamentals of the print process.

When a Windows user clicks the print icon, the following occurs:

1. The application generates an output file including document formatting called an enhanced metafile (EMF).

2. The EMF is sent to the local print spooler.

3. From the EMF file, the local print spooler generates a spool file using a print driver. The spool file includes printer-specific information needed by the printer to create the final document.

4. The print job is queued by the print spooler in the local spool folder and forwarded to the printer or print server where it is transformed from print commands to hard output.

In SBC environments the MetaFrame server acts like a regular client workstation during printing. The application running from the Terminal Server generates the EMF, the EMF file is sent to the local print spooler, and a spool file is generated. The spool file may then be sent directly to the printer, to the print server that holds the queue for that printer, or to a client connected to the MetaFrame XP server where it is re-spooled to the printer or print server.

The MetaFrame XP Print Architecture

Users in an SBC environment can print to the following types of printers:

▼ Printers connected to ports on the user's client device on Windows, WinCE, DOS, Linux, UNIX, or Mac OS platforms.

■ Virtual printers created for tasks such as printing from a PostScript driver to a file on a Windows client device.

■ Shared printers connected to print servers on a Windows network.

▲ Printers connected directly to MetaFrame XP servers.

The printer objects that ICA clients use can be categorized by connection types. There are three kinds of printer connections in a MetaFrame XP server farm: client connections, network connections, and local connections. This chapter refers to printers in a server farm as client printers, network printers, and local printers, depending on the type of connection they have in the farm.

Client Printers

Client printers are defined differently depending on the ICA Client platform.

▼ On DOS-based and WinCE client devices, a client printer is physically connected to a port on the client device by a cable.

■ On UNIX and Macintosh client devices, a PC or PostScript printer connected to a serial port (or a USB port for newer Macintoshes) is considered a client printer.

▲ On 32-bit Windows platforms (Windows 9*x*, Windows NT, Windows 2000, and Windows XP), any printer that is set up in Windows (these printers appear in the Printers folder on the client device) is a client printer. Locally connected printers, printers that are connected on a network, and virtual printers are all considered client printers.

Network Printers

Printers that are connected to print servers and shared on a Windows network are referred to as *network printers*. In Windows network environments, users can set up a network printer on their computers if they have permission to connect to the print server. In a MetaFrame XP environment, administrators can import network printers and assign them to users based on group membership. When a network printer is set up for use on an individual Windows computer, the printer is a client printer on the client device.

Local Printers

A *local printer* is a printer created by an administrator on the MetaFrame XP server using the Add Printer Wizard from within the Printers applet in the Control Panel. Like a network printer, print jobs printed to a local printer bypass the client device and can be sent either to a Windows print server or directly to a printer, depending on how the printer has been created on the server. If the printer is added to the MetaFrame server with the port pointed to a share such as *printserver**sharename*, then the print job is sent to the print server before heading to the printer. The print queue can be Windows-, NetWare-, or UNIX-based. If the printer is added and the port specifies the actual printer itself (such as an lpr queue to the printer's IP address), then the MetaFrame server is essentially the print server, and the job is sent directly to the printer. Local printers are not typically utilized in an enterprise MetaFrame XP environment because of the need for the administrator to set up every printer in the environment on each MetaFrame XP server. However, local printers can be utilized successfully in smaller MetaFrame XP farms (three or fewer servers).

CLIENT PRINTER MAPPING

Client printer mapping allows a user to access client printers from within an ICA session. Client printers are mapped into the ICA session upon login and are called *auto-created printers*. They are automatically removed from the server upon session termination. Published applications often rely on auto-created printers to provide access to a printer as print management utilities may not be available from the application itself. Client printers are supported in different ways depending on the operating system of the client machine. MetaFrame XP servers are able to automatically map all printers that are installed locally on Windows 32-bit clients, provided a suitable driver is installed on the server. All other clients require manual intervention in the printer mapping process.

Auto-Creation of Client Printers

The auto-creation of client printers for Windows 32-bit clients is a complex process that allows for great flexibility in a MetaFrame XP print environment. The basic process is outlined next.

1. **ICA session initiation/login** When a user logs in, a series of programs are run, including the following:

- Login scripts (if available)
- Client drive mapping (if enabled)
- Printer auto-creation (if enabled)
- Application compatibility scripts (if present)

2. **User rights are evaluated and permissions checked**   The MetaFrame server determines if the user has the rights to auto-create each locally installed printer. These rights are set in the following places:

- Citrix User Policies
- MetaFrame XP farm settings
- Citrix connection configuration/Connection client settings
- For W2K, Active Directory users and computers (user properties) Environment tab

If the current user does not have the preceding rights, then no client printers will be mapped.

3. **Exact driver match**   Each user's print drivers are matched against the printer drivers installed on the MetaFrame server. If an exact match for the driver description is found, then the client printer is mapped.

NOTE: Additional spaces and other subtle differences, such as case sensitivity, in driver description will cause this check to fail. These differences can occur between the same printer drivers on different operating systems. For example, a client driver "HP LaserJet 4 – PCL" will not match a server driver "HP LaserJet 4."

4. **Translation match**   Printer driver descriptions are then matched against the mappings found in the IMA database, if it exists. The database contains mappings between client printer driver descriptions and printer drivers installed on the MetaFrame server.

5. **Create printer share**   The printer share for locally attached printers is created with the format *Client Name#ClientPrinterName*. Network-attached printers are created with the format *Client Name#\\PrintServer\ShareName*. For example, on a client computer named WS01, with a locally attached printer name of PRINTER1, a successfully created printer share on the MetaFrame server would be named WS01#PRINTER1. While its network-attached printer on \\PRNTSRV_01\PRINTER2 would be named WS01#\\PRNTSRV_01\PRINTER2.

6. **Additional printers**   Steps 3 through 5 are repeated for each client printer.

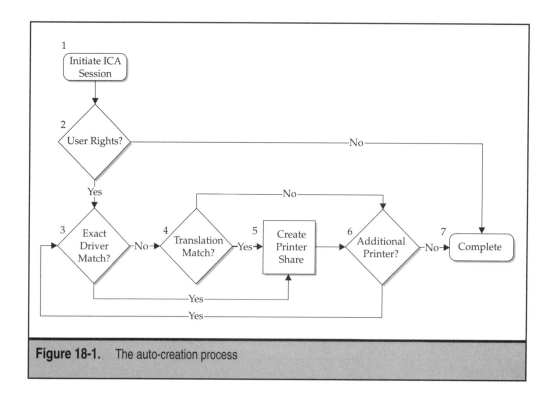

Figure 18-1. The auto-creation process

The auto-creation process is shown in Figure 18-1.

The path that a print job takes for auto-created client printers can change based on what type of printer it is and how the MetaFrame XP farm is configured.

Locally connected client printers always print through the ICA channel back to the client and are spooled locally on the client machine, as shown in Figure 18-2.

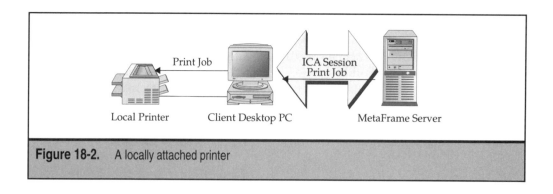

Figure 18-2. A locally attached printer

The behavior of network printers that are auto-created from the client can vary. If the network printer is auto-created as a client printer, the print job will spool back through the ICA channel to the client machine, then to the network print server, and then to the print device, as shown in Figure 18-3. This configuration is ideal for clients printing to network printers across a WAN link from the MetaFrame XP servers due to the print job being streamed within the ICA channel.

If the network printer is auto-created as a network printer then the job is spooled directly to the print server, as shown in Figure 18-4. This architecture is good when the network printer is on the same LAN as the MetaFrame XP server or where WAN bandwidth is not a limiting factor, as print speed will be faster and the ICA channel does not have to process the print information.

There are many pros and cons to using auto-created client printers.

Advantages of auto-created client printers:

▼ Seamless connection of printers.

■ Users see familiar printers.

■ All supported local printers are available.

■ Quick setup of existing client printers.

▲ Printer queues or permissions do not have to be configured on the MetaFrame XP server side.

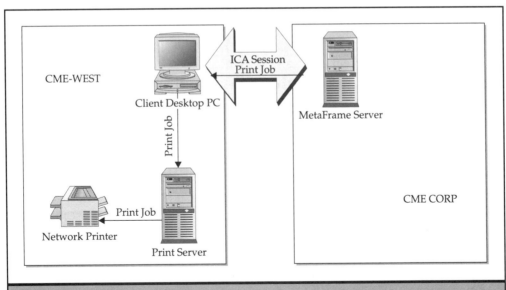

Figure 18-3. Network printer ICA

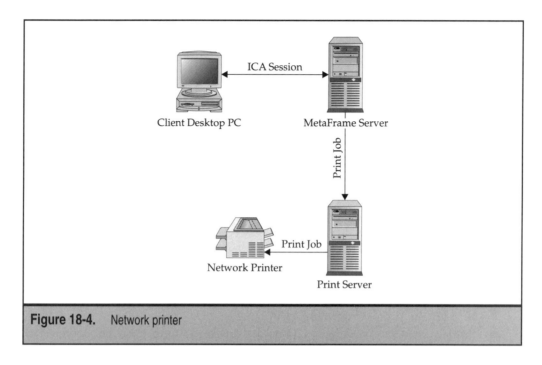

Figure 18-4. Network printer

Disadvantages of auto-created client printers:

▼ Increased bandwidth used by MetaFrame XP sessions.

■ Printing speed is usually decreased and higher resolution or color printers may overtax low-end client devices such as thin clients.

■ Printers must be installed and configured on each client.

■ Users can add, delete, update, or modify their printers in a way that breaks the auto-creation process.

▲ Driver management is necessary to ensure compatibility.

Windows Terminal Services Automatic Printer Redirection

RDP printer redirection is similar to client printer auto-creation in MetaFrame XP but is limited to locally attached (LPT, COM, or USB) printers and the local printer must use a driver installed on the server. There is limited support for print driver mapping functionality and no universal print driver setting. The automatic redirection of client printers is only available for Windows 32-bit operating systems. Windows-based terminals and 16-bit Windows clients can manually create queues but there is no support for any other operating system platforms.

MetaFrame XP Auto-Created Client Printing

Client printer auto-creation can be configured at the following levels:

▼ **Per MetaFrame XP farm**   This is configured in the CMC by selecting Printers in the left pane of the Printer Management Properties.

■ **Per Server**   This is configured by clicking Client Settings in the Properties of the ica-tcp connection in Citrix Connection Configuration.

▲ **Per User**   This is configured by Citrix user policies within the Policies section of the CMC.

Per MetaFrame XP Farm   The farm settings are configured from the Citrix Management console by right-clicking Printer Management and clicking Properties. In the Printer Management Properties dialog box, select Printers from the left pane as shown in Figure 18-5.

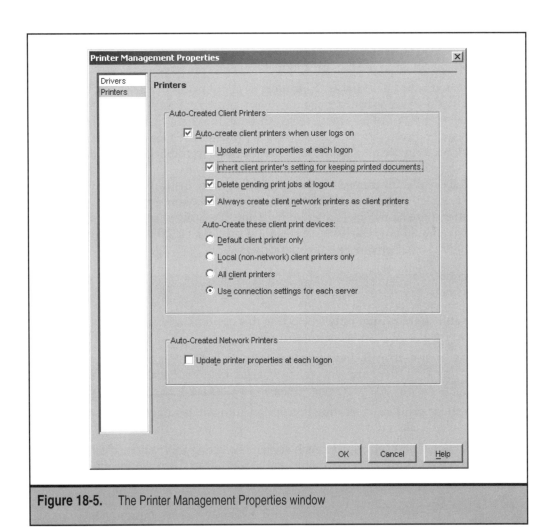

Figure 18-5. The Printer Management Properties window

The Auto-Created Client Printers section of this page has many options. If auto-creation of client printers is to be the default operation for users in the farm, make sure the box is checked next to Auto-create Client Printers When User Logs On. There are several options for how an auto-created printer acts under this section.

▼ **Update printer properties at each logon**   Selecting this option pulls the printer settings from the client at every logon. When selected, any user changes made to printer settings while in an ICA session are temporary and will not be retained.

■ **Inherit client printer's settings for keeping printed documents**   Selecting this option forces the use of the client printer's settings with regard to printed documents.

■ **Delete pending print jobs at logout**   Selecting this option deletes pending print jobs on auto-created client printers when a user logs out of the ICA session. Do not select this option if you want the pending print jobs to be available when a user logs on again.

▲ **Always create client network printers as client printers**   Selecting this option forces the server to connect client network printers as auto-created client printers so all print jobs are directed through the client (using the ICA channel) instead of directly printing to a network printer. When this option is selected, printing from MetaFrame XP servers to network printers that are auto-created by a client is faster over WAN connections. This is due to the fact that data sent to the client is compressed within the ICA session, instead of directly queuing the print job to the printer. Additionally, if two network printers have the same printer share name, the printer on the same network as the client is used. This option should not be selected if you want print jobs to be sent directly from MetaFrame XP servers to network printers.

This section also lets us specify which client devices the client machine attempts to create at logon.

▼ **Default client printer only**   Selecting this option auto-creates only the printer set as the Win32 client's default printer.

■ **Local (non-network) client printers only**   Selecting this option auto-creates only the local client printers on a user's client device. Locally attached client printers are physically connected via an LPT, COM, USB, or other local port.

■ **All client printers**   Selecting this option auto-creates all of the client printers on a user's client device.

▲ **Use connection settings for each server**   Selecting this option selects which client printers are auto-created using the settings in Citrix Connection Configuration.

Per Server   The per server printer auto-creation settings are found in the Citrix Connection Configuration program. They are held in the Client Settings under the Properties of the ica-tcp connection. These settings apply to any client connected to this server unless they have an overriding Citrix User Policy or auto-creation is turned off at the farm level. The key options in this section are

- ▼ **Connect client printers at logon**   Selecting this option automatically maps client printers during session logon.

- ■ **Default to main client printer**   Selecting this option forces the default printer on the server to be the client's default printer.

- ■ **Inherit user configuration**   Selecting this option uses the individual user's settings in Active Directory instead of settings in the connection configuration.

- ■ **By default, connect only the client's main printer**   Selecting this option only maps the client's default printer.

- ■ **Disable Windows client printer mapping**   Selecting this option turns off client printer mapping on the server. If this setting is turned on, it will override any settings configured on the MetaFrame XP farm level.

- ▲ **Disable Client LPT port mapping**   Selecting this option disables LPT port mapping on the server.

Per User   The use of Citrix user policies is the only way to effectively manage auto-created printer settings for different users or user groups. An example was given in Chapter 15 for creation of a Citrix user policy. The policy settings that are relevant to auto-created printing are under Client Devices in the Client LPT Ports and Client Printer sections. The pertinent policy settings are

- ▼ **Turn off client LPT port mapping**   When set to Rule Enabled, client LPT port mapping is disabled.

- ■ **Connect client printers**   When set to Rule Enabled, client printers are connected through the ICA channel. Once this rule is enabled, it is also necessary to select which client printers to connect upon logon.

- ■ **Default to client's main printer**   When set to Rule Enabled, the clients local default printer is set as the default in their ICA session.

- ▲ **Turn Off Client Printer Mapping**   When set to Rule Enabled, all client printers are disabled for the user and all other settings are ignored.

NOTE: Citrix User Policies override all other printer auto-creation settings configured at the server or farm level.

Universal Print Driver Configuration

The Universal Print Driver (UPD) is a Citrix-provided driver that uses PCL4 or PCL5c for Windows 32-bit and Macintosh clients, and PostScript for other clients. The UPD is discussed later in the chapter in more depth. It is important to remember that the UPD is only used for client auto-created printers. The UPD configuration is accessed by logging in to the CMC, right-clicking the Printer Management folder and clicking Properties. The UPD settings are located in the Drivers section. There are four settings for the UPD, as shown in Figure 18-6.

▼ **Native driver only**   Never uses the UPD.

■ **Universal driver only**   Always uses the UPD.

■ **Use universal driver only if native driver is unavailable**   Uses the UPD only for printers that do not have a native driver or a mapping to another print driver already in the CMC.

▲ **Both universal and native drivers**   Creates each printer with the UPD and a separate printer using the native driver or mapping (two instances of each printer).

This section of the properties also contains a check box to Automatically Install Native Drivers For Auto-created Client And Network Printers. This box should be checked if native drivers are being used and you want to automatically install and use native operating system drivers if they exist.

Driver Compatibility

Driver compatibility is a configurable option from within MetaFrame that allows administrators to specify either a list of acceptable (allowable) drivers for printer auto-creation or a list of incompatible drivers that are not to be mapped when presented to the MetaFrame server by the client (Never Create). Incompatible drivers would typically be ones such as Fax drivers, Adobe distillers, and so on. The interface for entering and managing these lists is accessed by

1. Logging in to the CMC.
2. Opening the Printer Management section.
3. Right-clicking Drivers and selecting Compatibility.

The Driver Compatibility console has several options, as shown in Figure 18-7. The server platform for the drivers can be selected. The primary choice is Allow Only Drivers In The List (Allowable) or Allow All Drivers Except Those In The List (Never Create). Drivers are then added to or removed from these lists with the Add and Remove buttons. The driver name can be either typed in manually or selected from a list of drivers already installed on the MetaFrame XP servers.

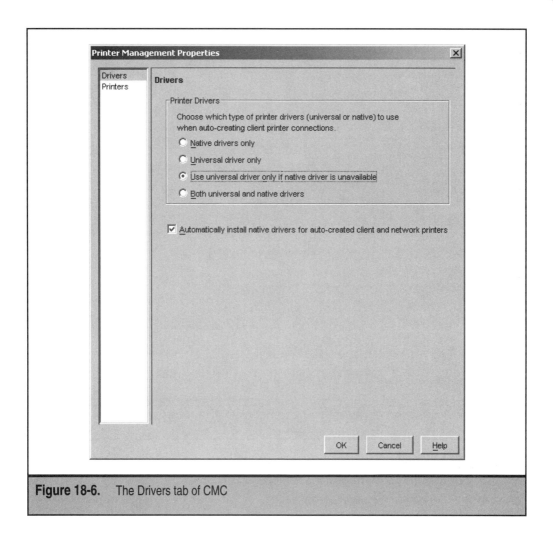

Figure 18-6. The Drivers tab of CMC

Print Driver Mappings

Print driver mappings are integral to a successful implementation of client auto-created printers. By using print driver mappings, an administrator can create mappings between known compatible drivers on the server- and client-side drivers that are not compatible or do not exist on the server. The Driver Mapping console provides a graphical interface to map client printer drivers to server printer drivers. The list of mappings is held in the data store so it is available to all servers in the farm. To access the Driver Mapping console:

1. Log in to the CMC.

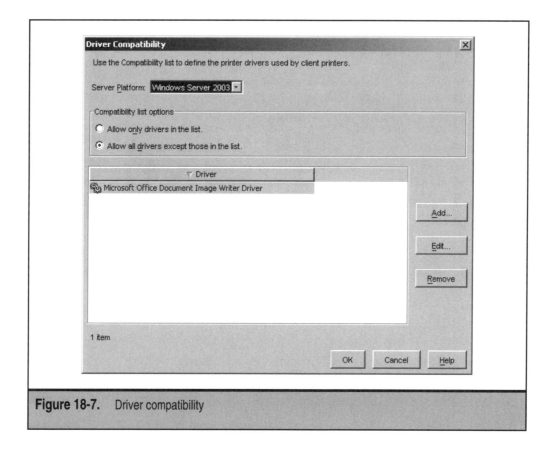

Figure 18-7. Driver compatibility

2. Open the Printer Management section.

3. Right-click Drivers and click Mapping.

The Driver Mapping console shown in Figure 18-8 allows you to enter, remove, or edit driver mappings. A driver mapping is created by clicking Add and then typing the exact client-side print driver. Afterward, choose an existing server driver from a drop-down box. It is important to test the mapping to make sure the print driver prints properly to the client printer. An administrator could map a client dot matrix printer to a server color laser driver, but print output would not be usable.

NOTE: Only an "allowable" or "never create list" can be created.

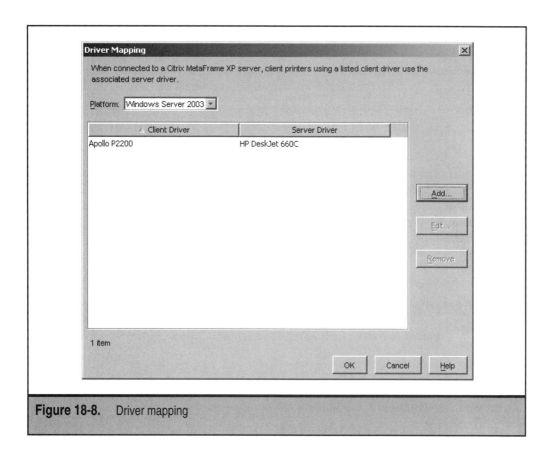

Figure 18-8.   Driver mapping

Printer Bandwidth Management

MetaFrame XP has built-in functionality to manage printer bandwidth within an ICA session. When a print job is transmitted through the ICA channel, it leads to increased bandwidth consumption. Failure to control printer bandwidth leads to slow or unresponsive sessions during printing. If the bandwidth is managed, the print jobs take longer to complete but the user's session is not adversely affected. The bandwidth that print jobs are allowed to consume in the ICA channel can be configured either on the per-server level or on a user level. The following formula is a guideline for using printer bandwidth management:

$$BandwidthLimit = \frac{BandwidthAllocatedforICA - (AveragePerSessionBandwidth)(NumberofConcurrentUsers)}{NumberofConcurrentUsers}$$

▼ **BandwidthAllocatedforICA**   This value is the bandwidth size allocated for ICA traffic across a specific WAN link.

- **AveragePerSessionBandwidth**   This is the average bandwidth used per ICA session.

▲ **NumberofConcurrentUsers**   This value is the number of concurrent users that access the MetaFrame XP servers through the connection link.

NOTE: If this equation results in a negative number, set the bandwidth available for printing to 5Kb.

For example, if there were a T1 from site to site with a 500Kb allocated partition for ICA and 10 concurrent users that use 30Kb per session, then we would limit the user printing bandwidth per session to 20Kb.

As mentioned earlier, the settings for printer bandwidth management can be configured on a per-server or per-user basis.

$$20\text{Kb} = \frac{500\text{Kb} - (30\text{Kb})(10)}{10}$$

Server-Level Setting   The server level setting can be configured in the properties of the individual server, or it can be done in the Printer Management section of the CMC. The following steps are used to configure the bandwidth setting for an individual server:

1. Log in to the CMC.
2. Click Printer Management.
3. Click the Bandwidth tab in the right-hand pane.
4. Right-click the server to be configured and click Edit.
5. Click the radio button next to Limited and enter the number of Kbps that are appropriate for that server. Click OK.

NOTE: The setting for a server can be copied to other servers in the environment by right-clicking the server and then selecting the servers in the dialog box that would be appropriate for that setting.

User-Level Setting   The user-level settings for printer bandwidth are set within Citrix user policies. The settings in the policy override anything set at the server level. For instructions on the creation of Citrix user policies, please refer to Chapter 15. The policy settings for bandwidth are held in the Client Devices section of the policy under Client Printers | Client Printer Bandwidth. The policy should be set to Rule Enabled and the appropriate Kbps input in the box for that user or group.

Thin-Client Printing

Thin clients do not have the ability to auto-create printers. If a printer is locally attached to a thin client, the ICA Client Printer Configuration utility or the Client Printers dialog box in the CMC must be used to create the printer within the user's ICA session.

ICA Client Printer Configuration

The ICA Client Printer Configuration utility allows users to control the creation, deletion, connection, and disconnection of ICA client printers in a session. The utility is used by client machines that do not have a native Windows Print Manager, such as the ICA DOS client or a Windows CE–based thin client. The ICA Client Printer Configuration utility must be run from inside an ICA session. If users do not have access to this program from a published desktop, publish the ICA Client Printer Configuration utility as a separate published application to allow users to view or configure client printers.

To create a new printer with the ICA Client Printer Configuration utility:

1. Select the Printer menu and click New or press the INSERT key.

2. This launches the Add ICA Client Printer Wizard, which uses dialog boxes to prompt the user for a printer type (driver name), the client port to which the printer is connected, and a name to use for the printer. These dialog boxes are similar to the ones used when adding a printer on a Windows 95 or Windows NT workstation.

3. Once all of this information is obtained, the utility will send a request for information to the client about the printer properties and any information necessary for creating the printer. On a DOS machine, this information is written to the printer.ini file so when this client connects again, the printer is created in the ICA session.

Client Printers

The Client Printers dialog box within the CMC allows for client printers to be created based on client name.

To add a client printer from the CMC:

1. Log in to the CMC.

2. Open Printer Management.

3. Right-click Printers and click Client Printers.

4. Click the Add button.

5. Enter the ICA Client name and the printer name, and then select the driver and the port that should be used for the printer.

UNIX Client Printer Auto-Creation

The default auto-created printer for the UNIX client can be set on either a user or machine level.

1. Edit the configuration file, wfclient.ini:
   - For a single user this should be *$HOME*/.ICAClient.
   - For all users of a machine, *$ICAROOT*/Config will work.

2. In the [WFClient] section of the file, type

   DefaultPrinter=*PrinterName*
   DefaultPrinterDriver=*PrinterDriverName*

   where *PrinterName* is a name for the chosen printer, and *PrinterDriverName* is the name of the Microsoft Windows driver for the printer.

3. Save and close the file.

Macintosh Client Printer Auto-Creation

No special configuration is needed to set up local printers to print during an ICA session for MAC clients. Users can change their local print settings during the session.

To print a document during an ICA session:

1. Make a connection to a server and open the application you want to use. When you are ready to print, from the Citrix ICA Client File menu choose one of the following two printing settings.
   - **Print Automatically**   Prints (using the current printer settings) when you select the printer and click Print.
   - **Print With Dialog**   After you select the printer and click Print, you see the standard Macintosh Print dialog box where you can change printer settings. Click the setting you want to use.

2. From the application's File menu, choose Print.

3. In the Print dialog box, select the printer: Client*username*#\\Mac Printer or Client*Macintosh ICA Client*#\\Mac Printer and click Print.

Java Client Printer Auto-Creation

The ICA Java Client must pass three values for auto-creation to be successful.

- ▼ **Printer name**   A locally significant name to identify the printer.
- ■ **Port name**   A file name, port name, or printer IP address and print queue.
- ▲ **Driver**   The printer driver. The driver name must match the driver name on the MetaFrame XP server exactly.

The Java parameter name to use when passing the printer name to the ICA Java Client is user.localclientprinters. The port name uses the Java parameter user.*printername*.port where the *printername* is the same as that specified in user.localclientprinters. The driver is passed by the parameter user.drivername.driver, where *drivername* is also the name specified in user.localprinters.

NETWORK PRINTERS

Auto-created network printers allow an administrator to import available printers from network print servers. The import process will install, if it is not already installed, the print driver from the network print server onto the MetaFrame XP server when a user logs in. Once the printers are imported, an administrator can assign users or groups to have that printer auto-created automatically. Additionally, it is possible to set basic default print properties for that printer. Users can be given the ability to then change those print settings or the administrator can push those settings back down to the user at each user logon.

Advantages of network auto-created printers:

▼ Printers can be auto-created for users on a per-user or group basis.

■ Printer settings can be set for the user.

■ MetaFrame XP integration with network print servers is seamless.

▲ Network traffic is minimized by taking the client out of the print process.

Disadvantages of network auto-created printers:

▼ There is no way to specify which printer is set as default for users that have multiple printers created.

▲ Users cannot utilize local printers unless client auto-creation is also used.

Importing Network Print Server

The import of Network print servers is rather simple.

1. Log in to the CMC.
2. Right-click Printer Management.
3. Click Import Network Print Server.
4. Enter the NETBIOS name or IP address of the print server in the Server field, then enter an account that has full permission to all printers on that server and click OK.

The printers from that server should now appear under Printers in the Printer Management section of the CMC.

Configuring Network Printer Auto-Creation

Users must be assigned permissions to imported network printers in order for them to appear in their ICA session. The process for assigning user permissions to these printers is quite simple.

1. Log in to the CMC.
2. Open Printer Management.
3. Click Printers (available printers will appear in the right-hand pane).
4. Right-click the printer to be configured and click Auto-Creation.
5. Add users or groups by selecting them and clicking Add. Then click OK, as shown in Figure 18-9.

NOTE: Printing preferences such as paper size, copy count, print quality, and orientation can be set for a printer by clicking the Printing Preferences button on the Auto-Creation screen.

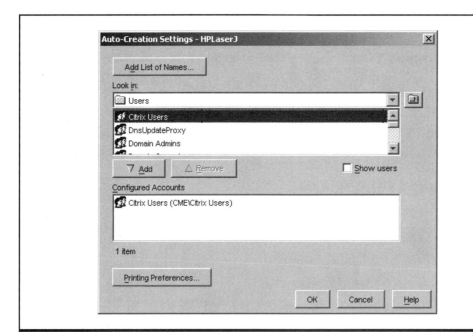

Figure 18-9. The Auto-Creation Settings dialog box

NOTE: Auto-created network printer settings can be updated at each logon by selecting the Printers section of the Printer Management Properties in the CMC. This should be selected if auto-created network printers are to be updated with settings assigned in the Management Console. Any changes made by users are replaced with the assigned settings every time the users log on. Do not select this option if you want to retain the changes that users make during ICA sessions to their network printer settings.

Printer Default

The Windows Printers folder may need to be published to end users to allow them to set a default printer if only network printers are utilized. The Printers folder is traditionally in the Control Panel or is accessible from the Start menu, but if users are using a locked-down desktop or only published applications, they need a way to manage their own default printer. The best way to accomplish this is to give the user a published application of the Printers folder.

The Printers folder is a shell extension that usually resides off the Control Panel. A globally unique ID (GUID) declares shell extensions. Printers are a Control Panel extension in the registry under HKEY_CLASSES_ROOT\CLSID\ {2227A280-3AEA-1069-A2DE-08002B30309D}. This generated identifier represents the extension and points to the proper DLL to run it. It defines the icon, the folder name, and so on. Using this extension with its default name value (Printers), you can run the extension independently in an Explorer instance. For example:

1. Create a new folder on the desktop and name it **Printers, {2227A280-3AEA-1069-A2DE-08002B30309D}**. When you press ENTER after you create this folder, you will notice that the folder icon changes to the Printers folder icon. If you open the folder, you will see your printers.

2. Create this new folder in the All Users profile folder in the Start menu.

3. Publish the folder as a published application.

   - Copy the \Windows\explorer.exe program to a new location with a new name (for example, C:\Print\explorerp.exe).

   - Rename it so that it runs as a unique process.

   - Publish the function using the new Explorer instance.

   - Name the application Print and use the following command line (assuming you created the Printers folder on the root drive C): **C:\print\explorerp.exe n,/ root,C:\Printers.{2227A280-3AEA-1069-A2DE-08002B30309D}**.

LOCAL PRINTERS

In smaller environments (less than three MetaFrame XP servers) local printers can provide a robust printing environment without requiring a large amount of administration to maintain them. All MetaFrame XP servers in this configuration become print servers and need individual print queues to each network printer used by clients. There are utilities such as the Print Migrator 3 from Microsoft (found on the Windows 2000 resource kit) that assist with propagation of printers from one server to another, but in larger farms this process becomes very time intensive. When a new printer is introduced to the environment, the administrator needs to configure the printer on each Terminal Server in the environment.

Advantages of local printers on a MetaFrame XP server:

▼ Excellent LAN printing performance.

■ Reliable.

▲ Printer setup per user is very controlled.

Disadvantages of local printers on a MetaFrame XP server:

▼ Additional overhead for MetaFrame XP server to process print jobs.

■ No local printer support.

■ Poor WAN printing performance.

■ Users must browse the network for printers they need that are not configured.

▲ Printers must be configured on all servers in the farm.

Printer Driver Selection

Driver selection is a critical decision for SBC printing. It is important to have a print driver that will be compatible with the multiuser environment and at the same time provide the printing functionality that is required by the users. While things have come a long way from the Windows NT 4.0 Terminal Server Edition's "blue screen of death" and limited support from third-party providers, drivers are still a paramount concern of printing in the SBC environment. The following driver selection topics are explained and their advantages and disadvantages discussed: the printer manufacturer native driver, the Microsoft operating system native driver, and the Citrix Universal Print Driver.

The Printer Manufacturer Native Driver

The *printer manufacturer native driver* is a print driver included with the printer or downloaded from the printer manufacturer's web site.

Advantages of printer manufacturer native drivers:

▼ All features of the printer are included with the driver (printing to mailboxes, two-sided printing, collating, stapling, and so on).

Disadvantages of printer manufacturer native drivers:

▼ The drivers are often not written for a multiuser environment and may cause the spooler service to crash any time a user prints with that driver.

■ Although they may be certified as multiuser-compliant, some advanced features still may not function properly (graphics printing, landscape, duplex, watermarks, and so forth).

▲ Drivers are not designed for a network environment and often have additional components that are not desirable (control panels, print monitors, and others).

Printer manufacturer native drivers have become better over time in terms of supporting the Terminal Services structure, but there are still many inherent problems. Windows Server 2003 drivers have improved due to more multiuser compatibility requirements by Microsoft. There will always be issues with drivers written by third parties due to the complexities involved in the print subsystem and the reluctance of some third-party providers to correctly code and test drivers for Terminal Services.

Microsoft Operating System Native Driver

Microsoft operating system native drivers are the built-in drivers that ship with the Windows operating system. Windows 2000 Server included drivers for over 2800 devices and Windows Server 2003 natively supports over 3800 devices.

Advantages of Microsoft native drivers:

▼ Drivers are included with the operating system.

■ Drivers are written as a part of the operating system so there will be fewer incompatibility problems.

▲ Many driver features are still available.

Disadvantages of Microsoft native drivers:

▼ Advanced printer features are not always supported (printing to mailboxes, stapling, and so on).

▲ Printers that are newer than the operating system do not have drivers.

This driver option is usually preferred because it is specifically written for compatibility with Terminal Services and still has many of the required printer features.

The Citrix Universal Print Driver

The Citrix Universal Print Driver (UPD) was first introduced in MetaFrame XP Feature Release 1. The new UPD version 2, included with MetaFrame XP Feature Release 3, has support for monochrome or color printing as well as 600-dpi resolution. The driver uses PCL4 or PCL5 for Windows 32-bit and Macintosh clients. Linux clients and PostScript-compatible printers use PostScript.

NOTE: The extended features (color, 600 dpi) are achievable only with the 7.0 version of the Win32 and Linux ICA Clients. The original UPD is available to Win32 and Macintosh OS X clients on version 6.30 or later.

Advantages of the Universal Print Driver:

▼ There are no additional print drivers to install on MetaFrame XP servers.

■ It is a very stable print driver.

▲ It is included with MetaFrame XP software.

Disadvantages of the Universal Print Driver:

▼ It is only supported on Win32, Mac OS X, and Linux clients.

■ Windows printers that cannot print using PCL 4 or PCL 5c will not work.

■ Advanced printer features such as duplex, stapling, and watermarks are not supported.

■ It is limited to 600 dpi.

▲ Large print jobs due to the rasterization of the EMF file before it is processed by the local print driver.

PRINT DRIVER MAINTENANCE

The proper installation and removal of print drivers is an important part of managing the printing environment. If the driver is not installed or removed properly it can cause printing system instability in the SBC environment. It is also important to make sure that the print drivers are consistent throughout the environment.

Driver Installation

The proper way to install print drivers is to use the Print Server Properties dialog box. It can be found by going to Start | Settings | Printers. In the Printers window, select File, then choose Server Properties. On the Drivers tab, administrators can see all the print drivers installed on the server. They can also add, remove, and update drivers, as shown in Figure 18-10.

Drivers can also be installed using the Add Printer Wizard. The Add Printer Wizard method installs the printer as on a normal workstation. An unused local port is selected during the installation of the printer. The printer is then deleted manually leaving the print drivers behind for use in auto-creation. The preferred method for adding print drivers is the Print Server Properties dialog box. A few quick tips for driver installation:

▼ Only install print drivers for printers that will be used by ICA Clients in the farm.

■ Always install print drivers on the same MetaFrame XP server and then replicate the drivers to the other servers in the farm.

▲ If possible, install print drivers that work for multiple printer types. This limits the number of required print drivers in the environment.

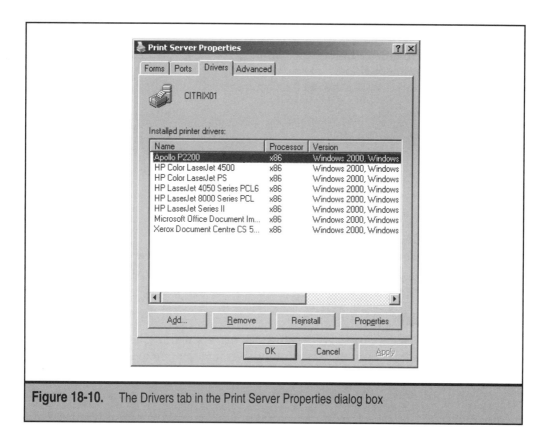

Figure 18-10. The Drivers tab in the Print Server Properties dialog box

Driver Removal

Print drivers can be removed from the server Operating System in a similar fashion to installation. The Driver section of the Server Properties dialog box (shown in Figure 18-10) has a Remove button for the removal of print drivers. It is best to remove any unneeded print drivers. Print drivers causing printer spooler instability should be removed immediately.

Driver Replication

Driver replication allows for print driver installation on multiple servers without having to visit each server and manually install the driver. It is important to only replicate Windows 2000 drivers to other Windows 2000 servers and only Windows 2003 drivers to Windows 2003 servers. There are two built-in ways to handle driver replication in a MetaFrame XP environment:

▼ MetaFrame XP manual driver replication

▲ MetaFrame XP auto-replication

MetaFrame XP Manual Driver Replication

Manual replication requires administrator input to invoke the process, which then runs without further user intervention.

Manual replication is started by the following steps:

1. Log in to the CMC.

2. Open Printer Management.

3. Click Drivers.

4. Select the driver or drivers to be installed on the right-hand side. (Hold the CTRL key for multiple select.)

5. Right-click a selected driver and click Replicate Drivers.

6. Click Yes to the warning message.

7. Select whether you want to replicate to all the same platform servers or if you want to select the servers, and also choose whether to overwrite any existing drivers that may have existed (as shown in Figure 18-11).

MetaFrame XP Auto-Replication

The automatic replication process is designed for drivers that frequently change in the environment. Automatic replication requires no user intervention to start the replication process but it can cause longer IMA service start times as well as increased CPU and network traffic loads.

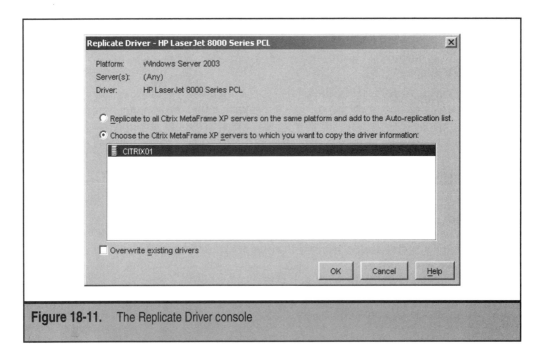

Figure 18-11. The Replicate Driver console

Auto-replication is configured using the following steps:

1. Log in to the CMC.
2. Open Printer Management.
3. Right-click Drivers and click Auto-replication.
4. Choose the operating system platform of the drivers to be configured and then click the Add button to add the drivers that should be auto-replicated.

NOTE: The Print Migrator 3 utility included with the Resource Kit media for Windows 2000 can also be used to replicate print drivers. The only advantage of this utility over the MetaFrame XP utility is its ability to replicate drivers from servers that are not part of the MetaFrame XP farm. The Print Migrator 3 must only be used during scheduled maintenance times, as it stops the spooler service during the replication.

TROUBLESHOOTING

Troubleshooting printing problems in the SBC environment can be complex and exasperating. The following section outlines a methodology to solve the most common printing problems. Most printing problems can be avoided or fixed by investigating a number of basic areas such as printer settings configuration, client-side printer drivers, server-side printer drivers, printing permissions, printer driver names, and client name.

Printer Settings Configuration

There are several locations in the SBC environment where printer settings can be configured. Any one of these areas can contribute to printer problems so they are a great place to start when troubleshooting printing problems.

Citrix Policies

Check any defined Citrix Policies to ensure that the resultant policy allows for the auto-creation of client printers. Citrix Policies will override all other printer configurations listed in this section, so they are, in turn, the first place to check when problems occur. The settings in question are located under Client Devices | Client LPT Ports and Client Printers. To ensure functionality, make sure that the Turn Off Client LPT Port Mapping option is not enabled under the Client LPT Ports section. Enabling this option causes any locally attached printer to not auto-create in a user's session. Ensure that in the Client Printers | Connect Client Printers dialog box, if it is Rule Enabled, the Connect Client Printers At Logon option is checked and appropriate settings below are set, and that the option is not Rule Disabled.

Farm Settings

The next place to verify configurations is the Farm settings for printer configuration. Open the CMC and right click the Printer Management listing. The settings will reside under both the Drivers and Printers sections. Common problems under the Drivers section include having the option Native Drivers Only checked and not having the Automatically Install Native Drivers For Auto-created Client And Network Printers option unchecked. This will cause any printers in which native drivers were not already loaded on the server to fail. Common problems in the Printer section are not having the Auto-create Client Printers When User Logs On option set or isolating printers to be mapped to only the default client-side printer. The former will cause no printer to be created; the latter will cause only one printer to show up (the clients' default).

Citrix Connection Configuration

The Citrix Connection Configuration administration program (found on the ICA Administrator toolbar or by choosing Start | All Programs | Citrix | Citrix Connection Configuration) also has settings that can define whether printers are auto-created or not. Double-click or right-click and select Edit on the protocol listener (ica-tcp, ica-ipx, and so on) to configure the settings. Select the Client Settings button and ensure that the Connect Client Printers At Logon option is checked if the Inherit User Config check box is not selected. Also, ensure that the following boxes are not checked under the Client Settings Area:

▼ Disable Windows Client Printer Mapping

▲ Disable Client LPT Mapping

Active Directory Users and Computers

In Active Directory Users and Computers, check the user's account settings by double-clicking the user account. Ensure that Connect Client Printers At Logon is selected on the Environment tab. This setting is applied if the Inherit User Config check box is set in the Citrix Connection Configuration administration program.

Client-Side Drivers

The next area to investigate if printers are not correctly showing up for users is the client-side driver. Verify that the latest and correct manufacturer's driver is loaded for the specific printer having problems. It is also essential at this point to make sure the local print subsystem is working. Test local printing with Notepad or another locally installed application to the printer in order to verify basic local printing functionality. Printing in the SBC environment will not be successful if the local subsystem is not operational. Problems at the local level must be solved before additional troubleshooting steps are taken.

Server-Side Drivers

Beyond the client-side drivers and local printer subsystem problems, the MetaFrame XP servers must also have a locally installed driver that matches the client-side driver for auto-creation to succeed. The match must be exact or a mapping must be created through the CMC. The drivers installed on a MetaFrame server can be verified in two ways.

The first is through the Server Properties dialog box which can be accessed by going to Start | Printers | File | Server Properties. The Driver tab shows a list of current drivers installed on the server. The second method is to view the following registry location:

HKEY_LOCAL_MACHINE\SYSTEM\CurrentControlSet\Control\Print\ Environments\WindowNT x86\Drivers\Version-3

This key contains subfolders for all the printers installed on the server. The proper method for installing additional printer drivers is detailed in the "Print Driver Maintenance" section of this chapter. Follow this procedure to ensure the MetaFrame XP server will have a suitable driver for auto-creation to succeed.

Printing Permissions

After ensuring that there are no printer settings causing printers not to create, and verifying both client and server drivers, the next thing to attack is permissions. Sufficient rights must be granted to the user to enable them to create and eventually print to the printer. A quick test of whether permissions are causing problems with the creation or access to printers is to log in to the MetaFrame XP server with an administrator level login from the end user's client. If the printer successfully auto-creates in this case, a permissions problem is most likely the cause.

In order to auto-create a printer successfully, a user must have access to certain files and directories on the server. For printer auto-creation, there are two important permissions that must be set. A user should have at least Read, Write, Execute, and List Folder Contents permissions to the directory *%systemroot%*\system32\spool. Users should additionally have Read, Write, Execute, and List Folder Contents permissions to the file *%systemroot%*\system32\printer.inf.

Assigning user permission to Imported Network Print Server(s) through the CMC does not automatically grant the user the right to actually print to the printer. This permission set merely auto-creates the printer within the user's profile. This information is located in the following registry keys in the profile:

▼ HKEY_CURRENT_USER\Printers\Citrix\NetworkPrinters

▲ HKEY_CURRENT_USER\Printers\Connections

Finally, verify that the user has at least Print permissions on the print server. This may be explicit (named user) or implicit (group membership).

Printer Driver Names

Printer driver names also play an important part in the auto-creation process. The problem stems from the fact that different operating systems have different named drivers for the same printer. For example, an HP LaserJet 5 printer has a driver name of "HP LaserJet 5P" in the Windows 2000/2003 operating system environment (MetaFrame XP server) and "HP LaserJet 5P/5MP (HP)" on a Windows 95/98/Me environment (typical client PC).

This fundamental difference will cause the printer auto-creation to fail. As far as the MetaFrame XP server is concerned it does not have an exact driver match.

For this reason, it is critical to know the exact printer driver name used on both the client and server. This information is used to create a mapping entry in the CMC to ensure proper auto-creation. As explained earlier in this chapter, a mapping defined in the CMC determines what driver is used when a user tries to connect.

Client Name

Another item that can cause printer problems is the client name that the local ICA Client uses. The setup program for the ICA Client asks for a client name during installation and defaults to the local NetBIOS name. An alternate name may be specified. This setting has an effect on printing if all client PCs do not have unique client names. When a printer is auto-created on a MetaFrame XP server it includes the client name as part of the path in the format *clientname#printername*. For example, if a PC with the name PC215 connects to a MetaFrame server with an HP LaserJet 4 attached, the printer will be mapped as PC215#HP LaserJet 4. If two machines connect to the same MetaFrame XP server with the same client name and printer, the server will have problems figuring out where to send print jobs since the queues will have the same name. This leads to user print jobs being sent to another user's printer, the correct printer, or nowhere at all. Always use unique client names on users' systems to avoid this pitfall. Chapter 17 discusses naming conventions to ensure unique client names.

It is also important to note that if a user creates or changes the ICA Client name and places a comma in that name, auto-creation of printers will no longer function for that client. The comma must be removed for Client Printer Auto-creation to work. The client name is also limited to 20 (single-byte) characters.

Additional Troubleshooting Topics

The previous sections addressed the most common problems but there are many other obscure pitfalls. This section details additional items that could lead to problems.

Updating Server Information

If you add or remove a printer on a network print server, update the print server information to ensure that the console displays the available printers on the Printers tab. Select a print server and use the Update Network Print Server command from the right-click menu, the toolbar, or the Actions menu. This is a manual process since print server information does not update automatically.

When changing the driver on the print server, remove the object from the print server, refresh the printer node within the Citrix Management Console, and ensure the printer is removed. Log on as a user and then log off after verifying the printer is successfully deleted. Add the printer with the new driver to the print server, refresh the print server within the Citrix Management Console, add the user to the imported print server, and re-test with the previous logged on/off user.

Changing the share name of a network printer deletes all usernames entered in the auto-creation list for the printer in the Citrix Management Console. These assignments are written to the datastore and associated with the share name of the network printer. When you make changes to the printer on the network print server, make sure the usernames are reassigned to the printer in the Citrix Management Console.

Removing a print server removes all of its printers from the farm. This is the opposite of importing a network print server. If you remove printers, ICA Client users cannot print to them. If you want to do this, select the print server to remove, and then choose Discard Network Print Server from the right-click menu, the console toolbar, or the Actions menu. After you confirm the command, the print server no longer appears on the Network Print Server tab and its printers aren't displayed on the Printers tab.

This process also removes the object from the user's profile at the next logon. Ensure users are not reconnecting to a disconnected session when troubleshooting this issue.

Third-Party Ginas

No, third-part ginas does not refer to Geena Davis, but instead to other third-party vendors such a Novell (Nwgina.dll) or PCAnywhere (AWgina.dll) that may block the Citrix Gina (Ctxgina.dll) from accomplishing its task of auto-creating printers. The primary operating system Gina is specified in the following registry key:

**HKEY_LOCAL_MACHINE\SOFTWARE\Microsoft\WindowsNT\
CurrentVersion\Winlogon\GinaDll**

By default, initial installations of Microsoft operating systems do not show this value and Msgina.dll is considered the default Gina. Third-party vendors such as Citrix (Ctxgina.dll), Novell (Nwgina.dll), or PCAnywhere (AWgina.dll) modify this winlogon key and add the GinaDll value. When MetaFrame XP is installed, if the GinaDll value is not Msgina.dll, Citrix adds a new value in the registry:

**HKEY_LOCAL_MACHINE\SOFTWARE\Microsoft\WindowsNT\
CurrentVersion\Winlogon\ctxgina.dll**

Potential problems can occur if another application is added after MetaFrame that overwrites this Gina. If you continue to have printing problems after checking the previous topics then look into this registry key to make sure the Citrix Gina is the primary Gina used by the system.

Important Files

There are several files that are critical for successful printer functionality in the SBC environment. Corruption of any of the following files can lead to complications with printing.

▼ Cdmprov.dll (located in the *%systemroot%*\Program Files\Citrix directory) enumerates printers during the login process.

▲ Cpmmon.dll (located in the *%systemroot%*\Program Files\Citrix directory) is used during the printing process back to the client.

Compatibility Lists

Make sure that any Driver Compatibility settings are not causing problems with the printers that are not working successfully. In CMC | Printer Management, there is a Drivers section. Right-click the Drivers entry and select Compatibility to display the Compatibility dialog box. Ensure that if Allow All Drivers Except Those In The List is selected, that the printer driver name for the client currently having difficulties is not listed. If it is listed, then this setting is blocking the auto-creation of the printer. If the Allow Only Drivers In The List option is selected, make sure the driver being used is present in the list.

The Lexmark Z2 Driver

If Lexmark Z2 printers are present in the environment, provide a mapping to use another driver when printing to this printer. The Lexmark Z-series monolithic driver is linked to the Lexmark installer and may cause the auto-creation process to function improperly.

The Spooler Service

Although it sounds basic, ensure that the spooler service is running and no event viewer messages indicate spooler problems. If the spooler service is stopped on a MetaFrame server, all connected users will lose their sessions printers. Restarting the spooler will correct the problem. On the Windows 2000/2003 server, adjust the spooler service to restart automatically after failure. This can be accomplished through Start | Control Panel | Administrative Tools | Services. Locate the Print Spooler service, right-click it, and select Properties. On the Recovery tab set the options for First, Second, and Subsequent failures to Restart The Service. Set the Restart The Service After field to one minute.

Thin Clients

Windows CE–based thin clients will not auto-create printers in the same way workstations do because printer drivers do not exist locally on the thin-client device. The ICA Client Printer Configuration program or the Client Printers section of the CMC should be used to initially connect and troubleshoot thin-client printing. Double-check the client names specified in the Client Printers section if this utility is being used, or select New from the Printer menu to create an initial mapping in the ICA Client Printer Configuration program. Additionally, contacting the specific OEM device manufacturer for support regarding the appropriate printing support in SBC environments can provide insight into problems.

THIRD-PARTY VENDOR PRINTING SOLUTIONS

Even with all of the advancements and improved functionality, there are still times when a third-party application is needed to optimize printer management. Third-party printing tools can reduce administrative load, increase performance, and simplify operation for end users. The Citrix Universal Print Driver (UPD), first released with FR1, was Citrix's first major step toward simplified printing. With the release of FR3 Citrix has improved the UPD. This section discusses the Citrix UPD along with the following third-party printing solutions:

▼ ThinPrint v5.5

■ triCerat Simplify Printing v2

▲ FutureLink UniPrint XP Server v2.24

The Citrix UPD is a PCL4 or PCL5 printer driver implementation that also works with non-PCL printers such as PostScript and proprietary printers. Print jobs are rasterized by the UPD's Interpreter on the client side and are subsequently processed by the native printer drivers.

FutureLink UniPrint XP Server v2.24

The UniPrint XP Server provides universal printing capability by generating PDF files and sending them to the local client for printing. The UniPrint XP Server component is installed on the Terminal Server and the UniPrint client, and Adobe Acrobat 4.0 or later and the ICA Client are installed on the client machine. The server component installs a Universal Print Driver that has a user-selectable virtual printer. Once a print job is submitted to the UniPrint UPD, the server component converts this print job to PDF format, sends it to the client, and uses the client's locally installed print driver to print using the client's default local printer.

UniPrint XP Server provides three PDF compression techniques when creating print jobs. Note that the supported compression techniques are susceptible to degradation of image quality. This is most noticeable when printing documents that are rich in color. Additionally, font consistency can be a problem whenever the destination client does not have the document's required fonts causing font substitution. To avoid this, turn on UniPrint's embed font property to convert the text to an image. The caveat is that rendering text as an image will increase print job size. For more information on UniPrint XP Server, visit www.futurelink.net.

ThinPrint v5.5

ThinPrint provides core printing functionality along with print job compression and session-based, bandwidth control driver-free printing via its ThinPrint Output Gateway (TPOG) printer module. The TPOG printer on the server is mapped to remote client printers automatically with ThinPrint AutoConnect by defining a template definition, class definition, or manually by renaming the TPOG printer name to explicitly point to a specific remote-client printer. ThinPrint's patented Driver Free Printing technology makes it possible to transmit print data without a printer driver installed on the server. The TPOG simulates a printer driver and sends compressed print data in a printer-dependent format to the local print system. There, the print data is rendered by the local printer driver. The advantages to this technology are obvious: central administration no longer needs to change printer drivers when client printers are added or changed; printer driver conflicts with the deployed software platform no longer occur; CPU load is reduced because of print job rendering; all printers on all ports are supported. Thus both users and administrators benefit from considerable improvements. ThinPrint also allows the use of a print server in your server farm even when the client is separated from the host by NAT and firewall issues with the Virtual Channel Gateway. Additionally, over 90 percent of the thin client manufacturers (as well as many print server, network printers, PDA, and cell phone manufacturers), embed the ThinPrint client directly into their hardware.

triCerat ScrewDrivers v2

Simplify Printing v2™ is based on the well-known ScrewDrivers™ architecture. It is a universal printer driver that hooks into the Windows Print Spooler Service to provide full functionality of local printers. It sends print jobs in the EMF format, which is the native Windows Spooling format. Once the job is compressed and sent to the client side plug-in, it is decompressed and rendered to the local client printer.

On the Terminal Server, the ScrewDrivers printer driver mimics the standard Windows printer options and capabilities of the client printer, such as resolution, paper size, and available trays. Printers are built automatically and allow users to have a seamless printing experience.

Simplify Printing builds printers seamlessly during login and reconnection to sessions through a query of the local client printers. On logout/disconnect, printers are automatically deleted. Administrators can specify whether only the client's default printer is built, or if a set number or all of the client's printers are built. Users can specify which printers they want to have priority, as well as which printers they do not want built. Users are never required to do any administration if the default options are acceptable. Other options such as bandwidth control can be set on a server-wide or connection-specific basis through the server and/or client control panel. For more information, visit www.tricerat.com.

Table 18-1 provides a comparison of third-party print utilities.

Deciding on the Best Third-Party Printing Utility

The only way to select the most suitable solution for a target environment is to perform a similar performance analysis of the solutions being considered. However, based on the results of our tests, the following guidelines can be used:

▼ Allocate sufficient bandwidth for printing as it will help reduce sporadic and poor response times due to printing. Use the equation located in the "Printer Bandwidth Management" section, earlier in this chapter.

■ Use PostScript Level 2 or PCL 6 printers whenever possible as these formats generate smaller print jobs.

■ Use black-and-white or grayscale as the default color for colored printers.

■ Configure the defaults of all printers to run at low resolution unless the application requires high-resolution prints.

■ For a small footprint (system and network overhead) solution, consider using UniPrint XP Server since it generates small print jobs.

■ For a practical solution, consider using Citrix UPD. At no cost, Citrix UPD provides good performance with support for printing-related bandwidth management.

▲ For good cross-platform support, consider using ThinPrint since it supports Linux, UNIX, OS/2, and Win16 operating systems.

Features	Citrix UPD	Simplify Printing v2	ThinPrint v5.5	UniPrint XP Server v2.24
Resolution	600 dpi	Any (based on printer manufacturer driver)	Any (printer manufacturer driver)	Up to 1200 dpi
Metafile Support	PCL4, PCL5c, or PostScript Metafile	EMF	EMF	PDF
Color Support	Yes	Yes	Yes	Yes
Network Protocols	ICA	ICA, RDP5, Native TCP/IP	ICA, RDP5, Native TCP/IP	ICA, RDP5, Native TCP/IP
Compression on transmission	ICA-based compression	Yes	Yes	Yes
Printer Auto-Creation	Yes	Yes	Yes	No
Supported Client Platforms	Win32 ICA Clients (Win95, 98, Me, NT, 2000, Windows XP) version 6.20 or later. Feature Release 1 is required on the server. Macintosh OS X is supported on client version 6.30 and Linux clients are supported with ICA client 7.00.	95/98/Me/ NT/2000/ XP/2003, some embedded NT/XP	Windows 3.1, 95/98/Me, NT, 2000, CE, XP, Linux, UNIX, OS/2 (Win16), Smartphone, PocketPC 2002, Symbian	Windows 95, 98, NT, 2000, XP, Embedded NT and XP, and Macintosh

Table 18-1.   Third-Party Printing Utility Summary

Features	Citrix UPD	Simplify Printing v2	ThinPrint v5.5	UniPrint XP Server v2.24
Client-Side System Requirements	ICA Client version 6.20 or later. 600 dpi and color are not available until the 7.00 client version.	ICA 6.X and higher (ICA 4.x on request), RDP 5.0	Valid ThinPrint client for selected OS. Win32 OS is required for "Driver Free Printing"	ICA Client version 6.20 or later, PDF reader
Server-Side System Requirements	Terminal Services, MetaFrame XP FR3	Terminal Services, MetaFrame optional (1.8 and later supported)	Terminal Services, MetaFrame (any version supported)	Terminal Services, MetaFrame optional (1.8 and later supported)
Bandwidth Control	Yes—Global setting	Yes—Global	Yes—Global and per port	No
Size of Spool File	Large	Small	Small	Medium

Table 18-1.   Third-Party Printing Utility Summary *(continued)*

CASE STUDY

CME, our case study company, did an audit of their print environment before they implemented MetaFrame XP. The firm had each department list its currently used printers complete with driver names. Once the list of printers was determined, a MetaFrame XP server was set up to test the print drivers by installing the Microsoft operating system native driver and then printing to the driver from two client machines simultaneously. If no Microsoft native driver for the printer was available, it was then tested with the Citrix Universal Print Driver unless additional print features beyond the UPD's abilities were required. If advanced features were required past the UPD or Microsoft drivers, the print manufacturer's drivers were installed and tested. If a printer did not print in the proper format or caused the print spooler to crash, the printer was put into a Drivers Compatibility list for incompatible drivers. All printers on this list will have to be replaced rather than risk having a bad printer in the environment. Once a list of good printers was determined, a short list of supported printers was created for the procurement department to use when purchasing new printers. Design goals required at least one printer each for low-volume client printing, high-volume network printing, low-volume color client printing, and high-volume color printing. The audit of the environment also verified that all departments used the corporate asset number for the machine name so that the client name will be unique and appropriate for all clients within the corporate environment.

CME uses Microsoft Native drivers any time there is a Microsoft native driver for the printer or if there is a driver that can be mapped to the current client driver. The UPD will be used for client auto-created printers and some printers that remain in the environment waiting to be replaced. The print device manufacturer's print driver will be used for a few limited machines in marketing and engineering that require additional print features.

The print drivers will all be loaded onto one MetaFrame XP server initially and then replicated from that server to all other servers using MetaFrame XP manual driver replication. Future drivers will be tested first on one MetaFrame test server farm before replication to the production farm.

The printers will be provided to the users by using auto-created network printers for users at corporate sites with a print server(s). Roaming sales personnel, FAT clients, and executives that have a locally attached printer or that connect from home will use auto-created client printers. Citrix User Policies will set the client auto-creation settings. The options in the Printer Management properties of the CMC for Always Create Client Network Printers As Client Printers and Delete Pending Print Jobs At Logout will be selected in addition to the default settings.

The printer bandwidth between sites will be managed by the Packeteer for Network auto-created printers and each user that has auto-created client printers will have bandwidth restrictions specified within a Citrix User policy.

The Printers folder will be published for the users so they can set their default printer. The other major print management steps CME is taking is to train all of their managers on printer management and policies so that end users will have an immediate place to go for common support early in the process. An e-mail will be sent to the enterprise explaining how to set a default printer and how to acquire the necessary printers.

CHAPTER 19

Disaster Recovery and Business Continuity in the SBC Environment

Disaster recovery and business continuity jumped into the spotlight in the wake of the September 11 terrorist strikes, 2001 California power outages, and 2003 East Coast blackout. Unfortunately, many people think of these events and assume that it will never happen to them. Indeed, statistically, most organizations will never experience a major geopolitical or natural disaster. On the other hand, the likelihood of business interruption due to normal day-to-day activities such as employee turnover, database maintenance, power fluctuations, file maintenance, and component failures is nearly guaranteed. We see customers almost daily who have experienced significant loss due to these far more common occurrences.

A large number of studies have been published on this topic, with some very interesting statistics emerging. Some of the more telling statistics are

▼ A Gartner report estimates that two out of five companies that experience a disaster will go out of business within five years.

■ 43 percent of companies experiencing disasters never reopen, and 29 percent close within two years (McGladrey and Pullen).

■ One out of 500 data centers will have a severe disaster each year (McGladrey and Pullen).

▲ Most companies value each 100 megabytes of data at more than $1 million (Jon Toigo).

With this much industry agreement, the question is not whether to plan for disaster, but rather how to plan for disaster, and how much to spend on the plan. This chapter will focus on how to utilize a server-based computing environment to provide full disaster recovery and business continuity within the realm of business possibility for large and small businesses alike.

It is important to note that even smaller organizations will benefit from the discussion in this chapter. Many small companies feel that they cannot afford server redundancy, let alone data center redundancy. Although this chapter will focus more on a mid-size organization plan, these same best practice approaches will apply to even the smallest customers—just on a lesser scale. Even a home-based workstation with a large hard drive configured to mirror data from the main corporation, stationed next to a single MetaFrame server to handle remote access will dramatically reduce the risk of severe business loss in most disaster scenarios.

DISASTER RECOVERY VS. BUSINESS CONTINUITY

Most organizations today have a disaster recovery (DR) plan in place, although very few have thought it out thoroughly, and even fewer have it documented or tested on a consistent basis. Most DR plans for smaller organizations consist of a tape backup and maintain the assumption that anything further will cost more than the statistical chance of downtime. The challenge is that although a tape backup does provide potential recovery, it does not provide business continuity (BC). A *business continuity* plan is an all-encompassing, documented plan of how an organization will return to productive activity within a pre-defined period of time. This not only includes IT services, but also telecommunications, manufacturing, office equipment, and so on. It is important to understand that recovering from a disaster is a subset of business continuity. Although DR is the most important part of business continuity, just having the ability to recover mission-critical data (or never losing it in the first place) is not sufficient to return most organizations to even a minimum level of productivity. Additional concepts such as end-user access and offsite storage locations are critical for a full return to productivity. In the same light though, without recovery of the data, access is a mute point. Most organizations today could not re-create such electronic information as accounting and e-mail data in the event that computer records are lost or corrupted, or recovery from tape backup fails (a significant statistical probability).

Business continuity planning should be broken into two phases:

▼   Minor disasters that do not involve a major facility problem (data base corruption, temporary power loss, server failures, virus outbreaks, and so on)

▲   Major disasters that may require relocation (natural or geopolitical disasters, for example)

From these phases, documentation can be built to describe the risk mitigation procedures, as well as recovery procedures required to maintain business productivity.

When creating a business continuity plan, the following aspects should be considered:

▼   What defines a minor and major disaster, and what are the critical points at which a BC plan will be enacted?

■   What applications, key business systems (including non-IT–based systems), and employees are defined as critical?

■   Where will employees be housed if their main location is unavailable?

■   What time period is acceptable for mission-critical systems to be down, and what is an acceptable time to enact the BC plan?

■   How will access to critical data, business systems, and applications be provided within the predefined time period following a disaster?

▲   Who will be responsible for enacting and maintaining the BC plan?

From the preceding list, it is clear that BC planning focuses primarily on two objectives: *recovery time* and *recovery point*. Put simply, an organization must ask the question "How long can we be down?" and "What do we need to have available after that time?" When initiating a DR/BC study, many companies start out with an attitude that the entire IT infrastructure has to be continuously available, or at least recoverable, in a very short time window, such as four hours. Without server-based computing though, few companies can afford this kind of high availability for the entire IT infrastructure. And even with SBC, an effort should be made to prioritize what must be recovered and how long it can take.

Recovery Time Objectives

When examining the disaster recovery needs of your organization, you will likely find differing service level requirements for the different parts of your system. For example, it may be imperative that your billing and accounting system come back online within two hours in the event of a disaster. While inconvenient, it may still be acceptable for the manufacturing database to recover in 24 hours, and it may be acceptable for engineering data to come back online in two weeks (since it may be useless until new facilities are in place anyway). A key to a successful BC plan is knowing what your recovery time objectives are for the various pieces of your infrastructure. Short recovery times translate directly into high costs, due to the requirements of technology such as real-time data replication, redundant server farms, and high-bandwidth WAN links. Fortunately, with MetaFrame and Terminal Services, you don't have to hunt down PCs across the enterprise to recover their applications; all of your application servers will be located in the data center. We recommend using a tiered approach when applications and users must be restored. Figure 19-1 shows an example of one company's top recovery time objectives.

NOTE: A continuity plan requires an ongoing process of review, testing, and reassessment, since most organizations will change sufficiently over the course of a year, thus making a two-year-old DR/BC plan useless.

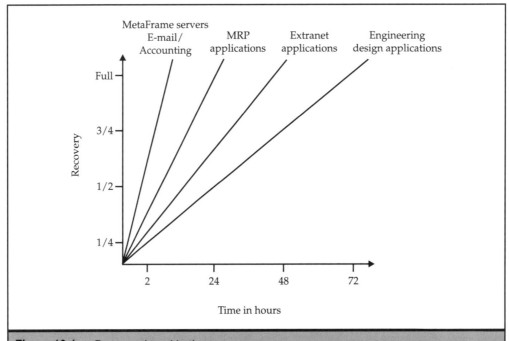

Figure 19-1.   Recovery time objectives

The SBC Solution to Business Continuity

A major theme throughout this book has been building robustness into an SBC infrastructure. Redundancy of the network, server, application, and data center has been discussed. We also made the assumption that on- and offsite tape backups are performed nightly. Most minor disasters can be mitigated by simply following the best practices in this book. It is impossible though to guarantee uptime for a single location, due to the large number of both internal and external risks. Additionally, the data center is not the only thing requiring redundancy—a workstation with access to the mission-critical applications and data for an employee to work from is also required.

Some of the more typical problems with a distributed environment that are solved with an SBC solution are listed here:

▼ Foreseeable disasters often entail evacuation of large numbers of workers, thus leading to the need to have total flexibility for where knowledge-based workers work, what device they are working from, and when they work.

■ Even if the workers are not displaced, if the data center is displaced, it is highly unlikely in a distributed environment that users will still have sufficient bandwidth to access the data at a new location. In an SBC environment, the bandwidth requirements are much lower and more flexible (we show later in this chapter that Internet bandwidth from any source is sufficient if the SBC environment is built properly).

■ The availability of specific replacement PCs on a moment's notice cannot be guaranteed, thus making it difficult in a distributed environment to guarantee that a user will have the necessary processing power to run their applications. In an SBC environment, a user's desktop CPU power and operating system environment are largely irrelevant, allowing the use of whatever hardware is on hand.

▲ The manpower required to quickly install and configure ten or more applications for hundreds or thousands of users is enormous in a distributed environment. In an SBC environment, the applications don't need to be installed or configured, as they are already on the server farm (or backup server farm).

With this clear advantage, many organizations today are embracing server-based computing as the only possible solution to IT business continuity.

Server-Based Computing Business Continuity Design

Conceptually, there are two simple approaches to fulfill immediate resumption failover requirements in an SBC environment—failover of the data center and failover of the client environment. If both are in place, under major disaster circumstances, an organization will simply switch the data center to another location, and then have users connect to the new data center from wherever they can get an Internet connection. Of course the larger an organization is, and the more dispersed its users are, the more complex this task will be. Additionally, for small organizations, this solution may appear to be overkill, as the cost of the redundant data center may exceed the value of the data. Approaches to reducing the cost of business continuity in an SBC environment include

▼ Defining only a subset of users and applications that need access following a disaster, thus reducing the amount of redundant infrastructure.

■ Placing lower expectations when defining what is acceptable downtime, thus allowing the use of a cold backup rather than a hot backup.

▲ Increasing the acceptable amount of data loss. For example, if a full day of data loss is acceptable, then the main and redundant data centers require less bandwidth than if all data must be current to within 30 minutes.

From this list, it is clear that prior to implementing an SBC business continuity plan, we must answer the questions from the first section of this chapter regarding how long we can be down, and who needs to have access. In order to provide guidance in this process, we will call upon our case study, CME Corp, again.

The CME Business Continuity Plan

CME's infrastructure, as described in the Introduction to Part III of this book, is similar to many mid-sized and enterprise organizations. CME has multiple locations, a large number of mission-critical applications, and the perceived need for immediate recovery from data loss. In Chapter 17, we defined that CME will have one central data center to reduce complexity and cost, and allow for central management. Although we will define some IT resources and equipment at CME-WEST in Seattle, CME-WEST users will access their applications and data at CME Corp in Chicago, since that is where the live, up-to-the-minute data resides, and also because it is very costly to maintain the bandwidth required to real-time mirror database and files between two geographically disparate locations.

The apparent downside to this approach though is that all of CME's eggs are in one basket—at the CME Corp headquarters data center. Should a natural, accidental, or geopolitical disaster occur on or near this site, all 3000 users will lose access, potentially forever. To resolve this problem, CME has defined a remote backup site, CME-WEST, as the hot backup site. In order to minimize costs, CME will only replicate a subset of the corporate data-center hardware to permit rapid recovery of mission-critical services and applications and allow managers to make an informed decision regarding permanent rebuilding of the entire corporate data center at the alternate site. In order to achieve this objective, CME has defined a pre-positioned hot backup at CME-WEST for initial reconstitution (8–24 hour survivable), which provides immediate access for a subset of users while the corporate staff is moved to CME-WEST.

CME's IT staff have met with CME's executives and answered the questions posed earlier in this chapter. Table 19-1 shows the results:

Business Continuity Question	CME's Answer
What applications are defined as critical, and what is acceptable downtime for them?	CME has determined that not all applications and users have the same requirement for access and availability in the case of a major disaster. As such, CME has defined three tiers of availability:
	1. Tier one requires application availability and user access within two hours, regardless of cause, Tier two requires application availability and user access within 24 hours, and Tier three requires application availability and user access within two weeks. The Tier-one applications include Microsoft Exchange e-mail, and Microsoft Great Plains accounting software (including payroll, human resources, and accounts receivable/payable functions).
	2. Tier-two applications include the Oracle-based Manufacturing (including production schedules, bill of materials, supply chain information, inventory, and so on).
	3. Tier three includes all remaining applications. Note that this timeline has been set at two weeks to allow for a temporary facility move.

Table 19-1.   CME's Business Continuity Definitions

Business Continuity Question	CME's Answer
Who are the key personnel requiring access at each tier?	1. Tier-one key personnel who require access include all top-level managers/directors, critical IT staff, and a limited number of predefined support staff (about 50 people total). It is important to note that some of these key users must be located at CME-WEST to provide skillset redundancy in the case of a major disaster in Chicago.
	2. The key personnel to which access must be guaranteed grows in Tier two to include a larger set of personnel (about 500 people total) across all CME locations required to operate these key systems. These additional personnel include accountants, human resource managers, remaining IT staff, key manufacturing and development engineers, and lower-level managers.
	3. Tier three includes all remaining personnel.
What defines a major disaster and what are the critical points at which a business continuity plan will be enacted? Note that CME Corp data center has internal data redundancy, including redundant network core components, bandwidth, servers, HVAC, and power. Thus, the business continuity plan only calls for a data center failover in the event of a major disaster in which the determination that more than eight hours of localized downtime will occur (this may be a guess or a well-known fact, depending on the type of disaster and available information).	Any event that will cause a minimum of eight hours of downtime at the Chicago data center will enact the data center failover. Examples of this include a major server hardware or network infrastructure failure, which, due to delays in getting replacement equipment, causes an outage at the data center for more than eight hours; a malicious ex-employee sabotages the infrastructure; a government organization confiscates servers and data due to illegal employee activity. Examples of less common disasters might include a severe snowstorm that renders major utilities offline or causes structural damage to the building; a train derailment at the nearby depot forces evacuation due to a hazardous spill; a localized geopolitical disaster renders the facility unusable.

Table 19-1.   CME's Business Continuity Definitions *(continued)*

Business Continuity Question	CME's Answer
How long is acceptable before enacting the business continuity plan and who is responsible for enacting the BC plan?	Once notification of a major outage has been issued, a decision will be made by the BC team (which consists of the CIO, CTO, CEO, CFO, and their support personnel) within one hour regarding whether to failover to the CME-WEST data center. Note though that this provides only one hour of time to accomplish the actual failover of the data center within the specified two-hour window.
How will access to critical data and applications be provided within the predefined time period following a disaster and where will employees be housed if their corporate headquarters location is unavailable?	Employees required for Tier-one and Tier-two continuity must have broadband or dial-up Internet connectivity from home and must complete the BC training and maintain the accompanying BC documentation at their residences. CME will provide the broadband connectivity and a thin client or corporate laptop for the 50 Tier-one designated employees. Tier-two employees will use existing employee-provided hardware and Internet connectivity to connect from their residences or other CME branches. These Internet connections will provide full access to the Tier-one and Tier-two applications. Tier three will utilize a makeshift facility if required, in addition to any home-based access.

Table 19-1. CME's Business Continuity Definitions *(continued)*

With the business continuity requirements documented and defined, CME's IT group is now able to create the technical portion of the document to ensure that the requirements will be met.

AN INFORMATION TECHNOLOGY PLAN TO MEET BUSINESS CONTINUITY REQUIREMENTS

CME's server-based computing environment makes the implementation of these requirements possible. CME-WEST, as the recovery site for Tier one and Tier two, will need to have hot support for 500 users. These users will require the defined Tier-one data, applications, and access through the Internet. We assume that Tier three will either be implemented back at the Chicago facility or that a temporary facility (which could be CME-WEST) will be used. During the two-week window between Tier two and three, CME IT will have to work feverishly to acquire all of the required hardware to replace any hardware lost in the disaster.

Hot Backup Data Center Design

A *hot backup data center* is a backup data center with real-time servers, ready to be used at a moment's notice. The advantage of a hot backup data center is that it provides a fast resumption plan. The disadvantage is that it requires redundant hardware that generally remains idle except to receive updates and periodic testing.

The most important element of the data center design is geographical location. In order for the backup data center to truly provide resumption, the data center must be located a significant distance from the main data center, and it should not be subject to the same disasters as the main data center (for example, both data centers should not be close enough that a single hurricane could render them both useless).

The rest of the data center design components should mimic the main design center. In the case of CME, we have defined that the backup data center only needs to support 500 users, so the data center will be much smaller than the corporate data center that supports 3000 users. Additionally, there is no need to replicate the testing and training environment, or some of the redundancy that exists at the main data center. Thus, the CME-WEST hot backup data center will be about ten percent of the size and cost of the main data center.

Backup Data Center Components

Although the backup data center is much smaller than the main data center, defining the critical components is still an important part of the business continuity plan to ensure that everything will work upon failover. Although the list of required hardware and software for most organizations will differ, studying the components required at the CME data center and comparing these to the headquarters' data center will allow you to extrapolate what is needed for your organization.

CME's backup data center will require the following components:

▼ Ten Citrix MetaFrame XP servers imaged from the CME headquarters data center to support the 500 possible users required upon failover.

■ A DMZ-based Secure Gateway/Web Interface Server and an internal Web Interface.

■ One Secure Ticket Authority server

■ One Oracle Database server

■ One Microsoft SQL server

- One Microsoft Exchange server

- The LAN and WAN networking components defined in Chapter 17

- Internet connectivity utilizing a separate ISP than what is used at the Chicago data center

- A firewall with DMZ and VPN hardware

- An Internet-based secondary mail server to queue mail in case the Exchange server is offline

- Internal and Internet DNS servers

- Storage area network solution (SANS)

- Appropriate tape backup units to facilitate the recovery of archived data and any information not located on the SAN

▲ UPS backup generator power for the data center

Hot Site Data and Database Resumption

The most critical part of the business continuity plan is the ability to recover the file and database data (the disaster recovery section of business continuity). Even if the full business continuity plan is not enacted, the recovery of data is critical. For example, if the Oracle data becomes corrupt or the Oracle cluster should completely fail, even though this does not constitute a disaster, it is critical that the data be recovered quickly and easily. Worse yet, if a government seizure should happen, there must be a plan to restore the data to non-seized hardware in a timely manner. In order to service this, all databases, files, and e-mail data must be copied to the backup data center nightly at a minimum. Although this is easy to accomplish with file data, doing this with database and e-mail data is more difficult. The larger SANS vendors (HP, EMC, and LeftHand Networks) all support a snapshot technology to effectively copy Exchange and database data across a WAN to another similar SANS device. There are also some non-hardware–based technologies such as NSI Software's Double Take that mirror Microsoft Exchange and other database software. Note that in the CME scenario we are only copying the data at night. Thus, if a disaster happens late in the day, requiring failover to CME-WEST, all data created in the course of the day will be lost. If your organization requires less data loss risk than this, the solutions from LeftHand, EMC, HP, and NSI can provide up-to-the-second transaction redundancy (typically called double-commit), but the dedicated bandwidth requirements and associated costs increase dramatically. Chapter 17 defined that, for CME, 6 MBit of their 12-MBit dedicated pipe will be partitioned at night to support the data mirroring.

Restoration of the Applications and User Access

For any environment that wishes to have a robust, fast resumption plan, all applications requiring immediate availability and flexible user access following a disaster must be installed in a server-based computing environment at the backup data center. In CME's case, all applications required for Tier-one and Tier-two business continuity are installed on the SBC server farm at CME-WEST. Thus, failover of the applications simply requires repointing users from the CME Corp data center to the CME-WEST data center Secure Gateway/Web Interface server. The Web Interface server and MetaFrame farm will be configured identically to the larger farm at CME corporate. All applications, load balancing services, and user services supported from the corporate MetaFrame farm will be fully supported from the CME-WEST farm, with no additional configuration or work following the failover.

User access to these applications becomes the remaining hurdle. As seen in Figure 19-2, all CME remote offices have an Internet/VPN connection, with the exception of the American sales offices. CME has also defined that all of the Chicago Tier-one and Tier-two users who may have been displaced from the disaster will have access from their home Internet connections (assuming, of course, that Chicago's Telco infrastructure has not been rendered unavailable by the disaster). Thus, with the exception of the American sales offices, all users will have full access to the CME-WEST backup data center through the Internet. The BC plan calls for all Tier-two employees at the American sales offices to utilize Internet connections (home based, coffee shop based, and so on) for connectivity until their frame relay connections can be repointed to the DS3 ATM in Seattle (about 72 hours typically).

All Tier-one users will be trained to use a backup URL to access Internet-based MetaFrame Secure Gateway resources at CME-WEST. This provides for immediate access and allows for propagation delays in "repointing" both public DNS resources and BGP routing tables to claim the corporate identity at CME-WEST, as discussed in Chapter 17. Within the 24-hour window, the BGP and DNS changes will have propagated, allowing Tier-two users access through the standard Internet accessible URL.

It is important to note that this entire business continuity plan hinges on the Internet connectivity at CME-WEST. Chapter 17 specifies that CME-WEST has a DS3 line with a 1.5MB virtual circuit that can be increased in a 24-hour period to 15 Mbit. This bandwidth increase will be required to support the 500 Tier-two users needing access over the Internet, and eventually, retermination of the VPN-connected branch and regional offices. Manual BGP failover will provide a seamless failover for all Internet-based connectivity (including VPN connections and Internet e-mail) between CME Corp and CME-WEST (the CME-WEST firewall will be reprogrammed to serve as the CME Corp firewall after BGP convergence to allow IPSec connections without changing the remote sites). All directly connected networks (Seattle and American sales offices) will use an Internet connection in the case of ATM or frame relay failure. If the ATM at CME Corp will be down for an extended period of time, the frame relay links in the American sales offices can be repointed to CME-WEST over the private WAN ATM DS3 within 72 hours.

In addition to remote user access, some employees will need co-located office space. CME-WEST was designed with sufficient capacity in the form of WLAN hardware and prepositioned access switches (see Chapter 17 for further discussion) to support temporary users from other locations.

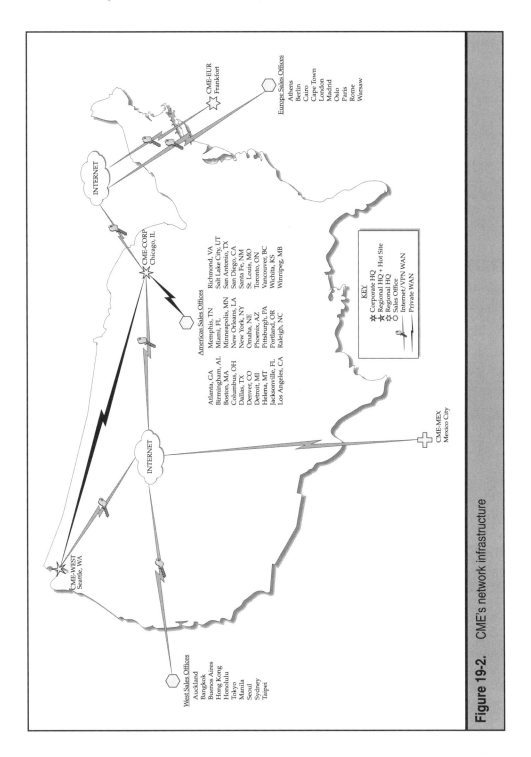

Figure 19-2.   CME's network infrastructure

Full Restoration Plan

Following a major disaster, and an accompanying failover to CME-WEST, and if the disaster requires a new facility, there is a risk that restoration of the original Chicago location may not happen within two weeks or not at all. As such, the Tier-three plan may require either enhancing the temporary infrastructure at CME-WEST and salvaging the Chicago site (to make CME-WEST the new corporate home) or rebuilding a new CME Corp data center in Chicago or some other location to house and support all the CME Corp users long term.

Again, if the CME Corp facility is rebuilt and the server and network infrastructure restored and tested, a period of downtime (usually 24 hours) must be planned to manually fail back the BGP and DNS to point back to the primary location and to return users to that facility.

Documentation

Now that CME's plan is falling into place, an all-inclusive document needs to be created. This document should, at a minimum, include the following:

▼ Emergency phone numbers for all manufacturers and support vendors

■ Names and contact information for the 50 Tier-one people

■ Specifics on how the plan will be implemented, and who will implement it

■ Network diagrams

■ Security policies

▲ Emergency IT response information

This document should be reviewed and updated twice per year by the BC committee. Additionally, the 50 Tier-one employees should receive formal training annually to keep them updated with policies and procedures. Tier-two employees should receive a yearly e-mail or other document to keep them updated on the procedures.

Maintenance of the Hot Backup Data Center

Although the hot backup data center will not be used for general day-to-day activity (other than the storage area network that will receive the backups every night), in order to guarantee two-hour failover, the backup data center must be maintained. The same maintenance items that are logged to the main data center must also be replicated to the backup site. Items such as service packs, hotfixes, application updates, security updates, and so on must all be kept up-to-date. A simple approach to keeping the MetaFrame and Windows 2003 servers up-to-date is to use the imaging procedures discussed in Chapter 11 to image the backup site servers monthly. Additionally, the SANS should be checked weekly to ensure that the data being copied over every night is indeed current and usable.

Test of the Business Continuity Plan

Twice a year (for example, once during a summer break and once during a winter break), the business continuity plan should be tested. It is imperative that all Tier-one personnel be included in this test. The test should ensure successful connectivity, availability, and data integrity, as well as confirm that everyone knows how and when to set procedures in motion.

DISASTER RECOVERY SERVICE PROVIDERS

It is important to note that everything discussed in this chapter can be outsourced to myriad providers, although your organization will still have to set the parameters of Table 19-1 and follow through with yearly testing and updating. It is important that whoever is chosen understands your organization's environment and can accommodate the SBC infrastructure portion of the solution.

CHAPTER 20

Migration to Windows 2003 and Citrix MetaFrame XP

Given the improved functionality, stability, and performance available in a server-based computing paradigm founded on Windows Server 2003 and Citrix MetaFrame XP, most businesses will want to upgrade as soon as possible. Like any major overhaul of the corporate infrastructure, migrating to the Windows Server 2003/Citrix MetaFrame XP environment is not without its limitations and pitfalls.

INTRODUCTION TO MIGRATION

This chapter addresses upgrade and migration concepts and considerations, both from an OS (Windows server) perspective, and from the server-based computing (Terminal Services/Citrix MetaFrame) perspective.

Why Migrate?

The benefits of migrating away from Windows NT 4.0 are well documented and plentiful. Heading the list are the dependency on NetBIOS name resolution services and the lack of integrated directory services. Given that most organizations will migrate away from versions of the Windows operating systems with a finite life expectancy, the benefits of migration in a server-based computing network are simple: Windows 2000 Server and Windows Server 2003 domains provide the extensible global structure that works hand-in-hand with the global deployment of server-based networks. MetaFrame XP and Windows Server 2003 provide greater fault tolerance, resilience, manageability, and flexibility. They also offer a licensing model more appropriate to a computing paradigm that is no longer tied to the user's workstation, and provide superior accessibility, scalability, and security.

That said, large-scale migrations and upgrades are never easy and are always subject to long nights and unforeseen problems. To that end, a combination of Microsoft best practices for upgrading the operating system and domain, as well as Citrix best practices for MetaFrame XP migration are needed. A subset of Microsoft's strategies related to server-based computing is covered in the "Migration Limitations and Restrictions" section that follows. However, administrators should develop a specific project plan detailing all of the Microsoft-centric steps required for domain and server upgrades. From the Citrix perspective, Citrix Consulting Services (CCS) developed a specific philosophy for managing migration.

CCS Citrix Migration Methodology

The CCS migration methodology is made up of the following five main phases:

▼ Analysis

■ Design

■ Implementation

■ Readiness

▲ Production rollout

In addition to the five main phases, a management checkpoint is included at the end of each phase to review deliverables and assess overall project status. Project management is also required throughout each phase. The CCS migration methodology is depicted in Figure 20-1.

The five phases of the CCS methodology are explained in the following sections.

Analysis   The analysis phase is broken down into four segments:

▼ Project scope
■ Project plan
■ Infrastructure assessment
▲ Proof of concept

The following deliverables are created during the analysis phase:

▼ Project plan
▲ Infrastructure assessment

In addition, if a proof of concept is conducted, those results are also published during the analysis phase.

Design   The design phase includes the following segments:

▼ Native MetaFrame XP architecture
■ Identification of migration strategy
▲ Migration architecture

The following deliverables are created during the design phase:

▼ Native MetaFrame XP architecture design
▲ Migration architecture design

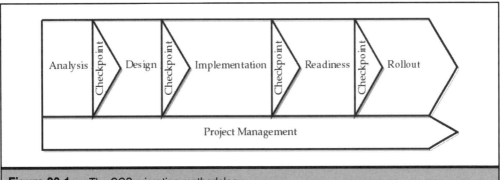

Figure 20-1.   The CCS migration methodology

Implementation   The implementation phase includes the development and testing of any components or scripts that were identified and planned during the design phase. Examples of implementation phase deliverables include

▼ Unattended Installation scripts used to build a new server, including the operating system, MetaFrame, and user applications and configurations

■ Logon/logoff scripts used to customize the user's environment

■ Components needed to integrate published applications into a web portal using MetaFrame Web Interface and MetaFrame Secure Gateway

▲ Customized Web Interface web pages

Readiness   The readiness phase consists of the following two main segments:

▼ Testing

▲ Pilot

The testing and pilot segments are used to verify that the native MetaFrame XP architecture and the migration architecture will scale to support production users.

Production Rollout   The production rollout phase consists of the installation and configuration of the non-pilot portion of the production environment. This includes the rollout of the migration architecture that will evolve into the native MetaFrame XP architecture.

MIGRATION LIMITATIONS AND RESTRICTIONS

Table 20-1 highlights the possible upgrade paths. Within the table, Windows NT 4.0 Terminal Server Edition and all Windows 2000 versions are assumed to use Microsoft's native RDP-based services only (no Citrix software).

Upgrading the Domain

Upgrading the domain is a significant first step, especially when upgrading from Windows NT 4.0. The next few sections discuss the required steps to perform the upgrade from a variety of operating systems.

Upgrading from Windows NT 3.51 Server

Although strictly speaking, an upgrade path from Windows NT 3.51 to Windows 2000 is possible, the authors strongly recommend it not be taken. The upgrade process is both inconsistent in its results, and unpredictable in terms of stability owing to the significant incompatibilities in hardware abstraction layers (HAL) and drivers. In rare cases where the network is trapped in a dependency on a legacy NT 3.51 domain controller, a rolling upgrade to Windows NT 4.0 and/or Windows 2000 may be needed. This should be viewed as a transitional upgrade only, with the upgraded server gracefully demoted and removed from the domain as soon as possible.

Upgrade From	Upgrade To	Upgrade Possible	Recom-mended	Caveats
Windows NT 3.51 Server	Windows 2000 Server	Yes	No	Hardware limitations drivers Legacy settings and files Service Pack 5 (required)
Windows NT 3.51 Server	Windows Server 2003	No	No	
Windows NT 4.0 Server	Windows 2000 Server Windows Server 2003	Yes	Yes	Legacy settings and files Service Pack 5 (required) Service Pack 6a (recommended)
Windows NT Server Enterprise Edition	Windows 2000 Server Windows Server 2003	Yes	Yes	Must use equivalent versions Legacy settings and files Service Pack 5 (required) Service Pack 6a (recommended)
Windows 2000 Server	Windows Server 2003	Yes	Yes	Must use equivalent versions
Windows NT 4.0 Terminal Server Edition (TSE)	Windows 2000 Server Windows Server 2003	Yes	No	Must use equivalent versions Legacy settings and files Service Pack 5 (required) Service Pack 6a (recommended) Licensing changes
Windows NT 4.0 TSE MetaFrame 1.0	Windows 2000 Server Windows Server 2003	No	No	Uninstall Citrix MetaFrame Licensing changes
Windows NT 4.0 TSE MetaFrame 1.8	Windows 2000 Server Windows Server 2003	No	No	Reinstall Citrix MetaFrame 1.8 Licensing changes
Windows 2000 Server MetaFrame 1.8	Windows Server 2003	No	No	Not supported by Citrix
Windows 2000 Server MetaFrame XP	Windows Server 2003	Yes	Yes	Licensing changes

Table 20-1.   The Operating System and MetaFrame Upgrade Matrix

Upgrading from Windows NT 4.0 Server

The upgrade path from Windows NT 4.0 to Windows 2000 Server or Windows Server 2003 is more linear. The fundamental Microsoft restrictions must be met in terms of hardware capability, and application and driver compatibility. In addition, the primary domain controller (containing the read/write copy of the accounts database) must be upgraded first. Although NT 4.0 Service Pack 5 is the stated minimum requirement, Service Pack 6a provides greater stability and the same NTFS version compatibility as Service Pack 5 (NTFS version 5). Note that NTFS 5 compatibility does not allow a Windows NT 4.0 server to access all of the features of Windows 2000 NTFS, specifically: release points (also called mount points or junction points), Encrypting File System (EFS), and disk quotas. Finally, all upgrades from version to version are limited to upgrading to an equivalent, or later, operating system. For example, you cannot upgrade from Windows NT 4.0 Enterprise Edition to Windows Server 2003, you must use Windows Server 2003 Advanced Server.

Experience has shown that a transitional upgrade is by far the preferred method to migrate a domain from Windows NT 4.0 to Windows 2000 Server or Windows Server 2003, with or without Active Directory. In this context, transitional means the upgraded server platforms (PDCs and BDCs) exist only long enough to allow their roles to be moved to a new "clean install" server. Any upgrade from Windows NT 4.0 to Windows 2000 or later is imperfect, and legacy files and settings derived over the lifecycle of the original server are carried forward to the "new" domain model. The simplified transitional upgrade process is

▼ Validate to legacy NT 4.0 PDC based on Microsoft's upgrade recommendations.

■ Install and configure a new NT 4.0 Interim server as a BDC with all required patches and services packs. This may be a high-end workstation rather than a server platform.

■ Promote this interim BDC to PDC. This may be either a logical promotion using dcpromo to simultaneously demote the old PDC, or a ruthless promotion with dcpromo where the old PDC is offline and inaccessible.

■ Verify that the read/write copy of the SAM database is completely replicated before proceeding.

■ Upgrade the Interim server (now PDC) to Windows 2000 or Windows Server 2003 and install Active Directory as a mixed mode domain.

■ Verify that all services (WINS, DNS, file replication) are working correctly.

■ Verify that the upgrade is properly acknowledged by member servers. This may require a reboot of Windows 2000 or later member servers to re-register DNS and services in Active Directory.

■ Remove the Legacy BDC (old PDC) from the domain and rebuild as Windows 2000 Server or Windows Server 2003, rejoin the domain, promote to domain controller, and verify services and synchronization.

■ Once the rebuilt Domain Controller is stable, transfer the operation's master roles as necessary and reverify services and synchronization.

■ Continue rebuilding the remaining Legacy BDCs as required.

▲ Demote and remove the Interim Domain Controller if appropriate.

Although this process may seem more cumbersome than the textbook Microsoft upgrade, consider the complexity of trying to configuration manage a directly upgraded server:

▼ Which files and versions are Legacy and not used by the current OS? Which registry entries are no longer valid?

■ Which profile information must be managed? The information in *%systemroot%* profiles*%username%* or that in Documents And Settings*%username%*?

▲ Which profile elements are still linked?

Additional limitations, such as how to overcome the boot partition size limitation of Windows NT 4.0 (4.0GB native, 7.6GB maximum), are not always considered during an in-place upgrade.

One of the most commonly overlooked upgrade caveats deals with the Microsoft Terminal Services Licensing service. In a Windows NT 4.0 domain with Windows 2000 or Windows Server 2003 member Terminal Servers (with or without Citrix MetaFrame), the Licensing Service must be installed on a Windows 2000 or later member server. As soon as the domain is upgraded to Windows 2000 or Windows Server 2003, Terminal Services Licensing can *only* run on a domain controller. Terminal Services breaks immediately upon upgrade and remains so until it is deinstalled from the member server and reinstalled and relicensed on the Domain Controller.

Upgrading from Windows 2000 Server

The Windows 2000 to Windows Server 2003 upgrade is seamless and subject only to the previously discussed hardware, application, and version limitations. One notable exception is Novell Netware integration. If your environment requires interoperability with Novell over IPX/SPX (NWLink), you cannot use the 64-bit version of Windows Server 2003. Additionally, Windows 2003 Server–based domains can operate in one of three modes: Windows 2000 Mixed Mode (NT 4.0 compatible), Windows 2000 Native Mode (no NT 4.0 domain controllers), or Windows Server 2003 Mode (all domain controllers must be Windows Server 2003). Table 20-2 lists the features available for each mode.

Domain Feature	Windows 2000 Mixed	Windows 2000 Native	Windows Server 2003
Domain controller rename tool	Disabled	Disabled	Enabled
Update logon timestamp	Disabled	Disabled	Enabled
Kerberos KDC key version numbers	Disabled	Disabled	Enabled
User password on InetOrgPerson object	Disabled	Disabled	Enabled
Universal Groups	Enabled for distribution groups. Disabled for security groups.	Enabled. Allows both security and distribution groups.	Enabled. Allows both security and distribution groups.

Table 20-2. The Windows Server 2003 Domain Mode Feature Matrix

Domain Feature	Windows 2000 Mixed	Windows 2000 Native	Windows Server 2003
Group Nesting	Enabled for distribution groups. Disabled for security groups, except for domain local security groups that can have global groups as members.	Enabled. Allows full group nesting.	Enabled. Allows full group nesting.
Converting Groups	Disabled. No group conversions allowed.	Enabled. Allows conversion between security groups and distribution groups.	Enabled. Allows conversion between security groups and distribution groups.
SID History	Disabled.	Enabled. Allows migration of security principals from one domain to another.	Enabled. Allows migration of security principals from one domain to another.

Table 20-2.   The Windows Server 2003 Domain Mode Feature Matrix *(continued)*

Upgrading Terminal Servers

Operating system upgrades based on Microsoft's best practices allow administrators to migrate from one Terminal Server OS to the next. Upgrade considerations for Windows NT 4.0 TSE and Windows 2000 are listed next. While these upgrades are possible, administrators should consider the implications of moving multiple disparate OS versions to a common standard. Although the benefits of having all Terminal Servers running the same (modern) OS are obvious, configuration control and management may be lost. A Windows Server 2003 Terminal Server built from the ground up will be radically different from a server that was migrated from Windows NT 4 to Windows 2000 to Windows Server 2003. If a precise configuration control and management process requires servers to be identical, do not upgrade, rebuild.

Upgrading from Windows NT 4.0 TSE

The TSE-to-Windows 2000 Server (Terminal Server) or TSE-to-Windows Server 2003 (Terminal Server) upgraded path is subject to the same limitations discussed in the "Migration Limitations and Restrictions" section. Although not addressed as a critical consideration in that section, administrators must be aware that the upgrade also upgrades Internet Explorer. Any Terminal Service applications dependent upon IE functionality must be compatible with IE 5.01 or later. Additionally, licensing based on the old Operating Systems Equivalency provision (if a user ran Windows 2000 Professional on their desktop, they did not need a Terminal

Service Client Access License) has been removed. All users (either by device or by user) must have a Windows Server 2003 CAL.

Upgrading from Windows 2000

The Windows 2000 to Windows Server 2003 upgrade is seamless and subject only to the previously discussed hardware, application, license, and version limitations.

Upgrading Citrix MetaFrame

Upgrading existing Windows 2000 servers that are already running MetaFrame XP is a straightforward Microsoft-centric in-place upgrade. Conversely, upgrading both the OS version and the Citrix MetaFrame version requires special considerations.

Upgrading from Windows NT 4.0 TSE and MetaFrame 1.8

Microsoft documentation indicates Citrix MetaFrame 1.8 must be deinstalled prior to upgrading to Windows 2000. This is not strictly true, and although not a recommended upgrade path, it is a viable subject for several restrictions:

▼ The operating system must be upgraded first.

■ After the OS upgrade, Citrix MetaFrame 1.8 for Windows NT will show as "installed" but will not function, and error messages will indicate a new version of Citrix MetaFrame is required.

■ Reinstall Citrix MetaFrame 1.8 for Windows 2000.

▲ This upgrade process preserves all published applications and MetaFrame settings.

Upgrading from Windows 2000 and MetaFrame 1.8

Migration from MetaFrame 1.8 to MetaFrame XP on Windows 2000 is intended to be a transitional strategy, not a permanent fixture. During the migration process, the MetaFrame server farm must run in Interoperability mode, which limits the use of some MetaFrame XP advanced features. The following general limitations apply:

▼ Upgrade Citrix MetaFrame from 1.8 to XP first.

■ Migration licenses are required.

■ Avoid leaving the farm in Interoperability mode for an extended period.

■ The MetaFrame XP server farm must have the same name as the MetaFrame 1.8 server farm. When you install MetaFrame XP on the first server in the farm, name the server farm at the same time you create the data store.

NOTE: ICA Clients see the MetaFrame XP and MetaFrame 1.8 farms operating in mixed mode as a single farm. However, they are actually two separate farms.

- Management Utilities are different.

  - MetaFrame XP farms and MetaFrame 1.8 farms are managed by separate utilities. You can manage a MetaFrame 1.8 farm using MetaFrame 1.8 utilities including Citrix Server Administration (mfadmin.exe) and Published Application Manager (appcfg.exe). You should use the updated versions of these tools that are installed on each MetaFrame XP server. We do not recommend running previous versions of these tools from the existing MetaFrame 1.8 servers.

  - Use the Published Application Manager utility to configure and modify published applications for MetaFrame 1.8 servers. Use the Citrix Server Administration utility to configure options on MetaFrame 1.8 and MetaFrame XP servers. Note that the settings on MetaFrame XP servers take effect only when the server farm is operating in mixed mode.

  - Use the Citrix Management Console to manage a MetaFrame XP farm. Published Application Manager cannot be used to manage applications migrated to MetaFrame XP servers.

- When MetaFrame XP is configured for mixed mode operation, MetaFrame 1.8 farms and MetaFrame XP farms appear unified because ICA browsers in both farms pool information. A MetaFrame XP server becomes the master ICA browser of both farms. The new master ICA browser holds information about the published applications available on each server.

  MetaFrame XP mixed mode operation requires two types of network traffic. Both MetaFrame 1.8 servers and MetaFrame XP servers communicate via UDP Port 1604 for MetaFrame 1.8 server communication. In addition, IMA TCP Port 2512 traffic exists between all MetaFrame XP servers for MetaFrame XP server communication. Operating in MetaFrame XP mixed mode results in increased network traffic and can affect network scalability.

  ▲ For additional details, refer to the Citrix XP Migration whitepaper at http://support.citrix.com/servlet/KbServlet/download/30-102-7632/XP_Migration_Whitepaper.pdf

During the transitional phase (before all servers are moved to MetaFrame XP), the following functional limitations exist:

  ▼ In mixed mode, the XML Service connects to the Program Neighborhood Service using Program Neighborhood Named Pipes. In native mode, the XML Service connects to the IMA Service using an IMA Remote Procedure Call (RPC).

  - The ICA Client uses the Program Neighborhood virtual channel to connect to the Program Neighborhood Service in mixed mode, and to the Program Neighborhood subsystem in native mode.

  - The ICA Client uses the ICA browser protocol (UDP Port 1604) to connect to the ICA browser service in mixed mode, and to the browser subsystem in native mode.

- In mixed mode, the Program Neighborhood and ICA browser services exist and are enabled, while the Program Neighborhood and browser subsystems are disabled. The Program Neighborhood and ICA browser services interact with the local Windows Registry.

- In mixed mode, Citrix Server Administration (mfadmin.exe) makes RPC connections to all MetaFrame 1.8 and MetaFrame XP servers. It also connects to Termsrv via Winstation API (RPC). In native mode, Citrix Server Administration makes RPC connections only to MetaFrame 1.8 servers.

- In mixed mode and in native mode, Published Application Manager (appcfg.exe) reads application information only from MetaFrame 1.8 servers. Published applications for MetaFrame XP are managed only through the Citrix Management Console.

▲   The IMA service exists in both modes of operation. It communicates with other servers via the IMA protocol over TCP Port 2512. It also connects to Termsrv via Winstation API (RPC), the local host cache via ODBC, and the data store via ODBC. The IMA service interacts with the local Windows Registry only in mixed mode.

This upgrade process preserves all published applications and MetaFrame.

Licensing Considerations

One of the most confusing parts of upgrading a Citrix MetaFrame farm is the limitations imposed by Microsoft's Terminal Services licensing, which varies based on the domain environment and the operating system used for the Terminal Servers. Table 20-3 summarizes the licensing server options.

Domain	Terminal Server OS	Licensing Server
Windows NT	Windows NT TSE	Windows NT member server, Windows 2000 member server, or Windows Server 2003 member server
	Windows 2000	Windows 2000 member server or Windows Server 2003 member server
	Windows Server 2003	Windows Server 2003 member server
Windows 2000	Windows NT TSE	Windows 2000 domain controller or Windows Server 2003 member server
	Windows 2000	Windows 2000 domain controller or Windows Server 2003 member server
	Windows 2003	Windows Server 2003 member server

Table 20-3.   Microsoft Terminal Services Licensing

Domain	Terminal Server OS	Licensing Server
Windows 2003	Windows NT TSE	Windows Server 2003 member server
	Windows 2000	Windows Server 2003 member server
	Windows 2003	Windows Server 2003 member server

Table 20-3.   Microsoft Terminal Services Licensing *(continued)*

For Windows Server 2003 Terminal Servers, a new licensing server is required (Windows 2000 will *not* support Windows Server 2003 Terminal Services licensing). However, a Windows Server 2003 licensing server will support Windows 2000 and Windows 2003 licensing as well as legacy Windows NT TSE licensing. On the plus side, a Windows Server 2003 license server does not have to be a domain controller, and when installed in a Windows 2000 domain, eliminates the former restriction that Windows 2000 Terminal Services Licensing Service *must* reside on a DC. During migration to Windows Server 2003, the first step is to install a new Windows Server 2003 license server.

Finally, the Windows Server 2003 licensing server must be configured as a license server compatible with Windows 2000 server, as discussed in the Microsoft KnowledgeBase article Q278513.

CHAPTER 21

Ongoing Administration of the Server-Based Computing Environment

The goal of ongoing administration is to ensure that IT services are delivered according to service level requirements that are agreed to by IT management and other relevant decision makers within a company. The day-to-day operations of an IT department should be proactive and require that the proper products, services, and infrastructure are in place to identify and prevent potential problems. This chapter provides guidance on how to manage and troubleshoot server-based computing environments. Through these methodologies, achieving reliable, available, supportable, and manageable solutions built on Microsoft and Citrix products and technologies can be attained.

This chapter also examines the need to develop dedicated support systems to track and facilitate end-user problems, perform maintenance on infrastructure, track service level agreements, and communicate to the end-user community IT progress and relevant problems. In some companies this may be any combination of help desk, service desk, operations, or call center services. Regardless of what it is called or how they are combined, the need and function of these critical components must be analyzed for successful management and operation of the SBC environment.

SCHEDULED MAINTENANCE ACTIVITIES

There are specific tasks that should be performed on a daily, weekly, monthly, and quarterly interval to ensure service levels are being met. General tasks are outlined in this section to provide a guide for MetaFrame XP administrators. It is very important to schedule time at defined intervals to ensure maintenance activities happen and any administrative actions are documented for reference later. Daily issues and maintenance should be tracked and reviewed so persistent problems can be identified and a timeline can be created for resolving them.

On a quarterly basis, a baseline comparison should be conducted against the information monitored and gathered throughout the period. This will identify any inconsistencies that may need to be addressed. Performing a user load trend analysis will help administrators determine proper use of server resources. If trending indicates degradation of server performance due to overload of users, expansion of the MetaFrame environment (such as adding additional load balanced servers) may be necessary. A project, which includes analysis of infrastructure and design, should be initiated and subsequent requisition of hardware, software, and resources scheduled.

Daily Maintenance Activities

Daily maintenance activities are centered on the essential tasks needed to ensure the Citrix farm is highly available and is servicing the end-user needs. These tasks should include, but not be limited to, the following:

▼ **Back up the datastore**   A Microsoft Access–based datastore (DS) can be backed up either using the **dsmaint backup** command utility or by copying the backup datastore file (mf20.bak) that is created every time the IMA service is stopped to a network share. This task is most commonly executed daily with a scheduled script. Third-party datastores (SQL or Oracle) require additional configurations from within SQL or Oracle management software to ensure proper backup of the datastore. See Figure 21-1 for a sample reboot script that copies the backup datastore file to a network share.

■ **Reboot servers** Servers should be rebooted frequently to eliminate any "hung" processes or memory leaks. A simple reboot script like the one shown in Figure 21-1 can be used as a scheduled task to reboot servers with MetaFrame XPs or XPa. MetaFrame XPe has reboot functionality included and can be scheduled from the server properties in the CMC.

CAUTION: Do not reboot more than ten servers every ten minutes. Rebooting more than ten servers at a time can cause severe load on the datastore, prompting delays in IMA service start times.

NOTE: Sleep.exe is part of the Windows 2000 Resource Kit and the Windows Server 2003 Resource Kit.

■ **Verify that all servers are communicating properly with the datastore** This can be done either by running **qfarm** from the command line with the **/app** and **/load** extensions to make sure all servers are showing up and load values are appropriate, or by viewing the status of the server from the CMC. **qfarm** with the **/app** switch will detail which servers are providing which applications, checking to make sure all servers and appropriate applications are listed to verify communication. **qfarm** with the **/load** switch will detail all servers and their associated load levels. Load levels should be within zero to 9999 at all times. A load level of 10000 indicates a server is reporting maximum load on a particular load evaluator. If the load level is above 10000, it indicates a problem with load balancing or the datastore. **qfarm** used with the **/online** or **/offline** switch will display which servers are currently online or offline in the farm.

```
change logon /disable
msg * Please log off and save your work. The server is going down in 5 mins.
sleep.exe 5
net stop spooler
sleep.exe 30
del c:\WINNT\System32\spool\PRINTERS\*.* /q
REM ** unremark the next three lines if you are using Microsoft Access as the IMA datastore.
REM net stop "independent management console"
REM sleep.exe 30
REM copy C:\Program Files\Citrix\Independent Management Architecture\mf20.bak \\backupserver\share
sleep.exe 30
tsshutdn.exe /REBOOT
```

Figure 21-1. Sample reboot script

■ **Perform a thorough review** Review any Resource Manager performance alerts, virus notifications, and datastore backup logs or scripts for proper execution. Notifications should be configured for these whether they are e-mail or SNMP traps.

■ **Assess event viewer errors** Event logs should be checked daily on all servers to ensure that the operating system, applications, and system security are functioning normally. Microsoft Operations Manager is a great utility to view event logs centrally but other event log consolidation tools exist that can dramatically simplify the daily task of checking each event log by providing a unified interface, such as the products made by RippleTech (see bw.rippletech .com for more information), Sentry Pro (see www.sentry-pro.com for more information), or Gravity Square (see www.gravitysquare.com for more information).

■ **Troubleshoot problems** Troubleshoot daily user problems and handle emergency hardware issues such as failed hard drives, network cards, and so on.

▲ **Check for session states using Citrix Management Console** Reset lengthy disconnected sessions if disconnect times are not enforced. Record and trend the number of disconnected, idle, and active sessions to help refine the MetaFrame session disconnect settings.

Weekly Maintenance Activities

Weekly maintenance activities focus on proactive tasks that are aimed at keeping both the farm and servers healthy. These actions should include, but not be limited to, the following:

▼ **Verify concurrent user need does not exceed current purchased licensing** The **clicense connections** command provides an overview of current usage of all Citrix products. Look for a low number of available licenses to determine when there is need for additional licensing.

■ **Check free space** Check free space on all servers to ensure sufficient space is available for proper operation. Once a server gets below ten percent of total disk space available, the performance of the server will be affected.

■ **Ensure antivirus definitions are up-to-date**

■ **Generate reports** Create reports on downtime/uptime, performance problems, and lingering issues to understand and react to problems in the environment. Update the user community on current problem resolution and uptime of environment through e-mail, intranet (MSAM covered in Chapter 16 can provide a great solution for end-user communication), or other means.

▲ **Review and apply any critical Windows, application, or Citrix updates/hotfixes** It is critical to stay up-to-date with the latest patches or fixes to prevent unnecessary problems. The changes should be applied to a test server first to verify operability before rollout to production servers.

Monthly

Monthly maintenance activities focus on high-level farm administration and housekeeping. These tasks should include, but not be limited to, the following:

▼ **Monitor bandwidth utilization for ICA sessions**   Review current bandwidth versus bandwidth needed to support printing, session responsiveness, and potential growth.

▲ **Update printer drivers, and driver mappings, and remove unused drivers** The latest versions of the drivers should be used, all servers should contain the same drivers, unused drivers should be removed, and driver mappings and compatibility lists should be updated.

Quarterly

Quarterly maintenance activities focus on reviewing current farm design and monitoring performance levels. These tasks should include, but not be limited to, the following:

▼ **Analyze usage and growth patterns**   Analyze farm usage and future growth patterns to estimate requirements for expansion of the MetaFrame XP environment, then perform budgetary and growth planning.

■ **Run defrag and chkdsk on all drives**   Third-party defragmentation utilities, such as Executive Software's Diskeeper, should be utilized to facilitate scheduled and robust defragmentation.

■ **Perform test restores of the datastore from tape backup to an isolated testing environment**   Since the DS is an important component of the MetaFrame environment, we recommend performing periodic restores from tape backup. This restore should follow established procedures. The DS should be restored onto equipment similar to that in the production environment. To avoid network conflicts and the risk of affecting the production environment, the restored DS should be in an isolated test network (as discussed in Chapter 10). Administrators should check the operability of the restored datastore by adding a MetaFrame server into the farm and connecting to an application.

▲ **Perform baseline comparisons against previous baselines**   Baseline comparisons indicate whether the current sizing of the farm is adequate. If performance problems are identified, additional hardware and software will need to be purchased and implemented.

FARM MANAGEMENT

Farm Management is required to verify that the farm continues to meet the needs of the MetaFrame XP environment. Servers should be monitored to verify that the load is appropriate. Too many users, runaway processes, memory leaks, and poor applications on a server can lead to poor performance.

The Citrix Management Console (CMC) is the central program used to monitor and manage MetaFrame XP servers and server farms. The CMC is a Java-based program that ships with MetaFrame XP. Each Citrix product (such as Installation Manager) adds software modules (Java Applets) to the CMC to provide controls and other features for those products.

The Citrix Management Console

The Citrix Management Console allows the MetaFrame XP administrators to do the following:

▼ Configure servers and farm settings from any connected workstation.

■ View information about current sessions, users, and processes.

■ Set up and manage printers for ICA Client users.

■ Publish applications and monitor application usage.

■ Enter, activate, and assign MetaFrame XP licenses.

■ Monitor, reset, disconnect, and reconnect ICA Client sessions.

▲ Send messages to ICA Client users and shadow their ICA sessions.

Each MetaFrame XP server has the CMC installed by default. However, the MetaFrame XP CD-ROM can be used to install the CMC on other Windows workstations. This enables the MetaFrame Operations Group to manage Citrix server farms from non-MetaFrame computers. Only users in the Citrix Administrators group are authorized to use the CMC.

The CMC queries the Zone Data Collector (or a server you select) for information such as running processes, connected users, and server loads. Depending on the size of the server farm, the console might affect performance in the server farm. It is best to open only one copy of the CMC at a time and connect it to the Zone Data Collector (ZDC) so the console can query data directly. Auto refresh of the CMC should not be used in most situations due to the additional strain it places on the ZDC server.

Controlling Access to the Citrix Management Console

The CMC uses a standard Windows logon and user account authentication to grant access to designated Citrix administrators. Access to the CMC must be granted by adding a user or group to the MetaFrame XP Administrators section of the CMC. A MetaFrame XP administrator with CMC read-write privileges can add MetaFrame XP administrators from within the Citrix Management Console. To add a Citrix administrator, right-click the MetaFrame XP Administrators node in the console tree in the left-hand window pane and choose Add MetaFrame XP Administrator. In the dialog box that appears, select the user and group accounts that will be added to the Citrix Administrators group in the console and click Next. The Select Tasks dialog box now appears. Select the appropriate access level for the new administrator and click Next. The access granted to an administrator is fully customizable. There are options for View Only, Full Administration, and Custom. Custom permissions can be used to create level-one help desk personnel access, which only allows for administration of user sessions. All levels of the CMC have their own access rights, so it is possible to create administrator logins for managers such that they have access only to the areas they need to perform their job, but little else beyond that.

Using Server and Application Folders Within CMC

The CMC provides the ability to group servers and applications into folders. There is no correlation between CMC folders and Program Neighborhood folders displayed within application sets. The CMC folders help to manage a large number of servers and increase the performance of the CMC because the CMC only queries data for the servers or applications in the current folder view. One way to increase the response time of the CMC is to divide the list of servers into folders based on their zones.

Managing Zones

In a MetaFrame XP server farm, a *zone* is a grouping of MetaFrame XP servers that share a common data collector, which is a MetaFrame XP server that receives information from all the servers in the zone. A zone in a MetaFrame XP server farm elects a Zone Data Collector for the zone if a new server joins the zone, a member server restarts, or the current ZDC becomes unavailable. A ZDC becomes unavailable if the server goes down or is disconnected from the network, or if you move the server to another zone.

When a zone elects a new ZDC, it uses a preference ranking of the servers in the zone. You can set the preference ranking for the servers in a zone on the Zones tab in the server farm's Properties dialog box. Each zone has four levels of preference for election of a ZDC. The preference levels, in order from highest to lowest preference, are

- ▼ Most Preferred
- ■ Preferred
- ■ Default Preference
- ▲ Not Preferred

All servers in a zone are assigned to one of the four election preference levels. When the zone elects a new ZDC, it tries to select a server from the first preference level. If no servers at this level are available, the zone selects a server from the second level, and so on.

When you create a farm, the election preference for all servers is Default Preference, except for the first server added to the zone, which is set to Most Preferred and is the initial ZDC.

On the Zones tab in the console, a colored symbol appears next to each server name to indicate the election preference setting. You can change the default election preference to designate a specific server as the data collector. To do this, set the election preference for the server to Most Preferred. If you do not want some servers to be the ZDC, set the election preference for those servers to Not Preferred.

Managing Users and ICA Sessions

Some of the main tasks of a MetaFrame XP administrator revolve around management of users and sessions. If a server has a problem or needs to be taken down for maintenance, then logons must be disabled and later reenabled. Sessions will also need to be reset, logged out, or disconnected for users so they can get back into the system with a clean start.

To View Current Users

Current users with sessions on a server can be viewed from the Users tab either of the server's folder or by selecting the individual server in the server's tree from within the CMC. The Users tab on the server's folder level allows an administrator to view all of the sessions in the farm. The following information for each session is shown:

▼ **User**   The name of the user account accessing the system

■ **Server**   The name of the MetaFrame XP server for the session

■ **Application**   The Published Application name for the application running in the session

■ **Client Name**   The name given to the ICA Client device in the ICA Client software

■ **Session**   Displays the type of session and a session number

■ **Session ID**   The numeric identifier of the session on the host server

■ **State**   The current status of the ICA session

▲ **Logon Time**   The time the user logged on to the server

Selecting an individual server only shows the sessions on that server. There is an additional column for Idle Time when sessions are viewed from the server level. This column shows the time that a session has been active, but not interacting, with the application.

The current users logged on to a server can also be viewed from a command prompt with the **query user** command. The **query user** command only shows the users on the current server, unless another server is specified with the /server:*<servername>* parameter. It does not return the application or client name information from the command line.

To Enable or Disable Logons

To enable or disable logons from the CMC, do the following:

1. Right-click a server in the tree in CMC and choose Properties.
2. To disable logons by ICA Client users, clear the Enable Logons To This Server check box on the MetaFrame Settings tab.

3. To restore the ability of ICA Clients to connect to the server, select Enable Logons To This Server on the MetaFrame Settings tab.

Logons can also be disabled from the command prompt using the **change logon** command. The command has three options: enable logons, disable logons, or query what the current logon state of the server is.

Managing ICA Sessions

User's sessions can be managed from the CMC by viewing the users either at the server level of the CMC or by choosing the individual server under the server's tree. Many options are available by right-clicking the individual user.

▼ **Connect**   This allows an administrator to connect to a user's disconnected session. If a user is disconnected, this allows an administrator to connect to the user's session and both close applications and save documents.

■ **Disconnect**   This allows the administrator to manually disconnect a user's session, letting the user be gracefully disconnected without closing any applications. They can then be reconnected from another client.

■ **Send Message**   This permits messages to be sent to the client side of the ICA session. Users can be notified of new applications, upgrades, or system shutdowns.

■ **Shadow**   This option allows shadowing of the selected session as long as the CMC is being run from an ICA session. Shadowing cannot be initiated this way from the console of the server.

■ **Reset**   Resetting a session terminates all processes that are running in the session and can cause applications to close without saving data.

■ **Status**   This shows incoming and outgoing traffic as well as compression taking place on the inbound and outbound ICA traffic.

■ **Logoff Selected Session**   This option closes applications and attempts to save changes to information before terminating the session.

▲ **Session Information**   Gives detailed information about the ICA session such as session processes, color depth, client IP addresses, screen resolution, encryption, DLLs in use, and client caches.

Managing Application Access

Management of application access is an important day-to-day task. Users or servers may need to be added or removed from individual applications at any time. A user may need one-time access to a specific application or an application may stop functioning correctly at any time.

Adding and Removing Users from a Published Application

Although applications do not have to be published for ICA Clients to access them, publishing provides management benefits and makes application access easier for end users. Applications can be centrally managed from the CMC on any server.

To give a user access to a published application, open the CMC and do the following:

1. Right-click the Published Application and select Properties.
2. Click Users in the left column.
3. Select a domain, and add the users or groups by clicking the Add button.

To remove a user, access the same user tab, highlight the user or group that should be removed and click the Remove button.

If access is given to an Active Directory group, administrators can grant access to new users by adding the user account to the Windows 2000 Group.

Adding and Removing a Server from a Published Application

The CMC can be used to add and remove servers from a published application. Once a server has been added to a published application, users can connect to the published application on the newly added server.

To add or remove a server from a published application:

1. Open the CMC.
2. Click the Applications folder on the left pane to view published applications.
3. Right-click the published application and select Properties.
4. Click Servers in the left column.
5. To add a server, highlight the server from the list in the left pane and click the Add button.
6. To remove a server, highlight the server in the list in the right pane and click the Remove button.

BASIC TROUBLESHOOTING TECHNIQUES

Although troubleshooting any distributed system can be challenging and time-consuming, applying a structured methodology to troubleshooting can help sort through possible causes and reveal the root cause of most problems.

This section includes troubleshooting procedures for some of the more common problems found in an SBC environment.

Connections

One of the most common problems in the SBC environment that requires troubleshooting involves connectivity. When users cannot connect to the MetaFrame servers, there are numerous possibilities to consider.

▼   **The ICA Client is not configured properly**   This is often the problem if only one user cannot connect to the farm. If the user is using Program Neighborhood, check the server location address by selecting the connection, right-clicking, and selecting the Properties option. The proper server location address should be entered in the Address List box by clicking the Add button. Note that if TCP/IP + HTTP is the protocol being used, the appropriate XML port must be entered when adding the server location. If the Program Neighborhood Agent is being used, make sure the Web Interface URL is correct.

■   **The MetaFrame server is not accepting any more connections**   Check to make sure logons have not been disabled by launching the CMC, highlighting the server(s) in question, right-clicking, and selecting Properties. Next, click the MetaFrame XP Settings option and make sure in the Control Options section that the Enable Logons To This Server check box is selected.

■   **The MetaFrame server's load level is too high**   If the load level of a server is too high, new sessions will not be directed to the server. Check the load on the server from within the CMC. Highlight the server(s) in question and click the Load Manager Monitor tab. If the server is reporting a full load, check the Load Evaluators to make sure they are appropriate. This can also be checked by running **qfarm /load** from a command prompt. A server at maximum load will report load as 10000.

■   **The listeners are down**   Listeners (both ICA and RDP) are the control mechanism by which new sessions are established to MetaFrame XP servers. The state of the listeners can be checked from the CMC. Click the server(s) in question and select the Sessions tab. The listeners for both ICA (ICA-tcp) and RDP (RDP-Tcp) will be shown and should be in a listen state. If either is in a down state, new connections cannot be established to the server, and the listener should be reset by right-clicking the listener and selecting Reset. If this does not bring the listener back to a listen state, reboot the MetaFrame server. Also verify that nothing else is using port 1494. A common way to check connectivity to the MetaFrame servers is to run the following from a command prompt:

telnet <insert server name> 1494

The response should be △△ICA△△ICA△△ICA, which is an ICA Banner from the Citrix server. This output will continue until the Telnet session is broken or times out. If this does not appear there may be a problem with the listeners.

■   **There are not enough idle sessions available**   By default, there are two idle sessions available for logons. If more than two connections are made before one of the idle sessions frees up, an error is received on the client when trying to connect. Typically, if the user attempts to connect again, they will be able to log on. If errors of this nature occur during peak login times, increase the number of idle sessions by editing the HKLM\System\CurrentControlSet\Control\Terminal Server\ IdleWinStationPoolCount registry key.

- **There are network issues present**   This could be on the server or client side of the network. The main items to verify include the following: are the server's network cards functioning properly; are routers and switches between the client and server configured correctly; are firewall settings blocking ICA traffic; and are client network cards configured and functioning properly. As mentioned earlier, one of the best ways to establish connectivity to the Citrix server is to run the following from a command prompt:

  telnet <insert server name> 1494

  The response should be △△ICA△△ICA△△ICA, which is an ICA Banner from the Citrix server. If this does not appear and the ICA listener is up and running, then something is blocking communication from the client to the server.

- ▲ **Core services not functional**   Both the Independent Management Architecture (IMA) and Citrix XML services must be running for a MetaFrame XP server to function properly. Check both of these service states by selecting Control Panel | Administrative Tools | Services to ensure they are both in a *Started* state. If their status shows blank, right-click the service and select the Start option.

Shadowing Users

Many end-user problems can be resolved without physically visiting the user by utilizing the shadowing technology included with MetaFrame. Permissions for shadowing are best set up in a Citrix Policy and only granted to administrators and managers within the company. Shadowing rights enable the control of a user session to instruct the user on how to perform a certain function, troubleshoot client-side problems, or promote general education about applications, printing, and system orientation. There are a couple of ways to initiate shadowing. One can be started from within the CMC by right-clicking the user sessions to be shadowed and selecting the Shadow option. Another method is to use the Shadow Taskbar found on the ICA Administrator Toolbar. A popular way to give managers access to shadowing without giving them permissions to the CMC is to publish the Shadow Taskbar program as a published application.

Troubleshooting the SQL Datastore

If you are utilizing a SQL Datastore there are several troubleshooting tips that can assist the administrator in discovering and fixing connectivity problems. The following list consolidates the most common problems encountered with the SQL Datastore and how to correct the issues.

- ▼ **The wrong credentials are supplied for SQL authentication**   During the configuration of a SQL Datastore, a username and password are entered, which are used for accessing the Datastore database. If this username or password is changed without updating the DSN used to connect to the Datastore, connectivity problems will be encountered.

■ **The DSN is configured for NT authentication not SQL authentication**
Ensure that the DSN file is configured for the proper method of authentication by opening the Data Sources (ODBC) from within Control Panel | Administrative Tools.

■ **The network connection between the SQL server and the MetaFrame server is down**   Test connectivity by using Data Sources (ODBC) utility from within Control Panel | Administrative Tools by selecting the DSN and clicking the Configure button.

■ **Log space**   Ensure you have the Truncate Log At Checkpoint option selected or have adequate backups scheduled to ensure that the logs do no grow unnecessarily.

▲ **Worker threads**   In larger farms (greater than 256 servers), the number of worker threads needs to be increased for proper operation. This can be achieved by using the SQL Server Enterprise Manager, right-clicking the server name, selecting properties, then clicking the Processor tab and changing the Maximum worker thread count from 256 to a number greater than the number of servers in the farm.

Troubleshooting IMA

The IMA service and underlying subsystems are the core of MetaFrame XP and must be running on all farm servers for proper operation. The following list consolidates the most common problems encountered with the IMA service and how to correct the issues.

▼ If an error is received after booting a MetaFrame server that states one or more services failed to start, and the non-starting service is the IMA service, allow the service more time to start since the initial load on the IMA service will cause delays past the default six-minute timeout of the service manager.

■ If a direct connection to the DS is being used, verify that ODBC connectivity exists.

■ If the Local Host Cache (LHC) (imalhc.mdb) is missing, corrupt, or provides incorrect information, start by refreshing the LHC and then move on to re-creating the LHC. To refresh the LHC, run the following from a command prompt: **dsmaint refreshlhc**. If this fails, re-create the LHC with the following command: **dsmaint recreatelhc**.

▲ Review the Event Viewer logs for any errors, and research the Citrix Knowledge Center (support.citrix.com), or contact your local Citrix reseller to assist in troubleshooting.

If the ODBC Connection Fails

If using direct mode connections to the DS, ODBC connectivity is required for proper operation of the IMA service. If ODBC issues are suspected, try the following:

▼ Verify the name of the DSN file the IMA service is using by looking in the registry setting HKEY_LOCAL_MACHINE\SOFTWARE\Citrix\IMA\DataSourceName.

■ Reinstall the latest compatible version of MDAC to verify that the correct ODBC files are installed.

▲ Enable ODBC tracing for further troubleshooting.

Other Common Problems

Other common problems revolve around licensing, such as when servers will not accept product licenses. If problems do occur while adding product licenses to a MetaFrame XP server, connect to the CMC, right-click the server, and select the Set MetaFrame Product Code option. Verify that the appropriate code is set for the server. Once this is verified, run the **clicense refresh** command from a command prompt to refresh active licensing. If there are still problems, stop and restart the IMA service.

OPERATIONS SUPPORT

Whether a network includes server-based computing or not, it is critical to have a support methodology and their appropriate systems in place to ensure user issues can be tracked, resolved, and communicated to those necessary in an appropriate amount of time.

The role that IT support plays in providing efficient and effective customer assistance is continually evolving. Whether a company has a service desk, help desk, or call center, this service is key to bringing customer service to a higher level. Through proper staffing, process development, and use of tools and technology, the IT support organization must handle the day-to-day problems of the user community, administer the environment, and report back to the business the uptime of the network.

IT management should be treated like a business entity even if it is not revenue-generating. Customers, whether internal staff or outside interests, judge the quality of the entire IT organization by the service they provide. Most companies utilize a three-tier approach to supporting its user community. The first level is the initial point of contact for user problems. At this level, the support staff should have a basic understanding of Citrix administration. They should be able to log and track problems, provide basic problem resolution (reset sessions, create printer mappings, and so on), notify the company of system outages, and be able to escalate to the second level of support.

The second tier of support is mainly concerned with the day-to-day operation of the MetaFrame environment. At this level, periodic checks of the system are performed, event logs are processed, backup and core services are verified, licensing levels are monitored, advanced problems are resolved, and the installation and rebuilding of servers is performed. Coordination with the first level of support, and escalation of irresolvable problems to the third level of support are also performed. The third level of support ensures the MetaFrame environment meets the business needs of the organization and adheres to the service level agreements (SLA) in place for the company. They are concerned with capacity planning, advanced problems resolution, ensuring service packs/hotfixes are applied to the environment, reviewing business needs, and escalating problems to authorized Citrix resellers when needed.

It is important that both informal and formal customer surveys be performed regularly to gather objective data about each tier of support. Systems, people, and processes can then be changed and new customer data gathered to ensure constant improvement.

PART IV

Appendixes

APPENDIX A

Internetworking Basics

The server-based computing (SBC) paradigm is heavily dependent upon the capacity and performance of the internetwork that connects client nodes to the SBC server farm. In larger companies and enterprise environments, workload and associated technical expertise are typically divided among a number of "experts" or teams of specialists (network, database, mail server, web servers, and so on). At smaller companies on the other hand, there may be one or two experts responsible for all aspects of the organization's IT infrastructure. In either case, the focus of IT staff members charged with making the SBC network work is usually server-centric, in spite of the dependence on network services. These same systems administrators still need a clear understanding of networking to be able to plan and design (as discussed in the second section of this book), and then implement, operate, maintain, and troubleshoot (as discussed in the final section). This appendix provides a low-level networking introduction to provide common ground for discussing issues and concepts with other IT staff members, vendors, and service providers.

THE OSI MODEL

The Open Systems Interconnection (OSI) model was originally developed by the International Standards Organization (www.iso.org) in 1974 to establish a standardized model for interconnecting networks and computers using multivendor networks and applications. Although originally envisioned as a formal standard, it has become less of an implementation standard and more a benchmark model. The principles applied when creating the OSI model were

▼ A layer should be created where a different level of abstraction is needed.

■ Each layer should perform a well-defined function.

■ The function of each layer should be chosen with an eye toward defining internationally standardized protocols.

■ The layer boundaries should be chosen to minimize the information flow across the interfaces.

▲ The number of layers should be large enough that distinct functions need not be thrown together in the same layer out of necessity, and small enough that the architecture does not become unwieldy.

The resulting effort defined a seven-layer model (Figure A-1) that allows information to be passed up and down through the hierarchy, layer to layer, such that each layer needs to only provide a standards-based interface to adjacent layers and has no dependence on non-adjacent layers. In simple terms, the network layer does not need to know anything about the physical media or the application data being transported, it only needs to know how to pass the information down to the data link layer or up to the transport layer.

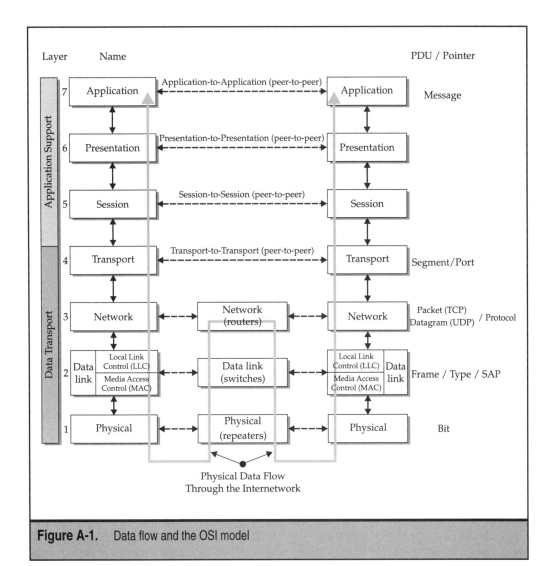

Figure A-1.   Data flow and the OSI model

OSI Model Layers

Each of the layers defined by the OSI model (keep repeating—it's only a model, it's only a model) performs specific functions to allow applications to ultimately transmit data over the physical media. The model's seven layers (commonly a protocol stack) are used extensively to define equivalency of function in other protocol stacks such as the Internet Protocol Suite. Although most other protocol stacks do not have a one-to-one mapping to the OSI model's layers, the actual protocols are referred to by their OSI equivalent function. For example, Novell's Sequenced Packet Exchange (SPX) protocol does not fully map to the OSI model transport layer, but it is still functionally referred to as a transport-layer protocol.

Within the model, layers 1 through 4 (the "lower" layers) support data transport between end nodes or devices while 5 through 7 (the "upper" layers) deal with application support.

The Application Layer

At the top of the "stack" is the application layer. It supports application and end-user processes. Communication partners are identified, quality of service is identified, user authentication and privacy are considered, and any constraints on data syntax are identified. Everything at this layer is application-specific. This layer provides application services for file transfers, e-mail, and other network software services. Telnet and FTP are applications that exist entirely in the application level.

The Presentation Layer

The presentation layer provides independence from differences in data representation by translating from application to network format, and vice versa. The presentation layer works to transform data into the form that the application layer can accept. This layer formats and encrypts data to be sent across a network, providing freedom from compatibility problems. It is sometimes called the syntax layer.

The Session Layer

The session layer establishes, manages, and terminates connections between applications. It also sets up, coordinates, and terminates conversations, exchanges, and dialogues between the applications at each end.

The Transport Layer

The transport layer provides transparent transfer of data between end systems, or hosts, and is responsible for end-to-end error recovery and flow control. It ensures complete data transfer. The OSI model defines different transport services, four connection-oriented and one connectionless.

The Network Layer

The network layer provides switching and routing technologies, creating logical paths, known as virtual circuits, for transmitting data from node to node. Routing and forwarding are functions of this layer, as well as addressing, internetworking, error handling, congestion control, and packet sequencing. Note that the term "switching" refers to path switching and has nothing to do with Ethernet switches. For any protocol stack to be viable in an enterprise environment, it must have a routable address at this layer.

The Data Link Layer

At the data link layer, data frames are encoded and decoded into bits for the physical media. This layer furnishes transmission protocol knowledge and management and handles errors in the physical layer, flow control, and frame synchronization. The data link layer is divided into two sublayers: the Media Access Control (MAC) layer and the Logical Link Control (LLC) layer. The MAC sublayer controls how a computer on the network gains access to the data and permission to transmit it (CSMA/CD for Ethernet) as well as logical addressing (MAC address). The LLC layer controls frame synchronization, flow control, and error checking.

The Physical Layer

The physical layer conveys the *bit stream*—electrical impulse, light, or radio signal—through the network at the electrical and mechanical level. It provides the hardware means of sending and receiving data on a carrier, including defining cables, cards, and physical aspects. Fast Ethernet, RS232, and ATM are protocols with physical layer components.

OSI Model Data Flow

Understanding data flow through the OSI model, particularly the lower layers, is key to understanding network design, performance, and troubleshooting. Figure A-2 shows the process of data encapsulation from Layer 7 down to transmission on the wire at Layer 1. The original application message is encapsulated at each successive layer by appending and in some cases prepending the lower layers' protocol information to the payload. This layered functionality is what allows a single workstation to log on to a Novell server over IPX and a Windows server over TCP/IP.

Referring back to Figure A-1, the logical communication is peer-to-peer at the same layer. The Telnet client application on one host communicates to the Telnet server application on another host. The data link layer on one device communicates with the data link layer on another device. The physical data flow is up and down the protocol stack.

Intermediate nodes (the three-layer stack in the middle of Figure A-1) may only need functionality at the lower three layers, as they need not be aware of communication at the upper layers. As an example, a Telnet session from Dallas to Chicago may transit many

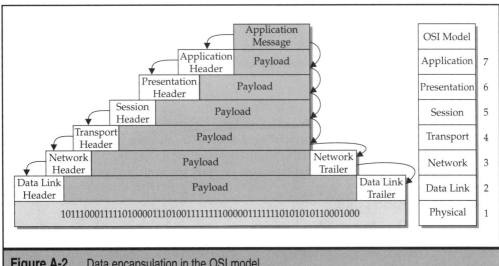

Figure A-2.   Data encapsulation in the OSI model

intermediate nodes over the Internet. At each of those sites, data needs to be deencapsulated only as far as the network layer to allow path selection and forwarding.

From a LAN standpoint, a Layer-1 device refers to a device that functions at the physical layer. Repeaters and multiport repeaters (LAN hubs) are Layer-1 devices. They regenerate and retransmit an electrical signal consisting of ones and zeros.

A Layer-2 LAN device works at the data link layer, meaning it is protocol-aware at Layer 2 and recognizes Layer-2 frame formats and addresses (MAC addresses). LAN switches are Layer-2 devices; they forward (directed) or flood (broadcast) frames on the network, but each port is independent of the electrical signal and physical media on any other port.

Classifying a device as a Layer-3 device means the device works at the network layer and recognizes network layer addressing and protocol. Routers and Layer-3 LAN switches are at this layer. Communications between dissimilar LAN technologies such as between Token Ring and Ethernet requires Layer-3 functionality. For example, in a network with a Token Ring segment and an Ethernet segment, the Layer-2 frame formats are incompatible. To communicate from one segment to the other, the frame formats and media access control methods from one segment must be "stripped away" to allow the data to be reencapsulated in the correct format for the other segment.

The OSI Model as a Benchmark

Figure A-3 shows a greatly simplified correlation of the OSI model to common protocol stacks. Note that the Internet Protocol stack defines only four layers and that common network operating systems consistently have a clear separation between Layers 5 through 7 functions and Layer 4, primarily driven by the ubiquitous nature of TCP/IP.

THE INTERNET PROTOCOL

The Internet Protocol suite (commonly referred to as TCP/IP) comprises the essential protocol stack for modern networks. To effectively plan or manage a network based on TCP/IP, one must understand the network addressing methodology.

The IP Protocol Stack

As mentioned previously, the Internet Protocol stack consists of only four layers. It does not define the physical layer connectivity as in the OSI model, but it allows connectivity to the same types of physical media through compatibility at the "link" layer. Of the four layers, the transport and network layers are of primary interest.

The IP Application Layer

The IP protocol classifies all application (user-oriented) protocols into a single layer. IP is primarily concerned with internetworking so these protocols are handled monolithically.

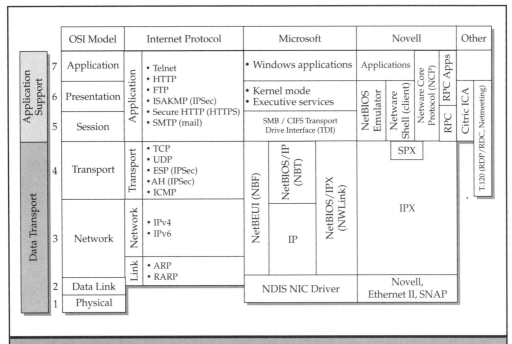

Figure A-3.   Common protocol suites versus the OSI model

The IP Transport Layer

The IP transport layer consists of two primary services: connection-oriented (session) service via TCP, and connectionless service via UDP. TCP is used for guaranteed delivery by tracking individual segments in sequence. UDP provides less overhead and "faster" service, but does not guarantee delivery. Connection-oriented service is used for most data transfer needs while connectionless service is used extensively for voice over IP (VoIP) and similar needs. To understand the difference, envision two environments: First, a Citrix session (ICA) where video display data is transported to and from a server—because data integrity is more important than speed, the key-clicks and resulting screens must be accurately represented, and second, a VoIP call—the talker is not subject to flow control and a listener must receive most of the data in a contiguous flow to hold a conversation. As a result, they cannot wait for the missing pieces of the conversation to be retransmitted and reassembled, even over a poor quality path. Data flow is more important than integrity.

The IP Network Layer

The IP network layer consists of the addressing and routing protocols needed to get IP packets across the Internet.

The IP Link Layer

The IP link layer (also called the network access layer) employs industry standard drivers and OSI-compatible data link layer services (Ethernet, Token Ring, and so on).

IP Addressing

The textbook for one 300-level college course attempts to teach IP addressing logic by jumping straight into binary math, espousing the mathematical concept of a "bitwise AND." For those unaccustomed to IP addressing, this explanation immediately falls in the range between voodoo and techno-babble. Nonetheless, binary math is the key to really understanding IP addressing. A "bitwise AND" means, given two expressions (IP address in binary and mask in binary), the bitwise AND result returns a 1 if both expressions have 1s in a bit position, otherwise the result is 0. This is the logical process used to derive the network (or subnet) from an address and mask combination. The first example under the upcoming "Address Classes" section illustrates the bitwise logic.

Addressing Basics

Standards define IP addresses by "class" and further define reserved and private address ranges. Reserved addresses are not usable by host devices, while "private" addresses are private in the sense that they are not routable over the Internet and must undergo network address translation (NAT) to a registered public IP address when traversing the Internet. Table A-1 lists the IP address allocations and classes.

Decimal Range	Class	Default Mask/Length	First Octet
1.0.0.0–126.255.255.255	Class A	255.0.0.0/8	0$xxxxxxx$
128.0.0.0–191.255.255.255	Class B	255.255.0.0/16	10$xxxxxx$
192.0.0.0–223.255.255.255	Class C	255.255.255.0/24	110$xxxxx$
224.0.0.0–239.255.255.255	Class D (Multicast)	None	1110$xxxx$
240.0.0.0–255.255.255.254	Class E (Experimental)	None	11111xxx
	Special Address		
10.0.0.0–10.255.255.255	RFC 1918	255.255.255.0/8	
127.0.0.0–127.255.255.255	Reserved - Loopback		
169.254.0.0–169.254.255.255	Automatic Private IP Addressing	255.255.0.0/16	
172.16.0.0–172.31.255.255	RFC 1918	255.255.0.0/12	
192.168.0.0–192.168.255.255	RFC 1918	255.255.255.0/16	

Table A-1.   IP Address Allocations

Address Classes   Class A networks encompass 126 networks, each with over 16 million unique addresses. The decimal values specified are based on the underlying binary values such that the first eight bits (octet) of the address defines the class.

▼   Class B networks encompass over 14,000 networks, each with over 65,000 addresses.

■   Class C networks encompass some two million possible networks of 254 addresses each.

▲   Class D networks are used for multicast services (including many dynamic routing protocols), while Class E networks are reserved.

Each of the first three classes carries a presumed (default) self-encoded mask. This is evident when entering an IP address on most network hardware; once the address is entered, the default mask automatically populates. As an example, in the IP address 10.10.10.1:

Decimal:	10.	10.	10.	1
Mask (decimal):	255.	0.	0.	0
Binary:	00001000	00001000	000010000	00000001
Mask (binary):	11111111	00000000	000000000	00000000
Bitwise AND:	00001000	00000000	000000000	00000000
Network (decimal):	10.	0.	0.	0

The first octet starts with the binary sequence $0xxxxxxx$, making it a Class A address.

Binary Basics   The binary values of each octet reveal the structure of the IP address. Use a simplified conversion table to convert decimal to binary. In IP addressing, the default mask can be modified to reduce (subnet) or expand (supernet) existing networks. In common notation, the mask is expressed either in decimal format (255.255.255.128) or as a number of 1s in the mask (/25). In the following example, the binary values use the same address (10.10.10.1) with different subnet masks. To determine the "size" of the network (number of hosts), use the formula 2^n-2. When determining the maximum number of hosts on a given subnet, n represents the number of 0s in the binary mask. When determining the number of possible subnets, n is the number of 1s added to the default mask.

Decimal:	10.	10.	10.	1
Mask (decimal):	255.	0.	0.	0
Binary:	00001000	00001000	000010000	00000001
Mask (binary):	11111111	00000000	000000000	00000000

The address and mask define one network (no bits added to the default mask). There are 24 0s in the mask, so the network has $2^{24}-2$ host addresses (16,777,214). The two excluded addresses (the –2) are the host address of all zeros (10.0.0.0), which defines the network, and the host address of all ones (10.255.255.255), which defines a broadcast to all hosts on this network.

In a routed environment, addresses at each end of the link must be different (different networks or subnet). To use the 10.*x.x.x* address space, subnetting is required to define smaller networks.

Decimal:	10.	10.	10.	1
Mask (decimal):	255.	255.	254.	0
Binary:	00001000	00001000	000010000	00000001
Mask (binary):	11111111	11111111	111111110	00000000

The address and mask define multiple networks (15 bits were added to the default mask). The original network has been subnetted to produce $2^{15}-2$ individual (32,766) subnets. There are nine 0s in the mask so each subnet has 2^9-2 host addresses (510). The two excluded addresses are the host address of all zeros (10.10.10.0), which defines the network, and the host address of all ones (10.10.11.255), which defines a broadcast to all hosts on this network.

Why Binary?   Until IP addressing becomes second nature, only the binary values can reveal problems with the addressing scheme. From the last example, the host A at 10.10.10.1 with a mask of 255.255.255.240 needs to communicate to host B plugged into the same hub with an address of 10.10.10 21 and a mask of 255.255.255.240. All appears well, but they cannot communicate over IP.

Decimal (A):	10.	10.	10.	1
Decimal (B):	10.	10.	10.	21
Mask (decimal):	255.	255.	255.	240
Binary (A):	00001000	00001000	000010000	00000001
Binary (B):	00001000	00001000	000010000	00010101
Mask (binary):	11111111	11111111	111111111	11111000

The bits in the host address that correspond to the ones in the mask must match for both devices to be on the same logical network. In this case, host A is on network 10.10.10.0 while host B is on network 10.10.10.16. Even though they share the same Layer-1 electrical signal and they can see each other's MAC address at Layer 2, they cannot communicate without a router.

IP Protocols and Ports

Referring back to Figure A-1, note that at both the transport and network layer, services are keyed to specific protocols (of which IP is one) and ports (such as TCP port 23 for Telnet).

Literal	Value	Description
ip	0	Internet Protocol
icmp	1	Internet Control Message Protocol, RFC 792
igmp	2	Internet Group Management Protocol, RFC 1112
ipinip	4	IP-in-IP encapsulation
tcp	6	Transmission Control Protocol, RFC 793
igrp	9	Interior Gateway Routing Protocol
udp	17	User Datagram Protocol, RFC 768
gre	47	General Routing Encapsulation
esp	50	Encapsulated Security Payload for IPv6, RFC 1827
ah	51	Authentication Header for IPv6, RFC 1826
eigrp	88	Enhanced Interior Gateway Routing Protocol
ospf	89	Open Shortest Path First routing protocol, RFC 1247
nos	94	Network Operating System (Novell's NetWare)
pcp	108	Payload Compression Protocol

Table A-2. Common IP Protocols

Numerous web sites have extensive lists of both well-known and not-so-well-known ports and protocols. The partial lists in Table A-2 (protocols) and Table A-3 (ports) covers the majority of values common in modern networking. Table A-4, meanwhile, lists Internet Control Message Protocol message types and codes.

In Table A-2, the literal value is the common name. When defining access control lists or firewall rules to control access to the corporate data center, some protocols are generally "safe" and can be permitted (such as esp, the encrypted traffic in IPSec)

Literal	Protocol	Value	Description
ftp-data	TCP	20	File Transfer Protocol (data port)
ftp	TCP	21	File Transfer Protocol (control port)
ssh	TCP	22	Secure Shell

Table A-3. Common TCP/UDP Ports

Literal	Protocol	Value	Description
telnet	TCP	23	RFC 854 Telnet
smtp	TCP	25	Simple Mail Transport Protocol
domain	TCP/UDP	53	DNS (Domain Name System)
bootps	UDP	67	Bootstrap Protocol Server
bootpc	UDP	68	Bootstrap Protocol Client
tftp	UDP	69	Trivial File Transfer Protocol
gopher	TCP	70	Gopher
finger	TCP	79	Finger
www	TCP	80	World Wide Web
pop3	TCP	110	Post Office Protocol — Version 3
ntp	TCP	123	Network Time Protocol
netbios-ns	TCP	137	NETBIOS Name Service
netbios-dgm	TCP	138	NETBIOS Datagram Service
bgp	TCP	179	Border Gateway Protocol, RFC 1163
ssl (https)	TCP	443	Secure HTTP (secure sockets layer)
smb	TCP	445	Microsoft SMB
isakmp	UDP	500	ISAKMP
syslog	UDP	514	System Log
lpd	TCP	515	Line Printer Daemon — printer spooler
rip	TCP	520	Routing Information Protocol
mssql	TCP	1433	Microsoft SQL
citrix-ica	TCP	1494	Citrix ICA
sqlnet	TCP	1521	Structured Query Language Network
radius	TCP	1645, 1646	Remote Authentication Dial-In User Service
rdp	TCP	3389	Microsoft RDP

Table A-3. Common TCP/UDP Ports *(continued)*

while others may need to be restricted (such as gre, to prevent non-approved tunneling through the network).

Individual ports at the transport layer are a more granular way of controlling, monitoring, and managing traffic flows. Both Citrix (ICA, TCP port 1494) and Microsoft (RDP, TCP port 3389) use defined ports that can be easily managed to restrict traffic.

ICMP Type	Message	Code	Code Meaning
0	Echo Reply		
3	Destination Unreachable	0	Net unreachable
		1	Host unreachable
		2	Protocol unreachable
		3	Port unreachable
		4	Fragmentation needed and Don't Fragment was set
		5	Source route failed
		6	Destination network unknown
		7	Destination host unknown
		8	Source host isolated
		9	Communication with destination network is administratively prohibited
		10	Communication with destination host is administratively prohibited
		11	Destination network unreachable for type of service
		12	Destination host unreachable for type of service
		13	Communication administratively prohibited
		14	Host precedence violation
		15	Precedence cutoff in effect
4	Source Quench		
5	Redirect	0	Redirect datagram for the network (or subnet)
		1	Redirect datagram for the host
		2	Redirect datagram for the type of service and network
		3	Redirect datagram for the type of service and host
8	Echo		
11	Time Exceeded	0	Time to live (TTL) exceeded in transit
		1	Fragment reassembly time exceeded
12	Parameter Problem	0	Pointer indicates the error
		1	Missing a required option
		2	Bad length
13	Timestamp		
14	Timestamp Reply		
15	Information Request		
16	Information Reply		
17	Address Mask Request		
18	Address Mask Reply		

Table A-4.   ICMP Types and Codes

ICMP messages are included as a reference for two reasons: First, some ICMP messages are essential to a well-behaved network (unreachables), while others are essential troubleshooting tools (echo, echo-reply, traceroute); second, the remaining messages will propagate through the network and create a security and denial-of-service (DoS) risk if not controlled. As an example, mask reply messages can be used for fingerprinting the network, redirects can be used for DoS attacks, and echo requests should not be allowed "in" from the Internet.

APPENDIX B

Creating an On-Demand Enterprise Financial Analysis Model

Every organization's financial analysis will involve unique variables and methods of calculation, but you can use the model presented in this appendix as a framework for creating your own SBC financial evaluation. This model defines a method for identifying common costs and savings involved when migrating to enterprise server–based computing.

> **TIP:** The Citrix ACE Cost Analyzer (www.acecostanalyzer.com) is a great tool for providing a quick, high-level analysis of the type of savings that can be expected from deploying SBC. We contributed to both the concept and development of the ACE Cost Analyzer and frequently recommend it to our clients. The model we present here is intended as a more rigorous drill-down into specific anticipated product costs and benefits in order to present a compelling return on investment (ROI) to the key financial decision makers.

BUILDING A SPREADSHEET MODEL

We recommend creating a spreadsheet that calculates both expected server-based computing costs and savings over a three-to-five-year time frame. The savings come from reducing the costs involved in a client-centric computing environment. These costs include both existing expenses and anticipated future expenses. For instance, if SBC enables you to eliminate the requirement to upgrade PCs as part of a regular refresh cycle, then the cost of purchasing and installing the PCs becomes an annual average savings under server-based computing.

It is not necessary to be creative when financially justifying an enterprise SBC project. The hard quantifiable savings alone should easily pay for the project and also provide a good return on investment. We recommend quantifying soft savings, such as reduced user downtime, and then listing these savings independently of the return on investment calculation. Although the value of certain benefits from implementing SBC can exceed that of the combined savings, we still recommend listing benefits separately as well. Taking this conservative approach makes a very strong statement to management about the overwhelming value of the project. It also helps the feasibility committee defend their evaluation against anyone who tries to poke holes in the financial analysis.

An effective financial model utilizes a multidimensional spreadsheet that isolates the different variables involved. This makes the spreadsheet both easy to follow and easy to adjust for different assumptions. We recommend creating a spreadsheet with four tabs: Demographics, Logistics, Costs, and Report.

Information entered into the Demographics, Logistics, and Costs sections will come from assumptions and research by the feasibility committee. The Report section will show the results of calculations derived from information entered into the other three sections.

In order to simplify the model, do not bother listing costs that are equivalent under both server-based and client-centric scenarios. For instance, if you plan to purchase new Windows Server 2003 file servers regardless of whether you build an on-demand enterprise or not, do not list the cost of these servers in your financial model.

> **NOTE:** This model is only a starting point for providing a thorough SBC financial analysis. When engaged to prepare an analysis for a client, we inevitably add many more detailed calculations based upon discovery of the specific organizational environment.

Demographics

The number of users and remote offices participating in the SBC project are identified and categorized along with salary information for both IT staff and non-IT employees. Figure B-1 shows a Demographics spreadsheet example.

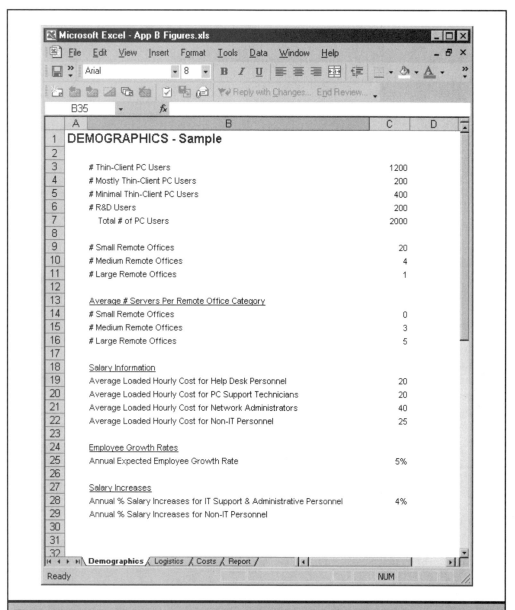

Figure B-1.   Demographics section of a financial justification model

Number of Users

Whether employees or contractors, the number of expected SBC users should be estimated and categorized as to what degree of hosted applications they are likely to require. Common categorizations include thin-client, mostly thin-client, minimal thin-client, and other.

▼ **Thin-client**   These users will run their entire desktops from the Citrix server farm. They will either use Windows terminals or PCs configured as Windows terminals with local drive mapping disabled.

■ **Mostly thin-client**   These users run the majority of applications from the Citrix server farm, but may still run some applications locally. Certain laptop users and users requiring unique applications often fall into this category.

■ **Minimal thin-client**   These users primarily operate in client-centric mode and will use server-based computing selectively. This group might include headquarters employees who use client-centric PCs at work, but who like to dial into the network from home. It might also include salespeople who are often on the road, but who need to access corporate applications and databases. It might include remote PC users who simply like to save time by accessing their e-mail through MetaFrame XP Presentation Server rather than downloading it.

▲ **Other**   This category will differ by organization. It might include R&D engineers who want to run Windows applications on their UNIX workstations. It might include customers who run applications as anonymous Internet browsers utilizing Secure Gateway. Or it may be limited to a single company executive who insists on continuing to run the majority of his applications on a Mac.

Remote Offices

The composition of remote offices will have a big impact on the design of the server-based computing architecture. We recommend different categorizations such as home office, small office, medium office, large office, jumbo office, and regional office. Some general parameters follow, though of course they will be different for almost every organization.

▲ **Home office**   The home office is the new branch office. Telecommuters typically dial into the network or come in through the Internet. They sometimes use their own PCs and sometimes use company-issued PCs or laptops. If the organization implements a server-based computing environment, telecommuters are good candidates for inexpensive Windows terminals.

■ **Small remote office**   Generally, these offices range from one to five users and have only low-bandwidth connectivity to headquarters, if any.

■ **Medium remote office**   These offices range from 5 to 14 users. They sometimes have their own file and e-mail servers. Limited bandwidth connectivity is often in place.

■ **Large remote office**   These offices range from 15 to 39 users. They often have their own servers and will sometimes have their own network administrators on staff. They frequently have high-speed bandwidth connections to headquarters.

- ■ **Jumbo remote office**   These offices range from 41 to 200 users. They almost always have multiple servers and often have local network administrators in addition to high-speed bandwidth connections.
- ▲ **Regional office**   These offices have over 200 users along with IT support staff onsite.

Salary Information

Salary information should be listed for all categories of IT staff and should be loaded for FICA, workers compensation insurance, vacation, and so on. The average hourly loaded cost for non-IT personnel should also be listed. Include projected annual salary increase percentages as well.

Employee Growth Rate

The expected employee growth rate should be obtained from management. For simplicity, we usually assume that this growth rate will apply across the board to all categories of employees and to all locations. Of course, you may wish to fine-tune your spreadsheet with more specific calculations if appropriate. This information will be utilized to project increased IT resource demands.

Logistics

The Logistics spreadsheet section is for making assumptions about how usage and growth variables will impact users and equipment. Where appropriate, the logistics should reflect the specific user or remote-office categories defined in the Demographics section of the spreadsheet. Figure B-2 shows a Logistics spreadsheet example.

Internal Cost of Capital

The feasibility committee should obtain the organization's internal cost of capital from finance. This figure will be used to calculate the present value of both project costs and savings.

Usage

An SBC environment often enables economies in licensing, infrastructure requirements, and support because the number of concurrent users tends to be less than the number of total users. In some cases, this discrepancy can be very large. A multinational manufacturer based in California, for instance, saves a great deal of money on Citrix MetaFrame XP Presentation Server licenses because their users around the world operate in different time zones. The figures relating to user, server, and electricity usage include the following:

- ▼ **Concurrent users by category**   List the expected concurrency percentage for each category of users.
- ■ **Server usage**   Calculate the number of users per MetaFrame XP Presentation server, which will enable you to calculate the total number of servers required in the Report section.

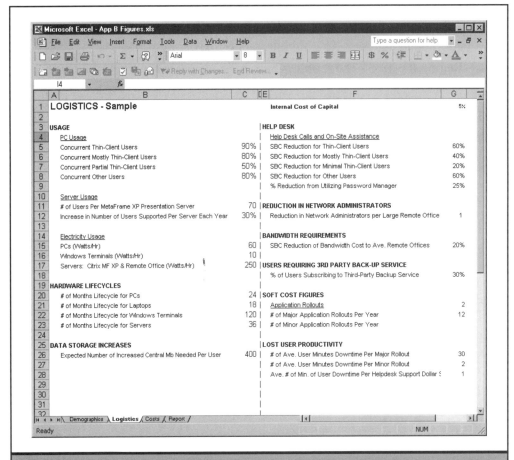

Figure B-2. Logistics section of a financial justification model

- ■ **Increase in supported users each year** As servers continue to become more powerful, they will be able to support much larger numbers of users. Estimating this percentage enables you to more accurately forecast the number of new and replacement MetaFrame servers required in the years ahead, which will continue to fall relative to the number of users accessing them.

- ▲ **Electricity usage** Different manufacturers and products have a different KWH usage for their PCs and Windows terminals. HP currently has wattage requirements posted on their web site. Windows terminals commonly require up to 85 percent less electricity than PCs.

Hardware Life Cycle Estimates

In order to build a realistic financial model, the feasibility committee should estimate life cycles for PCs, laptops, Windows terminals, and servers. These figures should reflect the number of expected months of use for each device, like those listed next:

▼ **Personal computers** The average realistic PC life cycle in most organizations seems to range between two and four years, though some organizations keep them even longer.

■ **Laptops** The average laptop's life expectancy is generally around two thirds that of PCs.

■ **Windows terminals** Since Windows terminals tend to have mean times between failure measured in decades, and since processing takes place on the MetaFrame servers, the Windows terminals' expected life cycle should easily exceed the time frame of the financial analysis.

▲ **Servers** The life cycle for servers tends to range between two and four years. The increasing power of servers should also be considered when used to operate MetaFrame XP Presentation Server because it means that fewer servers can handle more employees. This makes it more economically compelling to centralize computing.

Data Storage
If appropriate, an estimate should be made for the increased centralized storage that will be required for each category of user once users become SBC clients.

Reduction in Help Desk Calls/Personnel
The feasibility committee should estimate the impact an SBC will have in reducing either help desk support calls or support personnel—depending upon how their organization accounts for this expense. For instance, IT may already charge users $100 per month for both phone and technician support. The feasibility committee might estimate that under server-based computing, support calls will decrease by the following amounts per category of user: thin-client, 80 percent; mostly thin-client, 60 percent; minimal thin-client, 20 percent; other, 80 percent.

Reduction in Network Administrative Personnel
This figure should reflect the lower number of administrators required as a result of eliminating servers in remote offices.

Bandwidth Considerations
Estimate bandwidth requirements for both a PC-based and server-based computing environment. These depend upon the applications utilized, the size of the remote offices, and the extent to which users are full thin-client users.

Third-Party Backup Subscriptions
Most PC-based computing environments allow users to maintain data on their local hard drives. If IT already backs up this data, then additional storage may not be required. If users are required to back up their own hard drives, then include this time as a soft cost for lost productivity. If a third-party service is utilized, include the percentage of users who subscribe to this service.

Soft Cost Figures

Soft costs are those costs that are harder to quantify, but that still clearly impact the organization.

Application Rollouts   The estimated number of application upgrades or rollouts is used to calculate their costs, assuming that excess personnel or contractors are required to accomplish them. If your organization simply forgoes most application upgrades because of the huge cost of performing them within a PC-based computing environment, then having the latest software can be identified separately as a server-based computing benefit on the Report spreadsheet section.

▼ **Number of major application rollouts per year**   Rollouts of new application packages or operating systems

▲ **Number of minor application rollouts per year**   Software version upgrades

Lost Productivity

Estimate the amount of user productivity lost each year due to downtime and PC-based computing limitations such as inaccessibility to required corporate data.

▼ **Number of average user minutes downtime per rollout**   The expected length of downtime suffered by users for both major and minor rollouts.

■ **PC upgrades**   The expected downtime users undergo when they receive a new PC.

▲ **Help desk delays**   The expected lost productivity time while waiting for the help desk to resolve a PC problem.

Costs

Estimated costs for both the existing PC-based computing environment and the proposed SBC are entered into the Costs section of the spreadsheet. Figure B-3 shows a Costs spreadsheet example. Where appropriate, modify costs to reflect the specific user category as defined in the Demographics section of the spreadsheet.

An SBC Data Center

As discussed in Chapter 5, building an on-demand enterprise will involve configuring one or more data centers to support enterprise server–based computing. This is likely to require a more robust and redundant architecture than that of most existing PC-based computing environments. You may be able to upgrade your existing data centers, or you may wish to build new ones or co-locate them with a third-party service such as AT&T or Verio. The feasibility committee needs to choose a preliminary strategy, including the number of data centers, and assign appropriate costs for the model.

MetaFrame Servers   Include both the cost and installation expense for each server.

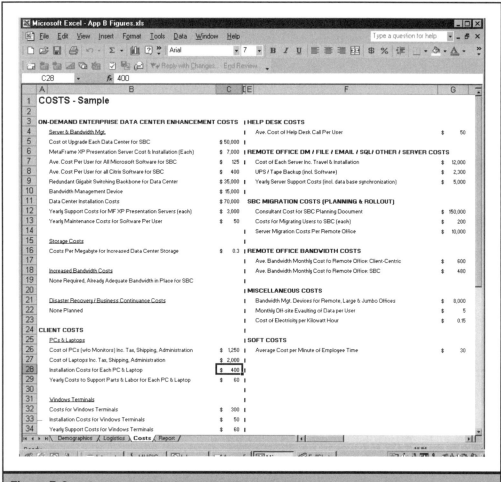

Figure B-3.   Costs section of a financial justification model

Windows Server 2003 Software   Microsoft licenses Windows Server 2003 Terminal Services on either the basis of total number of users or devices. See Chapter 2 for licensing details.

Citrix Software   Citrix software is licensed on a concurrency basis, as explained in Chapter 3. In addition to the basic MetaFrame XP Presentation Server licenses, most organizations also purchase at least some of the other MetaFrame Access Suite components, including MetaFrame Secure Access Manager, Password Manager, and Conferencing Manager.

LAN Backbone   As discussed in Chapter 6, an SBC data center requires a very robust LAN backbone. This usually means a minimum 100MB switching configuration and may include FDDI or gigabit switching for larger implementations along with redundancy.

Bandwidth Management   If you have remote offices, you may want to consider utilizing bandwidth management, as discussed in Chapter 6. One good solution is to use a bandwidth management device such as Packeteer's PacketShaper. These units can easily pay for themselves by increasing the utilization of available bandwidth from 40 to 80 percent.

Installation   Ensure enough money is allocated to properly install all of the data center components. Remember that much of the work may have to be done during off-hours in order not to disrupt your current environment.

Maintenance and Support   Include estimated costs for both annual maintenance and support of hardware and software.

Storage Costs

Estimate the cost per megabyte for required increased data-center storage to support the SBC users.

Electricity Costs

Include the company's average cost per kilowatt.

Increased Bandwidth Costs

Although the bandwidth costs to remote offices may fall under server-based computing, the data center bandwidth requirements may increase.

Disaster Recovery/Business Continuance

The feasibility committee needs to determine the extent to which the SBC will include disaster recovery and business continuance. The associated costs should then be entered into the spreadsheet.

Client Costs

The cost for PCs and laptops includes sales tax, shipping, and administration. Software operating system costs are included along with annual hardware support costs. A realistic installation cost should reflect the hours it takes to configure each device. For most organizations, this ranges between three to eight hours per PC or laptop.

The lack of any moving parts makes the installation and annual support costs for Windows terminals minimal.

Help Desk Costs

Some organizations will show help desk costs as reductions in the number of support personnel required. Others might already have an assigned monthly support cost per user.

Remote-Office Server Costs

Servers in remote offices will usually be eliminated under an SBC scenario. It is therefore important to estimate the costs for these servers, including ancillary equipment such as tape backups, tape backup software, uninterruptible power supplies and software, network O/S software, and network management software. Include costs for installing new servers along with the costs for annual server maintenance.

Conferencing Costs

Several Internet conferencing programs charge fees to enable sharing of documents to both internal personnel and external clients. They typically charge by the minute. Exclusive of telecommunications costs, fees commonly range around .30 to .50 per minute, or about $50 to $150 per month per user.

Migration Costs

Estimate the costs for migrating PC users to server-based computing desktops, including the cost of migrating the data to the corporate data center. Four hours for migrating each PC is probably a reasonable figure. Include the estimated cost to migrate information from remote office servers back to the corporate data center. Also include the cost for preparing the project definition and planning documents, as well as the infrastructure assessment.

Remote-Office Bandwidth Costs

Compare the cost of bandwidth required for a PC-based computing environment with the cost for providing adequate bandwidth connectivity for a server-based computing environment. Both figures will depend upon the size of remote offices and the bandwidth medium. Using the Internet or a VPN is likely, for example, to be much less expensive than using a dedicated leased line or frame relay connection. Server-based computing could either reduce or increase the bandwidth cost to a remote office depending upon the number of users and applications required. Effective use of an ERP application in a remote office, for instance, may require much higher bandwidth under PC-based computing than under server-based computing.

Miscellaneous Costs

This category includes the miscellaneous additional costs for both the server-based and PC-based computing environments. Examples include costs for bandwidth management devices for the larger offices and the cost of using a third-party service to back up user hard drives.

Soft Costs

The cost of employee time shown on a minute or hourly basis should be entered into this part of the spreadsheet.

Report

The Report section pulls together all of the information from the Demographics, Logistics, and Costs sections of the spreadsheet. The end result is a net present value estimate for building an SBC and for the savings it is expected to generate over a three-to-five-year time frame. The present value of the total savings can then be divided by the present value of the total cost of the project to show the expected return on investment for the SBC initiative.

We like to list the categories in the first column and then the summarized costs for the ensuing years in the following columns, as seen in Figure B-4, which shows an example of a Report spreadsheet section over a three-year analysis period.

Demographics Summary

We find it useful to recap the total number of expected concurrent employees by year, along with the number of expected MetaFrame servers required in a demographics summary. Since technology is almost certainly accelerating faster than your employee growth rate, the number of servers required each year should actually decline.

SBC Costs

SBC costs are the summation of all the different components involved in constructing and maintaining an on-demand enterprise data center.

TIP: You may wish to break down costs and savings on a per-user basis in order to analyze the impact of an SBC from a different angle.

Data Center Costs   In the sample shown in Figure B-4, we consolidate the costs by hardware and installation, software, and support costs.

Migration Costs

Migration costs include the project definition, infrastructure assessment and planning costs, as well as the client migration costs and remote-office migration costs.

SBC Savings

As mentioned earlier in the appendix, the SBC savings equate to the money not spent that would have been required to sustain a PC-based computing environment.

PC and Laptop Savings   PC and Laptop Savings section summarizes the expected savings from less-frequent upgrades of PCs and laptops. The figures come from multiplying the total cost of the laptop or PC by 12 and dividing it by the life cycle of the device. For instance, suppose a PC costs $1250, including taxes, installation, shipping, and administration. If your company policy is to replace PCs every 18 months, then your annual savings by going to server-based computing will be $1250 × (12 / 18) = $833 per PC. If appropriate, the annual maintenance savings for PCs and laptops should also be reflected in this category.

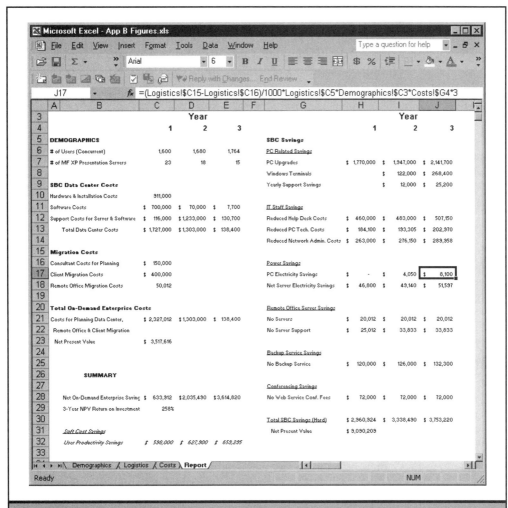

Figure B-4.   Report section of a financial justification model

Windows Terminal Savings   Windows terminal savings result from being able to purchase less-expensive Windows terminals rather than PCs for new users. In the example in Figure B-4, we assume that PCs will gradually be replaced with Windows terminals as they come up in their normal refresh cycle.

Yearly Support Savings   Yearly support savings are a result of using Windows terminals or from using PCs locked down like Windows terminals rather than fat-client PCs for new users.

IT Staff Savings

The amount of decreased help desk support, PC desktop support, and remote office network administrator support required under an SBC should be summarized by showing a decline in either the monthly charge per user or in a reduced salary cost for IT personnel.

NOTE: According to a 2003 Gartner Research Report, password-related help desk calls account for nearly 25 percent of call volume, on average. This means that implementing the Password Manager component of the MetaFrame Access Suite alone should generate significant reductions in help desk staffing requirements. User productivity will also be increased since users no longer will need to wait for the help desk to assist them with forgotten passwords.

Remote-Office Server Savings

Remote-office server savings result from no longer having to upgrade and maintain remote-office servers. The annual savings from not having to upgrade the servers are calculated in the same manner as the savings from not upgrading PCs and laptops.

NOTE: All servers in remote offices may not be eliminated under an SBC model, depending upon factors such as the size of the office and bandwidth availability. If any remote office servers will remain under SBC, then the calculations will need to be modified appropriately.

Power Savings

Electricity savings are included for the replacement of PCs with Windows terminals, and for the elimination of remote-office servers (adding back the increased electricity usage for the Citrix servers in the data centers).

Conferencing Savings

Citrix MetaFrame Conferencing Manager also enables real-time application sharing for both internal and external users, but at a one-time fixed fee that is included as part of the SBC software cost. Conferencing savings are therefore the annual expense of the organization's web-based conferencing service.

Backup Savings

Any hard backup savings such as the money that will no longer be required for third-party backup services are reflected here. Any soft backup savings are quantified apart from the ROI calculation.

Summary

Subtract the SBC costs from the anticipated savings to show the net SBC savings each year.

Calculate the expected ROI of an SBC by subtracting the net present value of the SBC costs from the net present value of the SBC savings. Then divide this figure by the net present value of the SBC costs.

Soft Savings

Show soft savings apart from the ROI calculation, and include savings from reduced user downtime and inaccessibility to required corporate data. Specific productivity savings can also be calculated from utilizing the Password Manager and Secure Access Manager components of the MetaFrame Access Suite.

Benefits

List the expected benefits from implementing an SBC along with the financial report. It might even be appropriate to quantify some of them, but excluding them from the ROI calculation should still leave a project savings easily large enough to justify the SBC implementation.

APPENDIX C

Creating an On-Demand Enterprise Subscription Billing Model

In most organizations, IT expenses are often allocated on the basis of somewhat arbitrary criteria, such as a percentage of sales. On the other hand, commercial Application Service Providers (ASPs) must charge their customers' fees that are clearly based upon usage of their application hosting services. By utilizing Citrix access infrastructure to create an on-demand enterprise, IT can become a corporate computing utility, provisioning software as a service. This enables them to apply a similar billing model as a commercial ASP to their organization's internal customers. The advantage is greater accountability as departments, offices, and users quickly understand the costs of IT resources they consume. By adjusting their consumption habits to minimize IT expenses, the entire organization benefits. This model also tends to spotlight the types of hidden IT costs that frequently plague many organizations utilizing a client-centric model of computing. For purposes of this model, we'll refer to accessing SBC as part of the on-demand enterprise as a Corporate ASP.

MONTHLY SUBSCRIPTION FEES

IT can charge users a monthly subscription fee structured like a cable company bill. Each user and each remote office is charged a basic monthly fee for utilizing the Corporate ASP. Additional fees cover supplementary applications, services, and changes. Account change fees help to ensure that users remain conscious of the administrative costs their requests for system modifications entail.

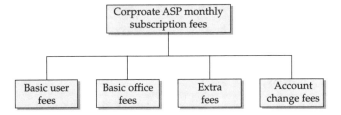

Basic User Fees

Basic user fees are monthly charges for products and services necessary for a user to access the Corporate ASP. For example, a department with ten user accounts would be charged a basic monthly fee for each of the ten named users to receive help desk support and the necessary hardware, software, and disk space.

▼ **Help desk support**   The basic user fee should include a charge for help desk support. SBC both greatly simplifies the user-computing environment and allows help desk personnel to "shadow" user sessions. When including Password Manager, which by itself should reduce the average help desk support requests by 25 percent, this charge should run far less than it would in a client-centric computing environment.

■ **Network device**   Users require a PC, laptop, Macintosh, UNIX Workstation, or Windows terminal in order to access the Corporate ASP. Although it probably makes more sense to let departments pay for their own equipment, IT does need to set a price for access.

■ **Disk space**   The basic subscription fee should include a certain amount of disk space in the corporate data center.

▲ **Basic software suite**   Users will have access to the standard corporate software suite such as Microsoft Office and e-mail. This suite should include virus-protection software and all licensing costs for accessing Terminal Services and MetaFrame XP Presentation Server.

Basic Office Fees

The monthly basic office fee covers the expense of putting a remote office onto the Corporate ASP. The charges might be categorized by size of office, as described in Appendix B and as shown here:

Office Type	Number of Users	Basic Monthly Fee	Shared Disk Space
Small	1–5	$ 50	500MB
Medium	5–14	$150	1GB
Large	15–30	$250	2GB
Jumbo	41–200	$900	10GB

▼ **Shared disk space in the corporate data center**   Remote offices may require shared disk space in excess of the amount for individual users.

■ **Bandwidth**   The monthly fee should include the cost of connectivity as well as the cost of bandwidth management and support.

■ **Printing**   Large remote offices often have print servers, and small offices use print management hardware at the corporate data center. General office fees should cover basic printing, using corporate standard printers.

▲ **Administrative support**   The monthly fee can also include a basic level of administrative support for each office.

Extra User Fees

As with a cable company, IT can tack on additional charges for additional services. The following table shows an example of basic and additional monthly subscription fees.

User Subscription Fees	Amount
Basic user fees	
Includes PC or Windows terminal, network and MetaFrame software licensing, MS Office, e-mail, antivirus software, 200MB data center storage	$150

User Subscription Fees	Amount
Additional user fees	
Laptop	$ 50
Extra 100MB storage	$ 10
Each extra 32-bit application	$ 10
Local printer (Terminal Server–supported drivers)	$ 5

Some of the categories of additional fees are as follows:

▼ **Nonstandard software**   Users requiring access to nonstandard corporate applications should pay additional fees. Unusually resource-intensive or 16-bit applications requiring separate MetaFrame XP Presentation servers will be more expensive.

■ **Hardware types**   It generally costs slightly more to maintain and support a PC configured as a Windows terminal than it does to support a genuine Windows terminal. A laptop user who runs applications both locally and through the Corporate ASP will likely require significantly more support. IT can tack on additional charges depending upon the type of hardware utilized and the degree to which the user operates in complete thin-client mode.

■ **Additional disk space**   IT can charge users extra for additional data storage requirements.

■ **Local devices**   Local devices such as printers and scanners can be charged appropriately.

▲ **Access from home**   A small charge might be levied for employees who want to work from home as well as from the office, though server-based computing makes this process relatively painless. IT may instead choose to bundle this service as part of the basic monthly user fees in order to encourage working from home.

Extra Office Fees

IT can charge extra fees to remote offices requiring additional storage space or printing requirements beyond the basics. New users or application changes also fall into this category.

Account Change Fees

In order to help foster computing efficiency throughout the organization, IT may wish to charge remote offices or departments for each account change. An account change is a new account setup or an addition or deletion to a user or office account. For example, adding or deleting a specific application to a user or group desktop would be an account change. An account change would also take place if an office decided to increase or decrease its shared disk space at the data center.

USING RESOURCE MANAGER FOR SPECIFIC USAGE BILLING

Citrix Resource Manager (RM) may be used to supplement the monthly subscription fee model by billing users for some applications per minute of connection time. It also enables billing by memory utilization and/or processor utilization. A semiconductor manufacturer, for example, might utilize a common manufacturing application requiring a huge amount of RAM per user. RM can add a supplemental fee for the inordinate amount of server resources that manufacturing users consume.

RM Billing

RM can create its own billing reports, which can be delivered directly to users or imported into another accounting or ERP application.

User Delineation

RM provides the capability of going through the domain structures and creating bills for users or groups. RM enables billing by user or by cost center using the Windows domain structure, or you can create your own cost center assignments. For example, you might bill by office or by department. Users in different geographical locations can automatically be charged in their own currency.

Billing Reports

Billing reports can be constructed to show resources used, session start time, session elapsed time, process loaded time, CPU time, memory utilized, and process active time. Figure C-1 shows a screen print from an RM report.

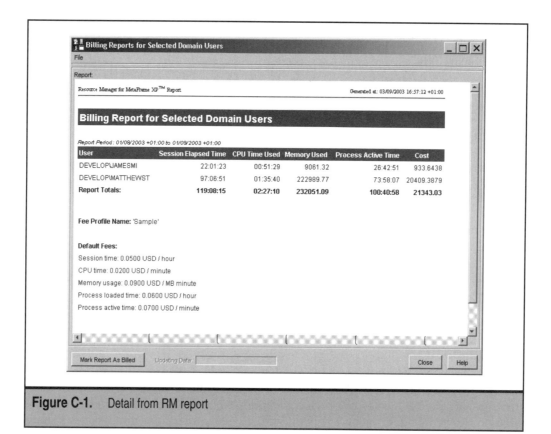

Figure C-1.   Detail from RM report

INDEX

E

F

X

Y

Z

INTERNATIONAL CONTACT INFORMATION

AUSTRALIA
McGraw-Hill Book Company
Australia Pty. Ltd.
TEL +61-2-9900-1800
FAX +61-2-9878-8881
http://www.mcgraw-hill.com.au
books-it_sydney@mcgraw-hill.com

CANADA
McGraw-Hill Ryerson Ltd.
TEL +905-430-5000
FAX +905-430-5020
http://www.mcgraw-hill.ca

**GREECE, MIDDLE EAST, & AFRICA
(Excluding South Africa)**
McGraw-Hill Hellas
TEL +30-210-6560-990
TEL +30-210-6560-993
TEL +30-210-6560-994
FAX +30-210-6545-525

MEXICO (Also serving Latin America)
McGraw-Hill Interamericana Editores
S.A. de C.V.
TEL +525-1500-5108
FAX +525-117-1589
http://www.mcgraw-hill.com.mx
carlos_ruiz@mcgraw-hill.com

SINGAPORE (Serving Asia)
McGraw-Hill Book Company
TEL +65-6863-1580
FAX +65-6862-3354
http://www.mcgraw-hill.com.sg
mghasia@mcgraw-hill.com

SOUTH AFRICA
McGraw-Hill South Africa
TEL +27-11-622-7512
FAX +27-11-622-9045
robyn_swanepoel@mcgraw-hill.com

SPAIN
McGraw-Hill/
Interamericana de España, S.A.U.
TEL +34-91-180-3000
FAX +34-91-372-8513
http://www.mcgraw-hill.es
professional@mcgraw-hill.es

**UNITED KINGDOM, NORTHERN,
EASTERN, & CENTRAL EUROPE**
McGraw-Hill Education Europe
TEL +44-1-628-502500
FAX +44-1-628-770224
http://www.mcgraw-hill.co.uk
emea_queries@mcgraw-hill.com

ALL OTHER INQUIRIES Contact:
McGraw-Hill/Osborne
TEL +1-510-420-7700
FAX +1-510-420-7703
http://www.osborne.com
omg_international@mcgraw-hill.com

99% of the *Fortune* 500 use Citrix.

Obviously, there's room for improvement

When it comes to customers, we set the bar very high. Sure, 99% of the *Fortune* 500 use our software to deploy applications centrally so their workers have secure, easy and instant access to business-critical information — anywhere, anytime, from any device, over any connection. But we won't be happy until the CIOs of every company are running their organizations as on-demand enterprises — realizing the benefits of saving millions on their IT costs, ensuring secure access to information, improving employee productivity and increasing their business agility. As more than 120,000 Citrix customers already do. To learn what we can do for your organization, visit www.citrix.com